Effective Depositions

Effective 2nd EDITION Depositions

HENRY L. HECHT

University of California, Berkeley
School of Law (Boalt Hall)

AMERICAN BAR ASSOCIATION
Section of Litigation

Cover design by ABA Publishing.

Henry L. Hecht, Scoops v. Business-Aide, Inc.: A Liability and Damages Case File (5th ed. 2009).

Printed in the United States of America.

14 13 12 11 5 4 3 2

Library of Congress Cataloging-in-Publication Data

Effective depositions / Henry L. Hecht.—2nd ed.
    p. cm.
  Includes index.
  ISBN 978-1-60442-906-0
  1. Depositions—United States. I. Hecht, Henry L.
  KF8900.E35 2010
  347.73'72—dc22

                          2010011166

DEDICATION

In loving memory of my parents, Isaac and Catharine,
who made so many things possible;
and to my daughter, Emily, who brings me such joy.

—H.L.H.

CONTENTS

ACKNOWLEDGMENTS

I have been a law teacher and continuing legal educator for more than twenty-five years. In that time, I have worked with thousands of law students and lawyers. I hope I have taught them well; I know I have learned from them. I begin by acknowledging their contributions to this book.

I also acknowledge the contributors, who took time from their busy lives to write—and rewrite—their chapters so that all of us could gain from their expertise and wisdom.

A project of this magnitude takes the support of a long list of people. At the top of the list is Larry Vilardo of the ABA Section of Litigation Book Publishing Board and Connors & Vilardo LLP. Larry's editing prowess improved every aspect of this book. Tim Brandhorst, Deputy Director of ABA Book Publishing, and Denise Eichhorn, Director of Marketing for ABA Book Publishing, provided encouragement and wise counsel throughout this project.

A special note of thanks goes to Paul Freeman, a professional editor and good friend, who has taught me much about the art of writing. Thanks also to Gregory L. Watts of Wilson Sonsini Goodrich & Rosati, who brought his practice experience to bear in helping draft Appendix 1, Sample Notice of Deposition and Request for Production of Documents, in order for it to reflect the world of electronically stored information; to the law firm of Shearman and Sterling LLP for permitting me to adapt its internal training memorandum in order to create Appendix 4, A Lawyer's Guide to Preparing a Deposition Witness; and to California Continuing Education of the Bar for permitting me to adapt its checklist on objections in state court practice in order to create Appendix 8, Objections at a Deposition in Federal Practice.

Finally, I acknowledge the support of the University of California, Berkeley, School of Law (Boalt Hall). Dean Rowan, Reference & Research Services Director, never failed to locate the sources I needed. Three research assistants, Elise Miller, David Keller, and

Chris Howard, used their considerable skills to ensure the accuracy of the text. And last, but not least, my two faculty support assistants, Steve Vercelloni and Wanda Castillo, tolerated my endless requests for revisions with grace and skill.

Henry L. Hecht

CHAPTER 1

The Role and Importance of Depositions

HENRY L. HECHT

"Raise your right hand."

To most people, these words conjure up an image of an anxious witness, hand on a Bible, preparing to testify at a trial. Yet to most litigators the words conjure up something quite different: the start of a deposition.

Since 1938, when the Federal Rules of Civil Procedure were adopted to eliminate "trial by ambush,"[1] discovery—particularly depositions—has been at the heart of dispute resolution. In fact, over 98 percent of all civil cases now resolve without being tried.[2] When a litigator questions a witness today, it is far more likely to be in a law office at a deposition than in a courtroom at trial.

The Essentials: Preparation and an Understanding of the Deposition Process

Much has been written about the rigors and sophistication of trial practice. But examining and defending witnesses at depositions can be just as complex and challenging as trying a case—and arguably more important to its resolution.

Experienced lawyers never try a case without doing a tremendous amount of preparation. You should adopt the same attitude for depositions. Furthermore, you should take every deposition seriously; even those that look simple and straightforward can turn into minefields when you are unprepared.

The time to start preparing for a deposition is long before a witness is asked to "raise your right hand." And to prepare properly, you need a thorough understanding of the deposition process. Without it, you can neither adequately take a deposition nor adequately prepare or defend a witness.

For proof of all this, consider the following exchange at a hypothetical deposition. The deponent is Terry Blake, a computer salesperson for Defendant Business-Aide, Inc. Blake allegedly misrepresented the suitability of computer software he sold to plaintiff Leslie Roberts, the owner of Scoops Ice Cream.

TAKER (Plaintiff Roberts's lawyer): Q. Let's turn now to your conversation with Ms. Roberts. Shortly after you met Ms. Roberts, you told her that you love Scoops ice cream, is that correct?

A. Well, I don't remember using those exact words.

Q. Did you say something to that effect, sir?

A. I probably did.

Q. Had you ever eaten Scoops ice cream before meeting Ms. Roberts?

A. Probably not.

Q. That was just a selling technique of yours?

DEFENDER (Defendant's lawyer): Objection. That question is argumentative.

TAKER: Q. Please answer my question, sir.

WITNESS: Do I have to answer?

DEFENDER: Go ahead and answer it.

WITNESS: A. I just wanted to make her feel comfortable.

TAKER: Q. When you first met Ms. Roberts, you told her that your boss, Maxine Waller, had told you all about Ms. Roberts's needs, is that correct?

A. You know, I don't remember that precisely.

DEFENDER: He's not asking you to guess. Just give him your best recollection. If you don't remember, say "no."

TAKER: Q. You had not spoken with Maxine Waller before meeting with Ms. Roberts, is that correct?

A. Well, I got her memorandum.

2

TAKER: Q. Let me repeat my question. You had not spoken with Maxine Waller before your meeting with Ms. Roberts, is that correct?

WITNESS: A. Just a minute.

TAKER: I'd like the court reporter to note for the record that the witness is conferring with his counsel. I object to the practice of conferring in the midst of a question.

WITNESS: A. Probably.

TAKER: Q. Is that what your counsel just told you to say?

DEFENDER: I'm going to instruct the witness not to answer that question. The question obviously invades the attorney-client privilege.

TAKER: Q. Are you going to follow the instruction given by your counsel?

WITNESS: A. Yes.

Even a short, apparently simple exchange like this one raises several key questions:

1. Why did the taker want to impeach the witness about whether the witness said he loved Scoops ice cream? Should the taker have saved the question for trial?
2. Did the defender successfully deflect that question by objecting to it as argumentative? Could the defender have done more? Should the defender have done more? What?
3. Did the taker respond appropriately to the objection?
4. Why did the taker ask whether Maxine Waller "told" the witness all about Ms. Roberts's needs? Was the witness's answer helpful? To whom?
5. What should the taker have done when the witness said, "I don't remember that precisely"?
6. May a witness confer with his defender while a question is pending? Was the taker's response appropriate? Should the taker have done more?
7. Was it proper for the defender to instruct the witness not to answer the question, "Is that what your counsel just told you to say"?
8. What should the taker have done in response to the instruction not to answer?

This book answers all these questions. It also raises and answers many other questions about depositions.

How the Book Approaches Depositions

As most lawyers realize, there is more to the deposition process than just the deposition. This book separates the deposition process into three distinct stages: (1) before the deposition, (2) during the deposition, and (3) after the deposition.

Every deposition is an interactive event with multiple players: the examiner, the witness, the defender, the court reporter, and possibly a videographer. Many of the chapters focus on one of the players at a time—first through the eyes of the examiner, and then through the eyes of the defender. At times, this approach can seem artificial. But it offers an enormous benefit: close scrutiny of each side's strategy. Whenever possible, the text merges the two perspectives and discusses them together.

Among the issues covered by the book are the following.

Stage One: Before the Deposition

The focus of this portion of the book discusses what the lawyers on each side must do to prepare.

- What are the examiner's purposes in taking a deposition? What other discovery methods should be used? In what order?
- How can a witness be compelled to attend the deposition? Where can a deposition be held? How many times can a witness be deposed? For how long?
- How does the examiner prepare to take a deposition? How does the examiner decide what topics to cover, what questions to ask, and in what order?
- How does a defender prepare herself and the witness? What should the defender say to a witness about a deposition and about how to answer questions? Are the guidelines for a deposition witness different from those for a trial witness?

Stage Two: The Deposition

The focus of this section is on questioning and defending techniques.

- When should the taker ask open-ended questions? What about narrow questions? What about leading questions? When should a combination be used?

4

- When should the taker use documents in questioning the witness? What is the most effective way to use documents at a deposition?
- How can the examiner exhaust the recollection of a witness? Where does the examiner draw the line before asking the ill-advised "one too many" question?
- How does the examiner handle an evasive witness? What can be done about an evasive witness after the deposition?
- How does an examiner or a defender deal with a witness who lied in the past or intends to lie at the deposition? What guidelines do the rules of professional conduct provide?
- What objections are available to the defending lawyer at the deposition? When should they be made? How should they be stated?
- When may the defender instruct the witness not to answer? How should the instruction be stated?
- What should the taker do in response to a defender's tactics?
- How should the examiner deal with an obstreperous defender during the deposition? After the deposition?
- When should a defender advise her witness to take the Fifth? What should the taker do in response?
- How does an examiner question an expert? What role does the defender play?
- When should a deposition be video recorded? Does video recording change the role of the examiner, defender, or witness?
- How can realtime transcription be used effectively? By the taker? By the defender?

Stage Three: After the Deposition

This section covers everything from getting a deposition transcript reviewed, corrected, and signed to using it at trial.

- What should the examiner, defender, witness, and court reporter do after the deposition?
- Is it useful to have the deposition summarized? By whom? In what format?
- What use can be made of deposition testimony? By whom?

5

- How can the testimony be used in motion practice?
- How can it be used at trial?

In addition to the foregoing list, the book covers a number of other problems that can surface in depositions.

The Use of the *Scoops* Case

From time to time, the book uses a hypothetical case: *Scoops v. Business-Aide, Inc.*[3] (The deposition exchange a few pages earlier is from this hypothetical case.) Here are the facts of the *Scoops* case you need to know.

Leslie Roberts owns Scoops, the "best little-known" ice cream shop in Cambridge, Massachusetts. Roberts has sued Business-Aide, Inc., a Boston retailer selling computer hardware and software, in connection with Scoops's purchase of accounting software from Business-Aide. The suit alleges intentional and negligent misrepresentation, breach of express warranty, and breach of the implied warranty of fitness for a particular purpose.

Roberts operates Scoops out of her own checking account. Because of Scoops's growth, she has had increasing difficulty tracking inventory and maintaining an accurate financial picture of the business.

Harold Jamison, Inc., is a New England chain of family restaurants and ice cream parlors. Two years ago, in October, Jamison offered to market Scoops's ice cream on a regional basis. However, the offer, which could prove lucrative to Scoops, was conditioned on Scoops' obtaining a line of credit sufficient to significantly increase its production capabilities. Jamison agreed to keep the offer open until January 15, one year ago.

Roberts then contacted Northeast National Bank about a line of credit. A loan officer told her to submit a loan application, including a financial statement. Aware that her business needed more financial sophistication, Roberts—a latecomer to technology—decided to buy a computer and accounting software. She reasoned that doing so would enable her to produce an accurate financial statement and monitor Scoops's inventory and cash flow.

Roberts asked one of her employees, Frank Fuller, to help Scoops find the right hardware and software. After talking with Maxine Waller, the owner of Business-Aide, Frank decided that Business-Aide could meet Scoops's needs. On November 12, Roberts met one of Business-Aide's salespersons, Terry Blake, at the store. After the meeting, Roberts purchased hardware and software from

6

Business-Aide. The purchase included an accounting program called "The Bottom Line." She used the program to prepare the financial statement required by Northeast National Bank for the line of credit.

At the time of her purchase, Roberts was unaware that The Bottom Line was designed only for cash-basis businesses. The software did not account for sales on credit (accounts receivable), purchases on credit (accounts payable), or prepaid expenses that benefit a business over time. Therefore, The Bottom Line was not appropriate for Scoops, an accrual-basis business with cash and credit sales as well as cash and credit purchases. As a result, the financial statement Roberts prepared using The Bottom Line substantially overstated Scoops's expenses and substantially understated its net income and assets. In other words, it made Scoops look less profitable (and less creditworthy) than it was.

Roberts submitted the misleading financial statement as part of her application for a line of credit. After reviewing it, the bank denied the application. By that time, it was too late for Roberts to reapply before the January 15 deadline. Consequently Scoops lost its potentially lucrative contract with Jamison. This lawsuit followed.

Roberts seeks damages of $250,000 for lost profits and $750,000 in punitive damages. Business-Aide denies liability.

Notes

1. Milton Pollack, *Discovery—Its Abuses and Correction*, 80 F.R.D. 219, 220 (1978) ("trial by ambush and secrecy were considered normal in courts of law" before adoption of Federal Rules of Civil Procedure).

2. *See* Admin. Office of the U.S. Courts, *Judicial Business of the United States Courts: 2006*, Table C-4A (only 1.3 percent of all civil cases in U.S. district courts reached trial in 2006), http://www.uscourts.gov/judbus2006/appendices/c4a.pdf. *See also* Marc Galanter, *The Vanishing Trial: An Examination of Trials and Related Matters in Federal and State Courts*, 1 J. EMPIRICAL LEGAL STUD. 459 (2004). The American Bar Association sponsored "The Vanishing Trials Project," which culminated in the ABA Litigation Section's Symposium on the Vanishing Trial in 2003. Marc Galanter's paper on the vanishing trial was presented at this symposium and later published in the *Journal of Empirical Legal Studies*.

3. HENRY L. HECHT, *SCOOPS V. BUSINESS AIDE, INC.*: A LIABILITY AND DAMAGES CASE FILE (5th ed. 2009).

CHAPTER 2

Discovery Methods, Discovery Planning, and Reasons to Take (or Not to Take) a Deposition

Henry L. Hecht

A case without a deposition seems unimaginable. Yet a deposition is only one of several fact-gathering devices available to a litigator through the pretrial civil discovery process. Therefore, depositions must be considered in the context of that process and in concert with other discovery devices.

The first part of this chapter provides an overview of discovery under the Federal Rules of Civil Procedure (FRCP), focusing on initial mandatory disclosures and the need for early, joint discovery planning. Next, the chapter reviews the five formal discovery methods under the FRCP, as well as limitations on their use. The chapter then suggests a step-by-step process for creating a discovery plan, using an example based on the *Scoops* case. Finally, the chapter looks at the special roles or purposes of depositions.

The Federal Discovery Scheme

Discovery is used to gather and preserve information about a case. The information helps a lawyer understand, evaluate, and manage the case. Used wisely, it can increase a lawyer's chances of success through settlement, dispositive pretrial motions, or trial.

The federal scheme envisions three distinct types of discovery. First, there are informal methods such as interviewing witnesses and requesting documents on a voluntary basis from nonparties. Because informal discovery is not subject to the FRCP, no formal notice is required.[1] Second, there are initial disclosures parties must make even though no formal discovery request has been made.[2] Third, there are five formal methods to discover additional matter from parties and nonparties.[3] One of the five is depositions.

Informal Methods of Discovery

Many lawyers think of discovery as an information-gathering process regulated by formal rules. Yet much information can be obtained informally—often before a lawsuit is even filed.[4] In fact, information gathered informally can help you and your client make an early evaluation of the case and decide whether to settle or continue to litigate.

The first and best informal step you can take is to interview your client and gather whatever relevant documents your client has. You should also review your opponent's pleadings, which presumably reflect her theory of the case and what she intends to prove.

Other informal steps that can yield useful information include (1) discussing the case with opposing counsel; (2) visiting a key location, such as the scene of an accident or the plant where a product was manufactured; (3) reviewing prior statements of your client and other parties, including testimony given in other cases; (4) interviewing third parties;[5] (5) conducting Internet-based research; (6) searching online databases; (7) reviewing trade and industry publications, which can be potential sources of standards or guidelines; and (8) hiring private investigators. Finally, there are the federal agencies.

They can be mother lodes of information, either in the form of data that is a matter of public record (Securities and Exchange Commission filings, for example) or data that can be accessed by request (Freedom of Information Act filings, for example).[6]

Informal discovery has numerous advantages. For one thing, it usually does not cost much. Most of the time, it can be done without an opponent's knowledge (though FRCP 26 may require you to divulge the identity of witnesses and documents that you discover informally). Furthermore, information gathered informally is controlled by whoever gathers it. Suppose you interview a witness in your office who makes statements unfavorable to your case. Although you may have to disclose the witness's identity, you are not required to send any summary of the interview to opposing counsel. With a deposition, on the other hand, each and every statement—even a damaging one—is preserved for your opponent.

The primary disadvantage of informal discovery is that information gathered informally may not be admissible at trial.[7]

Initial Disclosures Under the FRCP

FRCP 26 was radically amended in 1993. The amendments did not change the scope of discovery, which under FRCP 26(b)(1) remains extremely broad, covering

> any nonprivileged matter that is relevant to any party's claim or defense. . . . Relevant information need not be admissible at the trial if the discovery appears reasonably calculated to lead to the discovery of admissible evidence.[8]

But the amendments—which were initially controversial[9]—did change the nature of discovery by requiring parties to disclose certain information to their adversaries without a formal request and to confer with them to create a discovery plan for submission to the trial court. Thus, the amendments codified a trend toward greater case management by courts and expanded disclosure by parties at the start of a lawsuit. Through initial disclosures, information that once could be obtained only through potentially protracted and costly pretrial discovery, such as the names and location of witnesses and the identity of relevant documents, now must be provided early and automatically.

Information that parties must now automatically provide under FRCP 26, as amended in 2000, includes the following: (1) information about potential witnesses and documentary evidence "that the

11

disclosing party may use to support its claims or defenses, unless the use would be solely for impeachment";[10] (2) damage computations and the documents on which they are based; and (3) insurance agreements on which a judgment may be paid. In addition, after the initial disclosures, the parties must identify their expert witnesses and provide a detailed report signed by those experts who will testify at trial.[11]

In 2006, the FRCP were again amended to recognize the sheer volume of documents now generated and stored electronically (electronically stored information, or ESI). Indeed, the *ABA Journal* reported that major cases involve a terabyte of ESI that, if printed, would fill Chicago's Willis Tower (formerly known as the Sears Tower) four times.[12] The 2006 amendments require the parties to discuss issues related to the discovery of ESI, such as its source, whether it is reasonably accessible, how it will be produced, and arrangements for its preservation.[13]

The 2006 amendments also addressed the difficulty of guarding against waiver of privilege or work-product protection, a danger increased by the enormous volume of ESI being produced. As amended, FRCP 26(f) requires the parties to discuss issues related to the assertion of privileged or work-product–protected documents, including whether they can agree to procedures for asserting claims. The FRCP suggest two types of agreements:

1. A "quick peek" agreement, where the responding party provides certain requested materials for initial review without waiver, after which the requesting party designates the documents it wants produced. The responding party then screens only those documents actually requested and asserts privilege claims as provided in FRCP 26(b)(5)(A).
2. A "clawback" agreement, where production of privileged documents is made without waiving a privilege so long as the responding party identifies documents mistakenly produced. The recipient of those inadvertently produced documents then returns them.[14]

FRCP 37(e), as amended in 2006, also provides for a "safe harbor"; namely,

Absent exceptional circumstances, a court may not impose sanctions . . . on a party for failing to provide electronically stored information lost as a result of the routine, good-faith operation of an electronic information system.[15]

Before trial, the parties must disclose the evidence to be offered at trial.[16] FRCP 26(e)(1) creates a duty to supplement or correct both FRCP 26(a)-required initial disclosures and responses to the formal methods of discovery in a timely manner

> if the party learns that in some material respect the disclosure or response is incomplete or incorrect, and if the additional or corrective information has not otherwise been made known to the other parties during the discovery process or in writing; or as ordered by the court.[17]

From the outset, as explained in the 1993 advisory committee's note, a major purpose of the amendments was "to accelerate the exchange of basic information about the case and to eliminate the paperwork involved in requesting such information." Furthermore, the Rules were "designed to eliminate certain discovery, help focus the discovery that is needed, and facilitate preparation for trial or settlement."[18] This duty to exchange does not make previously protected material discoverable. But the amendments force the parties to produce certain information earlier and without a formal discovery request.[19] And, as noted above, the Rules require parties to confer in an attempt to reach an agreement on how to protect against waiver.

The Rules now require a new degree of cooperation between parties as well as greater court involvement. FRCP 26(f) requires parties to confer and develop a proposed joint discovery plan for submission to the court before the parties appear at an FRCP 16(b) scheduling conference.[20] After this conference, the court then issues a scheduling and planning order.[21] The discovery plan helps the court ensure that the timing and scope of disclosures, including limitations on the type of discovery and the methods to be used, are tailored to the case. At the scheduling conference, the court can help the parties identify pertinent issues and focus their discovery.

If a party fails to provide the information or the identity of a witness as required by FRCP 26(a), or fails to supplement as required by FRCP 26(e), the party is precluded from using that information unless the failure was substantially justified or is harmless.[22] FRCP 37(c)(1) also sets forth other sanctions in addition to or instead of preclusion. In addition, FRCP 37(c)(2) addresses the consequences of a failure to admit in response to an FRCP 36 request when the requesting party later proves a document to be genuine or the matter true.[23]

Formal Methods of Discovery

Once the parties agree upon a discovery plan as required by FRCP 26(f), they have available five formal methods to discover additional matter from parties and nonparties: (1) interrogatories, (2) requests for production, (3) depositions upon oral examination or written questions, (4) requests for admissions, and (5) physical and mental examinations.[24] The methods may be used in any sequence and combination. No party has priority in the use of the methods, and one party's ongoing discovery cannot delay the discovery of any other party.[25]

Advantages and Disadvantages of Formal Discovery Methods

Each formal discovery method has advantages as well as disadvantages.[26]

Interrogatories

FRCP 33 interrogatories are written questions sent to an opposing party. The responses must be signed by the party under oath. Alternatively, when the answer can be derived from documents and the burden of deriving the answer is substantially the same for both parties, the responding party can simply designate the documents responsive to the question.[27] Absent leave of court or written stipulation, there is a limit of twenty-five interrogatories, including all discrete subparts.[28]

Interrogatories are useful for gathering hard data; for example, names, addresses, document identification, corporate organization, and damage calculations. They also tend to be relatively inexpensive. For these reasons, interrogatories are often the starting point in a discovery plan and are frequently used to find out what witnesses to depose and where to locate documents. However, because the mandatory disclosures required by FRCP 26(a)(1)–(3) should include much of the information previously obtained through interrogatories, there should be less need for them.[29]

Although relatively inexpensive, interrogatories have serious disadvantages. They may be sent only to parties; they do not allow for follow-up; and they are limited in number. In addition, although the answers are signed by a party, they are typically drafted by the party's lawyer—with the resulting potential for the narrowest response or broadest objection.[30]

Requests for Production

Requests for the production of documents or tangible evidence, or for the inspection of land, can be addressed to parties through FRCP 34 and to nonparties, including expert witnesses, through FRCP 45.[31] The producing party can choose to produce the documents either as they are kept in the usual course of business or corresponding to the categories in the request. However, formal requests may not be required, because documents are often produced for inspection and copying without a formal request, even though FRCP (26)(a)(1)(A)(ii) requires parties only to initially identify documents.

FRCP 34(b) was amended in 2006 to permit the requesting party to specify how it wants electronically stored information produced.[32] If the requesting party does not specify a format, the responding party must state the format it intends to use.

For a deposition, you almost always want to obtain any documents about which you plan to question the witness. If you have not obtained them before the deposition, you can combine a document request with your deposition notice or subpoena. For a party, the request is made under FRCP 30(b)(2); for a nonparty, FRCP 45.[33] But as a practical matter, requesting documents in conjunction with a deposition notice usually does not work well. Documents requested by a deposition notice or subpoena are not required to be produced until the witness arrives for the deposition. That leaves little or no time for you to review the documents and incorporate their contents into your deposition preparation. This is an especially serious problem when documents play a pivotal role, such as in a breach of contract case where the documents bear on the contract's interpretation.

Compared with depositions, document requests are inexpensive, and they allow for production at a time and place convenient to the parties. In addition, there is no limit on the number of requests.

But document requests can backfire. Framed too narrowly, a request can miss key documents. Framed too broadly, the request becomes vulnerable to objection. An overly broad request can also lead to the production of everything—including the proverbial "kitchen sink," forcing you to conduct a time-consuming and expensive review.

Depositions upon Oral Examination and Written Questions

A deposition involves the formal questioning of a witness under oath. (The reasons to take and not to take a deposition are detailed in the last section of this chapter.) At a deposition, every party has an opportunity to examine the witness, and the testimony is preserved for possible use in pretrial motions and at trial. The deposition of a party is secured by notice under FRCP 30; for a nonparty, a subpoena under FRCP 45 is used.

At a deposition, you can confront a witness and ask follow-up questions. Depositions, however, can be time-consuming and expensive. Under the FRCP, a party can take only ten depositions, depose the same witness only once, and ask questions for no longer than one day of seven hours, unless otherwise stipulated or ordered by the court.[34]

Also available, but infrequently used, are depositions upon written questions under FRCP 31.[35] Attendance is secured by notice or subpoena. The questions are prepared in writing, read to the witness by another person, and answered under oath when read. No follow-up questioning is permitted.

Requests for Admissions

FRCP 36 allows a party to request that another party admit or deny the truth of "facts, the application of law to fact . . . and the genuineness of any described documents."[36] There is no limit on the number of requests you can make. Responses, which must be signed by the party under oath, are binding only for the pending action.

Any matter expressly admitted is conclusively established, absent court order on motion. Likewise, if a request is not timely answered or objected to, the matter is deemed admitted. FRCP 36 does not permit a party to deny a request in its entirety if in good faith the party can admit a part and qualify or deny the remainder.

Requests for admissions are usually made near the end of the discovery process, as the parties shape and limit issues for trial (or at least determine what is still in controversy). Requests for admissions can serve many purposes. First, if served late enough in the litigation, they can secure answers to key questions by eliminating the all-too-frequent objection that a response cannot be made due to ongoing investigation and discovery.[37] Second, they can help lay

16

a foundation for admitting documents or entering stipulations on documentary trial evidence.[38] They can be used, for example, to obtain an admission that a document is authentic or a signature is genuine.[39] Used in this manner, requests for admissions reduce the cost of trial and focus discovery planning. Third, requests for admission can fill gaps at the end of the discovery period, when formal discovery rules can limit the use of other discovery devices.

As with other discovery methods, the effectiveness of a request for admission depends on how carefully the request is drafted. It depends, too, on the good faith of the responding party's lawyer, who almost always prepares the responses.[40] When a response is inadequate, you can use FRCP 36(a)(6) to obtain sanctions against the responding party, including costs and attorney's fees, as well as an order declaring a matter admitted. Because of this potential, requests for admission can be a powerful discovery tool.[41]

Physical and Mental Examinations

A party's or real-party-in-interest's physical or mental condition can be examined by a qualified expert under FRCP 35(a) when those conditions are put into controversy. An order for an examination can be made "only on motion for good cause and on notice to all parties and the person to be examined."[42] The conditions for the examination must be specified in the order, and the resulting report must be available to all parties. The process results in an exchange of reports, if the person examined has been or will be examined for the same condition. This method is often used before the deposition of the complaining party or his expert.

Limitations on Discovery and Certification Standards

As the 1983 advisory committee noted, "the spirit of the rules is violated when advocates attempt to use discovery tools as tactical weapons rather than to expose the facts and illuminate the issues."[43]

Although the scope of discovery under FRCP 26(b)(1) is broad, the Rules place two limitations on the use of discovery methods to encourage an efficient, less abusive system.[44] Taken together, the two limitations—presumptive limits and the certification requirements—are "not meant to discourage or restrict necessary and legitimate discovery" but rather to obligate each lawyer to "stop and think about the legitimacy of a discovery request." [45]

Presumptive limits, as noted above, are placed on the number of interrogatories (twenty-five),[46] the number of depositions per side (ten)[47] and per person (one), and the length of a deposition (one day of seven hours).[48] These limits may be altered by stipulation or by court order. In determining whether to alter the limits, the court determines whether

> (i) the discovery sought is unreasonably cumulative or duplicative, or can be obtained from some other source that is more convenient, less burdensome, or less expensive; (ii) the party seeking discovery has had ample opportunity to obtain the information by discovery in the action; or (iii) the burden or expense of the proposed discovery outweighs its likely benefit, considering the needs of the case, the amount in controversy, the parties' resources, the importance of the issues at stake in the action, and the importance of the discovery in resolving the issues.[49]

FRCP 26 was amended in 1983 to add certification requirements similar to those required for the signature of other documents under FRCP 11.[50] In signing a discovery request, response, or objection, the party or attorney recognizes an affirmative obligation to engage in pretrial discovery in a responsible manner consistent with the spirit and purposes of the discovery rules.[51] At least one lawyer of record or the party, if unrepresented, must sign all discovery requests, responses, and objections.[52] By signing, the lawyer or party certifies "to the best of the person's knowledge, information, and belief formed after a reasonable inquiry" that the discovery request, response, or objection is (1) consistent with existing law; (2) "not interposed for any improper purpose, such as to harass, cause unnecessary delay, or needlessly increase the cost of litigation"; and (3) "neither unreasonable nor unduly burdensome or expensive" given the needs of the case and the discovery to date.[53]

FRCP 26(g) also provides mandatory sanctions for abuse. As noted by the 1983 advisory committee, "the premise of FRCP 26(g) is that imposing sanctions on attorneys who fail to meet the rule's standards will significantly reduce abuse by imposing disadvantages therefore."[54] But the rule makers were not naive. The 1983 advisory committee further noted that "(b)ecause of the asserted reluctance [of judges] to impose sanctions on attorneys who abuse the discovery rules . . . FRCP 26(g) makes explicit the authority judges now have to impose appropriate sanctions and requires them to use it."[55] If, without substantial justification, a certification violates the rule, the court will impose appropriate sanctions on the signer, his or her client, or both. These may include payment of the reasonable expenses and attorney's fees incurred because of the violation. [56]

FRCP 45 provides separate sanctions for abusive discovery practice.[57] The rule provides for sanctions against a lawyer who, in issuing a subpoena, imposes an undue burden or expense upon a person. The sanction may include payment of the third party's lost earnings and a reasonable attorney's fee.[58]

Like the FRCP, the Model Rules of Professional Conduct (Model Rules) provide limitations on abusive discovery practice. Model Rule 4.4 forbids a lawyer from using any practice, including a discovery request, that has no substantial purpose other than to embarrass, delay, or burden a third person.[59] Finally, a claim for tortious abuse of process may be available in connection with improper discovery.[60]

Creating a Discovery Plan

Regardless of your objective—making an initial evaluation of a case, deciding whether to settle early, obtaining evidence for a summary judgment motion, or preparing for trial—you need a discovery plan.

The plan is important for several reasons. First, having a discovery plan makes it easier to fulfill FRCP 26's joint planning and initial disclosure requirements. Second, because each discovery device has distinct advantages and disadvantages, a well-thought-out plan enables you to combine devices in a way that maximizes their usefulness. Finally, a good discovery plan helps you deal with limitations on discovery, such as the maximum of ten depositions per side and twenty-five interrogatories by one party to another.[61]

The first step in developing a discovery plan is to decide what information you need. Before you can make this decision, however, you must do both a legal and a factual analysis of the case.[62]

Legal analysis involves two tasks: (1) identifying the elements of the pleaded claims and defenses, and (2) deciding which party has the burden of proof on the elements. Legal analysis begins with a review of the pleadings to clarify the allegations of the parties. You then review the applicable jury instructions to determine what must be proven.[63] Factual analysis involves identifying those facts that either prove or contradict each claim or defense at issue.

Once you know what information you need, your next step is to decide which discovery devices will best help you obtain this information. To some extent, this decision depends on the probable source of the information. Is it likely to come from a witness? From a document? From answers to interrogatories? By judicial notice? Another important factor to consider is how persuasive potential sources of information are likely to be to a jury.

As a starting point, catalog information according to (1) what is available from informal sources, particularly your own client; (2) what is uncontested; (3) what is likely to be disclosed under FRCP 26; and (4) what can be established by stipulation or judicial notice.

A discovery plan should not be a "wish list" designed to unearth the proverbial "smoking gun." (The fact is, not every case has a proverbial smoking gun, or at least not one that can be found without a protracted, costly fight.) Instead, the plan should be the product of a careful cost/benefit analysis. The analysis should have a cost estimate for discovery, including the direct costs (such as legal fees, copying expenses, witness fees, and court reporter fees) as well as the opportunity costs. In addition, although the discovery process is theoretically cooperative and self-executing,[64] costs can rise exponentially if court enforcement is required.

In addition, other factors to consider include: How likely is it that the information sought will be found? Does it exist? Will the opponent produce it without a fight?[65] Is the probative value of the information worth the time and expense required to obtain it and present it at trial? Will a discovery request escalate the other side's discovery demands? Will the request provoke the opposition to object and move for a protective order or—even worse—provoke judicial displeasure and sanctions? Will the request educate the other side about your trial strategy? Will it create business risks for your client, such as forcing disclosure of trade secrets to a competitor?[66]

If your analysis is solid, you then should be in a good position to choose the appropriate discovery methods and the order in which they will be used. Remember, though, a discovery plan is only a general road map. It must be revisited periodically and revised, as new theories evolve, existing claims are narrowed, and more information is uncovered.

Example of a Discovery Plan in the *Scoops* Case

In *Scoops*, Leslie Roberts alleges that Terry Blake, a salesperson for Defendant Business-Aide, represented to her that The Bottom Line accounting software would meet her particular needs. The representation, she charges, constitutes negligent or intentional misrepresentation.

Suppose you represent the Plaintiff, Leslie Roberts. In developing a discovery plan for her misrepresentation claim, you first must decide what you need to prove. Assume it is the following: (1) that Blake made a material (or important) and untrue representation,[67] (2) with no reasonable basis for believing it to be true (or he made it recklessly without knowledge of whether it was true or false), (3) for the purpose of causing Roberts to rely on the representation, (4) which she justifiably did, and (5) thereby sustained damages.[68]

Now, assume you are considering the second element—that Blake had no reasonable basis for believing that his representation about the software was true (or that he acted in reckless disregard for the truth). How do you establish this element? One way is to show that Blake did not know the capacity of The Bottom Line accounting software.

Potentially valuable information relating to this second element might include (1) Blake's formal education about accounting principles; (2) his training on The Bottom Line; (3) his prior sales or use of accounting software, in general and of The Bottom Line in particular; and (4) employee evaluations bearing on his understanding of business applications software. Where might you find this information? Among other places, Business-Aide documents relating to (1) attendance records for training programs, (2) training materials distributed at seminars, (3) prior sales of accounting software, (4) customer complaints, (5) employee performance evaluations, and (6) employment policies.

As for potential witnesses, Blake is the most obvious. Maxine Waller, Business-Aide's owner, is a likely candidate, and so are other salespersons or training personnel.

Another potentially useful, though less obvious, source of information is third parties. Your discovery plan, therefore, might include contacting the company that makes The Bottom Line, to learn what training it offered for the product and whether any Business-Aide personnel, including Blake, took the training. You would also want to request any training materials the company used.

Once you know the information needed to prove the second element of your misrepresentation claim and where this information might be found, you must decide which discovery methods to use. Interrogatories could be used to identify Business-Aide's training policies and Blake's attendance at seminars. You then could follow up with a document request to obtain relevant documents, such as attendance records and copies of training materials. Your request, however, might trigger an objection that it invaded Blake's privacy, to the extent it sought his personnel records. As part of your plan, therefore, you may want your document request drafted narrowly enough to sidestep this objection and avoid a costly discovery battle. Alternatively, you must be prepared to defend the request in court.

After you receive the interrogatory responses and requested documents, your plan would probably call for deposition notices to be sent to Waller and Blake. You will need to decide in what order to depose these witnesses. Starting with Waller, the president of Business-Aide, may give you a chance to establish company policies on training and the knowledge it requires of its salespersons. Then you can depose Blake and contrast his training with Business-Aide's policy. As the deposition notices are being served, you might want to conduct informal discovery about accounting software sold by Business-Aide. This discovery could focus on issues such as competing products and training standards for sales personnel in Blake's position.

Like all discovery plans, this one should stay fluid. Suppose, for example, you learn during discovery that Blake had prior problems with other customers who bought business applications software, including The Bottom Line, from him. Given this information, you would want to interview or depose those customers.

Purposes of a Deposition

Too often, "deposition notices drop like autumn leaves," warned the former director of the Federal Judicial Center.[69] Before littering the litigation landscape with a deposition notice, you need to decide if the deposition is worth taking. An inappropriate deposition not only can be expensive; it also can damage your case. The material below catalogs some reasons to take—or not to take—a deposition.

Reasons for Taking a Deposition

Obtain Information from a Party

In *Scoops*, the core of Roberts's case is her claim that Blake orally misrepresented the capacity of The Bottom Line accounting software to fit her needs. Suppose you represent Business-Aide. You need to find out what Roberts contends Blake said to her and what she said to him. You could use interrogatories to do this. But the responses, even if verified, will come from Roberts's lawyer, not from her.[70] Furthermore, if the responses to your interrogatories are unsatisfactory, you must wait for another round of interrogatories—assuming you have not exceeded the limit—or move to compel further answers. That can be time-consuming and expensive.[71]

By deposing Roberts, you compel her to testify under oath about what she claims Blake said to her and she to him. You can ask follow-up questions until you exhaust her recollection. And these follow-up questions may produce discovery leads to other persons or documents. If her answers suggest that information is in the hands of an organization, you can use a deposition notice to locate the person in the organization—whether it is a party or a nonparty—who has the requisite knowledge.[72]

Obtain Information from a Nonparty

In *Scoops*, Frank Fuller, who once worked for Roberts but left the state where the case is pending, had a relevant conversation with Maxine Waller, the owner of Business-Aide. Suppose that as Business-Aide's lawyer, you believe that Fuller probably is willing to talk with Roberts and even testify on her behalf at trial, but that he will not speak with you voluntarily.[73] Understandably, you want to know what Fuller will say if he does testify at trial (and you hope the testimony will be favorable to your side).[74]

Because Fuller is not a party, you cannot serve interrogatories on him. But he can be deposed. In fact, the only way to force a nonparty like Fuller to testify under oath before trial is with a deposition. Even if a nonparty voluntarily speaks with you, the information you obtain is inadmissible hearsay.[75] But once a nonparty witness is deposed, the deposition can be offered into evidence if the witness becomes unavailable for trial.[76] If he testifies at trial, the deposition can be used as a prior inconsistent statement to impeach him.[77]

Preserve Testimony

As lawyers know all too well, the best-laid trial plans can be destroyed by unexpected events, including the unavailability of a key witness. By deposing a witness, you preserve the witness's testimony. Suppose that in *Scoops* you depose Fuller. His deposition testimony is favorable to your client, so you decide to use him at trial. Just before the trial begins, he unexpectedly dies. Because you deposed him, his testimony is available. Indeed, in the case of a nonparty, the deposition can be offered at trial *only* if the witness is unavailable. In the case of an adverse party, deposition can be offered at trial *for any purpose*, including impeachment.[78]

Support or Defend a Summary Judgment Motion

Deposition testimony can be particularly helpful when you are bringing or defending a summary judgment motion. (See FRCP 56, which refers to using deposition testimony as supporting evidence in motion papers.)[79]

"Lock in" Testimony

By careful questioning at a deposition, you can force the witness to testify to a particular version of events. It then becomes hard for the witness to surprise you at trial with newly found recollections—at least credible ones.

This point can be illustrated with an example from *Scoops*. One issue in the case is whether Roberts told Blake that she needed accounting software to create a financial statement for a bank loan application. Suppose that at her deposition Roberts says she cannot recall telling Blake this information.[80] If she tries to change her story at trial, she can be cross-examined and impeached with the deposition.

Attack a Witness's Credibility

On occasion, you may decide to use the deposition to impeach a witness and, thereby, attack credibility. The decision will be based on how certain you are the impeachment will succeed, how likely it is that the testimonial defect can be corrected, and whether the witness is likely to be available for trial. If successful, you may have prevented the witness from appearing at trial.

Obtain Documents

You can force a party to produce documents by using an FRCP 34 document request. With a nonparty, as noted earlier, the only way to have documents produced is with an FRCP 45 deposition subpoena. Contrary to what lawyers sometimes say, documents do not "speak for themselves." But when they are produced in connection with a deposition, you can question the witness about them. Being able to do this is essential when (1) the document was the product of several drafts or had multiple authors, (2) the document's routing is not apparent on its face, or (3) the document contains language that is not self-explanatory. You could try to obtain this kind of information with interrogatories after the documents have been produced. But considerable guesswork would be involved in drafting these questions, and it is unlikely the interrogatories would capture the same amount of useful information that a deposition would. Moreover, you may have wasted one of your twenty-five interrogatories.[81]

In *Scoops*, for example, Roberts sent a letter to Business-Aide describing her needs. Although she signed it, it was prepared by her then-employee Fuller. You would not know this without asking one or two deposition questions of either Roberts or Fuller.

Besides giving you an opportunity to explore a document, a deposition creates an opportunity to obtain the foundational testimony for a document you want admitted into evidence at trial.[82] Alternatively, a deposition can help you learn what more you need to lay the foundation or whether it will be impossible to do so.[83] For example, when a document is needed for a summary judgment motion, deposition questioning can let you know whether the document is admissible.

Help Make Sound Judgments

Many lawyers regard a deposition purely as a discovery tool. But it also can help you make judgments in evaluating your case and settlement proposals.

Scoops, for example, is essentially a credibility contest focusing on what Roberts and Blake discussed at a meeting. If you depose Roberts, you can use the deposition to evaluate her demeanor and credibility. You can try different styles of questioning—from friendly to aggressive—to find the most effective. And, by seeing how well prepared Roberts is in certain areas, you may learn something about her case and your opponent's concerns.

25

A deposition also allows you to evaluate the adversary's lawyer. For example, how well did she prepare her witness? Did she control the witness? How skillfully did she respond when you asked her to explain the basis for an objection? You may learn something, too, about how seriously the other side is taking the case. Was a senior partner sent to defend the deposition? A new associate? More than one lawyer?

Facilitate Settlement

As pointed out in the first chapter of this book, more than 98 percent of all civil cases are resolved short of trial.[84] Therefore, a deposition may wind up being the real "trial" in a case. Suppose you depose a key witness who makes a weak showing. Suddenly, the other side may become more amenable to settling on terms favorable to your client. Conversely, if you defend a witness who does poorly, your chances for a favorable settlement are likely to diminish.

Besides directly affecting settlement dynamics, depositions provide a forum for you to establish your credibility as a lawyer. Likewise, by noticing a particular deposition, you can send a message that your client is serious about the case and ready to spend money. Furthermore, a deposition gives you a chance to convey this message directly to the party witness at her deposition without the filter of her lawyer.[85]

Reasons Not to Take a Deposition

Though valuable as a discovery device, depositions have disadvantages.

Depositions Can Be Expensive

Regardless of your reason for taking a deposition, every deposition has direct and opportunity costs. Typically, the big-ticket item is legal fees. A lawyer must (1) prepare for and attend the deposition, (2) summarize the witness's testimony (often done by a legal assistant),[86] and (3) evaluate the testimony. With an hourly fee arrangement, these fees are easy to calculate; with contingency work, they are harder to calculate but no less real. The cost of transcription also can be significant. In a large metropolitan area, a reporter's fee for a full day's testimony can run over $1,000. If you wish to have a video record of the proceeding or if you want it transcribed using realtime technology, figure on spending even more.[87]

In addition, it is not unusual for a deposition notice to be reciprocated by the other side. When that happens, double your client's deposition costs for legal fees and add the opportunity cost for your client (typically in the form of lost time).

Depositions Provide Information to Your Opponent

The principal advantage of a deposition is that it enables you to gather information directly from party witnesses and nonparty witnesses. But this becomes a disadvantage if the information is valuable to your opponent who, but for the deposition, would not have been aware of the information or the witness's identity.[88]

Your Opponent May Be Able to Use the Preserved Testimony Against Your Client

A deposition not only provides information to the opponent; it also preserves it in a form that can be used against your client. Suppose you represent Business-Aide and you depose Roberts's former employee Frank Fuller because you assume he will not voluntarily speak with you. If his testimony damages your case, you have provided the other side with helpful testimony that it can use in a summary judgment motion or at trial.

The foregoing example suggests some ground rules:

1. Do not depose a friendly witness who has helpful and necessary testimony and is willing to testify at trial.[89] Depose such a witness to preserve the helpful testimony only if he is likely to be unavailable at trial—or if his testimony is needed in support of a pending motion.
2. Do not depose a hostile witness if the expected testimony will help the other side and the witness is likely to be unwilling and/or unavailable to testify at trial; all you will accomplish is to preserve potentially damaging testimony—though you cannot stop your adversary from deposing him.[90]
3. If you bring a lawsuit on behalf of an executor, do not depose a survivor in a state where a Dead Man's Statute disqualifies that person from testifying against the decedent's interests.[91] Otherwise, you may waive the statute's protection.

Your Opponent May Learn About Documents

Just as a deposition can generate testimony your opponent might otherwise not have obtained, it also can inform your opponent about documents that might otherwise not have been produced.

27

This happens most often with nonparty deponents. Additionally, a deposition can produce testimony that makes clear to your opponent that documents favorable to your position are inadmissible.

The Testimony Can Hurt Your Case

As noted above, one reason for taking a deposition is to obtain information that helps you evaluate a case and its settlement potential. When you take a deposition for that reason, however, you may not always be happy about the result. For example, an adverse witness may be more believable—and the testimony more damaging—than you expected.

And do not forget that when you depose a person, you also disclose your questions and questioning style for that witness and the defender lawyer. By the time of trial, the witness may be able to cure the testimonial defects uncovered at the deposition. If so, then any evaluation of the case you based upon the deposition becomes invalid. In addition, if you will be deposing several witnesses on the same subject matter, your first deposition has provided a road map for the witnesses who follow.

Depositions Can Have Unforeseen Consequences

True, a deposition can demonstrate your competence and diligent preparation. But if you do poorly at a deposition—and even the best lawyers have bad days—you can create the opposite impression. In addition, even a competently taken deposition can rebound against you. Seeing you shine, your opponent may be galvanized into a higher level of preparation. And your opponent may become educated about some aspect of your case that otherwise would not have been apparent.

Suppose that as Business-Aide's lawyer in *Scoops*, you decide to depose Roberts. At the deposition, you ask questions designed to show that she is incompetent (at least as to financial matters), did not articulate her needs, and therefore could not have relied justifiably on salesperson Terry Blake's representations. By asking these questions, you telegraph your trial strategy. In some situations, asking those questions can be a serious tactical error.

The risk of prematurely disclosing your trial strategy is even greater with expert depositions. Your questions can tell your opponent exactly what must be done to shore up the expert's opinion.[92]

In sum, never take a deposition without weighing the probable advantages and disadvantages. As a practical matter, of course, the balance often tips in favor of going ahead with the deposition. That is why, today, a case without a deposition is unimaginable.

Notes

1.   Although informal methods are not governed by the FRCP, the applicable rules of professional responsibility in each jurisdiction apply.

2.   Fed. R. Civ. P. 26(a)(1)–(4).

3.   See *infra* the section of this chapter entitled "Formal Methods of Discovery," which discusses each device and its advantages and disadvantages. The phrase "Methods to Discover Additional Matter" was the subtitle of former FRCP 26(a)(5). It was deleted by amendments to the Federal Rules of Civil Procedure that became effective Dec. 1, 2007 (the so-called "style" amendments).

4.   Some informal discovery must take place before a suit is filed to meet the certification requirements of FRCP 11.

5.   Model Rules of Prof'l Conduct R. 4.2 (2008) (restricting a lawyer, absent consent from the court or opposing counsel, from communicating "about the subject of the representation with a person the lawyer knows to be represented by another lawyer in the matter"); Model Code of Prof'l Responsibility DR 7-104 (1980) (placing limitations on contact with adverse parties known to be represented). See "Counsel's Communication with Employees of Adversary" in Chapter 6, discussing the prohibition on contact. See also Chapter 21, note 2, discussing the scope of adoption of the Model Rules.

6.   *See generally* Securities Exchange Act of 1934, 15 U.S.C. §§ 78a *et seq.* (1997); Securities Act of 1933, 15 U.S.C. §§ 77a-z, 77aa (2006); Freedom of Information Act (FOIA), 5 U.S.C. § 552 (2008).

7.   The out-of-court statement contained in a witness interview could be used to impeach a trial witness, to refresh recollection, or as past recollection recorded. See also Chapter 25, discussing uses of depositions at trial.

8.   Fed. R. Civ. P. 26(b)(1).

9.   "The proposed new regime does not fit comfortably within the American judicial system, which relies on adversarial litigation to develop facts before a neutral decision maker. By placing upon lawyers the obligation to disclose information damaging to their clients—on their own initiative, and in a context where the lines between what must be disclosed and what need not be disclosed are not clear but require the exercise of considerable judgment—the new Rule would place intolerable strain upon lawyers' ethical duty to represent their clients and not to assist the opposing side." Adoption of amendments to Federal Rules of Civil Procedure, 146 F.R.D. 507, 511 (1993) (Scalia, J., dissenting).

10.   This duty to disclose arises when a party's pleading alleges disputed facts "with particularity." But FRCP 8(a)(2) requires only "a short

and plain statement of the claim showing that the pleader is entitled to relief. . . ." FRCP 9(b) specifies that only claims of fraud and mistake must be pled with particularity. Thus, when the disclosures' requirements are triggered may be subject to dispute.

11. See "Mandatory Disclosure under FRCP 26" in Chapter 19, discussing expert disclosures.

12. Richard L. Marcus, *E-Discovery and Beyond: Toward Brave New World or 1984?*, 236 F.R.D. 598, 608 & n.53 (2006).

13. *See* FED. R. CIV. P. 26(b)(2)(B). Discussion of discovery of electronically stored information is beyond the scope of this book. The Advisory Committee Notes (2006) suggest "(t)he particular issues regarding electronically stored information that deserve attention during the discovery planning stage depend on the specifics of the given case. *See Manual for Complex Litigation* (4th) § 40.25(2) (listing topics for discussion in a proposed order regarding meet-and-confer sessions)." *See also* Barbara J. Rothstein, Ronald J. Hedges & Elizabeth C. Wiggins, *Managing Discovery of Electronic Information: A Pocket Guide for Judges*, FED. JUD. CTR. (2007).

14. FED. R. CIV. P. 26(f). *See also* FED. R. CIV. P. 26(f) advisory committee's note (2006) (discussing the problems of waiver and suggested agreements to meet those problems).

15. FED. R. CIV. P. 37(e).

16. FED. R. CIV. P. 26(a)(3).

17. FED. R. CIV. P. 26(e)(1). FRCP 26(e)(2) sets forth additional duties with respect to an expert whose report must be disclosed under FRCP 26(a)(2)(B):

> [T]he party's duty to supplement extends both to information included in the report and to information given during the expert's deposition. Any additions or changes to this information must be disclosed by the time the party's pretrial disclosures under Rule 26(a)(3) are due.

18. FED. R. CIV. P. 26(a)(1) advisory committee's note (1993).

19. *See* FED. R. CIV. P. 26(b) (regarding scope of discovery).

20. FED. R. CIV. P. 26(f)(1)–(2) (meeting shall be "as soon as practicable—and in any event at least 21 days before a scheduling conference is to be held or a scheduling order is due under Rule 16(b)[,]" and a written report outlining the plan is due within 14 days after the meeting). The parties are also required to discuss the possibility of settlement. *See also* FED. R. CIV. P., form 52, App. of Forms (Report of the Parties' Planning Meeting).

21. FED. R. CIV. P. 16(b). The parties are subject to sanctions for failure to participate in the framing of a discovery plan. FED. R. CIV. P. 37(f).

22. FED. R. CIV. P. 26(a).

23. FED. R. CIV. P. 37(c)(2).

24. FED. R. CIV. P. 26(a).

25. FED. R. CIV. P. 26(d).

26. *See* MARILYN J. BERGER, JOHN B. MITCHELL, RONALD H. CLARK & MONIQUE C.M. LEAHY, PRETRIAL ADVOCACY: PLANNING, ANALYSIS, AND STRATEGY (2d ed. 2007); ROGER S, HAYDOCK, DAVID F. HERR & JEFFREY W. STEMPEL, FUNDAMENTALS OF PRETRIAL LITIGATION (7th ed. 2008); THOMAS A. MAUET, PRETRIAL (7th ed. 2008).

27. FED. R. CIV. P. 33(d).

28. FED. R. CIV. P. 33(a)(1) (leave to serve additional interrogatories shall be granted to the extent consistent with the principles of FRCP 26(b)(2)'s limitations on discovery).

29. FED. R. CIV. P. 33(a) advisory committee's note (1993).

30. *See* Timothy C. Kienk, *Using and Abusing Interrogatories*, 11 LITI-GATION 25 (Winter 1985).

31. FED. R. CIV. P. 34(c) ("As provided in Rule 45, a nonparty may be compelled to produce documents and tangible things or to permit an inspection" with or without testimony). Rule 45 can also be used to obtain documents from experts who are considered to be nonparties.

32. *See* FED. R. CIV. P. 34(b). *See also* FED. R. CIV. P. 26(f) advisory committee's note (2006).

33. See "Obtaining Documents for Use at a Deposition" in Chapter 12. In the case of a nonparty, a subpoena can be used to secure documents without the necessity of a witness testifying.

34. See Chapter 3, discussing the presumptive limitations on the number of depositions per side, the number of depositions per person, and the length of a deposition.

35. See "Depositions on Written Questions" in Chapter 3.

36. FED. R. CIV. P. 36(a)(1).

37. FED. R. CIV. P. 36(a) ("The answering party may assert lack of knowledge or information as a reason for failing to admit or deny only if the party states that it has made reasonable inquiry and that the information it knows or can readily obtain is insufficient to enable it to admit or deny.").

38. See Chapter 13, discussing how to lay a foundation for a document's admissibility and the advisability of determining at a deposition whether a foundation cannot be laid.

39. *See* FED. R. EVID. 902 (self-authentication).

40. *See also* Edna Selan Epstein, *Rule 36: In Praise of Requests to Admit*, in THE LITIGATION MANUAL: A PRIMER FOR TRIAL LAWYERS 150 (John G. Koetl ed., 3d ed. 1999).

41. The provisions of FRCP 37(a)(5) apply to the award of expenses, including attorney's fees, incurred in relation to this motion, when the responding party fails to admit an FRCP 33 Request for Admission under specified circumstances.

42. FED. R. CIV. P. 35(a)(1).

43. FED. R. CIV. P. 26 advisory committee's note (1983). *See* FED. R. CIV. P. 26(g) advisory committee's note (1983), providing citations to studies of the sources and extent of discovery problems. *See also* PAUL W. GRIMM ET AL., DISCOVERY PROBLEMS AND THEIR SOLUTIONS (2005).

44. As noted in the 1983 advisory committee's note to FRCP 26, "[e]xcessive discovery and evasion or resistance to reasonable discovery requests pose significant problems." *See also* FED. R. CIV. P. 1 (stating that the goal of rules is "just, speedy, and inexpensive determination of every action and proceeding").

45. "The rule simply requires that the attorney make a reasonable inquiry into the factual basis of his response, request, or objection." FED. R. CIV. P. 26(g) advisory committee's notes (1983). FRCP 26(c) (protective orders) provides for the potential of other limitations on discovery. See "Task 11: Consider Whether You Need a Protective Order" in Chapter 4.

46. FED. R. CIV. P. 33(a)(1).

47. FED. R. CIV. P. 30(a)(2)(A), (B).

48. FED. R. CIV. P. 30(d)(1).

49. FED. R. CIV. P. 26(b)(2)(C).

50. FRCP 11 "does not apply to disclosures and discovery requests, responses, objections, and motions under Rules 26 through 37." FED. R. CIV. P. 11(d).

51. FED. R. CIV. P. 26(g) advisory committee's note (1983).

52. A similar certification obligation exists for all initial and pretrial disclosures mandated by FRCP 26(a)(1) and (3). The signature certifies that "to the best of the person's knowledge, information, and belief formed after a reasonable inquiry: with respect to a disclosure, it is complete and correct as of the time it is made. . . ." FED. R. CIV. P. 26(g)(1). If a request, response, or objection is not signed, it will be stricken unless it is signed promptly after the omission is made known, and a party is not obligated to take any action concerning the request, response, or objection until it is signed. FED. R. CIV. P. 26(g)(2).

53. FED. R. CIV. P. 26(g)(1).

54. FED. R. CIV. P. 26(g) advisory committee's note (1983).

55. *Id.*

56. FED. R. CIV. P. 26(g)(3). Unlike the provisions of FRCP 11, the signer's law firm is not subject to sanctions.

57. Sanctions under FRCP 37 do not apply to subpoenas. See "Subpoenas to Nonparties" in Chapter 3, discussing sanctions and subpoenas and the potential for motions relating to FRCP 45 being subject to the sanctions allowed by FRCP 11.

58. FED. R. CIV. P. 45(c)(1).

59. MODEL RULES OF PROF'L CONDUCT R. 4.4 (2008).

60. *See, e.g.,* Ginsberg v. Ginsberg, 443 N.Y.S. 2d 439 (1981) (allowing tort claim when repeated subpoenas were used to harass a spouse and exhaust her financial resources).

61. The limitations apply absent a court order or agreement of the parties. *See, e.g.,* FED. R. CIV. P. 30(a)(2) (limiting number of depositions); FED. R. CIV. P. 33(a) (limiting number of interrogatories), and FED. R. CIV. P. 30(d)(1) (limiting length of a deposition); FED. R. CIV. P. 29 (regarding stipulations).

62. See Chapter 4, discussing legal analysis in the context of an examiner preparing to question a witness.

63. *See, e.g.,* KEVIN O'MALLEY ET AL., FEDERAL JURY PRACTICE AND INSTRUCTIONS (6th ed. Supp. 2009); MANUAL OF MODEL CIVIL JURY INSTRUCTIONS FOR THE DISTRICT COURTS OF THE NINTH CIRCUIT (Ninth Circuit 2007).

64. The Honorable Wayne D. Brazil, *The Adversary Character of Civil Discovery: A Critique and Proposal for Change,* 31 VAND. L. REV. 1295 (1978).

65. *See* Marc B. Victor, *The Proper Use of Decision Analysis to Assist Litigation Strategy,* BUS. LAW., Feb. 1985, at 617 (discussing use of risk assessment).

66. See "Task 11: Consider Whether You Need a Protective Order" in Chapter 4.

67. For this brief analysis, the differences between statements of fact and opinion will not be considered.

68. *See, e.g.,* 2 CAL. JURY INSTRUCTIONS, CIVIL [BAJI] §§ 12.31–12.57 (9th ed. 2002 & Supp. 2004).

69. The Honorable William W. Schwarzer, *Mistakes Lawyers Make in Discovery, in* THE LITIGATION MANUAL: A PRIMER FOR TRIAL LAWYERS 127 (John G. Koetl ed., 3d ed. 1999).

70. Although the defending lawyer will likely have prepared the deposition witness for your questions, the give and take of a deposition means that no prewritten script can be used.

71. *See* Brazil, *supra* note 64.

72. See "Exceptions to the 'Only Once' Rule" in Chapter 3, discussing the use of an FRCP 30(b)(6) notice or FRCP 45 subpoena to an organization.

73. See "Other Issues Arising from Representation of Corporate Employees" in Chapter 6, discussing the propriety of contacting a former employee of an adversary.

74. *See infra* text accompanying note 89, discussing the danger a deposition will memorialize unfavorable testimony that might not have otherwise been available.

75. *See supra* note 7.

76. FED. R. CIV. P. 32(a)(4).

77. FED. R. CIV. P. 32(a)(2).

78. FED. R. CIV. P. 32(a)(2). See Chapter 25, discussing the uses of depositions at trial. If the deposition is anticipated to be used at trial, the nature of the questioning will change, as discussed in Chapter 11.

79. FED. R. CIV. P. 56(f) (if a party is unable to present facts in an affidavit to justify opposition to a motion for summary judgment, the court may order a continuance to allow depositions to be taken).

80. See "Witness's Lack of Recall" in Chapter 11.

81. *See* FED. R. CIV. P. 33(a)(1) (limiting number to "25 written interrogatories, including all discrete subparts"); *see also supra* note 28 and accompanying text.

82. See Chapter 13, discussing how to lay a foundation for a document's admissibility at trial.

83. See "Reasons to Establish a 'Negative Foundation' at a Deposition" in Chapter 13.

84. See Chapter 1, note 2.

85. A noted commentator on litigation practice, James W. McElhaney goes so far as to suggest that in order to get your settlement message to the represented party without improper communication, you ask the party deponent, "Would you rather settle this case without going to trial?" James W. McElhaney, *Discovery Is the Trial*, A.B.A. J., Aug. 2007, at 27.

86. See Chapter 24, discussing summarizing deposition testimony.

87. See Chapter 17, discussing the costs for a video recording combined with a stenographic transcript, and Chapter 18, discussing real-time transcription.

88. The mandatory initial disclosure requirements of FRCP 26(a)(1) require parties to disclose the identity of witnesses "likely to have discoverable information . . . that the disclosing party may use to support its claims or defenses. . . ." *See supra* text accompanying notes 2 and 10. Therefore, attempting to hide friendly nonparty witnesses until trial by not taking their deposition may no longer be an available stratagem. However, even if you need to disclose the identity of a friendly witness, you do not have to initiate a deposition. And even if you do, it is possible that the other side will fail to notice his deposition. *See also supra* text accompanying notes 22 and 23, discussing the duty to supplement and the sanctions for failure to do so.

89. You may want to interview a witness that you believe to be friendly in order to confirm that his testimony will be helpful.

90. On the other hand, unless you are convinced that witness will not be available at trial, you may prefer to depose a hostile witness in order to know what the witness will say.

91. *See McCormick on Evidence* § 65 (6th ed. 2006) (discussing "Dead Man's" Statute, sometimes called Survivors' Evidence Statute, and its variations and exceptions). *But see* FED. R. EVID. 601 (General Rule of Competency, which, except in diversity cases, abandoned the disqualification).

92. See Chapter 19, discussing expert depositions.

CHAPTER 3

Securing the Attendance of the Witness

HENRY L. HECHT

Once you decide to take a deposition, you must secure the witness's attendance. To do that, you must consider the following issues: (1) when formal discovery may be properly commenced in your case; (2) what form of notice is required (that is, deposition notice or subpoena); and (3) whether you want the witness to bring documents to the deposition. These issues are addressed by the Federal Rules of Civil Procedure (FRCP), local rules, and stipulations.

This chapter reviews the FRCP covering the attendance at a deposition of party witnesses and nonparty witnesses. The section entitled "Stipulations" explailns how most provisions of the FRCP relating to depositions may be modified by stipulation. The sections entitled "When Do Depositions Occur?," "How Many Depositions?," and "How Long May the Deposition Last?" describe limits on the timing, number, and length of depositions that apply in the absence of a stipulation or court order. The section entitled "Securing Attendance of the Deposition Witness" reviews the use of notices and subpoenas to secure the attendance of witnesses, including witnesses testifying on behalf of organizations and witnesses both within and outside the United States.[1] The next section,

"Requests for Documents," considers how document requests can be combined with a deposition notice or subpoena. The next section discusses the rules governing depositions before the commencement of an action or a pending appeal. The final section discusses depositions on written questions.

Stipulations

The Federal Rules of Civil Procedure provide a strict framework for deposition practice, yet they also give parties the flexibility to modify this framework in determining the timing, number, and length of depositions as well as the manner of conducting them.[2] In particular, FRCP 29 allows parties to stipulate in writing, unless otherwise directed by the court, that depositions may be taken "before any person, at any time or place, on any notice, and in the manner specified."[3]

Although this flexibility serves many purposes, the 1993 FRCP advisory committee emphasized two. First, stipulations allow counsel to "agree on less expensive and time-consuming methods to obtain information."[4] Second, when a complex case requires more depositions than allowed under the FRCP (as discussed below), or when more time is needed to complete a deposition than allowed, the parties can agree to the additional discovery and avoid the need for a motion to the court.[5] A court order will be needed only if a prior court order in the case already governs the procedure that the parties wish to alter.

Still, stipulations are not always an option. An intransigent adversary or your own tactics may make agreement unlikely. Furthermore, a stipulation may not be sufficient; it will not, for example, guarantee the attendance of a nonparty witness. Therefore, you need to be aware of the general "default" rules governing the timing, number, length, and noticing of depositions; that is, the rules that will govern when there is no stipulation (or in the absence of a court order).

When Do Depositions Occur?

Absent stipulation, local rule, or court order, no formal discovery may begin until a complaint has been filed and the parties have conferred about the discovery plan required by FRCP 26(f).[6] Under this rule, all parties to an action must confer at least twenty-one days before a scheduling conference is held with the court or before an FRCP 16(b) scheduling order is due.[7] When they confer, the parties must develop a discovery plan, including the timing and number of depositions, that will ultimately take the form of an FRCP 16(b) scheduling order. In most instances, the combination of a discovery conference and a scheduling order streamlines discovery and resolves any deposition timing or number issues.

By local rule, some courts permit or require earlier depositions. For example, when local rules require that a motion for class certification be filed shortly after a suit is begun, they typically permit or require early discovery on class certification issues.[8] However, absent agreement between the parties, you cannot take a deposition before you have conferred with all other parties.

As a practical matter, most depositions can be scheduled immediately after the parties confer. A notable exception is the deposition of expert witnesses. Typically, these occur late in the discovery process. The reason: Expert witnesses usually are not deposed until after the parties have made their mandatory disclosures regarding the identity of the expert witnesses expected to testify and the experts have produced their reports under FRCP 26(a)(2).[9] Although parties might disclose this information early in the case, the rules require only that, unless stipulated or ordered by the court, the disclosures must be made "at least 90 days before the date set for trial or for the case to be ready for trial."[10]

Former FRCP 30 placed a "hold" on discovery by a plaintiff. Absent leave of court, a plaintiff could not take a deposition until thirty days after service of the summons and complaint upon any defendant, unless the defendant sought discovery before that date.[11] As amended in 1993, the rules abolished the "priority," or sequence, of discovery. Once the parties have conferred (or commenced discovery by stipulation), formal methods of discovery may be used in any sequence, and the fact that one party has commenced taking depositions does not delay the other party's discovery.[12]

Finally, though most depositions occur while a lawsuit is pending, it is possible to take one before a suit is filed or when a trial court judgment is on appeal (as discussed in the next-to-last section of this chapter).

How Many Depositions?

As noted above, a primary reason both for stipulations and for the requirement to confer is to force parties to decide how many depositions will be taken. In the absence of a written agreement, a local rule, or leave of court, FRCP 30(a)(2)(A) limits the number of depositions to ten per side, even if there are multiple plaintiffs or defendants.[13] But FRCP 30's limitation on the number of depositions can be modified by local rule or court order. Some local rules permit a greater number of depositions,[14] and some district court judges limit the number of depositions more severely than FRCP 30.[15]

In a relatively small case, the ten-deposition limit may pose no problem. In a complex or multiparty case, however, the presumptive limit may be unrealistic. These types of cases (for example, financial fraud, class action, or product liability) often require dozens of depositions. And a large patent case may require ten depositions just to determine when an invention was conceived and reduced to practice.

In multiparty cases, you first should confer with all the parties on your side to agree on which depositions are needed most. Then you need to confer with the other parties. If you disagree, you might try to resolve this issue by limiting the total number of hours, rather than the total number of witnesses.[16] Ultimately, of course, if the parties cannot resolve the dispute, the court will. In some situations, you may want to ask the court at the FRCP 16 scheduling conference for a number of supplemental depositions to be taken by a particular party.[17]

Importance of Estimating Early

As soon as possible, estimate the number of depositions you expect to take, and then seek the written consent of the parties or ask for leave of court for depositions in excess of the presumptive limit of ten. Estimating the number of depositions, of course, can be difficult. For one thing, your opponent may be less than candid about identifying anticipated witnesses, and courts normally do not demand lists of probable deponents other than the identity of experts.[18]

Here is a good example of the problem of estimating the number of depositions you need to take: Plaintiffs' lawyers plan to depose a "whistleblower" witness unknown to defendants. The lawyers want to avoid revealing the name of the witness. They claim they have no obligation to do so because they did not know early in the case that the witness would be relevant and are excused from disclosure under FRCP 26(a)(1). Defendants, therefore, will not have included this particular deposition in their discovery plan. Confronted with this situation, in addition to relying on the mandatory disclosures required under FRCP 26(a)(1)(A), defendants' counsel should serve interrogatories early in the discovery period that seek to identify persons with knowledge of specific facts or contentions.

Another example of the problem of estimating the number of depositions: Your opponent tries to "bury" the identity of key witnesses in an overbroad list of "individual[s] likely to have discoverable information" disclosed under FRCP 26(a)(1)(A) and provides only a bland or incomplete recitation of what the witnesses may know. Because these disclosures do not fall under any requirement to confer (since they occur after an FRCP 26(f) meeting of parties), consider asking for greater specificity in the identification of witnesses at the time of the FRCP 16(b) scheduling conference. Doing so will help you avoid the possibility of a "surprise" witness.

Allowing for "Surprise" Witnesses

FRCP 30's limitation of ten depositions per side has ongoing, practical consequences as a case proceeds. Subsequent discovery may uncover additional, unanticipated witnesses to be deposed. Therefore, it may be prudent not to use all ten depositions at the outset. (As suggested above, the early use of interrogatories helps avoid "surprise" witnesses in many situations.) Sometimes, for example, a lawyer forgets to depose a witness (especially a third-party witness) to authenticate a key document, and a court then grants summary judgment at least partly because the lawyer cannot overcome a hearsay objection to the document.[19] The moral: Given the ten-deposition limit, be sure to take into account depositions needed to cure evidentiary objections.

Corporate Depositions

In response to a notice under FRCP 30(b)(6) (as discussed in the next section of this chapter), a corporation or other entity may designate more than one witness to testify on its behalf. But this designation will not necessarily affect the ten-deposition limit. The advisory committee's note to FRCP 30 indicates that an FRCP 30(b)(6) deposition should be treated as a single deposition for purposes of the limit, even if more than one witness is designated to testify.[20] But be aware that some courts may take a different approach.

Exceptions to the "Only Once" Rule

Absent written stipulation, local rule, or court order, a witness may be deposed only once under FRCP 30(a)(2)(A)(ii).[21] There are, however, three common exceptions to this rule.

The first is when a trial is bifurcated on separate issues, such as liability and damages. As long as the discovery is bifurcated as well, a person deposed once on issues relating to liability often can be deposed again on issues relating to damages.[22]

The second exception involves the question of whether the same witness may be deposed more than once in different capacities. For instance, suppose you deposed a witness pursuant to an individual notice. If an organization later designates the same witness to testify pursuant to an FRCP 30(b)(6) notice, can you depose the witness a second time? Or suppose you deposed a witness as an organization's designee under FRCP 30(b)(6). Can you depose the same witness a second time as an individual percipient-fact witness?

In either case, you should be able to take the second deposition without running afoul of the "only once" rule because the organization is responsible for the FRCP 30(b)(6) designation.[23] But you should be prepared for the organization to seek a protective order on the grounds that a second deposition of the same individual would be cumulative and burdensome. The organization's motion might be bolstered by the fact that at the first deposition, you were presumably free to cover a range of topics, not just those specified in the FRCP 30(b)(6) notice. And the organization might cite cases overruling objections that claimed that deposition questions exceeded the noticed scope of the examination.[24]

In practice, lawyers rarely treat an FRCP 30(b)(6) deposition as the only opportunity to depose a particular witness. Indeed, a second deposition may well be necessary because, as often happens during the FRCP 30(b)(6) deposition, you discover that the witness has relevant testimony on topics other than those delineated in the scope of the FRCP 30(b)(6) notice. In addition, FRCP 30(b)(6) itself seems to anticipate a second deposition. Although the rule states that a corporation "may set out the matters on which each person designated will testify," it does not state that these are the *only* topics on which the witness may testify or the only occasion when the witness may testify. Moreover, FRCP 30(b)(6) provides that it does not preclude taking a deposition by any other procedure authorized in the rules.

The third, final exception to the "only once" rule is when a witness is deposed before document discovery is completed and key documents are later produced that were unavailable for use at the witness's first deposition. This often happens because FRCP

26(a)(1)(B), requiring initial disclosure without a formal demand, permits a party to provide merely a "description by category and location" of relevant documents, and then only concerning those "things that the disclosing party has in its possession, custody, or control and may use to support its claims or defenses."[25]

How Long May the Deposition Last?

Prior to the 2000 amendments to the FRCP, it was common to notice a deposition "to continue from day-to-day until completed" without reference to any time limitations. The 2000 amendments, however, limited each deposition to one day of seven hours unless otherwise stipulated or ordered by the court.[26] Thus, the default is a deposition of one day, though the FRCP recognized that "[t] he court must allow additional time consistent with Rule 26(b)(2) if needed to fairly examine the deponent or if the deponent, another person, or any other circumstance impedes or delays the examination."[27] With respect to the all-important depositions of witnesses designated to testify on behalf of organizations under FRCP 30(b)(6), the 2000 advisory committee noted that "[f]or purposes of this durational limit, the deposition of each person designated under Rule 30(b)(6) should be considered a separate deposition."[28]

The seven-hour limit raises questions in at least two special situations. First, does the seven-hour time limit for an individual witness, who is noticed under FRCP 30(b)(1) and also produced as a corporate representative under FRCP 30(b)(6), apply cumulatively? In *Sabre v. First Dominion Capital*,[29] a federal district court concluded that such depositions are "presumptively subject to independent seven-hour time limits." Second, does the seven-hour time limit apply to a witness deposed in consolidated cases? In one such case, *Miller v. Waseca Medical Center*,[30] the district court found the decision depended on a showing of need. One plaintiff had filed separate actions against the same defendants, and the court consolidated the cases when the defendants sought two separate depositions of the plaintiff. The court found that the mere fact that the lawsuits might have proceeded separately did not entitle the defendants to depose the plaintiff for fourteen hours. The court also found that the consolidation did not mean that plaintiff's deposition could last more than seven hours. But, based on facts established by defendants, the court found that the need for additional time had been "amply demonstrated."

Securing Attendance of the Deposition Witness

Notice to Parties

The attendance of a deposition witness is secured either by notice or by subpoena, depending on whether the witness is a party or non-party.[31] Any party, including a party's officers, directors, and managing agents, may be required to appear at a deposition by notice alone.[32] Questions often arise concerning whether a witness is an "officer" or a "managing agent" of a party. Courts answer this question pragmatically based on the facts.[33] Among the facts courts consider are (1) whether the interests of the witness and the organization are aligned, and (2) the nature of the witness's functions, responsibilities, and authority regarding the subject matter of the lawsuit.[34]

Location of the Deposition

The notice may require a party to appear at a deposition in any "reasonable place." During the discovery conference required by FRCP 26(f), you should try to reach agreement on the location for anticipated depositions. Absent agreement, the party issuing the notice chooses the location by designating it in the notice. If your opponent objects, she can move for a protective order under FRCP 26(c).

Whether a deposition location is proper is in the discretion of the court, and each case is decided on its "own facts and equities."[35] Nevertheless, some general guidelines have emerged. First, an individual defendant usually should be deposed in the district of his residence.[36] Second, a plaintiff generally should be deposed in the forum where he filed suit.[37] Third, the depositions of corporate officers usually should occur in the district where the corporation has its principal place of business.[38] Finally, party deponents must pay their own travel costs to the deposition location.

These guidelines are flexible, however, and courts permit exceptions. In deciding whether to depart from the guidelines, courts consider many factors, including (1) which party is best able to pay for transportation; (2) the location of documents needed for the deposition; (3) the convenience of the deponent, parties, and counsel; (4) the location of physical evidence; (5) the location of prior depositions; and (6) which court is best able to supervise the deposition.[39] One federal district court,[40] for example, required two officers of a defendant corporation to appear in Chicago even though the corporation's principal place of business was Toronto. The court based its decision on the following facts: (1) the lawyers for the parties were located in Chicago, (2) the corporation had considerable business interests in Chicago, and (3) the corporation was able to bear travel costs better than the plaintiff.[41]

Contents and Timing of the Notice

The notice must include (1) the time and place for taking the deposition, (2) the name and address of each person to be examined, if known, and (3) the manner in which the deposition will be recorded.[42] If the name or address of the witness is not known, then the notice should include a general description "sufficient to identify the person or the particular class or group to which the person belongs."[43] A notice, for instance, that named "the Captain" of a specific vessel was found to be a sufficient identification.[44] But a notice that named a certain officer "and perhaps others" was insufficient for any officers other than the named one.[45]

As for timing, the Rules do not specify how many days before a deposition the notice must be received by the party witness and each other party; they state only that reasonable written notice is required.[46] What qualifies as "reasonable written notice" varies from case to case. In one case, two days' notice was held insufficient for the deposition of a third-party witness, even though opposing counsel could have attended the deposition. The court reasoned that the defender deserved time to clear his schedule and prepare for the deposition.[47] In another case, six days' notice was found to be reasonable, largely because the opposing party did not explain why more time was needed.[48]

The Fourteen-Day Notice Guideline

There are two reasons why—whenever possible—you should give at least fourteen days' notice.

First, FRCP 32(a) provides that any party receiving less than fourteen days' notice may prevent that deposition from being used against it if (1) the objecting party filed a motion for a protective order requesting that the deposition not be held or be held at a different time or place; (2) the motion was pending at the time the deposition was scheduled; and (3) the deposition nevertheless took place. Any party can file this motion even a party that will not give the deposition testimony. As a practical matter, therefore, any short-term benefit gained from minimal notice may be more than offset by a long-term cost; that is, the inability to use the deposition at trial against the party that moved for the protective order.

43

Second, although there is no relevant 2009 Advisory Committee Note for guidance, the 1993 Advisory Committee Note to prior Rule 32(a), which addressed the previous eleven-day guide, is instructive. The 1993 Advisory Committee Note suggests that when less than eleven days' notice is provided, a pending motion for a protective order constitutes "just cause" excusing a witness's failure to appear.[49] In other words, if you provide only minimal notice, you run the risk that the witness may not show up at the deposition. (The nonappearing party nevertheless risks FRCP 37(d) sanctions. And, notwithstanding the Advisory Committee's suggestion, a court may not look kindly on the nonappearing party's self-help.) To further complicate the analysis, the 1993 Advisory Committee Notes point out that "[i]nclusion of this provision is not intended to signify that 11 days' notice is the minimum advanced notice for all depositions or that greater than 10 days should necessarily be deemed sufficient in all situations."[50]

Serving the Notice

Written notice of the deposition must be served not only upon a party witness but also upon every party to the action. The notice must be signed (or signed promptly after an omission of signature is called to the attention of the party requesting the deposition). Until the notice is properly signed, the responding party is not obligated to take action.[51] The failure to sign and the resulting sanction can be significant if the noticing party is facing a discovery cutoff and therefore cannot serve a new, timely notice.

Notice must be served upon a party witness's lawyers unless a court orders service upon the party itself. Service is accomplished by delivering a copy to the lawyer (or to the party, if appropriate) or by mailing it to that person's last known address. If no address is known, then under FRCP 5(b)(2)(D) service can be made by leaving the notice with the clerk or other person in charge. Service by delivery is complete upon (1) handing the notice to the lawyer or party; (2) leaving it at the lawyer's or party's office with a clerk or in a conspicuous place; or (3) leaving it at the person's dwelling with someone of suitable age and discretion, if that office is closed or there is no office.[52] Service by mail is complete upon mailing.[53]

Subpoenas to Nonparties

The attendance of a nonparty witness is secured by subpoena.[54] Lawyers may obtain signed but otherwise blank subpoenas from the court clerk. As an officer of the court, the lawyer issues the subpoena on behalf of the court for the district in which the deposition will occur.[55] As the 1991 Advisory Committee Notes points out, "Any attorney permitted to represent a client in a federal court, even one admitted *pro hac vice*, has the same authority as a clerk to issue a subpoena from any federal court for the district in which the subpoena is served and enforced."[56] Through proper service of a subpoena, personal jurisdiction may be obtained over a witness who resides in any federal jurisdiction.

Location of Deposition

FRCP 45 limits the place of attendance for a nonparty deposition. The subpoena may require a witness to appear at a location up to one hundred miles from the witness's residence, place of employment, or place where the witness "regularly transacts business in person."[57] A subpoena requiring more than one hundred miles of travel can be quashed or modified and cannot be the basis for a contempt sanction for noncompliance.[58] Furthermore, a subpoena generally must be served within the district of the issuing court or within one hundred miles of the place of the deposition.[59]

If a dispute arises about compliance with a subpoena, courts require the parties to confer.[60] Initially, FRCP 45(c)(1) requires the party who issues the subpoena to "take reasonable steps to avoid imposing undue burden or expense" on the witness to be deposed. Once a defect is brought to the attention of the party issuing the subpoena, the party should correct the defect. If the party fails to do so and a motion to quash is filed, the issuing party risks monetary sanctions under FRCP 45(c)(1) and 45(c)(3).[61]

Failure to Obey a Subpoena

Although FRCP 45(e) provides that a party's unexcused failure to obey a subpoena may be contempt of court, the 1991 Advisory Committee Note states that "[b]ecause the command of the subpoena is not in fact one uttered by a judicial officer, contempt should be very sparingly applied when the nonparty witness has been overborne by a party or attorney." Considering the less drastic (and previously mentioned) methods for resolving subpoena disputes, a court will rarely hold a witness in contempt for failure to comply with a deposition subpoena.

Designating the Proper Court

When filling out the subpoena form, be sure to correctly designate the issuing court. In one case,[62] the issuing lawyer wanted

45

to depose a witness in a lawsuit filed in the Southern District of Georgia. Because the deposition was to take place in Pennsylvania, the subpoena should have been issued from the Eastern District of Pennsylvania. But the lawyer incorrectly filled out the form to issue from the Georgia court.[63] The witness did not appear for the deposition, and the issuing lawyer moved to enforce the subpoena and hold the witness in contempt. The witness did not claim that he was unable to appear or that appearing would have been unduly burdensome. Instead, pointing to the incorrect designation of the issuing court, he argued that the subpoena was a nullity. The Pennsylvania District Court agreed, holding that it lacked jurisdiction to enforce a subpoena issued from the wrong court.[64]

Reasonable Time for Compliance

The subpoena must give the witness "reasonable time to comply."[65] There is no standard for what constitutes reasonable time; instead, what is reasonable varies with the facts. At a minimum, the witness should be given adequate time to adjust his schedule and appear or file a formal objection to the subpoena before the date set for compliance. In one case,[66] when no discovery deadline had been set and there was no need for urgency, the court invalidated a subpoena that gave only a week's notice.

In determining what constitutes reasonable notice, always remember that inadequate notice carries an added risk: FRCP 45 allows a witness to recover lost earnings and reasonable attorney's fees if the lawyer issuing the subpoena has not taken reasonable steps to avoid imposing an undue burden or expense on the witness.[67]

Finally, do not forget about other parties: The party issuing the subpoena must give reasonable written notice of the deposition to every other party.[68] Reasonable notice, as discussed above, may mean notice of at least fourteen days. If less than fourteen days' notice is given, an objecting party may be able to prevent the nonparty witness's deposition testimony from being used against it at trial.[69]

At least one federal district court has laid down a practical rule for ensuring that the scheduling of a nonparty witness's deposition will not raise a conflict between the parties. The court granted the plaintiff a protective order to stay the deposition of a nonparty witness because defendant's counsel had scheduled the deposition for a date inconvenient to plaintiff's counsel.[70] After granting the motion, the court instructed that as a matter of professional courtesy and to avoid conflict, counsel for both sides should place a joint telephone call to the nonparty witness to schedule the deposition; and if the witness refuses to cooperate, counsel should jointly agree on a deposition date before the noticing party issues the subpoena.[71] Although this procedure is not required by every court, following it will avoid many unnecessary discovery battles.

Serving the Subpoena

Unlike a notice, a subpoena usually must be personally served on the person named.[72] FRCP 45(b)(1) requires service be made by "delivering a copy to the named person." Most federal courts have construed this requirement literally: The subpoena cannot just be left at the person's home or with the person's lawyer.[73] The subpoena may be served by any person who is not a party and is at least eighteen years old.[74]

Some federal district courts have departed from this traditional, personal-service requirement and approved the service of a subpoena by mail.[75] Noting that FRCP 45(b)(1) does not expressly require in-hand, personal service, one court concluded that delivery by certified mail was sufficient, provided the mail carrier was a nonparty and at least eighteen years old. It remains to be seen whether this interpretation of FRCP 45(b)(1) will be followed; in the meantime, personal service is the prudent method.

When the subpoena is served, fees for one day's attendance and mileage, set by statute, must be given to the witness.[76] A subpoena served without the attendance and mileage fees can be ignored.[77]

Failure of Noticing Party or Witness to Attend

Carefully calendar each deposition you schedule by notice or subpoena. FRCP 30(g)(1) provides for sanctions if the party noticing the deposition fails to attend. And FRCP 30(g)(2) provides for sanctions if the party noticing a deposition fails to serve a subpoena upon the witness, and, because of such failure, the witness does not attend. In both instances, the court may order the noticing party to pay, to each party attending, the reasonable expenses incurred in attending by these parties and their lawyers, including attorney's fees.

Securing the Attendance of a Corporate Witness: FRCP 30(b)(6)

Discoverable testimony often resides within a corporation or other organization. Because corporations and other organizations only speak through living persons, to learn what an organization knows, you must depose the officers, managing agents, or employees. And you must know the rules for deposing such representatives.

Pre-1970 Procedure

Before 1970, the procedure for taking the deposition of an organization was to name a specific official to be deposed on behalf of the organization.[78] This procedure, however, had several disadvantages for both the noticing party and the responding organization. First, it was often difficult for a noticing party to determine who was a "managing agent" who could speak on behalf of the organization.[79] Second, the noticing party often faced a situation in which each person designated by the responding organization would disclaim knowledge of facts and claim that someone else in the organization was the proper person to depose.[80] Third, because the noticing party frequently did not identify the correct officer, the organization could be burdened by unnecessary and unproductive depositions.[81]

How FRCP 30(b)(6) Works

To eliminate these problems, FRCP 30(b)(6) was added in 1970. It provides an optional discovery device to supplement the existing practice of notice or subpoena to an officer, director, or managing agent under FRCP 30(b)(1).[82] Under FRCP 30(b)(6), you name the entity you want to depose.[83] Then, you describe with "reasonable particularity" the matters on which examination is requested, but you do not specify any particular person as a witness. After being served, the organization must designate an individual or individuals to testify on its behalf. If the organization designates more than one person, it may set forth the matters on which each person will testify.[84] The organization must ensure that each person it designates is adequately prepared to testify about all matters "known or reasonably available to the organization" that relate to the examination.[85]

FRCP 30(b)(6) can be much more effective than serving a notice on a named individual. Suppose you want to obtain testimony about a large corporation's accounting practices, and you notice the deposition of a specific named individual in the accounting department who you think has the information. Naming the witness, however, may not work for one or more reasons.

First, you may guess wrong, and the witness named in your notice may show up at the deposition only to inform you that the person you really need to examine is someone else in his department. Second, you may obtain relevant testimony from the named witness, but then realize that this testimony is not sufficient. Third, you may discover during the deposition that the named witness, although possessing relevant information, does not qualify as an officer, director, or managing agent, so the testimony cannot be used against the corporation at trial.[86] In all of these situations, you will be forced to notice more depositions. Not only will the additional depositions cost more money, but they also may cause problems under FRCP 30's ten-deposition limit.

By proceeding under FRCP 30(b)(6), you avoid all these risks. Your notice to the corporation specifies that you want to obtain testimony about its accounting practices and describes with reasonable particularity the scope of the examination. The notice might even describe the exact accounting practices, transactions, or time periods on which the examination will focus. Then you sit back and wait for the corporation to designate one or more witnesses to testify on its behalf. As discussed above, no matter how many witnesses the corporation designates, depositions noticed under FRCP 30(b)(6) usually count as only one deposition for purposes of the ten-deposition limit. Furthermore, regardless of a witness's title or authority, under FRCP 32(a)(3), the testimony of a witness designated under FRCP 30(b)(6) is treated as that of an adverse party and, therefore, can be used by you at trial for any purpose.

Problems with FRCP 30(b)(6)

Lower-Level and Former Employees

But FRCP 30(b)(6) is not problem-free. Recall that the organization chooses whom to designate to satisfy an FRCP 30(b)(6) request; indeed, an FRCP 30(b)(6) notice or subpoena naming a person as a witness is improper.[87] Typically, an organization designates an officer, a director, or a managing agent. It might also choose to designate a lower-level or former employee, but it is not obligated to do so—even if that person is the one most knowledgeable about the relevant subject matter.[88] In fact, before the organization may designate a lower-level or former employee, it must obtain that individual's consent. However, the organization may be reluctant to seek consent because once the consent is obtained and the individual designated, the organization waives its right to treat the witness as a nonparty witness.[89] In addition, the would-be witness may be reluctant to consent because by doing so she waives the right to be called by subpoena rather than by notice. If attendance is secured by notice, the witness cannot collect attendance and mileage fees, and the witness is not protected by the one-hundred-mile geographical limit.[90]

Because an organization is not obligated to designate a lower-level or former employee, do not rely on an FRCP 30(b)(6) notice to obtain testimony from these individuals. If you want to take the deposition of such a person, subpoena that person directly in his individual capacity.

Witnesses Without Adequate Knowledge

Another problem with FRCP 30(b)(6) is that it does not require the organization to designate the "best witness" or the one most knowledgeable about the subject matter of the examination.[91] But the witness whom the organization designates must be prepared to give "complete, knowledgeable, and binding answers,"[92] which must reflect "the information the deposed party possesses, after due inquiry."[93] If the designated witness cannot adequately respond to questions, the organization must immediately designate another witness or properly prepare the original witness.[94]

Scope of Investigation Required of the Responding Organization

Some lawyers have interpreted an FRCP 30(b)(6) notice as imposing broad obligations on the responding party to conduct an investigation into a particular subject matter. There are practical difficulties with this view. In many cases, important witnesses are no longer employed by the organization and thus not within its control. In such circumstances, courts may not impose a burden on the company to contact and interview such persons. Moreover, if a corporation claims not to have an "officer, director, or managing agent" who is knowledgeable on the subject, or claims that relevant facts are not "reasonably available," an order compelling the corporation to conduct an investigation may be difficult to obtain.

Nevertheless, a corporation should be careful when claiming ignorance about a particular subject matter specified in an FRCP 30(b)(6) notice. Such a claim may result in an order precluding the corporation from later offering exculpatory testimony that was "reasonably available" [95] to it at the time of the deposition, either as a sanction under FRCP 37(a)(2) and 37(b)(2) or in response to a motion *in limine* at the time of trial.

Defining the Examination's Scope and Anticipating Objections

As with many discovery requests, the effectiveness of FRCP 30(b)(6) depends not only on the responding party's good faith, but also on the noticing party's ability to craft the scope of the notice or subpoena. As noted above, the rule requires the noticing party to describe with "reasonable particularity" the matters on which examination is requested. The "reasonable particularity" standard suggests that you can provide a less than precise definition, but when you draft a Rule 30(b)(6) notice, disclose the scope of examination with as much clarity and specificity as possible. If you do not, you are likely to get only general testimony—which may not be useful—together with objections to the overbroad scope of the noticed subject matter. In addition, broad examination topics give an organization an excuse for producing an inappropriate witness.

Consider, for example, a suit by XYZ Corporation claiming damages for lost profits. If you serve a deposition notice using a broad, generic subject matter description such as "facts supporting XYZ Corporation's damages theories," the corporation may object because (1) the notice prematurely calls for expert opinion testimony, and (2) the information sought is known only to the noticing party. A more effective request might be drafted as follows: "All facts showing how XYZ Corporation computed pretax profit on the sale of widgets during the period from three years ago to one year ago," or "All facts indicating all sales allegedly lost by XYZ Corporation to ABC Corporation during the period from three years ago to one year ago."

But just as an overly broad request can be a problem, so can an overly specific one. Such a notice may unintentionally limit an organization's responsibility to prepare a witness fully. Consider the request in the previous paragraph for "all facts showing how XYZ Corporation computed pretax profit on the sale of widgets during the period from three years ago to one year ago." Suppose XYZ Corporation does not have an officer, a director, or a managing agent familiar with the details of how XYZ's profits were, or are, computed for widgets. Or suppose XYZ did not during the relevant time period, and does not now, compute such profits. In that case, XYZ may simply produce a witness who will testify that XYZ does not compute profits on the sale of widgets—and say nothing more. Obviously, this testimony will not be helpful. You might have avoided this problem by making the request more general; for example, by excluding the phrase "on the sale of widgets" from the original notice.

Though an organization is obligated to provide a witness who is prepared to answer questions regarding only those matters described in the FRCP 30(b)(6) notice, you may want to ask the designated witness questions beyond the matters described in the notice. Even if your questioning exceeds the scope of the notice, opposing counsel should not have any basis for objecting. As a Florida district court explained,[96] FRCP 30(b)(6) does not limit what can be asked of a designated representative at a deposition. The rule, the court pointed out, is a rule of specification, not limitation. Therefore, the court noted, if the examining party asks questions outside the scope of the notice, general deposition rules apply and the witness is entitled to no special protection just because the deposition was noticed under FRCP 30(b)(6).

But as a practical matter, having the right to ask questions about a broad subject area may not yield the desired result. Suppose an officer is designated by an organization to testify about its accounting practices. You may also ask her questions about manufacturing or marketing. But because she is required to be prepared to testify only about accounting practices, she is not required to answer questions about other topics unless she has personal knowledge of them. Depending on her title and authority, her testimony about these other topics may not qualify as being "on behalf" of the corporation; in that case, it will not automatically be admitted into evidence at trial under FRCP 32(a)(2).[97]

As discussed above, questioning beyond the scope of the notice also may trigger disputes about whether the FRCP 30(b)(6) deposition now counts as two depositions toward the ten-deposition limit, and whether the examining lawyer should be precluded from re-noticing the deposition of the designated witness in an individual capacity in violation of the "only once" rule.[98] Be forewarned: if you ask extensive questions beyond the scope of the specified topics in an FRCP 30(b)(6) notice, some courts will prohibit a second deposition.[99]

Even though lawyers should not object to questions beyond the scope of the notice, they frequently do.[100] To avoid these disruptive objections to your questions, consider including general topics in the notice, supplemented by more specific subtopics.[101] That way, if your examination strays beyond any noticed subtopic, you can respond to an objection that the question is beyond the scope of the notice by pointing to the more general topic designated in the notice. As noted above, however, the broader the topic, the more objectionable it may be, and your opponent may object that the witness is being offered to testify only about the more specific subtopics. Your opponent may also object that the witness is not qualified to testify on other general subjects and, for each such topic, is not testifying "on behalf" of the corporation. On that basis, your opponent may argue that the testimony is inadmissible against the corporation.

To prevent such objections, you can "double notice" the deposition. Here is how this tactic works: Once you learn that a certain witness has been designated to represent the organization at an FRCP 30(b)(6) deposition, you send that person a second notice or subpoena—for the same date and time—naming the witness in his or her individual capacity.[102] Then, if your opponent objects that the examination is moving beyond the scope of the original FRCP 30(b)(6) notice, you can rely on the second individual notice, leaving it for the court to decide later which portions of the testimony have been given on behalf of the organization (and are thus admissible under FRCP 32(a)(2)). Note, however, that by "double noticing" you may be charged with two depositions toward the ten-deposition limit.

In sum, the FRCP give you two options for obtaining testimony from an organizational witness: (1) FRCP 30(b)(6) (notice directed to the organization), and (2) FRCP 30(b)(1) (notice to a named officer, director, or managing agent).[103] In either case, make clear in the notice or subpoena whether you are relying upon FRCP 30(b)(6) or FRCP 30(b)(1), so that both you and your opponent understand what will constitute a proper response.[104] Furthermore, clearly state in the notice that the witness is being summoned to testify in a representative capacity. Then, whichever option you choose, the testimony will be "on behalf of" the organization and available to be used at trial for any purpose.[105]

Deposing a Chief Executive Officer (CEO)

As discussed in the preceding chapter in the context of discovery planning, the Federal Rules of Civil Procedure were amended in

1983 to impose an affirmative duty on parties to use pretrial discovery in "a responsible manner that is consistent with the spirit and purposes of Rules 26 through 37."[106] The 1983 Advisory Committee Note adds that the certification requirement of FRCP 26(g) obliges each lawyer "to stop and think about the legitimacy of a discovery request."

Given that obligation, it may be improper to notice the deposition of a corporation's CEO—particularly the CEO of a large corporation. In the past, lawyers frequently attempted to depose CEOs, even when lower-level corporate agents could provide adequate testimony. One reason for noticing the deposition of a CEO—even one lacking firsthand knowledge of the case—was to harass the corporation and its officers as well as to force a settlement.

Since 1983, however, FRCP 26(g) has required the court to limit discovery of a CEO if it determines, among other findings, that the discovery sought can be obtained from another source that is more convenient, less burdensome, or less expensive.[107] Thus, when the deposition of the CEO is noticed today, the corporation's lawyer often can make a persuasive motion for a protective order. When considering such a motion, some courts have required that other discovery proceed first so that the need for the CEO's testimony can be reevaluated after preliminary discovery.[108] Similarly, some courts have required that written interrogatories precede any deposition of a CEO.[109] Similar limitations apply to the depositions of high-ranking government officials.[110]

Although a corporation's lawyers will usually want to prevent a CEO from being deposed, that is not always the case. Having a CEO testify at trial can humanize a large corporation for a jury. If, in response to a deposition notice, you have argued that the CEO is either too important or too busy to be bothered with a deposition, at trial, the CEO may face a difficult cross-examination about her earlier refusal to be deposed. Therefore, in appropriate cases, you may want to allow the CEO to be deposed even though you might have prevailed on a motion for a protective order.

Witnesses Outside the United States

Depositions of witnesses outside the United States pose unique problems.[111] A federal statute provides for service of a subpoena outside the United States, but only on a person who is a "national or resident" of the United States and only upon court order.[112] Although used infrequently in civil cases, the subpoena may issue if it is in the interest of justice and if it is impossible to obtain the same testimony in admissible form without the personal appearance of the prospective deponent. When a subpoena does issue, it is backed by contempt punishment under 28 U.S.C. § 1784, which includes *in rem* proceedings against the witness's local property as a means of requiring attendance.

This subpoena must be served in the manner specified for foreign service in FRCP 4(f). Typically, FRCP 4 requires compliance with the manner of service specified in an international agreement, such as the Hague Convention on the Service Abroad of Judicial and Extrajudicial Documents.[113] If no international treaty applies, FRCP 4(f)(2) specifies several alternative methods of service. In any event, the person serving the subpoena must also tender the estimated travel and attendance expenses. [114]

Requests for Documents

Both party witnesses and nonparty witnesses may be required to bring documents or other tangible items to their depositions.[115] FRCP 30(b)(2) provides that the notice of deposition to a party deponent may be accompanied by a request to produce documents, and that the request is governed by the same procedures that generally apply to FRCP 34 document requests. The documents to be produced must be listed individually or by category, and each must be described with reasonable particularity.[116] The request may be made in the body of the notice itself; but if the list of documents is lengthy, it usually is attached to the notice in the form of a separate schedule. If a schedule is used, the notice should state that the documents listed in the schedule must be produced when the witness appears.

A notice that includes a document request should be served on a party deponent at least thirty days before the deposition. The reason: FRCP 34 gives the party upon whom the request is served thirty days to serve written objections.[117] A party who is not given the full thirty days may appear at the deposition without the documents and serve written objections on the noticing party at that time. If such an objection is raised with respect to documents that were to have played a central role in the question, the deposition may have been wasted—and reopening the position after receipt of the desired documents may be difficult.

Because FRCP 30(b)(2) and FRCP 34 provide alternate means for obtaining documents from a party, you must consider the tactical advantages of each. If you wish to examine a deposition witness about many documents, using FRCP 34 may be preferable because the deponent can be required to deliver the requested documents *before* the deposition.[118] On the other hand, if you use FRCP (30)(b)(2)'s procedure, the witness is not required to produce the documents, absent agreement, until the deposition. In that event, having to review voluminous documents for the first time at the start of a deposition may create unnecessary delays—to which the witness may strenuously object—and which may use up valuable time in light of the seven-hour limit.[119]

In deciding whether to use FRCP 34 or FRCP 30(b)(2), you also should consider FRCP 45. Although only a deposition notice can require a party to bring documents to a deposition, an FRCP 45 deposition subpoena can command either a party or a nonparty to bring documents or other tangible items within the witness's possession, custody, or control to deposition.[120] As amended in 1991, FRCP 45 authorizes three different types of subpoenas: (1) a subpoena requiring only testimony, (2) a subpoena requiring both testimony and the production or inspection of documents, and (3) a subpoena requiring only the production or inspection of documents.[121] Thus, an FRCP 45 command to produce documents may be combined with the command to appear at the deposition, or it may be issued separately. A copy of the subpoena's designation of items to be produced must be attached to, or included in, the notice served on every party to the action.[122]

One advantage to using an FRCP 45 subpoena duces tecum (a subpoena requesting both documents and the deponent's appearance) is that it may require less advance notice for a document request than an FRCP 30(b)(2) notice. After being served with a subpoena duces tecum, the person named in the subpoena must object within fourteen days or before the time specified in the subpoena for compliance, whichever is shorter.[123] Hence, by using FRCP 45 to require a person to testify and produce documents at a deposition, you may be able to obtain documents in less than half the thirty days' notice required by FRCP 34, as incorporated in FRCP 30(b)(2).

Using a subpoena duces tecum to secure documents from a party may have advantages over using FRCP 30(b)(2) or FRCP 34; however, there is risk. Some courts will take a dim view of serving a subpoena duces tecum on a party.[124] If, because of an emergency or for other good cause, you need documents from a party in fewer than the thirty days required by FRCP 34, you may want to file an application for an order permitting expedited discovery.

You should also consider the technical distinctions between notice and subpoena. First, a witness objecting to an FRCP 30(b)(2) request for documents must provide a written explanation setting forth the reasons for any objection. In contrast, although FRCP 45 also requires a written objection, it does not require a statement of reasons for the objection unless there is a claim of privilege or work-product protection.[125] Second, an FRCP 30(b)(2) request entitles the noticing party to recover expenses, including reasonable attorney's fees, if it must seek a court order compelling production from a party who unjustifiably refuses to cooperate. FRCP 45, on the other hand, contains no such provision. Finally, if production by a party is commanded by an FRCP 45 subpoena duces tecum rather than by an FRCP 30(b)(2) notice, and if a court order is ultimately required to gain compliance, the order must issue from the court that issued the subpoena.[126] And that court may not be the court in which the action is pending and may, therefore, be an inconvenient forum.

Depositions Before Action or Pending Appeal

Occasionally, depositions may be taken at the extremes in the life of a suit—either before a suit is filed or when a trial court judgment is on appeal. In both situations, depositions are used to preserve testimony that might be lost during an unavoidable lapse of time. For obvious reasons, you cannot schedule these depositions during the FRCP 26(f) scheduling conference. You can, however, use FRCP 27.

Before a Lawsuit Is Filed

Under FRCP 27(a), a party planning to file a suit in federal court can petition for leave to take a prefiling deposition. Generally, the petition is granted only when the suit cannot be filed, and there is a risk that the witness may die, become incompetent, or otherwise be unavailable before a deposition can become taken in the normal course.

This happened in *In re Ernst*.[127] The petitioner wanted to sue the Internal Revenue Service over an estate-tax assessment, but could not do so until a statutory six-month waiting period expired. Because material testimony might have been lost during that waiting period, the court allowed the petitioner to take depositions—before the action was filed—of persons with knowledge about the facts supporting a challenge to the estate-tax assessment.[128]

To take a deposition before filing suit, you must first file a verified petition in the district court of the residence of anyone expected to be a party.[129] Before a court will grant the petition, it must be satisfied that the deposition is necessary to prevent a failure or delay of justice.[130] Some courts have held that the sheer lapse of time is sufficient reason for preserving the testimony.[131] Under this view, a petitioner makes a sufficient showing merely by demonstrating that she is prepared to bring a federally cognizable claim, but is barred from presently doing so. The petitioner need not show that the witness is likely to become unavailable in the interim. The *Ernst* court, which took this view, explained a showing of imminent loss of testimony due to the age, health, or general status of the witness is helpful but not necessary, as "it is common knowledge that the lapse of time is replete with hazards and unexpected events."[132]

Other courts have given less weight to the general risk that testimony might be lost before an action is filed and, therefore, have required the petitioner to show that testimony would be lost for some specific reason, such as the witness's advanced age, serious illness, or threat to leave the country.[133] Because courts differ on the required showing, it is prudent to identify in your petition all the reasons why testimony may be lost.

FRCP 27(a) is intended only to preserve testimony or other evidence that might be lost and not to circumvent FRCP 26, which sets the usual timing for discovery.[134] FRCP 27(a) therefore requires the petition to explain why it is impossible to bring suit now; it is not enough that filing suit may be inconvenient or difficult.[135]

In addition, the petition must include a showing that the petitioner expects to be a party in a federally cognizable action.[136] FRCP 27(a) may not be used solely to determine whether a person has grounds for a lawsuit or to determine against whom the action should be brought.[137] For example, in a case in the District of Columbia, a petitioner wanted to depose her former employer to determine whether she had been unlawfully dismissed. The court denied her petition for a prefiling deposition, pointing out that "[n]othing in the Rule or the cases construing it would lead to the conclusion that a person may require others to submit to depositions in order that such person may ascertain whether, under law, she has a cause of action."[138]

Some courts even require a showing that in the planned lawsuit the expected testimony will be both material and competent in the lawsuit that will be filed.[139] The Ninth Circuit, for example, denied a petition to preserve testimony when the petition failed to set forth the substance of the testimony that the petitioner expected to elicit. The court said that FRCP 27 cannot be used to discover unknown information the petitioner hopes will be useful.[140]

Pending Appeal

FRCP 27(b) allows depositions to be taken after a judgment has been rendered. Why might you need to take a deposition at this point? Because you might need to preserve testimony pending an appeal so it will be available in the event of a remand. Imagine, as just one example, that your case has been dismissed on jurisdictional grounds. While appealing the dismissal, you may want to preserve testimony on the merits of the action that you fear might otherwise be lost during the sometimes lengthy appeal process.[141] FRCP 27(b) is the answer.

To take a deposition pending appeal, a party must make a motion in the district court that rendered the judgment. The motion may be made after an appeal has been taken or before the time in which an appeal can be taken has expired.[142] The motion is noticed and served in the same manner as if the action were still pending in the district court.[143] "The motion must include (1) the name, address, and expected substance of the testimony of each deponent; and (2) the reasons for perpetuating the testimony."[144] The contemplated testimony must be for "use in the event of further proceedings in [the district court]."[145] The petition will be granted if the deposition is necessary to avoid a failure or delay of justice.

Depositions on Written Questions

FRCP 31 provides for taking a deposition upon written questions. This procedure may be used to depose any person, including any party.[146] A deposition on written questions counts against the ten-deposition limit, and, absent a stipulation or court order, the procedure cannot be used to depose a previously deposed person.[147] A nonparty's attendance must be secured by subpoena.[148]

A notice of deposition on written questions must be served upon every party and must include (1) the name and address of the person who is to answer the questions, (2) the name or descriptive title and address of the officer before whom the deposition is to be taken, and (3) a copy of the questions themselves.[149] Within fourteen days after the notice and written questions are served, any party may serve cross-questions upon all other parties. Redirect and recross questions may then be served within respective seven-day intervals.[150]

In addition, the noticing party must deliver the written questions to the officer designated in the notice. The officer will then promptly take the testimony of the witness in the same manner as that provided for the taking of oral depositions in FRCP 30.[151]

Depositions upon written questions are used infrequently. As one commentator has observed, "[w]ritten . . . interrogation is not as an effective method as oral or confrontory interrogation for obtaining discovery, especially when the deponent is an adverse party or hostile witness."[152] Depositions upon written questions are used most often when the witness is friendly, in a foreign country, or expected to respond to questions by asserting a Fifth Amendment or other privilege.[153] The procedure may also be useful when there is a great need to reduce costs or when an examination is expected to cover a very limited scope.[154]

Conclusion

Once the date, time, and location for a deposition are set, you—whether taker or defender—need to prepare. How to prepare is addressed in the next chapter.

Notes

1. This chapter focuses on the requirements of the FRCP and does not address the mechanics of preparing and serving a notice of deposition or subpoena. For a step-by-step guide to preparing and serving a notice or subpoena with a request for production of documents, see Henry L. Hecht, *How to Prepare and Serve a Notice of Deposition or Subpoena in Federal Practice (With Forms)*, *in* 18 PRACT. LITIG. 9 (Nov. 2007).

2. FRCP 29 was revised in 1993 to "give greater opportunity for litigants to agree upon modifications to the procedures governing discovery or to limitations upon discovery." FED. R. CIV. P. 29, advisory committee's note (1993).

3. FED. R. CIV. P. 29. The rule further specifies that depositions taken pursuant to such stipulations "may be used in the same way as any other deposition." *Id.*

4. FED. R. CIV. P. 29, advisory committee's note (1993).

5. *Id.*

6. FED. R. CIV. P. 26(d). FRCP 26(d) makes an exception for the proceedings "exempted from initial disclosure under Rule 26(a)(1)(B)." Additionally, the rules allow a party to take a deposition before the time specified

in FRCP 26(d) without a stipulation or court order when the party certifies in the notice of deposition that the witness is expected to leave the United States and be unavailable for examination in this country. FED. R. CIV. P. 30(a)(2)(C). See also "Creating a Discovery Plan" in Chapter 2.

7. Under FRCP 16(b)(2), a scheduling order must be issued by the court "as soon as practicable, but in any event within the earlier of 120 days after any defendant has been served with the complaint or 90 days after any defendant has appeared."

8. FED. R. CIV. P. 23(c)(1)(a) (certification decisions should be made "at an early practicable time.") See Newton v. Merril Lynch, Pierce, Fenner & Smith, 259 F.3d 154, 166 (3d Cir. 2001) ("[I]t may be necessary for the Court to probe behind the pleadings before coming to rest on the certification question.") (quoting Gen. Tel. Co. of Sw. v. Falcon, 457 U.S. 147, 160 (1982)).

9. FED. R. CIV. P. 26(b)(4)(A). See "Mandatory Disclosure Under FRCP 26" in Chapter 19, discussing expert disclosures.

10. FED. R. CIV. P. 26(a)(2)(C). If the evidence is offered solely to contract or rebut evidence on the same subject by another party, the disclosures by the rebuttal expert must be made within thirty days after the disclosure by the other party. Id.

11. "[I]t is only in the exceptional case . . . that plaintiff will be granted leave of court [to file notice of depositions] within the twenty-day period [from commencement of action as provided by federal rule of civil procedure]." Carribean Constr. Corp. v. Kennedy Van Saum Mfg. & Eng'g Corp., 13 F.R.D. 124 (S.D.N.Y. 1952) (discussing twenty-day hold found in FRCP before 1970). The thirty-day hold introduced in 1970 has given way, as described in the text, to a schedule based on a discovery planning conference by the parties and a court scheduling order. See FED. R. CIV. P. 26(f) and 16(b).

12. FED. R. CIV. P. 26(d)(2).

13. FED. R. CIV. P. 30(a)(2)(A). Both oral and written depositions count equally against this limit. The rule refers to a limit of ten depositions taken "by the plaintiffs, or by the defendants, or by the third-party defendants." The 1993 Advisory Committee Notes say merely that in multiparty cases, the limit is "presumptive" and may be modified to permit additional depositions. See also infra note 23 and accompanying text, discussing FRCP 30(b)(6) depositions.

14. See Bell v. Fowler, 99 F.3d 262, 271 (8th Cir. 1996) (district court did not abuse its discretion in limiting party to twelve depositions); Rosen v. Reckitt & Coleman, Inc., No. 91 Civ. 1675 (LMM), 1994 WL 652534, at *4 (S.D.N.Y. Nov. 17, 1994) (granting defendant 49 depositions in a class-action employment-discrimination suit.

15. In Raniola v. Bratton, 243 F.3d 610 (2d Cir. 2001), the district court limited the plaintiff to three depositions, instead of the presumptive ten, and then further reduced the number to two when defendants failed to

61

produce a subpoenaed witnesses. After reversing on other grounds, the Second Circuit determined that "[t]he record before us does not permit us to rule on [plaintiff's] claim that discovery was impermissibly limited." *Id.* at 628.

16. "Given the national rule, the former authorization for local rules regulating deposition duration was withdrawn." 8A Charles Alan Wright & Arthur R. Miller, Federal Practice and Procedure, Civil § 2104.1 (2d ed. 2009). See also *infra* section entitled "How Long May the Deposition Last?," discussing the presumptive seven-hour limitation under FRCP 30(d)(1).

17. Fed. R. Civ. P. 30(a)(2)(A) advisory committee's note (1993).

18. *See* Fed. R. Civ. P. 26(a)(2)

19. *See, e.g., In re* Seagate II Sec. Litig., No. C-89-2493(A)-URW, 1995 WL 66841 (N.D. Cal. Feb. 8, 1995) (statements in analyst reports and press articles excluded as inadmissible hearsay). See also "Requests for Admissions" in Chapter 2, discussing the use of requests for admissions as one way to lay the foundation for a document's admissibility.

20. Fed. R. Civ. P. 30(a)(2)(A) advisory committee's note (1993).

21. Fed. R. Civ. P. 30(a)(2)(A)(ii). See also "Reopening the Deposition" in Chapter 23.

22. Hall v. Nw. Airlines, No. 03-2004-MLV, 2004 WL 179311, at *2 (W.D. Tenn. Jan. 6, 2004) (permitting witness to be redeposed upon showing of good cause).

23. *See, e.g.,* Williams v. Sprint/United Mgmt, Co., No. 03-2200-JWL, 2006 U.S. Dist. LEXIS 4937, at *1–3 (D. Kan. Feb. 8, 2006). In *Williams*, the court found that although plaintiff had previously deposed a person as defendant's 30(b)(6) witness, plaintiff could redepose that same witness in his individual capacity without first seeking leave under Rule 30(a)(2). *Id.* The court, however, cautioned plaintiff against asking the witness "questions that they had previously asked during his Rule 30(b)(6) deposition in that such questions would be unreasonably duplicative and thus subject to the limitation of Rule 26(b)(2)." *Id.* at *4.

24. *See, e.g.,* Cabot Corp. v. Yamulla Enters., 194 F.R.D. 499, 500 (M.D. Pa. 2000) (holding that in a deposition noticed under Rule 30(b)(6), the scope of discovery is governed by Rule 26(b)(1)); U.S. E.E.O.C. v. Caesars Ent., Inc., 237 F.R.D. 428, 433 (D. Nev. 2006) (FRCP 30(b)(6) does not limit what can be asked of a designated representative at the deposition); see also *infra* notes 88–92 and accompanying text, concerning the scope of questioning in FRCP 30(b)(6) depositions.

25. *See* Fed. R. Civ. P. 30(d)(1) (formerly 30(d)(2)) advisory committee's note (1993) (stating that additional time should be allowed when justified under the principles regarding limitations on frequency and extent of discovery stated in Rule 26(b)(2)).

26. FED. R. CIV. P. 30(d)(1). The 2000 Advisory Committee note to former 30(d)(2), currently 30(d)(1), states that "[t]his limitation contemplates that there will be reasonable breaks during the day for lunch and other reasons, and that the only time to be counted is the time occupied by the actual deposition."

27. *Id.* See also "Task 12: Consider Whether to Seek an Order for the Deposition to Be Extended Beyond the Presumptive Seven-Hour Limitation" in Chapter 4, discussing seeking an extension order and the factors suggested by the Advisory Committee Notes for seeking such an extension.

28. FED. R. CIV. P. 30(d)(1) (formerly 30(d)(2)) advisory committee's note (2000).

29. No. 01CIV2145BSJHBP, 2001 WL 1590544, at *2 (S.D.N.Y. Dec. 12, 2001) (reasoning that if "a person who is both an individual witness and a 30(b)(6) witness were presumptively subject to a single seven-hour deposition there would be substantial potential for over-reaching").

30. 205 F.R.D. 537 (D. Minn. 2002).

31. A sample notice with a request for the production of documents at the deposition is found at Appendix 1. The sample notice reflects extensive revisions to the FRCP Rules 26, 34, and 45, as amended effective December 1, 2006, regarding discovery of electronically stored information. *See also infra* note 54 and accompanying text, discussing subpoenas to nonparties.

32. In some states, notice might also be sufficient to secure the attendance of an employee if the employee is the one most qualified to testify on behalf of the organization regarding a certain matter. *See, e.g.,* CAL. CIV. PROC. CODE § 2025.230 (West 2005) (deponent shall designate and produce at deposition "those of its officers, directors, managing agents, employees, or agents who are *most qualified* to testify on its behalf") (emphasis added).

33. United States v. The Dorothy McAllister, 24 F.R.D. 316, 318 (S.D.N.Y. 1959) (determining that both a chief boatswain's mate alleged to have been master of a tug, as well as a commander of the United States Navy alleged to have been the command duty officer on a warship, were managing agents because the ultimate determination as to whether the party could be bound by their testimony is to be made by the trial court). *See also* United States v. Afram Lines, 159 F.R.D. 408, 413 (S.D.N.Y. 1994) (finding that the examining party satisfies its burden by producing "enough evidence to show that there is at least a close question whether the proposed deponent is the managing agent").

34. Tomingas v. Douglas Aircraft Co., 45 F.R.D. 94, 96 (S.D.N.Y. 1968); *see also The Dorothy McAllister,* 24 F.R.D. at 318. For guidance, counsel may look to decisions under Rule 801(d)(2) of the Federal Rules of Evidence,

addressing admissions of a party, because interpretation of that rule sometimes involves similar issues concerning the authority of an employee to
speak on behalf of the corporation. However, most practitioners would
argue that the status of "managing agent" for purposes of FRCP 30 contemplates a higher level of authority than would necessarily be sufficient
for a witness to qualify under the Federal Rules of Evidence. To determine
whether a witness is a "managing agent," courts look at several factors:
(1) whether the individual is invested with general powers allowing him
to exercise judgment and discretion in corporate matters; (2) whether the
individual can be relied upon to give testimony, at his employer's request,
in response to the demands of the examining party; (3) whether any person
or persons are employed by the corporate employer in positions of higher
authority than the individual designated in the area regarding which the
information is sought by the examination; (4) the general responsibilities
of the individual "respecting the matters involved in the litigation"; and
(5) whether the individual can be expected to identify with the interests of
the corporation. *Id.*

35. *Tomingas*, 45 F.R.D. at 97.

36. Fausto v. Credigy Servs. Corp., 251 F.R.D. 427, 429 (N.D. Cal.
2008).

37. Food Gourmet v. Little Lady Foods, 2007 U.S. Dist. LEXIS 5430,
5 (N.D. Ill. 2007); Dalmady v. Price Waterhouse & Co., 62 F.R.D. 157
(D.C.P.R. 1973).

38. *See* Dwelly v. Yamaha Motor Corp., 214 F.R.D. 537, 541 (D. Minn.
2003) (declining to deviate from the general rule and holding that depositions should be held at corporate headquarters in Japan rather than in
the United States); Moore v. Pyrotech, 137 F.R.D. 356, 357 (D. Kan. 1991)
(ruling that officer of defendant must appear at defendant's principal
place of business in Kansas even though officer resides in Vancouver).

39. Jeffrey S. Kinsler, *The Proper Location of Party-Depositions Under
the Federal Rules of Civil Procedure*, 23 MEM. ST. U. L. REV. 763 (1993).

40. Kasper v. Cooper Canada, Ltd., 120 F.R.D. 58, 59 (ND. Ill. 1988).

41. *Id.* at 59–60. When the corporation's principal place of business
is located in a foreign country, courts may be prone to require corporate officers to travel to the forum because the court would be unable to
supervise depositions adequately in the foreign country. *See, e.g.*, Mill-
Run Tours, Inc. v. Khashoggi, 124 F.R.D. 547, 551 (S.D.N.Y. 1989); *see also*
Kinsler, *supra* note 39, at 767.

42. FED. R. CIV. P. 30(b)(1). *See also* FED. R. CIV. P. 30(b)(3)(A) and
"Virtues of Using Video Pretrial" in Chapter 17.

43. FED. R. CIV. P. 30(b)(1).

44. Shenker v. United States, 25 F.R.D. 96, 98 (E.D.N.Y. 1960).

45. Wagner Mfg. Co. v. Cutler-Hammer, 10 F.R.D. 480 (S.D. Ohio
1950); *see also* Struthers Scientific and Int'l Corp. v. Gen. Foods Corp., 290

F. Supp. 122 (S.D. Tex. 1968) (condemning attempts at "catchall" phrasing in deposition notice).

46. FED. R. CIV. P. 30(b)(1).

47. C & F Packing Co., Inc. v. Doskocil Cos., Inc., 126 F.R.D. 662, 679 (ND. Ill. 1989). *See also* Judicial Watch, Inc. v. U.S. Dep't of Commerce, 34 F. Supp. 2d 47 (D.D.C. 1998) (holding that nonparty deponent was entitled to object to subpoena served only one or two days before her scheduled deposition). The amount of advance time that constitutes reasonable notice may be specified by local court rules. *See, e.g.*, D. Kan. R. 30.1 ("reasonable notice for the taking of depositions shall be five days."). *But see* Vardon Golf Co., Inc. v. Supreme Golf Sales, Inc., 1989 U.S. Dist. LEXIS 13183 (N.D. Ill. 1989) (finding four days' notice unreasonable when the deposition was to be held in a distant location); Harry A. v. Duncan, 223 F.R.D. 536, 538–39 (D. Mont. 2004) (finding two weeks' notice unreasonable for 85 depositions); *In re* Sulfuric Acid Antitrust Litig., 231 F.R.D. 320, 327–28 (N.D. Ill. 2005) (finding ten business days' notice unreasonable when the noticing party waited until the end of the discovery and "even then languished in inaction" after opposing counsel's response to their notice).

48. Pearl v. Keystone Consol. Indus., Inc., 884 F.2d 1047, 1052 (7th Cir. 1989).

49. FED. R. CIV. P. 32(a) advisory committee's note (1993).

50. *Id.*

51. FED. R. CIV. P. 26(g)(2).

52. FED. R. CIV. P. 5(b).

53. FED. R. CIV. P. 5(b)(2)(C). Note that in at least some state jurisdictions, service by mail extends the time for the party receiving the notice to comply or respond. For example, in California state court, service by mail within the state extends the time by five days, while service by mail to an address outside the state extends the time by ten days. CAL. CIV. PROC. CODE § 1013(a) (West 2002).

The FRCP also contemplates delivery by electronic means if the person consented in writing. FED. R. CIV. P. 5(b)(2)(E). If consent is given, then "service is complete upon transmission, but is not effective if the serving party learns that it did not reach the person to be served." *Id.*

54. The form for a subpoena to testify at a deposition and/or produce documents in a civil action in federal court is reproduced in Appendix 2-A. The form for a subpoena to produce documents, information, or objects, or to permit inspection of premises, is reproduced in Appendix 2-B. *See also* Federal Judiciary, Form AO 88A and Form AO 88B, *available at* http://www.uscourts.gov/forms/uscforms.cfm?ShowAll=Yes. Because an expert witness is not a party, an expert's attendance is secured by subpoena unless agreed otherwise. See Chapter 19, discussing securing the attendance of an expert at a deposition.

55. FED. R. CIV. P. 45(a)(3)(B).

56. FED. R. CIV. P. 45 advisory committee's note (1991).

57. FED. R. CIV. P. 45(c)(3)(A)(ii). The one-hundred-mile limit is measured "as the crow flies"; that is, by straight line from point to point. Cook v. Atchison, Topeka & Santa Fe Ry. Co., 816 F. Supp. 667, 669 (D. Kan. 1993); Hill v. Equitable Bank, 115 F.R.D. 184, 186 (D. Del. 1987).

58. FED. R. CIV. P. 45(c)(3)(A)(ii); FED. R. CIV. P. 45(e).

59. FED. R CIV. P. 45(b)(2). For a thorough discussion of the sometimes complicated issue of where to serve a deposition subpoena, see David D. Siegel, *Federal Subpoena Practice Under the New Rule 45 of the Federal Rules of Civil Procedure*, 139 F.R.D. 197 (1992) ("The most demanding questions that arise under [FRCP 45] are those that begin with 'where' or the equivalent.").

60. FED. R. CIV. P. 37(a)(1) ("[A] party may move for an order compelling disclosure or discovery. The motion must include a certification that the movant has in good faith conferred or attempted to confer with the person or party failing to make disclosure or discovery in an effort to obtain it without court action.").

61. The party does not, however, risk FCRP 11 sanctions because that rule does not apply to discovery. FED. R. CIV. P. 11(d) (specifically excluding "disclosures and discovery requests, responses, objections, and motions under Rules 26 through 37" from its reach).

62. Kupritz v. Savannah Coll. of Art & Design, 155 F.R.D. 84 (E.D. Pa. 1994).

63. *Id.* at 86–87.

64. *Id.* at 88.

65. FED. R. CIV. P. 45(c)(3)(A)(i).

66. Mann v. Univ. of Cincinnati, 824 F. Supp. 1 190, 1202 (D. Ohio 1993).

67. FED. R. CIV. P. 45(c)(1).

68. FED. R. CIV. P. 30(b)(1).

69. *See supra* text accompanying notes 48–50.

70. Seabrook Med. Sys., Inc. v. Baxter Healthcare Corp., 164 F.R.D. 232 (S.D. Ohio 1995). *See also* Koninklike Philips Elect. N.V. v. KXD Tech., No. 2:05-cv-1532-RLH-GWF, 2007 WL 311248, at *17 (D. Nev. Oct. 16, 2007) ("The failure to meet and confer in scheduling a deposition, however, is a factor in deciding whether a protective order should be granted.").

71. *Seabrook*, 164 F.R.D. at 233.

72. FED. R. CIV. P. 45(b)(1). Circuits are split on whether service under Rule 5 meets the requirements of Rule 45. *Compare* Harrison v. Prather, 404 F.2d 267, 273 (5th Cir. 1968) (service of subpoena must be on person named therein; service on his attorney is not sufficient) *and* FTC v. Compagnie de Saint-Gobain-Point-A-Mousson, 636 F.2d 1300, 1312–13 (D.C. Cir. 1980) (service on a person of suitable age and discretion at the deponent's residence is not valid service of a subpoena) *with* Ultradent Prods., Inc. v. Hayman, 2002 WL 31119425, at *3 (S.D.N.Y. 2002) (service of subpoena on

registered agent of corporation or by certified mail satisfies Rule 45); Cordius Trust v. Kummerfeld, 2000 WL 10268, at *2 (S.D.N.Y. 2000) (service by certified mail satisfies Rule 45); *and In re* Shur, 184 B.R. 640, 642 (Bankr. E.D.N.Y. 1995) (Rule 45 does not require personal service).

73. Service upon an agent of a corporation, however, is sufficient. *See Ultradent*, 2002 WL 31119425, at *3.

74. Fed. R. Civ. P. 45(b)(1).

75. Hall v. Sullivan, 229 F.R.D. 501, 505 (D. Md. 2005) (service by Federal Express is sufficient because it reasonably ensures the witness will receive the subpoena and because personal service of subpoena not required by Rule 45); Doe v. Hersemann, 155 F.R.D. 630 (N.D. Ind. 1994).

76. 28 U.S.C. § 1821 (2005). The mileage allowance must be equal to that prescribed by the United States Administrator of General Services and should be made on the basis of a uniform table of distances adopted by the Administrator. Note that although only one day's fee must be tendered with the subpoena, you must ultimately pay the witness for each day's attendance, including time spent going to and from the place of examination. *Id.* These "witness fees" are distinct from the additional fees that typically must be tendered to experts to compensate them for time spent in responding to discovery. *See* Fed. R. Civ. P. 26(b)(4)(C).

77. Tedder v. Odel, 890 F.2d 210 (9th Cir. 1989); Robertson v. Dennis, 330 F.3d 696, 704–05 (5th Cir. La. 2003) (subpoena not properly served when attendance fee and mileage allowance not tendered). *But see* Cal. Civ. Proc. Code § 2020.230(a) (West 1995) (allowing attendance and mileage fees to be paid either at time of service or at time of attendance).

78. Mitsui & Co. (U.S.A.), Inc. v. P.R. Water Res. Auth., 93 F.R.D. 62, 64 (D.P.R. 1981) ("Rule 30(b)(6) was designed as an optional discovery device to supplement 'the existing practice whereby the examining party designates the corporation (or agency) official to be deposed.").

79. Cates v. LW Aerospace Corp., 480 F.2d 620, 623 (5th Cir. 1973).

80. The FRCP Advisory Committee referred to this practice as "bandying." Fed. R. Civ. P. 30(b)(6) advisory committee's note (1970).

81. *Cates*, 480 F.2d at 623.

82. *Id.*

83. Both party-organizations and nonparty-organizations are subject to FRCP 30(b)(6) requests. Consistent with deposition practice generally, notice is sufficient to require a party-organization to make the designation. For nonparty-organizations, a subpoena issued in accordance with FRCP 45 is required. The subpoena must state the obligation of the organization to designate appropriate witnesses.

84. Neither the rule nor the advisory committee's note specifies the manner of designation by the responding party.

85. Fed. R. Civ. P. 30(b)(6).

86. See "Legal Requirements" in Chapter 25, discussing the use of deposition testimony at trial under FRCP 32(a)(2).

87. Operative Plasterers & Cement Masons' Int'l Ass'n v. Benjamin, 144 F.R.D. 87, 89–90 (N.D. Ind. 1992); Cleveland v. Paimby, 75 F.R.D. 654, 657 (W.D. Okla. 1977).

88. Tailored Lighting v. Osram Sylvania, 255 F.R.D. 340, 349 (W.D.N.Y. 2009) ("the deponent must make a conscientious good-faith endeavor to designate the persons having knowledge of the matters sought by [the party noticing the deposition] and to prepare those persons in order that they can answer fully, completely, unevasively, the questions posed . . . as to the relevant subject matters"); Mitchell v. Am. Tobacco Co., 33 F.R.D. 262, 263 (M.D. Pa. 1963) (officer who retired before date set for deposition could not be compelled by notice).

89. Joseph R. Re, *Using Rule 30(b)(6) for Corporate Depositions*, 2 PRAC. LITIG. 83, 89 (July 1992).

90. The 1970 advisory committee's note to FRCP 30(b)(6) also recognizes that a witness can refuse to testify on behalf of the organization if the witness has an "independent or conflicting interest in the litigation— for example in a personal injury case."

91. FRCP 30(b)(6) witnesses need to prepare for the deposition and may rely upon information from others. Thus, objections based on lack of personal knowledge or hearsay are generally misguided. *See* Re, *supra* note 89, at 90. In contrast to the federal rule, some states may have a rule of civil procedure that specifically requires the designation of the "best" witness. *See, e.g.*, CAL. CIV. PROC. CODE § 2025.230 (West 2005) (organization must designate "most qualified" person).

92. Marker v. Union Fid. Life Ins. Co., 125 F.R.D. 121, 126 (M.D.N.C. 1989). *See also* Starlight Int'l, Inc. v. Herlihy, 186 F.R.D. 626, 638 (D. Kan. 1999).

93. Mitsui & Co. (U.S.A.), Inc. v. P.R. Water Res. Auth., 93 F.R.D. 62, 66 (D.P.R. 1981).

94. *Marker*, 125 F.R.D. at 126; R.J.F., Inc. v. United States, 657 F. Supp. 1291, 1294 n.6 (Ct. Int'l Trade 1987).

95. FED. R. CIV. P. 30(b)(6).

96. King v. Pratt & Whitney, 161 F.R.D. 475 (S.D. Fla. 1995).

97. *Id.* at 476.

98. *See supra* text accompanying notes 20–24.

99. Williams v. Sprint/United Mgmt., Co., No. 03-2200-JWL, 2006 U.S. Dist. LEXIS 4937, at *4 (cautioning examiner against broadening the scope of questions asked previously to the witness in a Rule 30(b)(6) re-deposition).

100. Note, however, that it is usually improper to object on the basis that the examination is beyond the scope of the notice. Paparelli v. Prudential Ins. Co. of Am., 108 F.R.D. 727, 729–31 (D. Mass. 1985). *But see* Detoy v. City & County of San Francisco, 196 F.R.D. 362, 367 (N.D. Cal. 2000) ("If Defendants have objections to either questions outside the scope of the 30(b)(6) designation or a question whether certain conduct

falls inside or outside Departmental policy, counsel shall state the objection on the record and the witness shall answer the question, to the best of the witness's ability.").

101. Re, *supra* note 89, at 87.

102. *Id.* at 87.

103. Operative Plasterers & Cement Masons' Int'l Ass'n v. Benjamin, 144 F.R.D. 87, 90; Moore v. Pyrotech Corp., 137 F.R.D. 356, 357 (D. Kan. 1991); GTE Prods. Corp. v. Gee, 115 F.R.D. 67 (D. Mass. 1987).

104. *Operative Plasterers*, 144 F.R.D. at 90.

105. *Id.*

106. FED. R. CIV. P. 26(g) advisory committee's note (1983). FRCP 26(g) was added to parallel the requirements of FRCP 11. See "Limitations on Discovery and Certification Standards" in Chapter 2, discussing certification requirements for propounding and responding to discovery requests.

107. *See* FED. R. CIV. P. 26(b)(2)(C)(i).

108. *See, e.g.*, Reif v. CAN, 248 F.R.D. 448, 454 (2008) (denying, without prejudice, plaintiff's request to take the deposition of his employer's CEO before lower-level employees had been deposed or served interrogatories).

109. For example, in *Mulvey v. Chrysler Corp.*, plaintiffs attempted to depose Lee Iacocca, Chrysler's chairman. 106 F.R.D. 364 (D.R.I. 1985). The court ordered that interrogatories be propounded instead, without prejudice to the plaintiffs' ability to depose Mr. Iacocca later if still warranted. *Id.* at 366.

110. *See* Alan N. Salpeter & Richard A. Salomon, *Discovery Rule Changes End Open Season on CEOs*, NAT'L L.J., May 13, 1985, at 15.

111. *See* Victoria E. Brieant, *Techniques and Potential Conflicts in the Handling of Depositions (Part 2) (With Forms)*, *in* 20 PRAC. LITIG. 9 (Jan. 2009), discussing issues surrounding securing the attendance of noncitizen witnesses in foreign countries. *See also* Ronald E. Myrick, *Obtaining Evidence Abroad for Use in United States Litigation*, 15 SUFFOLK TRANSNAT'L L. REV. 1 (1991); Mark A. Dombroff, *Taking Depositions Abroad*, 267 PLI/LIT 9 (1984).

112. 28 U.S.C. § 1783 (2005).

113. FED. R. CIV. P. 4(f)(1).

114. 28 U.S.C. § 1783(b) (2005). The court predetermines these expenses and states the amount in the order issuing the subpoena.

115. Discussion of the request for, and the production of, electronically stored information is beyond the scope of this book. See Chapter 2, note 13 and accompanying text.

116. FED. R. CIV. P. 34(b).

117. *But see supra* note 53 and accompanying text (regarding jurisdictions that extend time for compliance with a notice that is served by mail).

118. FED. R. CIV. P. 30(b)(5) advisory committee's note (1970).

119. A party-witness, in receipt of an FRCP 30(b)(5) notice requesting documents, might seek an order that requires proceeding under Rule 34 alone to avoid unreasonable delay at the deposition. *See* FED. R. CIV. P. 30(b)(5) advisory committee's note (1970). See also "Administrative Details" in Chapter 12, suggesting that the taker seek an agreement to provide documents before the deposition, even if not required, can be advantageous.

120. FED. R. CIV. P. 45(a)(1)(A)(iii); *see also* Cunningham v. Conn. Mut. Life Ins., 845 F. Supp. 1403 (S.D. Cal. 1994).

121. FED. R. CIV. P. 45(a)(1)(B)–(D). A subpoena for production or inspection of premises that is separate from a subpoena commanding attendance must be issued by the court for the district in which the production or inspection is to be made. FED. R. CIV. P. 45(a)(2)(C).

122. FED. R. CIV. P. 30(b)(2); 4A MOORE'S FEDERAL PRACTICE § 34.02. (3d ed. 1997, updated Apr. 2009).

123. FED. R. CIV. P. 45(c)(2)(B).

124. Wiwa v. Royal Dutch Petroleum Co., 392 F.3d 812 (5th Cir. 2004) (a subpoena duces tecum may be squashed if compliance would be unreasonable and oppressive); Hecht v. Pro-Football, Inc., 46 F.R.D. 605 (D.D.C. 1969) (a subpoena duces tecum that sought disclosure of documents unrelated to the sale at issue was oppressive and unreasonable).

125. In any event, it might be prudent to state the reasons in the objection as well as in the papers opposing a motion to compel.

126. *Supra* note 123.

127. *In re* Ernst, 2 F.R.D. 447, 451 (S.D. Cal. 1942).

128. *Id.* at 451–52 (testimony taken before action filed concerned motive of testator in disposing of substantial part of his estate by means of earlier inter vivos gift and trust).

129. FED. R. CIV. P. 27(a)(1). FRCP 27 is not the exclusive means by which to take a deposition before filing. FRCP 27(c) explicitly provides that a party also can proceed by an "old-style" action to perpetuate testimony—the common-law device after which FRCP 27 is patterned. *See* FED. R. CIV. P. 27 advisory committee's note (1937) ("This preserves the right to employ a separate action to perpetuate testimony under [28 U.S.C. § 644] (Depositions under dedimus potestatem and in perpetuam) as an alternate method.").

130. FED. R. CIV. P. 27(a)(3).

131. *Ernst*, 2 F.R.D. at 451.

132. *Id.*

133. *See In re* Boland, 79 F.R.D. 665, 667 (D.D.C. 1978) (order denied when no showing that prospective witness was aged, gravely ill, or threatening to leave country); Lombard's, Inc. v. Prince Mfg., Inc., 753 F.2d 974 (11th Cir. 1985) (motion denied when it alleged only that witnesses were not immune from the uncertainties of life and death and that plaintiffs feared evidence might be destroyed).

134. *See, e.g.*, State of Nevada v. O'Leary, 63 F.3d 932 (9th Cir. 1995); *In re* Gary Constr., Inc., 96 F.R.D. 432 (D. Colo. 1983) (petition for preaction depositions denied when petitioner merely attempts to conduct early discovery rather than preserve testimony).

135. Shore v. Acands, Inc., 644 F.2d 386, 388 (5th Cir. 1981); Gary Constr., 96 F.R.D. at 433 (court denied petition when only reason petitioner had not yet filed suit was that it could not currently anticipate its total damages).

136. Fed. R. Civ. P. 27(a)(1).

137. *Boland*, 79 F.R.D. at 668. *See also In re* MacCormack, 2000 U.S. Dist. LEXIS 5812, at *4–5 (D. Kan. 2000) (refusing a request under Rule 27(a) when deposition needed to assist party in writing their complaint).

138. *Boland*, 79 F.R.D. at 667–68.

139. *See, e.g., In re* Ferkauf, 3 F.R.D. 89 (S.D.N.Y. 1943) (testimony must be material and competent); *In re* Hopson Marine Transp., 168 F.R.D. 560, 565 (E.D. La. 1996) (requiring materiality and competency under Rule 27).

140. Nevada v. O'Leary, 63 F.3d 932 (9th Cir. 1995).

141. *See* Nevada v. O'Leary, 151 F.R.D. 655, 657 (D. Nev. 1993), citing W.H. Elliott & Sons, Inc. v. E. & F. King & Co., 22 F.R.D. 280 (D.N.H. 1957).

142. Fed. R. Civ. P. 27(b)(2).

143. *Id.*

144. *Id.*

145. *Id.*

146. Fed. R. Civ. P. 31(a).

147. Fed. R. Civ. P. 31(a)(2); *see also supra* note 47 and accompanying text.

148. See *supra* section of this chapter entitled "Subpoenas to Nonparties."

149. Fed. R. Civ. P. 31(a)(3).

150. Fed. R. Civ. P. 31(a)(5).

151. Fed. R. Civ. P. 31(b).

152. 4A Moore's Federal Practice § 31.02 (3d ed. 1997, updated Apr. 2009).

153. *See* Stephen P. Groves, *Procedure: Before and After the 1993 Amendments*, 29 Torts & Ins. L.J. 483, 492–93 (1994); *see also* Gastoil, Inc. v. Forest Hill State Bank, 104 F.R.D. 580 (D. Md. 1985) (witness expected to assert privilege); United States v. Salim, 855 F.2d 944 (2d Cir. 1988) (foreign witness).

154. Groves, *supra* note 153, at 492–93; *see also* DBMS Consultants Ltd. v. Computer Assocs. Int'l, Inc., 131 F.R.D. 367 (D. Mass. 1990) (used to reduce costs); Conkling v. Turner, 883 F.2d 431 (5th Cir. 1989) (used to inquire into limited area).

CHAPTER 4

Preparing to Take or Defend a Deposition

HENRY L. HECHT

As discussed in Chapter 2, depositions can be used to achieve many different objectives; therefore, they figure prominently in virtually every lawsuit. The key to doing well at a deposition is adequate preparation. This chapter explains what you need to do to prepare for a deposition, whether you are taking or defending it.

This chapter assumes that you have analyzed your case—at least to the extent necessary to put together a discovery plan.[1] The first half of the chapter looks at preparation from the taker's perspective; the second half from the defender's. When you defend a deposition, of course, you not only must prepare yourself; you must also prepare the witness. This subject is covered extensively in Chapters 5, 7, 8, and 10.

Preparing to Take a Deposition

A deposition has been described as an event that "only the taker can win, and only the witness can lose." Although this may be true, a taker cannot hope to "win" without adequate preparation.[2]

Set forth below is a step-by-step guide for preparing to take a deposition. There are two caveats about the guide. First, the suggested steps can be time-consuming and expensive. Therefore, for every deposition, you should do a cost/benefit analysis to determine what preparation is warranted. Second, although the guide consists of a series of steps, you might assume that the steps are sequential. As a practical matter, though, the steps are interrelated. Thus, their order depends on the circumstances of the deposition.

Task 1: Ask Yourself Why You Are Taking This Deposition

Your objective in taking a deposition—and often you will have more than one[3]—affects your preparation and, ultimately, the questions you will ask. Is your objective primarily discovery? If so, think in broad terms and plan to examine the witness on all the elements of the case. Is your objective to preserve the testimony of a witness who is not expected to be available at trial? Then use carefully worded questions that comply with the rules of evidence and produce answers that will be admissible at trial.[4] Is your objective to establish an element of the case that you need in order to prevail on a summary judgment motion? Then keep your focus narrow and the questions specific. Is your objective to secure documents and have the witness lay a foundation for their admissibility into evidence? Then before the deposition, review the foundational evidentiary requirements.[5]

Task 2: Review (Again) the Pleadings

Before you question a witness, you want to make sure that you understand the claims and defenses involved in the case. As you review the pleadings, consider what information the deponent might have about these claims and defenses.

Task 3: Review (Again) the Elements of Proof in the Case and Do Any Additional Necessary Research

As explained in Chapter 2, you must analyze the case before you can create a discovery plan.[6] In part, this involves understanding the elements of the claims and defenses at issue. It also involves determining who has the burden of proof on each element, a determination often best made by reviewing the relevant jury instructions.[7]

Revisiting your legal analysis will also help you anticipate the evidentiary objections that your opponent may raise at the deposition or eventually at trial. For example, suppose you anticipate an objection to a line of questioning that is based on a claim of privilege. You may need to do research to determine whether the objection is valid and what arguments you can use to defeat it.[8]

Task 4: Determine the Facts Needed to Establish a Claim or Defense

As explained in Chapter 2, part of your analysis involves identifying the facts required to prove or disprove the elements of a claim or defense. Presumably, you made this analysis when preparing your discovery plan. Nevertheless, it is a good idea to review it now.

The reason can be illustrated using the *Scoops* case. The core claim in that case is Leslie Roberts's contention that Terry Blake misrepresented the capacity of the accounting software he sold her to meet her needs. Suppose you represent Roberts and plan to depose Blake. Reviewing the factual analysis will remind you that a critical area about which you need to examine Blake is what he claims Roberts told him about her needs and what he told her when they discussed the accounting software she ultimately purchased.

Task 5: Review Prior Discovery in This and Other Litigation for Statements or Documents Related to the Witness

Reviewing prior discovery serves two purposes. First, prior discovery is likely to reveal information the witness has that would help to prove or disprove a necessary element of the case. Second, prior discovery can be a source of material for impeachment.

Review prior depositions for any mention of the witness. For example, if the witness is one of four witnesses to a conversation and the other three have already been deposed, review those transcripts to see how they described the event.[9] Also, review all documents, whether or not produced by the opposing party, that the witness authored or received or that mention the witness.[10] Do not limit your review to documents that have the witness's name in them. Include as well any documents bearing on subjects about which the witness might testify, regardless of whether you have any reason to believe the witness saw the documents. Why? Because at this point, you do not want to make limiting assumptions about the usefulness of documents. Instead, you want to learn what, if anything, the witness knows about the documents.

When reviewing prior discovery, do not overlook verified responses to interrogatories under Federal Rules of Civil Procedure (FRCP) 33[11] or sworn affidavits filed with motions. If your case is pending in a jurisdiction in which pleadings are verified by the parties, determine if the witness verified the complaint or answer, as it is another sworn statement by the witness.[12]

Do not limit your review to the instant litigation; instead, seek information about the witness—especially prior sworn statements by the witness—in other litigation. You can discover whether a witness was involved in prior litigation by using a court index of suits or through an Internet-based search. If the witness was involved in other lawsuits, ask opposing counsel in those cases for copies of transcripts and other discovery that may name the witness. Even if opposing counsel refuses to provide these materials, she should at least be willing to provide the name of the court reporter who transcribed testimony at a relevant deposition. You can then try to obtain a copy of the transcript from the reporter, assuming it is not sealed pursuant to a protective order.[13] As an alternative, consider asking the attorneys for other parties in the earlier case whether they will provide you with the material as a professional courtesy.

As you collect documents, create a witness file for the documents you plan to use at the deposition.[14]

Task 6: Decide If Additional Investigation Is Required

At this point, you may feel you have sufficient information to formulate your questions. If not, conduct whatever additional investigation is needed. If the case involves an accident, perhaps you need to visit the accident site before deposing the witness. Or you may need to talk first with—or perhaps depose—other witnesses. You may even need to hire an expert to help you prepare for the deposition.[15] In *Scoops*, for example, you might want to talk with an expert on accounting software before deposing Blake.

When the witness is a professional or public figure, background research on the Internet or in public records can be useful.[16] For example, suppose you represent the plaintiff in a legal malpractice case. Before deposing the defendant, you should find out if other clients complained about him to the state agency regulating lawyers, and, if they did, whether he was sanctioned.

Task 7: Think About Broad Themes Before Specific Questions

Outlining your questions might seem like a logical next step. Before you do that, however, focus on the theory or theme you want to develop as the discovery progresses. To try a case successfully, you need a logical, plausible, and commonsense theory to explain to the jury what happened. A deposition can provide one or more building blocks for your theory or may provide information that will cause you to alter your theory.

Suppose that in *Scoops* you represent the plaintiff, Leslie Roberts. Your theory might be that Blake was more concerned about earning commissions than meeting customer needs and that Business-Aide's commission structure gave him an incentive to sell expensive hardware instead of less-expensive software. You theorize that he pushed expensive hardware—which yielded a higher commission—and left Roberts, who had a limited budget, to buy software unfit for her needs. Keeping this theory in mind as you prepare for Blake's deposition will help you formulate questions that not only address the legal elements, but also create a picture that will provide a motive for Blake to misrepresent the capacity of the accounting software he sold Roberts.

You usually will want to develop more than one theory, particularly at the beginning of a case when it is hard to know what the best theory ultimately will be. In *Scoops*, for example, an alternative theory for Roberts's lawyer could be this: Blake did not understand the accounting software he was selling but was too embarrassed to reveal his lack of knowledge to Roberts, particularly because doing so would have jeopardized his making the sale.

Task 8: Develop a Questioning Approach

Long before you start questioning a witness, organize your questions. There is no right or wrong way to do this; in fact, often during a deposition you need to modify your initial approach. At least initially, how you organize usually depends on the following factors:

- The purpose in taking the deposition: Discovery? Preservation of evidence? Admissions?
- The nature of the witness: Is the witness a party? A nonparty? How experienced is the witness at testifying? Will the witness be available at trial?

- Experience with the opposing lawyer: Does the opponent thoroughly prepare witnesses? Is he generally obstreperous at a deposition? If you have never faced your opponent at a deposition, might other lawyers you know have information about him?
- The subject matter of the deposition: For example, are you interested in a single meeting attended by the witness? A series of meetings? Particular topics or subject matter?

There are two basic ways to organize questions: chronologically and topically.

Chronological Approach

As the name implies, this approach involves tracking a series of events (it could be meetings or letters or steps a witness took after an automobile accident) in the sequence in which the events occurred. The chronological approach is by far the most common organizational scheme. There are several reasons for this. First, takers—even less experienced ones—can more easily master the chronological approach. Second, it helps ensure complete coverage of all relevant events, a primary goal of a discovery deposition. Third, it works well when a deposition is offered at trial because chronological testimony is easy for a jury to follow. Finally, a chronological approach can fix a story line in the witness's mind, which is helpful to your case.

On this last point, suppose you are deposing Roberts, the plaintiff in *Scoops*. You may want to ask questions designed to produce a step-by-step chronology of her interest and activities in acquiring accounting software. In addition, you may want to ask questions designed to show that at each step she had questions about the capability of the accounting software, yet never tried to have them answered. You could then use her testimony to prove that her reliance on Blake, Business-Aide's salesperson, was unjustified.

Despite its value, the chronological approach has one big weakness: predictability. Once a witness—particularly a well-prepared one—realizes you are using a chronological approach, the witness probably will gain confidence about her preparation, her ability to testify, and her lawyer's predictions about what she would be asked. The witness's growing confidence in her attorney will make it harder to drive a wedge between the two and shake the witness from a "rehearsed" script.

Topical (Subject Matter) Approach

With a topical approach, you move from one topic or event to another without regard to time sequence. Its value to the taker is its unpredictability. Even a well-prepared witness will not know what you will ask next. Such uncertainty increases the likelihood of catching the witness off guard and obtaining damaging testimony that the witness might not have given if a chronological approach had been used.

A topical approach usually is most effective with a witness who is inadequately prepared, such as an executive too busy to prepare or a salesperson too cocky to be concerned about preparation. The topical approach also works well with a witness who, though prepared, is easily flustered, such as a lower-level employee who has never been deposed and feels his job is on the line. With all these witnesses, the randomness of the topical approach gives you more control of the deposition.

On the other hand, the topical approach may not be as effective when your primary objective is discovery. Although skipping around keeps a witness off balance, it increases the risk that you will overlook an important area of inquiry or not cover it thoroughly enough. When that happens, unpleasant surprises can occur at trial because you did not get the full story. To minimize this risk, use the topical approach only when you are confident that your outlining system is reliable and you can be certain you have covered all your bases.[17]

The topical approach is also problematic when your objective is to obtain a transcript that can be read at trial in lieu of live testimony. The more "random" the questions, the harder it is to organize a transcript that a jury can understand. Of course, this may not be a problem if your objective is a transcript that will be used for a pretrial motion or read to a jury only on specific points.

For obvious reasons, you should not use the same approach for every deposition, especially when a number of party witnesses are represented by the same opposing lawyer.[18] Try the chronological approach with one or two witnesses, then, with the next witness, shift to a more random approach. Make it difficult for a defender—and witness—to anticipate your questions.

Task 9: Consider the Type of Witness You Will Face

Find out as much as you can about the witness. The more you know about a witness, the more effective your questions will be.

As discussed above, review the pleadings, prior discovery, and documents naming the witness; all can tell you something about the witness. So can talking with other witnesses and even opposing counsel. And, as suggested above, conduct Internet-based research ("surf the net").

Once you have a sense of the witness, you can plan your questioning approach, as well as decide what type of questions to use. For a talkative witness, open-ended questions that encourage expansive answers should work well. With a well-prepared witness, you might try a sequence of topics and questions different from the one the witness is likely to expect, or start with a difficult and unanticipated question in the hope of catching the witness off guard. If you suspect that a witness is likely to be "forgetful" or even fabricate answers, decide whether to let the witness "hang himself" or to impeach the witness at the deposition.[19]

Task 10: Outline the Anticipated Questions

As a general rule, you should outline your questions instead of writing them out. There is a saying that "the less experienced the examiner, the more detailed the outline." But even if you do not have much deposition experience, an overly detailed outline can create multiple problems.

First, with a detailed outline, there is a tendency not to listen to the witness's answer; that—for obvious reasons—is one of the worst mistakes a taker can make. Second, when you write out questions and read them, your spontaneity suffers. Third, when you read a question from an outline, the witness is going to suspect that it is an important question and be more careful in responding. Fourth, a detailed outline may tip off a witness or her counsel about where the questioning is going and how much is left to cover. Fifth, if you need to keep looking at your outline, you cannot look at the witness—which means possibly missing an extraordinary amount of nonverbal information.[20]

To the rule against writing out questions there are two exceptions. First, written questions may be advisable when a deposition is used to obtain testimony for a pending motion or presentation at trial—particularly if you suspect the witness will later be unavailable. In that situation, the questions must be carefully worded to elicit the answers you need for the motion or trial. Second, when an expert witness is asked a hypothetical question, it must include all the desired elements; otherwise it will be vulnerable to objection. Therefore, hypothetical questions should usually be written out.[21]

Set up an outlining system that allows you the most flexibility. Questioning a witness is like exploring a river: Your overall goal may be to go straight down the river from the head to the mouth. But once the trip is under way, you might want to branch off into a side tributary. In fact, an unplanned side trip may turn out to be the best—and perhaps the only—route to the final destination. Because the course of a deposition may be uncertain, your note-taking system must be capable of letting you take side trips with a witness and then return easily to the main stream.

One system uses a three-ring notebook that has the outline on one side of a page and a blank space for notes on the other. As you question the witness, you mark off the areas covered (or, when you leave a subject before completing it, you make a note to come back to that spot). Some lawyers use different colored pens: a blue pen to draft the original outline and a red pen to note (1) responses requiring follow-up questioning before moving on to a new topic, and (2) the place where they leave the main subject to follow a lead. With the advent of realtime transcription, more and more attorneys are using the transcript appearing on their laptop computer to follow the questions and answers.[22]

When preparing an outline, some lawyers use the outlining feature of their word processing software. Not only does this feature make it easier to prepare the outline, but it also enables you to add marginal notes to the outline both before and during the deposition.

You can minimize outline preparation time by using standard opening remarks and question formats.[23] Opening foundational questions such as "State your full name for the record" and "Do you understand you are under oath?" easily lend themselves to standardizing. So do many of the questions typically asked when a witness is being examined about a conversation or a document.[24] Simply include a copy of the appropriate standard materials with your outline.[25]

Task 11: Consider Whether You Need a Protective Order

You might need a protective order under FRCP 26(c), either for your own needs or as a preemptive strike to counter an expected motion by the deponent or another party. (Because it is usually the deponent who makes this motion, the different situations for seeking an FRCP 26(c) protective order are discussed later in this chapter in the section on a defender's preparation.)

Task 12: Consider Whether to Seek an Order for the Deposition to Be Extended Beyond the Presumptive Seven-Hour Limitation

Before the deposition, you might want to seek an agreement with the other party extending the time for the deposition beyond the presumptive one-day-of-seven-hours limit (excluding breaks and lunch), mandated by FRCP 30(d)(1). The other side may agree, hoping for reciprocity. Failing agreement, you may want to move for a court order extending the time. In fact, the Advisory Committee Notes to FRCP 30(d)(1) set forth various factors that might lead you, before the deposition commences, to seek an extension of time:[26]

- The examination will cover events occurring over a long period of time;
- The witness will be questioned about numerous and lengthy documents;[27]
- The witness was provided with documents by the taker before the deposition, but did not read them;
- Documents were requested but not produced;
- In a multiparty case, each party needs to examine the witness;[28]
- The lawyer for the witness wants to examine the deponent;
- The examination is of an expert, even after submission of the report required by FRCP 26(a)(2)(b);
- The deponent, another person, or any other circumstance impedes or delays the examination;[29] and
- The witness needs an interpreter.

Task 13: Decide Whom You Want Present at the Deposition

First, consider whether you want your client present when you take a deposition. Some lawyers worry about suffering from "performance anxiety" if their own client attends. Yet there are many situations in which it makes good sense to have your client present. One is when your client has unreasonable expectations about the case. A deposition lets her see firsthand the strengths—and, yes, the weaknesses—of the other side's witnesses and evidence, an experience that may provide your client with a sobering dose of reality.

Having your client present can also be helpful when the case involves a credibility dispute, as in, for example, *Scoops*. Your client may be the best person to evaluate the deponent's credibility. Similarly, a client's presence can curb a witness's tendency to overreach when testifying. For example, if the other party to a conversation (your client) is sitting across the table at a deposition, the witness may not try to embellish testimony. (On the other hand, if you want the deponent to "overreach," thereby creating the potential for subsequent impeachment, you may not want your client present.)

When deposing the other side's expert, you may want to have your own expert present, regardless of whether you plan to have that expert testify.[30] Because expert testimony may be highly technical, having another ear to listen to the expert's answers and another mind to help you formulate questions can be useful. An expert's presence, like a client's presence, may also restrain the other side's expert from overreaching in her testimony—again, assuming you want to curb this tendency.

Finally, when a case is complex and the documents at the deposition numerous, consider having a legal assistant present. Besides keeping track of exhibits, a legal assistant gives you another pair of eyes and ears for observing the witness.[31]

Task 14: Arrange for a Deposition Officer, Court Reporter, Videographer (If Needed), and Room

The taker is responsible for arranging for a deposition officer who administers the oath and a court reporter who "records the testimony."[32] Typically, the reporter serves in both capacities[33] and, though retained by the taker, must be neutral, present to assist both parties.

The notice will have already specified the means of recordation, which under FRCP 30(b)(2) may be by sound, sound-and-visual, or stenographic means, unless the court orders otherwise.[34] If a stenographic record will be created, the choice of a court reporter is not a mere administrative detail; it is a critical one. First, by selecting a reporter you know is good, you can be sure of having an accurate transcript. Second, if the case involves technical terms, you can select a reporter with experience reporting in that area—again, reducing concern about whether the transcript will be accurate.[35] Third, if you choose a reporter with whom you have experience, not only will the reporter be familiar with your manner of speaking and pace, but you will be comfortable with the reporter's habits, such as a need for frequent breaks. Fourth, you can select a reporter who offers any special services you require, such as realtime transcription or a transcript provided both as an electronic file and in "hard copy."[36]

The taker also selects the location for the deposition, typically the taker's office. In some circumstances, it may be advantageous to select a different site—for example, the office of a third-party witness for the convenience of that witness or the office of an expert to reduce costs and make access to the expert's records easier. (As a defender, you may want to object to a deposition in the office of your expert for this very reason.) Another advantage of having witnesses testify in their own offices is that people tend to remember better when questioned in the place where the event occurred or where they are comfortable.[37]

Having selected the location for the deposition, the taker is also responsible for securing an appropriate room for the deposition. It should be situated to minimize interruptions. It should also have enough chairs, including a proper one for the reporter. (Most reporters prefer chairs without arms.) If the deposition is to be video recorded, the appropriate arrangements must be made.[38] All these details should have been attended to when the deposition was noticed. If not, they should be handled well before the day of the deposition.

Task 15: Pack a Bag Carefully

Make sure you take the following items with you to the deposition:[39]

- Caption page for the court reporter;
- If the deposition is a continuation, notation for the court reporter of the date of the last deposition and the final page number of the last transcript;
- If realtime transcription is being used, a laptop and appropriate software, cables, and connections;
- Instructions for the court reporter on when, where, and how (that is, in what format) to deliver the transcript, including any request for expedited service;
- Glossary of relevant terms and the spelling of difficult words to which the court reporter can refer (for example, in the *Scoops* case, which involves computer hardware, a glossary of technical terms such as "ROM" for read-only memory and "RAM" for random-access memory);

- Applicable rules of civil procedure and evidence, as well as any local rules and standing orders governing discovery;
- Contact information (typically a telephone number) for the judge, magistrate judge, or discovery special master who will decide discovery disputes (having this number handy will give added credibility to any threat you make during the deposition to call the judge for a ruling when, for example, the defender gives an improper instruction not to answer a question or uses disruptive defense tactics[40]);
- Available dates for discovery motions to be heard (having these dates handy will again give added credibility to any threat you make to file a motion to compel when, for example, an improper instruction not to answer has been given);
- Your own calendar, so you can schedule a continued deposition, the production of documents, or hearings on motions related to the deposition;
- Text of any proposed stipulations;[41]
- Outline of questions, including the appropriate "standard" questioning formats;
- Documents you plan to use at the deposition, placed in a witness folder[42] (bring at least three copies: an annotated copy for your use when questioning the witness, a copy that can be marked and attached to the transcript, and a copy for opposing counsel);
- Copy of the notice, subpoena, written stipulation, or court order that secured the attendance of the witness (often marked as an exhibit to the deposition);
- Copy of the pleadings (to question a witness and to respond to objections that your questioning is beyond the scope of permissible discovery);
- A standard English dictionary (an effective tool for a "dumb" witness who tries to avoid answering your questions by claiming not to understand common terms[43]); and
- Copy of any discovery orders, including protective orders that apply to the deposition.

Preparing to Defend a Deposition

As noted at the outset of this chapter, the prevailing wisdom is that "only the taker can win, and only the witness can lose" at a deposition. Nevertheless, a defender can do much to prevent or minimize damaging testimony. In fact, if you prevent a witness from giving testimony that seriously damages your side, you "win" the deposition.

To defend a deposition successfully, both you and the witness must be prepared. Some lawyers think that the most critical aspect of the preparation process is witness preparation, a subject covered in the next chapter. Those subscribing to this view point to the limitations on defenders imposed by the FRCP and many states.[44] For example, in some jurisdictions, once a deposition begins, conferences between witness and defender are prohibited except to determine whether to assert a privilege.[45] Some jurisdictions even forbid conferences during breaks—again, except to determine whether to assert a privilege.[46]

But before you can prepare a witness, you must prepare yourself by completing three tasks, discussed in turn below.

Task 1: Review the Notice and/or Subpoena for Procedural Compliance and Follow Its Commands

Unless a deposition schedule has been stipulated or court ordered,[47] the deposition process begins for a defender with the receipt of a deposition notice or subpoena. Review it for procedural compliance with the statutory requirements.[48] Some situations, for example, call for a subpoena, and a notice is legally insufficient. Confirm that the notice gives the witness sufficient time to appear, particularly if documents must be produced. In addition, confirm that service was proper. This step is important because "an objection to an error or irregularity in a deposition notice is waived unless promptly served in writing on the party giving the notice."[49]

Even if the notice or subpoena is procedurally defective and even if you promptly serve written objections, the witness may not simply refuse to appear.[50] Indeed, under the FRCP, you must either obtain a stipulation about the witness's appearance or move for a protective order to stop or modify the deposition as noticed.[51]

Whether or not the defect is curable, first try to resolve the conflict without judicial intervention.[52] Suppose the defect is curable because the notice was not timely, yet sufficient time remains for a proper notice to be served. Agreeing to a new date and time for the deposition, without requiring the other side to send a new notice, is good, cost-effective practice. In addition to holding down your client's legal costs, a cooperative approach can give you added leverage when negotiating the new date and location. Moreover, informal resolution encourages reciprocity when future disputes arise.

Suppose the defect apparently cannot be cured; for example, the witness is outside the subpoena power of the court. You should still try to resolve the matter without judicial intervention.[53] Of course, if your informal attempts prove futile, you should file a motion for a protective order or a motion to quash the subpoena. Then, even if your motion has not been heard and an order not yet issued by the time the deposition was scheduled to take place, your client should be safe in refusing to appear. Indeed, the advisory committee's note points out that when a motion for a protective order is pending, the witness would have "just cause" for failing to appear at the deposition.[54]

Even if you fail to stop the deposition, FRCP 32(a)(5)(A) gives you some protection.[55] The rule prohibits a deposition from being used against a party who,

> having received less than 14 days' notice of the deposition, promptly moved for a protective order under Rule 26(c)(1)(B) requesting that it not be taken or be taken at a different time or place—and this motion was still pending when the deposition was taken.[56]

If the witness whose deposition is noticed with insufficient time cannot be deposed at a later date and if the witness will be unavailable for trial, this provision can be extremely valuable. It is less valuable when the witness can be deposed at a later date or will be available for trial.

But, in either event, the victory may be Pyrrhic. Although under FRCP 32 a witness's deposition testimony cannot be used against a party who did not receive sufficient notice and filed a motion for a protective order, the testimony can be used against other parties. Furthermore, the taker may have been more interested in the discovery value of the deposition than in having the testimony admitted as evidence at trial.

Suppose the witness has no legal basis for failing to appear at a noticed deposition. If the witness then fails to appear, a court can impose the sanctions authorized by FRCP 37(d): (1) an order establishing certain facts; (2) an order prohibiting the disobedient party from supporting or opposing certain claims or defenses; or (3) an order striking pleadings, dismissing the action, or rendering a default judgment.[57] Note: These sanctions can be triggered even though no court order is violated; the witness's failure to appear is sufficient.[58]

Even if your witness must appear at a noticed deposition, the ultimate date, time, and location may be negotiable. Therefore, before committing to the appearance, clear the date, time, and location of the deposition with your witness, and remember to allow sufficient time for both you and the witness to prepare.[59] In addition, calculate the need for additional time if the notice includes a request for documents.[60] You will need time to review the document request for procedural compliance, serve a written response to avoid a possible waiver of objections, and comply with the demand for documents. With these time frames in mind, you are in a better position to try to negotiate the appearance date, time, and location if the original noticed date, time, and location are unsatisfactory.

How to comply with a request for documents is beyond the scope of this book. In general, however, you need time to determine the scope of the request, to gather and review the documents, and to make a strategic decision about the scope and date of production. Even if the notice calls for production at the time of the deposition, the taker would certainly prefer earlier production, a courtesy you may want reciprocated at a later date.[61]

When a document request is included with a notice of deposition (as authorized by FRCP 30(b)(2)), the procedure for objecting to this request is identical to the procedure for objecting to document requests under FRCP 34. The objection must be served in writing within thirty days of the request, unless the thirty-day period is modified by stipulation or court order.[62] This thirty-day period for party deponents contrasts oddly with the time given to witnesses—typically nonparties—served with a subpoena. FRCP 45(c)(2)(B) requires that a nonparty object to document production called for by a subpoena within fourteen days after service or before the time specified for compliance if such time is less than fourteen days.[63]

Suppose the notice requests an organization to designate a witness to testify on its behalf.[64] In that event, the organization—presumably with your help—must choose and identify the appropriate person (or persons) within the organization. When making the designation, an organization must make a "conscientious good-faith effort" to designate persons having knowledge of the matters at issue and must prepare the persons to answer "fully, completely and unevasively."[65] If more than one person in the organization can testify on the designated subject, it is generally not prudent to choose someone who is also a percipient-fact witness. Doing so may unnecessarily expose that person to more than one examination despite FRCP 30's limitation that a witness can be deposed "only once."[66]

An organization's choice of witness can be significant. Once designated by the organization, the witness speaks for it, and admissions by the witness become admissions by the organization.[67] Moreover, the deposition testimony may be used at trial by an adverse party, regardless of whether the designated witness is available at the time of trial.[68]

Another decision you must make after receiving a deposition notice or subpoena is whether to counterdesignate the method of recordation. Regardless of what method the taker designates, the defender has the right—with notice to the other parties—to designate another method of recordation. Remember, however, that the cost of the additional record or transcript must be paid by the counterdesignating party, unless a court orders otherwise.[69]

Task 2: Decide Whether to Seek a Protective Order

Given the broad scope of civil discovery,[70] the information sought at a deposition can be vexing for a deponent. As one commentator noted,

> In personal injury, matrimonial, and other noncommercial cases, discovery routinely trains its sights on private matters concerning a party's earnings, wealth, peccadilloes, or sexual habits. . . . That sort of thing also happens in commercial litigation. There, the parties—often competitors vying for business advantage—relentlessly pursue each other's trade secrets, technological know-how, customer lists, and marketing strategy.[71]

Obviously, most witnesses prefer to keep this kind of information "buried, or at least out of sight."[72]

If the taker at a deposition is likely to question your witness about sensitive issues, you must try to protect your witness. The relevant rule is FRCP 26(c). It permits a party or a person from whom discovery is sought to seek a court order to "protect [the] party or person from annoyance, embarrassment, oppression, or undue burden or expense."[73]

Eight different types of protective orders are listed in the rule. The list provides a useful framework for thinking about what type of protection you need.[74] For depositions, the list includes the following orders:

- The deposition not take place;
- The deposition take place only on certain terms and conditions, including a designated time and place;[75]
- Certain matters not be explored or the scope of inquiry about these matters be limited;
- The deposition be conducted with no one present except individuals designated by the court;
- The deposition be sealed and opened later only by court order; and
- Trade secrets or other confidential information not be disclosed or disclosed only in a designated way.

To obtain a protective order, you must show good cause.[76] In addition, you must certify that you conferred with your adversary in an attempt to resolve the dispute without judicial intervention. Your motion for the protective order will then be heard by the court in the district where the deposition is noticed.[77] Before filing an FRCP 26(c) motion, always remember that under FRCP 37(a)(5), a court can award reasonable expenses, including attorney's fees, to the prevailing party unless the court finds that either making the motion or opposing the motion was substantially justified or that other circumstances make an award of expenses unjust. If the motion is granted in part and denied in part, the court may apportion the expenses in a just manner.

There are other risks to filing a motion for a protective order. If the motion is denied in whole or part, the deposition goes forward. And—because you lost the motion—any objection at the deposition that revisits the issues you lost on the motion is unlikely to be sustained by a court.

Although an exhaustive treatment of protective orders is beyond the scope of this book, it is instructive to look at some common situations in which protective orders for depositions are sought.

Order That a Deposition Not Take Place

The prevailing standard is found in FRCP 30(a), which provides that a deposition of "any person" may be taken without leave of court.[78] Nonetheless, courts will issue a protective order to prevent a deposition from going forward when good cause is shown.[79]

The issue of "good cause" often arises when one party seeks to depose another party's lawyer.[80] For the court, the prospect of such a deposition raises two serious issues: (1) concern that the attorney-client privilege will be violated, and (2) concern that the lawyer testifying will no longer be permitted to try the case.[81]

Faced with such a situation, some courts refuse to stop the deposition until the lawyer refuses to answer questions. In other words, before a protective order will be issued, the lawyer must attend the deposition and invoke the attorney-client privilege.[82] Other courts, however, grant the order unless the party noticing the deposition shows that (1) there is no other way to obtain the information, (2) the information is relevant and not privileged, and (3) the information is crucial to preparation of the case.[83]

Under either approach, lawyers have been required to testify about nonprivileged conversations. They also have been required to testify when they were the best source of information on an issue, such as attorney's fees, or when the advice of counsel was a defense.[84]

Order That a Trade Secret or Other Confidential Information Not Be Disclosed or Disclosed Only in a Designated Way

An example from *Scoops* illustrates how a protective order can work in this setting. Assume you represent Business-Aide. Your client is worried that at the upcoming deposition of salesperson Terry Blake, questions may be asked about the company's business plans, customer lists, mark-up policy, and profit margins. Much of the information may be of little use to the plaintiff, Leslie Roberts, in pursuing her claim. But if the information is disclosed to Business-Aide's rivals, the company's competitive position could be seriously damaged.

As a first step, confer with Roberts's lawyer. Ask for a stipulation limiting both the scope of the deposition and any subsequent use of the testimony. If you obtain the stipulation, ask the court to issue it as an order.[85] Even when you are certain your opponent will not agree to such a stipulation, as noted above you must confer in an attempt to resolve the dispute before moving for a protective order, so the conference will not be wasted time.

Because the misrepresentation claims in *Scoops* appear unrelated to much of the business information that Business-Aide wants to protect, you may be able to obtain a protective order preventing

91

Roberts's lawyer from questioning Blake about confidential business information. If the court refuses to grant such an order, ask, in the alternative, for an order limiting the subsequent dissemination of the testimony.

When trade secrets or other confidential client information is involved, there are several tactical reasons why you should move for a protective order rather than wait until the deposition to object. First, you take the initiative in bringing your story before the court. If you can establish good cause for the order, the burden shifts to the noticing party to prove its need for the information. Second, in your moving papers you can ask for exactly the type of protection you need. In contrast, if you wait to object at the deposition or in response to a motion to compel, you are less likely to wind up with the specific protection your client seeks. Third, by filing your motion before the deposition, you avoid the appearance of stonewalling. Instead, you come to court as a lawyer seeking to protect a client's legitimate interests. Finally, if you lose the motion, you now know more about the discovery risks you face and can better prepare the witness to respond. Note, however, that moving for a protective order can have a serious drawback: The motion may alert your opponent to an area of inquiry she might otherwise not have considered. Lose the motion and it is virtually certain your witness will be questioned about this area.

When fashioning a protective order concerning a witness's trade secrets or confidential business information, consider including provisions that do the following:

- Define what is confidential;
- Describe the persons who may have access to the transcript and any exhibits and in what manner;[86]
- Limit copying and distribution of the transcript;
- Seal the transcript and limit its use during the litigation to persons on an access list, thereby preventing access by other parties and the press; and
- Allow the confidential information to be used only for this case.

Order That Only Certain Persons Be Permitted to Attend the Deposition[87]

As a defender, you may want to prevent someone from attending a deposition. One common example: You want to exclude other potential witnesses whose testimony could be influenced by what your witness says. A second example: Your client is likely to be questioned about its trade secrets, and you do not want your client's closest competitor listening intently as this information is disclosed. A final example: Your client is a plaintiff in a sexual harassment case, and the last person you or your client wants at her deposition is the alleged harasser.

How hard is it to obtain a protective order excluding someone from a deposition? The starting point for answering that question is FRCP 30(c). As amended in 1993, the rule addresses the perennial problem of whether other potential witnesses may attend a deposition.[88]

For trials, the traditional rule specifies that potential witnesses will be excluded at the request of a party.[89] For depositions, FRCP 30(c) takes a different approach. It provides that "[e]xamination and cross-examination of a deponent proceed as they would at trial under the Federal Rules of Evidence *except* Rules 103 and 615."[90] Thus, Federal Rule of Evidence (FRE) Rule 615, which allows a party at a trial to exclude a potential witness on request, is inapplicable to depositions. The result: the only way for a defender to exclude a potential witness from a deposition is by stipulation or by moving for a protective order.

A court should look favorably upon such a motion. As the advisory committee's note to FRE 615 points out, "[t]he efficacy of excluding or sequestering witnesses has long been recognized as a means of discouraging and exposing fabrication, inaccuracy, and collusion."[91]

Of course, merely excluding a potential witness may not be sufficient. As the 1993 advisory committee's note went on to point out, a court should also consider "whether the excluded witnesses likewise should be precluded from reading, or otherwise being informed about, the testimony given in the earlier depositions."[92] Be sure to consider whether you want to seek this relief.

Suppose the person you want to exclude is also a party, as in the earlier example of plaintiff in a sexual harassment case who does not want the defendant at her deposition. An order excluding a party is more difficult to obtain than one excluding a nonparty. The reason: FRE 615, which permits automatic exclusion of potential witnesses at trial, does not authorize exclusion of (1) a party who is a natural person, (2) an officer or employee of a party that is not a natural person designated as its representative by its lawyer, (3) a person whose presence at the trial is essential to the presentation of the party's case, or (4) a person authorized to be present by statute.[93] But an exclusion order even for those persons is not impossible. For example, in *Gallela v. Onassis*,[94] a suit by a freelance photographer against Jacqueline Onassis, the Second Circuit Court of Appeals approved a trial court's order barring the photographer from Onassis's deposition. (The trial court had issued the order after deciding it was necessary to protect the former First Lady from embarrassment and ridicule.[95])

In some, perhaps even many, situations, you will not win your motion to exclude a party from a deposition. As a fallback position, consider seeking an order that at least prohibits the attending person from speaking to your witness. If your client is a plaintiff in a sexual harassment case, even this minimal protection will be appreciated.

At times, you may want to prevent an unrelated third party— such as a competitor or the media—from attending a deposition. As pointed out in the advisory committee's note, the 1993 amendments addressed only the issue of attendance by potential witnesses; the amendments did "not attempt to resolve issues concerning attendance by others."[96] The United States Supreme Court has addressed this issue. In *Seattle Times v. Rhinehart*,[97] the Supreme Court held that there is no constitutionally protected right of open access to a deposition. The Court also ruled that a district court judge has broad discretion when deciding whether someone seeking a protective order for a deposition has shown good cause.

Sometimes, it is difficult to convince a trial court that there is "good cause" to exclude someone from a deposition. Consider a case involving Glenn Robinette, a figure in the Iran-Contra scandal of the late 1980s.[98] Robinette tried to bar the press and public from his civil deposition. (Traditionally, access by the press had been limited only to the written transcript.) He argued that the presence of the press could unnecessarily embarrass him and damage his reputation. This argument failed to impress the court; the press was allowed to attend. In its ruling, the trial court found that the witness had already received extensive publicity in his public congressional testimony and failed to show good cause for a protective order excluding others.[99]

Task 3: Prepare to Meet the Witness

As noted above, some lawyers consider witness preparation the most important part of a defender's preparation process. At the first meeting, it is not enough to say, "Tell me what happened," and then listen passively. Instead, be prepared to (1) explain the deposition process to the witness, (2) explain the ground rules for responding to questions,[100] (3) review the questions likely to be asked at the deposition, and (4) evaluate the witness's responses to them.[101]

To prepare properly for your first meeting with the witness, you need to do much the same work the taker does to prepare for the deposition.[102] For example, you must analyze the case to determine the elements of the claims and defenses as well as the facts needed to prove or disprove those elements.[103] Without this analysis, it is virtually impossible for you to develop your theory of the case, anticipate what questions will be asked, and decide what objections you may want to make. Therefore, before your initial witness meeting, review the taker's preparation steps covered in the first part of this chapter.[104]

In addition, you need to answer the following questions:

- When should I meet with the witness?
- Where should we meet?
- How long should the meeting be?
- How often should we meet?
- Who else should be present when we meet?

The issues raised by these questions, as well as a number of other issues that should be considered when you prepare a witness, are covered in the next several chapters.

Notes

1. See "Creating a Discovery Plan" in Chapter 2.

2. "If you fail to plan, you plan to fail." James W. McElhaney, *The Deposition Notebook*, 27 LITIGATION 55, 57 (Summer 2001) (quoting Brian Tracy, a time-management expert).

3. See "Purposes of a Deposition" in Chapter 2.

4. When taking an "evidence" deposition and faced with an objection, you may want to rephrase a question to cure the defect in the question. If discovery was your only—or primary—objective, you might not need to rephrase. See "Reactions by the Taker to the Defender's Tactics" in Chapter 14.

5. See Chapter 13, discussing evidentiary foundations for documents at a deposition.

6. See "Creating a Discovery Plan" in Chapter 2, discussing a system for case analysis during discovery planning.

7.   See Chapter 2, note 63 and accompanying text, discussing sources of jury instructions.

8.   See Chapter 6, discussing attorney-client privilege and work-product protection.

9.   See "Using Litigation Support and Transcript Management Software to Manage Deposition Transcripts" in Chapter 24, discussing the use of computers to search deposition testimony and create litigation databases. See also Chapter 18, discussing the ability of realtime transcription software to assist in searches.

10.   See "Formal Methods of Discovery" in Chapter 2, discussing methods of obtaining documents from both parties and nonparties.

11.   At the deposition, you may want to inquire about whether the witness helped to prepare the responses to interrogatories, even if the witness did not verify them. See FED. R. CIV. P. 26(g) (listing the signature requirement for discovery responses, the consequences of failing to sign, and the sanctions for improper certification). See also "Limitations on Discovery and Certification Standards" in Chapter 2.

12.   See, e.g., CAL. CIV. PROC. CODE § 446(a) (West 2004) ("When the complaint is verified, the answer shall be verified.").

13.   Depositions are no longer filed with the court as a matter of course. FED. R. CIV. P 5(d)(1). Instead, they are filed only when used in a proceeding or by court orders. Id.

14.   See "Selecting Documents to Use (or Not to Use) at a Deposition" in Chapter 12.

15.   See "The In-House Expert" in Chapter 19, discussing the discoverability of the identity of nontestifying consultants.

16.   See Chapter 2, note 6, discussing methods of gaining access to public records.

17.   See "Examination Techniques" in Chapter 11.

18.   See also "Organization of Questions" in Chapter 11.

19.   See Chapter 15, discussing dealing with evasive and fabricating witnesses.

20.   See "Nonverbal Communication" in Chapter 11.

21.   See "Hypothetical Questions" in Chapter 19, discussing the objections to hypothetical questions posed to an expert.

22.   See Chapter 18, discussing effective use of realtime transcription by the taker.

23.   See "Opening Remarks and Stipulations" in Chapter 11.

24.   See Appendix 6 and Appendix 7.

25.   Some lawyers create a deposition notebook for use at every deposition, to which they add the outline and documents for the pending examination. See discussion infra on "Task 15: Pack a Bag Carefully," listing items to be included in a deposition notebook.

26.   FED. R. CIV. P. 30(d)(2) advisory committee's note (2000) (addressing current Rule 30(d)(1)).

27. *Id.* (suggesting that the taker send copies of such documents to the witness in advance of the deposition so that the witness can review them). See also Chapter 12, note 12 and accompanying text, discussing this suggestion.

28. *Id.* (suggesting that "duplicative questioning be avoided and parties with similar interests should strive to designate one lawyer to question about areas of common interest").

29. Another factor that might warrant an extension but would not be known until the time of the deposition is when the deponent, another person, or any other circumstance impedes or delays the examination. FED. R. CIV. P. 30(d)(1) ("The court must allow additional time consistent with Rule 26(b)(2) if needed to fairly examine the deponent or if the deponent, another person, or any other circumstance impedes or delays the examination.").

30. By having a nontestifying consultant present, you will reveal the identity of someone whose identity might not otherwise be revealed. See "The In-House Expert" in Chapter 19, discussing discovery of the identities of nontestifying experts.

31. See also "Rule 7: Be Tough, but Build the Deponent's Confidence" in Chapter 8, discussing the value of using a second lawyer in preparing a witness to testify.

32. See "Contents and Timing of the Notice" in Chapter 3, discussing the need to designate the manner of recordation in the notice. *See also* FED. R. CIV. P. 30(b)(3)(A). A deposition taken within the United States must be taken before "an officer authorized to administer oaths either by federal law or by the law in the place of examination; or a person appointed by the court where the action is pending to administer oaths and take testimony." FED. R. CIV. P. 28(a)(1). The officer may also be designated by the parties under FRCP 29 (Stipulations About Discovery Procedure). FED. R. CIV. P. 28(a).

33. FED. R. CIV. P. 30(c)(1).

34. FED. R. CIV. P. 30(b)(3)(A) (noticing party shall state method by which the testimony shall be recorded). Under FRCP 30(b)(3)(B), "[w]ith prior notice to the deponent and other parties, any party may designate another method for recording the testimony in addition to that specified in the original notice. That party bears the expense of the additional record or transcript unless the court orders otherwise."

35. See the next section of this chapter, "Task 15: Pack a Bag Carefully," which suggests providing a glossary to assist the court reporter.

36. See Chapter 24, discussing summarizing depositions and the appropriate computer software, and Chapter 18, discussing realtime stenographic services.

37. Michael Owen Miller, *Working with Memory, in* THE LITIGATION MANUAL: A PRIMER FOR TRIAL LAWYERS 342 (John Koeltl ed., 3d ed. 1999).

38. See Chapter 17, discussing the logistics of a video deposition and the advisability of having a simultaneous stenographic record. If the

deposition is to be taken by telephone or other remote electronic means under FRCP 30(b)(4), appropriate arrangements will also have to be made.

39. See Appendix 3. The defender will want to bring many of the same items, as well as any written response to a document request pursuant to a FRCP 30(b)(2) deposition notice or a FRCP 45 subpoena and any documents to be produced at the deposition. *See also* James W. McElhaney, *The Deposition Notebook*, 27 LITIGATION 55 (Summer 2001).

40. See "Problem Situations for the Examiner and Suggested Responses" in Chapter 15.

41. See "Opening Remarks and Stipulations" in Chapter 11, discussing stipulations and suggesting that you have the text of proposed stipulations available.

42. See Chapter 12, discussing use of documents at a deposition.

43. See "You May Embarrass the Witness and Help the Taker" in Chapter 14, discussing the use of a dictionary in questioning an evasive witnesses.

44. See, e.g., Chapters 14 and 15, discussing limitations on how objections may be stated.

45. *See, e.g.*, Hall v. Clifton Precision, 150 F.R.D. 525, 527, 531 (E.D. Pa. 1993) (collecting cases); see also "Explaining the Deposition Process" in Chapter 7, discussing the propriety of witness and lawyer conferences during a deposition; "Breaks" in Chapter 11, discussing witness/lawyer conferences from the taker's perspective; and "Taking Care of the Preliminaries" in Chapter 14, discussing witness/lawyer conferences from the defender's perspective.

46. *See, e.g., Hall*, 150 F.R.D. at 529, 531–32; Aiello v. City of Wilmington, 623 F.2d 845, 858–59 (3d Cir. 1980). *But see* In re PSE & G S'holder Litig., 320 N.J. Super. 112, 117–18 (1998) (forbidding discussion at recesses during the day but allowing a defending attorney to prepare a witness at the end of the day for the next day's deposition).

47. Under FRCP 29, the parties may stipulate to a discovery schedule. In the alternative, under FRCP (16)(b), a scheduling order may have established the deposition schedule after a mandatory FRCP 26(f) discovery conference by the parties.

48. See "Securing Attendance of the Deposition Witness" in Chapter 3. In some jurisdictions, additional procedural requirements must be met; for example, in California state court practice, the service of a subpoena duces tecum is invalid unless a copy of the affidavit upon which the subpoena is based is served on the person served with the subpoena. CAL. CIV. PROC. CODE § 1987.5 (West 2005).

49. FED. R. CIV. P. 32(d)(1). FRCP 32(d)(1) does not define "promptly served," and the time within which objections will be permitted will vary with the circumstances. It has been held, however, that a stipulation to the adjournment of a deposition, without raising objections to notice,

constituted a waiver of objections to notice. Ehrlich v. Inc. Vill. of Sea Cliff, No. CV04-4025, 2007 WL 1593241, at *4 (S.D.N.Y. June 1, 2007) (citing Republic Prods., Inc. v. Am. Fed'n of Musicians, 30 F.R.D. 159, 162 (S.D.N.Y. 1962)). Similarly, objections to notice may not be raised for the first time on appeal. Peitzman v. City of Illmo, 141 F.2d 956, 961 (8th Cir. 1944).

50. FED. R. CIV. P. 37(d)(2) ("A failure to act [appear] described in Rule 37(d)(1)(A) is not excused on the ground that the discovery sought was objectionable *unless* the party failing to act has a pending motion for a protective order under Rule 26(c).") (emphasis added).

51. *See* FED. R. CIV. P. 29, 26(c); see also "Initial Disclosures under the FRCP" in Chapter 2, discussing the likelihood that under the Federal Rules, as amended in 1993, discovery conferences and scheduling orders may reduce disputes about notices.

52. *But see infra* text accompanying note 54 (discussing FED. R. CIV. P. 32(a) advisory committee's note (1993)).

53. A motion for a protective order must "include a certification that the movant has in good faith conferred or attempted to confer with other affected parties in an effort to resolve the dispute without court action." FED. R. CIV. P. 26(c)(1). The 1993 advisory committee's note to FRCP 26(c) suggests that "(i)f a movant is unable to get opposing parties even to discuss the matter, the efforts in attempting to arrange such a conference should be indicated in the certificate." A failure to confer as required by FRCP 26(c) will provide the court with adequate grounds to deny the motion for a protective order. Valencia v. Colo. Cas. Ins. Co., No. 06-12592007, 2007 WL 6585360, at *6 (D.N.M. Dec. 8, 2007) (granting "all of the Defendant's motions for protective order, because [Plaintiff] failed to confer in good faith regarding the scheduling of the notice").

54. "Although the revision of Rule 32(a) (discussed hereafter) covers only the risk that the deposition could be used against the nonappearing movant, it should also follow that, when the proposed deponent is the movant, the deponent would have 'just cause' for failing to appear for purposes of Rule 37(d)(1)." FED. R. CIV. P. 32(a) advisory committee's note (1993). *See also supra* note 52 and accompanying text.

55. See also "Exceptions to the 'Only Once' Rule" in Chapter 3, discussing the danger, for the noticing party, of proceeding with a deposition when a motion for a protective order is pending.

56. FED. R. CIV. P. 32(a)(5)(A). To satisfy the notice requirement, the notice must be in writing and properly served, regardless of whether the deponent or the deponent's lawyer already actually knew of the scheduled deposition date. See Lauson v. Stop-N-Go Foods, Inc., 133 F.R.D. 92, 94 (S.D.N.Y. 1990) (interpreting older versions of FRCP 30); Nuskey v. Lambright, 251 F.R.D. 3, 10–11 (D.D.C. 2008).

57. FED. R. CIV. P. 37(d), 37(b)(2). Additionally, rules of professional conduct forbid a lawyer from failing to "make reasonably diligent

effort[s] to comply with a legally proper discovery request by an opposing party." MODEL RULES OF PROF'L CONDUCT R. 3.4 (2002).

58. Note, however, that contempt of court is not a permissible sanction under FRCP 37(d). 8A CHARLES ALAN WRIGHT ET AL., FEDERAL PRACTICE AND PROCEDURE § 2291 (Supp. 2008).

59. See "Preparation Sessions: When, Where, How Often, and with Whom" in Chapter 5, discussing the need to confirm the availability of the witness, as well as how much time is needed to meet with and prepare the witness.

60. See FED. R. CIV. P. 30(b)(2), 45(b); see also "Request for Documents" in Chapter 3, discussing the use of a notice or subpoena to request documents.

61. See "When to Show a Document to a Witness" in Chapter 12, discussing reasons why a taker wants documents produced before the deposition and the defender's interest in reciprocity.

62. Absent a stipulation or court order, a party-deponent apparently cannot be required to object in fewer than thirty days from the date of a FRCP 30(b)(2) document request. But a subpoena might be used to shorten the time for production. See "Request for Documents" in Chapter 3, discussing the use of a subpoena as an alternative method to a notice requiring production by a party.

63. FRCP 45(c)(3)(A)(i) provides the nonparty some protection from this potentially harsh fourteen-day rule. Under that provision, the court may quash a subpoena that does not provide the nonparty with "reasonable time to comply." See also Chapter 3, discussing the timing requirements for the production of documents at a deposition, whether pursuant to a notice or subpoena.

64. See FED. R. CIV. P. 30(b)(6); see also "Requests for Documents" in Chapter 3, discussing the strategy of the noticing party in drafting a FRCP 30(b)(6) notice.

65. Ledbetter v. Wal-Mart Stores, No. 06-cv-01958, 2008 WL 697361, at *2 (D. Colo. Mar. 13, 2008). See also CAL. CIV. PROC. CODE § 2025.230 (West 2005) ("the deponent shall designate and produce at the deposition those of its officers, directors, managing agents, employees, or agents who are *most qualified* to testify on its behalf as to those matters to the extent of any information known or reasonably available to the deponent.") (emphasis added). See also "Securing the Attendance of a Corporate Witness: FRCP 30(b)(6)" in Chapter 3, discussing the duty of the responding organization.

66. FED. R. CIV. P. 30(a)(2)(A)(ii). At a minimum, the presence of a FRCP 30(b)(6) designated witness who is able to testify on matters beyond the scope of the notice provides the examiner with a potentially unexpected opportunity for additional discovery. See also "Scope of Investigation Required of the Responding Organization" in Chapter 3.

67. FED. R. CIV. P. 30(b)(6), 32(a)(3).

68. *See* FED. R. CIV. P. (32)(a)(2) ("Any party may use a deposition to contradict or impeach the testimony given by the deponent as a witness, or for any other purpose allowed by the Federal Rules of Evidence.").

69. FED. R. CIV. P. 30(b)(3)(B). See also Chapter 17, discussing the reasons to (and not to) video record a deposition.

70. See Chapter 2, discussing the broad scope of discovery.

71. Dan Levitt, *Keeping Secrets Secret, in* THE LITIGATION MANUAL: A PRIMER FOR TRIAL LAWYERS 264 (John G. Koeltl ed., 3d ed. 1999).

72. *Id.* Once discovery is filed with the court, it is available to the public, absent a protective order.

73. FED. R. CIV. P. 26(c)(1).

74. The starting place in your thinking, of course, is your interview of your own client.

75. See Chapter 3, discussing limitations on the number, length, and location of depositions.

76. FED. R. CIV. P. 26(c)(1); *see also* Cipollone v. Liggett Group, Inc., 785 F.2d 1108, 1121 (3d Cir. 1985) ("Broad allegations of harm, unsubstantiated by specific examples or articulated reasoning, do not satisfy the Rule 26(c) test."); Alexander v. FBI, 186 F.R.D. 71, 74–75 (D.D.C. 1998) ("The moving party has a heavy burden of showing extraordinary circumstances based on specific facts that would justify such an order.").

77. FED. R. CIV. P. 26(c)(1).

78. See Chapter 3, discussing who may be deposed and how to secure attendance of a witness.

79. See "Deposing a Chief Executive Officer (CEO)" in Chapter 3, and Chapter 19, discussing the categories of experts who may be deposed.

80. *See* Cornelia H. Tuite, *Block That Deposition*, A.B.A. J., July 1991, at 88 (noting rise in requests for depositions of lawyers as one that parallels increase in grand-jury subpoenas of lawyers).

81. *See* MODEL RULES OF PROF'L CONDUCT R. 3.7 (2002) (prohibiting lawyer from trying case in which lawyer will testify, except when providing testimony about uncontested issues or value of services rendered, or if disqualification would work substantial hardship on client).

82. *See* Qad, Inc. v. ALN Assoc., Inc., 132 F.R.D. 492 (N.D. Ill. 1990); Scovill Mfg. Co. v. Sunbeam Corp., 61 F.R.D. 598 (D. Del. 1973); *see also* Taylor Mach. Works v. Pioneer Distrib., No. 06-1126, 2006 WL 1686140, at *2 (C.D. Ill. June 19, 2006) (summarizing two approaches to resolving disputes about deposing attorneys).

83. *See* Shelton v. Am. Motors Corp., 805 F.2d 1323, 1327 (8th Cir. 1986). *But see* Pamida v. E.S. Originals, Inc., 281 F.3d 726, 730 (8th Cir. 2002) ("*Shelton* was not intended to provide heightened protection to attorneys who represented a client in a completed case and then also happened to represent that same client in a pending case where the information known only by the attorneys regarding the prior concluded case was crucial.").

101

84. Even if the deposition of a lawyer is ordered, the deponent or a party can still move for a protective order to limit the scope of the deposition as specified in FRCP 26(c)(1)(D).

85. Having a stipulation in the form of a court order will give you access to supervision and enforcement by the court. In addition, FRCP 30(c)(2) gives you a basis to instruct the witness not to answer. See "What Happens After an Instruction" in Chapter 14.

86. As pointed out by Levitt, *supra* note 71, limiting access from clients and experts can make defending a case difficult.

87. *See also supra* "Task 13: Decide Whom You Want at the Deposition."

88. Courts have disagreed about who may attend, some holding that witnesses should be excluded through the invocation of Rule 615 of the evidence rules, others holding that witnesses may attend unless excluded by an order under Rule 26(c)(5). FRCP 30(c)(2) provides that other witnesses are not automatically excluded simply by the request of a party. Exclusion, however, can be ordered under Rule 26(c)(1)(E) when appropriate. FED. R. CIV. P. 30(c) advisory committee's note (1993).

89. FED. R. EVID. 615 ("At the request of a party, the court shall order witnesses excluded so that they cannot hear the testimony of other witnesses.").

90. FED. R. CIV. P. 30(c) (emphasis added). FRE 103 (Rulings on Evidence) is not relevant for this discussion of who may be present at a deposition.

91. FED. R. EVID. 615 advisory committee's note (1972).

92. FED. R. CIV. P. 30(c) advisory committee's note (1993).

93. FED. R. EVID. 615.

94. 487 F.2d 986 (2d Cir. 1973).

95. *Id.* at 997 ("The grant and nature of protection is singularly within the discretion of the district court and may be reversed only on a clear showing of abuse of discretion.").

96. FED. R. CIV. P. 30(c) advisory committee's note (1993).

97. 467 U.S. 20, 32–33 (1984). *See also supra* text accompanying note 87.

98. Oliver North hired Robinette, a retired C.I.A. officer, to install a private security system. Robinette testified before Congress that North prepared false bills for the security system to hide that the origin of the funds was in profits generated by the secret sale of arms from the United States to Iran. Fox Butterfield, *Money from Iran Said to Buy Alarm for North's Home*, N.Y. TIMES, June 24, 1987, at A10.

99. Avirgan v. Hull, 118 F.R.D. 252 (D.D.C. 1987) (trial court noted that Robinette still had option of a motion to limit scope of deposition or to seal transcript if good cause could be shown). *But see* Kimberlin v. Quinian, 145 F.R.D. 1,2 (D.D.C. 1992) (distinguishing *Avirgan* as a "unique" case and noting that attendance of the press at a deposition is an "unorthodox practice"); 8 CHARLES ALAN WRIGHT ET AL., FEDERAL

PRACTICE AND PROCEDURE at § 2041 ("[I]t has been held that neither the public nor representatives of the press have a right to be present at the taking of a deposition.").

100. See Chapter 7, discussing "procedural" preparation.

101. See Chapter 8, discussing "substantive" preparation.

102. *See supra* "Preparing to Take a Deposition," discussing the taker's preparation for a deposition and the caveats concerning that step-by-step approach.

103. See "Rule 1: Give the Deponent the Big Picture First" in Chapter 8, discussing how a lawyer's theory and a witness's recollection must work together.

104. *See supra* "Preparing to Take a Deposition."

CHAPTER 5

Meeting the Witness

PAUL C. PALMER
G. RICHARD DODGE, JR.

Introduction

Some lawyers believe that when defending a deposition, nothing is more important than the time spent *before* the deposition preparing the witness. Even lawyers who do not subscribe to this view concede that witness preparation has become far more important in recent years. The reason is that most jurisdictions now limit the defender's ability to protect a witness once a deposition begins.

A lawyer "has the right, if not the duty, to prepare a client for a deposition,"[1] as one federal district court noted. But "[o]nce a witness has been prepared and has taken the stand, that witness is on his or her own"—whether the witness is testifying in a civil trial or a deposition.[2] Although a defending counsel may object to particular questions at a deposition, the Federal Rules of Civil Procedure require objections to be "stated concisely in a nonargumentative and nonsuggestive manner."[3] In addition, some courts have prohibited conferences between a witness and his or her counsel once a deposition has commenced[4] or during breaks,[5] other than for purposes of determining whether a privilege should be asserted.

The importance of witness preparation cannot be overemphasized. During the preparation session, you can evaluate how the witness fits into the case, preview the witness's testimony, and protect the witness's interests in ways that may not be possible at the deposition itself. The preparation session also gives you the chance to build rapport with the witness.

Initial Contacts with the Witness

Promptly after reaching agreement on the deposition schedule with opposing counsel or the issuance of a court order as to a discovery schedule, defending counsel should arrange a meeting with the prospective witness to begin preparing for the deposition.[6]

If defending counsel represents the witness's employer, it may be helpful to have the employer make this initial contact with the witness. The employer can (1) alert the witness that the deposition has been noticed, (2) make the initial introductions, and (3) help schedule the initial meeting between the witness and the lawyer. If the employer has its own in-house counsel, that lawyer often handles this initial contact with the witness. Having the employer or the employer's in-house counsel contact the witness can have a number of advantages. These include (1) reassuring the witness, (2) addressing any concerns the witness may have about the competing demands of the witness's work schedule and deposition preparation, and (3) explaining the defending lawyer's role.

Defending counsel should emphasize to the employer, however, that any communications between its nonlawyer employees and a prospective witness are likely to be discoverable.[7] Even if the substance of those discussions was not discoverable, the fact that they took place would likely be discoverable, and could leave the impression that the witness is not independent or that the witness's answers are contrived. For these same reasons, as discussed below, defending counsel should at the earliest opportunity instruct the witness to avoid discussing the case with anyone other than counsel. The witness should always lay the "blame" for this instruction squarely on counsel and be certain to follow it.

From the outset, as defending counsel, you should impress on the witness the importance of the deposition and the resulting need to devote sufficient time and attention to preparing for it. At the same time, you should attempt to reassure the witness, who may be disturbed and intimidated by the prospect of being deposed. You should find out as soon as possible whether the witness has any problem with the date noticed for the deposition so that you can take steps to reschedule it if necessary.[8] You also should find out whether the witness has any other questions about the deposition, such as how much time it will take or how to prepare for it. If the witness does have questions, you can point out that one of the primary purposes of meeting face-to-face will be to discuss all of the witness's concerns in detail.

Unless you have a specific reason to the contrary, you should advise the witness not to prepare any notes or other materials for discussion at the initial meeting, to avoid unnecessarily creating evidence that might be subject to discovery.[9] If the witness nevertheless feels the need to make notes to organize his or her thoughts in preparation for this initial meeting, you should advise the witness to label those materials "Privileged and Confidential" and "Prepared for Purposes of Discussion with Counsel." If you ask the witness to prepare any notes or other materials relating to the case, you should instruct the witness to label those materials "Prepared at the Request of Counsel." Labeling materials in this manner, whether in these words or similar ones, will reduce the risk that other parties or the court will later second-guess whether those materials are attorney-client privileged or work product.

You also should advise the witness not to review any existing documents, conduct any research, or talk to anyone else in preparation for the deposition. Of all these admonitions, the hardest one for most witnesses to understand and obey is to avoid talking with others about the case. Particularly when there are multiple witnesses to the same facts who know and work with each other, there tends to be a natural curiosity about what other witnesses recall and think about the situation. A witness might also be in contact with others who have a direct stake, or merely an interest, in the subject matter of the litigation and who might question the witness about it. In some instances—for example, when the witness's boss asks the questions—the witness may find it difficult to resist getting involved in such discussions.

Nevertheless, there are at least two compelling reasons for a witness to avoid discussing the facts with anyone other than the witness's lawyer.[10] First, the lawyer needs the witness's own recollections and understanding of the facts unaffected by external factors. Consciously or unconsciously, exposure to additional information or perceptions about the case that were not previously known to the witness can affect the substance or strength of the witness's testimony. The lawyer might find, for example, that otherwise strong and helpful testimony by the witness has been undermined by unnecessary exposure to uninformed perspectives or false or misleading evidence. Worse yet, the lawyer might never even learn that this change has occurred.

Second, any such discussions between the witness and third parties are likely to be discoverable if they are not privileged.[11] Discovery of these conversations by the opposing party could open up additional areas of questioning at the deposition and compromise the witness's testimony. If the witness's statements to the third party—made before the witness met with counsel and possibly before the witness's recollection was refreshed by documents reviewed with counsel—differed from the witness's ultimate testimony, that discrepancy might be used at trial to attack the witness's credibility. Even if the opposing party did not discover any substantive discrepancies between the witness's statements to third parties and subsequent testimony, the witness's admission that he or she had discussed the evidence with other interested parties might enable opposing counsel to suggest to the jury that the witness's testimony was contrived.

Sending the Witness Materials for Review Before the First Meeting

Some lawyers send more or less standardized letters or checklists to their clients, outlining the nature of the deposition process and various "ground rules" for how to be an effective deposition witness.[12] Advocates of this approach feel that it can expedite the deposition preparation process and leave the witness with a simple and concise reference sheet to review before the deposition. If such a letter is kept confidential, it likely will be protected by the attorney-client privilege. Aside from the risk of waiver of privilege (the consequences of which might not be great if the letter is worded carefully), the principal drawback of this approach is that the lawyer will not have the opportunity to gauge the witness's immediate reactions to these "ground rules" or to respond to any questions they might provoke as those questions arise. In addition, many lawyers feel that raising these kinds of issues in a letter to the witness—rather than in a face-to-face meeting—diminishes the lawyer's ability to "read" the witness's reactions accurately and to establish personal rapport. It also can make it harder to win the witness's trust and confidence.

Instead of a letter, some lawyers give an audio or video recording about the deposition process to their witnesses before the first face-to-face meeting. Alternatively, they may play these recordings at the beginning of the first preparation session. Video recordings are available from bar associations and other organizations; some lawyers also prepare their own customized videos.[13] These videos have most of the same advantages and disadvantages as the standardized client letter or checklist but can be more engaging and effective. They also can illustrate dramatically—through sample questions, answers, and follow-up questions—the reasons for the lawyer's guidelines.[14]

Finally, there are differing views on whether to send selected documents to a witness for review before the preparation session.[15] On the one hand, sending documents to the witness might save time because the witness will come to the preparation session familiar with the documents. On the other hand, the lawyer will not have the benefit of the witness's first reactions to those documents, nor the insights those reactions might offer.

Sending case-related documents to the witness in advance also prevents the lawyer from deciding, based on the witness's reactions to particular documents, whether to show the remaining documents to the witness (and, if so, when).[16] In addition, the contents of the documents might prompt a witness to inquire independently into the facts, or to form new opinions or conclusions, without the input of counsel. Intervening discovery requests to the witness also could pose difficult privilege issues.[17] These kinds of disadvantages often will outweigh any efficiencies resulting from providing documents to the witness before the preparation session.

Preparation Sessions: When, Where, How Often, and with Whom

The timing of preparation sessions with the witness, and how many sessions should be held, typically depend on a number of variables. These include (1) whether the witness has ever testified before, and if so, in what context, (2) the importance of the deposition to the case, (3) the deposition's potential scope, (4) the complexity of the issues likely to be covered, (5) substantive problem areas that become apparent during the preparation sessions, (6) how well or poorly the witness performs in the preparation sessions, (7) the availability of the witness for meetings, and (8) the health and personality of the witness—including whether the witness tends to be talkative, aggressive, or sarcastic, or otherwise requires special attention.[18] All too often, the witness's availability is the decisive consideration, and the lawyer must work within the limitations of the witness's schedule.

The witness's prior testimonial experience, or lack of it, may be important for several reasons. Obviously, you may have to spend more time, and go into greater detail, with a witness who has not previously been deposed than with a veteran deponent. Do not assume, however, that just because a witness has been deposed before, you need spend only a minimal amount of time reviewing deposition procedures. Perhaps the witness was not sufficiently prepared for that deposition, or so much time may have passed since the earlier depositions that a review of the basics is needed.

If possible, you should obtain transcripts of the witness's prior depositions.[19] You also may want to contact others familiar with the witness's prior testimony in order to assess the witness's performance and advise the witness how to avoid repeating any mistakes. In addition, you should find out whether the witness has testified in contexts other than depositions (such as at trial, in bankruptcy proceedings or examinations, or in administrative proceedings). Testifying in other contexts can result in misconceptions about the nature of the deposition process.

Preparation sessions should not be scheduled so far in advance of the deposition that the witness will forget the lawyer's guidance and instructions. Nor should they be scheduled so close to the time of the deposition that there is not adequate time to deal with any problems that might emerge. If the preparation sessions must take place significantly in advance of the deposition, it may be wise to schedule a brief "refresher" session closer to the deposition.[20]

To a large extent, the sensitivities of the witness and the realities of the witness's schedule and workplace may dictate where these preparation sessions should be held. They should be held in a comfortable setting where you and the witness will have privacy to talk freely and protect the attorney-client privilege, will not be unnecessarily interrupted, and will have access to any documents you need. The ability to control access to the session also is an important factor in selecting a site. Often the lawyer's offices will be the best location; in other cases it might be better to meet at the witness's office. Sometimes, however, the layout of the witness's office might make it difficult to obtain the necessary privacy, or the witness might be uncomfortable having private discussions with the lawyer in that setting. The witness might be more relaxed, and possibly more candid about coworkers and superiors, in a different environment. Preparation sessions away from the witness's office also might be preferable to avoid interruptions and the distractions of the telephone.

You must earn the witness's trust and confidence in order to ensure that the witness is completely candid in the preparation sessions. To encourage total candor, you should assure the witness of the confidentiality of these discussions. Confidential communications between a client and his or her lawyer in preparation for the client's deposition ordinarily are protected by the attorney-client privilege.[21] The work-product doctrine also may protect certain aspects of the deposition preparation process.[22] You should explain these privileges to the witness, emphasize that you will keep your discussions with the witness confidential, and advise the witness likewise to keep those discussions confidential to prevent any waiver of privilege.

Attendance at deposition preparation sessions should help to (1) avoid intimidating the witness, (2) encourage total candor, and (3) preserve all applicable privileges. No one should be present other than the witness, the preparing lawyer or lawyers, and (if necessary) persons assisting the lawyer, such as legal assistants or nontestifying experts engaged by the lawyer.[23] The attendance of third parties who are not jointly represented by the same lawyer in that matter would in most instances constitute a waiver of the attorney-client privilege.[24]

In some cases the sheer number of depositions noticed might suggest that it would be more efficient to prepare witnesses either collectively or in small groups rather than individually. There are compelling reasons, however, to avoid such group preparation.

Discussions with more than one witness at the same time may inhibit candor. The recollections and knowledge of the witnesses may be affected by their joint participation; witnesses might refresh each others' recollections, disclose information not known to others present, or attempt to convince other witnesses of their own versions of the facts (either during or after the joint preparation meeting). As a result, it may become impossible for witnesses to distinguish between what they knew personally and what others say occurred. The presence of multiple witnesses also can make it difficult for the lawyer to control the direction of the preparation session.

Moreover, the presence of other witnesses or representatives of another party (under a joint defense agreement) at a deposition preparation session is likely to be a discoverable fact. That fact could undermine the credibility of the witnesses' testimony by suggesting that they have collaborated to coordinate their stories. At the witnesses' depositions, for example, opposing counsel could ask each witness whether he or she met with anyone in preparation for the deposition, and, if so, with whom.[25] Opposing counsel also could ask each witness whether he or she discussed any of the facts of the case in the presence of other witnesses in preparation for the deposition. If any of these witnesses later testified at trial, opposing counsel might elicit this same information on cross-examination in order to suggest to the jury that the witnesses' trial testimony was not independent and, therefore, not credible.

Ideally, the same lawyer who will represent the witness at the deposition should prepare the witness from start to finish. This ensures that the defending lawyer has a full understanding of the scope and substance of the witness's knowledge of the facts, can anticipate the witness's answers during the deposition, and immediately can spot and address problems that might develop.[26] It also reassures the witness that the lawyer defending him or her understands the facts and the witness's concerns. In some cases, it is helpful to have a second lawyer participate in part of the deposition preparation session. The second lawyer can conduct a mock "hostile" examination without jeopardizing the principal lawyer's rapport with the witness.[27]

You may want to video record portions of the preparation session and review that footage with the witness. This allows the witness to see how she appears to others—including how her appearance, attitude, voice, behavior, mannerisms, and reactions enhance or detract from her testimony. These insights can help your witness testify more effectively. In addition, a witness who sees herself on video often is more receptive when the lawyer points out areas for improvement. Recording and reviewing practice questioning is an essential part of the preparation process when the deposition will be recorded on video.[28] Given the benefits of using video to prepare a witness and its relatively low cost, as well as the importance of depositions to the ultimate disposition of the case,[29] consider recording the deposition preparation session on video even when the deposition itself will not be taped.

Notes

1.   Hall v. Clifton Precision, 150 F.R.D. 525, 528 (E.D. Pa. 1993) (foot-note omitted). *See also* Chapters 7 and 8, discussing the importance of, and techniques for, witness preparation.

2.   *Hall*, 150 F.R.D. at 528.

3.   FED. R. CIV. P. 30(c)(2). See also "Making Objections" in Chapter 14, and "Problem Situations for the Examiner and Suggested Responses" in Chapter 15, discussing improper defense practices.

4.   *See, e.g., Hall*, 150 F.R.D. at 527, 531 (E.D. Pa. 1993) (collecting cases); E.D.N.Y. R. 30.6 (2007); *see also* "Explaining the Deposition Process" in Chapter 7, discussing the propriety of witness and lawyer conferences during a deposition.

5.   *See, e.g., Hall*, 150 F.R.D. at 529, 531–32; (consultations with counsel during breaks are prohibited). *But cf. In re* Stratosphere Corp. Secs. Litig., 182 F.R.D. 614, 621 (D. Nev. 1998) (consultations with counsel during periodic deposition breaks and more prolonged recesses are permitted).

6.   See "Task 1: Review the Notice and/or Subpoena for Procedural Compliance and Following Its Commands" in Chapter 4; *see also infra* note 8.

7.   See Chapter 6, discussing the attorney-client privilege.

8.   As a result of the 2000 amendments to the FRCP, the parties, unless exempted from initial disclosure under FRCP 26(a)(1)(E) or otherwise ordered, are required to confer and, among other things, develop a proposed discovery plan at least 21 days before a scheduling conference is held or a scheduling order is due under FRCP 16(b). FED. R. CIV. P. 16 and 26(f). If it then becomes necessary to reschedule a deposition within the time frame set by the court's scheduling order, such accommodations ordinarily are made by agreement of counsel. If opposing counsel is unwilling to reschedule the deposition, counsel representing the witness may move for a protective order or to modify or quash the subpoena (as appropriate). *See* FED. R. CIV. P. 26(c), 45(c)(3)(A).

9.   *See infra* notes 21–22 and accompanying text; *see also In re* Six Grand Jury Witnesses, 979 F.2d 939, 942–45 (2d Cir. 1992) (criminal proceedings; holding that notwithstanding attorney-client privilege and work-product claims, fact witnesses could be questioned about additional facts they learned and opinions they formed through analyses they undertook at the direction of counsel in connection with a federal investigation), *cert. denied*, 509 U.S. 905 (1993).

10.   A corporate deponent under FRCP 30(b)(6) may need the assistance of former or current employees of the corporation to prepare for the deposition. *See* Bank of N.Y. v. Meridien Biao Bank Tanzania, Ltd., 171 F.R.D. 135, 151 (S.D.N.Y. 1997) (corporate deponent must be prepared

"to extent matters are reasonably available, whether from documents, past employees, or other sources"). For instance, if the Rule 30(b)(6) deponent does not have personal knowledge of the matters noticed for testimony, it will be necessary for the deponent to obtain knowledge on those topics from documents and current or past employees. *See* PPM Fin., Inc. v. Norandal USA, Inc. 392 F.3d 889, 894 (7th Cir. 2004). A 30(b)(6) deponent may testify not just to matters within his or her personal knowledge, but to matters known or reasonably available to the organization. The presence of former or current employees of the company at a session to prepare a 30(b)(6) witness with company counsel does not waive attorney-client privilege. *See infra* notes 22–24 and accompanying text.

11.   *See infra* notes 21, 23–24 and accompanying text.

12.   These "ground rules" typically include, in somewhat condensed form, the kinds of advice and instructions discussed in "Twenty Guidelines for Deposition Testimony" in Chapter 7. See also Appendix 4 and Chapter 8, regarding substantive preparation.

13.   *See, e.g.,* DVD: Jan Mills Spaeth, You Will Be a Credible Witness at Your Deposition!: Witness Preparation for Deposition (Am. B. Ass'n 2008); DVD: Members of the St. Louis Bar, Deposition Preparation (Magic Lamb Prods. 2007); DVD: Dr. Noelle C. Nelson, How to Give a Good Deposition and Testify Well in Court (Mind Lab Pub. 2006).

14.   See "Twenty Guidelines for Deposition Testimony" in Chapter 7.

15.   Lawyers generally would agree, however, that documents should not be sent to a witness unless (1) they already have been, or will be, produced in discovery; or (2) the lawyer is otherwise prepared to allow them to be discovered. See Chapter 9, discussing discovery of writings used to refresh memory for the purpose of testifying.

16.   See Chapters 8 and 9, discussing the use and potential discoverability of documents used to prepare a witness.

17.   *See infra* notes 21–22 and accompanying text.

18.   There may be a number of ways for the lawyer to learn about the personality of the witness before they meet. If the lawyer also represents the witness's employer, the employer or its in-house counsel might be able to provide some insights. If the witness has testified in other proceedings, transcripts of that testimony might be available. A lawyer who represents multiple witnesses also might consider asking these other clients about the prospective deponent.

19.   Under the FRCP, a party is required to produce a list of any other cases in which that party's expert witness has testified as an expert at trial or by deposition during the previous four years. FED. R. CIV. P. 26(a) (2)(b). See also Chapter 19, discussing expert-witness depositions.

20.   This assumes, of course, that the lawyer will have interviewed the witness before the first deposition preparation session. If not, the lawyer should schedule such an interview first, or, if that is not possible,

plan on conducting separate "interview" and "preparation" phases in the initial meeting (and allow enough time for both).

21. *See, e.g., In re* Coordinated Pretrial Proceedings in Petroleum Prods. Antitrust Litig., 658 F.2d 1355, 1361 & n.7 (9th Cir. 1981), *cert. denied,* 455 U.S. 990 (1982). Under federal law, communications between an employee of a client and the client's lawyer, regarding matters within the scope of the employment and made at the direction of the client for purposes of enabling the lawyer to provide the client legal services or advice, ordinarily are protected by the attorney-client privilege. *See* Upjohn Co. v. United States, 449 U.S. 383 (1981). Under state law, however, the result may be different. *See, e.g.,* Consolidation Coal Co. v. Bucyrus-Erie Co., 432 N.E.2d 250, 254–58 (Ill. 1982) (limiting attorney-client privilege to communications with employees in client's "control group").

22. *See* Hickman v. Taylor, 329 U.S. 495 (1947); FED. R. CIV. P. 26(b)(3). A number of courts have held that the work-product doctrine precludes discovery of the specific questions asked by a lawyer in deposition preparation, the subject areas covered, and other matters tending to disclose the mental impressions, opinions, conclusions, or legal theories of the lawyer. *E.g.,* Russell v. Gen. Elec. Co., 149 F.R.D. 578, 581–82 (N.D. Ill. 1993); Hisaw v. Unisys Corp., 134 F.R.D. 151, 153 (W.D. La. 1991); Barrett Indus. Trucks, Inc. v. Old Republic Ins. Co., 129 F.R.D. 515, 519 (N.D. Ill. 1990); Protective Nat'l Ins. Co. v. Commonwealth Ins. Co., 137 F.R.D. 267, 280, 283 (D. Neb. 1989); Connolly Data Sys., Inc. v. Victor Techs., Inc., 114 F.R.D. 89, 96 (S.D. Cal. 1987); Ford v. Philips Elecs. Instruments Co., 82 F.R.D. 359, 361 (E.D. Pa. 1979). *But cf.* Barrett Indus. Trucks, Inc., 129 F.R.D. at 518–19 (work-product doctrine did not preclude questioning witness about facts disclosed to witness by counsel, identities of persons from whom counsel learned those facts, or existence or nonexistence of documents). The same principles have been applied in some cases to prohibit discovery of documents selected and compiled by the lawyer for use in deposition preparation. *See, e.g.,* Sporck v. Peil, 759 F.2d 312, 315–17 (3d Cir.), cert. denied, 474 U.S. 903 (1985); Omaha Pub. Power Dist. v. Foster Wheeler Corp., 109 F.R.D. 615, 616 (D. Neb. 1986); Bercow v. Kidder, Peabody & Co., 39 F.R.D. 357, 358 (S.D.N.Y. 1965). *But cf. In re* Minebea Co., 143 F.R.D. 494, 500 (S.D.N.Y. 1992) (compelling witnesses to answer questions "as to whether they reviewed documents in preparation for the deposition and questions as to the identity of those documents," but not questions "as to whether they were given the document(s) by counsel").

23. For the reasons discussed in "Confidentiality and Waiver of Privilege" in Chapter 6, experts who may testify at trial should never attend deposition preparation sessions conducted for other witnesses. *See* FED. R. CIV. P. 26(a)(2), 26(b)(4).

24. If the witness and the third party were participating in a "joint defense" or shared another sufficient "common interest," the third party's presence at the preparation sessions might not constitute a waiver of the

attorney-client privilege. *See* Hunydee v. United States, 355 F.2d 183, 184–85 (9th Cir. 1965). The third party's presence at those sessions nevertheless would be a discoverable fact, which could contribute to the perception that the witness's testimony was not independent.

In general, the presence of a third party at a deposition preparation session would constitute a waiver of work-product protection only if that party's presence was inconsistent with the adversary system. Permian Corp. v. United States, 665 F.2d 1214, 1219 (D.C. Cir. 1981). *See In re* Cendant Corp. Secs. Litig., 343 F.3d 658, 667 (3d Cir. 2003) (presence of trial consultant at a deposition preparation session does not constitute a waiver of work-product protection). As discussed above, however, the work-product doctrine might provide little, if any, substantive protection to the witness in this context. *See supra* note 22.

25. See Chapter 7, discussing examination regarding deposition preparation and standard questions regarding the witness's preparation.

26. See also "Rule 7: Be Tough, but Build the Deponent's Confidence" in Chapter 8, discussing use of a second lawyer to prepare a witness.

27. See also "Rule 6: Adapt the 'Do Not Volunteer' Rule to the Individual" in Chapter 8, discussing use of a second lawyer for practice questioning.

28. See "The Video Deposition" in Chapter 10 and Chapter 17, discussing video recorded depositions.

29. *See* Damaj v. Farmers Ins. Co., 164 F.R.D. 559, 560 & n.2 (N.D. Okla. 1995) (importance of depositions to disposition of cases). See also the discussion in "Facilitate Settlement" in Chapter 2. Obviously, the importance of the impression that a particular witness will make may vary with the importance of the witness to the defending party's case.

CHAPTER 6

Establishing and Preserving the Attorney-Client and Work-Product Privileges

Peter Gruenberger*

This chapter begins with a discussion of the importance of a deposition defender establishing an attorney-client relationship with a witness being prepared for deposition. The remainder of the chapter addresses the elements of the attorney-client and work-product privileges and provides practical suggestions about how best to preserve them. The chapter concludes with a discussion of ancillary issues that may arise when counsel for a corporation also represents corporate employees at their depositions.

Importance of Establishing an Attorney-Client Relationship

Witness preparation is usually the single most important step in ensuring a successful deposition.[1] The defending lawyer will want the preparation to be privileged in order to ensure that at the deposition the taker cannot inquire about communications between the defender and the witness at preparation sessions.[2]

The attorney-client privilege promotes and protects a full and frank discussion between the defender and the witness about the strengths and weaknesses of the case and the witness's role in it. The work-product privilege protects the thought processes of the attorneys working on the case. Conversely, absent these privileges, the questioner will be able to inquire into what was discussed between the defender and the witness at the preparation session. And this may enable the examiner to learn about legal theories or other impressions of the defender that otherwise would likely not be discovered through routine deposition questioning.[3]

Accordingly, there are multiple reasons for creating an attorney-client relationship between the defender and the witness. But even when the relationship exists, a defender must exercise caution in preparing the witness and always assume that the preparation session may become the subject of questioning at the deposition.[4] Indeed, prudent defenders always conduct preparation sessions as if they are being recorded. In addition, even when the attorney-client relationship exists, the defender must be careful in using privileged or work-product materials during preparation sessions given the potential for their discovery.[5]

Elements of the Attorney-Client and Work-Product Privileges

Attorney-Client Privilege

Generally an attorney-client relationship is created by some form of contract, whether formal or informal.[6] There are no "magic words" required, nor even the passing of money. The key is the intent and conduct of the parties. The attorney-client privilege has its roots in the common law, developed by the courts as a rule of evidence,[7] but some jurisdictions have made it the subject of statutes and court rules.[8]

As set forth in *United States v. United Shoe Machinery Corp.*, the attorney-client privilege "applies only if:

1. the asserted holder of the privilege is or sought to become a client;

2. the person to whom the communication was made (a) is a member of the bar of a court, or his subordinate and (b) in connection with this communication is acting as a lawyer;

3. the communication relates to a fact of which the attorney was informed (a) by his client (b) without the presence of strangers (c) for the purpose of securing primarily either (i) an opinion on law or (ii) legal services or (iii) assistance in some legal proceeding, and not (d) for the purpose of committing a crime or tort; and

4. the privilege has been (a) claimed and (b) not waived by the client."[9]

These elements, discussed below, vary from state to state, and there are differences between state and federal court practice.

In federal courts, the existence of the attorney-client privilege depends on whether the claim that is the subject of the litigation arises under federal or state law. For claims arising under federal law, the privilege is "governed by the principles of the common law as they may be interpreted by the courts of the United States in the light of reason and experience."[10] The federal common law similarly applies to cases where both federal and state law claims are asserted.[11] For claims arising in federal court under state law, state law governs.[12]

While a few courts have expressed some doubt about the two-way nature of the attorney-client privilege, most courts have ruled that it runs in both directions.[13] In other words, the privilege protects both communications from attorney to client and communications from client to attorney.[14] Hence, the privilege exists "to protect not only the giving of professional advice to those who can act on it but also the giving of information to the lawyer to enable him to give sound and informed advice."[15] And this protection applies whether or not the advice entails confidences of the client.[16]

The burden of establishing each element of the privilege is on the party asserting it.[17] In addition, many courts strictly construe the scope and application of the privilege.[18]

Work-Product Privilege

The work-product doctrine was first articulated and applied as a qualified privilege by the Supreme Court in *Hickman v. Taylor.*[19] In that case, the Court rejected "an attempt, without purported necessity or justification, to secure written statements, private memoranda and personal recollections prepared or formed by an adverse party's counsel in the course of his legal duties."[20] As the Court explained, unless a lawyer has the ability to maintain privacy from an adversary in the preparation of materials,

> much of what is now put down in writing would remain unwritten. An attorney's thoughts, heretofore inviolate, would not be his own. Inefficiency, unfairness and sharp practices would inevitably develop in the giving of legal advice and in the preparation of cases for trial. The effect on the legal profession would be demoralizing. And the interests of the clients and the cause of justice would be poorly served.[21]

Although the work-product privilege protects all documents prepared in anticipation of litigation, "[a]t its core, the work-product doctrine shelters the mental processes of the attorney, providing a privileged area within which he can analyze and prepare his client's case."[22] The documents prepared in anticipation of litigation do not, however, need to be created at the request of an attorney.[23] As codified in Federal Rule of Civil Procedure (FRCP) 26(b)(3), a lawyer's work-product typically may be discovered if

> the party [seeking discovery] shows that it has substantial need for the materials to prepare its case and cannot, without undue hardship, obtain their substantial equivalent by other means. [24]

In applying FRCP 26(b)(3), courts often divide a lawyer's work-product into two levels: factual work-product and opinion or "core" work-product. The latter, which encompasses a lawyer's "mental impressions, conclusions, opinions or legal theories," usually receives a heightened level of protection.[25]

The attorney-client and work-product privileges frequently overlap, but their thrusts differ.[26] In some respects the work-product privilege is broader than the attorney-client privilege; in other respects it is narrower:

- The attorney-client privilege encourages candid lawyer-client communications; the work-product privilege encourages thorough trial preparation by immunizing that preparation from discovery and by precluding "a learned profession [from] perform[ing] its functions either without wits or on wits borrowed from the adversary."[27]

- The attorney-client privilege protects only client communications; the work-product privilege protects all trial preparation.
- The attorney-client privilege applies regardless of the nature of the legal endeavor; the work-product privilege applies only to litigation.
- The quality of the protection differs: the attorney-client privilege is absolute; work-product protection is qualified.

Three conditions must be met in order to earn work-product protection. The material must be (1) a document or tangible thing; (2) prepared in anticipation of litigation; and (3) prepared by or for a party, or by or for his representative.[28] To determine whether the material was prepared "in anticipation of litigation," the focus is on whether the material was prepared (1) before or during litigation and (2) *because of* litigation and not for some other purpose.

Litigation need not have commenced for the work-product privilege to attach.[29] But if litigation has not yet begun, the party asserting work-product protection must be able to identify a tangible claim.[30] Some remote possibility of litigation is insufficient;[31] a clear resolve concerning litigation must exist.[32] As with the attorney-client privilege, the party asserting the work-privilege bears the burden of proof in both state and federal courts.[33]

The work-product privilege does not apply in nonadversarial proceedings[34] or apply to purely business advice.[35]

Applying the Attorney-Client Privilege When the Client Is a Corporation

When the client is an individual, whether the attorney-client privilege applies is relatively easy to ascertain. When the client is an organization, however, complexities arise. A lawyer representing an organization, such as a corporation, represents the juridical *entity*, not its constituents, whether shareholders, directors, officers, employees, or other agents.[36]

This section discusses the general rules applicable to current corporate employees. Special considerations applicable to former employees and employees of corporate affiliates are discussed in a separate section entitled "Other Issues Arising from Representation of Corporate Employees."

A corporation, like an individual, may assert the attorney-client privilege.[37] However, because a corporation can act only through its human constituents, a lawyer preparing a deposition witness employed by a corporation must decide whether the witness sufficiently personifies the corporation; only then will the preparation session be privileged.

For claims arising under federal law, determining who so personifies the corporation that they qualify as "clients" has evolved through case law.[38]

Before the Supreme Court's 1981 decision in *Upjohn Co. v. United States*,[39] federal circuit courts had split on the appropriate test for determining whether an employee's communications with counsel were privileged. Some circuit courts embraced the "control group" test,[40] which protected only the communications of senior management; others adopted a broader test, the "subject matter" test,[41] which encompassed certain communications of lower-level employees.[42]

In *Upjohn*,[43] the Supreme Court finally rejected the strict control-group test, but the Court declined to establish a bright-line test of its own. Instead, the Court held that the privilege should be determined on a case-by-case basis.[44] On the facts of *Upjohn*, the Court held the following factors to be persuasive in establishing the existence of the privilege:

1. the communications were made by employees to corporate counsel to secure legal advice for the corporation,
2. the employees cooperated with corporate counsel at the direction of corporate superiors,
3. the communications concerned matters within the employees' scope of employment, and
4. the information was not available from upper-echelon management.[45]

The lawyer for a corporation cannot assume, however, that the *Upjohn* test will necessarily determine the question of whether a particular corporate employee qualifies as a "client" because state law, rather than federal law, may be determinative on that issue.[46] Some states follow the *Upjohn* standard,[47] while others adhere to the control-group test.[48]

The Communication Must Be Made to an Attorney

For the attorney-client privilege to apply, the legal services, including deposition preparation, must be rendered only by a person qualified under applicable law to act as an attorney. When a lawyer is admitted to practice in some state or nation, membership in the bar where the services are performed "is not a sine qua non" of the privilege.[49] The prevailing view is that membership in the bar where the services are performed is merely one factor to be considered in determining whether counsel was acting in a legal capacity.[50] The attorney-client privilege applies equally to a corporation's inside counsel,[51] although there is a danger that a court might hold that inside counsel was providing business advice, which is not privileged, rather than legal advice.[52]

In addition, courts have recognized that to be effective, a lawyer must often rely on help from others, including "secretaries, file clerks, telephone operators, messengers, clerks not yet admitted to the bar, and aides of other sorts."[53] Thus, various categories of individuals working under the direct supervision and control of the lawyer are included within the scope of the attorney-client privilege.[54]

Similarly, the attorney-client privilege protects communications to and from outside consultants retained to assist the lawyer if the communication was made in confidence and to obtain legal advice from a lawyer.[55] Thus, the attorney-client privilege protects "information provided to an accountant by a client at the behest of his attorney for the purposes of interpretation and analysis . . . to the extent that it is imparted in connection with the legal representation."[56] Similarly, statements made by a client to a detective hired by a lawyer are protected by the privilege.[57]

It should make no difference whether the consultant is hired by the lawyer or the client, as long as the consultant's role is to assist the lawyer in rendering legal advice; however, as a practical matter, it may be more difficult to establish the privilege when the consultant is retained by the client independent of any request by the lawyer.[58] To increase the chances of retaining the privilege, the attorney, *not* the client, should retain the consultant/agent.[59]

There is a split in authority concerning communications with public relations firms. Some courts hold that the privilege may cover communications between a public relations firm and a client or the client's lawyers if the public relations firm is hired by the lawyers to help render advice related to the client's legal problems.[60] According to these authorities, an attorney's efforts to influence public opinion to advance the client's legal position are "legal services" and thus covered by the privilege. An alternative rationale for this view is that communications between a lawyer or client and a public relations firm to which the client gives decision-making authority may be privileged because the public relations firm is effectively incorporated into the client's staff and treated as an "employee" for purposes of the attorney-client privilege.[61]

Other courts, however, have ruled that the privilege does not protect communications between clients or their lawyers and a public relations firm because "the privilege protects communications between a client and an attorney, not communications that prove important to an attorney's legal advice to a client."[62] But even under this view, the communications may be protected under the work-product privilege.[63]

Communications Between an Attorney and Client Are Protected; Facts Are Not

The attorney-client privilege protects only a communication between the lawyer and the client from disclosure, not the underlying facts. As the Supreme Court stated in *Upjohn*,

> [T]he protection of privilege extends only to communications and not to facts. A fact is one thing and a communication concerning that fact is an entirely different thing. The client cannot be compelled to answer the question, "what did you say or write to the attorney?" but may not refuse to disclose any relevant fact within his knowledge merely because he incorporated a statement of such fact into his communication to his attorney.[64]

Furthermore, to be privileged, documents must be prepared and communications made in the course of rendering or seeking legal advice.[65] Thus, the attorney-client privilege applies to documents exchanged between corporate employees and copied to attorneys "if they contained communications intended to be confidential and a dominant purpose of the communication was to obtain legal advice."[66] If documents are "written for some other purpose than to seek legal advice and would have been prepared whether or not the attorney was sent a copy," they will not be covered by the privilege.[67] However, the privilege will apply if the document was sent in response to a request for information by "an attorney who was seeking information from his client to facilitate his representation of the client."[68]

Preexisting documents or documents edited by counsel but containing no legal advice are not covered by the attorney-client privilege.[69] Having counsel present at a meeting does not render the communications at that meeting privileged unless they are "related to the acquisition or rendition of professional legal services and must have retained a confidential character."[70] Nor does sending in-house counsel a copy of documents constitute a privileged communication. "A corporation cannot be permitted to insulate its files from discovery simply by sending a 'cc' to in-house counsel."[71]

An example of a communication that may fall outside the privilege is an investigative report prepared by a lawyer. It is not privileged merely because an attorney conducted the investigation. The critical question is whether the communication was made to render legal services.[72] When documents demonstrate that counsel was functioning in a scientific, administrative, or public relations capacity, the privilege does not apply. When the role assigned to attorneys can be performed by a panel of scientists, a doctor or scientist, or a tobacco company executive, it is not "primarily of a legal character" and falls outside of the attorney-client privilege.[73]

Legal Advice Distinguished from Other "Lawyer" Communications

The requirement that counsel be engaged to provide legal advice—as distinct from business advice—usually arises when a lawyer is advising a client about a transaction, which is typically not the situation in the context of a deposition. Nevertheless, a defender should explain to the witness the legal context of the preparation session, including such matters as the claims and defenses in the action, the nature of a deposition, and the rights and obligations of the witness. Such legal advice will help focus the witness on the purpose of the preparation session and better ensure the applicability of the privilege.[74]

The distinction between legal and business advice is not always clear. In *In re The County of Erie*, the Second Circuit recently applied a "predominant purpose" test in determining the boundaries between legal, business, and policy advice.[75] In *Erie*, the court described legal advice as occurring when a lawyer communicating advice interprets and applies "legal principles to guide future conduct or to assess past conduct."[76] The predominant-purpose test requires that the communication be made "for the purpose of securing primarily either (i) an opinion on law or (ii) legal services or (iii) assistance in some legal proceeding."[77]

In explaining the difference between legal advice and nonprivileged policy advice, the Second Circuit explained that a lawyer who recommends a "policy" to a client still can be rendering privilege-protected legal advice: "When a lawyer has been asked to assess compliance with a legal obligation, the lawyer's recommendation of a policy that complies (or better complies) with the legal obligation—or that advocates and promotes compliance, or oversees implementation of compliance measures—is legal advice."[78] In other words, when a lawyer assesses the law's requirements and how to comply with them, the lawyer is not providing unprotected general policy advice.[79]

The distinction between legal and business advice has special significance for inside counsel: The work-product privilege does not apply to materials that a lawyer routinely prepares or prepares for a business purpose, but only to materials "prepared principally or exclusively in anticipation of ongoing litigation."[80] However, a document "prepared to assist in the making of a business decision expected to result in litigation" is not necessarily excluded from protection.[81] In general, such documents will also be entitled to work-product protection if they can "fairly be said to have been prepared or obtained" in anticipation of litigation and not during the course of a routine investigation in the ordinary course of business.[82]

Dealing with the overlap between business advice and legal advice requires a pragmatic approach. "The mere fact that business advice is given or solicited does not . . . automatically render the privilege lost: where the advice given is predominantly legal, as opposed to business, in nature the privilege will still attach."[83] A lawyer's experience, education, and knowledge all factor into a lawyer's advice. "A lawyer's advice to his client 'does not spring from lawyers' heads as Athena did from the brow of Zeus.' . . . Indeed, the nature of a lawyer's role is such that legal advice may also include reference to other relevant considerations."[84] As long as the communication "concerns legal rights and obligations" and reveals "a lawyer's judgment and recommended legal strategies," the communication will retain its privilege.[85] Documents discussing financial questions and issues of commercial strategy and tactics are still protected by the attorney-client privilege when their contents make it evident that the attorney is presenting issues and analyzing choices based on his legal expertise and with an eye to the constraints imposed by applicable law.[86]

Crime, Fraud, and Fiduciary Exceptions to the Attorney-Client Privilege

"[C]ommunications in furtherance of contemplated or ongoing criminal or fraudulent conduct" are not protected by the attorney-client privilege.[87] The crime-fraud exception applies even if the attorney is not aware of the illegality involved. It is enough that the communication furthered, or the client intended it to further, the illegality.[88]

When a fiduciary retains an attorney to advise him in the exercise of his fiduciary duties, communications with the attorney are not absolutely protected from inquiry by the beneficiaries of the fiduciary relationship.[89] For example, shareholders suing derivatively are considered to be beneficiaries who, upon a showing of good cause, can override a corporate defendant's attorney-client privilege.[90] One court, however, refused to apply the fiduciary exception because courts "do not enjoy the freedom to restrict California's statutory attorney-client privilege on notions of policy or ad hoc justification."[91] In 2003, New York Civil Practice Law and Rules § 4503 abrogated the fiduciary exception to the attorney-client privilege as applied to confidential communications between an attorney and the representative of an estate.[92]

Confidentiality and Waiver of Privilege

Confidentiality

The confidentiality requirement for the attorney-client privilege to be attached to a communication rarely is a problem in the context of deposition preparation as long as a few commonsense precautions are taken. First, advise the witness that the preparation session is confidential and should not be discussed with others. Second, make sure the session is confidential by having present only people who fall within the privilege.[93] Finally, conduct the preparation session in a suitably private location, with no third parties within easy hearing distance.[94]

Waiver of Privilege

For the attorney-client privilege to attach to a communication, it must be and remain a confidential communication between client and attorney.[95] Voluntary disclosure of privileged attorney-client communications to unrelated third parties typically waives the privilege.[96] The privilege can be waived by the client or the client's personal representative but *cannot* be waived by the attorney.[97] In addition, conversations and agreements between lawyers adverse to each other are not privileged and must be disclosed if they are material.[98] But discussions or negotiations between opposing attorneys seeking to settle a controversy may be inadmissible under Federal Rule of Evidence 408.[99]

The privilege is lost once documents containing legal advice are made public.[100] Also, under the "at issue" doctrine, a waiver of the attorney-client privilege occurs when "the client places the subject matter of the communication *at issue*."[101] For example, when a proxy statement is disseminated with legal counsel's opinions regarding the tax consequences of a proposed merger, the disclosure to the public results in the waiver of the attorney-client privilege for *all* documents regarding the tax consequences of the merger.[102]

One type of waiver is known as "subject-matter waiver," a form of implied waiver based upon the fairness doctrine. Under this doctrine, the inquiring party can reach all privileged conversations about a particular subject once one privileged communication on the subject has been disclosed.[103] Fairness considerations dictate that parties should not be able to use communications both "as a sword and a shield."[104] This happens when a party discloses some useful documents but withholds "potentially adverse documents addressing the same subject matter."[105] When selective disclosure will prejudice an adversary at trial, "the remedy is to declare the privilege waived as to all other communications concerning the same subject matter."[106]

Fairness considerations also come into play where the party asserting the privilege makes factual allegations, the truthfulness of which may be assessed only by an examination of the privileged communications or documents. "[S]elective assertion of privilege should not be merely another brush on an attorney's palette, utilized and manipulated to gain tactical or strategic advantage."[107] For example, the attorney-client privilege may be found waived if a witness reviews privileged documents to refresh his recollection before testifying in a deposition.[108]

Like the attorney-client privilege, the work-product privilege can also be waived. "The court is not bound by the prohibitions contained in the Federal Rules of Evidence against the use of hearsay when making a determination regarding the existence and waiver of the work-product privilege."[109] Courts generally find work-product protection has been waived only when the disclosure substantially increases the likelihood that a potential *adversary* will secure the information.[110] Providing a cover letter describing aspects of a legal memorandum to an expert "is not an example of 'voluntarily disclosing the work-product in such a manner that is likely to be revealed to its adversary.'"[111] The mere mentioning of a document to a party or partial revelation of the document does not destroy work-product immunity.[112]

When there is a request for the production of documents, the Federal Rules require that privileged documents be listed in a privilege log, which "must be received either within thirty days of a request for documents or by a date that is either agreed to by the parties or determined by the court."[113] Failure to describe the subject matter of documents in the privilege log results in waiver because it "is the functional equivalent of no listing at all."[114] Also, the privilege log must be maintained in compliance with applicable local rules or else the "work product privilege may be waived."[115]

There is no waiver of either the attorney-client or the work-product protection when information is disclosed to a party or other person with a common interest. Whether parties share a common interest depends on whether they work together toward a common legal goal, not whether they theoretically share similar interests.[116] And a waiver does not arise when there is a distribution "within a corporation of legal advice received from its counsel."[117]

Prior to September 19, 2008, when Federal Rules of Evidence 502 was promulgated, inadvertent waiver of either of the two privileges may occur when the disclosing party uses inadequate precautions to maintain the confidentiality of the privileged communications, subject to the operation of the "clawback" provisions of the 2006 amendments to the Federal Rules.[118] Under Rule 502, disclosure of privileged documents may result in a waiver of privilege for those documents unless "(1) the disclosure is inadvertent; (2) the holder of the privilege or protection took reasonable steps to prevent disclosure; and (3) the holder promptly took reasonable steps to rectify the error. . . ."[119] Courts applying this rule have emphasized that the party asserting privilege must act promptly upon discovery of the inadvertent disclosure.[120] Hence, both before and after the promulgation of Rule 502, documents inadvertently disclosed in discovery or in court filings or during trial may waive the attorney-client privilege for those documents. But the inadvertent disclosure of one document protected by the work-product privilege usually does not result in a waiver of the privilege as to *other* documents or the waiver of the attorney-client privilege, or vice versa.[121] These rules encourage open communication between counsel and client, and also create "an incentive for counsel to take reasonable precautions in document production to avoid a waiver of privilege."[122]

Any analysis of waiver of the attorney-client privilege in the corporate context must begin with a proposition noted at the beginning of this chapter: The corporation is the client. If the corporation is the client, a document containing legal advice from counsel may be relayed among corporate employees to help them act according to that advice without waiving the attorney-client privilege.[123] A corporate officer testifying in his individual capacity before a grand jury, however, can impliedly waive the corporation's privilege without that entity's consent. To determine whether a corporate officer waived the corporation's privilege before a grand jury, a court will weigh the circumstances surrounding the witness's testimony, including the witness's motive to exculpate his own conduct and whether justice requires that the testimony should constitute a waiver.[124]

Communications also fall under the "at issue" doctrine "where invasion of the privilege is required to determine the validity of the client's claim or defense and application of the privilege would deprive the adversary of vital information."[125] But the attorney-client privilege is *not* waived when the party claiming the privilege did not need the privileged documents to sustain its cause of action.[126] One party cannot justify breaching the opposing party's privilege "by reason of [his] own pleading of an affirmative defense."[127]

Other Issues Arising from Representation of Corporate Employees

Counsel's Communications with Former Employees

It is not unusual for former employees of a corporation to be deposed. In *Upjohn*, the Court did not consider whether the attorney-client privilege extends to communications between a corporation's lawyer and its former employees. However, in the concurring opinion, Chief Justice Burger noted his approval of a rule that would treat communications between the lawyer and former employees as privileged in situations in which a "former employee speaks at the direction of the management with an attorney regarding conduct or proposed conduct within the scope of employment."[128]

The extension of the attorney-client privilege to include former employees promotes honest communication between former employees and a corporation's lawyer. Accordingly, many courts hold such communications privileged.[129]

Warnings to Corporate Employees Concerning Potential Conflicts of Interest

As a matter of ethics, a lawyer representing a corporation represents the corporate entity, not its directors, officers, managing agents, or employees.[130] When representing such corporate personnel—whether current or former—in a deposition, the corporation's counsel runs the risk that the deponent mistakenly may believe that corporate counsel represents her individually. If this happens, counsel could be disqualified if the interests of the corporation and the individual later diverge. Therefore, corporate personnel should be advised that corporate counsel does not represent them individually and of their right to obtain individual counsel.

Rule 1.13(d) of the Model Rules of Professional Conduct (Model Rules) provides some guidance on this issue, stating that "[i]n dealing with an organization's directors, officers [and] employees . . . a lawyer shall explain the identity of the client when it is apparent that the organization's interests are adverse to those of the [organization's] constituents with whom the lawyer is dealing." The comment to Model Rule 1.13(d) suggests that "care must be taken to assure that the individual understands that, when there is such adversity of interest, the lawyer for the organization cannot provide legal representation for that constituent individual, and that discussions between the lawyer for the organization and the individual may not be privileged." The comment goes on to add that whether such a warning should be given may turn on the facts of each case.

In addition to ethical considerations, there is another reason for providing appropriate disclosure to employees: the danger that a corporation's lawyer may be disqualified, as noted above, if a corporate officer does not understand the lawyer's role. That is exactly what happened in the seminal decision of *E.F. Hutton & Co. v. Brown*.[131]

In that case, Hutton's lawyer conducted an internal investigation that included interviewing various Hutton personnel regarding certain transactions. Afterward, the lawyer accompanied one of Hutton's officers to two hearings regarding the transactions. During both hearings, the officer told the judge that he was represented by the counsel for the corporation, and counsel did not take any steps to correct this mistake.[132]

In a subsequent suit by Hutton against the officer arising out of the same transactions, Hutton's counsel was disqualified. The court reasoned that the corporate officer reasonably believed that both he and Hutton were jointly represented by Hutton's counsel. The court stated that a lawyer's appearance on behalf of a corporate employee individually at a judicial proceeding raises a presumption of individual representation, which the corporation did not overcome.[133] Because of the subsequent conflicting interests between the employee and the corporation, the court required the lawyer to withdraw from the litigation.[134] The court was careful to note that

> [n]ot all corporate counsel appearing with corporate officers who are called to testify will risk disqualification. Only those counsel who permit the officer to believe that they represent him individually will disable themselves from appearing in subsequent litigation against him. And it is eminently proper to disqualify these, for they are the persons who are in a position, and have the obligation, to ensure that there is no misunderstanding by the officer.[135]

Counsel's Communication with Employees of Adversary

A related area of developing law has the potential to undermine the availability of the attorney-client privilege in the context of communications with lower-level, *former* employees of a corporate client. Ethics rules prohibit a lawyer from communicating directly with a party or other person who the lawyer knows is represented by another lawyer in the case without the consent of that person's lawyer.[136] To avoid such prohibited ex parte contact, it is important to determine which current or former corporate employees come under the corporate umbrella.

Courts appear to be taking a narrow view as to which employees fall within the corporate umbrella and thus may not be contacted ex parte by opposing counsel, limiting the kind of employees who qualify for the privilege. This trend runs counter to earlier cases that adopted a broader view about which employees are included within the corporation's attorney-client privilege.

With respect to *current* corporate employees, some courts take the view that the prohibition against counsel's communications with a represented "party" or person, extends only to employees with legal authority to bind the corporation.[137] The New York Court of Appeals has held that the prohibition also includes "the corporate employees responsible for actually effectuating the advice of counsel in the matter."[138] And the comments to the Model Rules state that the prohibition against ex parte contact applies to employees with "managerial responsibility"; that is, (1) those whose acts or omissions may be imputed to the corporation for purposes of criminal or civil liability, and (2) those whose statements might constitute admissions of the corporation.[139]

A minority of courts take a different approach. For example, in *Mompoint v. Lotus Development Corp.*,[140] a federal district court examined the propriety of counsel's ex parte interviews with employees of a corporate adversary. The court held that in every case it was necessary to consider the extent of a corporation's need to have its counsel present to ensure "effective representation" of the corporation.[141]

The Committee on Professional Ethics of the New York City Bar Association reached an even broader conclusion. In its view, a "corporation's right to effective representation can be guarded adequately only by viewing all present employees of a corporation as 'parties' for purposes of DR 7-104 where the proposed interview concerns matters within the scope of the employees' employment."[142] The Massachusetts Bar Association has also adopted this approach.[143]

Authorities seem to agree that the ethics rules do not restrain counsel from communicating with former employees of a corporate adversary.[144] The American Bar Association has issued a formal opinion to this effect. It provides that the Model Rules do not prohibit a lawyer from contacting former employees of an opposing corporate party without the consent of the corporation's counsel.[145] In *Siebert & Co v. Intuit Inc.*, the New York Court of Appeals found that allowing such contact with former employees strikes "a balance between protecting represented parties from making imprudent disclosures, and allowing opposing counsel the opportunity to unearth relevant facts through informal discovery devices."[146]

In *Merrill v. City of New York*, a district court stated that "the only policy arguably favoring some form of restriction on contact with a former employee would be if that former employee is in possession of information protected by a privilege that belongs to his former employer. That circumstance would counsel against allowing an attorney to inquire about such communications from the former employee, but it would not justify precluding any contact with that individual."[147] And the court in *Siebert* found that a disclosure by a low-level employee or former employee would not waive the corporation's privilege, where the employee was directed by the corporation's attorneys to avoid disclosing privileged or confidential information and no such information was disclosed.[148]

The same court held that the right to conduct ex parte interviews is not "a license for adversary counsel to elicit privileged or confidential information from an opponent's former employee."[149] Indeed, the court admonished counsel to take care to "steer clear of privileged or confidential information" and "conform to all applicable ethical standards."[150]

Given the rules against ex parte contact, corporate counsel should consider extending its representation to current and former corporate employees whose testimony may be significant. By doing so, the prohibition against ex parte communications by counsel for the adversary will apply if the employees are represented by corporate counsel. In seeking to create an attorney-client relationship, the corporation's lawyer must ensure that appropriate disclosure is made concerning potential conflicts of interest[151] and must guard against the possibility that the lawyer will be disqualified if a subsequent dispute between the corporation and the employee arises.[152]

Representation of Corporate Affiliates and Their Employees

Sometimes the witnesses in a particular matter include employees of corporate affiliates—parent corporations, subsidiaries, and sister corporations. In general, communications between corporate counsel and the employees of such affiliates are protected by the attorney-client privilege under one or more of four legal theories.

The first theory involves the situation in which the parties use the same counsel. In *United States v. United Shoe Machinery Corp.*,[153] a parent corporation and its affiliates and subsidiaries used the same inside and outside counsel. The court held that for purposes of the attorney-client privilege the "client" was the parent corporation and all of its related affiliates and subsidiaries.

The second theory involves situations in which the parent and subsidiary do not use the same counsel. In that situation, the "community of interests" test is used, as explained in a patent/antitrust case, *Duplan Corp. v. Deering Milliken, Inc.*[154] In *Duplan*, the court held that there was a sufficient community of interests between a French corporation (the patent holder) and some of its subsidiaries for the attorney-client privilege to apply.[155]

The third theory involves situations where communications between related corporations are considered privileged because the corporations are conducting a "joint defense."[156] This joint-defense privilege has also been applied in cases involving unrelated corporations that exchanged otherwise privileged communications.[157]

The joint-defense doctrine may allow for the presence of a co-defendant's lawyer to assist in the preparation of the witness. Under this doctrine, when two or more parties have a common interest, communications by one party to his lawyer in the presence of the other party are not discoverable by third parties.[158]

The protection afforded by this doctrine may be jeopardized in cases of multiparty cooperation if some of the parties to the joint defense later settle or other divergences of interest appear. To guard against possible defections, it is customary for the parties and their counsel to enter a written joint-defense agreement, spelling out the confidentiality agreements reached by the parties.[159] Ordinarily, however, in a subsequent dispute between two parties who were formerly part of a joint defense, either can compel disclosure of the confidential communication that passed between them and their respective lawyers.[160]

The fourth theory involves "joint clients" where one attorney simultaneously represents two or more affiliated parts; for example, a parent corporation and a subsidiary. Where there are joint clients who develop divergent interests in the course of the representation, the District of Columbia Circuit found that one client's attorney-client privilege should not be lost because the attorney wrongly continued to represent two entities with conflicting interests.[161]

Hence, information a parent company funnels through in-house counsel remains privileged against a subsidiary even though the in-house counsel worked on matters for both parent and subsidiary.[162] The subsidiary cannot waive the parent corporation's privilege without the parent corporation's consent.[163] The principle of attorney-client privilege in the joint-client context is that "when an attorney errs by continuing to represent two clients despite their conflicts, the clients—who reasonably expect their communications to be secret—are not penalized by losing their privilege."[164]

Notes

*Nancy E. Barton is owed a large debt for having authored the original Chapter 6 in the first edition of this book. Her scholarship appearing in that earlier work, *Establishing an Attorney-Client Relationship*, is the brick and mortar of this updated chapter.

Grateful acknowledgment also goes to Jennifer D. Larson, then a law student and now an associate at Weil, Gotshal & Manges LLP, for her contribution to these pages.

1. See Chapters 4 and 5, discussing the importance of witness preparation.

2. The attorney-client and work-product privileges protect against disclosure of communications, not against disclosure of the underlying facts by those who communicated with the lawyer. Upjohn v. United States, 449 U.S. 383, 395 (1981) (attorney-client privilege); FED. R. CIV. P. 26(b)(3) advisory committee's note (work-product privilege).

3. *See* FED. R. CIV. P. 26(b)(1) ("parties may obtain discovery regarding any matter, not privileged" as discussed in Chapters 2 and 3).

4. See "Initial Contacts with the Witness" in Chapter 5 and Chapter 6, discussing the lack of privilege when preparing a third party.

5. See Chapter 9.

6. *See, e.g.,* Nichols v. Keller, 19 Cal. Rptr. 2d 601, 608 (Ct. App. 1993), Foley v. Metro. Sanitary Dist., 572 N.E.2d 978, 984 (Ill. App. Ct. 1991); C.K. Indus. Corp. v. D.M. Indus. Corp., 623 N.Y.S.2d 410, 411 (App. Div. 1995), Parker v. Carnahan, 772 S.W.2d 151, 156 (Tex. Ct. App. 1989).

7. *See, e.g.,* Priest v. Hennessy, 51 N.Y.2d 62 (1980).

8. *See, e.g.,* N.Y. C.P.L.R § 4503(a) (McKinney Supp. 1988); CAL. EVID. CODE §§ 950–962 (Deering 1995); DEL. UNIF. R. EVID. 502 (1995); N.J. STAT. ANN. § 2A:84A-20 (West 1994); TEX. R. CRIM. EVID. 503(b) (1995).

9. United States v. United Shoe Mach. Corp., 89 F. Supp. 357, 358–59 (D. Mass. 1950). *See also* Bank Brussels Lambert v. Credit Lyonnais (Suisse) S.A., 220 F. Supp. 2d 283, 286 (S.D.N.Y. 2002) ("the attorney-client privilege is perhaps the oldest recognized common law privilege sanctioned by the courts").

10. *See In re* Crazy Eddie Sec. Litig., 131 F.R.D. 374, 377 (E.D.N.Y. 1990) (citing FED. R. EVID. 501).

11. *See* von Bulow v. von Bulow, 811 F.2d 136, 141 (2d Cir.), *cert. denied*, 481 U.S. 1015 (1987); Boss Mfg. Co. v. Hugo Boss AG, No. 97 Civ. 8495, 1999 WL 47324, at * 1 (S.D.N.Y. Feb. 1. 1999).

12. FED. R. EVID. 501.

13. *United Shoe Machinery Corp.* appears to suggest incorrectly that only communications by a client to an attorney are privileged.

14. Upjohn Co. v. United States, 449 U.S. 383, 395–96 (1981) (citations omitted). *See also* Johnson v. Sea-Land Serv., Inc., 2001 WL 897185, at *2 (S.D.N.Y. Aug. 9, 2001) (facts are not privileged, but descriptions of

those facts in response to an attorney's request for background information are privileged).

15.   *Upjohn Co.*, 449 U.S. at 395–96. Therefore, it is now well settled in New York and many other states and under federal common law that the privilege applies not only to communications by the client to the attorney but also to advice rendered by the attorney to the client, at least to the extent that such advice may reflect confidential information conveyed by the client. *See* Softview Comp. Prods. Corp, Inc. v. Haworth, Inc., 97 Civ. 8815, 2000 WL 351411, at *2 (S.D.N.Y. Mar. 31, 2000) (applying federal common law of privilege).

16.   *See* Rossi v. Blue Cross & Blue Shield of Greater N.Y., 73 N.Y.2d 588, 592 (1989) ("[W]hile the cases largely concern communications by clients to their attorneys, CPLR 4503 speaks of communications 'between the attorney . . . and the client,' and the privilege thus plainly extends as well to the attorney's own communications to the client." (citing authorities)). *See also* Stafford Trading, Inc. v. Lovely, 2007 U.S. Dist. LEXIS 13062, at *21–37 (D. Ill. 2007) (providing examples of documents in the case and explaining why each one is or is not covered by the attorney-client privilege).

Counsel in the few jurisdictions that may not clearly protect the lawyer's communications to the client should take special care to ensure the confidentiality of their advice by making explicit (rather than implicit) to the witness in preparation for a deposition the manner in which there is a relationship between the client's confidences and the lawyer's advice.

17.   *See von Bulow*, 811 F.2d at 146 (applying federal common law of privilege); Bowne of New York City, Inc. v. AmBase Corp., 150 F.R.D. 465, 470 (S.D.N.Y. 1993) (applying New York state law of privilege); Priest v. Hennessy, 51 N.Y.2d 62, 69 (1980).

18.   *See* N. Carolina Elec. Memb. Corp. v. Carolina Power & Light Co., 110 F.R.D. 511, 513 (M.D.N.C. 1986). *See also* Bristol-Meyers Squibb Co. v. Rhone-Poulenc Rorer, Inc., No. 95 Civ. 8833 (RPR), 1998 WL 474206, at *2 (S.D.N.Y Aug. 12, 1998) (applying federal common law of privilege).

19.   329 U.S. 495 (1947). *See also* United States v. Adlman, 134 F.3d 1194, 1196 (S.D.N.Y. 1998).

20.   *Id.* at 510.

21.   *Id.* at 511.

22.   United States v. Nobles, 422 U.S. 225, 238 (1975).

23.   *See In re* Copper Mkt. Antitrust Litig., 200 F.R.D. 213, 221; 2001 U.S. Dist. LEXIS 5269 (S.D.N.Y. 2001) (citing Bank of N.Y. v. Meridien BIAO Bank Tanzania, 1996 (S.D.N.Y. 1996)).

24.   FED. R. CIV. P. 26(b)(3). Several courts have declared that FRE 612 provides a basis for discovery of privileged documents wholly independent of the "substantial need" exception to the work-product doctrine.

See, e.g., Ehrlich v. Howe, 848 F. Supp. 482 (S.D.N.Y. 1994). State law also provides that the "work-product of an attorney shall not be obtainable." *See, e.g.,* N.Y. C.P.L.R. § 3101(c) (McKinney 1999).

25. *See, e.g.,* Curto v. Med. World Commc'ns, Inc., 2007 U.S. Dist. LEXIS 35464 (E.D.N.Y. 2007) (discussing the difference between fact work-product and opinion work-product and noting that the "distinction is relevant when a party seeks discovery of a work-product document because the classification of the document determines the showing necessary to warrant disclosure").

Some circuits have held the protection to be absolute; most have not. *See In re* Grand Jury Subpoena, 220 F.R.D. 130, 145–46 (D. Mass. 2004) (collecting cases).

26. *See, e.g., In re* Grand Jury Proceedings, 219 F.3d 175, 190 (2d Cir. 2000) (citing the Supreme Court's statement in *Nobles* that "the work-product doctrine is distinct from and broader than the attorney-client privilege") (citation omitted).

27. Hickman v. Taylor, 329 U.S. 495, 516 (1947) (Jackson, J., concurring).

28. *See* Stafford Trading, Inc. v. Lovely, 2007 U.S. Dist. LEXIS 13062, at *6 (D. Ill. 2007); Softview Comp. Prods. Corp, Inc. v. Haworth, Inc., 97 Civ. 8815, 2000 WL 351411, at *12 (addressing both attorney-client and work-product privileges).

29. *See, e.g.,* United States v. Adlman, 134 F.3d 1194, 1194–95 (S.D.N.Y. 1998); Maine v. United States DOI, 298 F.3d 60, 68 (1st Cir. 2002) ("In light of the decisions of the Supreme Court, we therefore agree with the formulation of the work-product rule adopted in *Adlman* and by five other courts of appeals. *See also supra* note 9 and accompanying text.

30. *See, e.g.,* United States v. KPMG LLP, 316 F. Supp. 2d 30, 41 (D.D.C. 2004) ("Mere mention of fear of being sued for an action or inaction is not the sort of 'anticipation of litigation' which is covered by the attorney work-product doctrine."); Coastal States Gas Corp. v. Dep't of Energy, 617 F.2d 854, 865 (D.C. Cir. 1980) (stating, in the context of a FOIA case, "the courts will not penalize litigants for doing initial preparation before filing a complaint, but we agree with the district court that at the very least some articulable claim, likely to lead to litigation, must have arisen").

31. *See In re* Grand Jury Proceeding, 2001 U.S. Dist. Lexis 15646, at *49 (S.D.N.Y Oct. 3, 2001) ("The party asserting the privilege must demonstrate that a 'substantial probability' of litigation existed at the time the material was created.") (citing Garrett v. Metro. Life Ins. Co., 1996 U.S. Dist. LEXIS 8054, *9 (S.D.N.Y. June 12, 1996)); Garfinkle v. Arcata Nat'l Corp., 64 F.R.D. 688, 690 (S.D.N.Y. 1974). *Compare* Burlington Indus. v. Exxon Corp., 65 F.R.D. 26, 42 (D. Md. 1974) ("[I]n order to satisfy the requirement that documents be prepared in anticipation of litigation, it is not necessary that the documents be prepared after litigation has been commenced. The work-product doctrine applies to material prepared when litigation

is merely a contingency."), *with* Sandberg v. Va. Bankshares, 979 F.2d 332, 356 (4th Cir. 1992) ("Although the general counsel's affidavit indicates the purposes of the . . . meeting, it does not indicate her purpose in making the notes. The mere fact that a lawsuit was pending does not transform an attorney's notes into material prepared in anticipation of litigation. Moreover, while a general counsel may be involved in litigation strategy and oversight, it is also possible that her involvement in the litigation is no different from that of other corporate officers. In either case, her purpose in taking the notes is not self-evident and we find that Bankshares has failed to satisfy its burden of proof on this issue.").

32.   Thus, work-product protection has been denied to an investigative report not directly linked to litigation. *See* Janicker v. George Wash. Univ., 94 F.R.D. 648, 650 (D.D.C. 1982) (holding that there must be "objective facts establishing an identifiable resolve to litigate prior to the investigative efforts resulting in the report . . . [w]hile litigation need not be imminent, the primary motivating purpose behind the creation of a document or investigative report must be to aid in possible future litigation").

33.   *See In re* Grand Jury Subpoena Dated Dec. 19, 1978, 599 F.2d 504, 510 (2d Cir. 1979); Granite Partners v. Bear Stearns & Co. Inc., 184 F.R.D. 49, 50 (S.D.N.Y. 1999) ("[P]arty must demonstrate both that the privilege exists and that it has not been waived.").

34.   *See In re* Grand Jury Subpoena Dated March 9, 2001, 179 F. Supp. 2d 270, 2001 U.S. Dist. LEXIS 20645, at *41 (S.D.N.Y Dec. 13, 2001) (finding the doctrine not applicable to efforts to obtain a presidential pardon because the process was not an adversarial one). *See also id.* at *35 ("[D]ocuments prepared in contemplation of ex parte proceedings before the Patent and Trademark Office are not entitled to work-product protection, unless they were prepared 'principally' for use in anticipated adversarial proceedings." (citing Golden Trade S.R.L. v. Lee Apparel Co., 1992 WL 367070, at *4 (S.D.N.Y. Nov. 20, 1992))).

35.   "[T]he fact that documents prepared for a business purpose were also determined to be of potential use in pending litigation does not turn these documents into work-product or confidential communications between client and attorney . . . 'business communications cannot be insulated from discovery by virtue of the mention of an attorney's name, or their being directed to an attorney.'" Hardy v. N.Y. News, Inc., 114 F.R.D. 633, 646 (S.D.N.Y. 1987) (citation omitted). Whether the privilege applies turns on whether the document would have been prepared irrespective of the expected litigation. *Id.* (citation omitted). "[I]t may well be said that the effect of *Adlman* is to enforce the work-product privilege even if there is a dual purpose for the creation on the materials." *Granite Partners*, 184 F.R.D. at 54.

36.   *See* MODEL RULES OF PROF'L CONDUCT R. 1.13; MODEL CODE OF PROF'L RESPONSIBILITY EC 5-18. Similarly, representation of other judicial entities such as partnerships, joint ventures, and associations does

not create an attorney-client relationship between the entity's lawyers and these constituents.

37.   *See, e.g.,* Commodity Futures Trading Comm'n v. Weintraub, 471 U.S. 343, 348 (1985) ("It is by now well established . . . that the attorney-client privilege attaches to corporations as well as to individuals."); Bell v. Maryland, 378 U.S. 226, 263 (1964) ("A corporation, like any other 'client,' is entitled to the attorney-client privilege."); *In re* Cendant Corp. Sec. Litig., 343 F.2d 658, 665–68 (3d Cir. 2003).

38.   The federal case law, to the extent that it has influenced state law, is relevant to the practitioner in resolving the scope of the privilege in a case applying state law. *See infra* note 30.

39.   449 U.S. 383 (1981).

40.   The control-group test requires that the person making the communication be "in a position to control or even to take a substantial part in a decision about any action which the corporation may take upon the advice of the attorney," or be "an authorized member of a body or group which has the authority." City of Philadelphia v. Westinghouse Elec. Corp., 210 F. Supp. 483, 485 (E.D. Pa.), *mandamus and prohibition denied sub nom.* Gen. Elec. Co. v. Kirkpatrick, 312 F.2d 742 (3d Cir. 1962). The control-group test was criticized as too restrictive because the lower-level employees most likely to have detailed factual knowledge are also least likely to be in a control position and thus least likely to have their communications protected. *See, e.g.,* Dennis J. Block & Nancy E. Barton, *Internal Corporate Investigations: Maintaining the Confidentiality of a Corporate Client's Communications with Investigative Counsel,* 35 BUS. LAW 5, 13–17 (1979).

41.   *See, e.g.,* Harper & Row Publishers, Inc. v. Decker, 423 F.2d 487, 491–92 (7th Cir. 1970), *aff'd by an equally divided Court,* 400 U.S. 348 (1971) (concluding that communications of noncontrolling employees with counsel are privileged when "the employee makes the communications at the direction of his superiors in the corporation and where the subject matter upon which the attorney's advice is sought by the corporation and dealt with in the communication is the performance by the employee of the duties of his employment").

42.   Later decisions approved in concept the greater flexibility afforded by the subject-matter test of *Harper & Row* but suggested additional criteria designed to curb the potential abuse of *Harper & Row* that might occur if employee communications were routinely funneled through counsel. *See, e.g.,* Diversified Indus., Inc. v. Meredith, 572 F.2d 596, 609 (8th Cir. 1978) (en banc) (making explicit a requirement that communications directed by corporate superiors and made by a lower-level employee must be made for the purpose of the corporation securing legal advice).

43.   449 U.S. 383 (1981).

44.   *Id.* at 396.

45.   *Id.* at 394.

46.   *See supra* note 14.

47.   *See also* D.I. Chabourne, Inc. v. Superior Court, 388 P.2d 700 (Cal. 1964) (adopting list of factors inquiring into reason why corporation required communication be made); Chicago Title Ins. Co. v. Superior Court, 200 Cal. Rptr. 507, 514 (Ct. App. 1985), Denver Post Corp. v. University of Colo., 739 P.2d 874, 880 (Colo. Ct. App. 1987); Wardleigh v. Nevada, No. 25190, 1995 WL 124120 (Nev. Mar. 22, 1995).

48.   *See* Snider v. Sup. Court of San Diego Cty., 7 Cal. Rptr. 3d 119, 131–132 (Cal. Ct. App. 2003) (collecting cases and analyzing different standards, including the "managing-speaking agent" test, the "case-by-case balancing" test, and the "alter ego" or "New York" test). *See also* Totherow v. Rivier Coll., 05-C-296, 3–6 (N.H. Feb. 20, 2007) (collecting tests).

49.   Zenith Radio Corp. v. Radio Corp. of Am., 121 F. Supp. 792, 794 (D. Del. 1954) ("Bar membership should properly be of the court for the area wherein the services are rendered, but this is not a sine qua non, e.g., visiting counsel, long distance services by correspondence, pro hac vice services, 'house counsel' who practice law only for the corporate client and its affiliates and not for the public generally, for which local authorities do not insist on admission to the local bar."). *But see* United States v. United Shoe Mach. Corp., 89 F. Supp. 357, 360 (D. Mass. 1950) ("The fact that [house patent counsel], though resident in Massachusetts and regularly working here, have never received a license to practice law here shows that these regular employees are not acting as attorneys for United.").

50.   Paper Converting Mach. Co. v. FMC Corp., 215 F. Supp. 249, 251 (E.D. Wis. 1963); *see also* Ga.-Pac. Plywood Co. v. United States Plywood Corp., 18 F.R.D. 463, 465 (S.D.N.Y. 1956).

51.   *See In re* County of Erie, 473 F.3d 413, 421 (2d Cir. 2007). *See generally* Garner v. Wolfinbarger, 430 F.2d 1093 (5th Cir. 1970). *But see* Bank Brussels Lambert v. Credit Lyonnais (Suisse) S.A., 220 F. Supp. 2d 283, 286 (S.D.N.Y. 2002) (describing "the general reluctance and narrow, grudging application of the privilege" in cases involving in-house counsel in law firms).

52.   The burden is on the lawyer to show that the communication concerned the rendering of legal, rather than business, advice. *See In re* Sealed Case, 737 F.2d 94, 99 (D.C. Cir. 1984) (in-house counsel who also had duties outside legal sphere bears burden to show that advice given in legal capacity). See also discussion in text accompanying notes 74–85.

53.   *See, e.g.,* United States v. Kovel, 296 F.2d 918, 921 (2d Cir. 1961).

54.   *Zenith Radio Corp.,* 121 F. Supp. at 794; FTC v. TRW, Inc., 479 F. Supp. 160, 163 n.7 (D.D.C. 1979) (citing 8 WIGMORE, EVIDENCE § 2301, at 583, § 2317, at 618 (McNaughton Rev. 1961)), *aff'd,* 628 F.2d 207 (D.C. Cir. 1980).

55.   *See* United States v. Schwimmer, 892 F.2d 237, 243 (2d Cir. 1989) ("The privilege also is held to cover communications made to certain agents of an attorney, including accountants hired to assist in the rendition of legal services.") *See also* United States v. Cote, 456 F.2d 142, 144–45 (8th

Cir. 1972) (test is "whether the accountant's services are a necessary aid to the rendering of effective legal services to the client"); FED. R. CIV. P. 26(b) (4). Chapter 19 discusses possible loss of privilege when the consultant is designated as a testifying expert.

56. *Schwimmer*, 892 F.2d at 243 (quoting United States v. Kovel, 296 F.2d 918, 922 (2d Cir. 1961)); *see also* Summit Ltd. v. Levy, 111 F.R.D. 40, 41 (S.D.N.Y. 1986). *See also* United States v. Bisanti, 414 F.3d 168, 170 (1st Cir. 2005) (noting that Congress passed a limited statutory accountant-client privilege, 26 U.S.C. § 7525(a)(1), but "the privilege only extends to communications that would be privileged were they between a taxpayer and an attorney"); *see generally* United States v. Torf (*In re* Grand Jury Subpoena), 350 F.3d 1010, 1015 (9th Cir. 2003) (noting that the attorney "hired Torf to help him assess the company's civil and criminal liability"). *But see* United States v. Frederick, 182 F.3d 496, 501 (7th Cir. 1999) ("But people who are under investigation and represented by a lawyer have the same duty as anyone else to file tax returns. They should not be permitted, by using a lawyer in lieu of another form of tax preparer, to obtain greater confidentiality than other taxpayers.").

57. John Doe Co. v. United States, 79 Fed. Appx. 476, 477 (2d Cir. 2003) ("Under certain limited circumstances, however, the attorney-client privilege may extend to communications with a third party, such as an accountant or private investigator hired to assist in the rendition of legal services.").

58. *Compare* United States v. Judson, 322 F.2d 460, 465–66 (9th Cir. 1963) (privilege applied to net worth statement prepared for IRS investigation by accountant hired by client at request of lawyer) *with* United States v. Brown, 478 F.2d 1038, 1040 (7th Cir. 1973) (privilege inapplicable to accountant's notes of meeting between client and lawyer when accountant's presence requested by client and not lawyer) *and Frederick*, 182 F.3d at 502 (stating that 26 U.S.C. § 7525 "does not protect work product").

59. *See* Hertzberg v. Veneman, 273 F. Supp. 2d 67, 77 n.4 (D.D.C. 2003). The *Hertzberg* court noted:

> If one wants to assure work product protection for factual or investigatory material or witness interviews, it surely is the better practice to have the agent who collects the information or conducts the investigation employed by the client's attorney rather than by the client directly because there is a stronger presumption that the work product of an agent of a lawyer retained for litigation or potential litigation (or the agent of an in-house or government agency lawyer with litigation responsibilities) was prepared "in anticipation of litigation."

Id. (citing *Nobles* but also pointing out that Rule 26(b)(3) does not require such an arrangement). *But see In re* Copper Mkt. Antitrust Litig., 200 F.R.D. at 219 (finding privilege where agent was retained by the client).

60.   *In re* Grand Jury Subpoenas, 2003 WL 21262645 (S.D.N.Y. June 2, 2003) (Martha Stewart case).

61.   *In re Copper Mkt. Antitrust Litig.*, 200 F.R.D. at 219.

62.   *See* Calvin Klein Trademark Trust v. Wachner, 198 F.R.D. 53, 54 (S.D.N.Y. 2000) (communications between a public relations consultant and counsel were found not to be protected under the attorney-client privilege but were nonetheless protected under the work-product doctrine). *See also* Haugh v. Schroder Inv. Mgmt., Inc., 2003 WL 21998674, at *5 (S.D.N.Y. Aug. 25, 2003) (same). The *Calvin Klein* court also found that even if the documents at issue had contained confidential communications from the client to the attorney, the disclosure of the documents to the public relations firm waived that privilege. Finally, the court noted that the public relations firm did not perform in a materially different way from the ordinary functions of a public relations firm. *Calvin Klein*, 198 F.R.D. at 54–55.

63.   Haugh v. Schroder Inv. Mgmt., Inc., 2003 WL 21998674, at *5 (S.D.N.Y. Aug. 25, 2003).

64.   Upjohn Co. v. United States, 449 U.S. 383, 395–96 (1981) (citations omitted). *See also* Johnson v. Sea-Land Serv., Inc., 2001 WL 897185, at *2 (S.D.N.Y. Aug. 9, 2001) (stating that facts are not privileged, but descriptions of those facts in response to an attorney's request for background information are privileged).

65.   Communications must be between the attorney and client, not merely any communication that might reveal the client's identity. Video recordings and unredacted photographs seized from an attorney's agent are not communications under the attorney-client privilege simply because they may lead to the discovery of the client's identity. Magill v. Superior Court of the County of Madera, 103 Cal. Rptr. 2d 355, 403 (Cal. Ct. App. 2001) (unpublished) (finding that photographs and videotape of client's car showing the license plate number did not amount to a privileged communication).

66.   U.S. Postal Serv. v. Phelps Dodge Ref. Corp., 852 F. Supp. 156, 163–64 (E.D.N.Y. 1994).

67.   *Id.*

68.   *See Johnson*, 2001 WL 897185, at *2 (quoting *United Shoe Mach. Corp.*, 89 F. Supp. at 358–59).

69.   *See In re* Grand Jury Subpoenas Dated Oct. 22, 1991, and Nov. 1, 1991, 959 F.2d 1158, 1166 (2d Cir. 1992) (stating that telephone records "though transmitted to Paul-Weiss, are not the client's confidential communications, are not within the privilege, and did not become exempt from discovery by that transmission."); *see also* Gould, Inc. v. Mitsui Mining and Smelting Co., 825 F.2d 676, 679–80 (2d Cir. 1987). *See Phelps Dodge*, 852 F. Supp. at 163 (if inside counsel edits a document but does not also render legal advice, no privilege applies).

70. Int'l Tel. & Tel. Corp. v. United Tel. Co. of Fla., 60 F.R.D. 177, 185 (M.D. Fla. 1973). *See also* Yang v. Reno, 157 F.R.D. 625, 636 (M.D. Pa. 1994) ("[T]he government has alleged no facts supporting the conclusion that at relevant meetings either Ms. Coven or other DOJ attorneys engaged in attorney-client communications with executive officials which were both confidential and necessary to enable them obtain informed legal advice.").

71. *Phelps Dodge*, 852 F. Supp. at 163–64.

72. *See* ECDC Envtl., L.C. v. N.Y. Marine and Gen. Ins. Co., No. 96 Civ 6033, 1998 WL 614478, at *9 (S.D.N.Y. June 4, 1998) (applying New York state privilege law).

73. *See* Sackman v. Liggett Group, Inc., 920 F. Supp. 357 (E.D.N.Y. 1996), *vacated on other grounds and remanded for reconsideration*, 167 F.R.D. 6 (E.D.N.Y. 1996), *reconsidered with pertinent reasoning aff'd*, 173 F.R.D. 358 (E.D.N.Y. 1997) (applying New York state privilege law).

74. See "Preparing the Witness: Rules for Reconstructing Reality" in Chapter 8, discussing how to best discuss the theories of the case.

75. *In re* County of Erie, 473 F.3d 413, 419 (2d Cir. 2007).

76. *Id.*

77. *Id.* at 420 n.7 (citing *In re* Grand Jury Subpoena, 204 F.3d 516, 520 n.1 (4th Cir. 2000)).

78. *Id.* at 422. *See also United Shoe Mach. Corp.*, 89 F. Supp. at 359 (D. Mass. 1950) ("[T]he privilege of nondisclosure is not lost merely because relevant nonlegal considerations are expressly stated in a communication which also includes legal advice.").

79. *County of Erie*, 473 F.3d at 422. (citation omitted).

80. *See* Resolution Trust Corp. v. Mass. Mut. Life Ins. Co., 200 F.R.D. 183, 188 (2001) (citing United States v. Constr. Prods. Research, Inc., 73 F.3d 464, 473 (2d Cir. 1996)). *See also* Hertzberg v. Veneman, 273 F. Supp. 2d 67, 75–82 (D.D.C. 2003) (evaluating the work-product privilege in the context of Exemption 5 of the Freedom of Information Act).

81. *See Resolution Trust Corp.*, 200 F.R.D. at 190 (citing United States v. Adlman, 134 F.3d 1194, 1199 (S.D.N.Y. 1998)).

82. "To meet this standard, a party 'must at least have had a subjective belief that litigation was a real possibility, and that belief must have been objectively reasonable' in the circumstances." *Hertzberg*, 273 F. Supp. 2d at 79. The court contrasted this "because of litigation" test with the "primarily to assist in litigation" test used other circuits, including the Second Circuit in *Adlman. Hertzberg*, 273 F. Supp. 2d at 79 n.5. The *Adlman* court approved of the formulation in Wright & Miller:

> The formulation of the work-product rule used by the Wright & Miller treatise, and cited by the Third, Fourth, Seventh, Eighth, and D.C. Circuits, is that documents should be deemed prepared in 'anticipation of litigation' and thus within the scope of the Rule,

if 'in light of the nature of the document and the factual situation in the particular case, the document can fairly be said to have been prepared or obtained because of the prospect of litigation' . . . The Wright & Miller 'because of' formulation accords with the plain language of Rule 26(b)(3) and the purposes underlying the work-product doctrine.

Adlman, 134 F.3d at 1202 (citing 8 CHARLES ALAN WRIGHT ET AL., FEDERAL PRACTICE & PROCEDURE § 2024, at 343 (1994)).

83. United States v. Davis, 131 F.R.D. 391, 401 (S.D.N.Y. 1990).

84. *ABB Kent-Taylor*, 172 F.R.D. at 57 (internal citations omitted) (applying New York state privilege law).

85. Rossi v. Blue Cross & Blue Shield of Greater N.Y., 73 N.Y.2d 588, 594 (1989).

86. *See* Note Funding Corp. v. Bobian Inv. Co., 1995 WL 662402, at *3 (applying New York state privilege law).

87. *See* Madanes v. Madanes, 199 F.R.D. 135, 147 (S.D.N.Y. 2001) (citations omitted). This exception ensures "that the 'seal of secrecy' does not extend to communications made for the purpose of the commission of a fraud or crime." *Id.* (citing United States v. Jacobs, 117 F.3d 82, 87 (2d. Cir. 1997)). "The crime-fraud exception places communications made in furtherance of a crime or fraud outside the attorney-client privilege. The exception is based on the recognition that the privilege necessarily will 'protect the confidences of wrongdoers.'" United States v. BDO Seidman, LLP, 2007 U.S. App. LEXIS 15796 (7th Cir. 2007) (citing United States v. Zolin, 491 U.S. 554, 562–63 (1989)).

88. Corporation v. U.S., 519 U.S. 945 (1996). *See also In re* Richard Roe, Inc., 68 F.3d 38, 39–40 (2d Cir. 1995); *In re* Grand Jury Proceedings, 87 F.3d 377, 381–82 (9th Cir. 1996), cert. denied sub nom.

89. Lawrence v. Cohn, 2002 WL 109530, at *3 (S.D.N.Y. 2002).

90. Garner v. Wolfinbarger, 430 F.2d 1093, 1097 n.11 (5th Cir. 1970).

91. Wells Fargo Bank v. Superior Court, 91 Cal. Rptr. 2d 716, 722 (Cal. 2000), citing CAL. EVID. CODE § 954 (2008).

92. *See* N.Y. C.P.L.R. § 4503(a)(2).

93. See *supra* text accompanying notes 55–56 concerning the types of assistants that counsel may employ without jeopardizing the privilege.

94. E.W. Schwartz v. Wenger, 124 N.W.2d 489, 492 (Minn. 1963) (attorney-client conversation in courthouse corridor waived privilege); People v. Harris, 442 N.E.2d 1205, 1208 (N.Y. 1982) (defendant's telephone conversation with counsel waived privilege when held in known presence of two third parties); Chandler v. Denton, 741 P.2d 855, 866 (Okla. 1987) (attorney-client conversation that took place at table at or near third parties waived privilege); Hofmann v. Conder, 712 P.2d 216, 217 (Utah 1985) (presence of hospital nurse did not waive privilege if

nurse's presence was reasonably necessary). See also "Preparation Sessions: When, Where, How Often, and with Whom" in Chapter 5, discussing strategic considerations on where to meet.

95. *See Priest*, 51 N.Y.2d at 68–69.

96. *See In re* Cardinal Health Inc. Sec. Litig., 2007 WL 495150 (S.D.N.Y. 2007). *See also In re* Currency Conversion Fee, 2003 WL 22389169, at *1 (S.D.N.Y. Oct. 21, 2003); Workman v. Boylan Buick, Inc., 36 A.D.2d 978 (N.Y. App. Div. 2d Dep't 1971).

97. *See* Carte Blanche (Singapore) PTE, Ltd. v. Diners Club Int'l Inc., 130 F.R.D. 28, 31 (S.D.N.Y. 1990); *In re* von Bulow, 828 F.2d at 100 (citations omitted). *See also In re* Estate of Nathaniel Colby, Deceased, 187 Misc. 2d 695, 698 (Sur. Ct. N.Y. County 2001) ("Since a client could have waived the [attorney-client] privilege to protect himself or to promote his interest, it is reasonable to conclude that, after his death, his personal representative stands in his shoes for the same purposes."). *See also In re von Bulow*, 828 F.2d 94, 100 ("[I]n appropriate circumstances" an attorney may have implied authority to waive the privilege (citing 8 J. WIGMORE, EVIDENCE § 2325 (McNaughton rev. ed. 1961).).

98. *See* Stefano v. C.P. Ward, Inc., 19 A.D.2d 473 (N.Y. App. Div. 3d Dep't 1963).

99. SEC v. Down, 969 F. Supp. 149, 159 (S.D.N.Y. 1997); *In re* Silverman, 13 B.R. 270, 272 (Bankr. S.D.N.Y. 1981) (stating that the public policy behind the rule is to encourage settlement discussions).

100. *See* Sullivan v. Bd. of Educ. of Eastchester Union Free Sch. Dist., 131 A.D.2d 836, 839–40 (N.Y. App. Div. 2d Dep't 1987), *related reference,* 154 A.D.2d 664 (N.Y. App. Div. 2d Dep't 1989).

101. N.Y. TRW Title Ins., Inc. v. Wades Canadian Inn & Cocktail Lounge, Inc., 225 A.D.2d 863, 864 (N.Y. App. Div. 3d Dep't 1996) (emphasis added). *See also* Resolution Trust Corp. v. Mass. Mut. Life Ins. Co., 200 F.R.D. 183, 191 (2001) (citation omitted).

102. *See In re* Pioneer Hi-Bred Int'l, Inc., 238 F.3d 1370 (2001).

103. *See* FED. R. EVID. 502, effective Sept. 19, 2008; FED. R. EVID. 502 advisory committee notes (2007) (noting that, under the new rule, subject matter waiver cannot result from "an inadvertent disclosure of protected information"); *see also* discussion, *infra*, of inadvertent waiver.

104. *In re von Bulow*, 828 F.2d at 101 (citation omitted). For a potential example of a selective waiver attempted after the promulgation of Rule 502, *see SEC v. Bank of America Corp.*, No. 09 Civ. 6829 (JSR), 2009 WL 3297493 (S.D.N.Y. Oct. 14, 2009).

105. Bristol-Myers Squibb Co. v. Rhone-Poulenc Rorer, Inc., 1997, WL 801454, at *3 (S.D.N.Y. 1997).

106. Madanes v. Madanes, 199 F.R.D. 135, 152 (S.D.N.Y. 2001) (citing *In re* Leslie Fay Co. Sec. Litig., 161 F.R.D. 274, 282)).

107. *See In re Leslie Fay Co.*, 161 F.R.D. at 283 (citing *In re* Steinhardt, 9 F.3d 230, 235 (2d Cir. 1993)).

108.   *See* Stafford Trading, Inc. v. Lovely, 2007 U.S. Dist. LEXIS 13062 (D. Ill. 2007) ("courts have reached varied results in assessing whether and when communications with a third-party consultant assisting the client results in waiver of the attorney-client privilege") (collecting cases). *See also* Suss v. MSX Int'l Eng'g Servs., Inc., 212 F.R.D. 159, 165 (S.D.N.Y. 2002). See also Chapter 9.

109.   Resolution Trust Corp. v. Mass. Mut. Life Ins. Co., 200 F.R.D. 183, 195 (2001) (citing Cooper Hosp./University Med. Ctr. v. Sullivan, 183 F.R.D. 119,129 (D.N.J. 1998)).

110.   *See, e.g., Resolution Trust,* 200 F.R.D at 188–89 (citations omitted); Music Sales Corp. v. Morris, 1999 U.S. Dist. LEXIS 16433, at *22–23. The case often cited for this proposition is *In re* Steinhardt Partners, 9 F.3d 230 (2d Cir. 1993), which held that voluntarily disclosing materials to the SEC during an investigation waived the work-product privilege for those materials. But the court did not establish a per se rule because a rigid rule would not be appropriate where the private party's interests aligned with those of the government.

111.   *Resolution Trust,* 200 F.R.D. at 196 (citing Bowne of New York City, Inc. v. AmBase Corp., 150 F.R.D. 465, 479 (S.D.N.Y. 1993)).

112.   *See Charter One Bank,* 2002 WL 262504, at *5. Similarly, forwarding protected work-product to one's child does not destroy work-product immunity. *See* United States v. Stewart, 2003 WL 22384751, at *7 (S.D.N.Y. Oct. 20, 2003).

113.   *Strougo,* 199 F.R.D. at 521; *see* FED. R. CIV. P. 26 (b)(5)(A).

114.   *Strougo,* 199 F.R.D. at 521 (citing Hurst v. F.W. Woolworth Co., 1997 WL 61051, at *6 (S.D.N.Y. Feb. 11, 1997).

115.   *Id.* at 521 (citing FED. R. CIV. P. 26 (b)).

116.   *Id.* at 520 (citing N. River Ins. Co. v. Columbia Gas. Co., 1995 WL 5792, at *4 (Jan. 5, 1995)).

117.   *Id.* (citing Upjohn Co. v. United States, 449 U.S. 383, 391–92 (1981)). *See also In re* Visa/Mastermoney Antitrust Litig., 190 F.R.D 309, 314 (E.D.N.Y. 2000); Will of Pretino, 150 Misc. 2d 371, 374 (N.Y. Surr. Ct. 1991). Joint defense is discussed in more detail in the last section of this chapter.

118.   *See* FED. R. CIV. P. 26(b)(5)(B) (a party making the claim of inadvertent disclosure of protected information may notify party receiving the information of a claim of privilege and its basis; after notification, the party receiving the information must return it or seek a court order resolving any disputes).

119.   FED. R. EVID. 502(b). Rule 502(a) and (b) govern disclosures made in federal proceedings. Rule 502(c) addresses disclosures made in state proceedings, mandating that such disclosures do "not operate as a waiver in a Federal proceeding" if, under either federal or state law, the disclosure "would not be a waiver."

120.   *See, e.g., Eden Isle Marina, Inc. v. United States,* No. 07-127C, 2009 WL 2783031, *22 (Fed. Cl. Aug. 28, 2009) (noting "defendant's failure to

take prompt, affirmative, curative action" and concluding that work-product protection was waived); *Synergetics USA, Inc. v. Alcon Lab., Inc.*, No. 08 Civ. 3669, 2009 WL 2016795, *1 (S.D.N.Y. July 09, 2009) (noting that the producing party "requested the return of documents promptly after it discovered the inadvertent production"); *see also Heriot v. Byrne*, 257 F.R.D. 645 (N.D. Ill. 2009) ("how the disclosing party discovers and rectifies the disclosure is more important than when after the inadvertent disclosure the discovery occurs") (emphasis omitted).

121.   *See* Resolution Trust Corp. v. Mass. Mut. Life Ins. Co., 200 F.R.D. 183, 194 (2001) (citing *In re* Pfohl Bros. Landfill Litig., 175 F.R.D. 13, 21 (W.D.N.Y. 1997)).

122.   *See In the Matter of Baker*, 139 Misc. 2d 573, 576 (N.Y. Surr. Ct. 1988); *see also Lloyds Bank PLC v. Republic of Ecuador*, No. 96 Civ. 1789 DC, 1997 WL 96591, at *3 (S.D.N.Y. Mar. 5, 1997). *See also Spieker v. Quest Chero-kee, LLC*, No. 07-1225-EFM (D. Kan. July 21, 2009) (stating that "reasonable steps to prevent disclosure" requires more than a wholesale production subject to a confidentiality or claw back order) (citing FED. R. EVID. 502).

123.   *See Charter One Bank, F.S.B.*, 2002 WL 262504, at *8–9.

124.   *See* U.S. v. John Doe, 219 F.3d 175, 186 (2d Cir. 2000) (holding that consideration of fairness may support a finding that a corporate offi-cer's testimony before a grand jury did not effect a waiver of the corpora-tion's attorney-client or work-product privileges).

125.   N.Y. TRW Title Ins., Inc. v. Wades Canadian Inn & Cocktail Lounge, Inc., 225 A.D.2d 863, 864 (N.Y. App. Div. 3d Dep't 1996).

126.   Mfrs. & Traders Trust Co. v. Servotronics, Inc., 132 A.D.2d 392, 397 (N.Y. App. Div. 4th Dep't 1987).

127.   *See Resolution Trust Corp.*, 200 F.R.D. at 192 (citing Chase Man-hattan Bank v. Drysdale Sec. Corp., 587 F. Supp. 57, 58–59 (S.D.N.Y. 1994)).

128.   Upjohn Co. v. United States, 449 U.S. 383, 403 (1981) (Burger, C.J., concurring).

129.   *See In re* Coordinated Pretrial Proceedings in Petroleum Prods. Antitrust Litig., 658 F.2d 1355, 1361 n.7 (9th Cir. 1981); Command Transp., Inc. v. V.S. Line (USA) Corp., 116 F.R.D. 94, 97 (D. Mass. 1987).

130.   *See* MODEL RULES OF PROF'L CONDUCT R. 1.13; MODEL CODE OF PROF'L RESPONSIBILITY EC 5-18.

131.   305 F. Supp. 371 (S.D. Tex. 1969).

132.   *Id.* at 390–91.

133.   *Id.* at 391.

134.   *Id.*

135.   *Id.* at 398. The court in another case, United States v. Keplinger, 776 F.2d 678 (7th Cir. 1985), followed the same type of analysis employed by the *Brown* court, but reached the opposite conclusion, holding that the individual corporate employees were not represented by the corporate counsel. The court based its conclusion on the fact that defendants did not

seek individual legal advice, did not inquire regarding individual representation, and did not indicate their belief that such a relationship existed. Moreover, the mere fact that the corporation's lawyer accompanied one of the defendants to a meeting did not support a finding that the defendant had a reasonable basis for believing that he was being represented individually.

136. *See* MODEL CODE OF PROF'L RESPONSIBILITY DR 7–104(A)(1); MODEL RULES OF PROF'L CONDUCT R. 4.2.

137. *See* Wright v. Group Health Hosp., 691 P.2d 564, 569 (Wash. 1984); Niesig v. Team I, 558 N.E.2d 1030, 1035 (N.Y. 1990).

138. *Niesig,* 558 N.E.2d at 1035.

139. MODEL RULES OF PROF'L CONDUCT R. 4.2. cmt.

140. 110 F.R.D. 414 (D. Mass. 1986).

141. *Id.* at 418.

142. Comm. on Prof'l Ethics of the Ass'n of the Bar of the City of New York, Op. 80-46 (1980).

143. Comm. of Prof'l Ethics of the Mass. Bar, Formal Op. 82-7 (1982). *See also* Cont'l Ins. Co. v. Superior Court, 37 Cal. Rptr. 2d 843, 855–56 (Ct. App. 1995) (noting California's adoption of a broad test, although not without some judicial concern).

144. *See* Siebert & Co. v. Intuit Inc., 868 N.E.2d 208 (Ct. App. 2007) (citing *Niesig,* 558 N.E.2d at 1035–36); *Cont'l Ins. Co.,* 37 Cal. Rptr. 2d at 858.

145. ABA Comm. on Ethics and Prof'l Responsibility, Formal Op. 359 (1991). *See* Valassis v. Samelson, 143 F.R.D. 118 (E.D. Mich. 1992). *Contra* Rentclub, Inc. v. Transamerica Rental Fin. Co., 811 F. Supp. 651 (M.D. Fla. 1992) (ex parte contacts with former employees should be barred if they might result in disclosure of privileged communications).

146. *Siebert,* 868 N.E.2d 208.

147. Merrill v. City of New York, 2005 U.S. Dist. LEXIS 26693, at *3–4 (S.D.N.Y.). *See also* Wright v. Stern, 2003 U.S. Dist. LEXIS 23335, at *3 (S.D.N.Y.) (directing "that plaintiff's counsel refrain from seeking to elicit from any present or former Department employee any attorney-client communications").

148. *Siebert,* 868 N.E.2d at 211.

149. *Id.*

150. *Id.*

151. *See* MODEL CODE OF PROF'L RESPONSIBILITY DR 5-105; MODEL RULES OF PROF'L CONDUCT R. 1.7. See also "Preparing a Nonparty Witness for Deposition" in Chapter 10, discussing the pros and cons of representing a nonparty.

152. Although Formal Opinion 359 and the majority of courts allow ex parte contacts with former employees, corporations have at their disposal tools to protect against such unwanted contacts. Two Model Rules police the actions of opposing counsel in dealing with an unrepresented person. Model Rule 4.3 imposes an affirmative duty on opposing counsel

to make clear to the interviewee the opposing counsel's role and bias in the matter. ("In dealing on behalf of a client with a person who is not represented by counsel, a lawyer shall not state or imply that the lawyer is disinterested.") Model Rule 4.4 requires the opposing lawyer to recognize and respect the rights of third parties. Furthermore, a corporation may seek protective orders or may use confidentiality agreements with former employees to prevent disclosure.

153. 89 F. Supp. 357, 358 (D. Mass. 1950).

154. 397 F. Supp. 1146, 1184–85 (D.S.C. 1974).

155. *See also* Roberts v. Carrier Corp., 107 F.R.D. 678, 687–88 (N.D. Ind. 1985) (finding privilege between related subsidiaries); Ins. Co. of N. Am. v. Superior Court of Los Angeles, 166 Cal. Rptr. 880 (Ct. App. 1980) (finding privilege between related corporations); Scott Paper Co. v. Ceilcote Co., 103 F.R.D. 591, 597 (D. Me. 1984) (finding privilege between parent corporation's in-house counsel and employee of defendant subsidiary).

156. *See* Weil Ceramics & Glass, Inc. v. Work, 110 F.R.D. 500 (E.D.N.Y. 1986) (related subsidiaries shielded by attorney-client privilege because they were codefendants).

157. *See, e.g.*, Cont'l Oil Co. v. United States, 330 F.2d 347, 350 (9th Cir. 1964); Transmirra Prods. Corp. v. Monsanto Chem. Co., 26 F.R.D. 572, 576 (S.D.N.Y. 1960) (patent infringement case involving communications between lawyers for corporations sued by common plaintiff decided on basis of work-product immunity analogous to cases using attorney-client privilege).

158. *See* United States v. McPartlin, 595 F.2d 1321, 1336–37 (7th Cir. 1979); Hunydee v. United States, 355 F.2d 183, 185 (9th Cir. 1965); *Cont'l Oil*, 330 F.2d at 350.

159. MANUAL FOR COMPLEX LITIGATION, 2D § 21.43 (Robert A. Cahn exec. ed., 1986).

160. *See* Medcom Holding Co. v. Baxter Travenol Labs. Inc., 689 F. Supp. 841, 844 (N.D. Ill. 1988); McCORMICK, EVIDENCE § 91, at 190–91 (Cleary ed. 1972). Similarly, a lawyer who represents two parties in a single matter may not assert the privilege in a later dispute between the clients. Quintel Corp., N.V. v. Citibank, N.A., 567 F. Supp. 1357, 1364 (S.D.N.Y. 1983).

161. *See* Eureka Inv. Corp. v. Chicago Title Ins. Co., 743 F.2d 932 (D.C. Cir. 1984).

162. *See* Teleglobe USA Inc. v. BCE Inc. (*In re* Teleglobe Commc'ns Corp.), 2007 U.S. App. LEXIS 16942 (3d Cir. 2007).

163. *See Teleglobe*, 2007 U.S. App. LEXIS 16942.

164. *Teleglobe*, 2007 U.S. App. LEXIS 16942 (citing the *Eureka* principle from Eureka Inv. Corp. v. Chicago Title Ins. Co., 743 F.2d 932 (D.C. Cir. 1984)).

CHAPTER 7

Procedural Preparation of the Witness

Paul C. Palmer
G. Richard Dodge, Jr.

Most prospective witnesses know little—if anything—about litigation in general, the particular case, or what to expect at a deposition. These uncertainties lead most witnesses to react negatively when they learn that their depositions have been noticed. As a result, to prepare a witness for the deposition, the defending lawyer must (1) place the deposition in context for the witness, (2) explain the deposition process, and (3) advise the witness on how to testify effectively.

Typically, the defending lawyer will review these procedural issues with the witness at the beginning of the preparation session before focusing on the substance of the witness's testimony. The primary reason for this sequence is that the witness is likely to be concerned about these procedural issues. The traditional wisdom also holds that the lawyer should give the witness some advice about how to testify effectively at a deposition before eliciting the witness's proposed responses to specific questions in order to assist the witness in framing that testimony.

But beginning the session with guidelines for testifying effectively may not be the best approach in every case for any number of reasons. First, you might conclude that a particular witness would be more likely to forget those guidelines if they are provided at the outset of the preparation session. Second, such guidelines might be meaningless to the witness out of context. Third, if you begin by advising the witness to provide only limited, carefully circumscribed answers to deposition questions and then question the witness regarding the substance of her proposed testimony, you might never learn the full extent of the witness's knowledge, as a result of the witness following your own rules for testifying.[1] Fourth, you might be concerned about conveying an improper and dangerous message to the witness: that he or she should withhold evidence from all concerned, including you.

Fortunately, a lawyer who wants to avoid the traditional approach of reviewing all procedural issues with the witness before beginning the substantive deposition preparation has several alternatives available. First, you might delay any discussion of procedural issues until the end of the preparation session, after the substance of the witness's proposed testimony has been fully explored. Second, you and the witness might begin with a selective overview of the kinds of questions likely to be asked and the witness's answers, and then turn to detailed procedural and substantive preparation. Third, you might interweave procedural and substantive preparation throughout the preparation session (a process that can be effective with some witnesses, but confusing to others). Fourth, you might begin the session by asking the witness about any concerns the witness would like to discuss, and then use those concerns, whether procedural or substantive, as the starting point. Particularly with an anxious witness, this last approach is recommended; otherwise the witness's concerns will permeate the session in any event.

You must decide which of the different approaches to deposition preparation is likely to be most beneficial for each particular witness. In the process, you should be flexible and attentive to the witness's needs and concerns. In many cases, open dialogue with the witness quickly will lead to a more or less traditional sequence of procedural preparation followed by detailed substantive preparation. You should not fall into that pattern thoughtlessly, however, simply because it is the traditional, familiar, or most comfortable approach.

Placing the Deposition in Context

At some point in the preparation process, every witness wants to know why his deposition has been noticed: What is this all about? Why have I been singled out? How does my deposition fit into this case? Even a witness who is a party to the litigation may have questions about the timing and purposes of the deposition. A witness may be somewhat apprehensive until he gets those answers. The witness may even seek the answers to these questions from others. To avoid these problems early in the preparation session, you should place the deposition in context for the witness.

Equally, if not more, important, you must educate the witness to some extent regarding the key issues and contentions of the parties in the case.[2] If the witness does not understand what each party is attempting to prove, she may become unfocused and rudderless during the deposition in the face of tough questioning by opposing counsel. She may not be alert to semantic traps and other pitfalls and may provide thoughtless testimony that has to be explained away later (with some loss of credibility in the process).

Similarly, if the witness does not understand the defending lawyer's goals in the deposition, the witness may not be much help when testifying. In most cases, you will need to disabuse your witness of the belief that the deposition is her chance to tell her story. In other situations, you may want your witness to go beyond a terse answer to a particular question to make a point.[3] You should anticipate this possibility and consider preparing the witness to give that kind of testimony if the opportunity presents itself. In some cases, however, you may conclude that the witness is not likely to be able to use any such opportunities effectively without opening up other areas for follow-up questioning. Or you may decide the witness is not especially capable. In those situations, you should advise the witness against trying to score points in his deposition testimony.

How much background information about the case and the parties' contentions you should provide to the witness depends on the witness, the case, and the witness's role in it. At one end of the spectrum—for a minor witness who can testify only about limited, straightforward issues—a general overview of the case and the probable focus of the deposition might suffice. At the other end of the spectrum—for a key witness or one who will testify about highly technical issues—it might be necessary to review the issues, allegations, and facts in considerable detail.

Explaining the Deposition Process

In addition to providing the witness with some information about the case, the lawyer should explain the nature of the deposition process. Most witnesses will be unfamiliar with that process. Even those who have been deposed before should be reminded of the nature of the deposition process and the roles of the various participants. You should never accept at face value a witness's claim that she knows all about depositions and does not need you to review deposition procedures—not even when the witness has testified previously. Instead, you should probe the subject diplomatically, to make sure you understand the witness's perceptions and the extent of the witness's knowledge regarding depositions. In the process, you can demonstrate your competence and help foster the witness's confidence in you.

You should emphasize that a deposition is a formal proceeding, although ordinarily no judge or magistrate judge will be present and it will not be conducted in a courtroom.[4] Explain who is likely to attend the deposition, including the court reporter or videographer, the witness, counsel for the witness and for other parties, and possibly representatives of the various parties. You may want to explain that a representative of a party may attend the deposition as a matter of right.[5] In appropriate cases, explore with the witness whether there is any need for a protective order to preserve the confidentiality of subjects likely to be raised at the deposition or to limit the scope of questioning.[6] If possible, provide the witness with specific information about those likely to attend the deposition, such as the demeanor and style of the lawyer taking the deposition, to help the witness feel prepared for this process.

Explain that the witness first will be placed under oath. You must then decide, on a case-by-case basis, how much to say about the oath. In some situations, a pointed explanation that the witness has a legal obligation to tell the truth, under penalty of perjury, might be perceived as insulting or intimidating. In other situations, however, you may want to emphasize those points.[7] Many lawyers always advise their witnesses that testimony under oath is given under penalty of perjury, placing greater or lesser emphasis on this point depending on their perceptions of the witness.

Explain that counsel for the party who noticed the deposition will conduct the direct examination and may show the witness copies of documents obtained through the discovery process, including documents from the witness's files. Reassure the witness that you are familiar with those document productions and do not expect to be surprised by any documents shown to the witness. You also should explain that you may object to certain questions asked by opposing counsel during the deposition (which the witness must nevertheless answer following the objections), and that you may instruct the witness not to answer certain questions (which the witness should then refuse to answer).[8]

Inform the witness that after opposing counsel has questioned her, you will have the opportunity to conduct "cross-examination," but that you are unlikely to do so because this could lead to further "redirect" by opposing counsel.[9] Emphasize that the entire proceeding will be recorded by a court reporter or videographer.[10] Also explain that the witness will have the right to review and correct the transcript or recording.[11] In most cases, the defending lawyer will advise the witness to request the opportunity to do so.

It may be helpful to show the witness a sample of an actual deposition transcript, preferably from an unrelated case. (This avoids altering the witness's knowledge of the facts and eliminates any possible inference that the witness has studied the other testimony to conform his or her own testimony to it.) A sample transcript can illustrate that pauses do not appear in the written transcript (as compared with the video record), that clear and audible responses are required, that complete questions and complete answers are essential, and that attempts at humor or sarcasm typically are not so funny (and may be confusing) in a transcript. As previously noted, there also are some excellent, professionally produced videos that can give the witness a better understanding of the deposition process.

Witnesses who do not fully understand the deposition process may misinterpret advice about how to testify effectively as a green light to withhold information properly sought in the deposition. To prevent any such misconceptions, it may be helpful to explain to the witness how our adversarial system works. For example, you might explain that each party is expected to present its case in the light most favorable to that party. Each party has the right to take depositions to strengthen its own case or probe the opposing party's case. The deposition is not intended to be a nonpartisan inquiry into the facts, nor a hearing on the merits. Instead, it is an opportunity for the examining party to obtain testimony that will be used to advance its goals in a partisan way. That party's counsel decides what questions to ask the witness. The witness must respond truthfully and completely to the questions asked at the deposition, but has no obligation to inform opposing counsel more generally about the facts.

As suggested above, you should also explain that in most cases, the deposition should not be viewed as the witness's own day in court.[12] As a result, the witness will not help his case by volunteering information, insights, or explanations, or by pointing out weaknesses in the opposing party's case.[13] To the contrary, that is precisely what opposing counsel would like the witness to do. Opposing counsel's goals in the deposition almost invariably include eliciting as much information from the witness as possible and freezing the witness's testimony to limit the possibility of a subsequent credible change in testimony. You should explain to the witness how opposing counsel might use the witness's deposition testimony in the case, including as substantive evidence when the witness is a party and for impeachment.[14]

Discuss the role that you will play in the deposition and the limits on what you can do and say. Make clear that a deposition is not intended to be an occasion for sparring between the parties' lawyers. Instead, explain that your primary goals at the deposition will be to (1) ensure that a clear and proper record is developed, (2) protect the witness against improper or unfair questions, and (3) preserve any applicable privileges. If you have not already done so earlier in the deposition preparation, review with the witness the attorney-client privilege and any other privileges that might be applicable.[15]

Explain that from time to time you may object to questions as unfair, confusing, or otherwise improper. Advise the witness to pay close attention to these objections because they signal problems with the questions or the assumptions underlying them.[16] You should explain that in most instances, the witness must answer the question (if the witness can) after the objection has been made,[17] but should consider the objection carefully before doing so. Also inform the witness that in some instances, you may instruct the witness not to answer a question, usually to protect an applicable privilege.[18] Advise the witness to follow all such instructions not to answer and not be alarmed or swayed if opposing counsel threatens to move to compel the witness's testimony or seek sanctions. You may also want to explain to the witness the procedure by which any resulting discovery disputes will be resolved.

Subject to any rules or orders of the court limiting consultation during the deposition,[19] you should encourage the witness to consult with you privately whenever the witness feels it necessary to do so. The witness should understand, however, that ordinarily it is not desirable to consult with counsel constantly throughout the deposition (particularly if the deposition is video recorded). Carried to an extreme, such extensive consultation can leave the impression that the witness's testimony is weak and contrived, and may provoke a motion to preclude such conferences.[20] You also should warn the witness that opposing counsel might try to discourage any consultation between the witness and you by objecting to such consultations, making remarks about them on the record, or using other tactics.[21] Advise the witness to ignore such attempts to stop consultation with you.

Encourage the witness to ask for a break in the proceedings whenever he feels the need for one, and not to be dissuaded from doing so by opposing counsel. Explain to your witness that you do not want him to testify for too long without taking a break because a tired witness can be a careless one. Advise your witness that some examiners wait until the witness appears to be tiring to ask the most difficult questions.

You also should explain that the examiner might ask whether the witness met with you to prepare for the deposition and what the witness did to prepare for it.[22] These questions often make witnesses uncomfortable, particularly if they are unprepared for them. Reassure the witness that there is no problem in truthfully stating (if asked) that the witness met with you and reviewed documents in preparation for the deposition. Lawyers taking depositions sometimes pointedly ask witnesses whether defending counsel told them what to say in their testimony (more in the hope of putting the witness on the defensive than of eliciting a positive answer). Some lawyers advise their witnesses to answer that question truthfully: "No." Others advise their witnesses to respond: "I was instructed to tell the truth." You should explain that because more substantive questions about deposition preparation—for example, regarding which documents were shown to the witness—may infringe upon the attorney-client privilege and work-product protection, you may instruct the witness not to answer them.[23]

Twenty Guidelines for Deposition Testimony

A deposition is not a conversation with opposing counsel; it is a means for opposing counsel to create a record.[24] As a result, it has more in common with the dictation of a legal document than with an everyday conversation where a person may feel more at ease to retract what was said.[25] Because a deposition is a formal, adversarial process, it requires a distinct—and often unfamiliar—manner of response from the witness.

Witnesses often are unaccustomed to the distinctions among different kinds of information that lawyers seek. For this reason, usually you will want to review with the witness the differences among personal knowledge, hearsay, inference, assumption, speculation, and opinion. Because these distinctions may seem elusive to witnesses, they are best explained with concrete examples.

One technique for illustrating these distinctions is to discuss the different sources of information the witness might have about the weather. For example, if the witness could see outside at the time of the deposition, the witness might be able to testify about the weather based on personal knowledge. But what if the witness were in a windowless room? In that case, the witness could not have *personal knowledge* of the weather outside at the time of the question. The witness might, however, have been told, overheard, or read that it was raining, and therefore have *hearsay* information about the weather. Alternatively, the witness might have seen people entering the building with wet raincoats and umbrellas, and *infer* from those facts that it was raining. The witness might recall that it had just started to rain when he or she entered the building, and *assume* that it was still raining. Or the witness might have no factual basis for testifying whether it was raining or not, but *speculate* one way or the other. If opposing counsel were to state that it was raining outside, the witness might, or might not, have an *opinion* about the accuracy of that statement. Hearsay, inferences, assumptions, speculation, and opinions might or might not be correct. In addition to using general examples along these lines, you might want to use specific examples from the actual case.

Whatever examples you use, make it clear that there is an entire spectrum of different information sources with varying degrees of probative value. An answer based on inferences, assumptions, speculation, or an opinion is not responsive to a question that asks for the witness's direct personal knowledge. It also may be misleading. A jury might not fault a witness for an inaccurate answer if the witness qualified the answer as an inference, assumption, speculation, or opinion. But a jury would probably discredit a witness who gave the same inaccurate answer without such a qualification.

Discuss with the witness the likelihood that he will have varying degrees of recollection, ranging from clear and definite recollections to only vague impressions. To again use an example relating to the weather, the witness might clearly recall that it was raining on a particular day (for example, on a day when there was flooding). Alternatively, the witness might only "think" (with a greater or lesser degree of certainty) that it was raining. The witness must be prepared to specify during the deposition how clearly or vaguely the witness recalls particular facts.

Also discuss with the witness the possibility that particular evidence might—or might not—refresh the witness's recollection. If the evidence triggers recollections, prompting the witness to recall facts the witness knew but had forgotten, the evidence has refreshed the witness's recollection. If the evidence does not bring back any memories, then it does not refresh the witness's recollection (regardless of anyone's expectations to the contrary). Advise the witness never to be defensive about an honest lack of recollection.

In many cases, the witness must be sensitized to the distinction between what the witness knew at the time of the events at issue and what the witness knows at the time of the deposition based on information obtained after the fact. You should tell the witness to make this distinction clear in his deposition testimony whenever necessary to avoid leaving a misimpression on the record.

There are a number of other guidelines to help witnesses testify effectively in depositions. These guidelines are all intended to protect the interests of the witness. They are not intended to "hide the ball" improperly, but rather to minimize the witness's exposure to partisan examination and ensure that the witness's testimony is clear, precise, accurate, and presented in the best possible light.

Twenty of these guidelines are set forth below.[26] Nearly all are variations or elaborations on a few basic rules: (1) always tell the truth, (2) listen to the question, (3) pause before answering, (4) make sure you understand the question, (5) do not guess, and (6) do not volunteer information.

1. Always Tell the Truth

Testimony in a deposition is given under oath under penalty of perjury. The witness must always testify truthfully and should never knowingly mischaracterize or exaggerate the facts.[27] The lawyer should explain that the truth consists of the facts as best the witness can recall them—without speculation or exaggeration.

Any deviation from the whole truth—or bending of the truth—could destroy the witness's credibility and jeopardize the entire case. Ordinarily, the witness should not worry about any seeming inconsistencies between the witness's own testimony and other evidence opposing counsel might bring up. Likewise, the witness should not try to reconcile the evidence, but just stick to the facts as the witness recalls them. The defending lawyer may want to reassure the witness that although the preparation process involves reviewing all the facts, the witness should not be unduly concerned about what the witness does or does not recall. A witness should not try to reconstruct facts he does not actually know and should not deny recalling facts he knows.[28]

2. Listen Carefully to the Question

The witness should pay close attention to each question. The witness should wait for opposing counsel to complete the entire question and be certain he has heard the question correctly. Only then should the witness answer. Witnesses often think they understand a question before it has been completed and proceed to answer. In doing so, the witness might mistake the point of the question, or answer it without regard to qualifications or limitations. This can lead to the witness volunteering information that would not otherwise have been elicited. It also can open up additional substantive areas for further questioning and seriously confuse the record.

For example, assume that a witness met with a Mr. Smith and that the meeting took place in December two years ago. The answer to the incomplete question "Did you meet with Mr. Smith . . ." might be "yes." But the answer to the complete question "Did you meet with Mr. Smith during October two years ago?" would be "no." Thus, if the witness answered "yes" before the examiner completed the question—and nothing was done by either the witness or the defender to clarify that answer—the result would be the following misleading transcript:

Q. Did you meet with Mr. Smith . . .
A. Yes.
Q. . . . during October two years ago?
Q. Did anyone else attend that meeting?

Although the truthful answer to the complete question is "no," the transcript would reflect incorrectly that the witness did attend the October meeting.

3. Pause Before Answering

Pausing before each answer has a number of advantages. First, it gives defending counsel a chance to state any objections to the question. Second, it gives the witness time to think about the question. Third, it gives the witness time to formulate an answer. Fourth, it ensures that the witness—not the examiner—controls the rhythm and pace of the deposition. Many lawyers ask their witnesses to wait a specific period of time (perhaps five seconds, which the witness can count silently) to ensure an adequate pause. Defenders may need to work with the witness during deposition preparation to help the witness develop greater awareness of the timing and pace of his testimony.

Reasonable pauses between questions and answers typically will not be reflected in the written record.[29] Showing the witness a sample transcript can help illustrate this point.[30] And advise the witness not to apologize for pauses, or even refer to them, because this would only create a written record when one would not otherwise exist. If opposing counsel comments on how long the witness takes to answer a question, the witness should respond that he wants to make sure the answer is accurate and complete.

Opposing counsel typically will want to push the witness into a fast-paced, unreflective dialogue. It is never in the witness's interest to allow that to happen. The witness should therefore resist any attempts by opposing counsel to hurry the witness along or to discourage pauses before answers. You should explain to the witness that as defending counsel, to some extent as you can help control the pace of the deposition by (1) objecting (when appropriate), (2) asking the reporter to read back certain questions before the witness answers them, and (3) asking if the witness would like to take a break at a particular point. Because you will interject yourself in this way only when it is in the witness's interest, the witness should be alert and responsive to your input.

4. Think About the Question

The witness should think about each question carefully and pay close attention to its wording. The wording should dictate the scope of the answer. Moreover, the very wording of the question may be problematic; it may assume facts not known to the witness, may be based on a false premise, or may misrepresent or mischaracterize earlier testimony. Unless the witness points out such problems on the record before answering, the witness may appear to accept or

161

endorse the question. Compound questions and questions including double negatives also can confuse witnesses and result in misstatements. Although you will have told the witness that you will object to the form of improper questions—alerting the witness to the potential problems in the process—you should advise the witness not to rely solely on you, but, instead, be alert for any problems the witness might spot on his own.

The witness should especially watch out for questions with loaded terminology. The term "agreement," for example, might be a loaded one when the parties disagree about whether a binding contract was ever formed. Certain adjectives—such as "important," "fast," "expensive," "frequent," "often," "excessive," "dangerous," or "high-level," among others—may also be loaded terms in some contexts.

A lawyer taking a deposition often will ask a witness to agree to the lawyer's own summary of the facts, which may or may not be precisely accurate and probably will be framed in a partisan way such as:

Q. Is it fair to say that you had a series of private meetings with your competitors to discuss pricing and other competitive issues?

The examiner who asks such a question usually is setting up the witness by attempting to develop the transcript in the way most useful to the examiner's client. The witness should never simply adopt such a characterization or reformulation of his testimony. Instead, if it does not fairly restate the facts (without partisan slant), the witness should say so. The witness also should be prepared to explain, if asked by opposing counsel, what is wrong with the summarization.

5. If Necessary, Ask for Clarification

The witness should make certain he understands each question. This includes (when relevant) the time frame addressed and any technical terms used (without definition), as well as any shorthand references. If the witness is uncertain about the question in any respect, the witness should ask for clarification. If the question is confusing, the witness should say so.

The witness should request clarification of any questions that are too vague, conclusory, or general. The witness also should ask opposing counsel to define terms that may be subject to varying interpretations. Explain to the witness, however, that opposing counsel may refer such inquiries back to the witness:

Q. Were there many reports of problems with that software?
A. Well, what do you mean by "many"?
Q. What did you consider to be "a lot" of reports of problems for software of that kind?

Similarly, a witness sometimes can steer the examination in a certain direction through the manner in which the witness responds to a vague question:

Q. Were there a lot of reports of problems with that software?
A. Do you mean more than 50?

In most cases, however, the witness should avoid this kind of dialogue with opposing counsel. It is not the witness's role to clarify questions, and doing so is likely to lead to follow-up questioning.

6. Ask to See Any Documents That Are Referenced

Lawyers sometimes ask questions about documents without first showing copies to the witness, hoping the witness's initial answers later will be proved wrong by the documents. They also ask questions about information contained in documents without showing the witness a copy. The witness usually can circumvent this game by simply asking to see a copy of any document referred to in a question before answering. The witness should then read the document in its entirety.[31] If the witness answers questions about a document without first reading it in its entirety, she should expressly note this in her testimony. Even if a document is not referenced by opposing counsel, you should ask to see a document if the question asks for recorded information—for example, "What was the patient's blood pressure at noon on that day?"

7. Do Not Assume That Documents Are Accurate

There is a natural inclination to assume that what is written in a document (particularly a business record) is true. In most cases, however, a witness should not assume that facts reflected in a document are accurate. Instead, a witness who has no knowledge of a document or its contents should make that clear in her testimony. Although that witness can then testify about what that document appears to be and say, such testimony will have little, if any, probative value. If the witness has no independent knowledge or recollection of the facts stated in a document, she should never respond to a question by reading into the record a seemingly responsive portion of that document or by agreeing in statements made in it. As the following example illustrates, this can leave the misimpression that the document refreshes the witness's recollection and that the witness agrees with its contents:

> Q. This letter of September 5th clearly indicates that she was relying on the company's advice. Is that correct?
> A. Yes.
> Q. And the company knew that.
> A. Yes.

The witness should understand that the better answer, if truthful, is simply: "The document says that, but I have no recollection of that."

8. Formulate a Complete Answer Before Beginning to Respond

A witness should never think out loud in a deposition as one might in everyday conversation. Instead, the witness should formulate each answer carefully before responding to the question. For some witnesses, it helps to think of answering a question in a deposition as dictating a document.[32] In both cases, it is only the written record that will count.

9. Answer Only the Precise Question Asked

Because the witness's goal is to provide only the information specifically requested during the deposition, the witness's answers should be carefully limited to the precise questions asked. The witness should not attempt to expedite the deposition by providing more focused or comprehensive answers than the questions require. Consistent with guideline 2 (listen carefully to the question), the witness should not try to second-guess what the questioner is trying to ask or anticipate subsequent questioning. Doing so is likely to open up additional lines of questioning and prolong the deposition unnecessarily. The witness should answer just the one question asked:

> Q. What is the color of your car?
> A. I have a green Prius.

The question asked is only about color. The truthful answer is "green" and nothing more.

10. Keep Your Answers Short

Ordinarily, if a yes or no answer will suffice, the witness should answer only yes or no and nothing more. If the witness does not know or cannot recall the answer to a question, the witness should say that and no more. The witness should avoid discursive, narrative responses. The witness should not elaborate unnecessarily on his answers—no speeches! To motivate the witness to keep the answer short, you should explain that the more the witness says, the more follow-up questions opposing counsel may have and the longer the deposition will last.[33]

Sometimes, however, it is in the witness's interest to testify somewhat more expansively in response to particular questions.[34] Unfortunately, it is usually very difficult for a nonlawyer witness to determine when (if ever) to deviate from the general rule that answers should be kept short. The witness's own instincts, which presumably will not be based on legal considerations, are likely to be dead wrong in this adversarial setting. You must therefore decide how to advise the witness on this issue. Typically, you can make that judgment only after gauging the personality and capabilities of the particular witness. Some witnesses should never attempt to score points in this way because they are unlikely to do so effectively. When you feel that a particular witness could elaborate on certain points effectively, you should review that area of testimony (including likely follow-up questions and answers) carefully with the witness. You also should advise the witness that when in doubt, he should keep his answers short and to the point.[35]

11. Choose Your Words Carefully

Even the most succinct answers can be overly broad or otherwise misleading if not worded carefully. The witness must be careful not only about how much to say, but also how to say it. If it is necessary to qualify or explain an answer to prevent it from being misleading, the witness should do so.[36] Witnesses should be particularly careful about testifying that something "always" or "never" happened, or about specific dates, precise words used, distances, speed, elapsed time, sizes, quantities, and similar matters. If the witness's recollection of any matter is not firm and clear, the witness should qualify testimony accordingly. The witness should never allow opposing counsel to pressure the witness into testifying in absolute terms.[37] The witness should not, however, unnecessarily hedge otherwise strong, direct answers.

165

12. Inferences, Assumptions, Speculation, and Opinions

A fact witness should stick to the facts personally known to that witness, including what the witness personally observed, thought, and believed. Under the liberal federal discovery rules, however, a deposition witness may be asked questions calling for hearsay or other evidence not admissible at trial.[38] It is therefore essential that the witness make clear in his testimony not only what he knows, but also how he knows it.[39] If the witness is required to testify regarding his inferences, for example, the witness should make clear that they are only inferences. If required to testify to hearsay, the witness should point out that it is only hearsay, and that he does not know whether it is true or false (assuming that is the case). The witness should always take care to avoid mixing personal knowledge, hearsay, and other sources of information indiscriminately in his testimony.

A lay witness ordinarily should resist answering hypothetical questions on the grounds that any answer would be speculative. You should advise the witness, however, that opposing counsel may press for speculation, or ask various foundational questions to try to establish that the witness is not speculating. For example, if the witness cannot recall what she did in a particular situation, opposing counsel might ask whether there was a practice the witness followed in such situations. If there was such a practice, the examiner would be likely to ask whether the witness has any reason to think she deviated from that practice in this instance.

Similarly, if a witness testifies that she cannot be sure whether a particular statement was correct, opposing counsel might ask whether the witness has any reason to doubt that it was correct.[40] The witness must, of course, answer such questions truthfully. In appropriate cases, however, the witness also may want to reemphasize that she has no personal knowledge or recollection of the facts.

When a witness does not know something, the witness should never allow opposing counsel to insinuate that the witness *should* know it. Otherwise, the witness will appear to have testified as though she *does* know it. Examiners often employ this tactic with executives and others with management and oversight responsibility, who may be reluctant to admit lack of knowledge of matters within their areas of responsibility. For similar reasons, lawyers, doctors, and other professionals often make poor witnesses.

13. Do Not Volunteer Information

As a general rule, the witness should not volunteer any information during the deposition.[41] Lawyers often play dumb when questioning a witness in the hope of prompting the witness to "help" them. Information a witness thinks should be given to opposing counsel—even though not requested—may lead opposing counsel on tangents and prolong the deposition. Witnesses also should avoid what are sometimes called "spaghetti answers"—rambling answers that provide different strands of information, each of which opposing counsel can then spend time pulling out.

A witness should never refer unnecessarily to any documents or other evidence that has not been put before the witness in the deposition, particularly if the witness knows the documents have not been produced in the litigation.[42] With some exceptions (see guideline 6), the witness should not volunteer that she could answer a question (or do so more accurately or completely) if the witness had additional records.[43] For example:

Q. When did you first meet her?
A. I really can't recall. I would have to check my office calendar.

This kind of answer is likely to lead to a request for the calendar and possibly for an additional deposition session.[44]

14. Do Not Try to Sustain a Dialogue

Often there are periods of silence during a deposition. Opposing counsel may pause and stare at the witness, hoping to unnerve the witness and induce the witness to say something more. It is human nature to want to fill such awkward periods of silence by saying something. The witness should resist that impulse. The witness should be prepared to sit silently for as long as necessary, waiting for the next question.[45]

15. Do Not Argue, Debate, or Lose Your Temper

Arguing or debating with opposing counsel is inconsistent with the goal of providing only narrow, carefully framed answers to specific questions. For that reason, it is precisely the kind of response examiners often try to provoke in depositions. A witness who debates or argues tends to become careless and say more than he should. Therefore, remind the witness that she is unlikely to persuade opposing counsel—an advocate for the opposing party—of anything in the process.

Lawyers taking depositions often alternate between "hostile" and "friendly" questioning in depositions in order to keep the witness off balance and cause the witness to open up or change her testimony. If the witness is satisfied with her testimony, she should stick to the previous answers and ignore these tactics.

16. Be Wary of Sudden "Recollections" During the Deposition

A witness may suddenly "recall" facts in the heat of a deposition. When that happens, the witness should consider carefully whether these recollections are valid. The witness also should confer with defending counsel privately about these newly recalled facts at the first opportunity. Counsel may have information bearing on the accuracy or inaccuracy of these recollections. Ultimately, however, only the witness can determine the extent, clarity, and truthfulness of her own recollections.

17. If You Make a Mistake, Correct It as Soon as Possible

After answering a particular question, a witness may later realize that the answer is inaccurate for one reason or another. In that situation, the witness should correct the answer at the first opportunity. Consistent with guideline 16 (be wary of sudden "recollections" during the deposition), if the correction is a significant one, the witness first should consult with defending counsel about the change. Defending counsel may then decide to raise the issue immediately (typically by having the witness state on the record that the witness would like to add something to earlier testimony). Alternatively, defending counsel may decide to wait until the conclusion of the direct examination to raise the issue on cross-examination.[46] The witness should not volunteer any explanation for the mistake, nor attempt to rationalize or defend it.

18. Do Not Get Involved in Case Management Matters

A witness should never agree to produce any documents, look up any facts, fill in any blanks in the transcript, or otherwise undertake any efforts at the request of opposing counsel. Nor should the witness enter into any other dialogue with opposing counsel regarding the status or progress of the litigation. Instead, the witness should refer all such matters to his lawyer.

19. Be Reasonably Polite and Formal at All Times

A witness should avoid obscenities, sarcasm, insults, jokes, and casual banter, and should not respond in kind if opposing counsel resorts to any of these tactics. In fact, if opposing counsel becomes insulting, sarcastic, or otherwise hostile, a witness should respond by becoming even more polite. A witness also should be wary of being drawn into informal, off-the-record discussions with representatives of other parties at any time. A witness always should be on his guard in the presence of opposing counsel, their staff, or other parties. Nothing at a deposition can be considered off the record.

20. Avoid Catch-All Answers

The witness should understand that the lawyer conducting the deposition may ask very broad, catch-all questions at the end of the deposition. Opposing counsel might ask, for example, if the witness has "any other information" on a particular subject. Lawyers also frequently ask, "Is there anything else that you haven't told me?" These catch-all questions are intended to draw out additional information. They also are designed to close the door on any further testimony by the witness in subsequent proceedings by providing a basis for impeaching the witness's credibility if the witness later testifies to facts not disclosed at the deposition. On cross-examination at trial, the witness who allowed opposing counsel to close the door in this manner would have to testify that he did not tell opposing counsel the additional facts testified to at trial when asked at the deposition. Whatever excuses the witness might make at trial, the implications of this cross-examination would be clear: Either the witness was lying at the time of the deposition or is lying now; either way the witness is a liar.

How the witness should answer these kinds of catch-all questions depends on how they are framed. If the witness has additional information responsive to the question, the witness must answer the question accordingly. If the witness is certain he has nothing to add, he should say so. In most cases, however, the witness should be wary of closing the door by answering that he does not "know anything else" unless very confident that is the case. Instead, the witness should respond that he has tried to answer fully the questions that have been asked to the best of his recollection. Instead of testifying that he "does not know" anything else about a subject, the witness should testify that he "does not recall" anything else. If the witness later recalls additional facts between the time of the deposition and trial, the witness would then at least not have to explain away prior testimony that he did not "know" anything else about the subject.

Most witnesses appreciate the insights and assistance these kinds of guidelines provide, particularly when they are illustrated with concrete examples. The lawyer must be careful, however, not to overwhelm or intimidate the witness with too many detailed guidelines. At the very end of the preparation session, the defending lawyer should reemphasize the few central rules, noted at the onset of this section, that will most help the witness during the deposition: (1) always tell the truth, (2) listen to the question, (3) pause before answering, (4) make sure you understand the question, (5) do not guess, and (6) do not volunteer.

Proper Practice Versus Improper Coaching

Preparing a witness to testify at a deposition is a proper and important function of counsel. There is a clear difference, however, between preparing a witness to testify effectively regarding the facts and altering the witness's testimony. Deposition preparation that crosses this line may be improper, unethical, and even illegal.

One federal court has noted pointedly that a principal purpose of depositions is to memorialize witnesses' recollections before they have faded or "been altered by intervening events, other discovery, or the helpful suggestions of lawyers":

> The witness comes to a deposition to testify, not to indulge in a parody of Charlie McCarthy, with lawyers coaching or bending the witness's words to mold a legally convenient record.[47]

On occasion, witnesses themselves also have questioned the propriety of deposition preparation by counsel.[48]

Even if the witness expressed no concerns about the deposition preparation process at the time it occurred, later events can alter the witness's perspective.[49] Lawyers should not count on confidentiality in such situations, particularly if the applicable attorney-client privilege is held (and waived) by the witness personally. Regardless of whether the client wishes to preserve that privilege, moreover, allegations of serious misconduct during deposition preparation can raise issues under the crime/fraud exception to the attorney-client privilege, potentially defeating such privilege claims.[50]

The applicable legal and ethical limits of proper preparation are reasonably clear. Under federal law, subornation of perjury is a criminal offense.[51] So is corruptly endeavoring to "influence, obstruct, or impede, the due administration of justice."[52] The federal witness-tampering statute makes it a crime to engage knowingly "in misleading conduct toward another person" with the intent to "influence . . . the testimony of any person" or to cause that person to withhold testimony in an official proceeding.[53]

The Model Rules of Professional Conduct provide that a lawyer "shall not counsel a client to engage, or assist a client, in conduct that the lawyer knows is criminal or fraudulent."[54] The Model Code of Professional Responsibility (Model Code) includes similar injunctions.[55] In an aspirational guideline, the Model Code addresses probing and developing the testimony of a witness concerning matters that are inherently subjective:

> Often a lawyer is asked to assist his client in developing evidence relevant to the state of mind of the client at a particular time. He may properly assist his client in the development and preservation of evidence of existing motive, intent, or desire; obviously, he may not do anything furthering the creation or preservation of false evidence. In many cases a lawyer may not be certain as to the state of mind of his client, and in those situations he should resolve reasonable doubts in favor of his client.[56]

The problem usually lies in identifying precisely where the line is to be drawn between properly developing a client's testimony and improperly "furthering the creation . . . of false evidence."[57]

Deposition preparation should include thoroughly exploring the witness's knowledge and recollection of the relevant facts. When necessary, it also should include testing and even challenging the validity of the witness's proposed testimony. In the process, the witness's recollection of the facts may change. That is a proper and desirable result when it leads to the truth. Intentionally or unintentionally, however, it also can have the opposite result.

This problem may be complicated by the process of recollection itself, as well as the witness's subconscious response to the questions asked by counsel:

> [T]he process of remembering is not one dependent upon "memory traces," which can be played back as if by placing a stylus into the groove of a phonograph record. Rather, the

171

process is one of active, creative reconstruction which begins at the moment of perception. The reconstructive process is significantly affected by the form of the question asked and by what we understand to be our own interest–even though, on a conscious level, we are responding as honestly as we possibly can. [58]

One result of this reconstructive process, it has been argued, is that a lawyer's "effort to obtain 'all the facts' is virtually certain to result in obtaining something very different from 'the *exact* facts.'"[59]

This may be true not only regarding the details of the witness's testimony, but also regarding whether the witness has any recollection at all of particular facts. As previously noted, proper deposition preparation may, and often does, include questioning the witness's recollections. When pressed, a witness might legitimately and correctly conclude that she has no reliable recollection of particular facts. [60] A witness also might conclude, however, that it is not in her interest to recall those facts, and fall back upon a convenient (and difficult to disprove) claim of lack of recollection. At some point, proper inquiry by the lawyer preparing the witness may become improper persuasion. As one federal judge observed some years ago,

> [t]he line is not easily drawn between proper review of the facts and refreshment of recollection of a witness and putting words into the mouth of the witness or ideas in his head. The line must depend in large measure, as do so many other matters of practice, on the ethics of counsel.[61]

Wherever the ethical line is drawn, "there will inevitably come a point at which the lawyer knows, to a moral certainty, that the client's ability to reconstruct in good faith has been fully tapped." [62] At that point, the lawyer "who continues to seek the desired testimony crosses the ethical line and enters upon active participation in the creation of perjury."[63]

Final Instructions to the Witness

At the end of the final preparation session, you should confirm that the witness knows the date, time, and place of the deposition. You should arrange to meet with the witness at a specified time and place on the day of the deposition, before it begins, to review some of the basic guidelines and answer any last-minute questions.

Unless there are compelling reasons to deviate from the following rules, you should advise the witness not to do any research regarding any of the matters involved in the case and not to talk to anyone else about it. You also should advise the witness not to bring to the deposition any materials in any way related to the case, such as documents, notes, calendars, address books, or a laptop, PDA, or BlackBerry.

In some instances, you may be reluctant to broach the subject of alcohol or drug use for fear of offending the witness or signaling distrust or lack of confidence in the witness. Nevertheless, you should explain that the examiner might ask about any alcohol consumption or drug use before the deposition. Witnesses often do not understand that they may be required to answer what they regard as very personal questions along these lines. As a result, failure to forewarn the witness could lead to damaging developments on the record.[64] Even an ultimately benign examination on these issues, if it catches the witness off guard, can embarrass and rattle the witness, undermining the witness's confidence and ability to deal with more substantive questioning. Depending on how you raise these subjects, you usually can alert the witness to these potential lines of questioning without overemphasizing them. In some instances, a casual reference is appropriate; in others, a more pointed discussion is needed.

You also may want to advise the witness tactfully about the witness's clothing and appearance (particularly if the deposition will be video recorded), considering the impressions of the witness that the opposing party and counsel (and ultimately the jury) will be forming.

Finally, you should make certain the witness knows how to reach you if she has any further thoughts or questions before the deposition. If the witness recalls any additional information or develops any other concerns in the interim, it is far better to address them before the deposition than at the last minute, when there may be little, if any, opportunity to do so.

Notes

1. Even assuming that the lawyer has interviewed the witness before the deposition preparation session, the lawyer will not necessarily have asked the precise questions that the lawyer would pose in the preparation session. Witness interviews typically focus simply on obtaining

information, while deposition preparation focuses more precisely on helping the witness to frame specific testimony.

2. *See* "Preparing the Witness: Rules for Reconstructing Reality" in Chapter 8, discussing how to place the case in its legal context.

3. *See also infra* note 9.

4. If a special master or discovery referee will attend the deposition, the lawyer should, of course, discuss that with the witness.

5. *See* FED. R. CIV. P. 30(c) (providing that the presumptive exclusion of other witnesses under Federal Rule of Evidence 615 does not apply to depositions).

6. *See* FED. R. CIV. P. 26(c) (court may issue a protective order limiting the scope of the deposition).

7. See Chapter 21, discussing perjury at a deposition; see generally Jonathan Liebman & Joel Cohen, *Perjury and Civil Litigation*, 20 LITIGATION 43, 43–46 (1994).

8. See the discussions of this issue later in this section.

9. Under the Federal Rules of Civil Procedure (FRCP), after opposing counsel calls a witness for examination, the witness's counsel has the opportunity for "cross-examination" (possibly followed by "redirect" examination by opposing counsel). FED. R. CIV. P. 30(c) ("The examination and cross-examination of a deponent proceed as they would at the trial under Federal Rules of Evidence, except Rules 103 and 615."). Although such follow-up examination of a witness by his or her own counsel may be cross-examination in form, it rarely is the kind of adversarial grilling usually associated with cross-examination. See "Examination of Your Own Client at the Deposition on Cross-Examination" in Chapter 10.

10. *See* FED. R. CIV. P. 30(b)(4); also see "The Video Deposition" in Chapter 10.

11. Under the 1993 amendments to the FRCP, if the witness or a party so requests before the completion of the deposition, the witness will have 30 days after notification of the availability of the transcript or recording to review that transcript or recording and make any corrections to it. FED. R. CIV. P. 30(e). *See infra* note 46 and accompanying text (strategic considerations in requesting an opportunity to review the transcript and making changes). See also Chapter 23, discussing the end of the deposition.

12. This is not true, of course, if you anticipate that the witness will not be available for trial. *See* FED. R. CIV. P. 32(a)(4). In that situation, counsel will need to elicit from the witness all the testimony that might be required at trial.

13. Limited exceptions to this general rule include (1) those rare instances in which counsel wants to "showcase" an exceptionally strong witness to enhance the likelihood of a settlement, (2) depositions in aid of settlement by agreement of the parties, and (3) instances in which the lawyer has prepared the witness to give specific testimony if the

opportunity presents itself. See the guidelines for testifying later in this chapter, and Chapter 8.

14. *See* FED. R. CIV. P. 32(a), and Chapter 25 on using depositions at trial.

15. In particular, if the witness will assert his Fifth Amendment privilege against self-incrimination, the lawyer should review this with the witness carefully in order to avoid any waiver of that privilege in the deposition. *See* United States v. Kordel, 397 U.S. 1, 7–10 (1970); United States v. White, 846 F.2d 678, 689–90 (11th Cir. 1988). See also Chapter 22 on the Fifth Amendment and civil depositions.

16. This is not to suggest that counsel should "coach" the witness through improper "speaking objections." *See* FED. R. CIV. P. 30(c)(2) ("An objection must be stated concisely in a nonargumentative and nonsuggestive manner."); Wilson v. Sundstrand Corp., Nos. 99 C 6944 & 6946, 2003 U.S. Dist. LEXIS 14356, at *35 (N.D. Ill. Aug. 18, 2003) ("The Federal Rules of Civil Procedure unambiguously prohibit 'speaking objections.'"). Instead, defending counsel has the right and (in many instances) the duty to make proper objections in the course of the deposition.

17. *See* FED. R. CIV. P. 30(c)(2) ("An objection at the time of the examination—whether to evidence, to a party's conduct, to the officer's qualifications, to the manner of taking the deposition, or to any other aspect of the deposition—must be noted on the record, but the examination still proceeds; the testimony is taken subject to any objection.").

18. *See, e.g.*, FED. R. CIV. P. 30(c)(2) ("A person may instruct a deponent not to answer only when necessary to preserve a privilege, to enforce a limitation ordered by the court, or to present a motion under Rule 30(d)(3) [relating to the manner in which the examination is being conducted].").

19. *See, e.g.*, Chapsky v. Baxter V. Mueller Div., No. 93 C 6524, 1994 U.S. Dist. LEXIS 9099, at *3 (N.D. Ill. July 5, 1994) ("private conferences during a deposition between a deponent and his or her attorney for any purpose other than to decide whether to assert a privilege are not permitted"); Hall v. Clifton Precision, 150 F.R.D. 525, 527, 531 (E.D. Pa. 1993) (same); E.D.N.Y. Civ. R. 30.6 (order number 13, stating that "An attorney for a deponent shall not initiate a private conference during the actual taking of a deposition, except for the purpose of determining whether a privilege should be asserted.").

20. *See supra* note 19.

21. These tactics also might include, for example, moving to present the fact of the conference between the witness and counsel in evidence at trial. *Cf. Chapsky*, 1994 U.S. Dist. LEXIS 9099, at *3 (denying motion "to bar plaintiff from testifying about a certain document because plaintiff changed her testimony midway through the deposition after consulting with her attorney" and stating that "the better approach would be to use plaintiff's prior inconsistent deposition testimony to impeach her at trial").

175

22. See discussion in Chapter 5, at note 22 and accompanying text.

23. *See supra* note 18 and accompanying text. See also Chapter 5, notes 21 and 22, and accompanying text.

24. See the discussion regarding the place of depositions within the adversary process earlier in this chapter. *See also* Appendix 4.

25. *See infra* note 32 and accompanying text (guideline 8, formulating complete answer before beginning to respond). *See also* FED. R. CIV. P. 30(e) (Review by the Witness; Changes); "Requesting Review of the Deposition Transcript" in Chapter 23, discussing the review and correction of the transcript.

26. *See also* Frederick S. Gold, *Preparing Your Client for Deposition,* TRIAL, Feb. 1993, at 57–62; James W. McElhaney, *Preparing Witnesses for Depositions,* A.B.A. J., June 1992, at 84–86; Tom H. Davis, *ABCs of Preparing Clients for Deposition and Trial,* TRIAL, Feb. 1992, at 42–47; David H. Berg, *Preparing Witnesses, reprinted in* ABA SEC. LITIG., THE LITIGATION MANUAL 466–76 (2d ed. 1989); Earl K. Cantwell & David M. Hehr, *Guidelines for Preparing Witnesses and Conducting Depositions,* N.Y. ST. B J., Jan. 1989, at 14–17; Brian M. Peters & Alan G. Rosenbloom, *Preparing the Medical Malpractice Defendant for Deposition,* PRAC. LAW., July 1988, at 71–83; Mark J. Valponi, *Preparing Novice Witnesses for Deposition,* TRIAL, May 1988, at 67–71.

27. A witness's obligation to tell the truth extends, of course, to his responses to questions as to whether he recalls particular facts. *See* United States v. Barnhart, 889 F.2d 1374, 1377, 1379 (5th Cir. 1989) (affirming perjury conviction of grand jury witness who testified that he did not recall making certain statements to government agents); Liebman & Cohen, *supra* note 7, at 43–46; also see Chapter 21, discussing perjury at a deposition.

28. *See supra* note 27.

29. The usual guidelines are somewhat different in a video recorded deposition, where hesitation in answering questions will be apparent to the fact finder and may affect the witness's credibility.

30. As noted above, however, the lawyer should be very circumspect about showing the witness transcripts of any depositions in the same case.

31. See Chapter 14, discussing defending counsel's role in the use of documents at the deposition.

32. When the witnesses are familiar with dictation, some lawyers have expanded this analogy by suggesting a comparison to a dictation machine without an "erase" button.

33. FRCP 30(d)(1) limits a deposition, unless otherwise stipulated or ordered by the court to one day of seven hours.

34. *See supra* note 13; see also "Examination of Your Own Client at the Deposition on Cross Examination" in Chapter 10.

35.   It may help to remind the witness that if there are any points that still warrant clarification or elaboration after the conclusion of the direct examination, defending counsel will have the opportunity to revisit those issues on "cross-examination." See "Examination of Your Own Client at the Deposition on 'Cross Examination'" in Chapter 10.

36.   As indicated under guideline 10 (keep your answers short), however, the witness generally should limit any explanation to that which is strictly necessary to prevent the answer from being misleading. The witness should avoid unnecessary digressions or extraneous matters. When in doubt, the witness should keep it short and to the point—and then consult with counsel privately if permitted to do so.

37.   For example, if the witness does not believe that a simple yes or no answer would be accurate, the witness should never provide such an answer. If, on the other hand, the witness believes that such an answer would be accurate, but could be misleading, the witness could give the simple answer and then elaborate to the extent necessary to ensure that this answer would not be misleading.

38.   *Compare* FED. R. EVID. 602 ("A witness may not testify to a matter unless evidence is introduced sufficient to support a finding that the witness has personal knowledge of the matter.") *with* FED. R. CIV. P. 26(b)(1) (permitting discovery of information that would not be admissible at trial, provided that it "appears reasonably calculated to lead to the discovery of admissible evidence"); *see also* FED. R. CIV. P. 32(d)(3)(A) ("An objection to a deponent's competence—or to the competence, relevance, or materiality of testimony—is not waived by a failure to make the objection before or during the deposition, unless the ground for it might have been corrected at that time.").

39.   See introductory discussion under the section of this chapter entitled "Twenty Guidelines for Deposition Testimony."

40.   See "Witness's Lack of Recall" in Chapter 11, and "Evasive Witnesses" in Chapter 15.

41.   Some limited exceptions to this rule do exist. *See supra* note 13; discussion under guideline 10 of this chapter.

42.   It is unnecessary to refer to such extraneous evidence if the witness can answer the precise question asked based on the witness's own personal knowledge or lack of knowledge. This would include, when appropriate, the simple response that the witness does not know or can not recall the answer to the particular question. In some instances, however, the witness will need to refer to extraneous evidence to ensure that his or her answer is not misleading. For example, the witness who has no firsthand knowledge of facts about which he or she is questioned, but who has reviewed business records of those facts, ordinarily should make clear in his or her testimony that those records are the source of the witness's information.

177

43. Compare this guideline with the discussion under guideline 6, which suggests that the witness ask to see documents that are referenced in a question.

44. See "Defender's Response to Document Requests During a Deposition" in Chapter 14.

45. Defending counsel may, of course, decide to break the silence in a particular instance by asking the examiner if a question is pending or otherwise pointing out the delay. Counsel may want to explain this to the witness during the preparation session. See also "Closure" in Chapter 11, discussing the examiner's use of silence.

46. The witness also will have an opportunity to correct any mistakes when the witness reviews the deposition transcript. *See supra* note 11 and accompanying text. Substantive corrections at that stage, however, can lead to a further deposition session. In addition, at trial opposing counsel may comment on the corrections. The witness, therefore, should never intentionally wait until that stage to make a correction to his or her testimony.

47. Hall v. Clifton Precision, 150 F.R.D. 525, 528 (E.D. Pa. 1993).

48. According to a plaintiff in one case, for example, an employee of the defendant reported "that defendant's attorneys had instructed him 'to change his story when responding to certain questions at [his] deposition,'" and that the employee "had followed the instructions [of defendant's lawyers] and had lied in response to [those] questions [at the deposition].'" *In re* Grievance Comm. of the United States Dist. Ct., 847 F.2d 57, 58 (2d Cit. 1988). The plaintiff's counsel testified, however, that "he felt that [the employee's] statements to [plaintiff] reflected nothing more than a 'layperson's [mis]interpretation of deposition preparation.'" *Id.* at 59; *cf. In re* Shell Oil Refinery, 812 F. Supp. 658, 663 (E.D. La. 1993) (quoting statements of former employee that before his deposition, lawyers for his employer "counseled me not to tell the truth in my deposition," and "prepared me for three days and coached me on how to avoid the truth").

49. *See, e.g.*, White v. Am. Airlines, Inc., 915 F.2d 1414, 1417–18 (10th Cir. 1990) (plaintiff sued former employer alleging he was wrongfully discharged for refusing suggestions by company counsel, during deposition preparation sessions, that he perjure himself in deposition; plaintiff never notified anyone at the company of these alleged attempts to suborn perjury).

50. Under the crime/fraud exception, the attorney-client privilege is inapplicable to communications that otherwise would be privileged, but that were undertaken in furtherance of future criminal or fraudulent conduct. *See, e.g., id.* at 1417–18, 1423–24 (communications between company counsel and employee during deposition preparation sessions, in which counsel allegedly urged employee to perjure himself in deposition, fell within crime/fraud exception to attorney-client privilege); *see*

generally United States v. Zolin, 491 U.S. 554, 562–63 (1989); 3 JACK B. WEINSTEIN & MARGARET A. BERGER, WEINSTEIN'S FEDERAL EVIDENCE ¶ 503(d)(1) (2007).

51. 18 U.S.C. § 1622 (2003).

52. 18 U.S.C. § 1503 (2000); *see* Tedesco v. Mishkin, 629 F. Supp. 1474, 1479–82 (S.D.N.Y. 1986) (finding that lawyer suborned perjury, aided and abetted his client in committing perjury, and obstructed justice in connection with deposition testimony of his client).

53. 18 U.S.C. § 1512 (2004).

54. MODEL RULES OF PROF'L CONDUCT R. 1.2(d) (2007); *see also id.* Rs. 3.4(a), 3.4(b), 3.4(f). *See also* "Ethical and Practical Constraints" in Chapter 8, on the practical constraints in the substantive preparation of a witness.

55. MODEL CODE OF PROF'L RESPONSIBILITY EC 7-5 (2005) (lawyer should not "knowingly assist the client to engage in illegal conduct," or "encourage or aid his client to commit criminal acts or counsel his client on how to violate the law and avoid punishment thereof"); *id.* DR 7-102(A)(6), (7) (prohibiting participation in creation or preservation of evidence that lawyer knows "or it is obvious" is false, or counseling or assisting client in illegal or fraudulent conduct).

56. *Id.* EC 7-6; *id.* EC 7-26 (lawyer should not present evidence that he "knows, or from facts within the lawyer's knowledge should know," is perjured).

57. *Id.* EC 7-6; *see* Geders v. United States, 425 U.S. 80, 90 n.3 (1976) (referring to "the important ethical distinction between discussing testimony and seeking improperly to influence it"); *see generally* John S. Applegate, *Witness Preparation*, 68 TEX. L. REV. 277–352 (1989). The District of Columbia Bar Legal Ethics Committee similarly referred to this line between proper and improper witness preparation some years ago, concluding that

> a lawyer may not prepare, or assist in preparing, testimony that he or she knows, or ought to know, is false or misleading. So long as this prohibition is not transgressed, a lawyer may properly suggest language as well as the substance of testimony, and may—indeed, should—do whatever is feasible to prepare his or her witnesses for examination.

D.C. Bar Legal Ethics Comm., Op. 79 (1979).

58. Monroe H. Freedman, *Counseling the Client: Refreshing Recollection or Prompting Perjury?, reprinted in* ABA SEC. LITIG., THE LITIGATION MANUAL—TRIAL, 357, 361 (John G. Koeltl & John Kiernan eds., 1999) (emphasis added). Professor Freedman cites one study finding that "witnesses' estimates of the speed of an automobile involved in an accident will vary with the verb used by the questioner in describing the impact: 'smashed' (40.8 mph), 'collided' (39.3 mph), 'bumped' (38.1 mph), 'hit'

(34.0 mph), and 'contacted' (31.8 mph)." *Id.; see also* Chapter 11 note 67 and accompanying text discussing this study on the effect of a question's wording; *see also* Applegate, *supra* note 57, at 308, 329–33.

59. Freedman, *supra* note 58, at 359.

60. In some cases, objective facts might rebut the client's initial "recollection." Failing to challenge the "recollection" under those circumstances might amount to malpractice on the part of the lawyer, and lead to the creation of impeachable testimony.

61. Hamdi & Ibrahim Mango Co. v. Fire Ass'n of Phila., 20 F.R.D. 181, 183 (S.D.N.Y. 1957) (van Pelt Bryan, J.); *cf.* United States v. Poppers, 635 F. Supp. 1034, 1037 (N.D. 111. 1986) (criminal prosecution for obstruction of justice; noting that "[t]here is a fine line between coaching someone to lie and coaching someone to present a story in the 'best' light").

62. Freedman, *supra* note 58, at 363.

63. *Id.*

64. Indeed, some answers could lead to the rescheduling of the deposition.

CHAPTER 8

Substantive Preparation of the Witness: Reconstructing Reality*

DENNIS R. SUPLEE
DIANA S. DONALDSON

"Rader and I had a dozen similar conferences over the next five months. 'Preparing testimony,' it was called. . . . I was fascinated by the testimony that was produced by our Socratic Dialogues. . . . There were qualifying phrases here and there . . . but there wasn't a single lie in it. And yet it wasn't the truth."

—P. Caputo, *A Rumor of War*, 329–30 (1977)

You represent Business-Aide, Inc. The other side has noticed the deposition of Terry Blake, defendant Business-Aide's employee who sold the accounting software to Leslie Roberts.

You understand from Maxine Waller, owner of Business-Aide, that Blake was unfamiliar with the differences between cash-basis and accrual-basis accounting at the time of the sale. Blake feels he is solely responsible for placing Business-Aide on the receiving end of a lawsuit. Blake has told Waller that although he does not actually remember whether Leslie Roberts told him anything about Scoops's special accounting needs, he was busy and distracted when he met her in the store, and he is convinced that she "must have" mentioned her accounting needs to him. His conviction is reinforced by an unfortunate earlier incident in which he also sold the wrong kind of business software to a customer. You have to prepare Blake to give his version of events at his deposition in a way that is as favorable as possible to Business-Aide's case.

* * *

What is the truth? Are litigators charged with finding it? These questions give you pause most often when you first encounter your own witnesses, usually with a deposition on the horizon.

You depend on the witness's memory. But human memory is frail and subjective. The typical deponent does not have a clear and specific recollection of all the events that the deposition will explore. A person who was involved in, or witnessed, an accident saw a thousand details in the blink of an eye. When the deposition is taken months—or even years—later, the witness will remember the details selectively, sometimes even unconsciously substituting inference or desire for memory. In a business case, the problem may be reversed. Not a thousand details in a dramatic flash, but a thousand details over an extended period of time, diluted by millions of intervening and mundane daily events.

Added to the difficulty of summoning a clear and coherent memory of past events is the elusive nature of the "truth" of those events. The 1950 Japanese movie *Rashomon*, directed by Akira Kurosawa and winner of an Academy Award for Best Foreign Language Film, shows four starkly different versions of the same crime as described by the three participants and one witness, thereby demonstrating that each person may have his or her own subjective truth. Similarly, the writer Lawrence Durrell recounts differing interpretations of the same events in *The Alexandria Quartet* to demonstrate "the difficulty of ever knowing . . . what has actually happened and what people's motives really are."[1] The Academy Award–winning movie *Crash* powerfully explores related themes.

Indeed, psychologists have shown that memory is a creative process of reconstruction, rather than the playback of a video recording or the process of recall of objective "facts."[2] And during that process of reconstruction, "[i]nvention is no less common than suppression."[3]

Nevertheless, a deposition requires the witness to testify under oath to his or her version of events. You will not get very far if you respond to a deposition notice by sending a philosophical letter to your opponent asking, "What can we really know about the truth?" Instead, you need to prepare the witness by reconstructing a reality based on what the witness remembers (or thinks he or she remembers) and can testify to with conviction (or at least with a modicum of assurance).

Witness preparation makes many lawyers squirm. Although lawyers have a professional obligation to prepare witnesses to testify, the process sometimes seems uncomfortably close to influencing the witness to shade the truth. Witnesses, for their part, sometimes believe that the preparation process is a not-so-subtle attempt to get them to lie.

This chapter discusses the issues and difficulties inherent in "reconstructing reality"—substantively preparing deposition witnesses to testify. It starts by discussing how to prepare a witness in an ethical manner. It concludes by suggesting two sets of guidelines or rules: one for preparing yourself to meet with the witness, and the other for handling the witness during the preparation session.

Ethical and Practical Constraints

Your job in preparing a witness for deposition, like that of a lawyer in preparing a witness for trial, is to help reconstruct the witness's memory of the facts—even though you do not know whether the witness's version amounts to the truth because you were not there (and, as discussed earlier, would arguably not know even if you had been there). In that sense, the preparation process from your standpoint is truth-neutral. What ethical and practical guidelines should you follow?

Some experienced litigators say that as an advocate, you should strive to elicit a reconstruction helpful to your client's position, regardless of your subjective view of the truth, as long as you do not offer evidence you know to be false. Indeed, your own view of the truth is irrelevant to preparing the witness to testify—unless, of course, you know that the witness is lying.[4] But you may feel this advice troubling because you have a problem being "neutral" about the truth. Indeed, you may question whether it is proper to assist a witness in reconstructing reality, rather than simply presenting the witness's testimony without prior rehearsal. And even if you overcome your ethical qualms, you still face the hard practical question: How far can you go in inviting the witness to adopt a version of the facts to which you do not subscribe?

Regardless of your questions or uncertainties about the propriety of substantively preparing a witness, you cannot avoid this task. Witness preparation is necessary—an indispensable part of a lawyer's ethical obligation to represent the client competently.[5] Because our truth-seeking process is adversarial, you have an ethical obligation both to your client and to the process itself to prepare the witness to participate effectively in that process. A District of Columbia bar ethics opinion expressly endorses witness preparation techniques such as suggesting alternate phrasing of testimony, advising what to include in the substance of the testimony, and practicing direct and cross-examination with the witness.[6]

Witness preparation has become even more essential because Federal Rule of Civil Procedure (FRCP) 30(c)(2) has circumscribed the defender's role at a deposition. There now are restrictions on objections and instructions not to answer, and some courts have imposed further limits on the defender.[7] Even Brendan V. Sullivan, Jr., known for his frequent off-the-record conferences with Oliver North during the Senate's Iran-Contra hearings in 1987, endorses restricting such conferences *during* depositions: "By the time you get to a deposition, the client should be prepared. If you have done your job, the lawyer should be able to sit back."[8]

You may gain some comfort from knowing that witness preparation is an ethical obligation. However, as commentators have observed, witness preparation "is hardly, under our adversary system, a public ceremony." Thus, it presents the opportunity of re-creating testimony "in an image closer to that which the lawyer desires than to that which the truth requires."[9] But lawyers are not left entirely without guidance. Certain ethical rules constrain the process to some extent. You should begin with them.

Three Model Rules of Professional Conduct (Model Rules) prohibit a lawyer from knowingly presenting false testimony.[10] Model

Rule 1.2(d) provides: "A lawyer shall not counsel a client to engage, or assist a client, in conduct that the lawyer knows is criminal or fraudulent. . . ." Model Rule 3.3(a)(3) is more specific: "A lawyer shall not knowingly. . . . offer evidence that the lawyer knows to be false. If a lawyer, the lawyer's client or a witness called by the lawyer, has offered material evidence and the lawyer comes to know of its falsity, the lawyer shall take reasonable remedial measures. . . ." And Model Rule 3.4(b) comes closest to covering the witness preparation session: "A lawyer shall not . . . falsify evidence, *counsel or assist a witness to testify falsely*, or offer an inducement to a witness that is prohibited by law. . . ." (emphasis added).

These rules are limited to a lawyer's knowing misconduct. When a lawyer assists a witness in giving testimony that the lawyer *knows* is false or fraudulent, the lawyer acts unethically under any of these three rules. The more difficult question arises when the lawyer does not know that the testimony is false, but either suspects or should know that it is and nevertheless assists in preparing it.[11] It is unclear whether the Model Rules prohibit sponsoring evidence you *suspect* might not be true or are against negligent or reckless witness preparation.

You now know that you have a professional obligation to prepare the witness and that you may refuse to help the witness prepare or present testimony you know is false. But that is not enough. You are not a philosopher. You are a lawyer (an ethical one, you tell yourself), alone in your office, struggling with the ultimate practical question: Can you really sell the fact finder a story that you do not buy, even if you cannot say with certainty it is false?

The answer for most lawyers is no, for a variety of reasons. We do not construe our ethical obligations so narrowly that we feel comfortable offering evidence we suspect is untrue. Not only are we constrained by our profession's ethical directives, but as advocates, we also know that it makes no sense strategically to encourage the witness to testify to a version of the facts that is implausible. The challenge, then, is to prepare the witness to tell a coherent and credible story that will not compromise the truth as the witness sees it, but that helps your case or at least minimizes any potentially damaging impact.

Preparing for Witness Preparation: Seven Rules

Each time you prepare a witness for deposition, remind yourself that effective reconstruction of reality is the goal. The following seven rules (or guidelines) should make it easier to assist the deponent to reconstruct reality.

Rule 1: Remember That Preparing a Deponent Is Harder than Taking a Deposition

To take a deposition, you need only develop an approach and ask questions to elicit the desired testimony. But to prepare a deponent, you must anticipate every plausible line of attack the interrogator may take—and sometimes even how individual questions may be worded.

When you take a deposition, you control the questions. But no matter how well you prepare your witness for another lawyer's anticipated questions, neither the actual questions nor the answers will come from you. And there is little room, as noted above, for corrective action once the deposition starts. Your only weapons are objections and (rarely given or permitted) instructions not to answer. Neither helps much in a surprise attack.

Rule 2: With Rare Exceptions, the Most Experienced Lawyer on the Team Should Prepare the Most Important Witnesses

Although it is much more difficult to prepare a witness for a deposition than to take the deposition, lawyers sometimes succumb to the feeling that being on stage is more important than being behind the scenes. Experienced litigators should know better. Overlooking a line of questioning or failing to follow up while taking a deposition is almost always much less damaging to the case than exposing an ill-prepared important witness to skilled (or even unskilled) interrogation by the other side. That is why the more experienced litigator on a case should allow an inexperienced lawyer to take a deposition of one of the other side's witnesses before allowing that lawyer to prepare an important witness to testify. The potential consequences are simply too great to justify the risk of letting an inexperienced lawyer prepare a key witness.

Client relations also dictate giving top priority to preparing and representing the deponent. If a client's employee performs badly at a deposition, the client will want to know where the senior litigator was and why a less experienced lawyer was assigned to prepare the employee. From the client's viewpoint, there are no satisfactory answers to these questions. Even if the presence of more experienced counsel would have made no difference, there is no way of proving that to an unhappy client.

The lesson is clear. If you are senior counsel on a case and the client or the client's employee may be bloodied at the deposition, make sure you—and not a less experienced lawyer on your team—prepare the witness.

Rule 3: Be Clear About Who Your Client Is and Why

Before meeting with the witness to prepare for the deposition, carefully consider whether you and the witness have an attorney-client relationship and, if not, whether you should try to create one.[12] Only if you have such a relationship are communications during the witness preparation session protected from discovery. (Of course, the fact that you and a witness met and the frequency and duration of the preparation sessions are not protected information, even if an attorney-client relationship exists.[13]) In addition, only if you represent the witness can you give an instruction not to answer at the deposition.[14] Otherwise, you may only suggest or request that the witness not answer.

As the lawyer for Business-Aide, your protected attorney-client relationship extends to an employee in a managerial position, or an employee whose act or omission may be imputed to the company for purposes of liability, or an employee whose statement may be an admission of the company.[15] Thus, your preparation session with Terry Blake should be protected because his statements and conduct during the transaction with Leslie Roberts were within the scope of his employment and may be imputed to Business-Aide. But you will want to clarify that relationship with Blake.

Suppose you represent Business-Aide and learn that Business-Aide terminated Terry Blake shortly after the lawsuit was filed.[16] Scoops has now subpoenaed Blake to testify at a deposition. As counsel for Business-Aide, you may be tempted to contact Blake and offer to represent him at the deposition and prepare him to testify. But before taking this course, consider the risks and benefits. If you act as Blake's lawyer, you may have sacrificed tactical advantages you could otherwise have gained from Blake's testimony—without regard to whether that testimony is helpful or harmful to Business-Aide.

First, suppose Blake's testimony is helpful to your side. When counsel for Scoops learns that you have met with Blake, have established an attorney-client relationship, and are representing him, Scoops's counsel can undermine any testimony by Blake favorable to Business-Aide by arguing that his testimony is biased toward his former employer and is entirely unreliable because Business-Aide's lawyer is also Blake's lawyer. If you had not become Blake's lawyer, you could have portrayed him as a reliable witness—indeed, one who would not be expected to have good feelings toward his former employer, yet testified favorably to Business-Aide.

This danger of making the witness your own—even if the testimony is helpful—is starkly illustrated by a real-life example. In a dispute about insurance coverage, counsel for the defendant-insurer in his opening statement portrayed a former employee as disinterested. This gambit was frustrated when opposing counsel called the witness as part of her own case and had the witness admit that the insurer's lawyer had represented the witness at the deposition for no fee and that the witness had followed several instructions by that lawyer not to answer deposition questions. The plaintiff's lawyer then sought and was granted leave to ask leading questions, on the ground that the former employee had become a witness "identified with an adverse party" under Federal Rule of Evidence (FRE) 611(c).[17]

On the other hand, suppose Blake's testimony as a former employee is harmful to your side of the case. If you had known before he testified that his answers would be harmful, you probably would decide not to form an attorney-client relationship with him. But in that event, if you decide to meet with him in advance of the deposition, your communications would not be protected by the attorney-client privilege. And if you did establish an attorney-client relationship, prepared him for the deposition, and appeared as his lawyer at the deposition, you would have a hard time arguing at trial that he is simply a disgruntled employee whose testimony should be disregarded.

If you do decide to enter an attorney-client relationship with a former employee of your client, be aware that your opponent may attack the relationship as not bona fide. Representation initiated at the last minute will be particularly suspect. To improve the chances of maintaining the relationship against attack, the offer of representation should be made to the former employee by your client, the employer—not by you. This will also avoid the awkward position of offering your services when you and the former employee first meet. Finally, before anyone offers anything, consider whether dual representation could create conflicts.[18]

Rule 4: Do Your Homework Before Meeting with the Deponent

Too often an inexperienced (or careless) lawyer begins the fact-gathering session with the witness by paging through the file for a quick reminder of what the case is about while simultaneously questioning the witness about where he fits into things.

Do not do it that way. Prepare.

First, review the file to get a firm grasp of the facts and your opponent's contentions. Review the chronology of significant events, copies of documents relevant to this witness (including those written by, addressed to, or received by the witness), key documents (even if the witness did not write or receive them), and a list of words and actions attributed to the witness by others.

Find out as much as you can about the witness. For example, in the *Scoops* case, you would talk with Maxine Waller about Terry Blake's background and personality; you also would want his employment history with Business-Aide, including his personnel file. You would pay close attention to any information sources relevant to the issue of Blake's weakness in understanding business and financial problems, including information about an incident in which he sold the wrong business software to an important customer. Such information might not otherwise emerge in the course of your preparation of Blake. Your research will also help you decide how to work with Blake during the preparation session.

Try to identify those subjects for which painstaking fact reconstruction during the preparation session is likely to be important. In a business case, for example, the deposition could turn on whether this deponent's recollection of what was said at a key meeting is consistent with that of others who attended the meeting. In any kind of case, the deposition could turn on contradictory—or apparently contradictory—documents or on conflicting versions of a conversation. For example, in the *Scoops* case, you would focus carefully—before meeting with Blake—on the details of his conversation with Leslie Roberts about Scoops's computer needs.

**Rule 5: Before Meeting the Witness, Plan Your Strategy
for Refreshing Memory, Including the Use of Documents**

If a witness does not recall certain events, you may decide to refresh the witness's recollection through documents or otherwise. Or you may be pleased with the witness's lack of recall, particularly if you believe the testimony would have been harmful. You have no obligation to refresh a witness's recollection. For example, in preparing former President Ronald Reagan for his videotaped testimony in the Iran-Contra trial of former national security adviser John Poindexter, the president's counsel apparently opted not to refresh recollection. President Reagan repeatedly answered questions by saying he did not recall and simply stressed that he relied on the expertise and good faith of his advisers.[19]

There is a practical reason to probe a witness's memory to test the claimed lack of recollection. If you do not, you run the risk that the examiner might jog the witness's memory at the deposition, triggering testimony that you have never heard and, therefore, never discussed with the witness. That unprepared deposition testimony will be a potent cross-examination weapon at trial if the witness—now prepared—tells a different story on the stand. Therefore, lawyers usually err on the side of refreshing recollection before a deposition, even if doing so reminds the witness of details that might otherwise not have been recalled.

Decide which documents to show the witness. This decision may be crucial. Under certain circumstances, FRE 612 (or a state analog) can require production of documents used before or during trial testimony to refresh a witness's recollection, and this requirement has been applied to depositions.[20]

Before meeting with the deponent, decide what strategy you will adopt to avoid or minimize the risks of refreshing memory. If you decide not to show a document to the witness, be careful not to describe it in such detail as arguably to bring it within the rule requiring production. If you do use the document, prepare the deponent to say (if it is true) that the document did not "refresh my recollection" of the facts in question.[21] By all means, advise the witness that such a question may be coming and explain why the examiner is asking it.

In addition, you may say at the deposition (if it is true) that the witness was not shown any documents that were not already produced; therefore, a second, repeated production is not "necessary in the interests of justice" under FRE 612. Another approach is to have the deponent review many documents at the preparation session, all of which were previously produced to the other side. That way, if production of the documents reviewed is required under FRE 612, opposing counsel will not learn what you think are the most important documents, as the important will be produced again with the unimportant.

Rule 6: Plan Fact Gathering and Witness Preparation as Two Stages

Fact gathering and witness preparation are different exercises. Some lawyers frequently confuse the two and, as a result, do neither well. On the one hand, in gathering the facts, you want the deponent to be expansive—to volunteer all possibly relevant information even if you have not specifically asked for it. Reconstruction of reality begins with memory dredging. On the other hand, in preparing a witness, you want the deponent to answer questions as she would at the deposition itself—briefly and to the point, providing no information beyond what the question requires.[22]

It can be difficult for you—and disorienting for the witness—to switch back and forth from fact gathering to witness preparation. Worse yet, when these functions are confused, one of two problems can arise. The witness may conclude he or she should provide expansive answers at the deposition. Or the witness may decide that it is important to be terse, and fail to reveal important facts to you, leading you to make reasonable—but false—inferences from what you are told. This second problem happened to a lawyer who represented the manufacturer of a prototype of a new surgical device, which was sold to a hospital and allegedly malfunctioned during surgery. The lawyer, who had conscientiously prepared the salesperson for deposition, initially was unfazed by a question at the deposition inquiring where the salesperson was during the surgery—even though the lawyer did not know the answer. The witness's answer at the deposition astonished the lawyer: "In the operating room. This was a new device, and I wanted to see personally how well it performed." Asked later why he had not mentioned this important fact in the preparation session, the witness replied, "When I met with you, you never asked me directly about it, and you told me not to volunteer." This example dramatically demonstrates the danger of mixing fact gathering and witness preparation in a way that confuses the witness about the different guidelines for those two approaches. To avoid confusion about when you are gathering facts and when you are preparing the witness, try to have two separate sessions. Or at least split your meeting with the witness into two clearly defined stages. Or consider

191

having a colleague join you for the second stage to play the role of the examiner.[23]

Rule 7: Carefully Control How and When the Witness Will First Recount Crucial Events

Despite your best efforts, it is not always easy to distinguish fact gathering from witness preparation, so remember: The first discussion of events, however denominated, is likely to be the critical one. The deponent is likely to stick to the version of the facts given at the first session. Your greatest challenge may be deciding how and when the witness will first tell you the facts from which reality will be reconstructed.

Therefore, *before* you have the witness say anything, be sure you know the trouble spots in the case and the witness's view of key events. With that knowledge firmly in mind, be sure you ask questions the first time around that do not invite, or stampede, the witness into an unhelpful narrative.

Preparing the Witness: Rules for Reconstructing Reality

After you have prepared yourself for the witness preparation session, you will then meet with the witness. The following rules provide guidelines for that meeting, which may, as discussed above, actually be two meetings or one meeting combining fact gathering and witness preparation.

Rule 1: Give the Deponent the Big Picture First

Start your fact-gathering session by giving the deponent a context. Explain to the deponent why the deposition is being taken and how the deposition process works.[24] If the witness is anxious about anything, including what a deposition is and why his testimony is important, the witness may be distracted and unable to concentrate at the deposition.[25]

Explain the setting of the deposition, including where it will be taken, who will probably be present, if it will be video recorded, and what the court reporter does. Describe opposing counsel and what you know about that lawyer's questioning style. Assure the witness you will be there to represent him, that you will focus later on rules of thumb for answering questions at the deposition, but that you would now like to move to the merits of the case if there are no pressing questions.[26]

Do not make the mistake of thinking a witness—even a main actor—knows the contentions of the parties or recalls the key facts in dispute. Months or years might have elapsed since the events leading to the lawsuit. Unlike you, the witness might not have been living with the case since the suit was filed—in fact, the witness might have preferred to put it out of his or her mind. State the major contentions of each side and the most important facts each relies on to support its position.

Providing the legal context helps the witness focus on what is relevant and, to that extent, furthers the fact-finding process. There is a risk, however: The witness may take it as a signal to conform testimony to a legal theory. Remember the "lecture" from *Anatomy of a Murder*.[27] Defense counsel's client has been charged with (and turns out to be guilty of) first-degree murder. Before going over his client's recollection of events, defense counsel purposefully describes the legal defenses to murder, including those available to his client given the facts of the case. In doing so, the lawyer intentionally suggests a version of the facts that might result in a verdict of not guilty by reason of insanity.[28]

Is this approach ethical? Is it proper to tell a witness in a civil case about the legal theories that the witness's testimony might support before reviewing the facts with the witness? The answer is yes, within limits. The witness needs information from his lawyer about the law applicable to issues that will be the subject of questions at the deposition. Otherwise, the witness might—consciously or unconsciously—mold his testimony to an uninformed, erroneous view of the law that may well result in victory for the other side. At the same time, the lawyer needs to be sensitive to the point at which the witness will pick up the wrong message and may begin to fabricate testimony to conform to the law as described by the lawyer. A lawyer should never go beyond that point.[29]

Rule 2: Next, Go Over the Facts Chronologically

After you have outlined the context, confirm with the witness the dates of the pivotal events in the case. In a contract case, for example, these might include the date that the contract was entered, the date on which the witness first learned that the scarcity of raw materials would make it hard to perform, and the date of the alleged breach.

Then learn what the witness knows about the relevant facts. Skipping randomly from event to event to learn what the witness knows increases the risk that you will miss something. A chronological review is easy for both you and witness to follow because most people remember chronologically. A chronological approach also reduces the chance of oversight—which is the reason it is typically used in examining a deponent. Later in the preparation process, you will focus on key events and key allegations. Now, you are just getting an overview. The chronological approach gives you and the witness a structure for the entire process.

When the sequence of events is important, it may help to have the witness consult a written chronology you have prepared of the most important events; but be sure the version the witness sees does not contain your comments. (As forewarned above, always assume and act as if opposing counsel could ultimately discover this document under FRE 612 or a similar state rule.) Take each key event in order, asking what, if anything, the witness knows about it and then asking appropriate follow-up questions. Then ask whether anything of importance happened between that event and the next one on the chronology you prepared. (Again, note the parallel to deposition questioning.)

Of course, you might vary the purely chronological approach by moving in chronological order within certain large topics. In the *Scoops* case, for example, you could review with Blake every opportunity he had to learn of Roberts's needs and then develop the facts chronologically as to each occasion when Blake learned of her needs.

A case loaded with documents requires an additional level of preparation. There is much to be said for presenting documents in chronological order. But during the first pass, it is too time-consuming and tedious to review the facts and documents at the same time. Worse, the big picture may be obscured by a mass of detail.

Instead, review the facts and perhaps the five or six most important documents. At the end of the chronological overview, review the main points with the witness to be sure that nothing has been overlooked. Then review all the documents separately. That way, the witness will begin reviewing the documents with a firm grasp of the facts, which will be reinforced during the review of individual documents.

Rule 3: Try to Get at the Facts from Different Angles

A chronological review is only the beginning. Follow up with more detailed questions about individual subjects or allegations.

For example, suppose that the plaintiff claims the defendant's employees fraudulently misrepresented the capabilities of the defendant's product. You are the defendant's lawyer. It is not enough to review with your client's employees the conversations that took place at each of the four meetings between the parties and then inquire about any interim contacts. Take a different tack by asking about misrepresentations: Do you personally now know any facts that might support the claim that the plaintiff was misled? Did you know any such facts at the time of those meetings? Do you know of anything an employee of the defendant might have said or done that supports the claim? Or failed to say or do? Or said or did unintentionally? Or said or did that could have been misunderstood? Have you heard anything from anyone else that could support the claim?

Explore even remote possibilities of knowledge. Continuing the misrepresentation example, now suppose you represent the plaintiff. Counsel for the defendant notices the deposition of the plaintiff's controller, presumably to learn about the plaintiff's damage claim. When you prepare the controller for her deposition, ask whether she knows anything about the key factual allegations. Even if she did not participate in the meetings at which the alleged misrepresentations were allegedly made, has she heard from others what was said there?

Few sensations are more unpleasant than the fear that will grip you if you have not covered a significant question in the preparation session and it is asked at the deposition. One such sensation is the remorse that washes over you when you hear the witness, unprepared, flounder when you know the witness could have testified confidently and effectively if prepared properly for the question.

Rule 4: Structure Your Questions Carefully

Fact reconstruction is the hardest part of fact gathering. What may be most important is the order in which you ask questions. The structure of questions for reconstruction will vary with the situation. Many cases will present fact-reconstruction challenges that become apparent only when you meet the witness.

Take, for example, a case in which your client's building has burned down. Whether the loss is covered by insurance depends on the reconstruction of a telephone conversation between the defendant insurer's agent and the employee in charge of insurance for your client. The insurance agent claims that he told your client's employee that he was issuing a requested property insurance binder on the recently acquired building, but that the insurance policy

195

would contain a sprinkler clause. The agent also claims that he told the employee that if there were a fire and the sprinklers were not operational, there would be no coverage. After the binder was issued, but before the policy itself was issued, fire destroyed the building, and the sprinklers did not operate. If the insurance agent's version of the telephone conversation is accurate, your client loses the case.

In the first fact-gathering session, your client's employee is candid: His recollection of the telephone conversation is hazy. He understood the agent to say that the sprinkler clause affected only the premium rate, not coverage. But because his recollection is shaky, he is hesitant to deny the agent's story.

How do you reconstruct this reality? Do not focus on the employee's doubt; you only will reinforce it. Instead, reconstruct by (1) re-creating the scene described by the agent, (2) describing the implications of the agent's version of the story, and (3) pressing the employee on what he would have done if things had actually happened the way the agent claimed. It might go this way:

1. **Re-create the scene.**

   Your boss has asked you to get insurance. You call the agent for the company's insurance carrier. You ask the agent to bind coverage for this warehouse that the company has acquired. The insurance agent takes the information and tells you he will take care of it.

   Now, you are sitting in your office. The phone rings. The insurer's agent tells you that he will issue the binder, but that it will be made subject to a sprinkler clause. He says that means that if the warehouse burns down because the sprinklers are not operational, you have no insurance.

2. **Describe implied conduct starkly and then explore its implications.**

   Does it make sense that you just said "thank you" to the agent, hung up, and went back to your paperwork?

   At the time of the call, did you know whether the sprinklers in that building were operational? Who did know?

   Well, if the conversation really had gone the way the agent says, what would you have done? Would you have checked whether the sprinklers worked?

196

Do you remember saying to yourself, "I should call Charlie Johnson to check if the sprinklers are operational," or anything like that?

What was the amount of this policy?

Do you recall deciding not to bother calling Charlie Johnson even though this was a $20 million policy?

Did you just decide to take a chance and hope for the best? What possible reason would there be to do that?

3. **Put your witness back in the scenario.**

Now, focus on when you first found out about the fire. Did this thought go through your mind: "My Lord! I wonder if we don't have any insurance because the sprinklers were not operational"? Or did you say to yourself, "Thank goodness we have insurance!"

Now think back to the original conversation about the binder. Did this guy really say to you, "If there's a fire and the sprinklers are not operational, you have no insurance coverage"?

If the employee now says that he is sure the agent did not say that the sprinkler would affect coverage, follow up with, "Do you feel comfortable with that? Is it the truth?" If it is not true, he will almost certainly answer one of these questions in the negative.

Then try various alternative formulations to find the most positive one the witness agrees with, which might be this: "To the best of my recollection, when we discussed the insurance policy, Mr. X mentioned only the premium, not the coverage," or "Although I do not recall the conversation verbatim, Mr. X said something to the effect that the clause concerned the premium rate. I feel certain that if Mr. X had mentioned that we would not have coverage if the sprinklers were not operational, I would remember that." And so on.

Rule 5: Take the Witness Through Practice Sessions "on the Stand"

Most lawyers give the witness a set of guidelines for answering questions at a deposition.[30] Whatever guidelines you use, remember that guidelines for being deposed are like instructions for swimming—easy to grasp in the abstract, but hard to apply in deep, choppy water.

After reviewing the guidelines with the witness, turn to the substance of the testimony and go through some dry runs. But be certain that both of you know when you are fact gathering as the witness's lawyer, and when, instead, you are playing the role of opposing counsel and interrogating the deponent as if in a deposition.

There are a number of devices you can use to let the witness know you are role playing as if it were the actual deposition. The simplest is to switch from first name to surname to signal that the role playing has begun. Before you question the witness as the taker, you might, say something like, "You're in the witness chair, Mr. Blake." To end the mock deposition, say, "We're off the record, Mr. Blake." Then switch to the deponent's first name: "Terry, we need to review some of your answers." Those cues should let the witness know at any given moment whether he is "on stage" and should follow the guidelines for testifying, or "off stage" conferring with his own lawyer and thus able to speak freely.

Also, consider video recording the mock deposition session and then reviewing the video with the witness. (Caveat: The video recording may be discoverable.[31])

Throughout the preparation session, warn the witness always to avoid shorthand references that could be dangerous. In one case, the witness had written a letter that ended by inviting questions about enclosed specifications. The other side had never responded to this invitation—yet later claimed the specifications were ambiguous. The invitation was clearly helpful to the witness's side of the case. When the witness's lawyer first asked in witness preparation about the closing line of the letter, the witness flippantly replied that the invitation was "sales garbage." Then, more seriously, he said he would have been glad to field any questions. The witness and the lawyer continued to banter about "sales garbage"—though they both knew better than to use that language at the deposition. You know the rest. When the invitation in the letter was mentioned at the deposition, the deponent—like Pavlov's dog stimulated by the ring of a bell—blurted out, "That was just sales garbage."[32]

Rule 6: Adapt the "Do Not Volunteer" Rule to the Individual

The most troublesome rule for the deponent is, "Answer only the question asked, nothing more. Do not volunteer."[33] Lawyers say it to keep deponents from rambling on—which is important—but they do not always mean what they say.

How do you explain to the witness when he should follow the "do not volunteer" rule and when he should answer expansively? The best you can do is to tell the witness to follow the general rule when in doubt, but to remember there are exceptions. Then try to give the exceptions life. An abstract discussion will not help. Instead, go "on the record" during your practice sessions and use some examples of lines of inquiry to which the deponent should respond aggressively expansively.

For example, in preparing Terry Blake, you might want him to volunteer that Leslie Roberts cut him off as he attempted to find out more about Scoops's financial accounting needs. The practice deposition session might go like this:

> Q. We're back on the record, Mr. Blake. Now, did you discuss with Ms. Roberts the accounting needs of Scoops?
> A. No.
> Q. Isn't it true that you sold Ms. Roberts "The Bottom Line" software without knowing what Scoops's accounting needs were?
> A. Yes.

Lawyer: Terry, let's go off the record. We've just found one of the rare exceptions to the "do-not-volunteer" rule. We can't leave your answer like that because it sounds as if you didn't care about Leslie Roberts's accounting needs and arbitrarily sold her cash-basis software. That isn't what happened here, according to what you've told me. So, in responding to a question at your deposition, you have to go ahead and explain that Leslie Roberts became defensive when you asked her questions and was not responsive. Now, let's try it again.

> Q. Back on the record. Mr. Blake, isn't it true that you and Ms. Roberts never even talked about Scoops's accounting needs?
> A. Well, I tried to talk to Ms. Roberts about Scoops's accounting needs, but when I asked her about that, she became really annoyed and acted like she didn't want to get into that.

Some witnesses never seem to get it. But most will find your examples useful, and some may develop an instinct for sensing approaches that call for aggressive or more expansive testimony.

Above all, consider the witness's personality—a personality you should have investigated before the meeting and will have now observed during the preparation session. A witness's personality will dramatically affect the "do-not-volunteer" rule. The distracted inventor, the busy executive, the angry plaintiff—each will hear and follow your instructions differently. And each will respond differently to the examiner's personality and style.

Rule 7: Be Tough, but Build the Deponent's Confidence

Prepare the witness by being harder on him or her than the examiner will be. Explain to your witness why you are being so harsh. But take care: Saying why you are doing it and retaining your client's trust are two different things.

Experiment with different ways of structuring the questions on a subject, though the examiner may try only one approach. But think twice about playing the hard-nosed examiner when the witness gives a wrong answer to a difficult question. At the deposition, of course, the examiner might ruthlessly pursue any opening. But one of your objectives in preparation is to give the witness confidence. Repeatedly forcing your own witness to the wall during preparation will not do that.

For several reasons, you might think about having another lawyer play the examiner while you serve as the defender. First, you are no longer in the uncomfortable position of beating up your own witness. Second, you can watch how your witness performs under interrogation. Third, your witness gets a taste of how it feels to be questioned by a stranger. Fourth, the witness will better understand your role as a defender, and your discussion of defense tactics will become more real. Finally, as a defender, you will be able to demonstrate your ability to assist the witness at the deposition and thus build your witness's confidence in you.

However you handle the session, do not deflate your witness. Give the witness a taste of the harsh realities of a deposition and then demonstrate how to cope with it. When the witness gives a bad answer, ask a few more questions to determine whether the witness will be able to fix the problem with the answer during the follow-up questioning. If not, then say "off the record" and explain the implications of the bad answer. Rattle off the next six or seven questions that opposing counsel would ask, but do not force the witness to answer them at that time. Leave the witness whole, and then replay the initial questioning to give the deponent a chance to do it right.

Rule 8: Continue Preparing the Witness Until the Deposition Is Over

Continuity is the key. Be in touch with, and attuned to, the witness—a living, changing person. Ideally, first meet the witness five to 10 days before the deposition. Then have a brush-up session on the morning of the deposition.[34] The timing of the initial meeting (or meetings, if the fact-gathering session will be separate) is important. It should not be so early that the witness forgets the lesson learned. But it should be early enough to let the fact reconstruction settle in. If the actual deposition starts too soon after the fact-reconstruction session, the deponent may still be tentative about the reconstructed facts.

In the interval between the fact-reconstruction session and the deposition, the witness may want to test the accuracy of the reconstructed facts by trying to recall additional details, speaking with others about events, or consulting documents that might verify the reconstructed facts. You probably want to caution against such unsupervised efforts to refresh recollection.[35] Recognize that by learning new information, the witness may be forced to give substantive answers to deposition questions instead of saying, "I do not know." Worse yet, the witness may consult with, and be tainted by, unreliable sources.

If you tell the witness it is all right to check other sources to confirm recollection, ask to be kept posted on what those sources disclose. Otherwise, on the morning of the deposition, the witness may arrive and announce, "I've figured it all out, and what I told you the other day is wrong."

Witness preparation does not end when the deposition starts.[36] Without coaching, or being obstructive under FRCP 30(c)(2), you can still gently remind the witness during the deposition about your guidelines. For example, if a deponent is asked about, and gives, the date of a meeting, in most jurisdictions you may cut off the witness's impulse to tell what was said at the meeting by reminding the witness not to volunteer or by saying, "There is no question pending." If a witness starts to answer a question by saying "I would guess," you may want to admonish your witness not to guess by saying: "Mr. Suplee, if you have information, Ms.

Donaldson is entitled to an answer, but she doesn't want you to guess." But remember: Local court rules and practice may vary on what you are permitted to say to your witness at a deposition.

On the other hand, if the deponent's terse answers may be misleading, you may want to encourage the examiner to follow up—encourage the deponent to be more forthcoming rather than waiting for the correct information to emerge hours later when it is your turn to examine the deponent. For example, say to the examiner, "Well, there's a lot more to it than that, as you will find if you ask a few follow-up questions." Again, whether this interposition is proper under FRCP 30(c)(2) may depend on local court rules and practice.

Rule 9: Use Fact Reconstruction to Free the Deponent's Memory from Emotional Blind Spots and to Clarify Intent

You do not need a psychologist to tell you that people remember things to fit their own needs. Effective fact reconstruction may counter that tendency.

Before Terry Blake enters your office for the first preparation session, you glance again at Maxine Waller's memorandum that she sent to Terry Blake to refer Leslie Roberts as a new client and to guide Blake's selection of hardware and software for Scoops. There is no reference in the memorandum to accrual accounting or to special accounting needs. You also review Leslie Roberts's letter to Business-Aide, which similarly makes no mention of Scoops's particular accounting needs.

You must help Blake reconstruct the facts. What did he understand about Scoops's accounting needs from looking at these documents? What did Leslie Roberts actually say to him? Did Roberts ever refer to sales or purchases on credit?

In this sea of questions you have posed, to yourself, one thing is clear: If you ask Blake without preamble whether Roberts ever told him that Scoops was on accrual-basis accounting, he may well say she probably did. After all, you know he feels responsible for the lawsuit and has told Maxine Waller that Roberts "must have" told him about Scoops's accounting needs. In addition, he is not familiar with accounting terms, and he is worried that Roberts told him and he just misunderstood. When answering your question, he may then refuse to budge from that position—even though there is evidence that Roberts never mentioned Scoops's accounting needs.

You need to plan your questions. You also need to plan which documents to show Blake and in what order.

* * *

You have prepared and now it is time to meet with Blake at your office. Although he is a computer whiz who can make neophyte customers feel comfortable with computers, he enters your office hesitant and nervous. You are in control because you know how to prepare a witness. You put him at ease. You establish the context, structure your questions, and finally—but cautiously—approach the big moment during the practice questioning. You start with the memorandum from Waller:

Q. Let me show you both the memorandum that Maxine Waller sent to you about her telephone conversation with Frank Fuller from Scoops and the letter from Leslie Roberts, which is attached. Did you read those documents when you got them?

A. Yes.

Q. Does the memorandum mention the accounting method used by Scoops?

A. No.

Q. Does the letter mention the accounting method used by Scoops?

A. No.

Q. Does the memorandum mention that Scoops had special accounting needs?

A. No.

Q. Does the letter mention that Scoops had special accounting needs?

A. No.

Q. When you spoke to Leslie by telephone before you met her in the store, did she say anything about having special accounting needs?

A. No.

Q. So, before meeting her in the store, did you have any reason to believe that Leslie Roberts had any special accounting needs?

A. No.

Q. When you met Leslie Roberts in the store, did she ever mention that Scoops had special accounting needs?

A. No. In fact, when I tried to talk to Ms. Roberts about Scoops's accounting needs, she acted really annoyed and brushed off my questions.

Q. Were you aware that The Bottom Line accounting software was less sophisticated than the Chief Financial Officer software?

A. Yes.

Q. Did you understand in what ways the two accounting programs differed?

A. No.

Q. Nevertheless, if you had ever learned that Scoops had special accounting needs, would you have sold Roberts The Bottom Line without asking more questions?

A. No.

Q. Did you tell Leslie Roberts that The Bottom Line was less sophisticated than the Chief Financial Officer?

A. Yes.

Q. Did she then choose to purchase The Bottom Line?

A. Yes.

Yes, that is about what you thought had happened. It is one of those good days when a deponent's reconstructed reality converges with your own sense of truth.

Notes

*This chapter is adapted from an article by Dennis R. Suplee and Diana S. Donaldson that first appeared as "Reconstructing Reality: Preparing the Deponent to Testify," LITIGATION, Fall 1988, at 19.

1. Lionel Trilling, *The Quartet: Two Reviews*, in THE WORLD OF LAWRENCE DURELL 56 (Harry T. Moore ed., 1962).

2. *See* Monroe H. Freedman, *Counseling the Client: Refreshing Recollection or Prompting Perjury?*, THE LITIGATION MANUAL 490, 492–93 (3d ed. 1999).

3. *Id.* at 492.

4. See Chapter 21, discussing perjury by your witness at a deposition.

5. *See* MODEL RULES OF PROF'L CONDUCT; District of Columbia Bar, Legal Ethics Comm., Op. 79, at 139 (1979) ("Indeed, a lawyer who did not prepare his or her witness for testimony, having had an opportunity to do so, would not be doing his or her professional job properly."); 3 WIGMORE ON EVIDENCE § 788 (1970) (witness preparation is an "absolute necessity"). For a thorough discussion of this issue, *see* John S. Applegate, *Witness Preparation*, 68 TEX. L. REV. 277, 286–89 (1989). See also "Proper Practice Versus Improper Coaching" in Chapter 7. Judicial approval of witness preparation is reflected in the scornful question from the bench,

most likely to come after the witness has given several unresponsive, rambling answers on direct examination, "Counselor, haven't you prepared this witness?"

6. District of Columbia Bar, Legal Ethics Comm., Op. 79, *supra* note 5, at 139.

7. A well-known decision is *Hall v. Clifton Precision*, 150 F.R.D. 525 (E.D. Pa. 1993), in which the judge prohibited conferences with the witness, even during breaks, except to assert a privilege. *See also* Southgate v. Vt. Mut. Ins. Co., 2007 U.S. Dist. LEXIS 45291, at *15–16 (D.R.I. June 21, 2007); Jones v. J.C. Penney's Dep't Stores, Inc., 228 F.R.D. 190, 196 (W.D. N.Y. 2005); Calzaturficio S.C.A.R.P.A. S.p.A. v. Fabiano Shoe Co., Inc., 201 F.R.D. 33, 40 (D. Mass. 2001) (counsel "not entitled to assist his witness during a deposition"); Mruz v. Caring, Inc., 107 F. Supp. 2d 596, 606 (D.N.J. 2000); Stempler v. Collect Am., Ltd., 2000 U.S. Dist. LEXIS 3313, at *3 (E.D. La. Mar. 15, 2000); Armstrong v. Hussmann Corp., 163 F.R.D. 299 (E.D. Mo. 1995); Paramount Commc'ns, Inc. v. QVC Network, Inc., 637 A.2d 34 (Del. 1994); DEL. R. CIV. P. 30 (d)(1) (prohibiting conferences between deponent and defender); E.D.N.Y. Standing Order on Effective Discovery in Civil Cases ¶¶ 12–13. Contra McKinley Infuser, Inc. v. Zdeb, 200 F.R.D. 648 (D. Colo. 2001) (refusing to adopt restrictions on conferences during breaks); Acri v. Golden Triangle Mgmt. Acceptance Co., 142 Pittsburgh Legal J. 225 (C.C.P. Pitts. 1994) (disagreeing with Hall deposition guidelines as relegating role of defense counsel to that of "a silent fly on the wall"). See also "Problem Situations for the Examiner and Suggested Responses" in Chapter 15 for an extended discussion on the limitations on defense tactics.

8. ABA Sec. Litig., *Comment on Hall v. Clifton Precision*, LITIG. NEWS, June 1994, at 3.

9. A. LEO LEVIN & HAROLD CRAMER, PROBLEMS AND MATERIALS ON TRIAL ADVOCACY 30 (1968).

10. *See* MODEL RULES OF PROF'L CONDUCT Rs. 1.2, 3.3, 3.4 (2007). See "ABA Model Rules" in Chapter 21 for an extended discussion of the applicable Model Rules in the context of perjury at a deposition.

11. See "Knowledge" in Chapter 21, discussing perjury at a deposition and the requisite standard of knowledge.

12. See "Elements of the Attorney-Client and Work-Product Privileges" in Chapter 6.

13. *See* United States v. Semel, 411 F.2d 195, 197 (3d Cir. 1969); Langer v. Presbyterian Med. Ctr., 32 Fed. R. Serv. 3d 56, at *36 (E.D. Pa. 1995); Condon v. Petacque, 90 F.R.D. 53, 54 (N.D. Ill. 1981).

14. See "Instructing a Witness Not to Answer" in Chapter 14.

15. MODEL RULES OF PROF'L CONDUCT R. 4.2 cmt. *See also* Upjohn Co. v. United States, 449 U.S. 383 (1981) (communications with employees concerning matters within scope of their duties protected by privilege). See also "Applying the Attorney-Client Privilege When the Client Is a

Corporation" and other sections in Chapter 6 for an extended discussion of who is the client.

16.   See "Counsel's Communications with Former Employees" in Chapter 6.

17.   FED. R. EVID. 611(c) ("Leading question. [W]hen a party calls a hostile witness, an adverse party, or a witness identified with an adverse party, interrogation may be by leading question.") See also "Warnings to Corporate Employees Concerning Potential Conflicts of Interest" in Chapter 6, further discussing the danger of a disqualifying conflict of interest created by representing a current or former employee.

18.   See "Warnings to Corporate Employees Concerning Potential Conflicts of Interest" in Chapter 6

19.   *See* Joe Pichirallo, *Reagan Says He Told Aides "We Don't Break the Law,"* WASH. POST, Feb. 23, 1990, at A1.

20.   FED. R. CIV. P. 30(c) ("The examination and cross-examination of a deponent proceed as they would at trial under the Federal Rules of Evidence, except Rules 103 and 615."). *See In re* San Juan DuPont Hotel Fire Litig., 859 F.2d 1007, 1018 (1st Cir. 1988); *but see* Sporck v. Peil, 759 F.2d 312 (3d Cir.), *cert. denied,* 474 U.S. 903 (1985). See also Chapter 9.

21.   See "How to Avoid Putting Privileged Documents at Risk" in Chapter 9 for an extended discussion of how to protect documents reviewed by a witness from disclosure.

22.   See "Twenty Guidelines for Deposition Testimony" in Chapter 7 for guidelines on preparing the witness.

23.   *See infra* section "Rule 7: Be Tough, but Build the Deponent's Confidence," discussing having another lawyer play the examiner while you serve as the defender.

24.   See "Placing the Deposition in Context" in Chapter 7.

25.   See "Explaining the Deposition Process" in Chapter 7 for suggestions on when to discuss with a witness the deposition process.

26.   Some lawyers like to save time by sending the deponent a letter covering these procedural points before the first meeting. But even if you send a letter, you should review these points in person. Many witnesses will not read your letter. Some who do may not understand it. See also "Sending the Witness Materials for Review Before the First Meeting" in Chapter 5, discussing the pros and cons of sending a letter or video recording to the witness in advance of the preparation session.

27.   ROBERT TRAVER, ANATOMY OF A MURDER (1958). The book was popularized in a movie directed by Otto Preminger, starring Jimmy Stewart as defense counsel.

28.   Note that the book involved a capital case, in which there may be more of a consensus that the defendant is entitled to know of the legal defenses available before discussing the facts.

29.   See "1. Always Tell the Truth" in Chapter 7, and Chapter 21, discussing deposition perjury by your witness.

30.   See "Twenty Guidelines for Deposition Testimony" in Chapter 7.

31.   See Chapter 10, note 34, and "A Video Recording Synchronized to the Transcript Can Be Used Throughout the Discovery Process" in Chapter 17, discussing the discoverability of a video recording of witness preparation.

32.   In an often-cited experiment, Russian scientist Ivan Pavlov, a Nobel Prize winner in Physiology or Medicine, demonstrated that environmental events that previously had no relation to a given reflex (such as a bell sound) could, through experience, trigger a reflex (such as salivation). This kind of learned response is called conditioned reflex, and the process whereby dogs or humans learn to connect a stimulus to a reflex is called conditioning. See Lotta Fredholm, Pavlov's Dogs, http://nobelprize.org/educational_games/medicine/pavlov/readmore.html (May 15, 2001).

33.   See "13. Do Not Volunteer Information" in Chapter 7, discussing when to ignore that rule.

34.   See also "Preparation Sessions: When, Where, How Often, and with Whom" in Chapter 5.

35.   See also Chapter 9.

36.   See also Chapter 14, discussing defending at a deposition and, in particular, limitations on defenders.

CHAPTER 9

Discoverability of Documents Used to Refresh the Recollection of a Witness: Federal Rule of Evidence 612[*]

PETER GRUENBERGER

The Perils of Ignoring Federal Rule of Evidence 612

A frequent scenario early in a deposition finds the witness being asked ostensibly routine questions regarding what the witness has done, if anything, to prepare for the deposition.[1] The defender becomes concerned, however, when the routine questions begin to get more specific and detailed. Before the defender figures out where it is all headed, the examining lawyer requests production of the documents the witness has just identified as materials he reviewed before the deposition—some, if not all, of which refreshed the witness's recollection or affected his testimony.

Worse, the witness has referred not only to documents produced to the other side but also to some of the defender's file memos. One of them consists of the defender's neatly packaged annotated chronology of key events and conversations. Another is the defender's "good facts/bad facts" memorandum analyzing the strengths and weaknesses of her client's case, with references to particular events and conversations.

Unfortunately, the defender now remembers giving these documents to her witness during the preparation session because time was limited and the witness's memory of key events and conversations was terrible. Because the witness would likely be a key trial witness, it was important that he remember by the time of the deposition rather than only later at trial.[2]

At this point in the deposition, the defender might reflexively respond to the request for documents by questioning the skill and experience of the examining lawyer and making disparaging references to his ignorance of the attorney-client and work-product privilege. The examining lawyer responds by politely suggesting that the defender reread Federal Rule of Evidence (FRE) 612 and Federal Rule of Civil Procedure (FRCP) 30(c), so that the time and expense of a motion to compel production can be avoided. The examiner then continues with the deposition, carefully leaving the record open pending either compliance with his demand for production or the filing of a motion to compel.

The defender returns to her office and, with hopeful skepticism, picks up her source materials for FRE 612 and FRCP 30(c). To her dismay, she finds that FRE 612 states:

> if a witness uses a writing to refresh memory for the purpose of testifying, either
>
> (1) while testifying, or
> (2) before testifying, if the court in its discretion determines it is necessary in the interests of justice, an adverse party is

entitled to have the writing produced at the hearing, to inspect it, to cross-examine the witness thereon, and to introduce in evidence those portions which relate to the testimony of the witness.[3]

FRCP 30(c) provides that at depositions, the examination and cross-examination of witnesses may proceed as permitted at trial under the provisions of the FRE.[4] A handful of courts have found FRE 612 inapplicable to deposition testimony on different theories.[5] Most courts, however, have found that FRCP 30(c) makes FRE 612 applicable to testimony given in a deposition and will, with the proper foundational showing, make privileged materials used to refresh recollection discoverable by the party taking the deposition.[6]

Of course, the defender's concern should go well beyond the disclosure and production of documents reviewed by the witness—both those previously produced to the other side and those prepared in anticipation of litigation but not yet produced. Just producing "core" work product (such as internal good facts/bad facts memoranda), which typically would be protected by FRCP 26(b)(3), can be highly damaging in its own right. It can also be damaging because informing the examiner which documents the defender has selected for witness preparation speaks volumes about the defender's theories. Recognizing this danger, some courts have afforded a higher level of protection to such types of lawyers' core work product.[7]

Given the potential for disclosure under FRE 612, the defender must be alert to the possible consequences of using particular documents to prepare a witness. Conversely, the examining lawyer must (1) carefully inquire regarding the preparation process and (2) create a sufficient record to meet the foundation requirements for production pursuant to FRE 612.

This chapter reviews the techniques that deposition takers can use to maximize the likelihood of discovering which documents a witness has reviewed and thereby gain access to documents not previously produced. It also reviews the strategies that defenders can use to prepare a witness adequately, while minimizing the likelihood that documents reviewed by a witness while preparing for a deposition—whether or not previously produced and whether or not privileged—will become discoverable by the examiner.

FRE 612 in Theory

To use FRE 612 effectively in a deposition—either offensively or defensively—lawyers must understand the reason for the rule. FRE 612 seeks to balance the traditional protections of privilege with the interests of fairness in allowing an examiner to conduct a cross-examination that can fairly test the nature and origins of the witness's memory.

Documents are generally protected from disclosure by two privileges. First, the attorney-client privilege protects confidential communications between lawyer and client for the purpose of securing legal advice. Second, the work-product privilege qualifiedly protects a lawyer's efforts in representing a party in contemplated or actual litigation.[8]

When documents—whatever their nature—are used by a witness to refresh recollection, the scope of both privileges is called into question. One view, as noted above, is that FRE 612 allows disclosure of otherwise nondiscoverable documents to ensure adequate cross-examination of a witness who may be relying on those documents rather than on memory.[9] Under this view, a balancing test must be applied to determine whether the protections against disclosure are outweighed by the needs for fair examination.

An alternative view is that disclosure is required when documents are used by a witness to refresh his recollection, even when those documents are privileged, because the privilege (attorney-client or work product) has been waived.[10] Under this waiver theory, balancing is not required. Which theory applies and how to balance the competing interests of protection and disclosure have been the subject of considerable jurisprudence.

FRE 612 in Practice

Whether an examiner's inquiries about documents reviewed in preparation for a deposition will require production of some or all of those documents depends on a number of variables. These include the identity of the witness, the type of material being reviewed, and the circumstances under which the witness reviews the material.

Who Is the Deponent?

The type of witness being prepared—lay fact (percipient) witness, lawyer, or nontestifying expert—may affect the extent to which documents are at risk of being discoverable.

The factors that might require document production from, or afford protection to, lay witnesses—even if they are lawyers—are not the same as those for experts.[11] When testifying experts are involved, FRE 612 must be read in conjunction with FRCP 26(a)(2)(B), FRCP 26(b)(4)(A), and FRE 705,[12] which require disclosure of the facts or data underlying a testifying expert's opinion as well as the opinion itself. Even with respect to non-testifying experts, FRE 612 still must be considered in connection with FRCP 26(b)(4)(B), which provides for discovery as provided in FRCP 35(b) or upon a showing of exceptional circumstances.[13]

The fact that a lay witness happens to be a lawyer will not affect a court's decision whether to grant access to documents. Even when a former lawyer testifies and refers to her notes, those notes may be discoverable under the same circumstances as materials referred to by nonlawyer witnesses.[14]

What Type of Material Is the Deponent Reviewing?

Another consideration that affects witness preparation is the type of material used to prepare the witness. Nonprivileged documents previously produced usually do not generate as much concern for the defender as privileged attorney-client communications. Nevertheless, defenders should guard against the disclosure at the deposition of which documents were reviewed by a witness. Even information about the selection of already-produced, nonprivileged documents shown to a witness may reveal to an adversary information about the strengths or weaknesses of the case or of the particular witness.

Work product is of special concern. Because so-called "ordinary" work product (that which does not involve the lawyer's mental processes)[15] is afforded considerably less protection than "core" work product (that which does involve the lawyer's mental processes),[16] a preparer needs to be especially careful not to increase the risk of making ordinary work product discoverable. As discussed below, once an examiner establishes that ordinary work product has refreshed the witness's recollection, a relatively simple showing of need in the interest of fairness will be sufficient to remove the document's work-product protection. Furthermore, core work product, though receiving greater protection and thus much less easily obtained by an adversary, is not wholly immune from the FRE 612 trap.

Under What Circumstances Is the Document Being Used?

There are two additional issues a defender must consider for in preparing a witness: (1) whether a document is really refreshing the witness's recollection, and (2) at what point it is being reviewed. If a document is used by a witness to refresh memory *during* a deposition, it *must* be produced to the opponent—even if it otherwise would be privileged.[17] (As noted above, disclosure is required to permit adequate cross-examination.) Therefore, to prevent disclosure, the defender should make certain that the witness does not bring to the deposition any documents related to the case that the witness might use while testifying.[18] A thornier issue, addressed below, is the extent to which a document must be disclosed if it refreshes a witness's recollection *before* testifying.[19]

Defending a Deposition: Structuring the Preparation

In a handful of jurisdictions, witness preparation carries the risk that any use of documents to prepare a witness will result in an automatic waiver of privilege.[20] This extreme view, however, is rare; most courts take a more measured, less mechanical approach to waiver.[21] Nevertheless, the careful practitioner should assume that the use of a document—whether or not privileged—to prepare a witness gives examiners ammunition for compelling production.

The fact that a witness looks at a document usually is insufficient to destroy any claim of privilege. The rationale for giving an examiner the right to obtain a document is that the examiner needs to see it in order to separate the witness's true memory from one suggested by a document. When a witness does not have a clear, independent recollection of events, reviewing documents may shade the witness's testimony. In that situation, the examiner is entitled to know which documents the witness reviewed and to have access to those documents in order to cross-examine effectively. But access will be granted only if there is evidence that the document or documents affected the witness's testimony; that is, the witness relied on the documents or disclosed a portion of them.[22]

Understanding the Tests

Courts have devised a number of tests for determining whether a document used in witness preparation must be turned over to an adversary.[23]

Most courts first apply a three-pronged test to determine whether a proper foundation has been laid for requiring disclosure

214

under FRE 612. The foundational elements are (1) the witness has a loss of memory, (2) the witness has used a writing to refresh that memory, and (3) the witness has relied on the reviewed material for the purpose of testifying. When these elements are met, most courts conclude that the material is discoverable in the interests of justice,[24] particularly when the requesting party has not had complete access to the information relied upon by the witness.[25]

But the party requesting disclosure must do more than establish these foundational elements. When deciding whether to order disclosure, most courts will also apply a three-factor balancing test. Under this test, courts consider (1) whether the opposing party exceeded the limits of preparation on one hand and concealment on the other, (2) whether the material sought contains fact or opinion work product (legal strategies and conclusions are absolutely protected), and (3) whether the requesting party is simply on a "fishing expedition."[26]

The balancing test first gained prominence in *Berkey Photo, Inc. v. Eastman Kodak*,[27] a case involving the preparation of experts for deposition. In that case, Kodak refused to produce four notebooks prepared by its counsel that were shown to its economic experts as background material during their deposition preparation. Kodak's counsel claimed the notebooks contained his "legal analysis, mental impressions and . . . legal judgment as to what facts were needed to be understood, mastered, and possibly presented at trial."[28] The experts testified that although they read the notebooks and the notebooks increased their appreciation of the photo-finishing industry, they did not use them to prepare their summaries of the factual support for their opinions. Overruling counsel's claim of work-product privilege, the magistrate judge ordered production of the notebooks under FRE 612.

In *Berkey Photo*, Judge Frankel—in what is considered a seminal opinion—phrased the issue as "whether the . . . notebooks . . . had sufficient 'impact' on the experts' testimony to trigger the application of Rule 612."[29] In his opinion, he acknowledged that the notebooks provided to the experts arguably affected the experts' testimony and had "the sound and quality of materials appropriate 'to promote the search of credibility and memory.'"[30] Judge Frankel found there might be an argument for allowing discovery either on a theory of waiver[31] or qualified privilege "where an attempt is made to exceed decent limits of preparation on the one hand and concealment on the other."[32] Nevertheless, he noted that in the instant case there was no "calculated plan" to prepare the experts and at the same time shield the material from discovery. Therefore, in balancing the request for discovery against the countervailing protections afforded by the work-product privilege, he denied Berkey's demand for production. He also considered that given the then paucity of law in the area, counsel might not have been aware of the consequences of assembling the notebooks for the experts' use.[33] But his opinion concluded with a sharp warning that in the future there would be "powerful reason to hold that materials considered work-product should be withheld from prospective witnesses if they are to be withheld from opposing parties."[34]

Several years later, the Third Circuit dealt with a similar problem but used a slightly different approach. In *Bogosian v. Gulf Oil Co.*,[35] plaintiffs appealed the trial court's order compelling production of memoranda prepared by counsel (and thus arguably protected by the work-product privilege) that were reviewed by expert witnesses before their depositions.[36] The case is noteworthy for its forceful stance supporting protection of core work product used to prepare experts:

> Examination and cross-examination of the expert can be comprehensive and effective on the relevant issue of the basis for an expert's opinion without an inquiry into the lawyer's role in assisting with the formulation of the theory. Even if examination into the lawyer's role is permissible, an issue not before us, the marginal value in the revelation on cross-examination that the expert's view may have originated with an attorney's opinion or theory does not warrant overriding the strong policy against disclosure of documents consisting of core attorney's work-product.[37]

A year later, the critical foundational elements for discovery under FRE 612 were extensively analyzed by the Third Circuit in *Sporck v. Peil*.[38] The case involved a discovery dispute over production of hundreds of thousands of documents. Before the deposition of Sporck, the defendant corporation's president, his counsel had prepared him with numerous documents that counsel had selected and compiled for that purpose. None contained work product. But counsel argued that his selection of documents should be protected under the work-product doctrine as it represented his legal opinion regarding the evidence relevant to the allegations and any potential defenses.[39]

At the deposition, the plaintiff's counsel asked Sporck if he had examined any documents in preparation for his deposition. After an affirmative answer, the taker moved to compel production of those documents. The lower court ordered production, and Sporck sought a writ of mandamus directing the court to vacate the order.

The Third Circuit held that counsel's selection of documents constituted highly protected opinion work product.[40] It then examined the elements of FRE 612, which require a showing either that the witness relied on the documents or that the documents influenced his testimony.[41] The court found that the taker's general question was insufficient to establish the necessary foundation for the production of the documents. The court explained that if counsel had first elicited specific testimony from Sporck and then questioned him about whether any documents refreshed his recollection or influenced his prior testimony, the selection of documents shown during witness preparation would not have constituted protected work product at all.[42]

As noted above, greater protection is afforded core work product—material that reflects a lawyer's thought processes.[43] Therefore, even when a court finds a waiver,[44] documents containing legal theories may warrant in camera inspection,[45] and the court may order that the documents be redacted to eliminate disclosure of the lawyer's mental processes or legal theories.[46] This approach is advocated by Judge Weinstein, who, in his evidence treatise, suggests that for core work product, a judge should examine the material in camera and permit its production only if the requesting party would be hampered in testing the accuracy of the witness's testimony without it.[47]

Proper deposition preparation requires a defender to be familiar with the approach used in the jurisdiction that governs the particular deposition. In most instances, the relevant case law will involve striking a balance among the following: protection of the attorney-client or work-product privilege, the question of waiver, fairness to the parties, and the identity of the witness.

How to Avoid Putting Privileged Documents at Risk

Avoiding the perils of FRE 612 requires planning and hard work by a defender. It also requires spending a considerable amount of time preparing a witness. It certainly is quicker and easier to draft factual summaries, prepare binders of information or highlights of critical points, and then give all of them to a client to review. But this shortcut can dramatically increase the risk of disclosure to an adversary.

Here are some approaches to avoiding the FRE 612 trap.

1. Spend a great deal of time talking with your client-witness in the days before the deposition. Because oral communications with the client are absolutely privileged, conversation is the safest way to refresh recollection. FRE 612 is concerned with writings; oral memory "jogs" are protected.

2. If you are concerned about your witness's mastery of the facts and you feel he needs a written summary as a crutch, write down only the undisputed facts and then orally supplement these facts with any additional information you want your client to have in mind. This method minimizes any damage if the written summary becomes discoverable.

3. If you must use documents to assist your client, use only documents that have already been produced. Although your adversary may learn that your witness reviewed a particular document, he will gain little from revelation. Another reason to limit preparation materials to documents already produced is that a court, when deciding whether to require disclosure of a selection of documents, may view disclosure as an unfair and unnecessary invasion of a lawyer's work product when the documents themselves have already been produced.

4. If information in privileged documents is essential to your preparation, discuss the contents of the documents with the witness, but do not show them to him.

5. Conduct your own balancing test. Decide whether your witness truly needs to see a document to refresh recollection. If you are worried about discovery of a particular document by the examiner, do not show that document to your witness unless the need to refresh recollection outweighs the danger of disclosure.

6. Explain to your witness the meaning of "refreshed recollection"—the foundational requirement for disclosure. Be aware that witnesses frequently misunderstand this concept. Before showing the witness a document that you do not want discovered, determine if the witness has

an independent recollection of the facts contained in the document. If the witness has an independent recollection, using the document for preparation is less problematic because there is less chance your adversary can make the required foundational showing that the document refreshed memory and thus must be produced.

7. If you must use core work product in preparing your witness, before showing a document to the witness redact those portions that are not essential to the preparation and would be highly damaging if discovered by your adversary.

8. Finally, tell your client to expect questions about what documents were reviewed and explain why you are spending so much effort to prepare him without the use of documents. The more your client understands about the deposition process—particularly the FRE 612 trap— the better prepared he will be to deal with the substance of the deposition and the taker's tactics.

How to Lay a Foundation at Deposition for the Discovery of Documents Used to Refresh Recollection

Before giving an examiner access to an adversary's privileged document under FRE 612, many courts require that the examining lawyer lay a proper foundation.[48] Failure to do so may be fatal to a demand for production.[49] Merely establishing that a witness looked at a document is not enough.[50] As discussed above, the examiner must also elicit explicit testimony that the document sought has both been reviewed and has refreshed the witness's recollection or otherwise "impacted" his testimony.[51]

Some courts may require more than a cursory inquiry into whether a witness's memory has been refreshed by a document.[52] In those jurisdictions, the courts may not require production unless the examiner has thoroughly questioned about the circumstances leading to the review and questioned the witness thoroughly about the extent or scope of the refreshing.[53]

Suppose you represent Leslie Roberts, the Plaintiff in the *Scoops v. Business-Aide* case. You are deposing Terry Blake, a former Business-Aide employee. You learn that more than a year ago Blake and his boss, Maxine Waller, met with Business-Aide's lawyer shortly after Leslie Roberts filed the lawsuit against Business-Aide. You want to find out if there are any notes of that meeting. If there are, you would like access to them, even though they are privileged. After establishing that the meeting took place, you might follow with a series of questions (objections omitted) like the following:

Q. Did you meet in preparation for this deposition today with anyone?

A. Yes.

Q. With whom?

A. My counsel, Ms. Jones.

Q. On what date?

A. February 3.

Q. Was anyone else present?

A. Yes, Ms. Waller.

Q. Were any notes taken at that meeting?

A. Yes.

Q. Who took those notes?

A. The lawyer.

Q. Did those notes summarize that meeting?

A. Yes.

Q. And did they contain comments about what you told Leslie Roberts in the Business-Aide store over two years ago about the capacity of the computer equipment that you sold her to meet her needs?

A. Yes.

Q. Did your attorney show you those notes?

A. Yes.

Q. Did you then review those notes with your attorney shortly after this lawsuit was filed?

A. Well, I looked them over.

Q. When you say you looked them over, did you read them?

A. Yes.

Q. How much time did you spend reading them?

A. Five or ten minutes.

Q. And was the reason you reviewed those notes because you were going to be deposed today?

A. I guess so.

Q. And before you reviewed those notes was your memory dim regarding what you told Leslie Roberts about the computer she ordered ?

A. Well, sort of. I remembered some of it.

Q. Did reviewing the notes help you remember additional portions of your conversation with Ms. Roberts?

A. Yes.

Q. What, specifically, did the notes refresh your recollection about? [Who was there? What was said?]

Once you establish that the witness's recollection was refreshed by the notes, ask that they be produced.[54]

In addition to having the notes produced, eliciting such testimony may be crucial in attempting to gain access to a group of documents reviewed by the witness whose selection may reveal the more highly protected lawyer's mental processes.[55] By asking questions about which documents refreshed the witness's recollection, the taker may be able to overcome a court's inclination against providing all of the documents selected by the defender.

Laying a proper foundation may ultimately make a significant difference in the outcome of the deposition, and of the case as a whole, depending on the importance of the witness and the documents discovered. If the required foundation has been established, production and inspection of the documents will be required. The documents may then be used in examining the witness, and relevant portions of the documents may be introduced into evidence.[56]

Even when documents are discoverable under FRE 612, the extent to which they are discoverable varies. An entire file reviewed by a witness may be discoverable if the examiner would otherwise be unable to obtain the "substantial equivalent" of its contents.[57] However, if the collection and organization of the materials would reveal opposing counsel's mental processes, some protection may be afforded.[58]

Under a more narrow interpretation of FRE 612, only a portion of the notes or materials reviewed may be required to be produced—limited to those portions used to refresh and referred to during the deposition.[59] Accordingly, although a document may need to be produced, it does not necessarily mean the taker will be permitted to inquire into the genesis of the document[60] or whether the document was given to the witness by counsel.[61] Moreover, disclosure will result only from voluntary use of a document for preparation. When, for example, a witness refreshes his recollection by reviewing privileged documents pursuant to a court order, the privilege is not waived.[62]

Notes

*Kevin P. Hughes and Laraine Pacheco, who coauthored the original Chapter 9 in the first edition of this book, deserve maximum credit for shedding light on this subject so masterfully. Their earlier work on discovery of Federal Rule of Evidence 612 documents is the foundation of this revised chapter.

Grateful acknowledgment also goes to Elana R. Pollak, then a law stdent and now an associate at Weil, Gotshal & Manges LLP, without whose help these pages could not have seen the light of day.

1.   A similar probe also may take place each time a document is marked or referred to during a deposition or when a particular topic is raised during the deposition.

2.   A sudden recollection at trial might be attacked during cross-examination as a recent fabrication and destroy the witness's credibility completely. See "Twenty Guidelines for Deposition Testimony" in Chapter 7 and "Rule 5: Before Meeting the Witness, Plan Your Strategy for Refreshing Memory, Including the Use of Documents" in Chapter 8, discussing the danger of answering, "I don't recall."

3.   FED. R. EVID. 612.

4.   Notably excepted from this portion of FRCP 30(c) are FRE 103 (rulings on evidence), which concerns the manner in which evidentiary rulings are handled by the court, and FRE 615 (exclusion of witnesses), which relates to the general practice of excluding witnesses from the courtroom during trial. Presumably these rules are excepted because they are inapplicable to depositions. But see "Task 13: Decide Whom You Want Present at the Deposition" in Chapter 4, and "Making Objections" in Chapter 14.

5.   See, e.g., Byme v. N.Y. Tel. Co., No. 87 Civ. 6874, 1989 U.S. Dist. LEXIS 11147, at *9 n.4 (S.D.N.Y. Aug. 9, 1989) (even when witness used document to refresh recollection, it makes "little sense" that access to privileged document by someone with right to access constitutes waiver); Omaha Pub. Power Dist. v. Foster Wheeler Corp., 109 F.R.D. 615 (D. Neb. 1986). See also Wentz v. Grubbs, No. 90–661, 1994 U.S. Dist. LEXIS 13628 (D. Or. Sept. 16, 1994) (even though defendant reviewed entire file to refresh his memory before deposition, interests of justice do not require that materials otherwise protected by attorney-client privilege be disclosed); Marshal v. Quinn-L Equities, Inc., No. 3-87-1384H, 1988 U.S. Dist. LEXIS 18541 (N.D. Tex. Dec. 30,1988) (when all documents protected by attorney-client privilege, application of FRE 612 would render privilege meaningless).

6.   See, e.g., In re Fedex Ground Package Sys., Inc., Employment Practices Litig., 2007 WL 733753 (N.D. Ind.); Heron Interact, Inc. v. Guidelines, Inc., 2007 WL 1991401 (D. Mass); see also cases collected at notes 9 and 10, infra. As one court has noted, however, the mere fact that a party may obtain a document if used to refresh a witness's recollection does not render that same document otherwise discoverable in the absence of

actual use in deposition preparation. *See* Banks v. Wilson, 151 F.R.D. 109 (D. Minn. 1993) (refusing to order production of defendant's statement when no deposition took place and not showing defendant unable to recall circumstances surrounding events at issue).

7. *See, e.g.*, Sporck v. Peil, 759 F.2d 312 (3d Cir. 1985); *see also* discussion in the section entitled "Understanding the Tests," *infra*.

8. See Chapter 6.

9. *See, e.g.*, Redvanly v. Nynex Corp., 152 F.R.D. 460, 464 (S.D.N.Y. 1993); Auto Owners Ins. Co. v. Totaltape, Inc., 135 F.R.D. 199 (M.D. Fla. 1990); Parry v. Highlight Indus., 125 F.R.D. 449 (W.D. Mich. 1989); *In re* Atl. Fin. Mgmt. Sec. Litig., 121 F.R.D. 141 (D. Mass. 1988).

10. *See, e.g.*, United States v. 22.80 Acres of Land, 107 F.R.D. 20 (N.D. Cal. 1985); Wheeling-Pittsburgh Steel Corp. v. Underwriters Labs., Inc., 81 F.R.D. 8 (N.D. Ill. 1978).

11. See "Privileges Relating to Expert Witnesses" in Chapter 19.

12. FRCP 26(a)(2)(B) requires that the disclosure of the identity of an expert shall be accompanied by a written report, signed by the expert, containing, inter alia, the data and facts relied upon by the expert in forming his or her opinions.

FRE 705 states that the expert may testify in terms of opinion or inference and give reasons therefore without first testifying to the underlying facts or data, unless the court requires otherwise. The expert may in any event be required to disclose the underlying facts or data on cross-examination.

13. Fed. R. Civ. Proc. 26(b)(4)(B)(i)-(ii) ("Expert Employed Only for Trial Preparation. Ordinarily, a party may not, by interrogatories or by deposition, discover facts known or opinions held by an expert who has been retained or specially employed by another party in anticipation of litigation or to prepare for trial and who is not expected to be called as a witness at trial. But a party may do so only as provided in Rule 35(b) or on a showing of exceptional circumstances under which it is impracticable for the party seeking discovery to obtain facts or opinions on the same subject by other means.").

14. *See, e.g.*, Redvanly v. Nynex Corp., 152 F.R.D. 460 (S.D.N.Y. 1993) (lawyer is like any other factual witness with information regarding critical events); Eckert v. Fitzgerald, 119 F.R.D. 297 (D.D.C. 1988) (lawyer's notes memorializing substance of settlement conference discoverable when lawyer became witness for his former client).

15. Such "ordinary" work product might include a chronology of events, an appointment diary of meetings with the client and witnesses, a calendar of meetings with co-counsel, or a book of already produced documents divided by subject matter.

16. The more highly protected "core" work product might include a good facts/bad facts memo; an outline of admissions at the plaintiff's deposition; a memorandum prepared by an associate outlining relevant

case law and assessing, on the facts of the case, the chances of prevailing; or notations on a contract regarding whether the witness complied with his or her contractual obligations.

17. *See* FED. R. EVID. 612(1). Note that documents reviewed *during* testimony are documents reviewed by the witness while he is being questioned, not documents reviewed after the deposition has begun. *See* Hiskett v. Wal-Mart Stores, Inc., 180 F.R.D. 403 (D. Kan. 1998).

18. See "Final Instructions to the Witness" in Chapter 7.

19. *See* FED. R. EVID. 612(2).

20. *See* Wheeling-Pittsburgh Steel Corp. v. Underwriters Labs., Inc., 81 F.R.D. 8 (N.D. Ill. 1978) (finding no distinction between refreshing one's recollection during testimony and before testimony). In stark contrast to *Wheeling, see* Derderian v. Polaroid Corp., 121 F.R.D. 13 (D. Mass. 1988) (refusing to require production of notes of meetings producible when requesting party had full access to persons with whom meetings held). The court in Derderian reasoned that Congress intended materials used to refresh a witness's recollection while testifying to be treated differently from those used to refresh recollection before testifying; the distinction between "while" and "before" in the rule would be lost if disclosure were always mandated.

21. *See* Bloch v. SmithKline Beckman Corp., No. 82–510, 1987 U.S. Dist. LEXIS 2795 (E.D. Pa. Apr. 9, 1987) (although witness's recollection refreshed by summary of interview with English counsel that was given to him for signature two weeks before his deposition, document not discoverable because, inter alia, not provided for purpose of preparing for deposition).

22. *See, e.g.,* Sporck v. Peil, 759 F.2d 312 (3d Cir. 1985); Bank Hapoalim B.M. v. Am. Home Assurance Co., No. 92 Civ. 3561, 1994 U.S. Dist. LEXIS 4091 (S.D.N.Y. Apr. 1, 1994); Baba-Ali v. City of New York, No. 92 Civ. 7975, 1993 U.S. Dist. LEXIS 14629 (S.D.N.Y. Oct. 18, 1993) (foundation must be laid to show that witness's responses informed by document); Baker v. CNA Ins. Co., 123 F.R.D. 322 (D. Mont. 1988); Leucadia, Inc. v. Reliance Ins. Co., 101 F.R.D. 674 (S.D.N.Y. 1983); *In re* Comair Air Disaster Litig., 100 F.R.D. 350 (E.D. Ky. 1983); *see also* Pack v. Beyer, 157 F.R.D. 226, 231 (D.N.J. 1994) (rejecting plaintiff's reliance on FRE 612 to gain access to privileged documents to which defendant was referring during hearing for purpose of determining whether documents privileged; "Rule 612 should not be viewed as a device which may be used to destroy the proper assertion of a privilege."). For an example of the type of testimony that would establish a right to discovery, see *infra* for a sample set of questions, illustrating how to lay a foundation for discovery of documents used to refresh recollection.

23. Although the case law most frequently deals with discoverability of work product, the reach of FRE 612 also extends to documents embraced by the attorney-client privilege.

24. *See, e.g., In re* Atl. Fin. Mgmt. Sec. Litig., 121 F.R.D. 141 (D. Mass. 1988).

25. *See In re* Comair Air Disaster Litig., 100 F.R.D. 350 (E.D. Ky. 1983) (accident report discoverable). However, it is not an abuse of discretion for the court to find that disclosure is not necessary in the interests of justice. *See* McKenzie v. McCormick, 27 F.3d 1415, 1420–21 (9th Cir. 1994); Smith & Wesson v. United States, 782 F.2d 1074 (1st Cir. 1986).

26. This test, adapted from *Berkey Photo, Inc. v. Eastman Kodak*, 74 F.R.D. 613, 614–17 (S.D.N.Y. 1977) was first articulated in *In re Joint Eastern and Southern District Asbestos Litigation*, 119 F.R.D. 4 (E. & S.D.N.Y. 1988) (if foundation laid to establish that witness refreshed his recollection by using product book, book discoverable). *See, e.g.*, Bank Hapoalim B.M. v. Am. Home Assurance Co., No. 92 Civ. 3561, 1994 U.S. Dist. LEXIS 4091 (S.D.N.Y. Apr. 1, 1994) (ordering production of specifically identified documents, reviewed for a number of hours by a witness whose testimony revealed that he relied on documents that would provide valuable sources for cross-examination). Regarding the necessity of the first factor in the balancing test, the court in *Joint Eastern* found it "disquieting to posit that a party's lawyer may 'aid' a witness with items of work product and then prevent totally the access that might reveal and counteract the effects of such assistance." 119 F.R.D. at 6 (citing *Berkey*, 74 F.R.D. at 616).

27. 74 F.R.D. 613 (S.D.N.Y. 1977).

28. *Id.* at 614.

29. *Id.* at 615.

30. *Id.* at 616.

31. Judge Frankel noted that given the trends favoring broad access to materials, it would be "disquieting" to think that a lawyer could assist a witness with work product and then deny his or her adversary access to the material that could counteract the effects of such assistance. Accordingly, he cautioned counsel to use other types of materials to prepare witnesses that could later be made available to the cross-examiner. When there is a choice, Judge Frankel reasoned, "the decision to give the work-product to the witness could well be deemed a waiver of the privilege." *Id.*

32. *Id.* at 617.

33. *Id.*

34. *Id.*

35. 738 F.2d 587 (3d Cir. 1984).

36. The Third Circuit resolved the issue by analyzing the interplay between FRCP 26(b)(3) (Trial Preparation: Materials) and FRCP 26(b)(4) (Trial Preparation: Experts), devoting only a footnote to FRE 612 analysis. *Bogosian*, 738 F.2d at 595 n.3.

37. *Bogosian*, 738 F.2d at 595. The dissenting judge rebuked the majority for failing to consider that the defendants might need to impeach the expert at his deposition because the plaintiffs could decide to introduce

the deposition in lieu of live testimony at trial. Thus, in the dissenting judge's view, this was not an ordinary discovery situation, and the real question was whether the defendants' interest in having the material for cross-examination of the expert at trial outweighed the plaintiffs' interest in protecting core work product. *Id.* at 597. This concern creates a dilemma for the trial judge who, while protecting a party's work product, must also ensure that the adversary is not denied the opportunity to cross-examine, rendering the opposing party's expert's deposition inadmissible pursuant to FRE 802 and FRE 804(b)(1).

38. 759 F.2d 312, 313–18 (3d Cir. 1985).

39. *Id.* at 313.

40. *Id.* at 316.

41. *Id.* at 318.

42. *Id.*

43. *See* Hickman v. Taylor, 329 U.S. 495 (1947).

44. *See supra* note 5 (regarding discussion of waiver).

45. *See, e.g.,* Parry v. Highlight Indus. Inc., 125 F.R.D. 449 (W.D. Mich. 1989) (reviewing core work product in camera and finding no evidence of witness coaching).

46. *See, e.g.,* Bogosian v. Gulf Oil Corp., 738 F.2d 587 (3d Cir. 1984); In re Atl. Fin. Mgmt. Sec. Litig., 121 F.R.D. 141 (D. Mass. 1988); Aguinaga v. John Momell & Co., 112 F.R.D. 671 (D. Kan. 1986).

47. WEINSTEIN'S FEDERAL EVIDENCE ¶ 1612[04] (2d ed. 1997); *see, e.g.,* Butler Mfg. Co. v. Americold Corp., 148 F.R.D. 275 (D. Kan. 1993) (to obtain work product, showing must be made that document actually influenced witness's testimony); Barrer v. Women's Nat'l Bank, 96 F.R.D. 202 (D.D.C. 1982) (memorandum used to refresh recollection would be ordered produced if in camera inspection revealed discrepancies between memorandum and deposition testimony); Al-Rowaishan Establishment Universal Trading & Agencies, Ltd. v. Beatrice Foods Co., 92 F.R.D. 779 (S.D.N.Y. 1982) (following Weinstein's approach, but finding document protected).

48. *See, e.g.,* Mead Corp. v. Riverwood Nat. Res. Corp., 145 F.R.D. 512 (D. Minn. 1992); *In re* Joint E. & S. Dist. Asbestos Litig., 119 F.R.D. 4 (E. & S.D.N.Y. 1988). See also Chapter 13.

49. *See* Sporck v. Peil, 759 F.2d 312 (3d Cir. 1985); Timm v. Mead Corp., No. 91 C 5648,1992 U.S. Dist. LEXIS 1411 (N.D. Ill. Feb. 7,1992) (transcript that revealed that witness only "glanced" at documents insufficient basis to invoke FRE 612).

50. Thus, even if a witness admits to having reviewed hundreds of documents in preparation for a deposition, documents that have not refreshed the witness's recollection need not be identified or produced.

51. *See* United States v. 22.80 Acres of Land, 107 F.R.D. 20 (N.D. Cal. 1985).

52. *See* Butler Mfg. Co., 148 F.R.D. 275.

53. *Id.*

54. See "Obtaining Documents for Use at a Deposition" in Chapter 12 and "Handling Documents at the End of the Deposition" in Chapter 23, discussing how to secure documents requested at a deposition.

55. *See* Sporck v. Peil, 759 F.2d 312 (3d Cir. 1985) (discussing the different types of work product).

56. Skill in this area may yield significant benefits if the witness will not be available to testify at trial. A deposition that has already concluded may be nevertheless reopened. *See* Nicholas J. Murlas Living Trust v. Mobil Oil Corp., No. 93 C 6956, 1995 U.S. Dist. LEXIS 3489 (N.D. Ill. Mar. 16, 1995) (permitting plaintiff to reopen witnesses' depositions once privileged documents disclosed pursuant to FRE 612 because defendant should have produced the documents at time of depositions and plaintiffs entitled to cross-examine on documents).

57. *See* Auto Owners Ins. Co. v. Totaltape, Inc., 135 F.R.D. 199 (M.D. Fla. 1990). *See also* Nicholas J. Murlas Living Trust, No. 93 C 6956, 1995 US. Dist. LEXIS 3489.

58. *See, e.g., Sporck,* 759 F.2d at 316–18; Stone Container Corp. v. Arkright Mut. Ins. Co., No. 93 C 6626, 1995 U.S. Dist. LEXIS 2400 (N.D. Ill. Feb. 22, 1995) (citing *Sporck* with approval and refusing to permit disclosure of counsel's selection of documents, particularly when documents had already been produced); *In re* Atl. Fin. Mgmt. Sec. Litig., 121 F.R.D. 141 (D. Mass. 1988) (deposition transcripts reviewed by witness discoverable, but lawyer need not reveal order in which provided). *But see* James Julian, Inc. v. Raytheon Co., 93 F.R.D. 138 (D. Del. 1982) (selection and ordering of documents assembled in binder for witness, even though work product, not protected because used to educate witness and may have affected witness's version of facts).

59. *See* S & A Painting Co. v. OWB Corp., 103 F.R.D. 407 (W.D. Pa. 1984) (portions of documents not used to refresh recollection "irrelevant" because "Rule 612 is not a mechanism for uncovering all prior inconsistent statements of a witness").

60. *See, e.g.,* Marshall v. United States Postal Serv., 88 F.R.D. 348 (D.D.C. 1980).

61. *In re* Application of Minebea Co., 143 F.R.D. 494 (S.D.N.Y. 1992).

62. *See* Laxalt v. McClatchy, 116 F.R.D. 455 (D. Nev. 1986).

CHAPTER 10

Special Witness Preparation Situations

PAUL C. PALMER

G. RICHARD DODGE, JR.

The twenty guidelines for witness preparation discussed in Chapter 7 address the most common situation: the preparation of a client, whose interests diverge from those of the examiner, for direct examination in a stenographically recorded deposition. Special circumstances sometimes call for deviations from these general guidelines and for special witness preparation techniques.[1]

Examination of Your Own Client at the Deposition on Cross-Examination

Defending counsel always has the right to cross-examine her own witness before the close of the deposition.[2] Counsel usually will forgo that opportunity. At times, though, it will be necessary for the defending lawyer to question her own client on cross-examination—

for damage control, to clarify important earlier testimony, or to draw out information not elicited on direct examination that defending counsel wants to have in the record.[3] When such cross-examination is necessary, lawyers typically limit it to the bare minimum, to avoid opening up additional avenues for questioning on redirect examination.

Obviously, as the defending lawyer, you should cross-examine your own client only when doing so is in the client's interest. Although it usually is not in the witness's interest to "help" opposing counsel on direct examination,[4] the opposite is true on cross-examination. The witness should understand the need to help if you cross-examine at the end of the deposition. This does not mean, however, that the witness should ignore all the usual guidelines for testifying at depositions and make casual and rambling statements or speeches. Instead, the witness should work with his lawyer during preparation to develop the desired testimony in a careful, methodical manner.

The witness should consider the point of the cross-examination questions carefully, attempt to understand where the lawyer is going with each question, and answer accordingly. This may lead to testifying somewhat more expansively than on direct examination. You also should explain that you might use leading questions on cross-examination to help focus the witness's testimony, even if they result in objections.[5] You should review examples of leading questions with the witness, illustrating how they keep the witness on track. But you also should make clear that you will use leading questions only rarely, if at all.

Even if you have prepared the witness for cross-examination before the deposition, you should, if permitted to confer with the witness during the deposition, again review the proposed cross-examination with the witness during a break or recess in the deposition.[6] You will want to alert the witness to the purposes of the cross-examination and any substantive areas you want to open up (or avoid) through your questioning. It may be necessary for you to ask the witness how he would answer a particular question in order to decide whether to ask it on cross-examination. To the extent possible, you should discuss with the witness the precise questions you will ask and the answers the witness will give. Because you are asking the witness to switch gears on cross-examination and testify more expansively, you should practice this cross-examination with the witness if at all possible.

Finally, you should prepare the witness for any redirect examination by opposing counsel. The witness must understand that he should respond to such redirect examination no differently than to direct examination. You should warn the witness not to allow the intervening cross-examination to lull him into carelessness.

Preparing a Nonparty Witness for Deposition

Many witnesses are neither parties to the litigation nor employed by a party. Such nonparty witnesses may include former employees of a party and current employees of a party's subsidiary if they are not in a privileged relationship with the lawyer.[7] They also may include fact witnesses who have never had any affiliation with either party and are, therefore, disinterested in the litigation.

If possible, you generally should interview such nonparty witnesses informally before their depositions.[8] If a witness is cooperative, you also may want to attempt to prepare the witness for the deposition. Preparation of the nonparty witness entails special risks, however, and therefore requires special attention.

A lawyer for a party must assume that any conversations she has with a nonparty witness may be discoverable.[9] Although some courts have concluded that confidential discussions between a lawyer for a corporation and a former employee of the corporation are protected by the attorney-client privilege (at least when those discussions involve matters within the scope of the former employment and are undertaken at the direction of the corporation for the purpose of providing it legal advice), other courts disagree.[10] Supporting a claim of attorney-client privilege in more attenuated situations, including those involving employees of a subsidiary, is even more problematic.[11] Moreover, work-product protection, if available at all, may not preclude the discovery of facts that the lawyer discloses to a nonparty witness.[12]

If a nonparty witness asks a party's lawyer to represent the witness for purposes of the deposition, that lawyer generally may do so, assuming there is no conflict of interests.[13] Indeed, a party might conclude that its interests would be best served by making its counsel available to represent the witness at the deposition. Strategically, however, representing the nonparty witness may be a mistake. For one thing, if the witness might otherwise be perceived to be neutral in connection with the litigation, representation of the witness would likely alter that perception, and possibly diminish the weight of the witness's testimony.[14] In addition, a party might want

231

to distance itself from an unattractive witness, thereby avoiding or minimizing any taint by association in the eyes of the jury.

If the party's lawyer does represent such a nonparty witness for purposes of the witness's deposition, the lawyer may prepare that witness directly under the protection of the attorney-client privilege. The lawyer must bear in mind, however, that this privilege is the witness's to assert or waive.[15] Even if the witness initially is inclined to preserve the privilege, the witness could always have a change of heart. If the witness chooses at some point to disclose the substance of his discussions with the lawyer in the course of the deposition preparation, the witness will be free to do so.

If the witness will be represented by his own separate counsel at the deposition, but is willing to cooperate with the lawyer representing a party, it may be possible for that lawyer to prepare the witness indirectly. In that situation, the lawyer would work directly with the witness's counsel, who in turn would prepare the witness in a privileged conversation.[16] Because the party's lawyer would not be directly involved in the actual deposition preparation, however, the lawyer would not have the benefit of the insights usually gained through that process. Similarly, the witness would not have the benefit of detailed preparation by the lawyer most knowledgeable about the case.

If the witness will not be represented by any counsel at the deposition, a lawyer for a party should consider carefully whether it is in the party's interest to attempt to meet with and prepare the witness at all. If the lawyer elects to meet with the witness, the lawyer should be extremely circumspect about any statements she makes to the witness, or any questions she asks. Because those discussions will not be protected by the attorney-client privilege, opposing counsel will be free to question the witness about them, and the witness will be free to volunteer whatever information the witness might choose to disclose. The lawyer should therefore avoid directly or indirectly revealing to the witness any facts, perceptions, opinions, or strategies the lawyer would not want the opposing party to discover. In particular, the lawyer should avoid disclosing any indications of the lawyer's level of confidence in the case, offering any views on the likelihood of settlement, or revealing the client's interest in reaching a settlement.

A nonparty witness who is willing to talk to lawyers for one party may also have had—or may have in the future—similar discussions with lawyers for other parties. When meeting with a nonparty witness, the lawyer generally should inquire about any such discussions or other contacts with other lawyers, including what questions were asked and what answers were given. Aside from the substantive information this might yield, it can provide a road map of the likely areas of questioning at the deposition.

Special ethical considerations may apply to communications with nonparty witnesses.[17] Under the Model Rules of Professional Conduct, for example, any request that the witness not volunteer information to the opposing party—a mainstay in the preparation of a client for a deposition—ordinarily would be improper.[18]

Nonparty witnesses who spend time and incur expenses preparing for depositions may ask for compensation. The extent to which a party may accommodate such a request will depend on the applicable rules in the particular jurisdiction.[19] Because any payment to a nonparty witness could undermine the credibility of the witness's testimony, it should be avoided if at all possible. In particular, a party should avoid making any payment to a witness above and beyond the reimbursement of nominal expenses.[20]

The Video Deposition

In many respects, video depositions have more in common with live testimony at trial than with traditional, stenographically recorded depositions.[21] If video excerpts from the deposition are offered at trial, the jury will see the deposition testimony for itself, in a way far more revealing than any recitation from a written transcript. The witness's appearance, demeanor, mannerisms, mode of testifying, and communications skills all can make as strong an impression on the fact finder as the substance of the witness's testimony.[22] As a result, some of the usual guidelines for witnesses must be altered when the deposition will be recorded on video, and an additional level of preparation is needed.[23]

If possible, preparation for a video deposition should include recording "trial runs" of examination of the witness, followed by review of the video with the witness.[24] This will allow both the lawyer and the witness to see how the witness appears on video. It also will provide them with a basis for working together to improve the witness's presentation. Reviewing the video with the witness will allow the "picture to speak for itself," minimizing the need for the lawyer to point out problems in a way that might harm the lawyer's relationship with the witness.

233

The witness's personal appearance is an important factor in a video deposition.[25] The witness should dress as he would for trial, be appropriately groomed, and avoid excessive jewelry or accessories. The witness should choose clothing not only for its suitability for trial, but also for its appearance on the screen of a monitor, which may blur or distort some colors and patterns.

The lawyer should point out to the witness any habits or mannerisms that might detract from the witness's testimony. The witness must avoid slouching, fidgeting, or any other behavior that might suggest the witness is uncomfortable and defensive. The witness also should be conscious of his manner of speech, tone of voice, and inflections throughout the deposition. Surprise, discomfort, and evasiveness may be readily apparent—and quite telling—on video.[26]

Eye contact is as important in a video deposition as at trial. Because the camera is a surrogate for the fact finder, lawyers often advise their witnesses to look directly at the camera when answering questions, and only occasionally at the questioner. Some experts believe, however, that although this approach works well for media professionals, it can cause the testimony of inexperienced witnesses to seem awkward and staged. The lawyer and witness should therefore experiment with different techniques during the preparation session and review the video of these trial runs to determine what works best for the particular witness. In addition, the witness should be instructed to avoid looking toward the witness's own counsel repeatedly during the deposition. Captured on video, this can create the impression that the witness is looking for help in answering the questions.

The usual rule that the witness should set his own pace when answering questions, taking as much time as he wants,[27] must be modified for a video deposition. Pauses count. Long delays between questions and answers are evident on video, and they can leave the impression that the witness is evasive and his answers contrived. The witness should instead try to respond at a reasonable pace, while still taking enough time to think about the questions and answers and allow the lawyer to object if necessary. The usual need for short deposition answers is even greater when the deposition is recorded on video. Lengthy answers on video rarely are effective before a jury.

If permitted, consultation with counsel[28] should be kept to a minimum and, if possible, take place off camera. The lawyer also may want to explain to the witness that the lawyer may choose to limit her objections during the video deposition in order to avoid the appearance of being obstructionist.[29]

The lawyer should review with the witness the logistics of a video deposition, including the placement of the camera, whether its focus will be fixed at all times or change from time to time, and any other arrangements in order to make the witness more comfortable with this process. If the lawyer anticipates either the use of demonstrative evidence or the reenactment of events by the witness during the deposition, these matters should be carefully rehearsed so they do not appear awkward or ineffective.[30]

Although some lawyers regard this kind of preparation as nonsubstantive stagecraft, it is an important part of the lawyer's job of preparing the witness for a video deposition. Appearance, demeanor, and other nonverbal factors all can make strong impressions on the viewer. Moreover, as noted above, it is always possible that portions of a video deposition will be used at trial. Careful preparation can help ensure that the witness's video testimony is as credible and effective as possible.[31]

Opinions vary concerning how the lawyer should deal with practice video footage after it has been reviewed with the witness. Such practice footage is a memorialization of statements made by the witness on matters relevant to the case. The phrasing and possibly even the substance of the witness's statements during such trial runs may differ in some respects from the witness's ultimate testimony.[32] Although that footage ordinarily is protected by the attorney-client privilege and the work-product doctrine, all or parts of it might be discoverable under certain circumstances.[33] For these reasons, some experts advise the lawyer to preserve that footage until the conclusion of the case in order to preclude any conceivable claim of destruction of evidence.[34] Absent an extraordinary coincidence, however, such as the service of a subpoena between the moments when the preparation video is created and erased, there is no legal obligation to preserve such video footage. Many lawyers therefore routinely erase all practice footage during or at the end of the preparation session, once they have reviewed it with the witness and it no longer is needed.

Notes

1. *See* Chapter 19.
2. *See* FED. R. CIV. P. 30(c).

3. Under the Federal Rules of Civil Procedure (FRCP), "cross-examination" at deposition is not limited to the scope of the direct testimony or matters affecting the credibility of the witness. *See generally* 8A WRIGHT, MILLER & MARCUS, FEDERAL PRACTICE AND PROCEDURE: CIVIL 2D § 2113 (2007). In most cases, however, the witness should be prepared to raise during the direct examination by opposing counsel any specific points that the witness and the witness's counsel want to include in the record. See Chapter 7, notes 12–13, guideline 10, "Keep Your Answers Short," and guideline 17, "If You Make a Mistake, Correct It as Soon as Possible." Waiting until after the direct examination to raise such additional points through questions by the witness's own counsel will only highlight those points and increase the likelihood of careful follow-up questioning by opposing counsel.

4. See "Explaining the Deposition Process" in Chapter 7.

5. Recognize, however, that the lawyer's cross-examination of his or her own witness by leading questions might not be admitted into evidence at trial if offered. *See* FED. R. CIV. P. 30(c)(1) ("The examination and cross-examination of a deponent proceed as they would at the trial under the Federal Rules of Evidence, except Rules 103 and 615."); FED. R. EVID. 611(c) (*"Ordinarily* leading questions should be permitted on cross-examination.") (emphasis added); *id.* advisory committee's note. The 1972 advisory committee's note on Federal Rule of Evidence (FRE) 611 explains that

> [t]he purpose of the qualification "ordinarily" is to furnish a basis for denying the use of leading questions when the cross-examination is cross-examination in form only and not in fact, *as for example the "cross-examination" of a party by his own counsel after being called by the opponent (savoring more of re-direct)* or of an insured defendant who proves to be friendly to the plaintiff.

Id. (emphasis added); *see* Oberlin v. Marlin Am. Corp., 596 F.2d 1322, 1328 (7th Cir. 1979) (affirming trial court's decision to admit into evidence portions of cross-examination of deponent by his own counsel through leading questions, but to exclude other portions; opposing party failed to object to leading questions at time of deposition, and deponent died before trial); Ward v. Freeman, Civ. No. 85–1254, 1990 U.S. Dist. LEXIS 14729, at *3 (E.D. La. 1990) (granting motion to exclude parties' cross-examination by leading questions of deponent aligned with those parties).

6. In some instances, rules or orders of the particular court may prohibit such discussions during a deposition or recess in a deposition, and make the substance of any such discussions discoverable. *See, e.g.,* Hall v. Clifton Precision, 150 F.R.D. 525, 528 n.5, 529 & n.7 (E.D. Pa. 1993); also see Chapter 7, note 19.

7. *See, e.g.,* Hohenwater v. Roberts Pharm. Corp., 152 F.R.D. 513, 517 & n.4 (D.S.C. 1994) (deposition witness employed by wholly owned

subsidiary of defendant was neither party nor employee of party to litigation).

8.   Whether a lawyer may contact a former employee of another party ex parte will depend upon applicable ethical guidelines. *See, e.g.,* ABA Comm. on Ethics and Prof'l Responsibility, Formal Op. 91–359 (1991) ("a lawyer representing a client in a matter adverse to a corporate party that is represented by another lawyer may, without violating Model Rule 4.2, communicate about the subject of the representation with an unrepresented former employee of the corporate party without the consent of the corporation's lawyer"). *See also* MODEL RULES OF PROF'L CONDUCT R. 4.2 cmt. 7 (2007) (the "consent of the organization's lawyer is not required for communications with a former constituent"); *accord* Brown v. St. Joseph County, 148 F.R.D. 246 (N.D. Ind. 1993); Goff v. Wheaton Indus., 145 F.R.D. 351 (D.N.J. 1992); Valassis v. Samelson, 143 F.R.D. 118 (E.D. Mich. 1992); DuBois v. Gradco Sys., Inc., 136 F.R.D. 341 (D. Conn. 1991). *But see* Rentclub Inc. v. Transamerica Rental Fin. Corp., 811 F. Supp. 651, 657–58 (M.D. Fla. 1992) (former employee who had access to privileged information held to be "party" for purposes of Rule 4.2 of the Model Rules of Professional Conduct), *aff'd,* 43 F.3d 1439 (11th Cir. 1995).

9.   Of course, in those jurisdictions that have not adopted an extension of the attorney-client privilege to corporate employees outside the "control group" (as provided in *Upjohn Co. v. United States,* 449 U.S. 383 (1981)), special care must similarly be taken in interviewing even current employees. *See* Chapter 5, note 19.

10.   In a concurring opinion in *Upjohn,* Chief Justice Burger suggested that under federal common law, the attorney-client privilege should extend to conversations between a corporation's lawyer and its former employees in certain circumstances. 449 U.S. at 402–03 (Burger, J., concurring). The Ninth Circuit agreed shortly thereafter, but that view has not been uniformly accepted. *Compare In re* Coordinated Pretrial Proceedings in Petroleum Prods. Antitrust Litig., 658 F.2d 1355, 1361 & n.7 (9th Cir. 1981) (attorney-client privilege protected lawyer's predeposition discussions with both current and former employees of client) *with* Clark Equip. Co. v. Lift Parts Mfg. Co., No. 82 C 4585, 1985 WL 2917, at *5–6 (N.D. Ill. Oct. 1, 1985) ("post-employment communications with former employees are not within the scope of the attorney-client privilege"). Courts similarly have reached differing results in cases decided under the substantive law of different jurisdictions. *Compare* Connolly Data Sys., Inc. v. Victor Techs., Inc., 114 F.R.D. 89, 94 (S.D. Cal. 1987) (under California law, no attorney-client privilege covering discussions with former employees) *and* Barrett Indus. Trucks, Inc. v. Old Republic Ins. Co., 129 F.R.D. 515, 517–18 (N.D. 111. 1990) (under Illinois law, same result) *with* Command Transp., Inc. v. Y.S. Line (USA) Corp., 116 F.R.D. 94, 97 (D. Mass. 1987) (under Massachusetts law, communications with former employee of client were attorney-client privileged).

11. *Compare* Hohenwater v. Roberts Pharm. Corp., 152 F.R.D. 513 (D.S.C. 1994) (corporation's attorney-client privilege was waived through disclosure of document to employee of wholly owned subsidiary) *and* Bowne of New York City, Inc. v. AmBase Corp., 150 F.R.D. 465, 490–91 (S.D.N.Y. 1993) (same result) *with* Admiral Ins. Co. v. United States Dist. Ct., 881 F.2d 1486, 1493 n.6 (9th Cir. 1989) (in light of *Upjohn*, "communications between employees of a subsidiary corporation and counsel for the parent corporation, like communications between former employees and corporate counsel, would be privileged if the employee possesses information critical to the representation of the parent company and the communications concern matters within the scope of employment") *and* United States v. Mobil Corp., 149 F.R.D. 533, 537 (N.D. Tex. 1993) (stating that rule articulated in *Admiral* "falls within the scope and spirit of the privilege"); *see also* Russell v. Gen. Elec. Co., 149 F.R.D. 578, 580–81 (N.D. Ill. 1993) (rejecting argument that "common interest" of lawyer's client and nonparty witness in validating work and credibility of witness was sufficient to prevent discovery of matters discussed between lawyer and witness before witness's deposition).

12. *See, e.g., Russell,* 149 F.R.D. at 582 (work-product doctrine did not prevent discovery of any facts that party's lawyer communicated to nonparty witness in meeting before his deposition, but did prevent discovery of matters reflecting lawyer's mental impressions of case); Stratagem Dev. Corp. v. Heron Int'l N.V., Nos. 90 Civ. 6328, 90 Civ. 7237, 1992 U.S. Dist. LEXIS 14832, at *25–28 (S.D.N.Y. Sept. 30, 1992) (work-product doctrine did not protect letters that party's lawyer sent to former employee of another party whose deposition had been noticed); *Barrett Indus. Trucks,* 129 F.R.D. at 518–19 (work-product doctrine did not preclude discovery of facts that party's lawyer disclosed to deponent).

13. *See, e.g.,* Polycast Tech. Corp. v. Uniroyal, Inc., 129 F.R.D. 621, 628–29 (S.D.N.Y.) (no ethical bar to one party's lawyers representing former employee of opposing party at his deposition), *aff'd,* 1990 U.S. Dist. LEXIS 15382 (S.D.N.Y. Nov. 15, 1990). The lawyer must take care, however, to abide by applicable ethical limitations on lawyer solicitation of clients. *See, e.g.,* MODEL RULES OF PROF'L CONDUCT R. 7.3 (2007); MODEL CODE OF PROF'L RESPONSIBILITY EC 2-3, EC 2-4, DR 2-103, DR 2-104 (2005); ABA Comm. on Prof'l Ethics, Informal Op. 828 (1965) (counsel for party may not "invite" former employees of that party to retain him to represent them in their depositions). *But cf. In re Coordinated Pretrial Proceedings,* 658 F.2d at 1361 ("in light of *Upjohn,* the definition of solicitation in the corporate-counsel context is altered").

14. *See also* FED. R. EVID. 611(c) (permitting leading questioning of "a witness identified with an adverse party").

15. Absent a sufficient "joint defense" or "common interest" between the party and the nonparty witness, disclosure of the party's attorney-client confidences to the nonparty witness in the course of the witness's

deposition preparation also would be likely to constitute a waiver of the party's attorney-client privilege. See Chapter 5, note 24.

16.   Although in theory communications with the witness's counsel might be no less discoverable than communications directly with the witness, in practice they may be less likely to be a focus of discovery. The party's lawyer ordinarily would have no guarantee, however, that communications with the witness's counsel would remain confidential and, therefore, should limit any such discussions accordingly.

17.   *See, e.g.*, MODEL RULES OF PROF'L CONDUCT R. 3.4 (2007) (fairness to opposing party and counsel); *id.* R. 4.1 (truthfulness in statements to others); *id.* R. 4.3 (dealing with unrepresented person); MODEL CODE OF PROF'L RESPONSIBILITY DR 7-102(A)(5) (2005) (false statements); *id.* DR 7-104(A)(2) (communications with person who may have adverse interests).

18.   MODEL RULES OF PROF'L CONDUCT R. 3.4(f) (2007) ("A lawyer shall not . . . request a person other than a client to refrain from voluntarily giving relevant information to another party unless: (1) the person is a relative or an employee or other agent of a client; and (2) the lawyer reasonably believes that the person's interests will not be adversely affected by refraining from giving such information."); *see* Harlan v. Lewis, 982 F.2d 1255, 1257–59 (8th Cir. 1993) (Model Rule 3.4(f) supported sanctions for counsel's suggestion to nonparty witness that he not speak with opposing counsel informally); *cf.* ABA Comm. on Ethics and Prof'l Responsibility, Formal Op. 93-378 (1993) (ex parte contacts with expert witnesses).

19.   *See, e.g.*, MODEL RULES OF PROF'L CONDUCT R. 3.4(b) cmt. (2007) ("it is not improper to pay a witness's expenses," but "[t]he common law rule in most jurisdictions is that it is improper to pay an occurrence witness any fee for testifying"); MODEL CODE OF PROF'L RESPONSIBILITY EC 7-28 (2005) ("A lawyer should not pay or agree to pay a non-expert witness an amount in excess of reimbursement for expenses and financial loss incident to being a witness"); *id.* DR 7-109(C) (allowing payment of "[e]xpenses reasonably incurred by a witness in attending or testifying," including "[r]easonable compensation . . . for his loss of time").

20.   Different rules apply to the payment of expert witnesses for the time spent preparing for depositions. See Chapter 19.

21.   *See* FED. R. CIV. P. 30(b)(2) ("Unless the court orders otherwise, [deposition] testimony may be recorded by audio, audiovisual, or stenographic means"); see Chapter 17.

22.   *See* Penasquitos Vill., Inc. v. NLRB, 565 F.2d 1074, 1085 (9th Cir. 1977) (Duniway, J., concurring in part and dissenting in part) (noting that "many trial lawyers, and some trial judges, will admit that the demeanor of a perfectly honest but unsophisticated or timid witness may be—or can be made by an astute cross-examiner to be—such that he will be thought by the jury or the judge to be a liar").

23. *See generally* David M. Balabanian, *Medium v. Tedium: Video Depositions Come of Age, reprinted in* ABA SEC. OF LITIG., THE LITIGATION MANUAL—DEPOSITIONS 95-105 (Priscilla Ann Schwab & Lawrence J. Vilardo eds., 2007); Fred I. Heller, *The Televised Witness: Preparing Videotaped Depositions*, TRIAL, Sept. 1992, at 50–55; Alexander R. Sussman & Edna R. Sussman, *Electronic Depositions*, LITIGATION, Summer 1989, at 26–30.

24. As discussed in "Preparation Sessions: When, Where, How Often, and with Whom" in Chapter 5, even if the deposition will not be recorded on video, the lawyer may still want to video record portions of the preparation session and review that footage with the witness.

25. *See, e.g.*, FED. R. CIV. P. 30(b)(5) ("The deponent's and attorneys' appearance or demeanor must not be distorted through recording techniques.").

26. *See* United States v. Tunnell, 667 F.2d 1182, 1188 (5th Cir. 1982) (noting that through use of video taped deposition, "[t]he trial judge was able to note [the witness's] attitude reflected by his motions, facial expressions, demeanor and voice inflections"); Weiss v. Wayes, 132 F.R.D. 152, 154 (M.D. Pa. 1990) (quoting *Tunnell*). See also "Nonverbal Communication" in Chapter 11, discussing the extent to which nonverbal communication conveys meaning.

27. See "3. Pause Before Answering" in Chapter 7.

28. See Chapter 7, note 19.

29. *Cf.* Mark A. Neubauer, *Videotaping Depositions*, 19 LITIGATION 60–69 (Summer 1993) ("an examining lawyer who anticipates obstructive objections should consider videotaping if for no other reason than to force her opponent to back off").

30. See FED. R. EVID. 801(a) (a "statement" may be oral, written, or "nonverbal conduct of a person, if it is intended by the person as an assertion"); *see also* Kiraly v. Berkel, Inc., 122 F.R.D. 186, 187–88 (E.D. Pa. 1988) (reenactment of accident); Roberts v. Homelite Div. of Textron, Inc., 109 F.R.D. 664, 667–69 (N.D. Ind. 1986) (same); Carson v. Burlington N., Inc., 52 F.R.D. 492, 492–93 (D. Neb. 1971) (same).

31. *See supra* notes 22 and 26.

32. The very purpose of deposition preparation is to improve the presentation of the witness's testimony and possibly refresh the witness's recollection in the process. See Chapter 8 and "Proper Practice Versus Improper Coaching" in Chapter 7.

33. For example, the client might waive the attorney-client privilege, intentionally or unintentionally.

34. Professor McElhaney has noted, for example, that one very experienced litigator who regularly recorded practice sessions on video always kept the video until after the conclusion of the case, "lest anyone accuse him of destroying evidence." James W. McElhaney, *Preparing Witnesses for Depositions*, A.B.A. J., June 1992, at 86.

CHAPTER 11

Taking the Deposition

HENRY L. HECHT

Assume you are the deposition taker and you are prepared—as well as you ever will be.[1] Your outline is in hand. The documents you intend to have marked are placed neatly in file folders.[2] You brought your business card and a caption page for the court reporter.[3]

Even after all this preparation, you still must resolve a number of issues. For example, where do you want people to sit at the deposition? How should you handle preliminary matters such as the required opening statement by the deposition officer? Are any stipulations needed? Should you be friendly or aggressive? In what order should you ask your questions? How should you respond if the witness claims lack of recall on a key issue?

Some of these issues can be decided—at least tentatively—before the deposition starts. Others can be addressed only after it is under way. The purpose of this chapter is twofold: (1) to review the issues a taker faces at the start of, and during, a deposition, and (2) to offer practical advice about resolving them. The chapter ends with a discussion of some social science research on questioning techniques and the importance of recognizing, using, and interpreting nonverbal signals. (Considerations at the end of the deposition both for the taker and the defender are covered in Chapter 23.)

To a great extent, resolution of these issues turns on three factors. The first is your purpose in taking the deposition. You approach a deposition taken primarily for discovery purposes differently than one taken primarily for evidentiary purposes. The second factor is the deposition environment—friendly or hostile—that you want to create. The third factor is your assessment of the witness and the defender; a hostile witness or defender cannot be handled in the same way as a friendly one.

Arranging the Deposition Room

Depositions are normally held in a conference room at the taker's office. Plan to be there early, before the other side arrives. That way, you can set up the room to suit your purposes. Research has shown that seating arrangements can affect how people communicate.[4] In general, the arrangement you choose depends on whether you want a friendly or a confrontational environment.

Most deposition rooms have a conference table and chairs. The typical seating arrangement is illustrated by Figure 1. The taker sits across the table from the witness, the defender sits at the witness's side, and the court reporter sits at the head of the table.

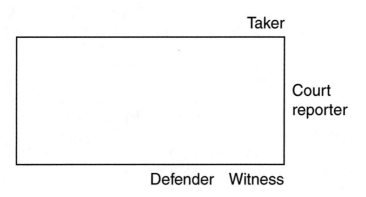

Figure 1
Typical Seating Arrangement for Deposition That Is Not Recorded on Video

Many court reporters prefer this arrangement because it enables them to see and hear everyone—particularly the witness and the questioner—as well as handle exhibits.[5]

Suppose instead of creating a traditional, confrontational arrangement you want an arrangement that fosters good rapport with a witness, such as a friendly, nonparty witness expected to give help-ful testimony or with a lower-level employee of an adverse party who has no visible, personal stake in the litigation. Then consider using the seating arrangement illustrated in Figure 2. It puts you at the head of the table, at a right angle to the witness; the court reporter sits to your right, and the defender sits on the witness's far side.

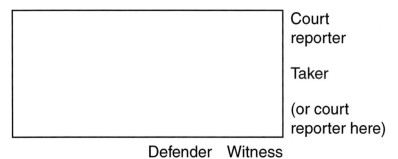

Court
reporter

Taker

(or court
reporter here)

Defender   Witness

Figure 2
Alternative Seating Arrangements

Why this arrangement? A study at a Canadian hospital found that when people sat at a rectangular table, cross-corner conversa-tions (people sitting at right angles) were six times more frequent than cross-table conversations (people sitting face-to-face).[6] Thus, a right-angle seating arrangement at a deposition may promote greater intimacy between you and the witness. It also may turn the defender into something of an outsider.[7] At a minimum, it removes the defender from your direct line of sight.

If the deposition room has a window—especially one with a view—you might try seating the witness and her defender so that they face it. The idea is to distract the witness—or her lawyer—in the hope that one or both will become more unguarded. Do not expect this to work, however, with a party witness or most law-yers. Most parties and their defenders are too focused to let them-selves be distracted by even a drop-dead view.[8]

One other point about seating: Like many aspects of a deposition, the room arrangement can be a battle. Defenders usually want the witness seated close to themselves and as far away from the taker as possible, so do not expect your preferences for seating to control. Thus, you will need to deal with the defender's and the court report-er's needs, and possibly those of a videographer as well.

Conferring with the Court Reporter

As the taker, you choose the court reporter.[9] Try to make the reporter's job easier. The reason: A happy reporter is more likely to accommodate your requests during the deposition. If you have not already done so, find out what type of chair the reporter prefers. Ask how often she needs a break, and discuss how long breaks should be. Also, see if she has time constraints. If so, and you plan to run late, arrange for a second reporter.

What you want first and foremost from a court reporter is an accurate record.[10] As part of that record, you may want (1) conferences between the witness and the defender to be noted whether or not you say anything about them on the record, (2) long pauses between questions and answers to be noted, and (3) nothing said during the deposition to be "off the record" unless you and the defender agree. If you want any of all or these understandings, be sure to ask the reporter to comply. Regardless of how many "understandings" you have, make sure the record accurately reflects what is happening at the deposition by verbalizing everything that occurs in the room. Absent a camera, only a word picture transcribed on the record will reflect the true picture.[11]

Opening Statement by the Deposition Officer

After the witness and her lawyer arrive and everyone is seated,[12] the deposition officer, who is usually also the court reporter, will ask the witness to raise her right hand and take an oath to tell the truth. At this point, you must decide how to handle certain preliminaries; namely, the deposition officer's opening statement, required by the Federal Rules of Civil Procedure (FRCP), and stipulations, if any, between you and the defender.

Be careful. First impressions at a deposition count just as heavily as they do at, say, a business meeting. And first impressions are made within "a blink of the eye."[13] How you handle these preliminaries can set the tone for the entire deposition. Handle them in a formal, unfriendly manner, and you are bound to have difficulty creating an informal, friendly environment. Approach these preliminaries as you did the seating arrangements: Decide what impression you want to make, and then act accordingly.

As for the deposition officer's opening statement, FRCP 30(b)(5) lays down the following requirement: Unless the parties otherwise agree, a deposition must begin with a statement on the record by the deposition officer. The statement must include the following: (1) the officer's name and business address; (2) the date, time, and location of the deposition; (3) the name of the deponent; (4) the administration of oath or affirmation; and (5) the identification of all persons present. Typically, the reporter asks the parties and attorneys to state their own appearances.[14] Ask those present whom you do not know to identify themselves.

To a witness—particularly one being deposed for the first time—the officer's statement can sound overly formal. To soften the formality—and the implicit reminder that the deposition is adversarial—ask the defender for a stipulation that the officer's statement need not be read but can be appended to the beginning of the transcript.[15] If the defender refuses, preface the reporter's opening statement with a comment such as: "Let me explain that before I start asking my questions the law requires the court reporter to make a few remarks about who is present and the like."

Opening Remarks and Stipulations

At this point, many takers turn to the defender and begin discussing stipulations. That can be a serious mistake. As a taker, your most important relationship at the deposition is with the witness. So, begin by speaking to the witness, introducing yourself, and telling the witness what to expect.[16] This can be accomplished in a few words.

> TAKER: Good morning. My name is Emily Carter and I represent Business-Aide, the Defendant. I am here to ask you questions about what you know regarding a purchase of computer hardware and software by Leslie Roberts, the Plaintiff in this case.

If you need to discuss stipulations with the defender, add the following:

> TAKER: Before we begin, your lawyer and I need to cover a few points about ground rules for this deposition.

Most of the stipulations discussed below are covered by the FRCP.[17] Nevertheless, stipulations remain an issue at many depositions.

Some takers deal with them by saying, "This deposition will be covered by the Federal Rules of Civil Procedure." After this statement, they may ask the defender, "Do you have specific stipulations to propose?" Other takers say nothing about stipulations.

Instead, they immediately start questioning the witness, leaving it up to the defender to raise the issue of stipulations.

Another way takers deal with stipulations is to ask, "Can we have the usual stipulations?" Every litigator has heard some story about an inexperienced lawyer at his first deposition who is asked this question by an experienced opponent. Not wanting to appear ignorant, the neophyte agrees. Only after returning to his office and reviewing the relevant rules does he realize, perhaps to his regret, what that agreement means.

Contrary to deposition folklore, there are no "usual stips." How then should you respond if your opponent asks you to agree to the "usual stipulations"? By saying, "I do not know what you mean by the usual stipulations. If you will state each one, I will let you know whether I agree." One last point on stipulations: If you do not reach any stipulations, say so on the record.[18]

In jurisdictions without the elaborate provisions of the FRCP, or when you want to customize the applicable rules, consider entering one or more of the stipulations reviewed below. In addition, given the limitation in federal practice to depositions of one day of seven hours absent a court order or stipulation, consider seeking any stipulations before the deposition to save valuable time for questioning. Then put the stipulations you reached in writing and mark it as an exhibit to the deposition.[19] If you want the same stipulations for later depositions, seek an agreement that the stipulations entered for one deposition shall be used throughout the case unless otherwise agreed.

As you review the following stipulations, consider which are likely to be of mutual interest to the defender. But keep in mind that takers and defenders often have different perspectives about the strategic value of any given particular stipulation.

1. *Stipulation that the deposition is taken by notice, subpoena, or agreement and all objections concerning notice of time and place of the taking of deposition are expressly waived.*

FRCP 32(d)(1) provides that "[a]n objection to an error or irregularity in a deposition notice is waived unless promptly served in writing on the party giving the notice." The rule, however, does not specify what form the objection should take or when it should be made.[20] As the taker, you can use this stipulation to foreclose a subsequent challenge that the deponent (or opposing party) was given inadequate notice. The stipulation is particularly useful if the witness is appearing by agreement, but you failed to get it in writing. In that case, the stipulation functions as the written agreement. In addition, if a party who received less than fourteen days' notice has moved for a protective order under FRCP 32(a)(4)(E) in the hope of preventing the deposition from being used against that party (and the motion has not been heard and, nevertheless, the witness is attending the deposition), offering this stipulation gives the objecting party a chance to reconsider and withdraw its motion.[21] If you enter this stipulation, mark the appropriate deposition notice, subpoena, or written agreement as an exhibit to the deposition.[22]

2. *Stipulation that the deposition may continue for more than one day of seven hours.*

FRCP 30(d)(1) provides that "(u)nless otherwise stipulated or ordered by the court, a deposition is limited to 1 day of 7 hours." In complex litigation, particularly cases involving a significant number of documents, the parties may find a stipulation to extend the deposition beyond this time limit of mutual benefit. Although a taker would likely want this stipulation, a defender may not want to agree in advance to lengthening the time for the deposition. A defender will likely want to defer a decision until later in the day when both the progress of the deposition and the ability of the witness to continue testifying can be better evaluated.[23]

3. *Stipulation that the deposition is being taken before a qualified deposition officer and reported by a qualified and disinterested shorthand reporter (or recorded by a qualified videographer).*

There seems little reason to agree in advance that the deposition officer and reporter are qualified. Indeed, FRCP 32(d)(2) provides:

An objection based on disqualification of the officer before whom a deposition is to be taken is waived if not made:

(A) before the deposition begins; or

(B) promptly after the basis for disqualification becomes known or, with reasonable diligence, could have been known.

As the taker, you should ask the reporter early in the deposition to read back at least one question and answer to make sure the transcript is accurate.[24] If it is not, suspend the deposition and seek another reporter.[25]

4. *Stipulation that all objections except those concerning the form of the question or the answer are reserved to the time the matter is offered in evidence.*

As discussed in the chapter on defending, under the FRCP there are two types of deposition objections.[26] The first type, such as objections to defects in the form of a question or answer (a compound question, for example), are waived if they are made at the deposition.

The second type of objection usually goes to the admissibility of the answer and involves such matters as the competency of a witness and the relevance of testimony. These objections do not have to be made at the deposition and are preserved until trial unless the evidentiary defect can be cured at the deposition. A good example: You ask a lay witness for a legal opinion. The defender objects to the question as improperly calling for an opinion of a lay witness. However, this defect can be cured at the deposition by establishing the witness's competency to answer. Therefore, the objection must be made at the deposition or it is waived.

In practice, the line between the two types of objections is often blurred. Deciding whether a question is objectionable because of form or because of a curable evidentiary defect can be difficult. By limiting the waiver to form objections, Stipulation 4 helps defenders avoid this dilemma. With this stipulation in place, even if a defender fails to object to a question with a curable evidentiary defect, the right to make the objection at trial is not forfeited.

The stipulation can also help takers. By reducing the need to object, the stipulation hampers a defender's ability to use frequent objections to interrupt questions and coach the witness.

But there is a downside for takers. Consider again the situation when you ask a lay witness for a legal opinion. The question has a curable defect. If Stipulation 4 is in effect, however, the defender need not object at the deposition. If he does not, the first time you become aware of the defect may be at trial, when you offer the question and answer into evidence and are met with an objection. But if the witness is not available, you will not be able to cure the defect in your question, the objection will be sustained, and the answer will not be admissible. None of this, of course, may concern you if your primary purpose for deposing the witness is discovery rather than obtaining admissible testimony.

5. *Stipulation that all objections shall be stated as "objection as to form" and nothing more shall be said by the objecting party unless the taker asks for an explanation of the grounds.*[27]

For a taker, this stipulation is a useful companion to Stipulation 4. By prescribing the format for form objections, Stipulation 5 should limit the use of "speaking" or coaching objections.[28]

In theory, Stipulation 5 should not be necessary given FRCP 30(c)(2), which requires objections to be stated "concisely in a nonargumentative and nonsuggestive manner." (The local rules of some jurisdictions have similar limitations on how objections may be stated.[29]) But in practice, this requirement is often ignored. Therefore, an express agreement about the allowable format of an objection can help the taker by setting a standard for judging the defender's conduct. Stipulation 5 can also help a defender by removing any doubt about how to state an objection properly.[30]

6. *Stipulation that if an instruction not to answer is given by the defender, the witness will follow that instruction and will be deemed to have failed to answer.*

Without this stipulation, a taker may not be able to establish the witness's failure to answer unless after each instruction the witness is asked whether she will follow the instruction.[31] If you expect the defender to frequently instruct her witness not to answer, ask for this stipulation at the start of the deposition. Otherwise, you may want to postpone asking for the stipulation until you decide it is needed.

For takers, the value of the stipulation is that it saves time. Yet it also reduces the opportunities a taker has to ask the witness questions such as: "Do you intend to follow the instructions given by your counsel? Do you understand I will seek a court order to compel you to answer? Do you understand I will also seek sanctions, including attorney's fees?" Sometimes just asking these questions causes a witness to answer.

7. *Stipulation that when one party objects to a question, the objection applies to all other parties unless a party opts out.*

This stipulation is useful in multiparty cases. It eliminates the disruptions caused by a chorus of lawyers parroting every objection made.

8. *Stipulation that the testimony, or a portion thereof, is governed by a protective order (or is to be sealed).*

If this stipulation is agreed upon, the relevant protective order should be marked as an exhibit to the deposition. In addition, the party seeking to invoke the order should clarify on the record the scope of the order (for example, the portion of the transcript it covers). and the protocol provided for handling the transcript, (for example, limiting its dissemination to those on an access list who have signed a copy of the protective order).

9. *Stipulation that the reading of the deposition to, or by, the witness and the signing thereof by the witness are waived.*

Under FRCP 30(e), a copy of the deposition transcript is provided to the witness for review only if the witness requests the opportunity to review it.[32] This stipulation makes clear that the witness does not seek review.

If review is requested, the rule gives a witness thirty days for the review after being notified by the deposition officer that the transcript is available. As the taker, you may want to use the transcript before the thirty-day period expires (for example, to support a summary judgment motion). (As an alternative, you may want a stipulation that the witness will have less than thirty days to review and sign the transcript.) In that event, this stipulation can be helpful. Still, from a taker's perspective, there is some value in having a witness review the transcript and make corrections. Should you wind up using the deposition to impeach the witness at trial, your impeachment will be more powerful if the witness read, corrected, and signed the transcript.[33]

When you are a defender, do not waive the right of review at the outset of a deposition unless your own need for a speedy transcript is compelling. Even then, wait until the end of the deposition to enter a stipulation so that you can make an informed judgment whether to waive review.

10. *Stipulation that the lawyer taking the deposition shall have custody of the original record of the deposition, including exhibits, and shall make it available for filing, if required.*

This stipulation reflects what FRCP 30(f)(1) mandates; namely, that the reporter delivers the transcript to the noticing party to be stored under conditions that will protect it against loss, destruction, tampering, or deterioration. Furthermore, the stipulation calls for the noticing party to make the transcript available for filing upon a court order to do so or when the transcript is to be used in the proceeding.[34]

11. *Stipulation that original exhibits be returned to the person producing them and copies be substituted after inspection of the originals.*[35]

Like Stipulation 10, this stipulation tracks a portion of FRCP 30(f)(2). Stipulation 11 eliminates problems created by witnesses and parties who object to having originals attached to the transcript. It prejudices neither side in its ability to inspect and use original documents or substitutes.

Opening Questions

After opening remarks and stipulations, you are ready to begin questioning the witness. At the extremes are two different approaches: (1) leading off with "foundational" questions that review the deposition process and (2) leading off with confrontational questions.

Foundational Questions

Starting with foundational questions is the more common approach. It uses a series of questions to explain the deposition process to the witness. You hope that after each question, the witness gives an affirmative answer. The questions are called "foundational" because together with the answers they create a basis or foundation for later impeachment at trial. In effect, they establish, among other things, that the witness understood the deposition process and the importance of the deposition and was prepared to testify. These admissions make it difficult for a witness to convince a judge or jury that she has a credible reason for later changing an answer.[36]

There are two additional reasons to start a deposition with foundational questions. First, because the questions are relatively straightforward and easy to ask, asking them can help put you at ease. Second, when asked in a friendly manner, the questions create the impression that you are fair and will conduct the deposition fairly, thereby building rapport with a witness. And that rapport can soften the witness's image—reinforced undoubtedly by the defender—that you are an adversary bent on harm. (Of course, your attempts at friendliness might reinforce a defender's admonition to a witness during preparation that you are a wolf in sheep's clothing.)

At some depositions, however, building rapport is less important than controlling a witness. When control is your primary concern, you may want to ask foundational questions in a harsher, more formal tone. Several model foundational questions and answers follow.

Prior Deposition Experience

Q. Have you ever had your deposition taken?
A. No.

NOTE: If the answer is "yes," you may want to preface the following questions with a phrase such as "I am sure that you understand from your prior deposition that. . . ." Obviously, prior deposition experience will cut against a witness's later claim that she did not understand the deposition process.

Represented by Counsel

Q. Are you represented by counsel today?
A. Yes.

NOTE: There are two reasons for asking this question. First, if the witness is represented by a lawyer at the deposition, it will be difficult for the witness to claim at trial that she did not understand the deposition process—especially if the same lawyer represents the witness at trial. Second, if the witness is not represented by a lawyer, it is less likely that opposing counsel will be able to instruct the witness not to answer a question.[37]

Q. And that is Ms. Carter, who is seated next to you?
A. Yes.

NOTE: As noted above, appearances by all the lawyers should have been stated on the record at the start of the deposition. Asking this question at the outset leaves no doubt on the record that the witness is represented, and by whom.

Q. Did you meet with your lawyer before coming to this deposition today?[38]
A. Yes.
Q. I am sure that your counsel has described the deposition process for you, but I want to make sure that you understand how we will proceed today.

NOTE: A general statement about a meeting between the witness and her lawyer to discuss the deposition process should not be objectionable, particularly because it is not asked as a question. Some lawyers do not bother to make this statement or ask the next several questions below about the witness's understanding of the deposition process. In their view, the fact that the witness is represented by a lawyer (as established by the earlier questions) provides a sufficient basis for subsequent impeachment.

Witness's Understanding of the Deposition Process

Q. Do you understand generally what the procedures for this deposition will be?

A. Yes.

Q. Do you understand that you have just taken an oath to tell the truth?

A. Yes.

Q. Do you understand that even though this is an informal setting, the oath that you took is the same as the one you will take as a witness if this case is tried?

A. Yes.

Q. Do you understand that the penalty for perjury applies to any false statements that you may make today just as if you were in a court of law?

A. Yes.

NOTE: If you want to establish a friendly tone, it may be best to omit the last question. The mention of perjury will reinforce the witness's hostile image of you. In addition, the question may draw an objection from the defender that you are harassing the witness. That objection will make it even harder to build rapport with the witness. The defender may even threaten to end the deposition and seek a protective order on the grounds that the warning about perjury is being given solely to annoy, embarrass, or oppress the witness.[39]

Questioning Process

Q. If you do not understand any question, will you tell me?

A. Yes.

Q. Then I will attempt to find out the problem with the question and rephrase the question. Is that satisfactory?

NOTE: Many lawyers do not like to make this offer. They feel that it cedes control to the witness and encourages both the witness and the defender to ask for questions to be rephrased.

A. Yes.

Q. If you do not hear any part of a question, will you tell me?

A. Yes.

Q. If you do not tell me otherwise, I will assume that you heard and understood my question. Is that satisfactory?

A. Yes.

NOTE: Whether this question and answer have any binding effect is debatable. It is doubtful that a witness can make this bargain before the questioning begins. In addition, defenders often object to the question as argumentative.

Q. If you realize during this deposition that an earlier answer was inaccurate or incomplete, let me know and I will give you a chance to correct it. Is that satisfactory?

A. Yes.

NOTE: This question can be useful when you later attempt to impeach a witness who claims that although she realized she gave an inaccurate answer at the deposition, she assumed it was too late to change the answer.

Q. Do you understand that your answers are being recorded by the court reporter and that you must give audible verbal responses?

A. Yes.

Q. Do you understand that the court reporter cannot record two people speaking at the same time so that you need to let me finish my question before you start your answer?

A. Yes.

NOTE: Court reporters appreciate these reminders. When asking these last two questions, consider a further attempt to build rapport by complimenting the witness on the good job she is already doing in responding audibly. But consider also that these questions, when directed to some witnesses, particularly those who have been deposed before, may seem condescending.

Q. Do you understand that you may request an opportunity to review the transcript that will be prepared by the court reporter from your testimony today?

A. Yes.

Q. Do you also understand that after your review, you may correct any errors you find in the transcript?

A. Yes.

Q. Do you also understand that if you do make any changes to the transcript, I will have an opportunity to comment upon those changes at trial?

A. Yes.

Ability to Testify

Q. Is there any reason at all why you feel you cannot testify fully and accurately today?

A. No.

NOTE: If the answer is "yes," ask follow-up questions to find out why. If the answers indicate that the witness cannot testify fully and accurately, you should consider adjourning the deposition to another day. Some lawyers use an alternative version of the question above, as follows:

Q. Are you aware of any physical or mental conditions that could interfere with your ability to testify today?

A. No.

Q. Are you are taking any medications that could interfere with your ability to testify?

A. No.

Q. Do you have any questions about the procedures that we will follow today?

A. No.

Additional Subjects, Including Breaks

How many other foundational subjects to cover will depend on your preferences as well as the witness being deposed. Spending too much time on foundational matters can irritate some witnesses and therefore be counterproductive.[40] But one additional area many lawyers cover at the start of a deposition is breaks.

Q. Do you understand that if you want to take a break, if you let me know, we will take one?

A. Yes.

NOTE: Asked in this manner, the question fosters a non-threatening environment. But it also gives the witness the option to take a break at any time based on your offer—even when a question is pending. In that event, during the break, the defender is likely to coach his witness. A better way to phrase the question is as follows:

Q. I plan on taking regular breaks during the deposition. Do you have any special needs for breaks that I should be aware of?

A. No.

NOTE: By asking the question in this manner, you stay in control while still appearing fair. If the witness has special needs (for example, a medical condition), ask follow-up questions to clarify what the needs are.

Q. Do you understand that although there will be breaks, there will be no break between a question and your answer?

A. Yes.

NOTE: A defender will often object to this question, stating that he and the witness will take breaks whenever they feel it necessary.[41] As taker, state your strenuous objection on the record and offer to break only after the witness answers your question.

Confrontational Questions

The confrontational approach can be illustrated with a *Scoops* example. Suppose you represent Plaintiff Leslie Roberts and are deposing Terry Blake, the salesperson for Defendant Business-Aide. You have a memorandum from Waller to Blake stating that a sale to Roberts will "catch up" Blake's commissions to the level of the other sales personnel. Instead of the usual foundational questions and stipulations, you begin with a tough, pointed question:

Q. Mr. Blake, you realized that if you made a sale to Leslie Roberts, your monthly commissions would catch up to those of other Business-Aide sales personnel, is that correct?

The defender well may object, complaining that the question lacks foundation. You should ignore the objection and demand an answer.

This approach lets you exploit your controlling role as taker: You noticed the deposition. You chose the time and place. Now you show the witness you mean business.[42] When should you use this approach? Usually, when your primary purpose is to catch the witness off-guard in the hope of obtaining damaging testimony. Confrontation can be particularly effective with a witness who has been told by a defender to expect a slow start to the deposition, marked by background questions and discussions between lawyers. If the confrontational approach produces an admission from the witness, stay with this style while you have the momentum.

Be aware, however, that a confrontational start can backfire. If the defender anticipates the tactic and prepares the witness for it, confrontation may make the witness more confident in her lawyer's predictions and in herself. Another problem: A confrontational start usually makes a witness more hostile—and more careful during the rest of the deposition. It also makes the defender more aggressive. Consequently, before deciding to use a confrontational approach, consider the following factors: (1) whether the witness has ever been deposed before and, therefore, may not be easily rattled; (2) whether the defender has previously seen you use the tactic; and (3) whether the witness has been prepared for confrontation (probably the case if defender has seen you use this tactic).

Questions About Witness Preparation

Regardless of the approach you use—whether foundational or confrontational—at some point during every deposition, you will likely want to question the witness about her preparation for the deposition. There are several reasons to do so. First, a witness who testifies to significant time in preparation will have a hard time later convincing a judge or jury that she did not understand the significance of the deposition. Second, such testimony can be used to impeach a witness who testifies to a lack of recall in spite of significant preparation before the deposition, but later at trial claims a newfound recollection.[43] Third, questions about preparation can produce testimony establishing a waiver of a privilege or the work-product protection. Fourth, as discussed below, the timing of a witness's preparation can help you decide how to organize your questions.

257

Model questions about preparation—none of which should be objectionable[44]—include the following:

1. Did you meet with your lawyer before the deposition for the purpose of preparing?
2. How many times?
3. When?
4. For how long?
5. Who was present?
6. Did you discuss this meeting with anyone else? If so, with whom?
7. Did you discuss the testimony you expect to give today with anyone other than your lawyer? If so, with whom?

Another area of questioning concerns documents reviewed for the deposition. This topic is covered in Chapter 9, Discoverability of Documents Used to Refresh the Recollection of a Witness: Federal Rule of Evidence 612.

If the witness is a not a party, the attorney-client privilege does not apply to discussions between that witness and a party's lawyer.[45] If such discussions occurred, ask about everything discussed and about any documents shown to the witness by the other party's lawyer.

Receipt of Documents

Suppose a notice under FRCP 30(b)(2) or a subpoena under FRCP 45 requests the production of documents at the deposition.[46] For two reasons, you should do everything possible to obtain those documents *before* the deposition. First, having the documents before the deposition will give you more time to review them and prepare. Second, given the one-day-of-seven-hours time limitation, you do not want to waste valuable time at the deposition reviewing documents for the first time.[47] But if you were unable to arrange for their production before the deposition, now is the time to receive them.[48] That means asking two or three questions along these lines:

Q. Were you served with a document request in this case?
A. Yes.

NOTE: Mark the request as an exhibit to the deposition.[49]

Q. Have you brought any documents with you today pursuant to that request?

NOTE: When a witness is represented by a lawyer, usually it is the witness's lawyer who produces any responsive documents. Look them over and decide whether to have each document marked now or later at a break.

After you receive the documents, ask about the production process, using the following questions as a guide:[50]

1. Ask the witness if additional documents will be produced pursuant to your request.
    a. If so, ask the witness to explain the delay.
    b. Demand a date certain for the production and reserve the right to reopen the deposition.[51]
2. Ask if any documents have been withheld.[52]
    a. If the answer is "yes," ask why the documents are being withheld.
    b. If the ground for withholding is privilege or work-product protection, ask for the information required by FRCP 26(b)(5), which requires the withholding party to describe the documents not produced and to identify the privilege or protection claimed for them.[53]
    c. If appropriate, ask additional questions to lay a foundation to overcome a claim of work product or privilege.[54]
3. Ask whether the witness is demanding the return of any documents inadvertently produced under a claim of privilege or work-product protection.[55]
4. Ask what role the witness played in gathering the documents that were produced.[56]
5. Ask where the documents were found.
6. If copies were produced, ask to inspect the originals. Make sure the copies are identical to the originals.[57]

NOTE: There are three common problems with copies. First, notes written in pencil on an original often reproduce poorly or not at all. Second, the use of different color marks or highlighting on a document will not show unless the copy is in color. Third, notes on the back page of an original often are overlooked and not copied. Therefore, make sure that everything on both sides of every page is copied and legible.

Organization of Questions

As discussed in Chapter 4, the taker typically organizes questions chronologically, topically, or sometimes both, depending on a variety of factors. A well-prepared taker will prepare questions long before the deposition, even though last-minute modifications often are necessary.

Sometimes, however, you do not have enough information before a deposition to decide what approach to use. When that happens, a good tactic to help you decide how to proceed is to question the witness early in the deposition about preparation, as discussed below. Find out how often, when, and how long she and her lawyer conferred. If they met several days before, and again on the morning of the deposition, the witness probably will be well prepared on key issues. In that case, you may want to put off questions about these issues until late in the day when the witness is tired or has forgotten the defender's coaching. On the other hand, if the witness and defender never met or met just briefly before the deposition, the witness may not be well prepared. Consider asking the tough questions early, before the witness can be further prepared at a break or the lunch recess.

In addition, occasionally mix up your approaches to avoid becoming predictable. Say you start with a chronological approach. After a break or lunch, ask a series of unanticipated questions. If you are lucky, you may catch the witness off balance and obtain damaging testimony.

Examination Techniques

How you question a witness is driven largely by your purpose in taking the deposition.[58] This section reviews questioning patterns for three different deposition purposes: (1) discovery, (2) admissions, and (3) impeachment. This section also looks at examination techniques common to every deposition. Because most depositions are taken for multiple purposes, frequently you will use more than one pattern.

Discovery

Gathering information is a key purpose for virtually every deposition—even when the witness is not a party. You want to learn everything the witness knows about certain subjects, even if the testimony is unfavorable. In addition, you want to lock the witness into a version of events that cannot be credibly changed at trial. You can accomplish this objective through a four-step approach that involves

(1) context, (2) content, (3) closure, and (4) corroboration.[59] (The mnemonic "CCCC" may help you remember the steps.) The following examples from the *Scoops v. Business-Aide, Inc.* case illustrate each of these steps, as well as what to ask when a witness claims a lack of recall.

Assume that you represent Leslie Roberts and are deposing Terry Blake. A key event in the case is Blake's meeting with Roberts in the Business-Aide store, more than two years before the deposition. Your client, Roberts, has told you that they discussed a number of points. One was Blake's recommendation that she buy a more expensive laptop computer rather than a less costly desktop model. The following example focuses on how you can learn Blake's version of what they discussed about the computer hardware he sold to Roberts. (The use of documents in questioning a witness is covered in Chapters 12 and 13. The role of the defender and the taker's response to the defender are considered in Chapter 14.)

Context

Everyone knows that journalists use open-ended questions to get people talking. Your instincts might tell you to use the same technique when you begin questioning Blake about the meeting. You could start with such questions as: "What did you say to Leslie Roberts when you first met her in the store?" Or, and more to the point, "What did you tell Leslie Roberts about the computer hardware that you sold to her?"

But your instincts would be wrong. Before asking Blake what was said at the meeting, put the event in context by asking about such details as the time, place, and location of the meeting. In effect, "set the scene" for the witness. There are five reasons to do this.

First, scene-setting takes the witness back in time and place. Studies show this helps a witness remember.[60]

Second, answers to scene-setting questions sometimes lead to additional discovery sources, such as people present at an event or a previously undisclosed document.

Third, the questions help you "read" a witness. Is he well prepared? Does he pause before answering a question? Does he answer only the question asked? Does he seem to have good rapport with his defender? Is he talkative? Is his memory of the event good?

Suppose Blake testifies that he cannot recall the day of the meeting, its duration, or who else was there. Later in the deposition, he testifies that he "clearly recalls" telling Roberts about the advantages of a laptop. Blake's uneven memory—which you may be able

261

to exploit at trial—suggests that he may not be telling the truth or at least provides the basis for an argument that his "clear recollection" is suspect.

Fourth, the information you learn can guide your later questions. For example, a sales meeting lasting one and one-half hours suggests that more was said than in a fifteen-minute meeting.

Fifth, before you start questioning a witness about a key point, you may want to build rapport with the witness. Scene-setting questions can do that by making the witness comfortable with you and your questioning style. (Of course, as noted above, the witness will likely have been warned during witness preparation that a deposition is not like "a normal" conversation, even if the taker tries to create that impression.)

Here are some model questions to ask Blake about the context of the meeting:

Q. Did you have any conversations, whether face-to-face or by telephone, with Ms. Roberts between October, two years ago, and today?
A. Yes.
Q. How many?
A. Two.

NOTE: It helps to first find out how many conversations there were. Once you know how many, you can explore them one by one, as follows:

Q. When was the first conversation?
A. In October, two years ago, I spoke with her on the telephone.
Q. Other than that telephone call, which we will explore later, when did you speak with Ms. Roberts?

NOTE: The example assumes that the first conversation over the telephone is not of interest at the moment and focuses only on the meeting between Blake and Roberts in Business-Aide's store. An effective note-taking system should allow you to return to the telephone call later in the deposition for further examination.[61] Alternatively, ask the court reporter to mark the place in the deposition where you want to return. Then, at a break, ask the reporter to identify the marked areas.

A. We spoke when we met face-to-face.
Q. Where was that meeting?

A. She met me in the Business-Aide store.
Q. Where in the store did she meet with you?
A. On the showroom floor, by the computers on display.
Q. Why did you meet with her?

NOTE: This question is not meant to establish the details of the meeting; instead, it is meant to put the witness back at the scene of the meeting.

A. I had telephoned her, as I mentioned, to set up a meeting. I was asked to do so in a memorandum I received from my boss, Maxine Waller. Her memorandum said that Ms. Roberts wanted to buy computer hardware and software for her business.

NOTE: You and everyone else at the deposition may know to which memorandum Blake is referring. But readers of the transcript may not, especially if there is more than one memorandum from Waller to Blake in the case. To clarify Blake's answer, ask a follow-up question.

Q. In referring to a memorandum from Maxine Waller, are you referring to Waller's memorandum to you dated November 4, two years ago, previously marked as Exhibit 8 to your deposition?
A. Yes.
Q. On what day did Leslie Roberts meet you in the store?
A. I do not recall specifically.

NOTE: Witnesses using phrases such as "I do not recall specifically" often have a general recollection. Follow up.

Q. Do you have a general recollection about the date?
A. The meeting was after I received the memorandum from Maxine Waller.
Q. Are you referring to Exhibit 8?

NOTE: At this point, there are at least five techniques you can use to establish the date of the meeting. First, if there is no dispute about the date (as in this case), ask for a stipulation that the meeting was on November 12. Second, represent to the witness that the meeting was on November 12, then ask if that refreshes his recollection. Third, show the witness a document indicating the date of the meeting, then ask whether the document refreshes the witness's recollection.[62] Fourth, ask the witness whether he knows of any documents that could set the date. Fifth, if all else fails, try to "bracket" the meeting between other dates known by the witness. For example, you could ask Blake whether the meeting occurred between the date of Waller's memorandum (November 4) and Thanksgiving. Sometimes, you can bracket with events in a witness's personal life—a birthday, promotion, or job relocation, for example—that you learned about earlier in the deposition during an examination about the witness's background.

Q. Was the meeting in the middle of November?
A. Yes.
Q. Did you prepare for your meeting with Ms. Roberts?
A. Yes.
Q. We will come back to your preparation later.

NOTE: Again, a question like this one highlights the need for a note-taking system that enables you to return to certain areas for further examination.

Q. How long was your meeting with Ms. Roberts?
A. I cannot recall.

NOTE: If a witness cannot recall the duration of a meeting, try a variation of bracketing technique discussed above. At Blake's deposition, for example, you could ask what he did right before and after the meeting and when. If he remembers, use the information to bracket his meeting with Roberts. On the other hand, when a witness recalls how long a meeting lasted, ask why he remembers its length. Often the answer runs something like this: "Because I marked the time in my personal calendar." Such a response provides an additional discovery source.

Q. What is your best estimate of the length of your meeting with Ms. Roberts?

NOTE: Questions asking for a witness's "best estimate" are another way to set a date or time frame. They often provoke a defender to object that the question calls for speculation. The taker, however, is entitled to an answer if the witness has any basis for estimating. Therefore, ignore the objection and tell the witness to answer. Some takers, in an effort to forestall the objection, preface a "best estimate" request by explaining that they want to know what only the witness knows and they are not asking for a guess. (A common example used to explain the difference between a best estimate and a guess is telling the witness that he could estimate the length of the room in which the deposition is being taken, but not the length of the taker's living room at home—unless, of course, the witness had been there.)

A. About one and one-half hours.
Q. Was anyone other than Ms. Roberts and you at the meeting?
A. No.

NOTE: If others were present, follow up with questions that identify them and help you locate them. If, on the other hand, the witness who is testifying about the meeting was not present, you need to ask the witness how he knows what happened at the meeting.

At this point, the scene has been set. You know the "where," "when," "how long," and "who" of the meeting—or at least some of these details. Equally important, you have focused Blake's attention on this event. Now it is time to find out about the "what" of the meeting.

Content

When you want to find out everything said or done at an event (like the meeting between Blake and Roberts), "T-funnel questioning" can be quite effective. Figure 3 illustrates this technique. You begin with open-ended questions, move to narrow questions, and then end with closure questions that finish the subject matter and exhaust the witness's recollection.[63]

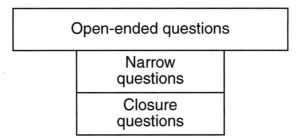

Figure 3
T-Funnel Questioning

265

Set forth below is a typical T-funnel questioning pattern. (Questions to gain closure and how to deal with a witness's lack of recall are discussed in the next two sections.)

1. What did you say about the topic at issue? (open-ended question, such as who, what, why, when, where, and how)
2. Did you say anything else about the topic? If so, what? (a foundational question, followed by an open-ended question)
3. Did you say X? (narrow question for elaboration and clarification)
4. You said Y, is that correct? (narrow, leading question suggesting what was said)
5. Other than X, Y, and Z, was anything else said? (closure question)
6. Are you aware of anyone else who knows anything about this conversation? (narrow question to help recall and provide closure)
7. Are you aware of any documents that refer or relate to this conversation? (another narrow question to help recall and provide closure)
8. All you said about the topic was X, Y, and Z; is that correct? (summary question to provide closure)

In short, you explore what the witness recalls, try to stimulate the witness's memory, and end with questions that close the topic and prevent later credible additions by the witness.

Suppose you want to use this technique to find out what Blake said to Roberts about the two available computers (PC TravelPro and PC DeskPro) when the two met in the Business-Aide store. Blake's deposition might look like this:

Q. Let's turn our attention to that part of the conversation during the November meeting in the Business-Aide store when you discussed the computers that Ms. Roberts might purchase.

NOTE: As a general rule, you do not want to telegraph to a witness what you will cover next. However, when you question a witness about a number of subjects tied to the same event, introducing each subject (sometimes referred to as "headlining" or "signposting") focuses the witness and enhances memory retrieval.

A. Uh-huh (or an affirmative nod).

NOTE: As pointed out earlier, an audible, verbal response is always required. Ask the witness whether the answer was "yes" or "no."

Q. What did you tell Ms. Roberts about the available computers?

NOTE: At this point, do not ask the witness for his exact words. (Many lawyers at this point ask the witness, "What did you say specifically?") Instead of a more limiting question, use a broad, open-ended question (like this one) that encourages the witness to give a narrative response. Then, zero in with questions about the witness's exact words.

A. I told her the computer hardware was the key and it must be able to handle her needs as her business grew.

NOTE: The witness has mentioned two separate points. Make a note of each so you can later follow up with questions using the witness's own words.[64]

Q. Did you tell her anything else about the available computers?
A. I told her that she would find a laptop far more convenient for her needs.
Q. Anything else?

NOTE: Although asking "anything else?" is more conversational in tone, you may want to use a longer, self-contained question that requires no reference to another part of the transcript, such as "What else did you say about the two computers?"

A. I think I said that the portability of the PC TravelPro would allow her to use her computer both at Scoops and at home.

NOTE: When a witness prefaces an answer with "I think," many defenders will interject and remind the witness not to speculate. Ignore the defender's interjection and ask the witness whether he recalls saying those words specifically or in substance. If the witness answers, "I can't recall for sure" or something to that effect, ask the witness whether he has any reason to doubt he made the statement.

Q. Anything else?
A. I told her that the price of the PC TravelPro was $2,345.
Q. Anything else?
A. I told her that the price of the PC DeskPro was $995.
Q. Anything else?
A. Not that I recall at this time.

Rather than following up at this point on the witness's claimed lack of recall (using the techniques discussed below), shift to narrow questions to try to find out exactly what was said on each topic mentioned so far. The advantage of immediate follow-up is that the witness's own words can be used while fresh in his mind. (The technique is commonly known as "looping" because the witness's own words were used in the next question.) Now you want to commit the witness to the specific words used.

Q. You said that you told Ms. Roberts that the portability of a laptop like the PC TravelPro gave that machine an advantage over the PC DeskPro, is that correct?
A. Yes.
Q. What did you say to her about this advantage?
A. I told her that a laptop was like having two computers for little more than the price of one.
Q. What did you mean when you said "it was like having two computers for little more than the price of one"?

NOTE: When forming a new question, as noted above, you often want to use the same words the witness just used in answering your last question. This shows the witness you are listening, makes it easier to frame the question, and encourages the witness to respond.

A. First, I meant she could easily take her laptop between Scoops and home.

NOTE: When a witness starts an answer with words like "first," as in the last answer, and "to begin with," implying there are other aspects, be sure to follow up.

Q. What are the other advantages you told her about?
A. I said that she might even enjoy taking her laptop with her when she traveled.
Q. Any other advantages?

NOTE: Again, as noted above, a question asking about "any other reasons" can create a record that is vague and hard to use. Therefore, ask complete (self-contained) questions that stand alone without reference to other questions or answers. For example, instead of the above question, you could ask: "Did you tell her any other advantages of a laptop?"

NOTE: Of course, by asking the more formal, complete question, you may sacrifice rapport.

A. No.

NOTE: Even when asking narrow questions, continue trying to exhaust the witness's memory. (Techniques for exhausting memory [closure] are, as noted above, covered later in this chapter.)

Q. When explaining the advantages of a laptop to Roberts, did you use the exact words, "First, owning a laptop is like having two computers for little more than the price of one."

A. Yes, or words to that effect.

NOTE: If possible, fix the exact words used. Do not, however, ask the witness, "Do you recall using those words?" Such an inquiry creates two problems. First, it can be answered with a "yes" or "no," thereby requiring a follow-up question. Second, it can encourage the witness to develop a sudden attack of lack of recall.

Q. Did Ms. Roberts have any questions about the two advantages you mentioned?

A. No.

An alternative way to question a witness about a conversation is by first asking what the witness said and then asking what the other party said in response. For obvious reasons, this alternating pattern of questioning is characterized as "he said, she said." Here is an example:

Q. What did you say to Ms. Roberts about the computers available for her purchase?

A. I told her the computer was the key; that it must be able to grow as her business grew.

Q. Did she say anything in response?

A. No.

Q. What did you say next?

A. I told her that she would find a laptop far more convenient for her needs.

Q. Did she say anything after you made that statement?

A. Yes. She asked me to show her the two machines.

NOTE: Witnesses with particularly good recall find this pattern very comfortable, and it can create a more accurate picture of the conversation. And, as noted above, you can get a sense of a witness's ability to recall during the first stage of the examination when you "set the scene."

Suppose you decide you have exhausted Blake's recollection of what he said about the two computers. Now is a good time to ask narrow, suggestive questions about issues Blake did not mention. There are two reasons for this step. First, the questions can stimulate Blake's memory. Second, they allow you to test your theory about what was said or—and this is key—what was *not* said at the meeting.

How do you know what other issues to cover? In *Scoops*, you may have learned about these issues from any number of sources. Among them: (1) your client's recollection of what was said at the meeting, (2) your own independent investigation (consultation with a computer expert, for example), and (3) earlier testimony by Blake about his usual practice when describing computer hardware to a customer.

Here are examples of narrow, suggestive questions about these other issues:

- Did you tell Ms. Roberts the amount of memory in the PC TravelPro?
- Did you tell her the potential for upgrading the PC TravelPro?
- Did you tell her the size of the hard drive in the PC TravelPro machine?

If Blake answers "yes" to any of these questions, follow up with additional questions. If he answers "no," ask him why he did not address these points. If Blake responds that he considered mentioning them but did not do so, ask him why.

Some takers shy away from "why" questions. They fear a response that might hurt their case, such as the following answer by Blake: "I tried to tell Roberts about a number of additional items so that she could make an informed decision. But she told me she did not want to hear any more; she had already made up her mind." Remember, when you depose someone for the purpose of discovery, you want to discover everything—both good and bad. In fact, it usually is better for the "bad" to surface before trial, when it may be possible to do something about it. At trial, it may be too late for corrective action.[65] (If the witness is not expected to be available at trial, you may want to ask more limited questions, rather than risk preserving damaging testimony.) Furthermore, as discussed below, narrow, suggestive questions can help you wrest admissions from a witness.

Closure

Closure is designed to exhaust a witness's recollection on a topic, thereby preventing a witness from later trying to credibly add to or change his testimony—or at least making it harder for a witness to do so.

Take Blake's deposition, for example. The simplest, most frequently used closure question is one along these lines: "As you sit here today, Mr. Blake, do you recall anything else that you told Ms. Roberts about the two computers?" After asking a question like this, be patient. Do not worry if the witness does not answer right away. Silence is your friend. It can make an inadequately prepared or nervous witness sufficiently uncomfortable to add something.[66]

If Blake answers "no" to a closure question and you believe your earlier questions were detailed enough to make any later changes in his testimony not credible, it is probably time to wrap up your questioning on this topic. But if his answer is "yes," follow up with the type of T-funnel questions described above in order to pursue what else, if anything, was said.

As an alternative to the closure question posed above, ask: "Did you say anything else to Ms. Roberts about the two computer units during the meeting in the store on November 12, two years ago, other than X, Y, and Z (repeating already-testified-to items)?" If the answer is "yes," then follow-up questioning is necessary.

A third way to close out a topic is to summarize a witness's responses in a single question that, when combined with a simple affirmative answer captures the essence of the witness's testimony on a particular point and makes for a readable question and answer at trial. Lawyers often launch a summary question this way: "Is it fair to say that. . . ?" Inevitably, the defender objects that the question is argumentative and mischaracterizes the witness's testimony. You can avoid this objection by asking the question in this form: "The only things you told Ms. Roberts during the meeting in the store on November 12, two years ago, about the two computers were X, Y, and Z (repeating already-testified-to items), is that correct?" If the witness answers "no," ask in what ways your summary is not correct, and then ask follow-up questions. If the witness answers "yes," your job is done.

Witness's Lack of Recall

Suppose, however, that a witness tries to hedge your attempts at closure by answering, "Not that I recall at this time" or words to that effect. What should you do?

It depends. If you believe that your earlier questions leave no room for the witness to develop a later, credible recollection about the subject, you probably should not pursue the recall issue. If, however, your thorough questioning has tied the witness to a lack of recall, your own client will be able to add helpful facts that the other side will not be able to contradict. But if you feel that the hedging witness may develop a later, additional recollection that you cannot attack, address the recall issue at the deposition. As a first step, clarify the meaning of the witness's testimony that he "does not recall."

Q. Does your answer "I do not recall" mean that you have no reason to believe you said anything else?

NOTE: If the answer is "yes," stop. If the answer is "no," follow up with the next question.

Q. Does your answer "I do not recall" mean that you have no current memory of saying anything else, but you may have said more?

There are at least three techniques for probing an apparently honest lack of recall. In addition to stimulating memory, these techniques are designed to prevent a witness from developing credible, newfound recollection at trial.

With the first technique, you begin by asking whether the witness is aware of anyone who could help his memory. Next, you ask whether there is anything (usually it will be a document) that could help the witness to remember.[67]

Once again, let's use Blake's deposition as an example. Suppose he tells you that a memorandum he prepared after his meeting with Roberts might help his memory. If you have the memorandum, show it to him and see whether it refreshes his recollection. If the memorandum is not available, ask for it to be produced and state that until it is, you will hold the deposition open.[68] If he mentions a person who could help him recall an important conversation, consider deposing that person.

A second technique, which can be used if the subject matter permits, is to compare and contrast what the witness recalls with his regular practice and custom. Suppose that early in Blake's deposition you asked him what information about computer hardware he provides to customers. To stimulate his memory, you could use his earlier testimony to pose questions that compare his usual practice with what he told Roberts.

A third technique is to show that the witness came to the deposition fully prepared to testify and thus has already explored all avenues that might prompt further recall. Questions about preparation, as suggested above, are often asked early in the deposition.[69] If your deposition questions establish that the witness met with his lawyer and spent a reasonable amount of time preparing for the deposition, including reviewing documents, you then can argue at trial based on your deposition questions that the witness was as prepared as possible and that his claim at trial to recall for the first time a new key fact is not credible.

Corroboration

The idea here is to ask a series of questions that might lead to the discovery of information either corroborating or discrediting a witness's testimony. The following questions were designed for Blake's deposition about his meeting with Roberts. With a little editing, they would work for most depositions:

1. Were notes taken at the meeting (or was the meeting recorded)? If so, by whom? Have these notes been produced? If not, why not? If the notes were not produced, follow up with a demand for production.

2. Were notes (or a memorandum) prepared after the meeting? If so, by whom? Have those notes been produced? If not, why not? If the notes were not produced, follow up with a demand for production.

3. Was any action taken as a result of the meeting? If so, by whom? What was done?

4. Was the action documented? If so, by whom? Has that document been produced? If not, why not? (If the document was not produced, follow up with a demand for production.)
5. Was the meeting discussed with anyone afterward? If so, with whom? Was the discussion documented? If so, by whom? Has that document been produced? If not, why not? (If the document was not produced, follow up with a demand for production.)
6. Who else has knowledge of the conversation? How do they know about it? How can they be located?

Some lawyers prefer asking these questions during the first stage of a discovery deposition when "setting the scene." There are two reasons for this approach. First, the questions can lead to additional discovery. Second, reminding a witness about the existence of independent sources against which testimony can be checked can curb a witness's proclivity for exaggeration. But there also is a logic to asking them during the corroboration stage since most of the questions concern actions taken during or after a conversation or meeting. In addition, asking them after an eager witness has expounded on what happened may lead to discovery of material for impeachment.

Admissions

At some point in most depositions your primary purpose shifts from discovering information to seeking admissions that support one or more legal theories and can be used in a pretrial motion or at trial. However, as noted below in the discussion on attempting to impeach a witness at a deposition, a decision to seek an admission at a deposition—particularly when the witness is expected to be available at trial—must be weighed against the risk that you will educate the witness. If the case does not settle, you will have given the deponent a dress rehearsal on what you hope to adduce from him at trial.

If you decide to seek an admission, remember that to be useful it must be part of an unambiguous set of questions and answers. The best way to get such a transcript is to use short (one fact per question), leading, unobjectionable questions.[70]

The *Scoops* case can illustrate this technique. Recall that Blake gave Roberts information about two computers, the PC DeskPro and the PC TravelPro. As Roberts' lawyer, one of your theories is that Blake, who lagged behind the other Business-Aide salespersons in earnings, was more concerned about his commissions than about Roberts's customer needs. You also theorize that Business-Aide's commission structure—9 percent for hardware, 3 percent for software—motivated Blake to sell hardware rather than software. You also suspect that Blake's desire for the larger commission for hardware led him to encourage Roberts to buy the more expensive PC TravelPro rather than the less expensive PC DeskPro. Because Roberts bought the more expensive laptop and because she had a limited budget, she wound up buying The Bottom Line accounting software, which was less expensive but not suitable for her needs.

Assume that earlier in the deposition you established Business-Aide's compensation scheme, its commission structure, and Blake's recent commission record. A leading examination of Blake in search of an admission that he had a financial interest in what Roberts purchased might look like this:

Q. You told Ms. Roberts that the computer was the key purchase and that it must be able to handle her needs as her business grew, is that correct?

A. Yes.

Q. You told her that she needed a machine with the features of the PC TravelPro, is that correct?

A. Yes.

Q. You told her that a laptop would be more convenient, is that correct?

A. Yes.

Q. You told her that having a laptop was like having two computers for little more than the price of one, is that correct?

A. Yes.

Q. You told her that the price of the PC TravelPro was $2,345, is that correct?

A. Yes.

Q. You told her that the price of the PC DeskPro was $995, is that correct?

A. Yes.

Q. You did not tell her that your commission on a hardware sale was 9 percent, is that correct?

A. No. I did not.

Q. You did not tell her that if she bought the more expensive PC TravelPro, you would earn more in commission than if she bought the less expensive PC DeskPro, is that correct?

A. No. I did not.

These admissions will not win the case. But they do support your theory about Blake's motivations and actions.

Impeachment

Most lawyers think of impeachment as something that happens at trial. Sometimes, however, you want to impeach a witness at a deposition. Whether—and when—to do this depends on several factors, such as:

- The likelihood that the deposition will encourage settlement (if not, you may want to save the impeachment for trial);
- The likelihood that the case will be tried (again, if so, you may want to save the impeachment for trial);
- The value of testing how the witness handles cross-examination;
- The likelihood that the witness can be rehabilitated by the time of trial, or at the deposition by the witness adding an explanation either during your examination or during follow-up examination by the witness's own lawyer (if so, you may not want to educate the witness and you may want to save the impeachment for trial); and
- The danger that premature cross-examination at a deposition will discourage the witness from willingly providing information during the rest of the deposition (if so, you may want to save the impeachment for either late in the deposition or for trial).

Successful impeachment requires the skillful use of leading questions. Recall the examination of Terry Blake in the first chapter:

Q. Let's turn now to your conversation with Ms. Roberts. Am I correct that you told Ms. Roberts shortly after you met her that you loved Scoops ice cream?

NOTE: Establishing that Blake told Roberts he loved Scoops ice cream, even though he had never eaten it, does not prove a material misrepresentation. But it tarnishes Blake's credibility.

A. Well, I don't remember using those exact words.

NOTE: Once again, the lesson for the taker is to listen to the witness. This answer suggests that Blake did, in fact, say something about Scoops ice cream.

Q. Did you say something to that effect, sir?

A. I probably did.

NOTE: You need to decide if the conditional answer by the witness is sufficient. If not, pin the witness down.

Q. In fact, you told her you loved Scoops ice cream, is that correct?

A. Yes.

Q. Had you ever had Scoops ice cream before meeting Ms. Roberts?

NOTE: This question is not leading, but it seeks an answer on which a leading question could be based. As Roberts's lawyer, you might want to wait until trial to pose the follow-up leading question asked below. But if you wait until trial to ask if he had eaten Scoops ice cream before meeting Leslie Roberts and guess wrong, your attack on his credibility will fail. Thus, as suggested above, use the deposition to gather information, whether good or bad.

A. Probably not.

Q. In fact, you never had Scoops ice cream before the meeting with Ms. Roberts, is that correct?

A. No. I had not.

The impeachment is complete. The witness admitted he "lied" to Roberts, although your question never used that term. Now you must decide whether to ask Blake why he said he loved Scoops ice cream. Asking this question may be risky because it gives Blake an opportunity to try to explain away his "lie."[71] (And he is likely to offer the explanation he and his lawyer worked out in witness preparation.) Nevertheless, ask the question. The usual rationale for not asking a "why" question after impeachment at trial does not apply at a deposition. Even if Blake's answer hurts your case, it is better to find that out at his deposition rather than at trial. In addition, given the position Blake is in, virtually any excuse he offers will be as troublesome to him as the impeachment. Suppose he tries to justify himself by saying, "I just wanted to make her feel comfortable." Now he has admitted lying to make a customer comfortable.

Suppose, at his deposition, Blake tries to fend off the impeachment by saying, "I do not recall saying I loved Scoops ice cream." For this type of answer, follow the approach described in the earlier discussion of lack of recall. First, as suggested above, clarify

277

what Blake means by "I do not recall." If he says it means he does not recall because he did not say it, you have a credibility dispute, and you may not want to pursue the recall issue. But if Blake waffles, saying something such as, "I do not recall saying it, but I may have," probe his lack of recall. And highlight his waffling with a series of questions such as:

Q. Are you denying you said, "I love Scoops ice cream"?
A. No, I just do not recall.
Q. Are you saying you never even mentioned Scoops ice cream?
A. No, I just do not recall.

Questions like these push a witness as far as possible concerning his recall. If you pursue this line of questioning and the witness still claims a lack of recall, it should be difficult at trial for this witness to "remember" this aspect of the conversation without serious, perhaps insurmountable, credibility problems.

Finally, remember that the order in which subjects are raised can help impeach a witness. Suppose you represent the defendant in a case alleging emotional distress. You suspect that the plaintiff's symptoms are not as serious as claimed and that at her deposition the plaintiff will exaggerate them. (You may even have some basis for this suspicion, such as medical records casting doubt on her case.)

When you start examining the witness about her symptoms, begin with open-ended questions. Make it easy for her to describe every symptom. Once she has, follow up on the nature of each symptom with T-funnel questions that seek to exhaust her recollection on the subject. Then, ask her what treatment she sought for each symptom. If she sought little or no treatment, the jury may infer that the symptom was not real or serious. On the other hand, if she sought extensive treatment, you have not lost anything because you have discovered useful—though admittedly unfavorable—information.[72]

Breaks

Unless a deposition is extremely short, at some point someone— you, the witness, the defender, the court reporter—will want a break.[73] As the taker, break when you feel the need to do so. Breaks give you a chance to rest, refocus your thoughts, organize documents for an upcoming series of questions, and review notes about areas requiring follow-up.[74] When a deposition is being recorded, use breaks to recheck the audio and video quality. If you have an ally—whether a colleague or a client—observing the proceedings, a break is a good time to discuss your ally's impressions. Finally, even if you do not need a break, the court reporter may. Giving her frequent breaks helps ensure the accuracy of the transcript.[75]

The witness or defender may also request a break.[76] Sometimes the request is legitimate; sometimes it is strategic, designed to halt a tough line of questioning until the defender can coach the witness. If you suspect that strategy is the motivation behind a break request, insist on completing your line of questioning before the break. (As noted earlier, you should have established this ground rule at the start of the deposition.) Although you can demand that no break be taken until a question or series of questions are answered, as a practical matter you cannot stop the witness and defender from leaving the deposition. If the witness and defender leave the room over your objection, state your objection on the record and make sure the videographer, if using one, keeps recording.

Before the deposition, you should have reviewed the applicable local rules about breaks and conferences. Some jurisdictions prohibit any conferences between a witness and his lawyer once the deposition begins, except to determine whether to assert a privilege.[77] In these jurisdictions, note your objection to the break and conference on the record. After the break, ask the witness if the purpose of the conference was to determine whether to assert a privilege. If not, ask what was discussed. If the witness is a third party, conferences with the defender are never privileged. If such a conference occurs, ask what was said during it.

After a break, takers often ask the witness the following questions:

Q. Do you understand you are still under oath?

NOTE: Though rather formal, the question serves as a good reminder. It probably is more appropriate to use after a lunch break.

Q. Do you wish to add to, or change, any of your prior testimony?

NOTE: Although sometimes asked, this question is dangerous. Even though a witness is free to amend an answer, why offer the witness an opportunity to explain away earlier, damaging testimony?

279

Q. Is there any reason why you cannot continue to give testimony today?

NOTE: If the witness gives some reason why he cannot continue, decide whether to recess until a later date. If you agree to recess the deposition, be sure to get an agreement on the record that it will be reopened.[78] If you continue the deposition in spite of the witness's request for a recess, the witness will have built in an excuse to explain away testimony unfavorable to his side of the case.

Eventually, you will want to end the deposition. Adjourning a deposition is covered briefly in Chapter 14, Defending the Deposition, and more extensively in Chapter 23, The End of the Deposition.

The "Science" of Asking Questions

When deciding what questions to ask a witness, how to word your questions, and in what order to ask them, many takers rely on their "gut." However, there is substantial social science research about questioning techniques, and even the most experienced deposition taker can learn from it.

Type and Sequence of Questions

In one study, researchers showed a two-minute movie to 151 subjects, who were men between the ages of 21 and 64.[79] The movie depicts two college students throwing a football outside a supermarket while a man and woman are leaving the store carrying groceries. The man says he forgot something and goes back to the store. As the woman continues walking, she is struck by a car. Her packages spill onto the ground. She and the driver of the car begin yelling at each other. Then her male companion returns and scuffles with the driver. The college students reappear. The scene ends with one of the college students running toward the supermarket to call the police.

After viewing the film, the subjects were asked to report on what they had seen. Three different types of questions were used:

1. Open or "narrative" questions (also called "free report form"), such as, "Tell us all you can remember."
2. "Controlled-narrative" questions, such as, "Tell me about the traffic and weather conditions."

3. Multiple-choice questions (also called "interrogatory report form"), such as, "Did the incident happen in a vacant lot, in a street, or on a sidewalk?"

In other words, the questions ranged from very open (called narratives in the study) to very narrow (called interrogatories in the study).

Here is what the researchers found: Narrative reports from those asked open-ended questions were the most accurate but the least complete. Reports from those asked controlled-narrative questions were less accurate than the narratives, but more complete. And responses based on interrogatories also were less accurate than the narratives, but more complete than the narrative or controlled-narrative responses. Other studies have yielded similar results.[80]

There is an important lesson here for deposition takers. If you are more interested in accurate answers than complete ones, ask broad, open-ended questions. If completeness is more important than accuracy, ask narrow or specific questions. Often, of course, you want both accuracy and completeness. Obviously, that means you should ask both broad and narrow questions. Does the order of the questions matter? Yes, it does. To maximize accuracy and completeness, allow a witness to first report freely (or in a controlled-narrative fashion). Then ask specific questions aimed at broadening the scope of the witness's report.

Reversing this process can produce inaccuracies. To understand why, assume that you are deposing Blake and that you are interested in learning what, if anything, he said to Roberts about the advantages of a laptop. Now consider two different scenarios.

In the first, you start with a general question: "Tell me everything you said at the meeting about laptops." Blake's answer includes nothing about the portability of a laptop. So you then ask a narrow question: "At the meeting, did you explain to Ms. Roberts how the portability of the PC TravelPro was an advantage?" This narrow question may cause Blake to remember whether he said anything about that subject, even though he did not mention this detail in his earlier response to your general, open-ended question.

In the second scenario, you begin with the narrow question about portability. Blake will probably answer "no," if he did not already mention portability. But later, when asked in an open-ended question to tell everything that he remembers he said about laptops at the meeting, Blake might think to himself, "Gee, I remember something about their portability. I guess I must have discussed it with Leslie Roberts." In other words, information included in a specific question can become part of a witness's memory when he is subsequently asked a general question—even when the information is wrong.

To recap: First, the form of a question can affect a witness's answer. General questions usually produce more accurate but less complete answers; narrow questions usually produce more complete but less accurate answers. Second, the way in which questions are sequenced is important. For both accuracy and completeness, begin with general questions that allow the witness to tell the story in his own words; then move to specific questions that increase the range or coverage of the witness's answers. This, of course, is exactly how the T-funnel questioning technique works.

Wording of Questions

Research has established that the wording of a question can also influence a respondent's answer. In one study,[81] for example, subjects were asked one of two questions about the height of a certain basketball player: "How tall is he?" or "How short is he?" Subjects who were asked the first question guessed the player's height at 79 inches; those asked the second question guessed it at 69 inches. Why the difference? The first question presupposed nothing about the player's height, but used the word "tall." By using the word "short," the second one presupposed that the player was short. The words used affected the answers to both questions.

In another study,[82] subjects participated in market research about certain headache products. Some were asked, "How many products have you tried other than the one in question? 1? 2? 3?" Other subjects were asked the same question except with the numbers 1, 5, and 10. The first subject group claimed to have tried an average of 3.3 other products; the second group claimed an average of 5.2 other products. Obviously, the numbers used in the questions affected the respondents' recollection of how many times an event (trying a product) had occurred.

The wording of a question can also affect an individual's recollection about whether an event even happened. Consider the study in which 100 subjects were shown a short film depicting a multiple-car accident.[83] After viewing the film, the subjects completed a questionnaire. Three of the questions asked about items that appeared in the film, while three others asked about items that did not. For half the subjects, the questions began with the words, "Did you see *a . . . ,"* as in, "Did you see a broken headlight?" For the rest of the subjects, the questions began with the words, "Did you see *the . . . ,"* as in, "Did you see the broken headlight?" Thus, the two questions differed only in the form of the article—"the" or "a."

The answers—"yes," "no," or "I do not know"—were tabulated. Subjects asked questions with "the" were much more likely to report seeing items that did not appear in the film. Subjects asked questions with "a" on the other hand, were more likely to respond, "I do not know" when asked about items that appeared in the film and items that did not. In addition, subjects with "a" questions responded, "I do not know" two to three times more often than subjects with "the" questions.

The results should make sense. A speaker uses "the" when he assumes that the referenced object exists and may be familiar to the listener. Thus, a lawyer who asks a witness at a deposition, "Did you see *the* broken headlight?" in effect says to the witness, "There was a broken headlight. Did you happen to see it?" The assumption built into this question will influence the answers of some witnesses. In contrast, the question, "Did you see *a* broken headlight?" includes no such assumption.

In addition to affecting memory, a questioner's choice of words can affect quantitative judgment. Take the study in which forty-five subjects were shown films of various automobile accidents.[84] Some were asked, "About how fast were the cars going when they *hit* each other?" Others were asked the same question, except that instead of the verb "hit," the researchers used "smashed," "collided," "bumped," or "contacted." Although all these verbs refer to the coming together of two objects, they have different connotations concerning speed and force of impact. Not surprisingly, they elicited different judgments about speed. Subjects who were asked the "smashed" question gave the highest speed estimates (40.8 mph). Those asked the "collided," "bumped," and "hit" questions gave progressively lower estimates (39.3 mph, 38.1 mph, and 34.0 mph, respectively). And those who were asked the "contacted" question gave the lowest estimate (30.8 mph).

In sum, researchers have established that a question's wording can influence the response. This phenomenon has been documented in a variety of contexts, such as when a person reports his own experiences, describes events recently witnessed, or answers a general question ("How short was the movie?") not tied to a specific incident.

For deposition takers, the lesson is obvious: Words count—even the article prefacing a word. Therefore, be careful when asking a question. Changing even a single word can significantly affect the answer.

Nonverbal Communication

That people communicate with more than words seems self-evident. Yet, when taking a deposition, many lawyers focus on a witness's words and largely ignore both their own and the witness's nonverbal signals. A big mistake. For at least the following five reasons, both your and the witness's nonverbal communication warrant close attention:

1. Nonverbal communication can be a highly reliable source of information because nonverbal signals are most often created at an unconscious, involuntary level.[85] Consequently, even skilled actors have trouble controlling or manipulating their nonverbal signals.[86]
2. Nonverbal signals can help you assess a witness's credibility.
3. Nonverbal signals can help you gauge the effect of your questions on the witness.
4. Your assessment of a witness's nonverbal signals can help you decide whether to probe further with questions or rephrase earlier ones.
5. Your nonverbal communication can be used to encourage a witness to answer your questions.

Nonverbal communication takes different forms. The purpose of this section is to identify some of the more common forms, discuss how to interpret nonverbal communication, and suggest ways to use this type of communication to your advantage. A caveat: Interpreting nonverbal communication can be difficult. For example, some witnesses try to use it to deliberately mislead a taker. Because of such problems, this section concludes with suggestions on how to check the accuracy of your interpretation, including the effect on the witness of your own nonverbal signals.

Nonverbal Communication in General

The term "nonverbal communication" describes anything that conveys information without words.[87] Gestures, facial expressions, body movements (kinesiology), spatial positioning, clothing, voice characteristics, and even body odor—all are forms of nonverbal communication.[88]

The study of nonverbal communication is still developing. Yet no one disputes the central role that nonverbal communication plays in exchanging information and in establishing rapport between humans.[89] As they do with words, people use nonverbal signals to influence others and to acknowledge attempts by others to influence them.[90] Indeed, some researchers have identified situations in which 55 percent of a spoken message's meaning depended on facial expression, 38 percent depended on tone of voice, and only 7 percent depended on verbal communication.[91]

The power of nonverbal communication was dramatically demonstrated by audience reaction to the first televised presidential debates in 1960, between John F. Kennedy and Richard M. Nixon. Those who heard the debates on the radio thought Nixon won; those who watched them on television thought Kennedy won.[92]

At times, nonverbal signals reiterate or reinforce a spoken message. A classic case: A baseball umpire yells "Out!" and simultaneously jerks his thumb skyward.[93] Often, nonverbal signals supplement the spoken word. But sometimes they can contradict the spoken message. Take the statement, "I really loved that speech." On their face, these are words of appreciation. Delivered with a grimace and eyes rolling upward, they become words of sarcasm.

The increasing use of video at depositions proves that many lawyers understand the importance of nonverbal communication.[94] They realize that a stenographic transcript may not convey the full scope of a witness's deposition testimony. A video recording of a deposition also allows you the luxury of reviewing a witness's nonverbal communication after the deposition Whether or not the deposition is on video, start studying the witness's nonverbal signals as soon as the deposition begins. Properly interpreted, these signals can make you a more effective examiner.

Facial Expressions

Facial expressions are probably the most frequently used channel for nonverbal communication.[95]

Although we have only a handful of words to describe different facial behaviors (smile, frown, wink, furrow, squint, etc.), our facial muscles are sufficiently complex to allow more than a thousand different facial appearances. In addition, the action of these muscles is so rapid that all the variations could be shown in less than a few hours' time.[96]

Facial expressions are more easily read than other forms of nonverbal communication. As early as 1872, Charles Darwin theorized that all humans, regardless of culture, share the same basic, innate facial expressions.[97] Darwin's theory has never been completely confirmed. Yet many sociologists believe that facial expressions are largely universal, and that only the frequency of these expressions is affected by nationality, ethnicity, and culture.[98] Consequently, these factors are usually not that important when interpreting facial expressions. It also is well established that even persons not trained to read facial expression can do so with a fair degree of accuracy.[99]

Facial expressions may be easy to read; they are also easy to manipulate. Many people can maintain a "poker face" in a variety of settings, including a deposition. Thus, a deponent whose face registers no surprise at a question may indeed be surprised. The lesson is obvious: When interpreting a deponent's facial expressions, be careful. Assume that some facial expressions will be manipulated.

Despite this problem, facial expressions are too valuable a source of information to be ignored. As you question a witness, study the deponent's face. Obviously, you cannot do this effectively if you keep your head buried to take notes, review your outline, look at the next document you intend to mark, or read a realtime transcript.[100] Therefore, come to every deposition so well prepared that you can give the deponent your full attention.

Gestures and Body Movements

Gestures and body movements contain a broad spectrum of expressive purpose and meaning. Some body movements, referred to as "emblems," communicate a specific message that can be readily translated.[101] One example is an "OK" sign, with thumb and forefinger together and the other three fingers extended (signifying acceptance in American culture); it has meaning even when unaccompanied by any words. (Note that the sign would not appear on a deposition transcript unless the taker states on the record that the witness made the "OK" sign or the deposition is recorded on video.) Other body movements, referred to as "adaptors," have no specific communicative purpose but can reflect an individual's inner thoughts or emotions.[102] Picking at one's face, bouncing one's leg, leaning back in a chair—all are adaptors.

Most people are not very conscious of their body movements, at least at the adaptor end of the spectrum.[103] According to Robert Harper, a frequent writer on the subject of nonverbal communication, the largely unconscious nature of these movements makes them harder to manipulate than verbal or facial expressions:

> Information that we may withhold verbally and fail to display in our facial expressions may be "leaked" through movements of our hands, legs, feet, and so forth, which are less under our conscious control and more likely to reflect our emotional state at the moment.[104]

Given this "nonverbal leakage," properly read body movements can offer a reliable window into a deponent's thoughts and emotions. At a minimum, they help you assess credibility.

The study of body movements has developed into its own unique discipline.[105] Although there is no agreement on the meanings of some movements, other gestures and mannerisms are so common that they usually can be interpreted with reasonable accuracy. Some examples:[106]

- *Wringing hands*: This shows anxiety or frustration. Tightly gripping the arms of a chair sends the same message.
- *Leaning back in chair with hands on back of head*: This movement is usually a sign of confidence or contentment.
- *Hands touching face or playing with glasses*: This indicates contemplation or thoughtfulness. (Compare this with picking at one's face, which can be a form of self-attack.)
- *Placing palm of right hand over heart*: People often do this when trying to convey sincerity or truthfulness.
- *Open or uplifted hands*: This is another common sign of sincerity or openness.
- *Covering and rubbing one's eyes*: This movement often signifies that the listener is rejecting or refusing to listen to the speaker.
- *Picking imaginary lint from one's clothing*: This is a sign of disapproval or discomfort.
- *Direct eye contact*: Although eye contact indicates forthrightness, prolonged eye contact or staring is considered an aggressive or combative act.
- *Head nodding*: This often is a sign of agreement. But rapid, repeated head nodding can indicate boredom or a wish for the speaker to get to the point more quickly.

- *Hand over mouth while speaking*: Most people know that lying is wrong. As a result, a lie is often accompanied by a "counter" gesture. One of the most common is a hand placed over the mouth just as the lie is uttered.

As a taker at a deposition, you are usually most interested in nonverbal signals that indicate the witness is lying or skirting the truth. One study found that when people lie, they nod less, gesture less, make fewer leg and foot movements, smile more, and assume more backward lean.[107] This study suggests that you should be wary when a witness prefaces a response by leaning back in his chair and becoming very still.

Also, be aware of your own body language—it can help (or hurt) you. Helpful body language can help you establish rapport, demonstrate interest, and encourage the witness to answer your questions. In one study,[108] participants were asked to judge the level of rapport between two people engaged in a problem-solving exercise. The participants saw the interaction on a video recording (without sound), heard it on audiotape, or read a transcript. Those who watched (without hearing) the interaction were best able to judge the level of rapport.

The lesson for takers: Both your words and, as discussed above, your nonverbal communication make a difference. To establish rapport and reflect an openness to what the witness is saying, try some of the following: smile (when appropriate); open your eyes a bit wider; lean forward (without invading the witness's sense of personal body space); nod (which also gives positive feedback); and assume an open, inviting posture, with arms uncrossed.

Paralanguage[109]

Another form of nonverbal communication is how the witness is speaking; that is, the witness's use of voice, including tone, volume, inflection, and pace (such as pauses). As with other forms of nonverbal behavior, carefully observe the witness's speech pattern. According to one expert on the detection of deception, the most common vocal clues to deception are pauses when a witness answers a question.[110] Pauses that are too long or too short can be caused by a witness's failure to work out his "lie" ahead of time.[111] Another study found that a speaker's pitch went up during deceit.[112]

Lawyers can also learn from sociologists who conduct interviews to support their empirical research. They spend time "watching" the inflection of the speaker (upward to indicate a question; downward to make a declaration), volume (louder for emphasis, softer for discomfort), and so on.[113]

When you are observing a witness's use of voice, be conscious about how you use your own voice. You want to do everything you can to encourage the witness—who has been told by his counsel that you are the enemy—to talk to you. Invite answers using some of the following techniques: an upward inflection when asking your question to indicate you do not have another agenda; a nonthreatening tone to foster rapport; and silence to convey interest in what the witness is saying. Even when you think you know what the witness will say, sound like you really are interested in the answer.

Finally, some practitioners suggest you "mirror" (match) the deponent's nonverbal behavior, including both body movements and voice, to build rapport. For example, if the witness leans forward, you lean forward. But beware: Others believe this technique will be intuitively recognized by a witness as an effort to manipulate and will end up sacrificing rapport. In addition, the effort required to mirror can cause you to lose focus on what a deponent is saying, which is, after all, the most important aspect of a deposition.

Dangers of Interpretation

Interpreting nonverbal communication is more art than science. As Edgar Jones, an experienced arbitrator once noted,

> [a]nyone driven by the necessity of adjudging credibility, who has listened over a number of years to sworn testimony, knows that as much truth must have been uttered by shifty-eyed, perspiring, lip-licking, nail-biting, guilty-looking, ill at ease, fidgety witnesses as have lies issued from calm, collected, imperturbable, urbane, straight-in-the-eye perjurers.[114]

The risks of misinterpretation can be minimized by following three basic steps, explored more fully below. First, consider the context of your interaction with the witness,[115] including the witness's individual traits and cultural background. Second, try to establish a baseline of the individual's behavioral repertoire. Third, test the nonverbal signs against other benchmarks. But, throughout the process, be sensitive to the fact that you may have your own biases. For example, you may distrust someone who does not look you in the eye, even though there may be a perfectly good explanation for that behavior.

Considering the Context and the Individual's Baseline Behavior

The context within which nonverbal communication occurs is affected by individual differences, gender, nationality, ethnicity, and culture.

Individual Differences

Accounting for differences between individuals can be challenging. It helps to keep four points in mind.

First, a body movement may be caused by a physical irritant and therefore lack any significant communicative intent. Suppose the witness keeps leaning back in his chair. You might, as suggested above, interpret this as a sign of deception or growing discomfort with your questions. But this interpretation would be wrong if the witness is leaning back in order to try to relieve a sore back. Similarly, a witness's constant rubbing of her eyes could signify her rejection of your message. But this behavior also could mean the witness has allergies or an irritating contact lens.

Second, certain personality types tend to display the same groupings of nonverbal cues. Friendly, outgoing people, for example, tend to smile often, look frequently at the other party, and lean toward that person.[116] These affiliative types look for opportunities to behave this way, so you would not expect their behavior to be much different at depositions. Likewise, high-strung people who tend to fidget constantly will probably do that at depositions, eliminating fidgeting as a meaningful form of nonverbal communication for them.

Third, some people are sophisticated at controlling or manipulating verbal and nonverbal messages. Consider the expert witness who is deposed frequently. Over time, this individual will become more skilled at giving answers, much in the same way that a lawyer taking depositions will become more skilled at asking questions.

Fourth, the range of nonverbal behavior among individuals differs. Therefore, you will want to develop an understanding of a witness's baseline behavior so that you can recognize deviations from that individual's normal nonverbal behavior (known as "tells" in poker).

Gender

Although the research on gender is inconclusive, it suggests that gender plays a role in nonverbal communication. There is evidence, for instance, that men shift seat positions more often and require more personal space than women.[117]

In addition, the taker's gender is as important to a deposition's context as the deponent's. A female deponent, for example, is likely to send different nonverbal cues to a female examiner than to a male examiner.[118]

Cultural Background

Facial expressions, as noted above, cut across cultural lines.[119] In contrast, body movements are heavily influenced by culture. Indeed, studies have confirmed the stereotype that Italians rely on demonstrative gestures far more than the "reserved" British.[120] In addition, the meaning of a gesture can change radically depending on cultural context. When used in Japan, the American "OK" sign, mentioned above, means "money." In Arab countries, the same gesture is usually accompanied with the baring of teeth and conveys extreme hostility.[121]

Testing Nonverbal Cues

As a taker, you want to test the witness's nonverbal communications in much the same way that you test the witness's words.

First, check the nonverbal signals for consistency with the verbal message. One way to do this is by asking the same question in more than one way or repeating it at different points during the deposition.

Second, evaluate the nonverbal communication in light of what you know about the witness. The more exposure you have to a witness, the better your understanding of the witness's baseline, which includes background, personality, and mannerisms. Toward the end of a long day, your interpretation of a witness's nonverbal communications should be more accurate than when the deposition began.

Third, recognize your own interpretative bias. If you have been conditioned to believe that direct eye contact indicates truthfulness, be aware of your assumptions.

Fourth, never stop probing. Treat ambiguous nonverbal responses as you would ambiguous verbal responses. Follow up with additional questions. Keep digging until you are confident that you can interpret the entire message. Only then should you feel safe in moving on to new subject matter.

291

Finally, recognize how difficult it is to pay close attention to a witness's words—let alone their nonverbal signals. As one frequent contributor in listening skills said:

> Listening is not easy, especially in conflict situations. One reason that listening is so difficult is that talkers are so slow (or perhaps listeners are too fast). Most people can listen at about 450 words per minute, but they can speak only about 175 words per minute. Therefore, listeners have a lot of extra time on their hands (and in their minds) when they are listening—time during which they evaluate what the other person just said, prepare their next response, or wander away in their minds to more interesting places.[122]

Conclusion

A deposition can be like a chess game, with at least three simultaneous players—taker, witness, and defender—each fighting over what the witness will say. As taker, you must make decisions constantly, from the opening words of the deposition to the reluctant "nothing more" at the end. And each decision must be made in light of many variables, including the stage of the lawsuit, the likelihood of settlement, the type of witness, the skills of the defender, and the purpose of the deposition. The suggestions in this chapter should help you make the best choices.

Notes

1. See Chapter 4.
2. See "Administrative Details" in Chapter 12, discussing the logistics relating to the use of documents at a deposition.
3. See "Task 15: Pack a Bag Carefully" in Chapter 4, discussing other supplies to bring to a deposition, and Appendix 3.
4. Edward T. Hall, the well-known writer on nonverbal communication, used the word "proxemics" to describe the way in which people use and relate to space. EDWARD T. HALL, THE HIDDEN DIMENSION (1992).
5. If the deposition is being video recorded, the videographer may have other needs that will affect the arrangement of the room. See "Depositions Made Easy: Noticing Requirements and Recording Logistics" in Chapter 17, discussing the logistics for video recording a deposition, and "Avoiding Distraction" in Chapter 18, discussing the arrangement of the deposition room when realtime transcription is used.

6. *See* HALL, *supra* note 4, at 108–09 (reporting study); GARY BELLOW & BEA MOULTON, THE LAWYERING PROCESS: MATERIALS FOR CLINICAL INSTRUCTION IN ADVOCACY, 175–76 (1978). For the study, observers watched people at a rectangular table in a hospital cafeteria and counted the number of conversations by persons seated in different positions. Whatever the reason, the study suggests that a cross-corner position made people feel more inclined to communicate.

7. See "Reactions by the Taker to the Defender's Tactics" in Chapter 14, discussing ignoring the defender as a strategy for a taker.

8. Some takers have even gone so far as to try to intimidate the witness by positioning themselves between the witness and the door.

9. See "Task 14: Arrange for a Deposition Officer, Court Reporter, Videographer (If Needed), and Room" in Chapter 4. See also "Avoiding Distraction" in Chapter 18, discussing additional logistics when using realtime transcription.

10. See Chapter 24, discussing how the court reporter's transcripts can be prepared to make summarizing, indexing, and searching easier, and Chapter 18.

11. See "Reasons to Have a Stenographic Record of a Video Deposition" in Chapter 17.

12. If the witness, subject to a proper notice, subpoena, or stipulation, does not appear, a record must be made of that fact. You will need to mark the document that set the appearance as an exhibit and then adjourn the deposition. Similarly, if a party noticing the deposition fails to appear or, having served a notice, fails to serve a subpoena on a nonparty deponent who does not attend, a record needs to be made. See "Failure of Noticing Party or Witness to Attend" in Chapter 3, discussing sanctions for failure to appear under FRCP 30(g).

13. *See* MALCOLM GLADWELL, BLINK: THE POWER OF THINKING WITHOUT THINKING 44, 50 (2005) (finding that first impressions are often made instantaneously or in as little as two seconds, and that these "thin slices of experience" can have enormous significance for our personal reactions in most situations).

14. "If the deposition is recorded nonstenographically, the officer must repeat the items in Rule 30(b)(5)(A)(i)–(iii) at the beginning of each unit of the recording medium. . . . At the end of a deposition, the officer must state on the record that the deposition is complete and must set out any stipulations made by the attorneys about custody of the transcript or recording and of the exhibits, or about any other pertinent matters." FED. R. CIV. P. 30(b)(5)(B)–(C).

15. You may want a similar stipulation in lieu of having the officer's statement repeated before each segment of a video deposition. *See also* *supra* note 14.

16. See the discussion later in this chapter concerning foundational questions of the witness that set the ground rules for the deposition process.

17. It is prudent to check the local rules, standing orders, and custom to determine whether you need any stipulations beyond the FRCP.

18. One danger of not specifying any stipulations you have reached is that a court reporter may assume unilaterally that certain stipulations will be used. If this happens, when you receive the transcript, you will find that it contains those stipulations the reporter assumed. Although reporters lack the authority to do this, some continue to do so—especially in jurisdictions with common stipulations. Also, note that some stipulations discussed in the text could be made at the conclusion of the deposition. See Chapter 23.

19. See "Task 15: Pack a Bag Carefully" in Chapter 4, suggesting you bring the text of any proposed stipulations to the deposition.

20. See "Defining the Examination's Scope and Anticipating Objections" in Chapter 3, discussing objection to the notice.

21. See *infra* "Opening Remarks and Stipulations," discussing a motion under FRCP 32(a)(4)(E).

22. See *infra* text accompanying notes 48–51 (discussing marking a notice or subpoena when documents have been requested to be produced at the deposition).

23. See also "Adjournment" in Chapter 14, discussing considerations for the defender in adjourning the deposition.

24. See "Adjournment" in Chapter 14, discussing the same suggestion from the defender's perspective.

25. The importance of having an accurate transcript is increased when technical terms are used, so you may need to hire a reporter with special expertise. See "Task 15: Pack a Bag Carefully" in Chapter 4, discussing the suggestion of providing a glossary to the court reporter.

26. See "Making Objections" in Chapter 14 and Chapter 16, discussing objections.

27. See "If You Decide to Object" in Chapter 14, discussing limitations on how objections may be stated and related strategic considerations.

28. See "Making Objections" in Chapter 14 and "Speaking Objections and 'Clarifying' Objectives" in Chapter 15, discussing speaking and coaching objections as well as limitations on defenders.

29. *See, e.g.*, D. MD. DISCOVERY GUIDELINES, guideline 5(b) ("Objections should be stated as simply, concisely and non-argumentatively as possible to avoid coaching or making suggestions to the deponent."); M.D.N.C. L.R. 30.1(2) ("Counsels' statements when making objections should be succinct, stating the basis of the objection and nothing more.") For further examples of local rules, see note 69 in Chapter 14.

30. See "Objections That Must Be Made at the Deposition or They Are Waived" in Chapter 14, discussing the form in which to state an objection. In addition, if the reason for making the objection does not have to be stated, any and all grounds may be preserved.

31. See "What Happens After an Instruction?" in Chapter 14 and "Improper Instructions Not to Answer" in Chapter 15, discussing the taker's options after an instruction not to answer.

32. See "Reviewing and Correcting the Transcript" in Chapter 23, discussing the pros and cons of reading, correcting, and signing a transcript.

33. *Id.*; see also "Using Depositions to Contradict or Impeach the Trial Testimony of a Witness" in Chapter 25, discussing how to impeach a witness who has read, possibly corrected, and signed a transcript.

34. FED. R. CIV. P. 5(d)(1).

35. See "Final Matters" in Chapter 23, discussing the handling of exhibits at the end of a deposition.

36. See "Using Depositions to Contradict or Impeach the Trial Testimony of a Witness" in Chapter 25, discussing the use of foundational questions from a deposition when impeaching a witness with prior inconsistent deposition testimony.

37. The rule previously allowed only a *party* to instruct a deponent not to answer. FRCP 30(c)(2), as amended, now provides that "[a] person may instruct a deponent not to answer." The 2000 Advisory Committee's note to FRCP 30, however, states that "[t]he amendment is not intended to confer new authority on nonparties to instruct witnesses to refuse to answer deposition questions." See also "Instructing a Witness Not to Answer" in Chapter 14.

38. See *infra* "Questions About Witness Preparation," for model questions about this subject.

39. *See* FED. R. CIV. P. 30(d)(3)(A).

40. In addition, foundational questions can use up valuable time in a deposition limited to one day of seven hours, as mandated by FRCP 30(d)(1).

41. See the section of this chapter entitled "Breaks," discussing the use of breaks as a defense tactic.

42. See "Surprise! You're on Candid Camera: Video Depositions Can Demand Different Techniques by Both the Examiner and Defender" in Chapter 17, discussing the taker's natural position of control.

43. See *infra* "Witness's Lack of Recall," discussing additional techniques for dealing with a witness's lack of recall.

44. See "Objections That Must Be Made at the Deposition or They Are Waived" in Chapter 14 and "Speaking Objections and 'Clarifying' Objections" in Chapter 15, discussing why these questions are not objectionable.

45. See "Preparing a Nonparty Witness for Deposition" in Chapter 10.

46. See "Requests for Documents" in Chapter 3.

47. See *infra* note 73 (the time spent reviewing documents at a deposition counts against the seven-hour limitation).

48. As a fallback position, you could seek the production on the morning of the deposition but before the time for questioning.

49. See "Administrative Details" in Chapter 12, discussing how to mark a document.

50. Questions to ask about the storage of electronically stored information are beyond the scope of this book. But see "Asking About a Document's Creation, Dissemination, and Accuracy" in Chapter 12.

51. See "Reopening the Deposition" in Chapter 23.

52. A written objection is required by FRCP 34 as incorporated into FRCP 30(b)(6).

53. FRCP 26(b)(5)(A) requires the party withholding documents to make its claim expressly and "describe the nature of the documents . . . not produced . . . in a manner that, without revealing information itself privileged or protected, will enable other parties to assess the claim."

54. See Chapter 6 and Chapter 9, discussing the nature of the work-product protection.

55. See FED. R. CIV. P. 26(b)(5)(B) (commonly known as the "claw-back" provision). The procedures for dealing with such materials is beyond the scope of this book.

56. *See also* Arthur H. Aufses, III, *Documents and Depositions: The Basics,* in THE LITIGATION MANUAL: DEPOSITIONS 7–8 (Priscilla Anne Schwab & Lawrence J. Vilardo eds., 2006) (suggesting additional questions about search and production of documents pursuant to FRCP 30(b)(5) notice to a party or FRCP 45 subpoena to a nonparty).

57. See *supra* Stipulation 11, concerning the custody of original documents at the end of a deposition.

58. See Chapter 2.

59. See Appendix 6.

60. *See* Michael Owen Miller, *Working with Memory, in* THE LITIGATION MANUAL: TRIAL 345 (John G. Koeltl & John Kiernan eds., 3d ed. 1999) (discussing acquisition, retention, and retrieval of memory).

61. See "Task 10: Outline the Anticipated Questions" in Chapter 4, discussing use of an outline for questioning and a system for note taking. See also "Interactivity with the Transcript—Quick Marks" in Chapter 18, discussing the use of realtime transcription as an aid to note taking.

62. A document used to refresh a witness's recollection does not have to be marked as an exhibit to the deposition, but most takers and defenders prefer a clear record about what has been reviewed by the witness. See "Using a Document to Refresh Recollection" in Chapter 12.

63. *See* David A. Binder et al., Lawyers as Counselors: A Client-Centered Approach 167–68 (2004) (discussing use of T-funnel technique in client interviewing).

64. See Chapter 24, discussing the use of realtime stenographic reporting and the use of computers by lawyers at depositions as an aid to note taking. See also Chapter 18, discussing the software available for realtime deposition transcription and annotation.

65. See "Reasons Not to Take a Deposition" in Chapter 2.

66. See "Twenty Guidelines for Deposition Testimony" in Chapter 7, discussing the defender's preparation of a witness to deal with a taker's use of silence.

67. When asking who or what might help the witness remember, avoid the lawyer-like phrase "refresh your recollection." Both the witness at the deposition and a jury hearing the question read back at trial will find your question of whether anything could "help the witness remember" far more friendly then asking "whether something could refresh the witness's recollection."

68. See "Obtaining Documents for Use at a Deposition" in Chapter 12 and "Continuing the Deposition for Specific Purposes" in Chapter 23.

69. See also "Twenty Guidelines for Deposition Testimony" in Chapter 7, discussing questions on witness preparation.

70. *See, e.g.*, William Alsup, *Getting the Truth from Adverse Witnesses*, 32 Litigation 17 (2006) (reviewing twelve questioning techniques).

71. See "Using Depositions to Contradict or Impeach the Trial Testimony of a Witness" in Chapter 25.

72. As an alternative, you may want to ask first about the treatment and then ask about the symptoms. If there was little treatment, the order of the questioning may compel the witness to limit what she says about the extent of her symptoms. Although this examination will not end the claim, it can make a difference.

73. Fed. R. Civ. P. 30(d)(1) advisory committee's note, 2000 Amendment ("This [seven-hour] limitation contemplates that there will be reasonable breaks during the day for lunch and other reasons, and that the only time to be counted is the time occupied by the actual deposition."). *See also* Fed. R. Civ. P. 30(d)(1) ("The court must allow additional time consistent with Rule 26(b)(2) if needed to fairly examine the deponent, or if the deponent, another person, or any other circumstance impedes or delays the examination.").

74. See Chapter 18, discussing the use of realtime transcription as an aid in reviewing testimony.

75. See also *supra* "Additional Subjects, Including Breaks."

76. See also "Strategies for Dealing with Conferences" in Chapter 15 and "Taking Care of the Preliminaries" in Chapter 14, discussing breaks from the perspective of the defender.

77. *See, e.g., Hall v. Clifton Precision,* 150 F.R.D. 525, 527, 531 (E.D. Pa. 1993) (collecting cases); *Aiello v. City of Wilmington,* 623 F.2d 845, 858–59 (3d Cir. 1980); *Standing Orders of the Court on Effective Discovery in Civil Cases,* 102 F.R.D. 339, 351 (E.D.N.Y. 1984) (prohibiting a defendant lawyer from "initiat[ing] a private conference with the deponent during the actual taking of a deposition except for the purpose of determining whether a privilege should be asserted"). See also "Explaining the Deposition Process" in Chapter 7 and "Lawyer/Witness Conferences" in Chapter 15.

78. See "Continuing the Deposition for Specific Purposes" in Chapter 23.

79. *See* ELIZABETH F. LOFTUS, EYEWITNESS TESTIMONY 90–94 (1996). Loftus's book reports several studies concerning questioning techniques; source citations in this chapter are to her book and not to the original studies.

80. In one such study, 151 subjects watched a film in which a man is shot and robbed in a park. With a narrative form, the test subjects were 91 percent accurate in the details, but with the interrogatory form, their accuracy score was only 56 percent. *Id.* at 92.

81. *Id.* at 94–97.

82. *Id.* at 94.

83. Elizabeth F. Loftus and Guido Zanni, *Eyewitness Testimony: The Influence of the Wording of a Question,* 5 BULL. PYSCHONOMIC SOC'Y 86–88 (1975), reported in LOFTUS, *supra* note 79, at 95.

84. Elizabeth F. Loftus and John C. Palmer, *Reconstruction of Automobile Destruction: An Example of the Interaction Between Language and Memory,* 13 J. VERBAL LEARNING & VERBAL BEHAV. 585–89 (1974), reported in LOFTUS, *supra* note 79, at 96.

85. ROBERT G. HARPER ET AL., NONVERBAL COMMUNICATION: THE STATE OF THE ART x–xi (1978) ("Information that we may withhold verbally and fail to display in our facial expressions *may be* "leaked" through movements of our *hands, legs, feet, and so forth, which are less under our conscious control* and more likely to reflect our emotional state of mind.") (emphasis added).

86. CHARLES B. CRAVER, EFFECTIVE LEGAL NEGOTIATION AND SETTLEMENT 48 (5th ed., 2005).

87. JOHN M. WIEMANN & RANDALL P. HARRISON, NONVERBAL INTERACTION 9 (1983).

88. *See, e.g.,* HARPER ET AL., *supra* note 85, at 304 (listing some of the forms of nonverbal communication).

89. *See id.* at viii; CRAVER, *supra* note 86, at 33; WIEMANN & HARRISON, *supra* note 87, at 9.

90. WIEMANN & HARRISON, *supra* note 87, at 9.

91. *See, e.g.,* Howard S. Friedman, *The Modification of Word Meaning by Nonverbal Cues,* in NONVERBAL COMM. TODAY 62 (Mary Ritchie Key ed., 1982) (after study in which subjects listened to neutral word

"maybe" combined with varying facial expressions and tones of voice, researcher concluded that perceived message depended 55 percent on facial expression, 38 percent on tone of voice, and 7 percent on verbal communication).

92. Sidney Kraus, *Winners of the First 1960 Televised Presidential Debate Between Kennedy and Nixon*, 46 J. COMM. 78, 80 (1996) ("[R]esearch showed that Mr. Kennedy was routed by Mr. Nixon on radio. In answer to the question who won the debates, 48.7% of the radio audience named Mr. Nixon and only 21% picked Mr. Kennedy. Among those who watched the debates on [TV], 30.2% named Mr. Kennedy the winner and 28.6% picked Mr. Nixon.").

93. HARPER ET AL., *supra* note 85, at 7.

94. See "Virtues of Using Video Pretrial" in Chapter 17.

95. HARPER ET AL., *supra* note 85, at 77.

96. PAUL EKMAN, TELLING LIES: CLUES TO DECEIT IN THE MARKETPLACE, POLITICS, AND MARRIAGE (4th ed. 2009); PAUL EKMAN, EMOTIONS REVEALED (2003).

97. CHARLES DARWIN, THE EXPRESSION OF THE EMOTIONS IN MAN AND ANIMALS (1872).

98. *See, e.g.*, HARPER ET AL., *supra* note 85, at 98–99 (cataloging researchers in support of Darwin's thesis).

99. HARPER ET AL., *supra* note 85, at ix.; CRAVER, *supra* note 86, at 49 (noting that persons who are not sensitive to nonverbal stimuli can easily enhance their ability to read these stimuli.)

100. See "Benefits for the Taker" in Chapter 18, discussing techniques to avoid this pitfall when using realtime transcription.

101. HARPER ET AL., *supra* note 85, at x; *see* Paul Ekman & Wallace Friesen, *The Repertoire of Nonverbal Behavior: Categories, Origins, Usage, and Coding*, in FROM SYNTAX TO COGNITION, FROM PHONOLOGY TO TEXT 833 (Mouton de Gruyter ed., 2002).

102. HARPER ET AL., *supra* note 85, at x; *see* Ekman & Friesen, *supra* note 101, at 854.

103. HARPER ET AL., *supra* note 85, at 132–33.

104. HARPER ET AL., *supra* note 85, at x–xi.

105. The study of body movements (kinesiology) was not officially recognized until its founder, Dr. George Goodheart, was able to make it a distinct discipline apart from chiropractics in 1963. Ass'n of Systematic Kinesiology, History of Kinesiology, http://www.systematic -kinesiology.co.uk/history-of-kinesiology.htm (last visited Mar. 26, 2009).

106. *See generally* CRAVER, supra note 86, at 51–66. (This section details common forms of nonverbal communication, both conscious and unconscious.)

107. HARPER ET AL., *supra* note 85, at 155.

108. Jon E. Grahe & Frank J. Bernierre, *The Importance of Nonverbal Cues in Judging Rapport*, 23 J. NONVERBAL BEHAV. 253 (1999), *reported in*

Charlotte Wortz, *Effective Communication with Deposition Witnesses*, 36 TRIAL 70, 73 (2000).

109.   Paralinguistics, in its current research tradition, began in the late 1950s, and the term 'paralanguage' was first introduced by A.A. Hill in 1958. WINFRIED NOTH, HANDBOOK OF SEMIOTICS 249 (1984); see also A.A. HILL, INTRODUCTION TO LINGUISTIC STRUCTURES 408 (1958). Paralinguistics refers to the study of paralanguage, which is defined as the "optional vocal effects (such as tone of voice) that accompany or modify the phonemes of an utterance and that may communicate meaning." Paralanguage, MERRIAM-WEBSTER DICTIONARY (2009), *available at* http://www .merriam-webster.com/dictionary/paralanguage.

110.   EKMAN, TELLING LIES, *supra* note 96, at 92.

111.   *Id.*

112.   Paul Eckman, Wallace V. Friesen & Klaus Scherer, *Body Movement and Voice Pitch in Deceptive Interaction*, 1976 SEMIOTICA 16, 23–27, *reported in* EKMAN, *supra* note 96.

113.   Interview with Kristen Luker, Elizabeth Josselyn Boalt Professor of Law and Professor of Sociology, Univ. of Cal., Berkeley, Sch. of Law (Mar. 24, 2009). Indeed, sociolinguistic scholars have an elaborate coding scheme to show changes in "normal" speech. *Id.* (coding scheme document available upon request).

114.   Edgar A. Jones, Jr., *Evidentiary Concepts in Labor Arbitration: Some Modern Variations on Ancient Legal Themes*, 13 UCLA L. REV. 1241, 1286 (1966).

115.   *See* Friedman, *supra* note 91, at 58 (explaining why the concept that "meaning depends on context" is a truism in psychology).

116.   *See* HARPER ET. AL., *supra* note 85, at 156; HARRY T. EDWARDS & JAMES J. WHITE, PROBLEMS, READINGS, AND MATERIALS ON THE LAWYER AS NEGOTIATOR 158 (1977).

117.   HARPER ET AL., *supra* note 85, at 154, 255–56.

118.   See "How Gender Differences in Verbal and Nonverbal Communication Affect Taking and Defending" in Chapter 16.

119.   See *supra* notes 97–98 and accompanying text.

120.   Adam Kendon, *Gesture and Speech, in* NONVERBAL INTERACTION 32 (Mary Ritchie Key ed., 1982).

121.   HARPER ET AL., *supra* note 85, at 164.

122.   John Barkai, *Teaching Negotiations and ADR: The Savvy Samurai Meets the Devil*, 75 NEB. L. REV. 704, 728 (1996).

CHAPTER 12

Using Documents at a Deposition

Henry L. Hecht

Experienced trial lawyers have a saying about documents: "Witnesses come and go, but documents stay in the jury room." The point, of course, is that documents can be powerful pieces of trial evidence.

Experienced trial lawyers also know that the time to focus on documents is long before trial. For one thing, it may not be possible to have a document admitted into evidence at trial unless it has been handled properly at a deposition. In addition, even if a trial never takes place—and, as noted at the outset of this book, most cases resolve before trial—documents are important. Among other things, they can identify information sources, help in the evaluation of a case, and decide the outcome of a critical pretrial motion.

This chapter examines the issues faced by you as a taker when using documents at a deposition. Those issues include (1) how to prepare to examine a witness about a document, (2) how and when to mark a document as an exhibit during the examination, and (3) how to question a witness effectively about a document. The next chapter examines how and when to lay a foundation for a document's admissibility at trial.

Obtaining Documents for Use at a Deposition

Normally, by the time a deposition is noticed, you have already used the discovery process to collect a number of documents from both parties and nonparties.[1]

But suppose the documents you need for a deposition have not been obtained before the date set for the deposition. In that event, you can use Federal Rule of Civil Procedure (FRCP) 30(b)(2) to require a party witness to produce them at the deposition; for a nonparty, you can use FRCP 45.[2] But, as discussed in Chapter 3, preparing properly for a deposition is difficult when the documents about which you plan to examine the witness are not produced until the deposition begins.[3]

Selecting Documents to Use
(or Not to Use) at a Deposition

As a first step, assemble all potentially relevant documents in your possession. Then decide which ones might either help you prepare for the deposition or be of use to you at the deposition. You probably will be most interested in documents authored or received by the witness, as well as documents referring to the witness.[4] Pleadings and discovery responses, such as answers to interrogatories or requests for admissions, also may be helpful, particularly when the witness signed them.

Next, photocopy the documents you have selected. There are two reasons for this. First, if any documents are originals, you do not want to lose those originals. Second, you want a set of exhibits that you can annotate as you prepare. If there are a relatively small number of copies, put them in a witness folder. Otherwise, the best filing system is usually chronological, though a topical or subject-matter system sometimes works better depending on how you plan to organize your questions.[5]

No matter what kind of filing system you use, keep the originals handy. At some point, review them to make sure that any handwritten notes, including those on the backs of pages, have been copied.[6]

As an alternative to copying the documents, you may want to scan and store them in an electronic file format.[7] But scanned documents are more difficult to search and/or annotate, so assume the electronic versions are primarily for storage. In addition, review each original yourself. Never rely on a summary of the document prepared by another lawyer in your office or by a legal assistant.

Now, decide which of the selected documents you might use at the deposition. In making your decision, focus on your purpose in taking the deposition. For example, if your purpose is discovery, you probably will want to use documents that, when coupled with the witness's answers, will help you understand what happened, provide additional information sources, or corroborate or disprove the witness's testimony. When a document has been prepared by the witness, you want to question the witness about its creation and meaning. When the witness received a document, you want to find out the circumstances surrounding its receipt and the witness's understanding of its contents.

Suppose that your purpose in taking the deposition is primarily evidentiary. In that event, documents used at the deposition should have evidentiary value, such as advancing a claim or a defense either on a motion or at trial. If so, at the deposition, you want to elicit testimony that will allow you to lay a foundation for the document's admissibility for a pretrial motion or at trial.[8] Even when a document has evidentiary value, the deponent-to-be may not be the only—or even the best—witness for laying a foundation. Another witness may be able to lay the foundation with fewer objections from the defender. But before deciding not to depose the first witness, make sure the other witness will be available either for a deposition or at trial.[9]

There are, of course, other reasons for selecting a particular document for use at a deposition—such as impeachment, or refreshing the recollection of a forgetful witness, or showing prior recollection recorded.

As you sift through documents, you usually will find some that are helpful to your understanding of the case but inappropriate for the deposition. One example is a document not relevant to the witness's testimony.[10] And even when a document is relevant, you may not want to use it at the deposition if you fear it will reveal your strategy for questioning another witness.

To illustrate: Suppose that in *Scoops* you represent Defendant Business-Aide and are preparing to depose Plaintiff Leslie Roberts. A key event is the meeting between Roberts and Terry Blake, Business-Aide's salesperson. Before the meeting, Maxine Waller, Business-Aide's owner, had a telephone conversation with Frank Fuller, Roberts's then employee. Fuller took notes on the conversation, and those notes were produced by Roberts's lawyer. (See Fuller's handwritten notes, Exhibit B at the end of Chapter 13).

303

What you do not know, however, is whether after the telephone call, Roberts discussed the notes with Fuller. After deposing Roberts, you next plan to depose Fuller about the notes.

Given these facts, you might not want to question Roberts about Fuller's notes if you fear doing so will telegraph your questioning strategy for an upcoming deposition of Fuller. Therefore, you may decide not to push hard on Roberts's knowledge of Waller's apparent representation—found in Fuller's notes—that Business-Aide was a "specialist for the small business" and would "tailor the plan to [Scoops's] computer needs." On the other hand, you may decide that using Fuller's notes to exhaust Roberts's knowledge of Fuller's telephone conversation with Waller may be more important than any risk in disclosing your questioning strategy.

Another reason for deciding not to question a deposition witness about an otherwise relevant document is if the document's only value is to prove undisputed facts. In *Scoops*, it is not disputed that Roberts purchased hardware and software from Business-Aide. If you depose Roberts, it may not make sense to spend time marking the sales invoice and asking her questions about it in order to prove that the sale took place. You can accomplish this objective by (1) a request for admission or (2) a pretrial stipulation putting the receipt into evidence. And those discovery methods will not eat into the presumptive seven-hour time limit on your deposition.

Yet another reason not to use a document at a deposition: You think the other side is unaware of the document's existence, and you want to keep it under wraps—at least for now. Note, though, that the FRCP makes it difficult to conceal a document's existence. For one thing, FRCP 26 requires parties to provide extensive voluntary disclosures at the beginning of a case, including the existence of documents "the disclosing party has in its possession . . . and may use to support its claim or defenses."[11] In addition, documents produced pursuant to a formal request must be provided to all parties. Finally, if you have a document you intend to use at trial and you fail to disclose it as required by FRCP 26(a)(1), and if the information is not timely supplemented as required by FRCP 26(e)(1), the document is presumptively subject to preclusion under FRCP 37(c)(1).[12]

A final reason for not using a document at a deposition is that it could alert the witness to a problem with her testimony or reveal damaging information about your client. This risk is usually outweighed by the need to obtain the witness's complete testimony at the deposition; otherwise, you face the potentially greater risk of being surprised at trial. In deciding whether to use a document at deposition, consider whether the needed testimony can be obtained with another document that presents less risk.

When to Show a Document to a Witness

Deciding when to first show a document to a witness depends on your purpose in taking the deposition and the document's contents and length.[13] Suppose discovery is your primary objective. Typically, you will want to first exhaust the witness's recollection and then use the document to aid her memory. That way, you test the witness's memory before influencing her with the document. (The same principle applies when you initially question a witness with general questions and then move to narrower, more specific ones.)[14] In addition, by waiting to show the document, there is the potential for impeachment if the witness's testimony is contradicted by the document.

Suppose you are taking Blake's deposition. In response to your initial questions, he testifies that Roberts seemed sophisticated in business matters. You then show him two documents: (1) a memorandum addressed to him from his boss, Waller, that describes Roberts as a woman "who seems to have little experience in managing a business or financial matters" and (2) a letter from Roberts, which Waller attached to her memorandum, in which she describes herself as "knowing almost nothing [about computers]." The two documents contradict Blake's claim that Roberts was sophisticated and undermine his testimony. By using the documents to impeach Blake at his deposition, you may curb later attempts by Blake to overreach.

If your purpose in taking a deposition is evidentiary, you may want to use a different approach. Suppose a document includes language (or characterizations) that you want the witness to adopt. In this situation, you may want to show the witness the document before eliciting any testimony. That way, the document may shape the witness's testimony in the direction most helpful to your case.

Documents can influence testimony because people perceive the written word as more accurate than the all-too-fallible human memory.[15] Consider a memorandum about an event prepared by a witness shortly after that event. Knowing the memorandum was created close to the time of the event, the witness likely will assume it is more reliable than her memory of the event. Furthermore, most witnesses are loath to admit that what they wrote was inaccurate.

Even a document that was received, though not authored, by a witness can have a persuasive hold if the witness did nothing after the document's receipt to contradict its contents.

To understand how the persuasive power of documents can be harnessed at a deposition, assume that you are taking Leslie Roberts's deposition. Roberts took notes when she went to a Chamber of Commerce meeting on the use of computers. (See Leslie Roberts's handwritten notes, Exhibit C at the end of Chapter 13.) The notes have question marks after the word "accrual." You believe the question marks show that Roberts did not know the meaning of the word accrual—at least when she made the notes. If so, she could not have adequately understood her business's need for accounting software or explained those needs to others. (The testimony will be even more powerful if you then establish by other questions that she still did not understand the meaning of accrual accounting two months later when she went to the Business-Aide store to meet with Blake.)

You could start by asking Roberts whether she understood accrual accounting. But a better approach would be to show her the handwritten notes first. Use their persuasive power to compel her to testify that she was confused about the meaning of accrual. (For an example of this questioning pattern, see the section on admissions below.)

The time to decide when to show the witness a document at a deposition is before the deposition. But you may need to rethink that decision depending on how well prepared the witness is—a subject most takers explore early in a deposition.[16] If the witness is well prepared, she probably reviewed the document when preparing for the deposition.[17] In that event, you may want to hold off using the document until later in the deposition, when the effects of preparation may—you hope—have "worn off."

Suppose that you decide you do not want to show a witness a particular document. Nevertheless, the defender may try to preempt your decision. To understand how to handle this situation, assume you are taking Roberts's deposition. You decide to question her about the Chamber of Commerce meeting before showing her the notes she took at that meeting. After you ask your first question about the meeting, the defender interjects, "Why don't you show Ms. Roberts her notes of that meeting that I provided to you, rather than conduct a memory test?"

What should you do? Ignore the defender. Introduce the notes only when you are ready to do so. You do not have to provide them just because the defender asked—maybe even demanded—you do so. If Roberts has been prepared well by the defender, she may be the one asking to see her notes. Again, you do not have to show the notes to her. However, before you withhold them, consider how this decision will affect any rapport with the witness that you have established or want to establish with the witness.

Administrative Details

Exhibit Numbering

Before the deposition, decide what numbering system you want to use for identifying exhibits. Suppose you have a case with one hundred documents, and some will be used with more than one witness. The easiest numbering system is one that marks the documents with numbers sequentially continuing from deposition to deposition, without reference to the deponent.

To understand why sequential numbering is a better system than numbering exhibits within each deposition with the deponent's name plus an exhibit number, consider the following scenario: At Roberts's deposition, a letter from Roberts to Waller is marked as "Roberts's Exhibit 5." Then, at Waller's deposition, the same letter is used. Marking it as "Waller's Exhibit 3" at the second deposition can be confusing. The confusion will be compounded if the same letter is also used at Fuller's and Blake's depositions and given new numbers after the witness's name.

Sequential numbering also has distinct advantages over a letter system. For one thing, using numbers is less complicated than using letters. Because there are only twenty-six available letters, in a document-laden case, you can wind up with numerous documents identifying an exhibit with something like "AAA." That can be confusing. In addition, if the same document is used with more than one witness, it is less confusing to have the same designated number each time the document is used.

When sequential numbering is used, a record must be kept at the end of the deposition of the last number used at the deposition. This is not a problem if the same court reporting agency is used for all depositions. When different agencies are used, however, the transcript from the last deposition may not be ready when the next deposition is taken. For that reason, at the end of each deposition, make yourself a note of the last exhibit number.

As an alternative, some lawyers use a system that marks exhibits "Plaintiff's Exhibit 1" or "Defendant's Exhibit 2," rather marking the exhibit with the witness's name. A problem with this approach is that it can subtly suggest that the contents of a document have been "adopted" by the side whose name is used to identify the document. Similarly, a system using numbers to identify the plaintiff's exhibits and letters to identify the defendant's exhibits can be confusing when the same exhibit is used for witnesses on both sides of the case.

Whatever system you want to use, you will want the other parties to agree to a single system. If there is no agreement you should seek a stipulation about one at the start of the deposition.

Using numbers also makes computer searches for documents easier—an important consideration in a case with numerous documents.[18] A further consideration: if the court permits the numbering system used during discovery to be used at trial, handling exhibits at trial will be easier.

Originals and Copies

You must also decide how many copies of a document to bring to the deposition. Typically, you need three: one to be marked by the court reporter, which is attached to the transcript and shown to the witness (it may be the original);[19] one for opposing counsel (for the reasons explained below);[20] and one (often annotated) that you will use to question the witness.[21] In a multiparty case, be prepared to provide one copy to each party's lawyer. Providing the defender with copies should prevent her from interrupting your examination with, "Where is my copy? I need to see the document before you ask any questions." In addition, providing the defender with a copy should remove any justification for the defender to lean toward the witness and point to parts of the document during your examination, thereby coaching the witness.

Premarking

A final decision is whether to have the reporter premark documents before the deposition begins.[22] Premarking can save time—an important consideration given the presumptive seven-hour time limitation on depositions.[23] With a consecutive numbering system, however, you will have gaps in the exhibit numbers if you decide not to use one or more premarked documents at the deposition. One option, therefore, is to wait to premark documents at various stages of the deposition, such as during a break or lunch, when you are more certain about which documents you will use when questioning the witness.

Sample Examination with a Document

Suppose you are deposing Leslie Roberts. Assume that you already examined her about the Chamber of Commerce meeting she attended two months before purchasing a computer from Business-Aide, but you have not yet shown her any documents related to that meeting. The seminar featured a speaker on the topic of "Computers as Managers." Roberts testified that she attended the meeting to learn how computers might help her manage her business more efficiently. She has also testified that she recalls the speaker discussing a few uses for computers, such as inventory control and check writing, but she recalls nothing else about the content of the meeting. Similarly, she testified that she "cannot specifically" recall the date of the meeting, except that it occurred in September after Labor Day.

At this point, you decide to mark a document that appears to be the handwritten notes Roberts took during the meeting. (See Roberts's handwritten notes, Exhibit C at the end of Chapter 13.) In the sample examination below, assume that you have multiple purposes: discovery, using the document to refresh recollection, and seeking an admission.

Marking a Document[24]

For this example, assume the parties have agreed to use sequential numbering and copies rather than originals.

Q. I would ask the reporter to mark for identification as Exhibit 1 a copy of a single page of handwritten notes with the date 9/14/YR-2 [two years ago] in the upper right-hand corner.[25]

NOTE: Documents are not admitted into, or excluded from, evidence at a deposition; rather, they are marked "for identification."[26] "Marking" refers to the reporter affixing some identification to the document, such as a sticker, stamp, or handwritten notation. The identification may include the name of the deponent, the date that appears on the document, and the designation given the document by the taker (in our example, "Exhibit 1"). The designation should not include anything about the document's contents, as it is the witness— not the taker—testifying under oath about the document. After marking a document, the reporter usually hands the document back to the taker unless asked by the taker to hand it directly to the witness. As an alternative to the question above, the taker could have premarked the exhibit, as suggested above. In that event, he would have said, "During the break, I had the reporter premark a document as Exhibit 1."

Q. Ms. Roberts, I am now handing you what has been marked for identification as Exhibit 1. Counsel, here is a copy for you.

NOTE: As discussed above, providing a copy to the defender may prevent an unwanted interruption. Because the record reflects only what is verbalized and then transcribed by the reporter, state on the record that you are providing the defender with a copy.

Q. Ms. Roberts, please review Exhibit 1 and tell me when you have completed your review.

NOTE: Asking the witness to read a document before answering questions about it prevents the defender from interrupting with a request that the witness be given a chance to read it. It also demonstrates your fairness. In addition, because the witness has just read the document, its language will be fresh in her mind when you ask questions. That can be important if, as discussed above, the document has language helpful to your case.

A. Uh-huh.

NOTE: As discussed in Chapter 11, a clear, unambiguous response is needed. Ask another question to clarify the answer.

Q. Does your response mean that you have completed your review of Exhibit 1?
A. Yes.

NOTE: If the document has multiple pages, you may want to direct the witness's attention to only a portion of the document. Given the presumptive seven-hour time limit on depositions, this may save time. But the witness and defender are not obligated to review only the portion you suggest. The defender may, therefore, remind the witness to read the entire document before answering your questions. If that happens, consider taking a break to give the witness an opportunity to review a lengthy document. After the break, confirm on the record that the witness did so.[27]

Q. Do you recognize Exhibit 1?
A. Yes.
Q. What is Exhibit 1?
A. The document has my handwritten notes taken at the Chamber of Commerce meeting.
Q. In your response, are you referring to Exhibit 1?
A. Yes.

NOTE: When questioning a witness about a document, you want to include an unambiguous reference, whether by number or other appellation, to the exhibit so that the questions and answers stand on their own without reference to other portions of the transcript.[28]

Q. Is all the handwriting on Exhibit 1 yours?
A. Yes.

NOTE: Whether to ask questions to authenticate a document as the first step in trying to lay a foundation for the document's admissibility into evidence is a judgment call. As noted in the next chapter, it is not necessary to lay a foundation at a deposition to question a witness about a document.[29]

Q. Did you take the notes on Exhibit 1 during the Chamber of Commerce seminar?
A. Yes.

NOTE: When taking a deposition, refer to a document consistently by its exhibit number rather than "the notes" or "this document" or the even more general "that." As noted above, you want an unambiguous, understandable record so that questions and answers stand on their own and do not need to be cross-referenced to another part of the transcript. In this example, you might refer to the notes contained in Exhibit 1 as the "notes of September 14, two years ago." (This identification assumes there are no other notes with that date.)

Q. Is Exhibit 1 a true and accurate copy of the notes you made during the September 14th meeting?

A. Yes.

Q. Are you aware of any changes that have been made on Exhibit 1 since you made these notes during the Chamber of Commerce meeting?

A. No.

NOTE: This series of questions should be sufficient to authenticate the document. Depending on the witness and the document, additional questions may be required to lay the foundation for the document's admissibility at trial.[30]

At this point, you may want to ask the witness whether she reviewed the document before the deposition and whether that earlier review refreshed her recollection.[31] If she answers "yes" to both questions, you may want to ask if the document she previously reviewed was an exact copy of the one marked as an exhibit.

Asking About a Document's Creation, Dissemination, and Accuracy[32]

Depending on the document, you may want to ask questions about its creation, dissemination, and accuracy. Such questions can help establish the reliability of the document and prevent a witness from trying to disown it by suggesting it was drafted inaccurately.

Questions for the (Apparent) Author of a Document

Ask the apparent author of a document questions such as the following:

1. When was the document prepared?

NOTE: If the witness does not recall when the document was prepared, follow up with questions about whether there is a regular practice or procedure concerning the preparation of such documents.[33]

2. Why was the document prepared?
3. Who prepared the document?
   a. If the named author did not prepare the document, who did?
   b. Did anyone help the author prepare the document? If so, who?

NOTE: Follow up with questions about whether there is a regular practice or procedure concerning document preparation, including who prepares such documents.

4. How was the document prepared?
   a. How much time was spent in its preparation?
   b. What were the sources of information used?
   c. Were any other documents used in preparing the document?
   d. If so, have those documents been produced? If not, why not? (Follow up with a document production request.)
5. Were there any prior drafts of the document?
   a. How many?
   b. Are there any underlying or related notes?
   c. If so, have those documents been produced? If not, why not? (Follow up with a document production request.)
6. Who reviewed the drafts?
   a. Were any comments made about prior drafts? Were the comments made in writing? Were they made by another means?
   b. Were the comments retained?
   c. If so, have those documents with those comments been produced? If not, why not?
7. Where is the original? If it is not available, why not?
8. To whom was the document sent?

NOTE: Follow up with questions about whether there is a regular practice or procedure for the distribution or routing of such documents.

9. What does the author mean by the words used in the document?

NOTE: Authors can testify as to meaning. As noted below, recipients of a document can only testify as to their interpretation of words used in a document.

Questions for the Recipient of a Document
1. When did the witness receive the document?
2. Was anything attached to the document?
   a. If so, have the attachments been produced? If not, why not? (Follow up with a document production request.)
   b. Is anything missing?

3. Did the witness read the document upon receipt?
   a. If the witness did not read it, when did the witness read it read?
   b. If not, why not?

NOTE: Follow up with questions about whether there is a regular practice or procedure for the distribution or routing of such documents.

4. Did the witness communicate with others after receiving the document?
   a. Did the witness document the communication?
   b. Has the documentation been produced? If not, why not? (Follow up with a document production request.)
5. Did the witness take any action after receiving the document?
   a. Was the action documented?
   b. Has the documentation been produced? If not, why not? (Follow up with a document production request.)
6. Was there a response to the document?
   a. If so, by whom?
   b. Was the response documented?
   c. Has the documentation been produced? If not, why not? (Follow up with a document production request.)
7. Is the document the witness received accurate?
   a. If not, in what way is the document inaccurate?
   b. Did the recipient make any corrections? In what manner?
   c. If the inaccuracies were documented, has the documentation been produced? If not, why not? (Follow up with a document production request.)
   d. Did anyone else find any inaccuracies?
   e. Was the author informed of the inaccuracies?
   f. By whom? In what manner?
   g. If the inaccuracies were documented, has the documentation been produced? If not, why not? (Follow up with a document production request.)
8. How does the witness interpret (understand) words used in the document?

NOTE: Recipients can testify as to their interpretation (understanding) of words used in a document authored by someone else, not to the meaning of the words.

Using a Document to Refresh Recollection

Q. The handwritten date at the top of Exhibit 1 is 9/14, YR-2 [two years ago], is that correct?

A. Yes.

Q. Does reading that date on Exhibit 1 refresh your recollection that the seminar was held on 9/14, two years ago?

NOTE: Recall for this example that Roberts testified she could not "specifically" recall the date of the meeting. This question uses the lawyer-like expression "refresh your recollection." As recommended in Chapter 11, it often is better to use a less formal expression, such as, "Does reading that date help your memory?"[34]

A. Yes.

NOTE: Before the witness can answer this question, many defenders will interject a reminder to the witness not to adopt a document's contents unless the witness has an independent recollection.[35]

Q. Your handwritten notes of September 14th also say at the top, "Chamber of Commerce—Mike Marshall," is that correct?

A. Yes.

Q. Does Exhibit 1 also help you remember that Mike Marshall was the speaker at the Chamber of Commerce meeting?

A. Yes.

Q. The first entry on Exhibit 1 says, "Computers as Managers," is that correct?

A. Yes.

Q. What does the entry "Computers as Managers" on Exhibit 1 mean?

A. The speaker said that computers can serve in a number of ways like on-site managers.

NOTE: The taker would then follow up with the T-funnel questioning technique, discussed in Chapter 11, to exhaust the witness's recollection on this subject. At this point, an aggressive defender might claim that the document "speaks for itself." That objection is not well taken. You are entitled to know what the author of a document meant by her own words. Similarly, when a document has been received by the witness, you are entitled to know the witness's interpretation or understanding

315

of its contents. However, questions about the meaning of a document that a witness has not previously seen (or written or received) call for speculation and are therefore objectionable.[36]

Roberts's notes have a list of topics after the heading "Computers as Managers."[37] A taker could use the list as the framework for a series of discovery questions about what was said at the seminar regarding the use of computers as managers.

Seeking an Admission

Q. I would like you to look at the fourth entry on Exhibit 1 under the heading "Computers as Managers." It says "accrual," is that correct?

A. Yes.

Q. There are two question marks after the word "accrual" on Exhibit 1, is that correct?

A. Yes.

Q. Why did you put the two question marks after the word "accrual" on your notes?

NOTE: Start with an open-ended question to obtain the information needed to set up the desired admission.

A. I did not know what the term "accrual" meant or what the accrual accounting method involved.

NOTE: Now use a leading question to capture the answer you want in a usable "sound bite."

Q. As of the time of this seminar on September 14, two years ago, you did not know what the accrual method of accounting was, is that correct?

A. Yes, that is correct.

Q. From the time the seminar was over until you applied for the bank loan using The Bottom Line accounting software, did you take any steps to find out what the accrual method of accounting was?

A. No.

NOTE: The taker could then follow up with a leading question, as suggested above, to capture the desired answer.

Discovery of Additional Documents During the Deposition

Often, the first time you learn of a document's existence is at the deposition. What should you then do? Consider the following example from the deposition of Leslie Roberts. The topic continues to be her attendance at the Chamber of Commerce meeting, two years ago.

Q. How did you learn about the seminar on computers at the Chamber of Commerce?

A. I received a flier in the mail.

Q. I do not believe that I have been provided with a copy of that flier. Do you still have the flier in your possession?

A. I do not know.

Q. If you had retained the flier, where would it be?

A. If I kept the flier, it would be in a file on my Chamber of Commerce membership.

Q. Where is the file on your membership located?

A. In a file cabinet in the back office of the Scoops ice cream shop.

NOTE: This series of questions creates a record that there would be little burden on the witness or her lawyer to locate and produce the document.

Q. At this time, counsel, I request that you search your client's files and provide a copy of the flier to me. The flier should already have been produced because it is responsive to our prior document request.

DEFENDER: I will take your request under advisement.[38]

NOTE: The defender's all-too-typical response is discussed in Chapter 14.

Q. Counsel, please be aware that I consider this deposition open until I receive the document and have an opportunity to question the witness about its contents.[39]

Finally, to ensure compliance with your request for the document, take these additional steps. First, ask the reporter—on the record—to mark the place in the transcript where the request for the document was made. Second, if you have not already done so, ask the reporter to prepare and attach to the transcript a separate list of all such requests. Finally, note the request in your deposition outline and, after the deposition, send either a letter request or a formal document request to the defender.[40]

As noted at the outset of this chapter, documents can play a key evidentiary role in any litigation. Thus, it is critical that you follow the steps above to locate and effectively use documents at a deposition.

Notes

1. See Chapter 2. Documents can be secured from parties by informal agreement, voluntary exchange after initial disclosures, or a formal document request. From nonparties, they can be secured by informal agreement or a subpoena *duces tecum*, with or without the necessity for testimony by the deponent.

2. See "Requests for Documents" in Chapter 3. Indeed, in some cases, the lawyer may be more interested in securing documents than in securing a witness's testimony.

3. See "Receipt of Documents" in Chapter 11; see also "Reopening the Deposition" in Chapter 23, discussing the discovery of additional documents during the deposition and the possible need to continue or reopen the deposition. In addition, the 2000 Advisory Committee Notes to then-numbered FRCP 30(d)(2) suggest "[i]f the examination reveals that documents have been requested but not produced, that may justify further examination once production has occurred." FED. R. CIV. P. 30 (2000) advisory committee's note.

4. See "Preparing to Take a Deposition" in Chapter 4, discussing the taker's preparation and review of documents.

5. See "Task 8: Develop a Questioning Approach" in Chapter 4 and "Questions About Witness Preparation" in Chapter 11, discussing the advantages and disadvantages of different organization systems for questioning.

6. See "Receipt of Documents" in Chapter 11, discussing the need to inspect originals produced in response to a request for the production of documents.

7. The most common format is as a pdf (portable document format) file, made using Adobe Acrobat.

8. For a discussion about why and how to lay a foundation at a deposition for a document's admissibility, see Chapter 13.

9. Some documents can be authenticated through the use of requests for admission; if so, deposition testimony may not be required for that purpose.

10. *See* FED. R. EVID. 401 (defining "relevant evidence" as "evidence having any tendency to make the existence of any fact that is of consequence to the determination of the action more probable or less probable than it would be without the evidence").

11. FED. R. CIV. P. 26(a)(1)(ii).

12. In addition, a party that fails to disclose required information can face sanctions, attorney's fees, and an adverse instruction to the jury. FED. R. CIV. P. 37(c).

13. This section of the chapter assumes you did send documents to the witness in advance of the deposition. Indeed, the 2000 Advisory

Committee Notes to then-numbered FRCP 30(d)(2) go further. They suggest "in cases in which the witness will be questioned about numerous or lengthy documents, it is often desirable . . . to send copies of the documents to the witness sufficiently in absence of the deposition so that the witness can become familiar with them." FED. R. CIV. P. 30 (2000) advisory committee's note.

14. See "The 'Science' of Asking Questions" in Chapter 11, discussing social-science research on the differing uses of open-ended and narrow questions and their effect on a witness's response.

15. Documents, of course, can also be fallible. During witness preparation, the defender should have discussed the fallibility of any documents likely to be used at the deposition and warned the witness not to adopt the contents of a document if it does not reflect the witness's recollection. See Chapter 7, "7. Do Not Assume That Documents Are Accurate."

16. See "Opening Questions" in Chapter 11, discussing questions about the witness's preparation.

17. See "FRE 612 in Practice" in Chapter 9, discussing inquiries about the use of documents to refresh recollection.

18. See "Using Computers to Index and Search Depositions" in Chapter 24.

19. FED. R. CIV. P. 30(f)(2). Originals may be marked for identification and then copies substituted after each party has an opportunity to inspect and copy the originals. *Id.* "Any party may move for an order that the originals be attached to the deposition pending final disposition of the case." FED. R. CIV. P. 30(f)(2)(B). See also "Opening Remarks and Stipulations" in Chapter 11, discussing suggested stipulations about the custody and retention of original documents marked as exhibits to a deposition.

20. One experienced lawyer has suggested that you notify the other parties if you intend to mark a very lengthy document (for example, a commercial lease agreement) so that they can make their own copies before the deposition and you do not need to make additional copies.

21. See "Task 15: Pack a Bag Carefully" in Chapter 4, discussing supplies to bring to a deposition. One experienced lawyer has suggested stapling your own annotated copy of a document to a folder containing the documents to be used at the deposition in order to reduce the danger of inadvertently handing the annotated copy to the witness or defender.

22. See "Receipt of Documents" in Chapter 11, discussing the marking of documents received at the start of a deposition pursuant to a Rule 30(b)(2) notice or an FRCP 45 subpoena.

23. *See supra* note 13, and accompanying text.

24. See also "Marking a Document" in Appendix 7.

25. Some documents bear identification numbers or marks added either at the time of production or after their receipt for easier reference

and retrieval. This procedure is commonly known as Bates numbering (or Bates stamping). The Bates Automatic Numbering Machine was patented in 1891–93 by the Bates Manufacturing Company of Edison, NJ.

26. See Chapter 13.

27. The 2000 Advisory Committee Notes state: "This [seven-hour] limitation contemplates that there will be reasonable breaks during the day for lunch and other reasons, and that the only time to be counted is the time occupied by the actual deposition." FED. R. CIV. P. 30 (2000) advisory committee's note. Thus, the time spent reading a document during a break would not count against the seven-hour time limitation.

28. See "Type and Sequence of Questions" in Chapter 11, discussing the importance of self-contained questions and answers.

29. In any event, the notes of an adverse party-witness are likely to be an admission and thus will not be hearsay. See "How to Lay a Foundation for the Admissibility (or Inadmissibility) of a Document" in Chapter 13.

30. See Chapter 13.

31. See Chapter 9.

32. *See* Arthur H. Aufses III, *Documents and Depositions: The Basics, in* PRISCILLA A. SCHWAB & LAWRENCE J. VILARDO, THE LITIGATION MANUAL: DEPOSITIONS 3 (2007).The subject of what to ask about the creation, retention (storage), and production of electronically stored information—so called "e-discovery" questions—is beyond the scope of this book. For a detailed guide to the questions to ask an organization's FRCP 30(b)(6) designated witness about the organization's information practices (that is, electronically stored information), see Joan Friedman, *Deposition Questions for the Custodian of Records*, 18 LITIGATION 7 (July 2007).

33. Aufses, *supra* note 32, at 9. Aufses suggests asking a series of questions on the witness's procedures for retention and destruction of documents, to make it difficult for a witness to explain the disappearance of a document.

34. See Chapter 11, note 67, discussing the phrasing of questions used to refresh recollection.

35. See "Twenty Guidelines for Deposition Testimony" in Chapter 7 and "Rule 5: Before Meeting the Witness, Plan Your Strategy for Refreshing Memory, Including the Use of Documents" in Chapter 8, discussing preparing witnesses to answer questions about documents.

36. See "The Question Calls for Speculation" in Chapter 14.

37. See Roberts's handwritten notes, Exhibit C in Chapter 13.

38. See "Defender's Response to Document Requests During a Deposition" in Chapter 14.

39. See "Continuing the Deposition for Specific Purposes" in Chapter 23, discussing keeping the deposition open pending receipt of requested documents.

40. See "Handling Documents at the End of the Deposition" in Chapter 23.

CHAPTER 13

Laying Foundations for Documents at a Deposition

DAVID A. SONENSHEIN

Documents are not admitted into, or excluded from, evidence at a deposition. Thus, no foundation for admissibility is needed to use a document in questioning a witness at a deposition.[1]

So why a chapter about foundations for documents in a book about depositions?[2] Here is why: Although a lawyer is not required to lay a foundation at a deposition, in some situations a lawyer should either do so or establish an opponent's inability to do so. The most common situation is when the witness who can lay the foundation for the document will not be available at trial. Counsel then must lay the foundation for that document; otherwise, the document—like the witness—may be unavailable for use at a later proceeding.

The first two parts of this chapter discuss the reasons why an taker may want to lay a foundation for a document at a deposition. They also discuss the circumstances in which the taker will want to establish a "negative foundation"; that is, demonstrate that a document is inadmissible. The third part of the chapter describes how to lay a foundation (and, by implication, how to decide whether a foundation is not possible), including how to handle the most common documents, at a deposition and trial. Finally, the fourth part provides two examples from the *Scoops* case: one in which the taker wants to lay the foundation for a document's admissibility, and one in which the taker hopes to establish a lack of foundation, thereby precluding future use of the document.

Reasons to Lay a Foundation for a Document at the Deposition

Before a deposition, a taker often suspects—or knows—that the witness will be unavailable for trial.[3] In that situation, the taker may want to offer the witness's deposition testimony at trial in lieu of live testimony.[4] In fact, if an unavailable witness is the best— or only—witness to lay the foundation for the admissibility of a document, a taker who wishes to use that document in a summary judgment motion[5] or at trial[6] should, at the deposition, properly lay the foundation for its later admission.

This assumes, of course, that the taker wants the document admitted. But if the taker does *not* want the document admitted and if the witness is the only person capable of laying the foundation, the taker should not ask the foundational questions that would make the document admissible if the witness is unavailable for trial.[7]

Reasons to Establish a "Negative Foundation" at a Deposition

In some situations, counsel should ask foundational questions for a completely different reason—to demonstrate that there is *no* foundation for admissibility, thereby strengthening the argument for not admitting the document at future proceedings. If the taker can establish a document's inadmissibility, the deposition record can be used to exclude the document in a summary judgment motion or motion in limine. Furthermore, establishing a document's inadmissibility allows the taker to prepare for trial knowing the document will not likely be admitted. With this assurance, there would be no need to account for the document in the theory of the case or to rebut it. Additionally, if the document is important enough, establishing a lack of foundation might even encourage settlement.

To obtain the information necessary to preclude the admissibility of a document, the taker should ask the witness questions that negate the requirements for admissibility. Even if the deposition questions do not prevent the document's admission, they may help determine what more needs to be done to oppose the document's admission at a later date or attack it during voir dire. Of course, if the deposition questioning reveals that the witness *can* lay a foundation for admissibility, the taker can plan evidence to rebut or explain the document.

One caveat: If a witness is not expected to be present at trial, there is risk in attempting to lay the "negative foundation." The questioning may inadvertently lay the foundation for a document the taker does not want admitted, and the document could be admitted by the opponent using the deposition transcript.

How to Lay a Foundation for the Admissibility (or Inadmissibility) of a Document

To lay the foundation for admission into evidence, the lawyer must be sure to cover all the following:[8] (1) preliminary matters, (2) authentication, (3) hearsay and its exceptions, (4) original-document ("best evidence") rule, and (5) relevance.[9]

Preliminary Matters[10]

The proponent of the document must

1. Mark the document as an exhibit either before the deposition begins or as each document is presented to the witness;
2. Give the marked exhibit to the witness and provide a copy to opposing counsel so that the witness and opposing counsel have no reason to use the same copy together;
3. Give the witness time to examine the exhibit and obtain the witness's admission on the record that she has had sufficient time to examine it;
4. Prevent counsel for the witness from conferring with the witness about the document;[11] and
5. Ask the witness to identify the document if she has not already done so.

Authentication

Authentication is the process by which the proponent of evidence demonstrates that an item of evidence is "what it purports to be." Federal Rules of Evidence (FRE) 901 through 903 set forth the requirement for authentication in a federal court. Generally, you authenticate a document by establishing the witness's familiarity with the document—for example, by authorship, receipt, observation of its preparation, or familiarity with the signature. For example:

Q. You have identified Exhibit 1 as a letter from your supervisor. How do you know that?
A. I recognize his signature.
Q. Have you seen his signature before?
A. Yes, many times.

If there is no witness who can claim familiarity with the document, the proponent may still demonstrate its authenticity by circumstantial evidence. For example, the fact that a document contains facts known only to the purported author of the document can demonstrate authorship. Likewise, showing that a second letter responds to an earlier letter sent to the purported author of the second letter demonstrates authorship of the second letter.

Hearsay and Its Exceptions

Any document is hearsay if its contents must be true or believed to be true to be relevant. If the document is offered for some relevant, nontruth, or nonhearsay purpose, no foundation for a hearsay exception is necessary. But if the taker wants to establish the admissibility of the document for its truth at trial, she must lay the foundation that the document is an admission or falls within a hearsay exception. Although the hearsay rule has many exceptions that apply to documents, only those most commonly used are discussed below.

Record of Regularly Conducted Activity (Business Record)

To lay the foundation for a record of regularly conducted activity under FRE 803(6), the proponent must establish the following elements:

1. The document is a memorandum, report, record, or data compilation, in any form,
2. of acts, events, conditions, opinions, or diagnoses
3. made at or near the time the acts or events took place
4. by, or from information transmitted by, a person with personal knowledge of the event or act

5. when such record is kept in the course of a regularly conducted activity, and
6. it was the regular practice of the business to make such record.

Note that under the fifth foundational element, the person who makes the entry in the record, or the person from whom the entrant receives the information for the entry, must have a "business duty"—that is, an employment obligation—to report or enter such facts into the record. This is the federal view, according to the advisory committee's note to FRE 803(6), which cites with approval *Johnson v. Lutz*. That case held that a police report incorporating a statement by a bystander does not qualify for admission, while a report incorporating a statement by a police officer is admissible. The police report in *Johnson* was inadmissible because the report was made from "hearsay statements of third persons who happened to be present at the scene of the accident when [the officer] arrived." Both the third persons and the police officer did not witness the accident, but merely reported what some others had told them.[12]

Finally, note that FRE 803(6) is governed by a trustworthiness proviso. That process allows a trial court to exclude a business record that otherwise satisfies the requirements of the business record exception when the source of information or the method or circumstances of preparation indicate a lack of trustworthiness.

Because of this proviso, counsel who want to oppose admission of the business record should explore with the witness any circumstances that might show a lack of trustworthiness. Perhaps the most common—and most important—of these circumstances would be the maker's knowledge of the existence of ongoing litigation that would be expected to involve the document.

Here is an example of a foundation that could be laid for an exhibit in the *Scoops* case. Assume that counsel for Business-Aide wants to lay a foundation for Maxine Waller's telephone log, which was prepared by Waller's secretary. (See Document D-7 from the *Scoops* case file, appearing as Exhibit A at the end of this chapter.) The secretary will be unavailable for trial, so the foundation must be laid by Waller during her deposition. Here is how the taker might lay the foundation:

Q. Please identify Exhibit D-7 (showing D-7 to the witness).
A. This is my telephone log of incoming phone calls for early October, two years ago. [Element 1]

Q. How are these phone logs made?

A. My secretary notes the name, time, and short message of every telephone call that she receives in my office. [Elements 2 and 4]

Q. When is the notation made?

A. Right at the time of the call. [Element 3]

Q. Why does your secretary make the entries in the log?

A. This is the standard practice in our office. All secretaries are required to keep phone logs in this way. [Element 6]

Q. What is done with daily phone logs at the conclusion of the day?

A. The logs are collected weekly and retained in a file for a period of six years. [Element 5]

Note that the elements of the foundation can be laid without using the precise language of FRE 803(6). Nevertheless, it is sometimes helpful to use the actual words of the rule to lay the foundation so that a court will have no doubt that counsel has "touched all the bases."

Public Records and Reports

To establish that a document is a public record or report under FRE 803(8), the proponent must establish that the document is a record, report, statement, or data compilation of a public office or agency, which sets forth either (1) the activities of the office or agency or (2) matters observed pursuant to a duty imposed by law to report such matters, excluding matters in criminal cases observed by law enforcement personnel.

Admission of such a report can lead to the admission of more than an agency's observations. For example, the Supreme Court ruled in *Beech Aircraft v. Rainey*[13] that when a public record is admissible, not only are its factual observations admissible for their truth, but the legal conclusions are admissible as well, provided that the conclusions are supported by factual findings or observations.

As with business records, the admissibility of a public report is also governed by a reliability (or trustworthiness) proviso, which excludes the contents of the record if it appears unreliable. The advisory committee and various courts have stated that the following four factors are indicia of reliability for public records, including "evaluative reports" that can be admitted under FRE 803(8)(C):

1. The timeliness of the investigation
2. The special skill or experience of the investigating official
3. Whether a hearing was held and the level at which it was conducted
4. Possible problems of bias or motive, such as whether the report was created with an eye toward litigation

Therefore, the proponent should ask the witness about such factors to determine whether the public record can be admitted at trial. The following questions deal with those factors in order.

- When did the investigation begin and end? How old was the evidence at the time of the investigation?
- What is the background and training of the official who conducted the investigation? What is the expertise and experience of those on whom the official relied?
- Was a hearing held to develop the facts of the investigation? If so, what was the nature of the hearing? Did the hearing comport with the minimum requirements of due process? What was the scope of the hearing compared with the scope of the investigation?
- What are the biases, interests, or organizational obligations of the official who conducted the investigation? What is the impact on the government agency of the outcome or conclusion of the investigation?

Recorded Recollection

To establish that a document is recorded recollection under FRE 803(5), the proponent must establish that the document

1. is a memorandum or record
2. concerning a matter about which the witness once had knowledge
3. but now has insufficient recollection to be able to testify fully and accurately; and
4. the document was made or adopted by the witness when the matter was fresh in the witness's memory; and
5. the document correctly reflects that knowledge.[14]

The taker should ask the witness about the time lapse between the time when the event happened and when it was recorded.

In addition, the taker should ask the witness the circumstances indicating that the document is correct.

Here is an example of how to lay the FRE 803(5) foundation for a document from the *Scoops* case. Assume that counsel would like to demonstrate the admissibility of the memorandum or notes created by Frank Fuller to memorialize the substance of his conversation with Business-Aide.[15] Counsel for Scoops should ask questions such as:

Q. Mr. Fuller, did you speak on the telephone with Maxine Waller of Business-Aide in October, two years ago?

A. Yes, I did. [Element 2]

Q. Mr. Fuller, do you remember the details of that conversation?

A. No, it's too long ago. [Element 3]

Q. Showing you Exhibit D-4 for identification, please tell us what it is.

A. These are the notes that I took during the conversation. [Element 1]

Q. How and why did you take the notes?

A. I listened carefully to what she had to say, and I immediately took down the important things that she said. [Element 4]

Q. Do you have any reason to believe your notes are accurate?

A. Of course. I was there to gain valuable information that would help Leslie's business succeed. [Element 5][16]

Former Testimony

To establish that the transcript of a deposition will qualify for admission as former testimony under FRE 804(b)(1), the proponent must establish the three following elements:

1. The declarant is or will be unavailable pursuant to FRE 804(a).[17]
2. The declarant's testimony is given at another hearing or deposition.
3. The party against whom it is offered had an opportunity and similar motive to develop the earlier testimony by direct, cross-, or redirect examination.

A sometimes neglected, but critical, issue can be the interplay of FRE 804(b)(1) with Federal Rule of Civil Procedure (FRCP) 32. FRCP 32(a)(1)(B) permits the deposition of a nonparty witness to be offered at trial for its truth "to the extent it would be admissible under the Federal Rules of Evidence if the witness were present and testifying" at trial. Yet, because a deposition transcript is an out-of-court statement, some courts require it to meet a hearsay exception if offered for its truth. Such courts require the proponent to demonstrate not only compliance with FRCP 32, but also compliance with the requirements of FRE 804(b)(1) (Former Testimony).[18]

Although deposition transcripts often satisfy the requirements of both rules, this is not automatic. For example, the definition of "unavailability" for purposes of FRE 804 is not identical to the definition of that term in FRCP 32; a witness who is one hundred miles from the courthouse is "unavailable" under FRCP 32(a)(4)(B) but if not "unavailable" under FRE 804.[19] Therefore, to be safe, counsel who want to offer the deposition transcript as former testimony should establish unavailability as defined by both rules.

In addition, a taker must establish the opponent's opportunity to examine his own witness, and must also establish that the opponent knows it is likely that his witness will be unavailable for trial. Establishing knowledge of the witness's unavailability is critical, so that the proponent can establish the third foundational element of evidence under FRE 804(b)(1); namely, that the opponent had the same motive to examine the witness at the deposition that she would have at trial (whether or not she did so at the deposition). Given this requirement, counsel who intends to offer the deposition of an absent witness should establish at the deposition the witness's prospective unavailability (for example, by asking the witness how far she resides from the courthouse or will at the time of trial). Counsel should also seek a stipulation from opposing counsel that the witness will not be available for trial.

Co-conspirator Statement

To establish that a document contains a co-conspirator statement, admissible under FRE 801(d)(2)(E), the proponent must establish the three following elements:

1. There is sufficient predicate evidence from which the court can find that reasonable jurors could find that a conspiracy exists.
2. The declarant and an adverse party are members of the conspiracy.
3. The declarant's statement was made in the course of, and in furtherance of, the conspiracy.

Numerous cases have held that conspiracy need not be alleged in the complaint for the proponent to be able to use the co-conspirator's statement as nonhearsay.[20] The co-conspirator exception is triggered in any civil case when the proponent can offer evidence of a combination of two or more persons for an illegal purpose. In *Bourjaily v. United States*,[21] the United States Supreme Court held that a hearsay statement a proponent wants to admit as a co-conspirator statement can itself be used—at least in concert with other evidence—in order to lay the foundation for its own admission.

The Residual Exception

To establish that a document qualifies for admission under the residual exception of FRE 807, the proponent must establish that the statement

1. is not covered by any of the other enumerated hearsay exceptions;
2. bears circumstantial guarantees of trustworthiness equivalent to those of the enumerated exceptions; and
3. is more probative on the point for which it is offered than other evidence that the proponent can procure through reasonable efforts.

The residual exception thus provides for the admissibility of hearsay that is both highly reliable and highly necessary. Many courts have held that reliability can be demonstrated by corroborating independent evidence, but the United States Supreme Court has called those holdings into question. In *Idaho v. Wright*,[22] the Supreme Court ruled that corroboration cannot be used to lay a foundation for reliability in the Confrontation Clause context in a case involving Idaho Rule 803(24). The language and reasoning of that case interpreting Idaho's residual exception can be applied to the identical residual exception found in the FRE.

Therefore, the only safe route is for the proponent to ask the witness about the circumstances surrounding the making of the statement that will provide indicia of reliability.[23] Indicia that courts consider include the following: (1) the statement is against the interest of the maker, (2) the maker has no motive to lie, (3) the statement is made under oath, and (4) the statement is not made to curry favor with the government.

In addition, courts have dealt with the so-called "near-miss" situation: the offer of hearsay under FRE 807 when the offered evidence—in different ways—just barely lacks a foundational element for the exception. Some courts have admitted near-miss hearsay on the theory that "close is good enough." But those rulings are subject to criticism because they effectively emasculate the rule and its exceptions. To be safe, assume that near-miss evidence, unless accompanied by additional indicia of reliability that compensates for the missing element, will be excluded.[24]

At a deposition, if you introduce a document that is lacking one of the foundational elements of a business record, ask the witness about other indicia of reliability that can make up for the missing element. For example, if the person making the entry in the record was not obligated to make the entry by a business duty to do so, but the entry was made under penalty of perjury, a court may admit the record under FRE 807.

Learned Treatise

To establish that a document is a learned treatise admissible under FRE 803(18), the proponent must establish through an expert that the book, article, or treatise is a reliable authority on a subject of history, medicine, or other science or art. When the material is offered on direct examination, the expert must testify that she relied on the treatise. When offered on cross-examination, the proponent simply needs to call the treatise to the expert's attention.

At a deposition that will be offered in lieu of live testimony— often the case with expert depositions—the proponent must lay a foundation for the admissibility into evidence of a learned treatise offer. Even if the expert deposition is taken for discovery only— and this may be difficult to predict at the time of the deposition— you should still inquire about the reliability of the treatise. That way, you will have a basis to ask about the treatise, either for purposes of admissibility or for impeachment at trial.

Original Document Rule

In addition to establishing that the document is authentic and admissible hearsay, the proponent must establish that under FRE 1001 the document is an original or its equivalent. If the original is unavailable, the proponent must explain its absence to overcome an objection based on the original-document rule, often referred to as the "best evidence" rule.[25]

The original-document rule applies when the facts contained in a document are directly in issue in the lawsuit, but not when the facts exist independent of the document. For example, in a case to determine the nature of a bequest in a will, the terms of the will are directly in issue and the bequest has no existence independent of the will. But in a case in which payment of a debt is the issue, the fact of payment exists, whether or not memorialized in a receipt. In that situation, the defendant need not produce the original of a receipt to prove payment.

Examples of Laying a Foundation for Admissibility and Inadmissibility

Example Number 1: Laying a Foundation When the Witness Will Be Unavailable for Trial

Suppose that as counsel for Defendant Business-Aide, you plan to take the deposition of Frank Fuller, the former employee of Plaintiff Leslie Roberts. Fuller now resides more than one hundred miles from the courthouse where the case will be tried. Therefore, he is not subject to the subpoena power of the trial court.[26] He cannot be compelled to attend the trial, and in all likelihood he will not voluntarily attend the trial.

In discovery, you received a document that contains Fuller's notes of a telephone conversation with Maxine Waller, the principal of Business-Aide.[27] (See Document D-4 from the *Scoops* case file, appearing as Exhibit B at the end of the chapter.) At the time of the conversation, Fuller was employed by Scoops. The document makes no mention of any discussion with Waller concerning the impending contract with Harold Jamison, the company that had offered to market Scoops's ice cream regionally; no mention of Scoops's application for a line of credit in order to increase its production capabilities, as Jamison required; and no mention of any specialized accounting needs of Scoops. As counsel for Business-Aide, you would like to establish the foundation for admissibility of this document because it supports your defense theory that Business-Aide was never informed of Scoops's need for accounting software for a particular purpose.

You are aware that Fuller may not be available at trial. To effectively plan your discovery and trial strategy, you need to know whether the document will be admitted into evidence. Therefore, you decide to try to lay the foundation at Fuller's deposition.[28] Before laying the foundation, however, you must determine on what basis the document, obviously an out-of-court statement and therefore hearsay, can be offered into evidence. You develop three different theories of admissibility.

One theory is that Fuller was the agent of Scoops, making his conversation and the notes of it admissible as an admission of Scoops.[29] Under this theory, you need to ask foundational questions of both Fuller (and later Roberts at her deposition) to establish Fuller's employment relationship with Scoops, his duties, and the terms of the directive from his supervisor, Leslie Roberts, to contact Business-Aide or other computer suppliers.

A second theory is that the document is recorded recollection, another exception to the hearsay rule.[30] To establish this exception, you need to demonstrate that Fuller has no independent recollection of the conversation, that the notes were made at the same time as the conversation (while the words were fresh in Fuller's mind), and that he wanted to record the contents of the conversation faithfully because it was important for the operation of Scoops's business.

Your third theory—a fallback position—is that the document is a business record.[31] This will require you to establish the six elements under FRE 803(6) of a business record, discussed above in the section "Record of Regularly Conducted Activity (Business Record)."

Example Number 2: Establishing the Lack of Foundation (a "Negative Foundation")

Suppose that as counsel for Defendant Business-Aide, you have in your possession Document D-1 from the *Scoops* file, which consists of the notes made by Plaintiff Leslie Roberts of matters discussed at the Chamber of Commerce seminar regarding the use of computers for a small business. (See Document D-1 from the *Scoops* case file, appearing as Exhibit C at the end of this chapter.) The document contains information indicating that Roberts knew very little about computers and accounting. These facts could support your opponent's case theory that Roberts was a business and computer novice who justifiably relied on the expertise of Business-Aide. Therefore, as counsel for Business-Aide, you make the decision that you would like to keep that document *out* of evidence at trial.

As counsel for Business-Aide, you know that you can offer the document as an admission if you choose, but you want to demonstrate that it is inadmissible if offered by Plaintiff Scoops.[32] To demonstrate the lack of a business record foundation, you need to ask questions of Roberts at her deposition that will show this document to be one-of-a-kind and that there was no regular practice of creating such documents.

As an alternative, in order to establish the lack of a foundation for a recorded recollection, you need to ask questions of Roberts at her deposition. Thus, you need to ask similar questions demonstrating one or more of the following:

1. A lack of a failure of memory by the witness regarding the seminar.
2. The notes were not intended to be complete.
3. The notes may not have been made while the seminar was fresh in the witness's mind.
4. Any other matters that negate the requirements of FRE 803(5).

With such a deposition record, you will have negated the two bases on which your opposing counsel could try to offer the notes at trial.[33]

Notes

1. "Relevant information need not be admissible at the trial if the discovery appears reasonably calculated to lead to the discovery of admissible evidence." FED. R. CIV. P. 26(b)(1).

2. Though the predeposition discovery of data through other discovery devices is not the subject of this chapter, it is worth noting that the amendments to Rule 26, effective December 1, 2006, provide for and describe the discovery of electronically stored information.

3. The witness does not have to be unavailable for the taker to plan to use the deposition testimony at trial. Some states have procedures for the noticing party to notice the deposition as an "evidence" deposition, allowing the deposition to be used at trial whether or not the witness is available. See ILL. S. CT. R. 202. ("Any party may use a video tape deposition of . . . any expert witness even though the deponent is available to testify if the deposition notice . . . reserved the right to use the deposition at trial."). The parties also may stipulate that the witness will be unavailable. See FED. R. CIV. P. 29 (Stipulations About Discovery Procedure).

4. See FED. R. CIV. P. 32(a); see also Chapter 25. If the document in question is a FRE 803(6) Record of Regularly Conducted Activity (a "business record"), an alternative to establishing a business record foundation at the deposition is the use of the business record "certificate" procedure provided in FRE 803(6), FRE 902(11), and FRE 902(12). This procedure permits the foundation for a business record to be established without the need for a live witness.

5. See FED. R. CIV. P. 56 (requiring that exhibits offered in support of, or in opposition to, a motion for summary judgment must be admissible as they would be at trial).

6. *See* FED. R. CIV. P. 32(a).

7. Of course, just because the noticing party chooses not to ask about a document does not prevent the defender from asking questions during cross-examination at the deposition.

8. For a more complete discussion of specific evidentiary foundations, *see* ANTHONY J. BOCCHINO & DAVID SONENSHEIN, A PRACTICAL GUIDE TO FEDERAL EVIDENCE (8th ed. 2007) and EDWARD J. IMWINKELRIED, FOUNDATIONS (6th ed. 2005).

9. Of course, to be admitted at trial, all evidence must be relevant under FRE 401 and FRE 402 or analogous state rules or law. The relevance of a document will generally be apparent from its contents and/or the circumstances of its preparation, delivery, or receipt. In addition, the document must not be privileged or there must be an exception or waiver of the privilege. *See* FRE 501; see also Chapter 6.

10. See Chapter 12 for a more detailed discussion of handling documents at a deposition.

11. Such conferences have been forbidden by a few federal courts that seek to minimize counsel's coaching of the deponent. *E.g.*, Hall v. Clifton Precision, 150 F.R.D. 525 (E.D. Pa. 1993). *Hall* and like cases prohibit conferences with a witness when a question is pending unless the conference addresses a matter of evidentiary or constitutional privilege, such as those discussed in "Elements of the Attorney-Client and Work-Product Privilege" in Chapter 6.

12. 170 N.E. 517, 518–19 (N.Y. 1930).

13. 488 U.S. 153 (1988).

14. Recorded recollection should not be confused with refreshed recollection. *See* FED. R. Evid. 612. Though both are triggered by a witness's inability to remember, recorded recollection is a hearsay exception that admits the contents of the document that recorded an event. Refreshed recollection is testimony given with the aid of a jogged memory. The contents of the refreshing document are not admitted into evidence.

15. See Document D-4 from the *Scoops* case file appearing as Exhibit B at the end of this chapter.

16. FRE 803(5) precludes the document containing recorded collection from being admitted as an exhibit at trial. Once admitted, the recorded recollection is published to the fact finder by reading its contents aloud.

17. Ordinarily, you will not know if the declarant is unavailable until the time of trial. Thus, this foundational showing will ordinarily be made at trial. However, in order to prepare for trial, it is prudent to ask questions at a deposition to determine if the witness anticipates being unavailable.

18. For a contrary view, *see* Scott F. Perwin, *Use of Depositions in Federal Trials: Evidence or Procedure?*, LITIGATION, Fall 1989, at 37, 39, in which the author argues that the hearsay rules and FRCP 32 provide alternative and independent grounds for the admission of deposition testimony.

In explaining his argument, Perwin notes that FRE 802 states that "[h]earsay is not admissible except as provided by these rules or by other rules prescribed by the Supreme Court pursuant to statutory authority or by Act of Congress." The advisory committee's note to FRE 802, in turn, specifically lists FRCP 32 as one of the "other rules prescribed by the Supreme Court."

19.   Pursuant to FRE 804(a), a witness is unavailable if the witness (1) is exempt from testifying due to privilege; (2) persists, despite a court order, in refusing to testify concerning the statement; (3) testifies to lack of memory of the subject matter of the statement; (4) is unable to testify because of death or physical or mental illness; or (5) is absent and the statement's proponent has been unable to procure his or her attendance or testimony by process or other reasonable means.

20.   *See* McCORMICK ON EVIDENCE § 259 (4th ed. 1992).

21.   483 U.S. 171 (1987).

22.   497 U.S. 805 (1990).

23.   *But see* United States. v. Valdez-Soto, 115 S. Ct. 1969 (Ninth Circuit ruled that despite *Idaho v. Wright, supra* note 22, it remained appropriate for district courts to use corroboration as basis for reliability.).

24.   David A. Sonenshein, *The Residual Exceptions to Federal Hearsay Rule: Two Exceptions in Search of a Rule,* 57 N.Y.U. L. REV. 867 (1982).

25.   Although many lawyers refer to the original document rule as the best evidence rule, the former is the appropriate term according to the 1972 notes to proposed FRE 1001; that term is also a more accurate description because the rule applies only to documents and not to other kinds of evidence.

26.   *See* FED. R. CIV. P. 32(a), 45(b)(2)(B); see also Chapter 3.

27.   *See supra* text accompanying notes 14–15.

28.   Although Fuller is not the only witness through whom the foundation could be laid, it may be easiest to lay the foundation through him. Leslie Roberts could also be used to lay the foundation based on the theories discussed in the text, but she may not be a cooperative witness.

29.   *See* FRE 801(d)(2) (admission by party-opponent). Note that under the Federal Rules of Evidence, admissions by a party-opponent are not considered hearsay, and hence technically are not an "exception" to the hearsay rule.

30.   *See supra* notes 14–15 and accompanying text (discussing recorded recollection).

31.   *See supra* text accompanying note 4 (discussing business records).

32.   An admission can be offered only by a party-opponent. FRE 801(d)(2). A party cannot offer its own statement as an admission; it must find some other basis for the statement's admissibility. FRE 802.

33.   *See also supra* text accompanying notes 4, 13–14 (discussing the types of questions necessary to establish the document as a business record or recorded recollection).

EXHIBIT A
Scoops v. Business-Aide, Inc.

DOCUMENT 7 (D-7)

BUSINESS-AIDE, INC.
INCOMING TELEPHONE CALLS _M W_

DATE	TIME	CALLER	REMARKS
10/29	9:00 am	Joyce Appleby (IBM)	
10/29	9:20 am	Chris Harkness	(Tennis) (MW busy with J.A. – will call back
10/29	10:00 am	Chris Harkness	Can you play tonight at 6:00 pm?
10/29	10:15 A.M.	FRANK FULLER (SCOOPS)	
10/29	10:35 A.M.	HAWLEY ELLIS (FIRST NATIONAL BANK)	
10/29	11:35 am	Chris Harkness	(MW busy with H.E. – told him you would call back
10/29	12:05 pm	Gail Severson (Boston Venture Capital)	
10/29	1:20 pm	George Harrow	
10/29	1:43 pm	Kevin	
10/29	2:20 P.M.	HAWLEY ELLIS (FNB)	
10/29	3:46 pm	Kevin	

EXHIBIT B

Scoops v. Business-Aide, Inc.

DOCUMENT 4 (D-4)

10/29/YR-2

BUSINESS-AIDE, INC.

— MAXINE WALLER
1209 APPLE ST., BOSTON 02118

— LOVES DOUBLE CHOCOLATE FUDGE

— SPECIALIST FOR THE SMALL BUSINESS
— TAILOR THE PLAN TO OUR COMPUTER NEEDS

— $4000 ?? -- NEED TO CALL BACK

— OFFER TRAINING

— HELPFUL — TALK TO LESLIE

EXHIBIT C
Scoops v. Business-Aide, Inc.

9/14/YR2

Chamber of Commerce — Mike Marshall

Computers as managers —

— inventory
— check writing
— cash flow
— accrual ??
— accounts receivable/payable ??
— spreadsheets (what are they??)
— projections
— $1250 (minimum) and up

"EASY SOFTWARE" ("user friendly")
Main thing is hardware — flexibility

CHAPTER 14

Defending the Deposition

Stuart W. Gold*
Henry L. Hecht

A deposition involves a struggle for control. At one level, this struggle is played out between taker and witness. But a deposition also pits taker against defender. To some extent a deposition is an event that "only the taker can win, only the witness can lose." Therefore, the defender's goal—with some exceptions[1]—is to have the witness testify as succinctly as possible, to minimize the likelihood of damaging testimony.[2]

As a defender, you must be particularly diligent and thorough when preparing your witness because federal and state discovery rules increasingly prevent a defender from playing an active role at a deposition.[3] Nonetheless, you still have many opportunities to "protect the record" and help the witness provide reasonable and accurate answers without hurting your case. At the same time, as a defender you must take care not to substantially obstruct the taker's examination or you open yourself and your client to serious sanctions.[4]

This chapter explores the defender's role—from the start of the deposition through adjournment. Although it focuses on the defender's use of objections and instructions not to answer, the chapter also discusses a taker's possible responses to a defender's tactics. Finally, the chapter looks at the use and misuse of the tools available to a defender, a subject also discussed in more detail in Chapter 15: Problem Counsel, Problem Witnesses.

Taking Care of the Preliminaries

Before the deposition, you should review the applicable rules, including any relevant local rules, governing depositions. In addition to the relevant Federal Rules of Civil Procedure (FRCP) and standing orders, at least eighteen federal district courts have adopted local rules regulating a defender's conduct. These rules often (1) prohibit a defender from initiating a private conference with a witness except to determine whether a privilege should be asserted, (2) prohibit speaking objections, and (3) require a defender to justify on the record any instruction not to answer.[5] However, local rules in a particular district may be more idiosyncratic. For example, the District of Maryland has a rule prohibiting smoking in the deposition room.[6] Furthermore, some of the local rules governing conduct at depositions can be quite extensive.[7] In addition to reviewing the local rules, you should review the standing order of, and decisions regarding deposition conduct by, the judge presiding in your case or by appellate courts in the jurisdiction, especially if you expect the deposition to be contentious.[8]

On the day of the deposition, plan to meet your witness at least thirty minutes before the two of you are due at the deposition site. Have that meeting near, but not at, the deposition site. Why? Because you do not want to leave your witness alone in the taker's office—where even idle conversation can cause problems.[9] A question in the reception area from the taker about what hotel the witness is staying at, and a failure by your witness to recall the name of the hotel, might lead your witness to make an offhand comment that she does not remember things as well as she used to. That in turn can lead to a significant question at some point during the deposition:

Q. How sure are you that the CFO discussed the cash flow situation at the board meeting last year?
A. I am positive about that.
Q. Didn't you tell me this morning when I first met you that you don't remember things as well as you used to?

At this meeting, ask the witness if she has any last-minute questions, and remind the witness of any important procedural and substantive points you want firmly planted in her mind.[10] This should be a relatively short list—rarely more than five items. Also, check to see if the witness brought anything you do not want in the deposition room, such as notes from the preparation sessions or a personal diary, PDA, BlackBerry, or calendar.[11]

Arrive early at the deposition. If you do, you may be able to choose the seats you and the witness prefer, although a competent taker will try to control who sits where.[12] It will also give you time to set up and test any needed laptop connection if realtime transcription is being used.[13] In addition, your timely arrival will hopefully ensure a timely end to the deposition, before your witness gets too tired.[14]

After arriving in the deposition room, give your business card to the court reporter. Obtain the names of everyone in the room, and get everyone else's business card, including the reporter's and the videographer's if one is present.[15] If there is more than one party or more than one lawyer on a side, establish who is going to examine the witness, in what order, and whom each lawyer represents. Before the deposition starts, confirm that only those allowed by the discovery rules or a court order are present.[16]

If you care about the order in which the examining lawyers question the witness, try to establish the rotation. However, absent a protective order, a defender cannot impose his rotation preference. More important than the rotation of questioners is what to do if more than one lawyer for a party intends to examine your witness. There is an element of unfairness in having multiple examiners.[17] However, because the Federal Rules do not expressly prohibit more than one questioner per side, you will probably have to live with the situation unless your witness is being harassed by the repetition of questions or subject matters.[18] At that point, you may be justified in suspending the deposition and seeking a protective order.[19]

If the deposition is being video recorded, review the witness's image on the monitor. Make sure there are no shadows or other problems that make the witness look less attractive or credible. At each break, recheck the monitor and ask for a playback to check the audio level and tone. All this can affect how your witness is perceived if and when the tape is played at trial or for a pretrial motion.[20]

Before the questioning starts, decide if you want any stipulations.[21] Do not stipulate to a preset number of breaks—one in the morning, one in the afternoon, for example—because you may find that you, and your witness, need more breaks than that. And rarely forgo a lunch break to speed things up. A deposition should never be an endurance contest. In fact, most witnesses cannot concentrate sufficiently at a deposition for much more than an hour. Staying alert can also be a problem for you because as the defender you may have little to do for long periods of time.

You can use breaks to confer with your witness, assuming conferences are not prohibited in your jurisdiction.[22] But remember not to overdo it, as the taker may seek additional time beyond the allotted seven hours under Federal Rule of Civil Procedure 30(d)(1) if excessive delay can be shown. Moreover, while conferences with your witness should be privileged, there is no guarantee that a judge will agree. Therefore, you should not say anything to your witness during a break that you would not want to be heard by the judge in your case.

If you need an accurate transcript and you do not already know the reporter's capability, ask for a "readback" early in the deposition to gauge how accurately the reporter is transcribing testimony.[23] But recognize that accuracy may not be as important to you as it is to the taker. In fact, if you do not expect to use the deposition at trial or in a motion for summary judgment, you may even prefer a garbled transcript because your opponent will have trouble using it effectively. On the other hand, during the deposition the witness may start testifying about issues you consider important, and you may then want an accurate record. If a couple of readbacks at that point indicate that the reporter is not accurate enough, ask for an adjournment to secure a better reporter. Your adversary may readily agree because, as noted, a taker almost always wants a readable transcript. However, before asking for an adjournment to get a new reporter, consider whether you are willing to bring the witness back another day if another reporter is not immediately available.

In addition to checking the reporter's accuracy, a readback can serve other purposes. For example, when a witness loses her train of thought or the meaning of the question, requesting a readback of the question and whatever answer the witness has given to that point can refocus the witness. Hearing the question again also can remind the witness to answer only the question asked and nothing more. And it can reestablish a desired rhythm that encourages the witness to pause before answering.

During the deposition, you may want to take notes. Note taking can help you stay alert—not an insignificant problem for a defender in a deposition that runs smoothly. The notes also can be a big help if you want to challenge the examiner on what he has asked and whether a question mischaracterizes a witness's earlier testimony. And during breaks, you can use the notes to identify areas where the witness is volunteering too much or speculating or otherwise having trouble.[24] By showing your witness what she just said, you are more likely to get the witness's attention; notes prevent "deniability" by your own witness. Finally, notes are useful if you want to examine your own witness after the taker is done. If you are using realtime, the electronic transcript can serve several of these functions.[25] But you may still want to take notes or at least note where in the realtime transcript you want to focus during your own examination, if any, of the witness. You should also consider that your notes are a more portable tool than your laptop to use during breaks.

Making Objections

The primary tool for a defender is the objection. In a trial, a lawyer often pays a price for objecting. For one thing, objecting can create the impression that the lawyer (or his client) is hiding, or at least wants to hide, something. In addition, if the objection is overruled, the lawyer can lose credibility with the judge and the jury even when the judge's ruling is not accompanied by some rebuke such as, "Sit down, counsel."

In contrast, at a deposition, no judge or jury is present to hear objections, which will not be ruled upon unless and until the deposition is offered as evidence at trial or on a pretrial motion. In addition, as detailed below, some objections must be made at a deposition or they are waived, while others, even though not made, are preserved for trial.

Because of the way objections work at a deposition, each time a question is asked, you as defender may need to resolve a number of questions simultaneously: Is the question objectionable? Do I need to object at the deposition or is my objection preserved? Do I want to object? How do I make my objection? And all these decisions must be made in a split second. (The average question lasts less than ten seconds).[26]

Is the Question Objectionable?

The Federal Rules of Evidence (FRE) apply to a deposition even though, as noted above, objections at a deposition will not be ruled upon until the deposition is offered into evidence at trial or as part of the record in a pretrial motion.[27]

FRCP 30(c)(2) requires the deposition officer to note "upon the record" more than just evidentiary objections:

> An objection at the time of the examination—whether to evidence, to a party's conduct, to the officer's qualifications, to the manner of taking the deposition, or to any other aspect of the deposition—must be noted on the record. . . . [28]

If the Federal Rules stopped there, the rules and strategy for objecting at a deposition would be no different than they are at trial. But the rules do not stop there. Instead, they treat deposition objections differently from trial objections in two significant respects. First, even when an objection is made at a deposition, the examination continues, with the testimony taken subject to the objection.[29] Second, certain objections, as noted above, are preserved for trial even if not made at the deposition, while others are waived if they are not made at the deposition.[30]

As for the first difference, a deposition witness is usually required to answer a question when an objection is made. The logic here is obvious. Because no judge is present, there is no one to rule on the objection at the deposition. If the witness were not required to answer, the deposition would be constantly halted to wait for a ruling. In addition, because a deposition is not a trial, there is no reason to exclude the answer because of concerns about admissibility of evidence. Nevertheless, some courts and even some individual judges invite counsel to contact them by telephone if an immediate ruling is needed.[31] There is another reason a witness is usually required to answer a question despite an objection. The primary purpose of a deposition is discovery, and the scope of that discovery is far broader than the scope of the admissibility standards used at trial. The Federal Rules permit discovery of "any nonprivileged matter that is relevant to any party's claim or defense."[32] Furthermore, "relevant information need not be admissible at the trial if the discovery appears reasonably calculated to lead to the discovery of admissible evidence."[33] Thus, requiring an answer, subject to objections, allows for open questioning leading to discoverable information, whether or not this information will ultimately be admitted at trial or a hearing on a pretrial motion. Only after the information has been gathered at the deposition are the FRE applied as if "the witness were then present and testifying."[34]

Even If the Question Is Objectionable, Should You Object to It?

There are, of course, a number of reasons why you should object to an improper question. The primary reason is that if you do not, and the objection is waived, you have lost the opportunity to protect the record. Also, you may not have protected your witness from an unfair or confusing question that could lead to a damaging answer. Or you may not have protected yourself in your struggle for control with opposing counsel. Nonetheless, there are at least eight reasons why you might *not* want to object to an improper question.

The Answer Does Not Damage Your Case

If the answer is going to be harmless, objecting to protect the record for a subsequent court ruling is of little concern. Furthermore, your objection could improve the examiner's question.

The Answer Is Not Useful to the Taker

Suppose a question is objectionable in form—a compound question, for example. Because of this defect, the answer may not be useful to the taker.[35] Consider the following compound question that is asked of Leslie Roberts, the plaintiff in *Scoops*, who claims she was sold accounting software that did not meet her needs. The question relates to her meeting with Terry Blake, a salesperson for defendant Business-Aide.

> Q. At the meeting, you did not mention your specific need for accounting software to prepare a financial statement for submission in a loan application, or did you?
> A. Yes.

The "yes" could refer to either part of the question. For this reason, the answer cannot be used later by the taker to show that the witness did not mention the specific need for the software. On the other hand, there may be reasons to object to the form of the question. For example, the ambiguity could be a problem if you need to show on a motion that the witness did mention her specific need for software to prepare a financial statement.[36] And, if the question and answer are read at trial without objection, the jury might interpret the answer adversely to your client's position.

You Can Hurt Yourself at Trial

Continually objecting, even though the questions may have minor technical defects in form, can cause you to lose credibility if your behavior is later scrutinized by a judge on a motion for a protective order, or if your comments are read to a jury.[37] Therefore, when defending a witness who handles even poorly worded questions without giving answers that might later prove problematic at trial, it is a good idea not to object. In fact, as a general rule, strive to be on the record as little as possible, by speaking only when necessary to protect the record or your witness from abuse.

You Can Upset the Witness

Constant objections can unnerve or break the concentration of a witness. (Of course, legitimate objections can also unnerve or distract the examiner.) Frequent interruptions for lawyer colloquy also can break a witness's confidence or concentration, particularly when the interruptions lead to lengthy discussions between the lawyers about evidentiary and procedural issues. During preparation, often you will have said something to your witness to this effect: "I'm sure you can handle the questions at the deposition. It's best if I am not on the record much. I will object only if I think there's something wrong with the question or if I want to warn you about a problem I see." At the deposition, if you start objecting frequently, your witness is likely to think, "What's going on here? My lawyer told me that she wouldn't object very often and now she's objecting constantly. I must be doing badly."

You May Embarrass the Witness and Help the Taker

An objection to a question may lead to your witness being embarrassed and forced to answer an even better-phrased question. Consider the following exchange at a deposition:

Q. Did you meet frequently with Jane during the month of November?

DEFENDER: Objection as to form. Vague and ambiguous as to "frequently." (Turning to the witness) You can answer if you understand the question.[38]

A. I don't understand the word "frequently."

Q. (To the witness) How would you define the word "frequently"?

[Or worse for the witness, the examiner asks the witness if he has ever used the word "frequently" himself. Or the examiner uses a dictionary to define the word.]

A. Three or more times.

Q. Fine. Using your definition of frequently, did you meet with Jane frequently during the month of November?

Your Objection Can Raise a Red Flag

Suppose you have been relatively quiet during the deposition. A sudden spate of objections can alert your adversary that his questions have begun to focus on an area of special concern to you and/or that you lack confidence in your witness in this area. Therefore, objecting only to the questions in critical areas may be counterproductive. It may be better to pace your objections throughout the deposition so they do not stand out in a critical area. That, however, does not mean you should abandon the earlier advice to limit how often you are on the record.

You Must Look Ahead

A deposition is not an isolated event. Aggressive or hypertechnical objections can create a "tit-for-tat" atmosphere, in which your adversary engages in similar behavior when you start asking questions at this deposition or take the deposition of your adversary's client.

Objections Have Ethical Implications

The purpose of discovery is to prevent "trial by ambush."[39] Objections are supposed to give notice to the taker about a defect and give her an opportunity to cure it; they are not supposed to harass the taker or frustrate disclosure.[40] For a defender, the critical issue should always be whether the question creates such an ambiguity about the meaning of the question or the answer that the question becomes unfair. If so, you should object to protect the record and your witness. Objecting solely to divert the taker's attention or coach the witness is improper.[41]

If You Decide to Object

As discussed above, there are two types of deposition objections.[42] The first type of objection must be made in a "timely" manner or it is waived; the second type is usually preserved for trial.

Regarding the first type, to preserve your right to use the objection when the objectionable testimony is offered at trial, you must object at the first available opportunity. That usually means objecting as soon as the objectionable question is asked (or objectionable conduct, such as conferring with a witness when a question is pending other than to determine if privileged information is sought, becomes known).[43] Occasionally, however, your witness will answer before you can object, either because your witness fails to follow your admonition to pause after hearing a question to give you time to object or because you do not realize the question is objectionable until after the witness begins to answer. Because your witness has answered before you can object, you are technically late; the objection is not "timely." Nevertheless, you should still object, because in a deposition, the timing of the objection is not as critical as it is at trial. Lodge your objection to the question, perhaps adding that you move to interpose the objection after the question and move to strike the answer. Though the objection may not be "timely made," the judge has discretion to grant your motion to strike. And because you made the objection—albeit after the answer—you can take the position that you gave notice to the taker of the question's defect and that the taker failed to rephrase it at her peril. All this may be "much ado about nothing" because once the answer is out, the questioner can rephrase the question.[44] But at least you have attempted to make and protect your record.

Also, although it is generally not good practice to interrupt your witness, if your witness is in the midst of a lengthy answer and/or you feel the answer is jeopardizing your case, you should consider interposing your objection before the witness finishes her answer. Alternatively, you may want to interrupt the answer with a comment. For example, if the question called for the witness to speculate and the answer commenced before you could object, you might comment: "I remind you not to speculate." Or you might comment: "I remind you to only answer the question asked." Or you might even say: "Excuse me, I do not believe you need to speculate for Mr. Taker."

Objections That Must Be Made
at the Deposition or They Are Waived

FRCP 32 establishes different timing requirements for the two types of deposition objections.[45] As for the first type of objections, those that are waived if not made at the deposition, FRCP 32(d)(3)(B) provides as follows:

> An objection to an error or irregularity at an oral examination *is waived if*: (i) it relates to the manner of taking the deposition, the form of a question or answer, the oath or affirmation, a

party's conduct, or other matters that might have been corrected at that time; and (ii) it is not timely made during the deposition.[46]

This rule is often discussed as if it applied only to objections about the impermissible way in which a question is asked. But the rule is far broader than that. It includes any "error or irregularity," such as defects in the oath, misconduct of the parties, and "other matters" that might be cured if an objection is promptly presented. Also covered by this rule, for example, are objections about the qualifications of the deposition officer, the right of someone to be present, the distortion by a camera or sound-recording device of the appearance or demeanor of deponents and lawyers,[47] and even an objection that the taker is providing the witness insufficient time to review exhibits before asking questions about them.

Objections of the first type (that is, those that are waived if not made at the deposition) are often easy to identify. Typically, they involve a defect in the question's structure or an imprecision that makes it unfair to require the witness to answer. The defect usually can be cured by rephrasing the question.

The material below discusses the most common of these "form objections." It also discusses two other objections that, though cast as form objections, often turn out to have little or no validity.

"The Question Is Ambiguous"

An ambiguous question uses terms that may be unfamiliar to the witness or are not specific enough. Take the question, "Did you inform Mr. Y about *the papers* you reviewed?" From the question, the witness cannot tell what "papers" the questioner has in mind.

"The Question Is Vague or Unintelligible"

This is a close relative of the previous objection. Two examples, with problem words emphasized, are, "Did you convey the *substance* of your conversation *directly* to Mr. X?" or "Did you find anything in the file that *piqued* your interest?" This objection typically arises when the question includes a word that may have different meanings for the taker, the witness, and the defender.

"The Question Is Argumentative"

Argumentative questions usually are asked when the taker becomes frustrated because she cannot obtain a desired response from the witness. Consider this sequence:

Q. You did not inform the plaintiff that the extended warranty was optional, did you?

A. I did inform Mr. X of that; I said it was optional.

Q. How did you say it?

A. "The extended warranty is optional."

Q. In those exact words?

A. Yes.

Q. You don't really remember your exact words, do you?

The last leading question is argumentative.

"The Question Is Compound (or Complex)"

A compound or complex question combines two or more questions into one. An illustration: "Did you write the letter, sign it, and mail it yourself?" These are three separate questions. A "yes" answer may refer to one or two or all three elements of the question. As a defender, you should consider objecting to such questions unless they are so innocuous that any resulting confusion is not meaningful or you want an unclear answer.[48]

"The Question Is Leading"

Leading questions suggest the answer and call only for a "yes" or "no" response. An illustration: "You agreed with the chairperson of company X that your company would hold the price of your Model T to $600, is that correct?" An objection to a leading question is inappropriate when the deponent is a hostile witness, an adverse party, or a witness identified with an adverse party.[49] An objection to a leading question is also generally inappropriate when the question may be necessary to develop the witness's testimony; that is, it is (1) designed to establish preliminary (or foundational) matters; (2) related solely to identifying exhibits (a preliminary matter); (3) designed to refresh recollection; (4) designed to aid a witness who needs help in testifying, such as a child or the infirm; or (5) directed to an expert witness as to undisputed preliminary matters. Conversely, such an objection is proper if the witness being questioned is the taker's client or not adverse to the taker's client.

"The Question Mischaracterizes the Witness's Prior Testimony"

This objection is appropriate when an examiner prefaces a question with a brief summary of prior testimony that you believe is inaccurate. Consider this question: "So after the chairperson reviewed your memorandum, he told you to contact the vice president of marketing at company Y, and what did you do?" It is objectionable if the witness testified previously only that she sent the memorandum to the chairperson and gave no testimony about his reviewing the memorandum or being asked to contact the vice president of marketing.[50] As in the example above, questions mischaracterizing a witness's prior testimony often begin with "so." Similarly, when a question is in the form "You testified x, y, and z, is that correct?" such phrasing should alert you to possible mischaracterization by the examiner and a corresponding objection.

"The Question Calls for a Narrative Response"

This objection is somewhat puzzling, particularly when used at a deposition. There is no rule of evidence that prohibits narratives; evidence rules are concerned with admissibility of evidence at trial. Most takers will argue correctly that this objection is inappropriate at a deposition because admissibility is not in issue. Therefore, if this objection is made, expect the examiner to persist in seeking a response.

"The Question Calls for Speculation"

This objection is proper when a question seeks information not in the witness's personal knowledge.[51] An example is a question calling for a witness's opinion about what someone else was thinking or for testimony about events at which the witness was not present or about which the deponent was not informed. Sometimes this objection takes the form of an objection that there is no foundation that the witness has knowledge about the subject under inquiry. The objection can also be used for questions calling for an improper lay opinion or conclusion or improper expert opinion or conclusion. Some defenders will also lodge this objection when the question is a hypothetical put to a fact/lay witness. However, the mere fact that a question is a hypothetical does not make it objectionable.

"The Question Has Been Asked and Answered"

No rule of evidence prohibits a taker from asking the same question more than once. Therefore, this objection is often inappropriate. It is valid only when the same question is asked so often that it becomes cumulative, burdensome, or repetitious, such that the witness is being harassed.[52]

353

"The Question Assumes Facts Not in Evidence"

Faced with this objection, a taker often will respond by arguing that no testimony or item is "in evidence" at a deposition. If, as a defender, you make this objection, expect an experienced taker to frame the same question carefully as a hypothetical to allow each element to be established at trial. Often the better phrasing of the objection is lack of foundation.

Objections That Are Preserved

As for the second type of deposition objections, the ones that are automatically preserved until the testimony is offered at trial or in a pretrial motion, FRCP 32(d)(3)(A) provides as follows:

> An objection to a deponent's competence—or to the competence, relevance, or materiality of testimony—is *not waived* by a failure to make the objection before or during the deposition, unless the ground for it might have been corrected at that time.[53]

These objections do not involve the impermissible way in which a question is asked, but instead are related to the impermissible nature of the testimony sought. Because the objections focus on the admissibility of testimony (rather than its discoverability), they typically—but not always—are preserved until the testimony is offered as evidence. Therefore, objections based on (1) hearsay, (2) offers to compromise, (3) relevance, (4) subsequent remedial measures, and (5) evidence of liability insurance generally should *not* be made at the deposition. However—and this is an important "however"—even this type of objection *must* be made at the deposition *if* the evidentiary defect presented by the question can be cured at the deposition.[54] Too many lawyers believe that they need to object only as to the form of a question, and that all objections regarding the question's substance are preserved. That is incorrect. As noted above, any defect that goes to the substance of the question (or the competency of the witness) and that can be cured at the deposition must also be met with an objection; otherwise it is waived.

Therefore, as a defender you may need to object to the competency of the witness, to questions that seek an inadmissible opinion or conclusion (for example, when a lay witness is asked for a legal conclusion), and to questions that lack foundation or are speculative, as noted above. For example, when a hypothetical posed to an expert is incomplete, a defender may make a foundation objection. The examiner will often respond by demanding that the defender state the missing elements of the hypothetical so that the defect can be cured. But that is not your role as defender. Rather you should continue to object if the question relates to materials the expert did not actually consult, consider, or rely on in forming an opinion.[55] (See the discussion later in this chapter on to whom an instruction not to answer is available.)

Even experienced practitioners have trouble drawing the line between objections that are waived and those that are preserved. Many litigators have at least one horror story about a judge finding a waiver for failure to object to questions when the defender was absolutely certain no objection was required.[56] The lesson: When in doubt, preserve the record.

One final point: When a question seeks to invade a privilege, object and instruct the witness not to answer. Otherwise, the privilege is waived.[57] An objection with an instruction not to answer should also be made to a question seeking information that may be protected from discovery by a court order,[58] or to stop harassing questioning in order to suspend the deposition to seek a protective order.[59]

If You Want to Object, How Do You Make the Objection?

If you decide to object or otherwise challenge a question, you must determine how to best accomplish this. FRCP 30(c)(2) mandates that "[a]n objection must be *stated concisely in a nonargumentative and nonsuggestive manner.*"[60] Although the rule refers only to objections, as a defender, before you object you may prefer to use an interjection instead.[61] Especially where speaking objections are prohibited, this approach may help the witness without causing an adverse response from the examiner.

For example, you may ask for a readback of the question to give yourself additional time to consider what to do. The readback also gives the witness time to consider the question and find any problems. After hearing the question a second time, you may decide to follow the adage, "If it ain't broke, don't fix it," and say nothing more. Indeed, if you do not have a good-faith objection, it may be improper to say anything more.[62]

Or, rather than objecting, you may ask for clarification. Be aware, however, that such a request does not protect the record against later use, because you have not made a formal objection upon which a judge can rule.[63] Still, you may prefer to avoid objecting. Consider the following question in a personal injury action:

Q. Was the car going very fast?
DEFENDER: Can you restate to clarify what you mean by "very fast"?

This request may be preferable to stating, "Objection as to form; vague and ambiguous." True, you have not preserved an objection for a trial court. But you have given "notice" to the examiner of the defect in the question and an opportunity to cure. Your comment serves a second purpose (as is true of every objection): the witness is alerted to your concern about the question. Even if the examiner stays with the question as asked, it is likely you will not mind the answer of your now alerted witness.

Another option is to suggest your own question, in the hope of moving the taker off her question. Consider again the same question in a personal-injury action:

Q. Was the car going very fast?
DEFENDER: Why don't you ask, "Was the car going faster than the posted speed limit of 35 miles per hour?"

As already discussed, the downside of such comments is they may help the taker to ask a better question. More often, they help you alert your witness to the defect in the question as well as its importance to the case.

If you decide to object on the record, you will want to put the objection into one of the following formats:

1. Objection without stating any ground; for example, "Objection."
2. Objection stating concisely the nature of the objection; for example, "Objection as to form."
3. Objection stating concisely the nature of the objection as well as the specific defect; for example, "Objection as to form; vague and ambiguous."
4. Objection with a longer discourse detailing the problem with the question, often referred to as a "speaking objection"; for example, "Objection as to form; vague and ambiguous. The term 'very fast' is ambiguous."
5. Objection with an even longer discourse detailing the problem with the question and alerting the witness to the taker's objective with the question; for example, "Objection

as to form; vague and ambiguous. The term 'very fast' is ambiguous. Do you mean to ask whether the car was going over the posted speed limit of 35 miles per hour?"[64]

How specific your objection should be depends on the circumstances and the relevant rules. Suppose you make a "general" objection that does not state a ground (option number 1, above). If the objection is overruled, it may be because you did not preserve the objection sufficiently for the judge to sustain it. If that happens, there may be no record of the basis for your objection that can be appealed.[65] Unless the nature of the objection is indisputably apparent from the context,[66] only a "specific" objection (that is, one that states the grounds for the objection) is sufficient to make a record. On the other hand, if a general objection is sustained, any basis that would support it is available on appeal.[67] (See the discussion below on rules limiting what you may say when you object.)

In some jurisdictions, it is clear that you must state the basis for certain objections—without making a speaking objection—because the objection is waived if no basis is stated.[68] This practice follows the logic of FRE 103, which requires you to state the "specific ground of objection, if the specific ground was not apparent from the context."

Similarly, if the taker asks for the basis of the objection, generally you should respond. Indeed, having asked for an explanation, the taker will be hard-pressed to dispute almost any legitimate explanation you provide (or stop you from speaking). Sometimes, you will not have developed the precise basis for an objection, at least initially, and therefore will not want to respond. In that event, you may be tempted to leave the objection open-ended. This is risky. Occasionally, however, it makes sense. For example, you may conclude that stating the basis for your objection discloses too much of your strategy.

Under the Federal Rules, certain local rules, and various judges' practices, speaking objections (option number 4 above) are clearly prohibited, although this does not stop the behavior.[69] Speaking objections are disfavored because they delay depositions and may be used to coach a witness. In some jurisdictions, even stating the nature of the objection (option number 2 above) is prohibited.[70]

Whatever the form of the objection, the witness must still answer unless you instruct the witness otherwise. As the defender, you should have covered this point in witness preparation. However, at the deposition, you may need to remind the witness of the need to answer the question by simply saying, "You may answer" after you object.[71] When a witness does not respond to the question, a taker often will chime in with, "You must answer the question." That can be helpful to the defender, because it reminds the witness that the taker is not a friend.

Objections to the Answer: By the Taker and the Defender

The taker has the right to object to an answer that is nonresponsive or otherwise defective. As a defender, you have this right as well,[72] though in some jurisdictions a defender can object to a nonresponsive answer only if it is otherwise inadmissible.[73] The reason for this rule, one commentator has explained, is that the taker may accept an unresponsive answer while the defender should be able to object only if the witness volunteers information without being asked a question or gives an answer objectionable on evidentiary grounds. The matter ultimately rests in the judge's discretion.[74]

Suppose that in a personal injury action a nonparty witness who is unavailable for trial is being examined by the defendant's lawyer:

Q. How old were you on the day of the accident?
A. The defendant ran a red light.

Absent an objection to the nonresponsive answer and a motion to strike, the objection will be waived and the answer may be admitted.[75] To prevent that, the taker needs to object and then move to strike the answer if offered into evidence.[76] Realize, however, that if at the deposition you, as a taker, say you plan to move to strike an answer, you can lose some rapport—assuming you had any—with a witness who finds both the formality and the message insulting. Therefore, after making the objection, the taker will often explain to the witness that the answer was not responsive and then either re-ask or rephrase the question.[77]

Besides objecting to nonresponsive answers, a taker should object to otherwise defective answers or risk the objection being waived. Consider again the deposition of a nonparty witness in a personal-injury action:

Q. How fast was the defendant going?
A. Based on what I was told, he must have been going seventy miles an hour.

This answer is not based on personal knowledge. It also is speculative. The taker should therefore object to the answer and move to strike it to prevent the answer from being admitted into evidence. The taker should then ask additional questions to establish whether the witness has personal knowledge. If so, the question can be rephrased to obtain the desired information.

When should a defender object to an answer and move to strike? When a witness gives a nonresponsive answer that has potentially damaging information—a rare occurrence if the witness has been properly prepared—you should object.[78] Even if you believe the answer is also irrelevant, you should object because a relevance objection that could be cured at the deposition must be made then or it is waived.[79] You will probably need to explain to your witness why you were objecting to her answers to reassure her that she has not damaged the case.

Continuing Objections

Another problem for a defender is whether to make the same objection more than once to a series of questions on the same topic. Consider the following exchange:

Q. What happened at the meeting between Mr. Blake and Ms. Roberts?

DEFENDER: Objection to form, the witness already said he was not at the meeting.

Q. What do you think happened at the meeting?

DEFENDER: Same objection; the answer would be speculation.

Q. Who else attended the meeting?

At this point, do you need to continue to object to every question about the meeting? Rather than issue a steady stream of objections, some defenders prefer to use a so-called "continuing (or standing) objection" to the entire line of questioning. And takers often accept the offer to avoid constant interruptions. This can be dangerous, because you, as the defender, cannot be certain that all the objectionable questions are covered by the continuing objection. If a specific objection is not made to a particular question, a court might find the objection to that question waived.

If you decide to make a continuing objection, be sure that the objection is both sufficiently precise and yet expansive. Avoid stock phrases such as, "I will make a continuing objection to any questions *in that area.*" Instead say, "I have a continuing objection to questions about this Blake/Roberts meeting." Rather than making a continuing objection, you might want to seek a stipulation that the initial objection will be deemed to apply to a specified line of questions and that the taker will not later argue that an objection to any one question was waived. Such a stipulation is usually in a taker's interest, because it eliminates the need for constant interruption. Another approach would be to make an objection after each objectionable question, but to use a less intrusive form of objection, such as, "Same objection."

Defending at a Nonparty Deposition

Suppose you represent a nonparty witness at a deposition. Just as when you defend the deposition of a party witness, you are limited to instructions not to answer on the basis of privilege, a limitation put in place by the court, and perhaps harassment.[80] But you cannot object to questions on evidentiary grounds.[81] Despite these limitations, you should still make sure your nonparty witness is treated fairly. You should be able to require that questions asked of the witness are reasonably clear. And you should be able to ask for clarification about such issues as time frame and definitions of words, as long as you act reasonably.

If you represent a party at a nonparty witness's deposition, you should object to the same extent as if you represented the witness. Keep in mind, however, that speaking objections may be scrutinized more closely when you are not representing the witness. You have the right to instruct the witness not to answer if she is in possession of information protected from disclosure by a privilege held by your client. Additionally, you might try to instruct the witness not to answer if the answer to the question is protected from disclosure by a limitation on discovery directed by the court or to stop the harassment of a witness if you intend to seek a protective order.[82] But the use of an instruction not to answer on these bases is more unusual if you are not representing the deponent.

Reactions by the Taker to the Defender's Tactics

A taker has a number of options when responding to the defender's tactics. Deciding which to use depends initially on whether, as a taker, you are concerned with the admissibility of the testimony or primarily with discovering information. You also must factor in the effect a response will have on the "turf battle" that occurs within each deposition.

Often, your best response is to ignore the defender. Even if the objection is proper, if your primary interest as taker is to obtain information, there is little reason to rephrase the question. Moreover, the defender may be deliberately trying to distract you, change the pace of the deposition, or move you on to another question or line of inquiry. If you like your question (or it serves your objectives), do not be diverted. After the defender's interjection, look at the witness and say, "You may go ahead and answer." Or look at the witness with an expectant glance and wait for an answer to fill the silence.

On the other hand, if you are a defender in this situation, you want to appear to be in control. Therefore, after objecting, you could say to your witness, "You may answer."[83] Or use the more aggressively phrased, "You may answer if you understand the question."

Often, witnesses will claim to have forgotten the question after an objection is lodged, especially if there is colloquy between the defender and taker. If you are the taker, you want the question answered. Ask the reporter to read it back for the witness or repeat the question yourself. (Just as the defender may have the question read back to decide whether to object, the taker may want a read-back to reconsider whether the objection is valid.)[84]

As a taker, you have at least two other options when one of your questions is met by objection. The first is to learn from your mistake and rephrase the question immediately, before the witness has time to answer. The second is to ignore the objection for the moment, get the witness's answer, and then rephrase. If you choose the second option, the defender may object that the question was asked and answered. Do not let the objection stop you from insisting the witness answer your rephrased question.[85]

If you see no defect in the question and the defender has not stated the ground for his objection, consider asking what it is. This technique can quickly silence those defenders who like to object but do not have good-faith grounds for their objections. Of course, by asking, you have now opened the door for the defender to speak, as discussed above. In any event, avoid being drawn into a debate about the merits of the question. No one is likely win that debate at the deposition, and the debate may well distract your attention away from the witness.

Though relevance is not a proper basis for an objection at a deposition, defenders often make this objection anyway, following it up with an offer to let the witness answer if you explain the relevance of the question. Faced with this response, you can simply ignore the defender. On the other hand, you may prefer to explain to forestall a fight and a possible instruction not to answer. But, to avoid telegraphing the intent behind your questions to the witness, consider discussing the relevance of your question out of the presence of the witness.

Instructing a Witness Not to Answer

An instruction to a witness not to answer a question is the defender's most potent weapon because absent such an instruction an answer must be given under FRCP 30(c)(2). Why? Because although all objections are noted on the record, "the examination still proceeds; the testimony is taken *subject to any objection*."[86] The instruction deprives the taker, at least temporarily, of an answer from the witness. At the same time, this course of action is fraught with danger for the defender. A miscall on an instruction not to answer can result in sanctions, ranging from recalling the witness for another session of the deposition, to paying the other side's fees and costs in moving to compel an answer, to vacating a summary judgment, awarding damages for deposition misconduct, including paying the costs of reconvening the deposition.[87] Obviously, a client dragged to a second deposition will not be happy. More important, a second deposition gives your adversary another crack at your witness beyond the seven-hour statutory limit.[88]

Because instructing a witness not to answer can have such dramatic consequences, it is not a step to be taken casually. In fact, before giving the instruction, you need to address and resolve a number of issues or questions, considered below.

When Can You Instruct?

FRCP 30(c)(2) sets forth only three circumstances when an instruction not to answer may be given:

1. to preserve a privilege;
2. to enforce a limitation directed by the court;[89] or
3. to present a motion under FRCP 30(d)(3) for a protective order against an examination conducted in bad faith or in a manner that unreasonably annoys, embarrasses, or oppresses the deponent or party.[90]

The logic of the first circumstance, which allows an instruction to preserve a privilege, is obvious. At a deposition there is usually no judge available to rule on the privilege issue. Unless the defender has the right to instruct the witness to refuse to answer, the privilege could be lost if the witness answers the question.[91] FRCP 26(b)(l) even explicitly excludes privileged information from the scope of discovery.[92]

If you are unsure whether the answer to the taker's question is privileged and the answer does not hurt your case, rather than risk an instruction that could result in a motion to compel the answer, you may be inclined to let the witness respond if you can obtain certain protections. This often involves a couple of options:

1. You can seek a stipulation that permitting the witness to answer does not waive any privilege that may apply to the answer and that the court will ultimately determine the privilege issues. This usually will not be accepted by the taker. If it is, you will need to make sure the transcript is either subject to a protective order generally or obtain an agreement that the question and answer be separately bound and retained by outside counsel, pending a ruling by the court on whether the answer can be used. The stipulation, though, will not bind the judge in your case or future cases where this testimony may be relevant as to whether a waiver has occurred; or

2. You can permit the witness to answer, without restriction on using the answer, but obtain an agreement from the taker that your permitting the witness to answer does not constitute a waiver of the privilege as to the subject matter of the answer *and* that neither the taker nor any other represented party will argue that permitting the answer waives the privilege as to the subject matter. You can often achieve this more narrow type of stipulation. While there is still no guarantee that the judge in the case will agree, most judges will abide by such an agreement.

The second part of the rule allows an instruction to enforce a court order placing limitations on the deposition.[93] Even without such an order, a defender may want to instruct a witness not to answer when a question calls for disclosure of trade secrets or other confidential information. Again, without the objection and instruction, this information would be disclosed. There is another option here for the defender: after instructing the witness not to answer, stipulate that the objectionable questions will be answered and the instruction withdrawn if the taker seals that portion of the record until a motion for a protective order can be heard. One advantage of allowing the testimony to go forward under seal is that you avoid the dilemma of instructing your client not to answer in an area and later being prohibited at trial from offering your client's testimony in that same area should this testimony become necessary. Additionally, if you let your witness answer, and the court eventually rules against you, the deposition need not be resumed because the testimony was preserved. Nonetheless, you still have to consider that you will be creating a written record of the answer.

The third part of the rule allows an instruction when the taker is harassing the witness and the defender wants to halt the questioning and move for a protective order.[94] FRE 403, which allows exclusion of relevant evidence on grounds of prejudice, confusion, or waste of time, supports the proposition that an instruction not to answer is proper when a question is put in bad faith or to annoy the witness. On its face, FRCP 30(c)(2) requires the defender to suspend the deposition. In practice, the instruction is often given with an understanding that the deposition may continue on other matters.[95]

Deciding what is, or is not, harassment is difficult. Is a wholly irrelevant question harassment? Does it make any difference if the question comes early in the day or near the end of the deposition? It should.

Some courts have permitted an instruction not to answer questions seeking irrelevant information.[96] Certainly, the isolated irrelevant question is not by itself a basis for the instruction. In sufficient numbers, though, irrelevant questions may justify an instruction. At some point, you must take a stand to protect your witness and maintain her confidence in you. And if a judge or magistrate is available by phone, you can likely resolve the issue at the deposition.[97] If an immediate ruling is not available, however, there is significant risk in instructing a witness not to answer on any ground other than the first two set out in FRCP 30(c)(2) unless you move for a protective order. In *Redwood v. Dobson*,[98] for example, the Seventh Circuit stated that "instructions not to respond that neither shielded a privilege nor supplied time to apply for a protective order were unprofessional and violated the Federal Rules of Civil Procedure as well as the ethical rules that govern legal practice." Indeed the court censured the defender for failure to suspend the deposition, even though it also censured the taker for his questions.[99]

What about a question that has already been asked and answered? Usually, that objection will not support an instruction not to answer.[100] However, suppose the question (and answer) could be critical to your side and has been directly answered two or three times already in a manner favorable to your client, and the taker is simply repeating it in the hope of getting the witness to change her answer. As a defender, you should consider risking an instruction not to answer unless you are confident your witness can see through the taker's scheme and re-answer the question without creating an inconsistency. Again, however, consider the potential consequence of not applying for a protective order. Unless the situation is clearly egregious, it will be difficult to obtain such an order. And an instruction without an application for a protective order runs the risk of sanctions from the court.[101]

Part of the process of deciding whether to instruct the witness not to answer without adjourning and seeking a protective order involves weighing the likelihood of the taker moving to challenge the instruction. If the harassment is sufficiently egregious, putting the burden of going to court on the taker may well result in no motion being made and the instruction prevailing. Even if the taker does make a motion to compel, you still have an opportunity to reconsider your stance and provide the requested information before the motion is heard—perhaps without even resuming the deposition.[102] As always, another part of your calculation is whether it is advisable to give the taker a chance to depose your witness beyond the seven hours allotted if your motion for a protective order fails.[103]

To Whom Is the Instruction Available?

An instruction not to answer is undeniably available to the witness's lawyer under the plain language of the Federal Rules of Civil Procedure. It is also available to other lawyers present if permitted by the rules.[104]

How to Instruct Not to Answer

Giving the instruction itself is simple. You should object to the question and state, "I'm instructing the witness not to answer." Usually, you should also state the basis for your objection and instruction.[105] In any event, the taker is likely to ask for the basis of the instruction, if not offered, because your response may help the taker rephrase the question and avoid another instruction. Stating the basis also helps the witness understand the danger in answering the question. If your instruction is on the basis of privilege, in certain jurisdictions you are required to state specifically the basis for your assertion of the privilege.[106]

Folklore has it that the reporter must "certify" the refusal, but the Federal Rules have no such requirement.[107] Still, the reporter can play a useful role by preparing a separate list indicating the page number at which each instruction and refusal to answer appears. Such a list will simplify the process of making a motion to compel because it eliminates the need to labor through a multi-page deposition transcript, trying to find each instance in which a witness was instructed not to answer.[108]

What Happens After an Instruction?

After the instruction, the taker typically asks the witness, "Are you going to follow your lawyer's instruction?" This is done for two reasons: (1) to make the refusal clear on the record, and (2) to pressure the witness. As the defender, you should prepare your witness for this question. It is up to the witness to decide whether to follow the instruction. Normally, the witness does. To avoid the taker's follow-up to the witness, you may want to seek a stipulation that if you give an instruction, it is deemed followed.[109] A taker may prefer not to so stipulate; that leaves the taker free to attempt to pressure the witness by telling her that by following the instruction, she can be subject to a motion to compel, a court hearing on the question, and a second deposition, and that she also may be required to pay any attorney's fees and costs that are incurred as a result.[110]

An instruction may also trigger a call to the court from the deposition if the court has indicated it will entertain such calls or the jurisdiction has a procedure for resolving such deposition disputes.[111]

After an instruction on one question, the taker may ask other questions in the same area to determine the scope of the instruction not to answer. By asking follow-up questions, the taker may learn that the privilege claimed was, in fact, waived.[112] Consider a supposedly privileged meeting: follow-up questions may show that because a third party attended, the privilege never attached to the discussion.

When faced with follow-up questioning, you, as the defender, need to decide whether to make a blanket instruction for the subject matter or require the examiner to ask each question with you then instructing after each one.[113] Usually you want to try to require the examiner to put each question to the witness. That way, if the taker later prevails on a motion to compel answers to the questions, the defender has a good argument that the resumed deposition should be limited to those questions and no others.[114] If, on the other hand, you use a blanket instruction and then lose the motion to compel, the court has no choice but to permit reexamination on the disputed subject without much limitation. Nevertheless, there are some situations where you can safely use a blanket instruction. A good example: when you have no doubt that the questions cover a privileged discussion between the witness and yourself, the witness's lawyer.

At the end of a deposition, revisit each instruction not to answer that you gave. Then decide if it now makes sense to withdraw any instructions. Three factors to consider are:

1. The likelihood that your adversary will move to compel,
2. The length of the deposition (have the statutory seven hours already run?), and
3. The time of day and the ability of your witness to field the questions adequately once the instruction is withdrawn.

If you withdraw an instruction, the taker should then re-ask the previously blocked question or questions.

How to Handle the Taker's Introduction of "Surprise" Documents

Prior to a deposition, a defender should have thoroughly reviewed all documents relating to the witness, so there will be no "surprise" exhibits introduced by the taker. However, in an era of e-discovery, the sheer volume of documents being produced increases the chance that an important document will be overlooked during witness preparation. In addition, the chances have increased that a document you have never seen before will surface at a deposition. Finally, the speed at which production can be accomplished electronically may shorten the time you have to review documents.

If you are confronted at a deposition with a document you have never seen before, you should first ask for a break so that you can briefly review the document and determine whether you need to talk to your witness about it. If there are potential privilege issues or you sense that you and the witness should talk about the document (for example, because you do not understand the document or you detect certain issues the witness may miss), you should go over the document with the witness. Also, you always should ask the witness if there is anything she wants to discuss or thinks you should know about the document. Of course, as noted above, many jurisdictions place limitations on conferences between counsel and witnesses during a deposition.[115] However, you clearly have a right to determine whether any privilege applies to the document or to testimony about the document. Moreover, you should have the right to discuss a document with the witness, just as you would in preparation. Nonetheless, a court may decide that you should have found the document and dealt with it in preparation, and may therefore impose sanctions for breaking a rule against discussing substance with a witness during the deposition. Therefore, you will have to weigh carefully the risks and benefits of discussing the "surprise" document with your witness if that discussion may violate a local rule.

Defender's Response to Document Requests During a Deposition

Similarly, the first time a taker learns about certain documents is sometimes at the deposition. The taker will then ask that the document be produced so the witness can be examined on it.

Faced with such a request, you must decide between at least two options. One is simply to take the request "under advisement," and then decide after the deposition whether to produce the document, assuming it exists.[116] The other option is to find the document and produce it at the deposition, thereby attempting to force the taker to question on the document at that time. This can be a good strategy when it appears likely that the taker will try to compel the witness back for another session beyond the seven-hour limitation based on the discovery of that document and you want to avoid that outcome. Quick production is also a good strategy if you want to force the taker to question on the document without having much time to review it. Obviously, you should not elect this option unless your witness can deal with questions about the document without extensive preparation.[117]

Examining Your Own Witness

Examining your own witness is the exception, not the rule.[118] If you take this step, after you complete the examination, the taker has the right to follow up and ask more questions—at least on any topic you have opened up. Questioning your own witness could also give the taker a good argument for extending the deposition beyond the seven-hour limit.[119] Your examination may also encourage the taker to consider whether he forgot to ask any questions. During the taker's renewed examination, those questions that were omitted can be asked, even if outside the scope of what you asked. You should still object, but that objection may not be sustained.

In at least two situations, however, you may need to examine your own witness. The first is when the taker's examination has produced an answer from your witness that is harmful or could be misinterpreted when offered into evidence unless it is clarified. Although you can provide the clarification by subsequent affidavit or by an explanation at trial, by that time it may seem fabricated.

In this situation, it is unlikely that you will have prepared the witness to be examined on this particular topic. Therefore, subject to local rules prohibiting discussions with the witness during breaks,[120] take a break to review with your witness your proposed questions and the answers she will give so you can evaluate whether your witness can be examined without undue risk of harmful answers. But be careful, because this kind of examination often occurs at the end of the day when a witness—and you also—may be tired. If you decide the examination is too risky, do not do it. Instead, fix the problem by having the witness later correct the deposition transcript.[121] A correction to the transcript, even though the other side is allowed to comment on it when offered in evidence at trial, may be better than having the witness correct her testimony for the first time before the jury.

The second situation in which you may want to examine your own witness is when you need the witness's testimony for a planned motion, and the taker's examination did not produce the testimony you need.[122] In this situation, you should have prepared the witness before the deposition on the subject about which you want to examine. Still, you must decide whether the witness is fresh enough at the end of the deposition to be examined further. If not, you can obtain the needed testimony for your planned motion by having the witness provide the testimony in an affidavit. Of course, an affidavit may be less effective than deposition testimony because affidavit testimony has not been subject to cross-examination. In addition, the affidavit may create an opening for another deposition session.

Adjournment

Witnesses can usually handle questioning that ends before 5:00 PM, except when a witness becomes ill before that time or eats inappropriately at lunch (for example, too much carbohydrates/sugar). In either event, insist on an immediate adjournment and agree on a date to resume. But depositions that run beyond 5:00 PM pose a problem for a defender. Although no one has done any empirical studies about post-5:00 PM depositions, there is little doubt that more damaging testimony comes late in the day. With the statutory seven-hour limit,[123] if you start promptly at 9:00 AM and take a relatively short lunch, you can conclude at 5:00 PM. But, depositions often start later, have longer than expected lunches and breaks, and hence proceed past 5:00 PM.[124] It is important as counsel for the deponent to arrive promptly before the scheduled start time to avoid giving the taker an excuse to extend the deposition until late in the day.

Suppose the examiner asks to go beyond the seven-hour limit. At that point, you must make some judgment calls. Start by asking the taker how late he wants to go and whether that will finish the deposition. If there is likely to be another session anyway (either because you agreed to a two-day deposition or because you believe the judge will grant a second session), you usually should adjourn the deposition *even if* your witness wants to continue. Why? Because by this time most witnesses, whether or not they realize it, are tired. Agree to continue past seven hours only when (1) you *want* to finish that day (for example, because you are concerned about the taker having more time to prepare if the deposition continues to another day), *and* (2) you obtain a commitment by the taker *on the record* to conclude the deposition on that same day. If no commitment is made, then you must decide whether it is realistic to expect the taker to finish. You also must consider whether, if the deposition continues, there will be enough time for you to examine the witness if that needs to be done, and how tired the witness may be at that point.

Takers like to keep their options open, so often a taker will not say on the record that the deposition is concluded. In fact, this may become a more widespread practice now that the Federal Rules provide for only one deposition of a person.[125] If you, as the defender, believe the deposition is over, say so on the record and prepare to leave with the witness. Even though that may not end the debate, once the witness has left, the burden shifts to the taker to seek an order for a continued deposition. If the taker claims that other areas of inquiry remain, ask that these be described on the record. You can use the taker's representations to attempt to restrict the scope of any further questioning if you allow the deposition to continue or the court orders another session.

Conclusion

Every deposition is a battle, with the taker and the defender as the combatants. As the defender, you will need to make many decisions, large and small. They often must be made quickly. Yet each decision also must be made in light of federal and local rules, standing orders, case law, and the attitudes and practices of the judge presiding over your case, as well as a complex blend of strategic factors.

Moreover, the decisions—and the judgments they involve—are ever changing. They vary with the case, the stage of the lawsuit, the type of witness, the skills of the taker, and the purpose of the deposition. Each decision is important, because what you decide affects your relationship with the witness and your adversary, the conduct of future discovery, and the view of the judge in your case.

Notes

*The authors gratefully acknowledge the contributions of Leslie O'Brien, an associate at Cravath, Swaine & Moore LLP, in helping them revise their chapter for the second edition.

1. For a discussion of a different view regarding the standard advice for defending a deposition, see Steven Lubet, *Showing Your Hand: A Counter-Intuitive Strategy for Deposition Defense*, 29 LITIGATION 38 (Dec. 2003).

2. As for how expansive the witness should be, that depends on the facts of the case, the purpose of the deposition, and the defender's level of confidence in the witness's ability. For example, to enhance the possibility of a settlement, a defender might want the witness to demonstrate her credibility, memory, and potential as a trial witness. In addition, if one wanted to have certain facts in the record by way of testimony subject to cross-examination (as opposed to by way of affidavit) to support later motions (for example, for summary judgment or motions in limine), that too would counsel a more expansive approach. See "Task 1: Ask

Yourself Why You Are Taking This Deposition" in Chapter 4, discussing how preparation strategies may differ depending on the perceived goals of the deposition.

3. *See infra* note 5 and accompanying text and Chapter 15, discussing the increasing number of restrictions on the defender at a deposition and problem defense counsel. See also "Ethical and Practical Constraints" in Chapter 8, discussing ethical restraints in preparing a witness to testify.

4. *See* FED. R. CIV. P. 30(d)(2) (court may impose sanctions, including costs and attorneys' fees, if a "fair examination" has been impeded, delayed, or otherwise frustrated); 28 U.S.C. § 1927 (expenses and attorneys' fees awardable against attorney if there has been unreasonable and vexatious multiplication of proceedings); Unique Concepts, Inc. v. Brown, 115 F.R.D. 292 (S.D.N.Y. 1987) (holding sanctions appropriate under 28 U.S.C. § 1927 and the "inherent power of the Court" where conduct of attorney defending at deposition "was undertaken in bad faith, intended to harass and delay, and reflected a willful disregard for the orderly process of justice"); see also "Federal Statutory Bases for Discovery Sanctions" in Chapter 15, discussing use of sanctions against problem counsel.

5. *See, e.g., infra* note 69 (local rules prohibiting speaking objections); local rules cited *infra* note 105 (local rules requiring basis to be detailed on claim of privilege); D. COLO. L. CIV. R. 30.3 (off-the-record conferences between counsel and witness, except for purpose of determining whether to assert privilege, and instructions not to answer, absent clear legal ground, are prohibited); S.D. IND. L.R. 30.1(b) (lawyer for deponent shall not initiate private conference with deponent regarding pending question, except to determine whether privilege claim should be asserted); M.D.N.C. L.R. 30.1 (counsel shall not engage in private off-the-record conferences with witness "while the deposition is proceeding in session," except to establish whether to assert privilege); E.D.N.Y. CIV. R. 30.6 (lawyer for deponent shall not initiate private conference with witness "during the actual taking of the deposition," except for purpose of determining whether to assert privilege); D. WYO. L.R. 30.1(d) ("Repeated directions to a witness not to answer questions calling for non-privileged answers are symptomatic that the deposition is not proceeding as it should."); *see also* M.D. ALA. GUIDELINES TO CIVIL DISCOVERY PRACTICE, guideline II; S.D. ALA. CIV. DISC. PRAC. 2.E.; M.D. GA. STANDARDS OF CONDUCT B.5.g.; D. KAN. DEPOSITION GUIDELINES, guideline 5; D. MD. DISCOVERY GUIDELINES, guideline 5; N.D. OHIO L.R. 30.1; D.S.C. CIV. R. 30.04; W.D. TEX. L.R. CV-30(b).

6. D. MD. CIV. R. 104.9.

7. *See, e.g.,* D. MD. DISCOVERY GUIDELINES (rules regarding speaking objections, repetitive or particularly personal questioning, attorney conversations with deponent during interrogation and breaks, claims of privilege, and proper recording of attorney misconduct); D.S.C. CIV. R. 30.04 (rules regarding preservation of objections, instructions not to

answer, speaking objections, attorney conversations with deponent during deposition and breaks, proper recording of attorney misconduct, and procedures for obtaining telephonic resolution of deposition disputes); D. WYO. L. CIV. R. 30.1. (rules regarding instructions not to answer, immediate rulings by magistrate judge, speaking objections, defending attorney conferences with nonparty deponents, and claims of privilege).

8. Although the United States District Court for the Eastern District of Pennsylvania did not have a specific rule governing conduct at depositions, the judge in *Hall v. Clifton Precision*, 150 F.R.D. 525, 531–32 (E.D. Pa. 1993) (Gawthrop, J.), entered an order governing counsel's conduct. See "Problems for the Defender in Controlling the Examiner" in Chapter 15, which discusses the *Hall* case as well as dealing with problem counsel at a deposition.

9. This discussion does not contemplate inappropriate contact with an adverse party known to be represented by counsel. *See* MODEL RULES OF PROF'L CONDUCT R. 4.2 (2008).

10. See Chapter 7, discussing witness preparation in general and final instructions to the witness.

11. Some lawyers refer to this practice as "stop and frisk." Also see Chapter 9.

12. See "Arranging the Deposition Room" in Chapter 11, discussing seating at a deposition.

13. See Chapter 18.

14. See *infra* section "Adjournment" for a discussion of the strategic considerations involved in continuing a deposition late in the day. See also Chapter 23.

15. At depositions, the usual practice is that the attorneys and everyone else present orally identify themselves on the video by name, affiliation, and whom they represent. See also Chapter 17 for a detailed discussion of video recorded depositions.

16. See "Task 13: Decide Whom You Want Present at the Deposition" and "Task 2: Decide Whether to Seek a Protective Order" in Chapter 4.

17. A related concern for the taker arises in a multiparty case when one lawyer represents the witness and numerous additional lawyers represent other parties. After an objection by the witness's lawyer, an entire procession of similar objections often follows. As a taker, you want to try to stop that practice because it uses up valuable time, especially in view of the federal seven-hour rule. *See* FED. R. CIV. P. 30(d)(1) and advisory committee's note, 2000 Amendment ("This limitation contemplates that there will be reasonable breaks during the day for lunch and other reasons, and that the only time to be counted is the time occupied by the actual deposition."). One solution is to seek a stipulation that an objection made by one will be deemed to apply to all. See "Opening Remarks and Stipulations" in Chapter 11.

18. *See* Rockwell Int'l, Inc. v. Pos-A-Traction Indus., Inc., 712 F.2d 1324 (9th Cir. 1983) (sanctions imposed on deponent for refusing to answer questions on the grounds that two lawyers were asking them on behalf of same party). However, where local rules specify that the examination of deponents is to proceed in the same manner as the examination of trial witnesses, and the examination of trial witnesses is limited to one attorney per party, an argument may be made that only one lawyer per party may examine a deponent. *See* CONN. SUPER. CT. R. 5-4, 13-30(a) (limiting examination and cross-examination of witness at trial to counsel who begins such examination and elsewhere providing that "[e]xamination and cross-examination of deponents may proceed as permitted at trial").

19. See "Task 2: Decide Whether to Seek a Protective Order" in Chapter 4.

20. See Chapter 17.

21. See "Opening Remarks and Stipulations" in Chapter 11.

22. See "Proper Practice Versus Improper Coaching" in Chapter 7 and "Lawyer/Witness Conferences" in Chapter 15, discussing improper witness conferences.

23. See "3. Stipulation that the deposition is being taken before a qualified deposition officer and reported by a qualified and disinterested shorthand reporter (or recorded by a qualified videographer)" in Chapter 11 for this and other suggestions from the taker's perspective. Although the court reporter is retained by the taker, the reporter is supposed to be a neutral entity, present to assist both parties. *See* FED. R. CIV. P. 28(c), 30(c)(1) (setting forth requirement for a disinterested deposition officer and requiring the deposition officer—or "person acting in the presence and under the direction of the officer"—to record the testimony of the witness).

24. However, some jurisdictions prohibit conversations between counsel and witnesses during breaks regarding the substance of deposition testimony. *See* D. MD. DISCOVERY GUIDELINES, guideline 5(g) ("During breaks in the taking of the deposition, no one should discuss with the deponent the substance of the prior testimony given by the deponent during the deposition."); D.S.C. CIV. R. 30.04(E) ("Counsel and witnesses shall not engage in private, 'off the record' conferences during depositions or during breaks or recesses regarding the substance of the testimony at the deposition, except for the purpose of deciding whether to assert a privilege or to make an objection or to move for a protective order."); DEL. CH. CT. R. 30(d)(1) (deponent's lawyer shall not confer with deponent during deposition—including during "recesses or continuances thereof of less than five calendar days"—about substance of earlier or anticipated testimony, except to determine whether to assert privilege or how to comply with court order, or suggest to deponent "manner in which any questions should be answered"); *see also* D. COLO. L. CIV. R. 30.3 ("Any off-the-record conference during a recess may be a subject for inquiry by the opposing counsel or pro se party, to the extent the conference is not privileged.").

Where the local rule's prohibition is limited to discussions regarding the "substance" of the testimony, the defender should be able to discuss procedural or stylistic issues such as volunteering information, speculating, not looking at the camera, or failing to read an entire exhibit before answering questions about that exhibit. Some local rules, however, do not appear to limit the prohibition to discussions relating to the "substance" of the testimony. *See supra* note 5.

25. "Realtime" reporting (when the transcript is being generated both in electronic format and on stenographic record) is being used with more frequency. Even if the court reporter is not providing an ongoing readout of the testimony, more and more computer-literate lawyers are using their own laptop computers to record the testimony unofficially. See "Realtime Recipient Software" in Chapter 18.

26. Steven Lubet, Modern Trial Advocacy: Analysis and Practice 263 (2004) ("A question [at trial] on either direct or cross examination typically lasts less than ten seconds; a long question will go on for no more than twenty seconds.").

27. FRCP 30(c) provides that "[t]he examination and cross-examination of a deponent proceed as they would *at trial under the Federal Rules of Evidence*, except Rules 103 and 615." (Emphasis added.) FRE 103, Rulings on Evidence, and FRE 615, Exclusion of Witnesses, are typically not at issue in depositions, absent a protective order. See "Task 2: Decide Whether to Seek a Protective Order" in Chapter 4.

28. Fed. R. Civ. P. 30(c)(2).

29. *Id.* The only time a question need not be answered is when an objection is joined with an instruction not to answer. *See infra* notes 86–90 and accompanying text (discussing instructions not to answer).

30. Fed. R. Civ. P. 32(d)(2)–(3).

31. Some local court rules specifically permit—or even require—attorneys to call a judicial official to get a telephonic ruling when deposition disputes arise. *See, e.g.,* S.D. Ind. L.R. 37.3 ("Where an objection is raised during the taking of a deposition which threatens to prevent the completion of the deposition and which is susceptible to resolution by the court without the submission of written materials, any party may recess the deposition for the purpose of submitting the objection by telephone to a judicial officer for a ruling instanter."); E.D.N.Y. Civ. R. 37.3 ("Where the attorneys for the affected parties or a non-party witness cannot agree on a resolution of a discovery dispute that arises during a deposition, they shall, to the extent practicable, notify the court by telephone and seek a ruling while the deposition is in progress."); *see also* D. Wyo. L. Civ. R. 30.1(d) ("Where a direction not to answer such a question is given and honored by the witness, either party may seek an immediate ruling from the Magistrate Judge as to the validity of such direction.").

32. Fed. R. Civ. P. 26(b)(1).

33. *Id.*

34. FED. R. CIV. P. 32(b) ("[O]bjection may be made at a hearing or trial to the admission of any deposition testimony that would be inadmissible if the witness were present and testifying.").

35. See *infra* section "Reactions by the Taker to the Defender's Tactics," discussing the taker's choices in the face of an objection. Who will benefit from an ambiguous answer is not always clear at the time of the deposition. If a defender knows the witness will be available at trial, he may not care. But even a defender who can secure the witness's presence at trial may prefer to have a clear answer on the record at the time of the deposition, rather than having to explain a deposition answer at a later date. See also *infra* section "Examining Your Own Witness" for a discussion of the decision to examine your own witness at a deposition.

36. Because it is your witness, you could submit an affidavit on a motion with more clear testimony.

37. See "Using FRCP 30 to Deal with Improper Objections" in Chapter 15 and "Depositions as Substitute Testimony" in Chapter 25, discussing reading of colloquy to a jury.

38. In some jurisdictions, however, this objection may be prohibited. *See infra* notes 69–70 and accompanying text (discussing prohibitions on "speaking" objections and stating the nature of an objection).

39. See Chapter 1, note 1.

40. MODEL RULES OF PROF'L CONDUCT R. 3.4(a) (2008) ("A lawyer shall not . . . unlawfully obstruct another party's access to evidence or unlawfully alter, destroy or conceal a document or other material having potential evidentiary value. A lawyer shall not counsel or assist another person to do any such act."). Also see "Ethical and Practical Constraints" in Chapter 8, discussing the ethical duty not to obstruct discovery.

41. See also "Problem Situations for the Examiner and Suggested Responses" in Chapter 15, discussing the judicial response to overly aggressive deposition defense counsel.

42. See Appendix 8.

43. *See* Rascon v. Hardiman, 803 F.2d 269, 277 (7th Cir. 1986) (failure to object to scope of testimony at deposition waives objection); Oberlin v. Marlin Am. Corp., 596 F.2d 1322, 1328 (7th Cir. 1979) (failure to object to form of question on cross-examination resulted in waiver); Bahamas Agric. Indus. Ltd. v. Riley Stoker Corp., 526 F.2d 1174, 1180–81 (6th Cir. 1975) (failure to object to form resulted in waiver, noting "[t]he focus of the Rule is on the necessity of making the objection at a point in the proceedings where it will be of some value in curing the alleged error in the deposition"); Raya v. Maryatt Indus. Corp., 1993 WL 515878, at *2 n.3 (N.D. Cal. Dec. 3, 1993) (failure to object to quality of translation of questions), *aff'd*, 67 F.3d 308 (9th Cir. 1995); Harb v. United Parcel Serv., Inc., 1985 WL 4850, at *3 (S.D.N.Y. Dec. 23, 1985) (failure to object to conduct of lawyers at deposition); *see also* Kirschner v. Broadhead, 671 F.2d 1034, 1038 (7th Cir. 1982) (failure to object to nonresponsive answers constitutes waiver).

44. See *supra* section "Even If the Question Is Objectionable, Should You Object to It?," discussing the timing of objections.

45. This discussion assumes that no stipulations are made to vary the FRCP, such as a stipulation that all objections, save as to form, are preserved until trial—which is broader than FRCP 32. See "Opening Remarks and Stipulations" in Chapter 11, discussing such a stipulation.

46. FED. R. CIV. P. 32(d)(3)(B) (emphasis added).

47. *See* FED. R. CIV. P. 30(b).

48. See *supra* section "Even If the Question Is Objectionable, Should You Object to It?" for a discussion of why you might not want to object to an improper question.

49. *See* FED. R. EVID. 611(c).

50. This question would also be objectionable based on a lack of foundation because there was no testimony establishing that the chairperson had reviewed the memorandum.

51. This objection is consistent with FRE 701, which limits the testimony of lay witnesses to those matters about which they have firsthand knowledge or that they have observed firsthand. *See* FED. R. EVID. 701 advisory committee's note (explaining that rule "is the familiar requirement of firsthand knowledge or observation").

52. *See* FED. R. EVID. 403, 611(a)(2)–(3); FED. R. CIV. P. 26(b)(1)–(2), 26(c).

53. FED. R. CIV. P. 32(d)(3)(A) (emphasis added).

54. *See* Cordle v. Allied Chem. Corp., 309 F.2d 821, 825–26 (6th Cir. 1962) (applying what is now FRCP 32(d)(3)(A)). An interesting question is whether the taker must object at the deposition if she believes a witness is intoxicated or on medication and cannot give accurate testimony based on that condition. If this is the case, an adjournment and rescheduling of the deposition will be required.

55. See Chapter 19, discussing defending at an expert's deposition.

56. *See Kirschner*, 671 F.2d at 1037–38; *supra* note 43 (citing other authorities).

57. FRCP 26(b)(1) states that discovery of privileged matters is not permitted. Under FRE 501, "the privilege of a witness . . . shall be determined in accordance with State law." Among the privileges protected by state law are attorney-client, work product (also see FRCP 26(b)(3)), physician-patient, spousal communications, trade secrets (also see FRCP 26(c)(1)(G)), penitent-clergy, and self-incrimination (also see United States Constitution, Amendment V). For a discussion of federal testimonial privileges generally, and the psychotherapist-patient privilege in particular, see *Jaffee v. Redmond*, 116 S. Ct. 1923 (1996). See also Chapter 6; FED. R. EVID. 502 (governing the scope of privilege waivers in federal proceedings); and "Improper Instructions Not to Answer" in Chapter 15. For a discussion of when and how to instruct a witness not to answer, see *infra* section "Instructing a Witness Not to Answer."

58. FED. R. CIV. P. 30(c)(2). See also "Task 2: Decide Whether to Seek a Protective Order" in Chapter 4, discussing the entry of protective orders to limit discovery.

59. FED. R. CIV. P. 30(c)(2).

60. FED. R. CIV. P. 30(c)(2) (emphasis added). Before the 1993 amendments to the FRCP, the rules did not state the manner in which objections were to be made. As always, it is important to consult any applicable local rules to determine whether there are specific requirements regarding how objections must be stated. *See, e.g.*, E.D. TEX. L.R. CV-30 ("Objections to questions during the oral deposition are limited to 'Objection, leading' and 'Objection, form.' Objections to testimony during the oral deposition are limited to 'Objection, nonresponsive.' These objections are waived if not stated as phrased during the oral deposition.").

61. See "Problem Situations for the Examiner and Suggested Responses" in Chapter 15, discussing improper defense tactics.

62. *See supra* note 40 and accompanying text (discussing ethical obligations).

63. *See* FED. R. EVID. 103(a)(1) ("Error may not be predicated upon a ruling which admits . . . evidence unless . . . a timely objection or motion to strike appears of record, stating the specific ground of objection, if the specific ground was not apparent from the context. . . .").

64. See "Coaching" in Chapter 15, discussing speaking and coaching objections by "problem counsel."

65. *See* On Lee v. United States, 343 U.S. 747, 750 n.3 (1952) (noting that general objection—"That is objected to"—is insufficient to preserve specific claim of violating constitutional provision); United States v. Hutcher, 622 F.2d 1083, 1087 (2d Cir. 1980) (where specific objection was unclear from context, general objection was insufficient to preserve claim for appeal under FRE 103(a)); Markel Serv., Inc. v. Nat'l Farm Lines, 426 F.2d 1123, 1127–28 (10th Cir. 1970) (finding appellant's general objections to memorandum introduced at deposition "insufficient to make the trial judge fairly aware of any foundational infirmities that had arisen during the deposition").

66. *See* FED. R. EVID. 103(a)(1).

67. Doe v. Johnson, 52 F.3d 1448, 1457 (7th Cir. 1995); Hutter N. Trust v. Door County Chamber of Commerce, 467 F.2d 1075, 1079 (7th Cir. 1972); 1 WIGMORE ON EVIDENCE § 18, at 827–28 (Tillers rev. 1983); 1 MCCORMICK ON EVIDENCE § 52, at 205 (4th ed. 1992). *But see* United States v. Walker, 449 F.2d 1171, 1174, 1176 n.5 (D.C. Cir. 1971) (sustained general objection would be affirmed only if "it clearly appears that the evidence is inadmissible under any circumstances"; dissent stated general rule).

68. *See* CAL. CODE CIV. PROC. § 2025.460(b) (West 2008) ("Errors and irregularities of any kind occurring at the oral examination that might be cured if promptly presented are waived unless a *specific* objection to

them is timely made during the deposition." (Emphasis added.)); Damaj v. Farmers Ins. Co., 164 F.R.D. 559, 561 (N.D. Okla. 1995) ("Counsel shall not make objections or statements which might suggest an answer to a witness. Counsel's statements when making objections should be succinct and verbally economical, stating the basis of the objection and nothing more."); McDonough v. Keniston, 188 F.R.D. 22 (D.N.H. 1998) (same); Zachariah v. Rockwell Int'l, 712 N.E. 2d 811, 814–15 (Ohio Ct. App. 1998) (defendant's general objections to expert's deposition testimony waived where objections stated without basis and basis indiscernible from context).

69. *See, e.g.*, FED. R. CIV. P. 30(c)(2); D. WYO. CIV. R. 30.1(e):

> Objections in the presence of the witness which are used to suggest an answer to the witness are presumptively improper. If the objection to a deposition question is one that can be obviated or removed if presented at the time, the proper objection is "objection to the form of the question," and the problem with the form shall be identified. If the objection is on the ground of privilege, the privilege shall be stated and established.

See also M.D. ALA. GUIDELINES TO CIVIL DISCOVERY PRACTICE, guideline 11(F) ("Lawyers should not attempt to prompt answers by the use of suggestive objections."); D. KAN. DEPOSITION GUIDELINES, guideline 5(a) ("Objections shall be concise and shall not suggest answers to or otherwise coach the deponent."); D. MD. DISCOVERY GUIDELINES, guideline 5(b) ("Objections should be stated as simply, concisely and non-argumentatively as possible to avoid coaching or making suggestions to the deponent."); M.D.N.C. L.R. 30.1(2) ("Counsels' statements when making objections should be succinct, stating the basis of the objection and nothing more."); N.D. OHIO L.R. 30.1 (b)(4) ("Speaking objections that refer to the facts of the case or suggest an answer to the deponent are improper and must not be made in the presence of the deponent."); D.S.C. CIV. R. 30.04(D) ("Counsels' objections shall be stated concisely and in a non-argumentative and non-suggestive manner, stating the basis of the objection and nothing more."); W.D. TEX. L.R. CV-30(b) ("Objections during depositions shall be stated concisely and in a non-argumentative and non-suggestive manner."); UNIFORM RULES FOR N.Y. STATE TRIAL COURTS § 221.1(b) ("Speaking objections restricted. Every objection raised during a deposition shall be stated succinctly and framed so as not to suggest an answer to the deponent. . . ."). Although speaking objections are prohibited in some jurisdictions, the practice does not necessarily result in sanctions. Flaherty v. Filardi, No. 03 Civ. 2167(LTS)(HBP), 2007 WL 2398762, at *4 n.2 (S.D.N.Y. Aug. 15, 2007) (noting instruction to counsel to refrain from speaking objections and commenting that "[s]peaking" objections should be avoided because they tend to prompt witnesses," but refraining from imposing sanctions); Cameron Indus., Inc. v. Mothers Work, Inc., No. 06 Civ.1999 (BSJ)(HBP), 2007 WL 1649856 (S.D.N.Y. June 6, 2007) (noting that counsel's speaking objections were inconsistent with rules governing depositions, but refraining from imposing sanctions).

70.   ALASKA R. CIV. P. 30(d)(1) ("No specification of the defect in the form of the question or the answer shall be stated unless requested by the party propounding the question."); ARIZ. R. CIV. P. 32(d)(3)(D) (same).

71.   In at least one jurisdiction, an attorney defending a deposition is under an affirmative duty to inform her client that, unless an authorized objection (for example, one based on privilege) is made, questions must be answered. D.S.C. CIV. R. 30.04(C).

72.   See FED. R. CIV. P. 32 (d)(3)(B) ("An objection to an error or irregularity at an oral examination is waived if (i) it relates to . . . the form of a question *or answer* . . . and (ii) it is not timely made during the deposition." (Emphasis added.)).

73.   See, e.g., Moultrie Nat'l Bank v. Travelers Indem. Co., 181 F. Supp. 444, 445 (M.D. Ga. 1959) (overruling objection to nonresponsive deposition answer, and agreeing with view that there is no per se error where deposition witness provides nonresponsive answer, but irrelevant facts included in such answer may be struck), *aff'd*, 275 F.2d 903 (5th Cir. 1960); Charlton Mem'l Hosp. v. Sullivan, 816 F. Supp. 50, 59 (D. Mass. 1993) (noting that while an interrogating counsel's objections to unresponsive answers will generally be sustained, other counsel's objections based solely on unresponsiveness will generally be overruled unless another valid basis for objection is added); *see also* 3 WIGMORE ON EVIDENCE § 785, at 200–02 (Chadbourn rev. 1970); Elyria-Lorain Broad. Co. v. Lorain Journal Co., 298 F.2d 356, 359 (6th Cir. 1961) ("Although it is true that the opponent may not object to a non-responsive answer on that ground alone, he may move to strike such an answer if it is objectionable for any other reason."). Some older decisions have held that only the examining lawyer may object to an answer, in the context of a trial, on the ground that it is nonresponsive. Page Steel & Wire Co. v. Blair Eng. Co., 22 F.2d 403, 406 (3d Cir. 1927) (holding that objection based on unresponsiveness of witness's answer was properly overruled "because the examiner alone had the right to object on that ground"); United States v. Schneiderman, 106 F. Supp. 892, 905 (S.D. Cal. 1952) (noting wisdom of rule that counsel not interrogating witness lacks standing to request that unresponsive answers be stricken based solely on ground of unresponsiveness, and denying defendants' motion to strike based on unresponsiveness of witness's answer).

74.   J. ALEXANDER TANFORD, THE TRIAL PROCESS: LAW, TRIAL TACTICS AND ETHICS 301 (1983).

75.   See, e.g., Kirschner v. Broadhead, 671 F.2d 1034, 1037–38 (7th Cir. 1982) (failure to object to nonresponsive answers waives objection); *see also supra* note 43.

76.   The answer is not, in fact, deleted from the deposition transcript or video record. The motion is recorded by the reporter for a later ruling.

77. If frustrated in getting an answer to an important question, you can file a motion to compel as a possible remedy. *See* FED. R. CIV. P. 37(a)(3)(B); also see "Improper Instructions Not to Answer" in Chapter 15, discussing motions to compel, and "Continuing the Deposition Pending a Court Order" in Chapter 23, discussing motions to compel at the end of a deposition.

78. *See Kirschner*, 671 F.2d at 1038 (noting that had plaintiff objected to defendant's answer as nonresponsive, the witness "would have conformed his answers to the questions" and "[t]he limited nature of such answers, in turn, would have alerted [defendants'] counsel to develop omitted portions of the story on cross-examination" rather than relying on the in-depth narrative already on the deposition record).

79. *See* FED. R. CIV. P. 32(d)(3)(A) ("An objection to . . . the competence, relevance, or materiality of testimony . . . is not waived by a failure to make the objection before or during the deposition, unless the ground for it might have been corrected at that time."); *Kirschner*, 671 F.2d at 1038 (noting that had the plaintiff objected to the deponent's testimony as irrelevant, defendants' counsel "would have been prompted to elicit relevant testimony favorable to their positions," thereby curing the relevancy objection).

80. *See* Fed. R. Civ. P. 30(c)(2) ("A person may instruct a deponent not to answer only when necessary to preserve a privilege, to enforce a limitation ordered by the court, or to present a motion under Rule 30(d)(3).") and advisory committee's note, 2000 Amendment ("The amendment makes it clear that, whatever the legitimacy of giving such instructions [not to answer], the nonparty is subject to the same limitations as parties."). Also see *infra* section "Instructing a Witness Not to Answer."

81. Women in City Gov't United v. City of New York, 112 F.R.D. 29, 32 (S.D.N.Y. 1986) (Nonparty witness's counsel is "not present to participate generally in the deposition" or to "object on evidentiary grounds," but does have standing to help deponent exercise testimonial privileges and may move to suspend deposition to prevent harassment); *see also* D. WYO. CIV. R. 30.1(f) ("An attorney defending at a deposition of a nonparty deponent shall not engage in a private conference with the deponent during the actual taking of a deposition, except for the purpose of determining whether a privilege should be asserted.").

82. *See infra* note 104 (discussing availability of instruction not to answer to attorneys not representing deponent).

83. Indeed, in at least one jurisdiction, you may be required as a defender to so inform your witness. *See supra* note 71.

84. See Chapter 18, discussing the uses by a taker and defender of realtime transcription.

85. See text above regarding the objection that the question has been asked and answered.

86. FED. R. CIV. P. 30(c)(2) (emphasis added).

87. See "Improper Instructions Not to Answer" in Chapter 15.

88. FED. R. CIV. P. 30(d)(1).

89. While the Federal Rules previously specified that instructions not to answer could be given to enforce limitations "on evidence," the Rules were amended in 2000 to delete references to "evidence." The current rule is meant to "apply to any objection to a question or other issue arising during a deposition, and to *any limitation imposed by the court in connection with a deposition*, which might relate to duration or other matters." FED. R. CIV. P. 30(d)(1) advisory committee's note, 2000 Amendment (emphasis added) (commenting on what is now FRCP 30(c)(2)).

90. FED. R. CIV. P. 30(c)(2).

91. *Cf.* CAL. CODE CIV. PROC. § 2025.460(a) (West 2008) (making waiver explicit: "The protection of information from discovery on the ground that it is privileged or that it is a protected work product under Chapter 4 (commencing with Section 2018.010) is waived unless a specific objection to its disclosure is timely made during the deposition.").

92. *See supra* note 57 and accompanying text (regarding other privileges such as physician-patient, spousal communication, clergy-penitent, and self-incrimination).

93. See "Task 2: Decide Whether to Seek a Protective Order" in Chapter 4, discussing seeking protective orders before the deposition.

94. *See also* FED. R. CIV. P. 30(d)(3) ("If the objecting deponent or party so demands, the deposition must be suspended for the time necessary to obtain an order [to terminate or limit the deposition]."). In contrast to the FRCP, the New York State Uniform Rules for the Conduct of Depositions do not require suspension of the deposition, but rather allow an instruction not to answer "when the question is plainly improper and would, if answered, cause significant prejudice to any person." UNIFORM RULES FOR N.Y. STATE TRIAL COURTS § 221.2.

95. In *Redwood v. Dobson*, 476 F.3d 462, 467–68 (7th Cir. 2007), the court adopted a strict enforcement of FRCP 30(d), the predecessor to FRCP 30(c)(2) and 30(d)(3). The court made clear that, where counsel believes a witness is being harassed, counsel may halt the deposition and apply for a protective order, "but must not instruct the witness to remain silent." *Id.* See also "Problems for the Defender in Controlling the Examiner" in Chapter 15, for a detailed discussion of this case.

96. *See, e.g.*, Kamens v. Horizon Corp., 81 F.R.D. 444 (S.D.N.Y. 1979) (denying motion to redepose defendant and rejecting contention that FRCP 30(c) "mandates that a deponent answer all questions"); *In re* Folding Carton Antitrust Litig., 83 F.R.D. 132 (N.D. Ill. 1979); *see also* Int'l Union of Elec., Radio, & Mach. Workers v. Westinghouse Elec. Corp., 91 F.R.D. 277, 280 n.5 (D.D.C. 1981) (exceptional situations when direction not to answer is appropriate may include questions concerning irrelevant information "directed to a sensitive part of the witness's past"). The more prevalent view appears to be that a witness must

answer even irrelevant questions or move for an order to terminate or limit the examination. *See, e.g.*, Ralston Purina Co. v. McFarland, 550 F.2d 967, 973–74 (4th Cir. 1977) (noting that the "action of plaintiff's counsel in directing the deponent not to answer was highly improper" and "[i]f counsel felt that the discovery procedures were being conducted in bad faith or abused in any manner, the appropriate remedy was to present the matter to the court by motion under Rule 30(d)"); Eggleston v. Chicago Journeymen Plumbers' Local Union No. 130, 657 F.2d 890, 903 (7th Cir. 1981) (questions should be answered subject to relevance objection unless they "unnecessarily touch sensitive areas or go beyond reasonable limits"); Quantachrome Corp. v. Micromeritics Instrument Corp., 189 F.R.D. 697, 700 (S.D. Fla. 1999) ("[I]f [defendant's] refusal to answer a question was based on a belief that the question was so far beyond the realm of possible relevance as to be abusive, [defendant] was then required to move for a protective order. . . ."); *Westinghouse Elec. Corp.*, 91 F.R.D. at 279–80 (ordinarily improper to direct witness not to answer on grounds of relevancy); Shapiro v. Freeman, 38 F.R.D. 308, 311 (S.D.N.Y. 1965) ("even if the plaintiffs' attorney believed the questions to be without the scope of the [court's] . . . order, he should have done nothing more than state his objections"). Similarly, a witness must answer questions that go beyond the scope of an FRCP 30(b)(6) deposition notice or move for an order to terminate or limit the examination. *See* Paparelli v. Prudential Ins. Co. of Am., 108 F.R.D. 727, 731 (D. Mass. 1985) (holding that instructions not to answer were improper where based on subject matter of deposition questions going beyond FRCP 30(b)(6) notice, and noting that proper remedy would have been to seek to adjourn deposition to make a motion pursuant to FRCP 30(d)(4) (now FRCP 30(d)(3))). *Contra* Detoy v. City and County of San Francisco, 196 F.R.D. 362, 366–67 (N.D. Cal. 2000) (noting that adjourning 30(b)(6) deposition "seems artificial and wasteful of both the parties' resources and the witness's time" and proper remedy for objections to questions beyond scope of 30(b)(6) designation is for counsel to note objection on record and witness to answer to best of witness's ability).

97. *See supra* note 31. Remember that if you want a transcript of the argument, you need to use a speakerphone, if available, and request that the reporter transcribe the argument. This is especially important if the ruling relates to a privilege question, where there is a greater probability of the ruling becoming subject to a later appeal.

98. 476 F.3d 462, 469 (7th Cir. 2007).

99. See "Problems for the Defender in Controlling the Examiner" in Chapter 15 for a detailed discussion of *Redwood v. Dobson*.

100. *See, e.g.*, First Tenn. Bank v. Fed. Deposit Ins. Corp., 108 F.R.D. 640, 640–41 (E.D. Tenn. 1985) (no right to instruct not to answer based on "asked and answered" objection); Hearst/ABC-Viacom Ent. Servs. v. Goodway Mktg., Inc., 145 F.R.D. 59, 63 (E.D. Pa. 1992) ("the fact that a

question is repetitive . . . is not an appropriate ground for instructing a witness not to answer a question").

101. Along these same lines, keep in mind that in at least one jurisdiction, if an attorney instructs a witness not to answer, he must subsequently move for a protective order or the objection is waived and the deposition may be reconvened. D.S.C. CIV. R. 30.04(C); see also *supra* note 95 and text accompanying notes 98–99 (discussing Redwood v. Dobson, 476 F.3d 462 (7th Cir. 2007)).

102. This approach may expose you and your client to the costs of making the motion even if you withdraw the motion before it is heard by the court.

103. *See supra* notes 87–88 and accompanying text (discussing possible negative consequences of a miscall on an instruction not to answer). When seeking a protective order on the ground of harassment, you should consider whether to request a special master as referee to sit at the deposition or to be available by phone to rule on objections and directions. *See, e.g.,* CAL. CODE CIV. PROC. § 639(a)(5) (West 2007) (reference to a referee on application of any party or the court's own motion). As an alternative to an instruction not to answer, it might be more appropriate to note improper examiner behavior on the record. *See* D. Md. Discovery Guidelines, guideline 7 (noting that person recording deposition shall enter on the record description by requesting person of conduct that violates guidelines). Later, this record may provide a basis for sanctions, particularly if there is no video record of the deposition. More important, it may put a stop to such behavior.

104. FED. R. CIV. P. 30(c)(2) ("A *person* may instruct a deponent not to answer only when necessary to preserve a privilege, to enforce a limitation ordered by the court, or to present a motion under Rule 30(d)(3)." (Emphasis added.)). However, some courts and commentators frown upon the practice of lawyers who do not represent the deponent giving instructions not to answer. *See, e.g., Shapiro,* 38 F.R.D. at 312 ("[party's lawyer] had no right whatever to . . . instruct the witnesses not to answer, especially . . . when the witnesses were not even his clients"); 2 JOHN M. CARROLL, ET AL., FEDERAL LITIGATION GUIDE ¶18.03, at 18–41 (1994); Gary S. Gilden, *A Practical Guide to Taking and Defending Depositions,* 88 DICK. L. REV. 247, 260 n.62 (1984). The deponent and any party always have a right to seek to suspend the deposition to make a motion pursuant to FRCP 30(d)(3). *See also Ralston Purina,* 550 F.2d at 973–74; *Shapiro,* 38 F.R.D. at 311–12. See also *supra* section "Defending at a Nonparty Deposition."

105. See M.D. ALA. GUIDELINES TO CIVIL DISCOVERY PRACTICE, guideline 1.I.4. (requiring that basis be detailed on claim of privilege); E.D.N.Y. CIV. R. 26.2(a) (same); S.D. ALA. CIV. DISC. PRAC. 1.K.3. (same); D. MD. DISCOVERY GUIDELINES, guideline 6(a)(i) (same); S.D.N.Y. CIV. R. 26.2(a) (same); N.D. W. VA. L.R. CIV. P. 26.04(2)(A) (same); D. WYO. L. CIV. R. 30.1(h) (same); UNIFORM RULES FOR N.Y. STATE TRIAL COURTS § 221.2

("Any refusal to answer or direction not to answer shall be accompanied by a succinct and clear statement of the basis therefor.").

106.   *See, e.g.*, S.D.N.Y. Civ. R. 26.2.

107.   *See* Gall v. St. Elizabeth Med. Ctr., 130 F.R.D. 85, 85–86 (S.D. Ohio 1990).

108.   Alternatively, if the transcript is available in an electronic format, a search can be performed. See Chapter 24, discussing computerized deposition transcripts, and "Interactivity with the Transcript—Quick Marks" in Chapter 18, discussing annotating a transcript when realtime is used.

109.   See "Opening Remarks and Stipulations" in Chapter 11, discussing such a stipulation.

110.   *See* FED. R. CIV. P. 30(d) and advisory committee's note, 1993 Amendment (noting that sanctions under this rule "may be imposed on a non-party witness as well as a party or attorney"); *supra* notes 4, 87, and accompanying text (discussing availability of sanctions where fair examination of witness has been delayed or otherwise frustrated).

111.   *See supra* note 31 and accompanying text (discussing telephonic resolution of deposition disputes and noting local procedures).

112.   *See* S.D. IND. L.R. 30.1(a) (allowing examiner "reasonable latitude . . . to question the deponent to establish relevant information concerning the legal appropriateness of the assertion of the privilege"); D. MD. DISCOVERY GUIDELINES, guideline 6(a)(ii) (same); W.D. TEX. L.R. CV-30(b) (same).

113.   See *supra* section "Continuing Objections" for a discussion of the problem with continuing objections.

114.   Nonetheless, it is possible that the court will permit reasonable follow-up questions at the resumed deposition.

115.   *See supra* note 24 (noting that some jurisdictions prohibit conferences between counsel and witnesses, even during breaks, regarding the substance of deposition testimony) and note 5 (citing local rules placing limitations on private conferences between counsel and witnesses "during the actual taking of the deposition," "while the deposition is proceeding in session," and "regarding a pending question"); *see also* UNIFORM RULES FOR N.Y. STATE TRIAL COURTS § 221.3 ("An attorney shall not interrupt the deposition for the purpose of communicating with the deponent unless all parties consent or the communication is made for the purpose of determining whether the question should not be answered [to preserve a privilege, to enforce a court-ordered limitation, or to prevent significant prejudice] . . . and . . . the reason for the communication shall be stated for the record succinctly and clearly.").

116.   Usually defenders prefer to have the deposition take place away from the deponent's office since it avoids business distractions (as well as easy availability of the deponent's files). Therefore, sometimes the defender's only option may be taking the request under advisement.

117. Also see "Requests for Documents" in Chapter 3 and "Obtaining Documents for Use at a Deposition" in Chapter 12.

118. See "Examination of Your Own Client at the Deposition on Cross-Examination" in Chapter 10, discussing preparing your own witness for examination on "cross."

119. The Advisory Committee's Note regarding the seven-hour rule indicates that the taker is entitled to use the full seven hours, though questioning by the lawyer for the witness and/or various other parties may support an extension of the time to complete the deposition. *See* FED. R. CIV. P. 30(d) advisory committee's note, 2000 Amendment ("Parties considering extending the time for a deposition—and courts asked to order an extension—might consider a variety of factors. . . . [S]hould the lawyer for the witness want to examine the witness, that may require additional time.").

120. *See supra* note 24 (discussing such restrictions).

121. This is usually inadequate, however, due to the constraints on what constitutes proper correction of a deposition transcript. See "Requesting Review of the Deposition Transcript" in Chapter 23, discussing corrections to a deposition transcript.

122. While as a general approach, you will instruct your witness to avoid volunteering information, there may be times when you have a *very able* deponent whom you will want to volunteer, if necessary, to make a record for a planned motion or to demonstrate to the other side that the facts of the case are not good for them and you have at least one "killer" witness. *See supra* note 2 for a discussion of factors to consider regarding how expansive a defender might want a witness to be.

123. FED. R. CIV. P. 30(d)(1).

124. Local rules impose additional restrictions beyond the seven-hour limit. *See, e.g.,* E.D. OKLA. L. CIV. R. 30.1(b) ("No deposition shall extend beyond seven hours in length, beyond 5:00 PM, or be taken on a weekend or holiday without agreement of all interested attorneys or court order); N.D. OKLA. L. CIV. R. 30.1(b) (same); E.D. TEX. L.R. CV-30 (deposition may be taken after 5:00 PM only "with approval of a judge or by agreement of counsel").

125. FED. R. CIV. P. 30(a)(2)(A) ("A party must obtain leave of court [to take a deposition] . . . if the parties have not stipulated to the deposition and . . . the deponent has already been deposed in the case. . . ."). See "Exceptions to the 'Only Once' Rule" in Chapter 3.

CHAPTER 15

Problem Counsel, Problem Witnesses

JEFFREY S. WHITE*
EVE T. SALTMAN

In a now-famous excerpt from a deposition, Texas lawyer Joe Jamail said to the examining lawyer, "Don't 'Joe' me, asshole. You can ask some questions, but get off of that. I'm tired of you. You could gag a maggot off a meat wagon."[1] Jamail's outburst was just one of a number of instances described by the Delaware Chancery Court addendum to its opinion as "rude, uncivil and vulgar" behavior by Jamail over the course of a deposition he defended.[2] Although Jamail was not a member of the Delaware bar, the Delaware court was so incensed at his behavior that it issued him an invitation for a "voluntary appearance"—so that he could explain to the court why he should not be barred from all future Delaware proceedings.[3]

This outburst of uncivil and unprofessional behavior during a deposition is not an anomaly. In December 2007, a New York judge ordered court supervision of a lawyer who engaged in objectionable conduct at a deposition.[4] According to the deposition transcript, instead of objecting to the form of the questions as being improper, the defending attorney suggested that the female examiner did not know how to take a deposition.[5] Not satisfied with this suggestion, the defender then stated, "This is not a white collar interview that you're sitting here interviewing something with your cute little thing going on."[6] And the defender continued to make gender-biased comments throughout the deposition in an attempt to intimidate the examiner and otherwise interfere with her examination.[7]

Lawyers are, of course, not the only participants in a deposition who sometimes behave badly. A prime example of a witness breaching all norms of common decency and decorum at a deposition occurred in a case involving the sale of residential mortgages.[8] Before the examining attorney was forced to adjourn the deposition,[9] the deponent "used the word 'fuck' and variants thereof no less than 73 times," while using the word "contract," a word particularly relevant to the case, only fourteen times.[10] When the examiner tried to question the witness about a loan applicant's background,[11] at first the witness refused to answer. Then he refused to review the provided loan file and stated, "Open it up and find it. I'm not your fucking bitch."[12] When the examiner again politely asked the witness to review the loan file, the response was even more caustic: "I'm taking a break. Fuck him. You open up the document. You want me to look at something, you get the document out. Earn your fucking money asshole. Isn't the law wonderful. Better get used to it. You'll retire when I'm done."[13] These outbursts, and others like it, led a federal district court judge to impose nearly $30,000 in sanctions jointly and severally against the deponent and his counsel.[14]

These decisions underscore the heightened sensitivity of state and federal courts in the past few decades to improper, abusive conduct at depositions and the negative effect of such conduct on the discovery process. But courts have been concerned about deposition abuse for much of the past century. In 1937, Rule 30 of the Federal Rules of Civil Procedure (FRCP) was adopted in part to safeguard and to protect people from unlimited discovery.[15] These safeguards proved to be inadequate as time passed, so additional restrictions were added in the 1990s and in the 2000 Amendments to the Federal Rules.[16] And attempts to curb deposition misconduct have not been limited to the federal rules, local rules, and court decisions, but have also been the focus of both national and local bar groups.[17]

Nevertheless, most litigators have at least one war story about outrageous conduct in a deposition—by the opposing lawyer, of course. Fortunately, there are ample ways to effectively deal with improper behavior by any participant at a deposition—the examiner, the defender, or the witness. This chapter explains how to deal with common problems by using familiar tools—available from the FRCP, other statutes authorizing sanctions, local rules, standing rules of the assigned judge, and case law.

Preparation

If you anticipate that a deponent or your opponent might try to undermine a deposition with incivility, there are several steps you should consider taking in advance to help ensure an orderly and fruitful deposition.

1. *Video record the deposition.* Attorneys are much less likely to misbehave, raise their voice, or use other intimidation tactics when they are being video recorded. In addition, a video record can help convince a judge to permit additional deposition time because of delaying tactics, evasion, and other inappropriate behavior.[18]

2. *Use a realtime transcription service at the deposition.* Realtime transcription services, such as LiveNote and Summation, permit a questioner to review the witness's answer immediately and ask any necessary follow-up questions. While this service entails extra cost, it often helps control counsel who dispute your recollection of questions. It also helps ensure that you have exhausted the witness's recollection of a topic and that you have a clear answer that can be used at trial if need be. Finally, a realtime transcription record may help convince a judge or magistrate judge that opposing counsel has acted improperly in those situations where a discovery dispute can be taken immediately to court.[19]

3. *Protective orders.* If you are defending a deposition and have good reason to believe that the questioner intends to ask about irrelevant sensitive information, consider moving for a protective order before the deposition begins.[20]

4. *Immediate rulings.* In extreme cases, determine whether the judge or magistrate judge will make herself available by telephone to rule on contentious issues. If so, take the appropriate telephone numbers with you to the deposition.

Problem Situations for the Examiner and Suggested Responses

Most examining lawyers would like defending counsel to act like a "potted plant."[21] Often, however, an examiner must expend time and energy contending with a defender who appears to be doing everything in her power to impede the examination.

Coaching

"Coaching" encompasses many different forms of behavior at a deposition, including improper objections, improper instructions, and repeated off-the-record conferences with the witness. The "coach," of course, is the defending lawyer who subtly—or not so subtly—attempts to manipulate the deponent's answers.

Speaking Objections and "Clarifying" Objections

Speaking objections are improper objections that are lengthier and more verbose than necessary to preserve the objection for trial.[22] They are used to convey information about the questions to a witness; they also may also be used to impede the flow of a deposition.

By using speaking objections, a defending attorney is trying to tell the witness how to answer a question. Before the deposition, the lawyer has told the witness that when she objects, the witness should listen to the objection carefully and then either incorporate the objection into his response or simply repeat the objection. For example, the defender tells the witness, "When I object to the question as vague, say to the examiner, 'I don't understand your question.'"

Every examiner is painfully familiar with the following examples of improper speaking objections:

Q. Did Ms. Jones say anything about the sales forecast?
DEFENDER: Counsel, I am going to object. You are asking the witness to guess and speculate about what was in the mind of someone else, which he cannot and will not do.

How can he know what was in the mind of Ms. Jones? You can ask him his understanding of the situation, but you cannot ask him what someone else might have said to anyone at anytime.

Or:

DEFENDER: Objection, vague and ambiguous as to "sales forecast." Also calls for speculation as to what Ms. Jones said at anytime to anyone about sales forecasts.

The subtexts here are obvious. In the first example, the defender is telling the witness to avoid disclosing anything the witness knows about how Ms. Jones was feeling or thinking about the sales forecast. In the second example, the defender is signaling the witness what the defender thinks is ambiguous about the question. In each example, the defender is coaching the witness to answer a question in a certain way.

Defenders often add the gratuitous comment—usually without even stating an objection—"If you recall" after a simple question such as, "What did Mr. Smith tell you about the software?" The comment has only one purpose: to encourage the witness to forget. Likewise, the interjections "If you know" or "Don't speculate" after a question such as, "What is the company's accounting system?" are intended to coach the witness to say, "I don't know" or "I would only be guessing."

"Clarifying" objections are a form of improper speaking objections. On the surface, they appear to ask for clarification from the examiner. But, like every speaking objection, their real purpose is to convey information from the defender to the witness. Usually, the defender's objection is something to the effect of, "I don't understand the question; therefore the witness doesn't understand the question."

The following are two examples of improper clarifying objections:

Q. Do you frequently meet with Mr. Smith?
DEFENDER: Wait a minute; [to the witness] don't answer the question. [To the examining lawyer] I don't understand what you are asking [the witness].
DEFENDER: Objection, do you mean at any time? What time period are you asking about?

391

Sometimes, clarifying objections take this form:

Q. What did Mr. Jones say to you during the telephone call in October, the year before last?

DEFENDER: Objection. Rather than having the witness play a memory-testing game, why don't you show the witness the notes he took of that telephone call?

Clarifying objections are improper: If the witness needs clarification, the *witness*, not her lawyer, should ask the deposing lawyer for clarification. A defender's purported lack of understanding is not a proper reason to interrupt a deposition. In *Hall v. Clifton Precision*, a federal district court judge held that lawyers are not permitted to state on the record their interpretations of questions because those interpretations are irrelevant and often suggest a desired answer.[23]

How to Respond to Improper Speaking and Clarifying Objections

The best way to stop a defender from coaching is to put the offending tactics on the record—both early and often. Making a record is essential for any future motion related to the offending conduct. A record made at the time of the deposition is far more persuasive than an affidavit prepared at the time of the motion.[24] In addition, an examiner who waits until the middle of a deposition—or even worse, until the end—to comment on the record about the opponent's tactics risks looking desperate or unprofessional.

Practical Strategies for Dealing with Improper Objections

Improper objections can be handled in several practical ways. Suppose you believe there is no need to explain your question to the interjecting defender. Or you do not want to rephrase it. Or you simply want to keep the deposition moving for strategic reasons. Then just look at the witness while ignoring the defender—which is good advice when dealing with any defender—and wait for an answer. Or look at the witness and add, "You may answer." Alternatively, while looking at the witness and continuing to ignore the defender, add, "Subject to your counsel's objection, go ahead and answer." And you can escalate your response by telling the witness, "You are required to answer my questions unless instructed not to do so by your attorney."

Suppose you believe your question is proper and does not call for speculation. You may want to explain this to the defending lawyer: "Counsel, I was not asking the witness to speculate on what Ms. Jones thought about the sales forecast. I asked him if Ms. Jones said anything to him about the sales forecast." After giving this explanation, you may want to re-ask the question as explained to the defender or ask the reporter to read back your question so that the question and answer appear on the transcript without the intervening objection or your reply.

Suppose opposing counsel objects that she does not understand your question; in other words, she is making a "clarifying" objection. Again, start by ignoring the defender, look straight at the witness, and ask, "Do you understand my question?" If the witness says "no," your next question should be, "What don't you understand about my question?" or "What word or words do you not understand?" Then follow up by asking, "Have you ever used the word '[word the witness says he does not understand]?'" and "What did you mean when you used that word?" Now a witness who parrots his lawyer's supposed lack of understanding will look foolish on the record when he needs to fabricate a reason why he does not understand the question. As stated in *Hall v. Clifton Precision*, "There is no proper need for the witness's own lawyer to act as an intermediary, interpreting questions, deciding which questions the witness should answer, and helping the witness to formulate answers."[25]

How do you handle the defender who keeps reminding a witness to answer only if the witness recalls? First, avoid beginning questions with phrases like "Do you recall." Such phrases may be seen by the witness as permission to forget. Second, if you believe before the deposition begins that the defender may adopt this tactic, consider starting the deposition by stating that your questions will ask only for the witness's knowledge. Ask the witness if she understands and agrees to this ground rule.[26] Answer only if you can then refer to this ground rule it whenever the defender interjects the phrase "if you recall."

In deciding how to respond to the defender who coaches, note any pattern to the improper objections. For example, do they seem to be made out of habit? Or as a matter of style? Or are they made only when a particular subject comes up? If the improper objections occur infrequently or in a noncritical area, you may want to ignore them. Ignoring a defender's interruptions may seem to conflict with the advice to make a record of the improper objections. But it also makes sense to be reasonable and not become aggressive until it matters.

No matter how intrusive a defender's objection, listen carefully to it. When a defender becomes obstreperous, it may signal that you have entered an area worth pursuing—especially if the defender was passive up to that point. In addition, objections—no matter how intrusive—sometimes can make you a better lawyer; they may help you to ask a better question than your original question.

Using FRCP 30 to Deal with Improper Objections

Several provisions of the FRCP provide ways to deal with speaking and clarifying objections.[27] FRCP 32(d)(3)(B) discusses objections during a deposition involving errors or irregularities relating to "the form of a question or answer, . . . a party's conduct, or other matters that might have been corrected at that time."[28] If these objections are not made during the deposition in a timely manner, they are waived. Under FRCP 32(d)(3)(A), objections to the competency of a witness or to the competency, relevancy, or materiality of testimony are not waived for failure to make them at a deposition, unless the grounds for such an objection could have been corrected at the deposition. And FRCP 30(c)(2) requires objections to be "stated concisely in a nonargumentative and nonsuggestive manner." Before the 1993 amendments, a deposing lawyer facing a difficult adversary had to make an FRCP 37(a) motion before seeking sanctions for inappropriate behavior.[29] As amended, FRCP 30(d) provides a separate basis for an examiner who needs relief from inappropriate speaking objections at a deposition.

As an initial step, at the start of the deposition, pull out your copy of FRCP 30 (or a comparable local rule), and then state on the record, "Counsel, I understand that you need to make your objections. However, our time is limited, and as you probably know, Federal Rule 30(c)(2) provides that objections shall be stated 'concisely in a nonargumentative and nonsuggestive manner.'" Do not let the defender draw you into a debate about how his objections do or do not contravene FRCP 30(c)(2). Instead, after making your statement, continue the examination. When facing a particularly obstreperous defender, you may want to read into the record FRCP 30(d)(2), which provides that a court may sanction anyone who "impedes, delays, or frustrates the fair examination of the deponent."

If the defender's coaching so "impedes or delays the examination" that it becomes impossible to proceed with questioning, you may want to adjourn the deposition and seek judicial intervention.[30] But beware: Such a motion probably will succeed only if you can show that the coaching prevented you from obtaining necessary information from the witness.[31] In *Johnson v. Wayne Manor Apartments*,[32] a federal district court judge found that on numerous occasions, "defense counsel improperly 'objected to the form of the question' by either suggesting what he apparently believed to be an appropriate answer to his client or [by] himself testifying."[33] After finding that the examining lawyer was effectively precluded from discovering what the deponent knew, the court awarded sanctions.

FRCP 30(d)(1) states that unless approved by the court or stipulated to by the parties, "a deposition is limited to one day of seven hours." But this rule also provides that, consistent with FRCP 26(b)(2), additional time must be granted "if needed to fairly examine the deponent or if the deponent, another person, or any other circumstance impedes or delays the examination."[34] You may find that additional time is needed due to either the seven-hour time limit or the discovery cut-off pending trial. If you believe that opposing counsel's speaking objections prevented you from finishing the deposition in seven hours or before the discovery cut-off pending trial, seek an order under FRCP 30(d)(1).[35]

To win an FRCP 30 motion, as noted above, you need a clear, persuasive record. That may mean ensuring that the record includes not only the number of speaking objections but also their duration. After the defender finishes his speaking objection, you might say, "I note for the record that counsel's sixth speaking objection took just over two minutes." Of course, your statement may lead to colloquy on the record, including a dispute about your characterization or your ability to keep accurate time, which can in turn waste more time. Yet having a record with such details may make your FRCP 30(d)(1) motion more persuasive: You can go through the transcript and calculate how much time the defender's speaking objections took and thus educate the court about how much time you lost because of your opponent's improper tactics. This calculation will not be clear on a traditional transcript; thus it is important to keep track of time during the deposition itself. Of course, if the deposition is video recorded, a record of the time and date will be available, and disputes over time will be avoided.[36]

If you have a video recorded deposition, consider compiling clips of the most egregious speaking objections. Then, with the court's permission, append this compilation to your motion papers to demonstrate the prejudice you suffered because of lost examination time.[37]

As an examiner, you also may want to terminate the deposition to move for sanctions, to compel further testimony, or for other relief.[38] Before you suspend or terminate the deposition, consider obtaining a telephone ruling from the judge, magistrate judge, or special discovery master handling overseeing discovery in the case. But understand that this tactic may be problematic for one or more reasons: (1) the judge or master must be available, (2) the record will be oral unless the reporter can prepare a transcript immediately,[39] and (3) it assumes the judge or master will hear the dispute without a noticed motion.

Under FRCP 37(a)(2)(B), the proponent of a question in a deposition may move for an order compelling a response, either after completing the deposition or after adjourning it for purposes of filing a motion. Given the risks of terminating the deposition and then losing this motion, give two or three "warnings" to the defender that his conduct may lead to termination of the deposition. In addition, state on the record the grounds upon which a motion for sanctions would be based. If you give such warnings, you will have to follow through to maintain your credibility. But the mere threat of a motion may solve your problem: FRCP 37(a)(5)(A) provides that the court "must" award the cost, including attorney's fees, of bringing a successful motion to compel the movant, unless the court finds that (1) the movant failed to first make a good-faith effort to resolve the problem before seeking court intervention,[40] (2) the opposing party's conduct was substantially justified, or (3) other circumstances make the award of expenses unjust.[41]

Federal Statutory Bases for Discovery Sanctions

In addition to the FRCP, other federal statutes authorize sanctions against both lawyers and parties for discovery abuses.

Section 1927 of Title 28

28 U.S.C. § 1927, which imposes liability for excess costs caused by counsel acting in bad faith, can be the basis for discovery abuse sanctions. This section authorizes an award of excess costs, expenses, and attorney's fees resulting from the unreasonable and vexatious

multiplication of proceedings. According to the Fourth Circuit in *Bakker v. Grutman,* "Section 1927 was intended to sanction conduct Rule 11 does not reach; i.e., protracting or multiplying the litigation to run up the opposing party's costs, remedied by awarding excess attorneys' fees and costs."[42] Section 1927 expressly authorizes sanctions to be imposed against "[a]ny attorney or other person admitted to conduct cases in any court of the United States."[43]

In *Unique Concepts, Inc. v. Brown,* a federal district court imposed sanctions and awarded costs because the case was "marred from its inception by incivility and a consistent lack of cooperation between counsel."[44] The motion that led to the imposition of sanctions involved a deposition at which plaintiff's counsel made several personal attacks on opposing counsel.[45]

In *In re Marker,* the court ruled that "[a] finding of bad faith on the part of the offending attorney is a prerequisite for awarding attorney's fees as a sanction under this provision."[46] But even a finding of bad faith does not guarantee sanctions. As the court stated in *Hackman v. Valley Fair,* "Once a finding of bad faith has been made, the appropriateness of sanctions is a matter entrusted to the discretion of the district court."[47]

In extreme instances, sanctions may include an award of the entire cost of defending a lawsuit.[48] Such a sanction might be awarded if there were persistent violations of the discovery rules throughout the litigation.

Before a court may impose a section under § 1927, due process requires that the offending attorney be given notice and an opportunity to be heard.[49] Furthermore, § 1927 sanctions are generally reviewed on appeal for an abuse of discretion.[50] And some courts apply a "clearly erroneous" standard to the district court's determination of bad faith, on the ground that "[b]ad faith is a factual determination."[51]

Courts' Inherent Authority

Courts may also award discovery sanctions against lawyer or parties.[52] The rationale for this authority is that courts must have the means to manage their affairs and achieve an orderly disposition of their calendars.[53] This inherent authority may be used to sanction lawyers or parties.[54] And as with sanctions under § 1927, law firms may be sanctioned for the conduct of their lawyers.[55]

A court using its inherent authority to impose sanctions must exercise discretion. As the Supreme Court stated in *Chambers v.*

NASCO, Inc., "Because of their very potency, inherent powers must be exercised with restraint and discretion. . . . A primary aspect of that discretion is the ability to fashion an appropriate sanction for conduct which abuses the judicial process."[56]

As with sanctions under § 1927, notice and a hearing are prerequisites for the imposition of sanctions under a court's inherent authority.[57] Similarly, the imposition of sanctions under a court's inherent authority will be reviewed on appeal for abuse of discretion.[58]

Improper Instructions Not to Answer

Under FRCP 30(c), objections during a deposition do not halt the examination; instead, the deposition continues with the testimony being "taken subject to any objections." But there is one mechanism by which a defender can stop an examination. FRCP 30(c)(2) provides that "[a] person may instruct a deponent not to answer only when necessary to preserve a privilege, to enforce a limitation [on evidence] directed by the court, or to present a motion under Rule 30(d)(3)."[59]

FRCP (30)(c)(2) spells out three specific circumstances for an instruction. It enlarged the situations where an instruction may be given. FRCP 30, as amended in 1993, was held to allow a lawyer to instruct a witness not to answer only when necessary to preserve a privilege.[60] Despite the unambiguous statement in amended FRCP 30(c)(2) of *three* circumstances in which instructions are permitted, an obstructionist defender will often direct his witness not to answer and see how far the adversary can be pushed.

Given the explicit language of FRCP 30(c)(2), repeated instructions not to answer on grounds other than those listed may be the basis for a motion for sanctions under FRCP 30(d)(2). That section permits, as noted above, sanctions for "impediment, delay, or other conduct that has frustrated the fair examination of the deponent." For repeated bad-faith violations, sanctions may also be imposed under § 1927 or a court's inherent authority.

When a lawyer instructs his witness not to answer because the questions call for privileged information, the examiner's follow-up questions should force the defender to state the basis for his claimed privilege.[61] It is the defender's burden to establish that the privilege applies.[62] If you are the examiner, be persistent until you completely understand what the defender believes is subject to privilege.

Because the attorney-client privilege is most likely to be claimed as the basis for an instruction, you should have at the deposition a copy of the relevant statute or case that lays out the elements of the attorney-client privilege.[63] You may also want to prepare a list of questions tracking those elements. At the deposition, you can use the questions to challenge the claims of privilege.

Suppose, for example, you ask the witness about a particular communication, and the defender objects on the grounds of attorney-client privilege. If you are convinced the communication was for a business purpose and not for legal advice, your list can help you ask the right questions to establish your position and defeat the claim of privilege.[64] It also can remind you of the questions you must ask if you are going to argue that the privilege was waived. (Were any third parties present during the allegedly privileged communication? Who were they? Did the witness communicate the substance of this communication to any third parties?)

If you suspect that your opponent will claim work-product protection, consider preparing similar questions dealing with that objection. You might want to ask, for example, whether the witness anticipated litigation at the time the document was created, and, if so, what litigation was anticipated.[65]

In addition to asking for the basis for the instruction not to answer, you may also want to ask questions about the particular subject that triggered the instruction. If those questions are met by similar instructions not to answer, you can ask the defender to stipulate that she will instruct the witness not to answer any question on the topic and that the witness will follow that instruction. But be sure you have a clear record of the questions for which you will seek responses in your motion to compel. And, as part of your motion papers, attach the appropriate portion of the deposition transcript and ask the judge or magistrate judge to order the witness to answer each question. Such follow-up questions will be important for any later motion under FRCP 37(a) to compel further testimony.[66]

Common sense dictates that you should not terminate a deposition unless a refusal to answer one or a series of questions prevents you from examining the witness effectively. Instead of terminating a deposition when a witness refuses to answer, it usually makes more sense to complete the deposition and then move to compel the desired answer or disclosure under FRCP 37(a)(3)(B). Be aware, however, that an outright refusal is not required for a motion to compel.

Under FRCP 37(a)(3)(B), the movant does not have to show bad faith on the part of the opposing party, but may simply terminate the examination until the motion compelling a response or further response is decided.

Finally, before terminating or adjourning a deposition because of an instruction not to answer, you may want to ask the defender to reconsider her instruction. Your offer gives the defender a chance to "save face" and avoid a motion. You might also try resolving any dispute about an instruction not to answer in an "off-the-record" discussion. In fact, you must do this in jurisdictions requiring you to "meet and confer" with your opponent before moving to compel. Although the Federal Rules contain no such expert requirement of a conference, such an off-the-record discussion would probably satisfy the requirement that you attempt in good faith to obtain the information before resorting to court action.[67] If you resolve the dispute, you then can go back on the record and re-ask those questions upon which instructions were given.

Lawyer/Witness Conferences

Different types of attorney-witness "conferences" may call for different reactions by the examiner. For example, the witness and her lawyer may have repeated "whispering" conferences that occur after a question is posed but before an answer is given. Or they may have repeated "off-the-record" conferences. Finally, they may confer both on and off the record about documents used as deposition exhibits.

Strategies for Dealing with Conferences

If the defender repeatedly whispers to her client in the middle of a question or after a question but before an answer, note the consultation on the record. Simply say, "Let the record reflect that counsel is conferring with her client while a question is pending." In addition, state for the record the amount of time the conference consumed.[68]

As an alternative, you may want to speak, on the record, directly to the defender: "Counsel, you know it is improper under FRCP 30(c)(2) to consult with your client while a question is pending." In *Eggleston v. Chicago Journeymen Plumbers' Local Union*, the Seventh Circuit Court of Appeals noted that plaintiffs and their counsel had held an estimated 127 private, off-the-record conferences, many of them while a question was pending. According to the court, "It is too late once the ball has been snapped for the coach to send in a different play."[69] In *Eggleston* the court suggested that

400

the trial court, "in view of the exceptional circumstances created by the past performances of counsel," appoint a discovery referee or special master under FRCP 53.[70] The court further noted that "[t]he costs of using this procedure will fall upon the parties and possibly serve as a deterrent to further abuse."[71]

For fast-moving litigation with numerous discovery disputes, both taker and defender may want to consider stipulating to a discovery referee who is available on short notice during depositions and for motions.[72] If you as examiner anticipate attorney-witness conferences, consider recording the deposition on video. In addition, when the defender and the witness confer, ask, "Counsel, why don't you state for the record what it is you need to tell your client before he answers my question?"

Also, note on the record every time the defender or the witness asks for a break "to confer." Keep track of who asks for breaks, when they are taken, their frequency, and how long they last. Your questions by themselves may inhibit the defender and witness from conferring. Or they may provide useful information for your motion papers. After a break, you may want to ask the witness on the record, "After conferring with your counsel, do you have any changes or additions to your testimony?" (An advantage to asking your question in this way is that your opening comment will be read to a jury as part of the question, whereas colloquy by counsel typically would not be read.)

The timing of a conference is also important. A request for a conference when no question is pending is usually less of a problem than a request made when a question is pending. Always insist on an answer to your question before allowing an off-the-record conference. And when there is a conference, you may want to ask why it is needed. If the witness or the defender claims that conference after conference is related to a privilege issue, but no privilege is asserted after the conference, you may want to note that fact on the record. You may also want to ask about the topic of the conference if no privilege is asserted.[73]

At the start of a deposition, many examining attorneys tell the deponent, "If you want to take a break at any time, let me know."[74] Instead of giving a witness the right to stop the deposition at any time, you may want to tell the witness that you control the deposition and will decide when breaks are taken. You might say, "If you would like to take a break, please let me know; and, if we are at an appropriate spot to take a break, we can do so." Alternatively, you may not want to say anything about breaks. If the witness asks for a "bathroom break" and you are in the middle of a critical examination area, you might say to the witness, "I will be finished with this topic area in ten minutes. Can you wait?" After each break, you may want to make a practice of asking the witness a series of questions about what she discussed with the defending lawyer during the break—even if the question brings an objection that the question calls for privileged information.

Some defenders like to take a break when the witness is shown a document and before the witness answers. Such breaks are usually not permissible. As the court stated in *Hall v. Clifton Precision*:

> When the deposing attorney presents a document to a witness at a deposition, that attorney is entitled to have the witness and the witness alone, answer questions about the document. The witness's lawyer, should be given a copy of the document for his or her own inspection, but there is *no valid reason why the lawyer and the witness should have to confer about the document before the witness answers questions about it.* . . . [T]here need not be an off-the-record conference between witness and lawyer in order to ascertain whether the witness understands the document or a pending question about the document.[75]

As with every conference during a deposition, note on the record a that a conference about a document has occurred. Some lawyers refuse to allow breaks during a deposition when a witness is being questioned about a document.[76]

Case Law and Local Rule Support for Dealing with Conferences

The Federal Rules do not explicitly address the issue of lawyer-witness conferences. But several courts have addressed the issue with local rules. The Eastern District of New York, for example, has a local rule prohibiting a defending lawyer from "initiat[ing] a private conference with the deponent during the actual taking of a deposition, except for the purpose of determining whether a privilege should be asserted."[77] And the Eastern District of Pennsylvania has ruled that lawyer-client conversations during a break in a deposition are not within the attorney-client privilege, except as related to whether a privilege should be asserted in response to a question.[78]

Many courts do not go as far as the *Hall* court. So it is always prudent to review local rules, standing orders of the assigned judge, and case law for support.

Problems for the Defender in Controlling the Examiner

Defenders have a unique problem. Besides trying to control depositions without appearing obstreperous, they must protect their witnesses from out-of-control examiners. As discussed above, given FRCP 30(c)(2) and 30(d)(2) as well as recent cases sanctioning lawyer misconduct, defenders—now more than ever before—must use careful advocacy rather than intimidation tactics or other inappropriate behavior.

The problems an examiner can present for a defender take several forms. For example, the examiner may ask a witness about personal habits or personal financial affairs that have nothing to do with the case. Or the examiner may repeat questions that the witness has already answered or argue with the witness: "Come on, isn't it true that you know your codefendant was lying to the plaintiff? Isn't it true you did nothing about it?"

As an initial step, warn the examiner that the questioning is becoming harassing or repetitive or is touching upon irrelevant topics. After giving a warning, you may want to ask the examiner, "Counsel, why is that information properly discoverable here?"—although you should not expect an answer.

Notwithstanding the FRCP 30(c) limitations on instructions not to answer, an examiner's questions may be so out of line that it is necessary to give such an instruction. In such a situation, you may want to instruct the witness not to answer by saying something like, "Counsel, your questions are inappropriate. They are irrelevant, abusive, and harassing. For these reasons I am going to instruct my witness not to answer." If the questioning is truly out of line, you will have a better record when responding to a subsequent motion to compel.

Another option for a defender is to terminate a deposition. FRCP 30(d)(3) provides that a party or the deponent may terminate a deposition to move for a protective order to stop the examination or limit its scope.[79]

Redwood v. Dobson illustrates when termination may be appropriate.[80] The deposition in that case was antagonistic from the start. It soon became harassing when the witness was questioned about his criminal record, primarily vehicular violations that had no bearing on the case and discipline by the state bar, another topic "whose relevance [w]as never explained."[81] The examiner asked whether the witness "had been ordered to obtain psychiatric counseling or anger-management therapy" and if he was "involved in any type of homosexual clique with any other defendants in this action."[82] Given those facts, the Court of Appeals for the Seventh Circuit found that the defender could have allowed the witness "to stalk out of the room" or could have ended the deposition and to stop the deposition in order for a protective order. But, the court pointed out, that the defender instead chose to instruct the witness not to answer.[83] The court found that the instruction violated both federal and ethical rules because it did not shield a privilege and was not done with the intent to obtain a protective order.[84] And the defender was subject to censure because he did not suspend the deposition and seek a protective order as required by FRCP 30(c)(2).[85] While termination is proper if a party or a deponent can show that the examination is being conducted in bad faith, or unreasonably annoys, embarrasses, or oppresses the witness, terminating a deposition is a serious matter. Before taking this step, make sure the record fully reflects the conduct that caused you to instruct the witness not to answer and stop the deposition. For example, say, "Counsel, you have asked the witness if she was drunk ten times, you have argued with her, and you are harassing her. This is improper. I have instructed the witness not to answer. And I am warning you that I will terminate this deposition if it continues." Creating a contemporaneous record on the transcript is far more credible than describing the examiner's misconduct in motion papers prepared after the deposition. Moreover, your timely warning gives the examiner fair notice and an opportunity to stop the abusive practice.

The downside to giving such a warning or instructing your client not to answer, as discussed above, is that failure to follow up by suspending the deposition and moving for a protective order can expose you to a motion to compel and sanctions, including censure. So use warnings and instructions sparingly, and only when you intend to terminate the deposition and seek a protective order if your warnings and instructions fail to stop the examiner.

As an alternative to terminating the deposition, you might suggest that the examiner move on to another line of questioning, saving for a later motion the disputed subject matter. But the Second Circuit Court of Appeals in *Redwood* criticized the idea of asking the examiner to move on to another topic.[86] Nevertheless a defender needs to be aware of the risks of stopping a deposition in order to move for a protective order. One risk is that a defender's motion for a protective order will elicit a countermotion by the examiner to compel and for sanctions. And then there is the added risk of an award of expenses under FRCP 37(a)(5) when a motion to terminate is made under FRCP 30(d)(3).

Problem Witnesses

Problem witnesses may require even more patience from the examiner than problem counsel. When challenged, witnesses can credibly plead ignorance of the rules for appropriate behavior at depositions; their lawyers, of course, have no basis for such a position. In addition, witnesses have no obligations of civility; their counsel must behave with civility because they are "officers of the court." Moreover, the examiner cannot expect help from the defender in dealing with a difficult witness. Indeed, if a defender believes her witness is frustrating the examiner so much that the examiner may give up, the defender is unlikely to make any attempt to control the witness.[87]

Before the year 2000, an examiner could usually count on the fact that the witness wanted the deposition to end as soon as possible. Therefore, the examiner would remind a witness that the more difficult he was, the longer the deposition was going to take and the more it was going to cost. But the 2000 amendments to FRCP 30(d)(1) now limit a deposition to one day of seven hours, unless otherwise stipulated or ordered by the court, so that the threat of keeping a deponent there all night if need be is no longer an option.[88] Nevertheless, the examiner is not without alternatives.

For example, FRCP 30(d)(1) states that "[t]he court must allow additional time ... if the deponent ... impedes or delays the examination." Furthermore, recent cases have extended the time allowed for a deposition when witnesses were uncooperative, improperly refused to answer questions, or otherwise hindered the examination.[89] This means that when faced with a "recalcitrant and uncooperative"[90] witness, an examiner can remind the witness that if the witness causes problems, the deposition can be extended beyond the seven-hour-one-day limit, further taking up the witness's and the defender's valuable—and costly—time.[91]

Witnesses can be problems for defenders, too. For example, a witness may tell one story during the preparation process, then suddenly change his story at the deposition.[92] Or a witness may begin volunteering information.

Evasive Witnesses

Every examiner has dealt with a witness who simply will not answer the questions posed. Many witnesses go to a deposition believing it is their job to avoid directly answering every question.

405

As one commentator has pointed out, "You should expect evasion. It's normal. And if you understand why witnesses do it, you are less likely to take it personally."[93]

When dealing with an evasive witness, tenacity is the key. You may want to put the witness off balance by sometimes being cordial and pleasant, and at other times being brusque and sharp. Once the witness realizes you will keep asking questions until you get a response, he will likely respond.[94]

Here are some other techniques you can use with an evasive witness:

- Make the questions as narrow as possible. That makes it difficult for the witness to avoid giving the response sought. For example, you can ask questions that call for only a "yes" or "no" response. Or you can ask the same question in different ways until you get a satisfactory answer. Persist even when faced with an "asked and answered" objection—the defender probably knows that the witness has not answered the question, and his objection probably is designed to prevent you from getting an answer.
- Remind the witness that he is under oath. Say to the witness, "Please remember that you are here under oath. You must answer all my questions unless your lawyer instructs you not to answer."
- If the deposition is being recorded on video, remind the witness that the jury is watching.
- Make the witness tell you exactly what he does not understand about your inquiry.[95]
- Make your persistence obvious. Tell the witness that if he remains uncooperative or impedes the deposition, the court will extend the seven-hour-one-day time limit and the deposition will be continued on another day. Then ask the same question again.

Some witnesses evade answering questions by claiming to know nothing at all. The answer to every question is "I do not recall" or "I do not know." This behavior may be "aided and abetted" by the defender's improper objections.[96] When examining such a witness, make a clear record of how little the witness claims to know. Ask the witness to describe in general terms his knowledge of the underlying facts. Then ask him to confirm that he knows only about subject A but not about subjects B through K. If you are deposing this witness because you believe he has information you need as part of your discovery plan, and not because you expect him to testify at trial, evasive answers are particularly frustrating.

Sometimes a witness with an "unusual" lack of recall actually benefits the examiner. If the examination forecloses the witness from having a newfound credible recollection by the time of trial, the witness can be eliminated as a trial witness. As a first step, ask the witness if there is anyone or anything—another person or a document—that might refresh the witness's recollection. If the witness says "no," the door on that subject is probably closed. A newfound recollection at trial will not be credible.[97]

But suppose the witness says that looking at certain documents or talking with certain people might refresh her recollection. You now have two options.

The first option is to try to refresh the witness's recollection at that point in the deposition. Show the witness each document that the witness has said might help her memory. Then ask the witness whether reviewing the document helps her recollection. If it does not, you have a record that should prevent later changed, credible testimony. If it does help her recollection, follow up.

The second option is to ask the witness to confirm that without reviewing certain documents she does not recall any information about each of the major topics in the litigation.[98] If the witness responds "yes" and you do not have the documents available to show the witness, recess the deposition until you have them. If the defender objects to continuing the deposition, advise your opponent that you will object to any testimony by the witness at trial on those subjects unless you are advised sufficiently in advance of trial of any newfound recollections.

In an extreme case—when a witness continues to claim no recall and you suspect the lack of memory is a ploy—warn the witness about perjury, and consider marking the perjury statute as an exhibit. Of course, expect the defender to object to this tactic.

If the witness continues to be evasive, you may want to terminate the deposition under FRCP 37(a)(3) and move to compel the sought-after response. In making this motion, you can use FRCP 30(d)(2), which provides for appropriate sanctions, including the reasonable expenses and attorney's fees incurred by any person "on a person who impedes, delays, or frustrates the fair examination." In some jurisdictions, as discussed above, you may also seek sanctions under 28 U.S.C. § 1927.

Fabricating Witnesses

Suppose you depose a witness who you are certain is lying.[99] Try to let the witness know that you think he is being untruthful. As an alternative, as discussed below, there may be advantages to waiting and confronting the witness at trial.

If you decide to confront the witness at the deposition, state the witness's position in the worst light possible. When the witness gives a particularly ridiculous response, repeat it back to him: "So, your testimony is that you had three or four drinks in the course of an hour, but you did not feel the slightest bit intoxicated; is that correct?" You may want to preface your questions with, "You realize that you are still under oath?" Or, if the deposition is being recorded on video, say: "You have now told the jury that you had three or four drinks in the course of an hour, but did not feel the slightest bit intoxicated; is that correct?"

Untruthful witnesses are often nonparties who do not have the same stake in the litigation as a party witness and have some unknown motive for falsifying testimony. Suppose you decide to depose a third-party witness whose prior witness interview with you produced potentially useful testimony. During that interview, the witness gave you one story. At the deposition, he changes the story.[100] Merely confronting the witness with the inconsistency—"When we met the other day, you told me X, and now you are telling me Y"—is unlikely to be productive. Instead, pause for a moment more and pull out your interview notes in a slow, deliberate way and study them. Then read—or at least act as if you are reading—from your notes and ask a series of questions that all begin with "Do you recall telling me that. . . ." The witness may fear answering "no" because he believes your interview notes will directly contradict him. Of course, if the witness answers "yes," you may need to follow up with other questions regarding that subject.

If you have material that impeaches the fabricating witness, the decision whether to use it at the deposition or wait until trial may be a difficult one.[101] Some of the factors to consider are (1) the availability of the witness at trial, (2) whether the impeaching material is really airtight, and (3) whether you can "close the door" on the witness's deposition testimony.

Impeaching at the deposition will give you the witness's explanation before trial, and you might be able to use this explanation against the witness at trial. Remember, though, to successfully impeach, you must eliminate any "wiggle room" for the witness. To close out the witness's deposition testimony in a way that will give the impeaching material a powerful impact at trial, ask the witness whether there is anything else he can tell you about the subject. In addition, you may want to summarize what the witness said in an "omnibus" question, and then ask if you fairly characterized everything the witness said. A disadvantage of impeachment at the deposition, however, is that you alert the witness (and his lawyer) to your plans and you lose the element of surprise at trial.

On the other hand, if you wait to impeach the witness at trial, you may not have an opportunity to impeach the witness. The reason: On the stand the witness may not give the testimony you are set to impeach, or he may change his testimony slightly in a way that makes it impossible for you to impeach it.

In some circumstances, you may want to pursue a witness for perjury. But convincing a prosecutor to indict a witness for perjury in a civil deposition is difficult. If you succeed, however, the rewards may be great. For example, you may be able to limit your opponent's ability to offer the witness or at least certain testimony of that witness. You may obtain leverage for settlement purposes. And you may obtain additional facts through a criminal investigation of the witness.[102]

Hostile Witnesses[103]

Many witnesses try to guess your objective in the deposition and then give answers that they believe thwarts the objective. What can you do if a deponent tries to undermine your examination in this fashion? One tactic: Use different inflections in your voice. Another: Structure your questions to disguise your objective, so the deponent thinks your objective is the opposite of what it is. For example, if you are trying to eliminate a witness from testifying at trial by confirming that the witness does not have any recollection, then to disguise this objective you might say, "I guess this will be a short deposition (or series of questions), because I take it you have little, if any, recollection. Let me just ask you a few quick questions for the record; then we can all go home." Using this technique leaves the record without the witness having an opportunity to claim newfound recollections in response to lengthy deposition questioning.

When dealing with a hostile witness, avoid becoming hostile yourself. When the examiner stays calm, an out-of-control deponent loses credibility—particularly on video. If a witness becomes abusive or rude, calmly state on the record that such behavior is unacceptable and ask the witness to stop being rude. The angrier and more abusive the witness becomes, the calmer you should be. Staying calm can be very challenging when the abuse is severe and constant, as it was against the examining attorney in *GMAC Bank v. HTFC Corp.*, discussed at the beginning of this chapter. In that case, the examiner was forced to endure nearly twelve hours of abuse that included descriptions such as "you're a piece of shit" and "fuck face," as well as tirades such as: "I'll make your life miserable. Trust me. You'll be drinking breakfast, lunch, and dinner every day. Start asking some real questions."[104] The reward for remaining calm even when the abuse is exceptionally denigrating is that a court can readily see who was acting improperly and who was behaving professionally. This improves the odds that the court will rule in favor of the examiner on a motion to compel and impose sanctions against a hostile witness (and his counsel).[105]

If a witness persists in such behavior, warn the witness that if the behavior continues, you will terminate the deposition and seek sanctions. To maintain credibility, never threaten action, including sanctions, unless you intend to follow through with the threat. You may also want to tell the defender to restrain his abusive client by reminding him that tacitly tolerating his client's behavior could be considered encouraging it, which could also lead to sanctions not only against the client but also against the defender for his inaction.[106]

"Rambling" or Volunteering Witnesses

Sometimes witnesses ramble:

Q. Did you ever complain to the defendant that his pricing policies were unfair?

A. Knowing the defendant's unsavory reputation and the vindictive temperament of its management, we decided that complaining would only provoke it to take further action to crush us.

Sometimes a witness's rambling benefits the examiner, such as when the witness volunteers helpful information. But when you are taking a deposition intended to be offered at trial, rambling answers like the one above may conflict with your purpose: to obtain usable answers to be read to a jury. When a witness rambles, tell the witness, "Please listen carefully to the next question. You will see that it can fairly be answered 'Yes' or 'No' or 'I don't remember.' Please answer it that way or let me know if you cannot answer it that way." The defender, who usually will have prepared his client to answer your questions and say no more, may even help you get a concise answer.

Send the witness a message by moving to strike the nonresponsive answer (indeed, a motion to strike is waived if not made at the deposition).[107] If you do not want to move to strike for fear it will break whatever rapport you have with the witness, wait for the witness to finish, and then say, "Ms. Witness, perhaps you did not understand my question. I am asking a much narrower question than the one you answered, and that is. . . ."

Sometimes a deponent's lengthy responses significantly slow down an examination. When that happens, you may want to say to the deponent, "I appreciate all the information you are giving me, but please listen to my question and respond only to that question." As an alternative, consider agreeing with the witness that she will give you a "yes" or "no" answer but should be well aware that you follow up the answer with additional questions, if needed.

If neither of these approaches work and it appears that the deposition cannot be properly completed within the time constraints of the seven-hour-one-day rule, remind the rambling witness that if he delays the examination with his answers, you will be able to get a court order to extend and continue the deposition. In addition, tell the witness that he may have to pay attorney's fees and other costs caused by his impeding the examination. When these warnings are ineffective, seek a court order extending the deposition, because "the court must authorize extra time" if a witness impedes or delays the opportunity for a "fair" examination.[108]

If the nonresponsive answers continue, you may want to take a break, prefacing the break with a comment such as, "I suggest that we take a break here. I would ask counsel for the witness to confer with him during the break and advise him of his duty to answer questions directly and without making speeches. If the witness continues to give the same kind of answers, I intend to seek the aid of the court." Again, do this only if you intend to follow through with your threat; otherwise, the threat will probably have little impact, and failure to carry it out will damage your credibility.

A volunteering witness can also be a problem for a defender. The first step in preventing a witness from volunteering is to educate the witness during the preparation session about the dangers of volunteering. If this advice is ignored during the deposition, take charge. At a break, give the witness examples of where he is going wrong, and reinforce the counterproductive nature of such conduct.[109] Remind your witness of the deponent who was so well prepared by his lawyer to answer questions "yes" or "no" that when asked, "Could you state your name for the record please?" the deponent answered, "Yes." A long silence ensued before the examiner realized that "yes" was the deponent's entire response.

As a defender, you should in general refrain from making his volunteering an issue with the witness, either on or off the record, while in the presence of the examiner or others. The witness may find this embarrassing. In addition, you risk losing the witness's trust and alienating him. Nevertheless, sometimes the only way to prevent volunteering and the resulting harmful testimony is by making volunteering an issue.

If you find yourself defending a witness who simply cannot follow your directions for answering questions, you may have no choice but to try to solve the problem on the record. There are several options to consider:

1. If the witness is answering too quickly without giving reasonable thought to the question, you may need to lodge legitimate objections to slow the pace down. As an alternative, you can periodically ask for readbacks of questions.

2. You may state on the record to the witness that the witness has answered the question (for example, "Excuse me, I believe you have answered the question" or "Ms. Witness, you should limit your answer to the question that the examiner is asking").

3. When a witness is not answering the precise question asked, interrupt and have the reporter re-read the question to the witness. Then ask the witness whether he understands the question.

4. If the witness is speculating, ask the examiner, "You do not want the witness to speculate, do you?" Or remind the witness of the examiner's preliminary instruction to the witness; namely, "Please don't speculate; just give your best recollection." If your statement does not convey the message to the witness, you may need to remind the witness on the record not to speculate by saying, "I suggest that you not guess at the answer; if you do not know, just say so."[110] But beware that the examiner may attack you for coaching, as discussed above.

If the behavior continues, ask for a break at an appropriate time. Then privately remind the witness to pause when answering and to not volunteer or answer questions not being asked.[111]

Conclusion

Increased awareness of abusive deposition practice has prompted additions to the FRCP, new case law, local rules, standing orders, new case law, and even local bar practice guidelines. All these provide a framework for efficient, amicable advocacy. And when lawyers and their clients fail to follow these rules, the remedy may be painful. Case law confirms that not only are courts becoming less tolerant of improper behavior, but also that clients and lawyers alike are availing themselves of the ample sanctions available to courts to facilitate discovery and curb improper behavior.

Notes

*The authors gratefully acknowledge the significant contributions of D. Barclay Edmundson, a partner, and Alyson C. Decker, an associate, at Orrick, Herrington & Sutcliffe LLP, in updating this chapter for the second edition.

1. *See* Paramount Commc'ns, Inc. v. QVC Network, Inc. (*In re* Paramount Commc'ns, Inc. S'holders' Litig.), 637 A.2d 34, 54 (Del. 1994) (addendum to opinion, excerpting portions of depositions). A few years after this exchange took place, the Eastern District of Texas modified its local rules and specifically listed what objections may be made by a defender at a deposition. E.D. TEX. L.R. CV-30 DEPOSITIONS UPON ORAL EXAMINATION ("Objections to questions during the oral deposition are limited to 'Objection, leading' and 'Objection, form.' Objections to testimony during the oral deposition are limited to 'Objection, nonresponsive.' These objections are waived if not stated as phrased during the oral deposition."). This rule is known locally as the "Jamail Rule." Excerpts from this infamous deposition, which almost escalated to physical violence, can usually be located on YouTube by simply typing in Joe Jamail and Texas deposition.

2. *Paramount Commc'ns, Inc.*, 637 A.2d at 54.

3. *Id.* at 56.

4. *See* Laddcap Value Partner, LP v. Lowenstein Sandler, PC, 18 Misc. 3d 1130(A), 2007 NY Slip Op. 52538(U) (2007).

5. *See id.*

6. *Id.*

7. *See id.*

8. GMAC Bank v. HTFC Corp., 248 F.R.D. 182 (E.D. Pa. 2008).

9. *See id.* at 196.

10. *Id.* at 187. The court stated, "This opinion quotes many of [the deponent's] uncensored remarks. While the use of profanity in the opinion is distasteful, it is necessary in order to capture the nature of the offensive conduct displayed by the deponent." *Id.* at 185 n.8. For the curious, the court noted that "[c]opies of the transcript and the video recording will be filed of record." *Id.* at 185 n.7.

11. *See id.* at 186.

12. *Id.*

13. *Id.*

14. *Id.* at 199 (awarding $13,026.00 in fees and expenses incurred by GMAC Bank in connection with its motion to compel and $16,296.61 in costs, as well as 75 percent of the fees incurred by GMAC Bank in connection with the two days of depositions to be paid jointly and severally by the deponent and his counsel, and ordering that another examination of the deponent take place at the courthouse before a magistrate judge). The court denied a motion by the deponent's counsel to reconsider its ruling sanctioning him for his conduct at the deposition based on counsel's claim of lack of procedural due process and lack of adequate notice of the sanctions being considered by the court. GMAC Bank v. HTFC Corp., No. 06-5291, 2008 U.S. Dist. LEXIS 62106 (E.D. Pa. Aug. 12, 2008).

15. FED. R. CIV. P. 30 advisory committee's note (1937).

16. *See* FED. R. CIV. P. 30 advisory committee's note (1993); FED. R. CIV. P. 30 advisory committee's note (2000). *See also* Judge Peter M. Lauriat, *Voice of the Judiciary: Rule 30(c): A Beginning to the End of Deposition Abuse*, 46 B.B.J. 8 (2002).

17. *See, e.g.,* Edmond M. Connor, *All's Fair in Love and Depositions in Orange County*, 40 ORANGE COUNTY LAW. 4 (1998) (discussing proposed Orange County Superior Court Rule regarding professionalism in depositions and other local rules); ABA Sec. Litig., *Guidelines for Conduct* (1998) (listing several guidelines for proper conduct in depositions). A number of courts have also adopted "civility rules" for attorney conduct. *See, e.g.,* C.D. CAL. CIVILITY AND PROFESSIONALISM GUIDELINES.

18. See Chapter 17.

19. See Chapter 18.

20. See "Task 11: Consider Whether You Need a Protective Order" in Chapter 4.

21. At the congressional hearings on the Iran-Contra matter, lawyer Brendan V. Sullivan objected on behalf of his client, Oliver North, to a question by Special Prosecutor Arthur Liman. The chair of the committee, Sen. Daniel Inouye, told Sullivan that "[the committee has] attempted to be as fair as we can. Let the witness object if he wishes to." To this comment, Sullivan replied, "I'm not a potted plant. I'm here as a lawyer. That's my job." *See Joint Hearings Before the Senate Select Comm. on Secret Military Assistance to Iran and the Nicaraguan Opposition, and the House Select Comm. to Investigate Covert Arms Transactions with Iran*, 100th Cong. 100-7 (1987) (testimony of

Oliver L. North). See also Chapter 8, text accompanying note 8, discussing Sullivan's views on defender-witness conferences during a deposition.

22. See Chapter 14, discussing objections at a deposition.

23. Hall v. Clifton Precision, 150 F.R.D. 525, 530 n.10 (E.D. Pa. 1993). Judge Gawthrop's opinion, while sometimes criticized as going too far, is considered a seminal case in setting guidelines as to the appropriate interjections a defender may make during a deposition. In fact, Rule 30(j) of the South Carolina Rules of Civil Procedure is derived from this opinion and is known as "one of the most sweeping and comprehensive rules on deposition conduct in the nation." *In re* Anonymous Member of S.C. Bar, 552 S.E. 2d 10, 16 (S.C. 2001).

24. *See* D. MD. DISCOVERY GUIDELINES, guideline 7 ("Upon request of any attorney . . . the person recording the deposition in accordance with Fed. R. Civ. P. 30(b) shall enter on the record a description by the requesting person of conduct of any attorney, party, or person attending the deposition which violates these guidelines, the Federal Rules of Civil Procedure, or the Local Rules of this Court.").

25. 150 F.R.D. at 528.

26. See "Opening Questions" in Chapter 11.

27. See Chapter 14, discussing proper defense practice.

28. An examining lawyer must preserve the record in connection with the witness's responses. For example, a motion to strike all or a portion of the witness's answer as nonresponsive must be made at the time of the response, or the objection is waived. *See* Kirschner v. Broadhead, 671 F.2d 1034, 1037–38 (7th Cir. 1982).

29. FRCP 37(a) provides procedures by which "a party may move for an order compelling disclosure or discovery." Many courts have local rules specifying additional procedures counsel must follow when filing a motion to compel. See also "Continuing the Deposition Pending a Court Order" in Chapter 23, discussing motions to compel.

30. *See* Phillips v. Mfrs. Hanover Trust Co., 1994 U.S. Dist. LEXIS 3748 (S.D.N.Y. Mar. 29, 1994) (finding FRCP 30, as amended, a more appropriate basis for sanctions than FRCP 37 in a case involving unreasonable behavior by opposing counsel at depositions, but sanctions were denied).

31. *E.g.*, Johnson v. Wayne Manor Apartments, 152 F.R.D. 56 (E.D. Pa. 1993) (motion to compel granted and further examination and sanctions found warranted).

32. *Id.*

33. *Id.* at 59 (granting sanctions under the equivalent of FRCP 37(a)(5)).

34. FRCP 26(b)(2) also allows courts to limit the duration of depositions.

35. FED. R. CIV. P. 30(d)(1); FED. R. CIV. P. 16(b)(3).

36. See "Time-and-Date Information" in Chapter 17, discussing video depositions and, in particular, time-and-date indications.

37. *See* Van Pilsum v. Iowa State Univ. of Sci. and Tech., 152 F.R.D. 179, 180–81 (S.D. Iowa 1993) (sanctions awarded against defending lawyer "personally" when court found that defending lawyer's improper objections and coaching unjustifiably monopolized 20 percent of deposition).

38. A motion for sanctions for impeding, delaying, or otherwise frustrating a deposition may be made under FRCP 30(d)(2). A motion to compel testimony when a deponent fails to answer a question after an improper instruction not to answer is given may be made under FRCP 37(a)(3)(B). Such a motion is further supported by FRCP 30(c)(2), which limits the instances in which an instruction not to answer may be given to only three situations: when the instruction is "necessary to preserve a privilege, to enforce a limitation directed by the court, or to present a motion under Rule 30(d)(3)." FED. R. CIV. P. 30(c)(2). A motion to compel may also be made where the answer is evasive or incomplete. FED. R. CIV. P. 37(a)(4). Additionally, the Federal Rules specifically allow the attorney taking the deposition to adjourn the examination before requesting an order to compel. FED. R. CIV. P. 37(a)(3)(C).

39. An oral record can lead to delay and a credibility dispute with opposing counsel pending the availability of a transcript. With the use of "realtime" reporting, in which a transcript is generated at the same time a stenographic record is being prepared, a transcript may be available for a telephone argument. See Chapter 18.

40. Many local court rules require the parties to meet and confer in good faith before filing a discovery motion. *See, e.g.,* C.D. CAL. L.R. 37-1 (requiring parties to discovery dispute to meet face-to-face, if located within the same county of the Central District, before filing any discovery motions).

41. *See* FED. R. CIV. P. 37(a)(5)(A) (requiring opportunity for parties to be heard). When faced with a motion to compel responses or further responses to questions posed in a deposition, defending counsel should consider making a cross-motion for a protective order to limit or completely avoid giving information on the subject matter. If the motion to compel is denied, the court may enter any protective order authorized by FRCP 26(c) (authorizing court to enter protective orders), and, after affording the parties an opportunity to be heard, "must" award expenses, including attorney's fees, to the opposing party unless the court finds that the motion was substantially justified or other circumstances make the award unjust. FED. R. CIV. P. 37(a)(5)(B). Finally, if the motion is granted in part and denied in part, FRCP 37(a)(5) allows the court to fashion a protective order pursuant to FRCP 26(c), and, after allowing the parties an opportunity to be heard, apportion reasonable expenses in relation to the motion. FED. R. CIV. P. 37(a)(5)(C).

42. 942 F.2d 236, 242 (4th Cir. 1991).

43. In addition to individual lawyers, law firms are subject to sanctions under 17 U.S.C. § 1927. *In re* Marker, 133 B.R. 340, 346 (W.D. Pa. 1991). Parties who are "willful participants" in an unreasonable and

vexatious litigation strategy also may be sanctioned under § 1927. Avirgan v. Hull, 932 F.2d 1572, 1582 (11th Cir. 1991) (upholding sanctions against party awarded, in part, on filing of affidavit purportedly outlining testimony of seventy-nine witnesses, twenty of whose names were unknown to affiant, several of whom had never spoken to the affiant or denied statements attributed to them, and remainder of whom furnished only inadmissible statements), *cert. denied*, Christic Inst. v. Hull, 502 U.S. 1048 (1992). *Contra* Browning v. Kramer, 931 F.2d 340, 344 (5th Cir. 1991) ("By its terms, § 1927 permits awards only against attorneys or other persons admitted to conduct cases before the court. It does not permit the court to sanction a party."). This section might also be used against a party-deponent appearing pro se. *See* Wages v. IRS, 915 F.2d 1230, 1235–36 (9th Cir. 1990) (upholding sanctions against pro se litigant who, following dismissal of her action against individual I.R.S. employees, filed substantially identical amended complaint), *cert. denied*, 498 U.S. 1096 (1991). *Contra* Sassower v. Field, 973 F.2d 75, 80 (2d Cir. 1992).

44.   Unique Concepts, Inc. v. Brown, 115 F.R.D. 292, 292 (S.D.N.Y. 1987) (awarding sanctions, under § 1927 and the court's inherent power, against defending lawyer whose "conduct was harassing, wasteful, vexatious and ruined the usefulness of the . . . deposition"). *See also* R.E. Linder Steel Erection Co. v. U.S. Fire Ins. Co., 102 F.R.D. 39 (Md. D. 1983) (ordering that each counsel would be required to forfeit five dollars for each interruption in future depositions and five dollars for each instance of extraneous remarks or ad hominem attacks on opposing counsel).

45.   In *Unique Concepts*, 115 F.R.D. at 293, the court noted that the following remarks were directed at the deposing counsel: "You are being an obnoxious little twit. Keep your mouth shut." and "You are a very rude and impertinent young man." When deposing counsel suggested that sanctions might be appropriate, plaintiffs' counsel went on to say, "If you want to go down to Judge Pollack and ask for sanctions because of that, go ahead. I would almost agree to make a contribution of cash to you if you would promise to use it to take a course in how to ask questions in a deposition." *Id.*

46.   133 B.R. at 346. *See also* Hackman v. Valley Fair, 932 F.2d 239, 242 (3d Cir. 1991) ("To justify the imposition of excess costs of litigation upon an attorney his conduct must be of an egregious nature, stamped by bad faith that is violative of recognized standards in the conduct of litigation.").

47.   *Hackman*, 932 F.2d at 242.

48.   *Avirgan*, 932 F.2d at 1581–82. *Cf. Browning*, 931 F.2d at 344–45 ("By its terms this statute does not authorize the wholesale reimbursement of a party for all of its attorneys' fees or for the total costs of the litigation. . . . Except when the entire course of proceedings were unwarranted and should neither have been commenced nor persisted in, an award under § 1927 may not shift the entire financial burden of an action's defense.").

49.   *In re Marker*, 133 B.R. at 350.

50. *Wages,* 915 F.2d at 1235.

51. *Hackman,* 932 F.2d at 242.

52. *See, e.g., Unique Concepts,* 115 F.R.D. at 293–94 (using inherent authority to award sanctions against lawyer defending witness at deposition and noting that "[c]ourts have drawn on their inherent authority to hold attorneys liable for the costs incurred by other parties due to discovery abuses"[citations omitted]).

53. *See* Chambers v. NASCO, Inc., 501 U.S. 32, 43–44 (1991).

54. *Chambers,* 501 U.S. at 41–42.

55. Kobleur v. Group Hospitalization & Med. Servs., Inc., 787 F. Supp. 1444, 1453 (S.D. Ga. 1991), *aff'd,* 954 F.2d 705 (11th Cir. 1992).

56. *Chambers,* 501 U.S. at 44–45.

57. W. Sys. v. Ulloa, 958 F.2d 864, 873 (9th Cir. 1992), as amended, 1992 U.S. App. LEXIS 14240 (9th Cir. Guam June 23, 1992), *cert. denied,* Ulloa v. W. Sys., 506 U.S. 1050 (1993).

58. *Chambers,* 501 U.S. at 55.

59. See "Instructing a Witness Not to Answer" in Chapter 14, discussing FRCP 30(c)(2).

60. *See* Standard Chlorine of Del., Inc. v. Sinibaldi, 1994 U.S. Dist. LEXIS 3388, at 15 (D. Del. Mar. 21, 1994) (stating that counsel's instruction not to answer deposition question on grounds of relevance was "manifestly at odds" with procedure set forth in amended FRCP 30). Before the 1993 amendments, when a court held that directing a witness not to answer on nonprivilege grounds was inappropriate, it usually did so in the context of a motion to compel pursuant to the then equivalent of FRCP 37(a)(3), which provides a mechanism for moving to compel for FRCP 30(c) violations. *See* Am. Hangar Inc. v. Basic Line, Inc., 105 F.R.D. 173 (D. Mass. 1985) (when witness does not answer because of erroneous instruction from her counsel, deposing lawyer should move to compel); First Tenn. Bank v. Fed. Deposit Ins. Corp., 108 F.R.D. 640, 641 (E.D. Tenn. 1985) (ordering witness to answer questions he had previously refused to answer due to counsel's instruction).

Even before the 1993 amendments, it was considered improper for a lawyer to instruct a deposition witness not to answer based upon objections such as relevance. Unless an objection to a deposition question was based on privilege and, in limited circumstances, violations of trade secrets, courts generally held that instructions not to answer were inappropriate. *See* Nat'l Microsales v. Chase Manhattan Bank, 761 F. Supp. 304, 307 (S.D.N.Y. 1991) (directions to witness not to answer are not permitted except when questions call for privileged information); Smith v. Logansport Cmty. Sch. Corp., 139 F.R.D. 637 (N.D. Ind. 1991) (it is improper for counsel to direct witness not to answer unless objection is based on privilege); *Am. Hangar,* 105 F.R.D. at 177 (instructions not to answer are improper except in very limited circumstances involving privileged matters and trade secrets).

61. The most commonly asserted privilege is attorney-client. Other privileges, such as the privilege against self-incrimination, may also be asserted. *See* FED. R. EVID. 501 (stating that privilege may be asserted in federal court based on the common law and in civil actions and proceedings governed by state law in accordance with state law). *See also* Pillsbury Co. v. Conboy, 459 U.S. 248 (1983) (holding that absent grant of immunity, deponent may properly assert Fifth Amendment privilege even when witness has testified regarding same subjects to grand jury). See also Chapter 22.

62. *See, e.g.,* Clarke v. Am. Commerce Nat'l Bank, 974 F.2d 127, 129 (9th Cir. 1992). *See also* Perrignon v. Bergen Brunswig Corp., 77 F.R.D. 455 (N.D. Cal. 1978) (employee's communications to in-house counsel were not privileged, as the statements were not made at direction of employer and did not pertain to employee's duties).

63. *See, e.g.,* CAL. EVID. CODE §§ 950 *et seq.* (West 2007); *In re* Fischel, 557 F.2d 209, 211 (9th Cir. 1977) (laying out elements of attorney-client privilege). See Chapter 6.

64. *See Fischel,* 557 F.2d at 212 (regarding lawyer notes, privilege can be maintained only upon proof that the notes "reveal communications of a confidential nature by the client to the attorney"). See Chapter 6.

65. Under federal law, the work-product doctrine covers only work product undertaken in anticipation of litigation. *See* Binks Mfg. Co. v. Nat'l Presto Indus., Inc., 709 F.2d 1109, 1118 (7th Cir. 1983) ("The mere fact that litigation does eventually ensue does not, by itself, cloak materials . . . with the protection of the work product privilege. . . ."). State laws may define the work-product doctrine differently. *See, e.g.,* CAL. CIV. PROC. CODE § 2018.030 (West 2007).

66. *See* FED. R. CIV. P. 37(a)(3)(C) (providing that if deponent refuses to answer question posed, examining lawyer may move to compel answer).

67. *See* FED. R. CIV. P. 37(a)(5)(A).

68. See *supra* section "Using FRCP 30 to Deal with Improper Objections" for a discussion on how to keep track of time on the record during a deposition.

69. 657 F.2d 890, 901–02 (7th Cir. 1981), *cert. denied,* 455 U.S. 1017 (1982).

70. *Id.* at 904. Going to court to seek the appointment of a special master or discovery referee should be a last resort in any problematic deposition situation. But the appointment of a special master to oversee discovery proceedings in cases where the parties are uncooperative and difficult has been met with approval by the judiciary. *See* Fisher v. Harris, Upham & Co., Inc., 61 F.R.D. 447, 449 (S.D.N.Y. 1973). In *Eggleston* the master was to act as an "on the spot referee" to settle deposition disputes as they arose in order to expedite discovery in general. 657 F.2d at 904. Special masters have also been appointed to deal specifically with such deposition tasks as ruling on objections to questions, ruling on the form of the questions, ruling on alleged violations of the Federal Rules, directing parties to answer proper

questions, and generally ensuring that the deposition progresses smoothly. *See Fisher*, 61 F.R.D. at 448–49; Omnium Lyonnais D'Etancheite et Revetement Asphalte v. Dow Chem. Co., 73 F.R.D. 114, 119 (C.D. Cal. 1977).

71. *Eggleston*, 657 F.2d at 904.

72. *See, e.g.*, CAL. CIV. PROC. CODE § 638 (West 2007).

73. A defending lawyer should expect an examiner to ask about communications between the deponent and his or her lawyer after breaks in the deposition. The defending lawyer should decide before the deposition how to handle these questions, weighing the force and effect of any relevant case law on this subject and how likely it is that the examining lawyer will make a motion, either to compel the testimony or for an order similar to the one issued by the *Hall* court, which allowed inquiry into the substance of the conference conducted during the deposition. *See infra* note 71.

74. See "Opening Questions" in Chapter 11, discussing the start of a deposition.

75. *Hall*, 150 F.R.D. at 529 (emphasis added).

76. As stated earlier in the text, an attorney can begin a deposition by explaining when breaks can be taken and thus take control of the situation before the problem arises. If this does not work and opposing counsel is determined to take a break to confer with his client about a document, one can refer to the *Hall* opinion as controlling such breaks.

77. E.D.N.Y. L. CIV. R. 30.6 (Conferences Between Deponent and Defending Attorney).

78. *Hall*, 150 F.R.D. at 528–29 n.7.

79. *See also* FED. R. CIV. P. 26(c) (providing for motion for protective order).

80. Redwood v. Dobson, 476 F. 3d 462 (7th Cir. 2007).

81. *Id.* at 467–68.

82. *Id.* at 468.

83. *Id.*

84. *Id.* at 469.

85. *Id.* at 470. Although this may appear to be a harsh result for an instruction not to answer obviously harassing questions that served no legitimate discovery purpose, the opinion emphasizes that adherence to the rules as well as professional and ethical standards during depositions is vital, especially in antagonizing situations such as this one. *Id.* at 469–70.

86. *Id.* at 467–70.

87. This passive approach, however, is not recommended, as it may lead to sanctions being awarded not only against the deponent but also against the defender who sits back and lets his client run amuck. For example, in *GMAC Bank*, federal district court jointly sanctioned both the deponent *and* the defending attorney because of the deponent's incorrigible behavior—including such choice statements as "I'm involved in flipping you" and "You want to know what color I wipe my ass with?"— and the defending attorney's inaction—including "silent toleration,"

snickering, and an occasional dare to opposing counsel to file a motion to compel. 248 F.R.D. at 188, 190, 194–99. *See also supra* note 14, detailing the award of monetary sanctions imposed jointly and severally against the deponent and his counsel and the order for a new deposition of the deponent to be taken in the courthouse before a magistrate judge.

88.   Another threat, one that affects the witness's financial interest, is that of sanctions. Under FRCP 30(d)(2), if a problem witness has impeded, delayed, or otherwise "frustrated the fair examination of the deponent" the court may impose "an appropriate sanction, including the reasonable costs and attorney's fees incurred by any parties as a result thereof."

89.   *See* LaPlante v. Estano, 226 F.R.D. 439, 439–40 (D. Conn. 2005); Calderon v. Symeon, 2007 U.S. Dist. LEXIS 18561 (D. Conn., Mar. 13, 2007). One does not need to show that the problem witness is acting in bad faith or intentionally impeding the deposition to be successful on an FRCP 30(d)(1) motion. *See* Gibbs v. Am. Sch. for the Deaf, 2007 U.S. Dist. LEXIS 25036, at *1–2 (extending the time limit for a deposition that "was slowed down and interrupted because of the need to use sign language interpreters").

90.   *See LaPlante*, 226 F.R.D. at 439–40 (D. Conn. 2005); *Calderon*, 2007 U.S. Dist. LEXIS 18561.

91.   In addition, if you succeed on an FRCP 30(d)(1) motion, you can ask the judge to create a set of guidelines for the deponent to follow when the deposition is continued. *See Calderon*, 2007 U.S. Dist. LEXIS 18561 (listing a set of guidelines for the witness to follow in further depositions, including that the witness must "allow the attorney to finish his question before beginning an answer and listen carefully to the question that is asked," give yes or no answers when the questions call for such answers, and answer questions in a "concise responsive manner," and providing that any further continuances would be at the witness's expense). In such a situation, you could also ask for a special master to be appointed as a referee. *See* Fed. R. Civ. P. Rule 53(3)(describing special master's duties).

92.   See Chapter 21, discussing how the defender should deal with perjury at a deposition.

93.   James W. McElhaney, *Evasive Witnesses*, LITIGATION, Spring 1994, at 48.

94.   When a deponent designated under FRCP 30(b)(6) is evasive and fails to have sufficient knowledge of designated topics, the questioner may be entitled to attorneys' fees as a sanction, in addition to a substitute witness, under FRCP 37(d). *See* Black Horse Lane Assoc., L.P. v. Dow Chem. Corp., 228 F.3d 275, 301–05 (3d Cir. 2000).

95.   See *supra* section "Practical Strategies for Dealing with Improper Objections" for a discussion of how to deal with a witness when the objection of vague and ambiguous has been raised as to a posed question.

96.   See *supra* section "Speaking Objections and 'Clarifying' Objections" for an example of improper objections made by a defender to encourage evasive answers.

97. See "Examination Techniques" in Chapter 11, discussing dealing with lack of recall.

98. See also Chapter 9. Federal Rule of Evidence 612 states that with regard to documents used to refresh a witness's memory prior to testifying, it is within the court's discretion to require that the documents be given to the adverse party "to inspect [them], to cross-examine the witness thereon, and to introduce in evidence those portions which relate to the testimony of the witness."

99. This section is written from the perspective of the examiner. See Chapter 21, discussing the issue from the perspective of the defender.

100. Needing to examine an unreliable third-party witness under oath is an excellent reason to have a second person attend a witness interview.

101. See "Using Depositions to Contradict or Impeach the Trial Testimony of a Witness" in Chapter 25.

102. *See generally* Jonathan Liebman & Joel Cohen, *Perjury and Civil Litigation*, LITIGATION, Summer 1994, at 43.

103. In this chapter, we are using the term "hostile witness" to describe a particular type of difficult deponent. Our use of the term should not be confused with the term of art that is used in reference to situations where it is permissible to ask a witness leading questions during direct examination at a trial. *See* FED. R. EVID. 611(c).

104. 248 F.R.D. at 186, 188, 193.

105. In *GMAC Bank*, the court made a point of commenting on the patience shown by examining counsel: "Counsel for GMAC exercised great restraint in the face of [the deponent's] persistent attempts to incite him to anger." *Id*. at 192.

106. *See id*. at 194–99. *See also supra* note 14 detailing the award of monetary sanctions imposed jointly and severally against the deponent and his counsel and the order for a new deposition of the deponent to be taken in the courthouse before a magistrate judge.

107. See "If You Decide to Object" in Chapter 14, discussing motions to strike an answer.

108. FED. R. CIV. P. 30(d) advisory committee's note (2000). *See also* FED. R. CIV. P. 30(d)(1).

109. See Chapter 14, note 122, discussing when, in contrast, a defender may want the witness to volunteer. See also "Twenty Guidelines for Deposition Testimony" in Chapter 7.

110. When using these techniques, however, a defender should be careful to avoid improper coaching and making unnecessary or improper speaking or clarifying objections. *See supra* section "Coaching" for examples of improper objections made by a defender.

111. If you confer with witness during a deposition, be aware that in some jurisdictions, as discussed in the text, that conversation may not be privileged.

CHAPTER 16

Issues for Women at Depositions

Lorna G. Schofield*

"I don't have to talk to you, little lady."
"Tell that little mouse over there to pipe down."
"What do you know, young girl?"
"Be quiet, little girl."
"Go away, little girl."[1]

Perhaps you think these quotations are the product of an overactive imagination. Guess again. They were made by a male lawyer to his female adversary during a deposition.[2] Such gender bias is not rare. Task forces in over forty states and five federal circuits have examined their court systems and found that gender bias against women lawyers, litigants, and court employees remains a pervasive problem.[3] Recent findings suggest that more than 8 percent of female litigators experienced unwanted sexual attention in the context of federal litigation in the previous five years, while less than 1 percent of litigators reported similar gender-related disrespect.[4] One study found that 74 percent of women have experienced some form of gender bias in the courtroom.[5] Respondents to task force surveys report that gender bias is even worse outside the courtroom at depositions and negotiations, where the rules of conduct are much looser.[6]

This chapter identifies some of the problems women litigators may face when trying to establish and maintain control at depositions. It offers practical suggestions for solving these problems. Controlling a deposition, however, is not a "woman's issue." Maintaining control is an issue at every deposition, regardless of the gender of the participant. Therefore, the suggestions in this chapter should be useful for all lawyers, but particularly those who may appear more vulnerable—women, minorities, gays and lesbians, and young or inexperienced lawyers.

The number of women in the legal profession is rising. As of 2006, women represented 30.6 percent of all attorneys and 48 percent of incoming law students.[7] In private firms, women constituted 44.1 percent of associates and 17.3 percent of partners.[8] Although only two of the nine United States Supreme Court justices are female, as of 2006 women represented 23.6 percent of federal circuit court judges and 23.3 percent of federal district court judges.[9] As women judges have become more visible, they have worked to bring public attention to the problem of gender bias in the legal system.[10]

Despite these advances, women face special difficulties. They are more likely than men to be the victims of sexist comments. And as discussed below, the way women traditionally communicate may hamper their ability to control a difficult witness or adversary. In addition, some women have little desire to engage in combative behavior. Those who do engage in it may not find the behavior innate or intuitive, but instead something they must learn through observation and reflection.[11] Thus, when there is a need for combative behavior, inexperienced women lawyers may be at a disadvantage.[12]

The first section of this chapter analyzes how gender differences in communication and sexist behavior can affect depositions. The second section suggests solutions for some of the problems a woman lawyer may encounter at depositions. The final section focuses on judicial and other official intervention to combat gender discrimination.

How Gender Differences in Verbal and Nonverbal Communication Affect Taking and Defending

Differences in Communication and Speaker Credibility

In our society, the image of authority often is associated with maleness.[13] Male lawyers often have the advantage of culturally recognizable symbols of authority such as height, heft, and a lower-pitched and deeper voice.[14] Although men on average are only 8 percent taller than women, the differences in size of the larynx between adult males and females are significant. The vocal folds of the larynxes of postpubescent males average about 50–60 percent longer than those of females of the same age.[15] These physiological differences not only create dramatic differences in pitch, but they even cause men and women to pronounce words slightly differently. For example, linguistics researchers have found that female speakers of English, German, and Swedish use greater vowel duration contrasts than men do.[16]

Recent linguistic research has focused on how issues of gender and sexuality complicate popular understandings of the differences between the sexes.[17] Gay men often are thought to exhibit "feminine" linguistic patterns, whereas lesbian women sometimes are thought to exhibit more "masculine" speech patterns.[18] Thus, stereotypes about "female" speech patterns apply equally to gays and lesbians whose speech may not conform to conventionally powerful male speech.

In addition to these physiological differences, research on gender and language suggests that sociobiological differences between the way men and women speak directly affect power relationships.[19] Studies report that men talk more than women and that male speech is more dominating and aggressive.[20] In addition, interruption can be a device for exercising power and control in a conversation, and studies show that males interrupt females more often than females interrupt males.[21] Based on such findings, one linguist concluded that men's language is the language of the powerful.[22] A 2007 study found that even though Hillary Rodham Clinton, at the time a U.S. senator and presidential candidate, worked to generate an image of a powerful female, her speech patterns conformed to stereotypical female speech patterns when compared with those of her husband and former U.S. President Bill Clinton.[23]

Because the medium of depositions is primarily speech, lawyers' speaking styles can determine who is in control. When women seek to assert control through their speech, they are not perceived in the same way as men.[24] Often their statements go unheard until made by a man or attributed to a man.[25] Because the manner in which women speak is viewed as less credible, their speech is not as powerful.[26]

425

With these differences in mind, both taking and defending a deposition can be analyzed in terms of the relationship between gender of the speaker and the perceived credibility of the speaker. Because a woman's manner of speaking affects her credibility, it also affects her ability to persuade and thus her effectiveness in professional settings.

Scholars have categorized speaker credibility into four dimensions. These are determined by the receiver's perception of (1) the speaker's focus on, and concern for, the other person ("goodwill and fairness"), (2) the speaker's overall knowledge and intelligence ("expertise"), (3) the credit or power other people give the speaker ("prestige"), and (4) the speaker's presentation skills ("self-presentation").[27] Studies indicate that women are perceived higher than men on only one of these dimensions: goodwill and fairness.[28] On the other three—expertise, prestige, and self-presentation—women are rated below men.[29]

Thus, when taking a deposition, a woman who questions an adverse witness in a hostile tone, rather than a helpful or curious one, may be giving up her only advantage—her perceived goodwill and fairness. On the other hand, if she adopts an approach that preserves the perception of goodwill and fairness, she may be ceding authority to a male adversary who adopts a stern, aggressive tone. The difficulty of choosing between these two options results from the conflict created by societal expectations of how a person in authority is expected to behave—with a hostile tone—and how a woman is expected to behave—with a tone conveying goodwill and fairness.[30]

As for expertise and presentation skills, the old adage applies: A woman has to be twice as good (and twice as prepared) as a man to get just as far. In fact, even when actual performance is held constant and the only variable is gender, numerous studies report that men and women are rated differently regarding expertise.[31] One study, for example, found that women who either argued without proper support or used "tag" questions (for example, "Don't you agree?") were viewed as less knowledgeable and intelligent than men who behaved similarly.[32]

When it come to prestige, it is hard for a woman to seize or retain power if she is assumed to be the least powerful person in the room. Indeed, what woman litigator can say that she has never been mistaken at a deposition for the (typically female) court reporter?[33]

"Sexual Trial Tactics"

The problems discussed in the previous section may not be connected to an adversary's inappropriate behavior. But women lawyers often are the victims of deliberate attacks. Some male adversaries challenge a female lawyer's authority at a deposition by trying to bully and intimidate her. They repeatedly interrupt or attempt to engage her in interminable colloquy or argumentation.[34] Other male adversaries use sexist behavior to undermine women lawyers.[35]

Deliberate efforts by opposing male counsel to undermine women lawyers on the basis of their gender have been called "sexual trial tactics." But they apply equally to depositions.[36] These tactics often take the form of verbal abuse,[37] or comments like, "Listen, babe" or "Where did you go to law school, sweetheart?"[38] Sometimes opposing counsel will refer to a female adversary by her first name while referring to males by their last.[39] Even women who are comfortable in the formal, rule-bound setting of the courtroom find greater difficulty asserting control in less-rule-bound settings like depositions and negotiations.[40]

The use of sexual trial tactics presents the question of how to define appropriate limits on zealous advocacy. Some lawyers, for example, may not view gender-biased conduct as the equivalent of a racist remark to a minority adversary.[41] Although the use of subtle and not-so-subtle sexist behavior may not break any formal rules, it crosses the line of acceptable professional behavior.[42]

Difficulties Taking a Deposition

A lawyer taking a deposition—whether a man or a woman—begins in a position of control compared with others present. The taker noticed the deposition; set the time and place (usually the taker's own conference room); chose the documents to be discussed; and asks questions the witness must answer. This control is essential to the questioner's goal of obtaining responsive, truthful, and, if possible, helpful answers from a reluctant or resistant witness defended by a lawyer.

Even though the taker starts with a natural advantage, it can be quickly lost if that lawyer does not speak in a way that highlights her power or if she permits an adversary to speak in a way that undermines her power.[43] For example, a male lawyer defending a deposition may comment to his client before the questioning begins, "Can you believe that this pretty little thing is opposing counsel?"[44] Or a male defender may repeatedly interrupt a female lawyer by objecting to every question, suggesting that she does not know how to ask a proper question, or by improperly instructing the witness not to answer.[45] "Rambo" deposition tactics among male attorneys may be designed to "demean[ ] inexperienced young women attorneys."[46]

Inappropriate physical behavior is another male intimidation tactic. Jacqueline Vitti Frederick, a Los Angeles litigator, recalled a deposition in which she faced six male opposing lawyers:

> They treated me very courteously while they were doing the questioning. But when I asked my first question, one attorney lurched across the table and shouted "Objection!" I responded, "I would like the record to reflect counsel just lurched across the table and screamed his objection." He was subdued after that, but the other five took up the tactic. It continued for eight hours on every question, and was obviously contrived to intimidate me.[47]

The video recording of depositions can help eliminate some sexual trial tactics by providing female attorneys with proof of inappropriate behavior.[48] Yet such tactics—which a judge may scrutinize when ruling on a motion for a protective order—may affect the immediate ability of the female lawyer to conduct the deposition effectively. They may delay or even prevent her from obtaining the information she needs. Worse, a witness who hears his male lawyer speaking disrespectfully to his female examiner also may also become uncooperative.

These dynamics are also affected by those attending the deposition. For example, a male lawyer defending a deposition with many female lawyers in attendance is less likely to employ such tactics—or to do so successfully.[49] Conversely, a woman taking a deposition in a room full of male lawyers is more likely to be attacked based on her gender.[50]

The gender of the witness also has an impact. A female witness may identify with a woman taker and therefore trust her more than a man. Alternatively, some women may resent women with authority and therefore be less cooperative than they would with a male questioner.[51]

A male witness, threatened by a female taker who is in a position of power, may become aggressive. Such aggressiveness might also surface if a male witness views the female lawyer as less intelligent and capable than himself or his male defender, as the speaker credibility studies discussed above indicate.

In sum, despite the authority a woman ought to wield when taking a deposition, her gender may significantly diminish the advantages associated with that authority unless she is prepared to deal with the gender problem.

Difficulties Defending a Deposition

Just as a woman's speaking style may create problems when she takes a deposition, her speaking style may create problems when she defends one. A defender must protect the record, protect the witness, and make the witness feel protected.[52] But a witness faced with an aggressive or abusive examiner may find it difficult to believe his female defender has the situation under control.

As noted in the previous section, a taker has a natural advantage over a defender. Therefore, a female defender must rely on other means to assert her power and control over the situation. But, as noted above, women are less likely to speak in a style that conveys authority.

Suppose an examiner is harassing or mistreating the witness. A woman defending the witness may decide not to intervene because of her judgment that the witness can handle the taker's behavior. However, that judgment may be influenced partly by the documented tendency, as noted above, of women to interrupt less than men.[53] In the same situation, a man might act differently. A male defender might intercede to counter the taker's authority or because of the greater tendency of males to interrupt. For a female defender, the best way to deal successfully with gender differences is to be vigilant not only about substantive issues but also about how a woman's actions affect her authority and control.

Given the results of speaker credibility studies, it is easy to see why a female lawyer might have difficulty winning the trust and confidence of the client or other witness she is defending, whether the witness is male or female.[54] The witness may be more accustomed to male lawyers or, because of gender stereotypes, may feel more "protected" by a male lawyer. For a variety of reasons, therefore, a witness may rate a female lawyer as inferior in terms of expertise, prestige, and preparation. This view may make relations between a female lawyer and the witness she is defending strained or even adversarial.[55]

429

How to Combat Difficult Adversaries and Witnesses

A female litigator should keep in mind the four elements of speaker credibility when planning her deposition strategy. In terms of expertise, she must strive to be consistently better prepared than her male adversary and the witness. For example, when taking a deposition, a woman needs full command of the facts so she is prepared to "discipline" a witness who strays from them. Having documents ready to contradict a witness's testimony is one example of how to maintain control. Similarly, knowing cold the rules governing permissible objections puts her in a better position to discourage an opponent from improper objections.[56]

In addition to being better prepared, a woman litigator must convey her intelligence and knowledge to both the witness and her male adversary. When preparing a witness, for example, she should take every opportunity to display her knowledge of the law and to mention her prior victories.[57] During a deposition, whether taking or defending, she should not shy from opportunities to engage her adversary in discussions on the merits (when appropriate), thereby communicating that she is not afraid to "take him on."

Whenever possible, she should speak in a manner to convey "goodwill and fairness" in order to enhance her perceived credibility. As taker, for example, she might use phrases like, "I want to make sure that you [the witness] understand my question" or "I want to make sure you [the witness] have a full opportunity to explain."

Similarly, a female litigator should plan for ways to enhance her prestige in order to gain power. For example, a more senior woman lawyer who has a younger male lawyer as her assistant conveys her relative prestige and power. A woman accompanied by a deferential senior partner (preferably male) is likely to have an easier time gaining the respect and cooperation of others in the room. On the other hand, a male colleague who interrupts and overrides a female colleague will undercut her authority, whether he is her junior or her senior.

By consciously improving her presentation skills, a woman can avoid many of the pitfalls of female speech. Affirmative statements should not be posed as questions, either in wording or inflection. Questions, particularly leading questions, should be phrased affirmatively. For example, "Is it correct you were driving a red car?" is more assertive than "Weren't you driving a red car?" (itself an improvement on "Isn't it true that you were driving a red car?"). Statements should be simply stated, not prefaced with

"I think." Furthermore, the speaker should not undercut her own statements—"I'm not sure but . . ." or "This may not be right but. . . ." She should speak clearly, audibly, and authoritatively. And she should try to modulate her voice so that it is not high-pitched or breathy. If needed and available, professional help from a voice coach can be a worthwhile investment.

When taking a deposition, a female litigator has several options for combating intimidating or inappropriate behavior by a male adversary. One is the following two-step approach: First, she should interpret the behavior as an assertion of authority and dominance and not as a personal attack (even though it may be one). Second, she should reciprocate with an equal or greater assertion of authority and dominance, but not necessarily in the same style or manner as the original attack.

Some women, instead of reciprocating by asserting their own authority, prefer to ignore the adversary and be calm, persistent, and respectful with the witness. This technique can be effective. For example, suppose an adversary engages in sexual trial tactics in the hopes of distracting a female litigator by making her angry. If the woman resists and is calm yet persistent, the adversary may give up his bullying.

But ignoring disruptive behavior may be interpreted as tacit acceptance arising from an unwillingness or inability to challenge the adversary, thereby inviting continued or escalating abuse. There is a fine line between being submissive and quietly effective. An effective response to an adversary's aggression must communicate that the woman will not accept inappropriate behavior. That does not always mean confrontation, but it does mean responding in some way. For example, if an adversary instructs the witness not to answer, the female litigator can calmly and respectively challenge the adversary's power by pointing to the Federal Rule of Civil Procedure that limits the grounds for instructions not to answer.[58] Such a response reinforces her expertise and, hence, her credibility.

Although passive female behavior can be dangerous, situations may arise in which the witness will cooperate with a beleaguered woman lawyer. A male witness may see the woman lawyer as a victim who needs to be rescued. A female witness may see her as a sympathetic ally. However, relying on this approach is highly problematic because it undermines a woman's images of strength and control. And, once lost, these images may be impossible to regain. Moreover, an image of weakness fostered by ignoring aggressive behavior may have consequences beyond the instant deposition. Clients may seek a different lawyer—one who is a stronger advocate (and probably male). In addition, seeing the effectiveness of such abusive behavior, adversaries are likely to continue to use it.

As a general rule, inappropriate behavior should not be ignored; instead, it should be challenged as soon as it occurs. The most direct challenge is to insist that the adversary stop the inappropriate behavior. A command to stop the behavior is likely to be more effective than a mere request.

As an alternative, a female taker might adopt a low-key but affirmative approach. She might, for example, look bored and avoid eye contact, shuffle documents, or stand up and walk around the room. She could inquire whether the reporter has recorded every word and then ask the adversary if he has finished. Or she could ask the defender whether he has instructed his witness not to answer. If the answer is "no," she could ask the witness to answer. In addition to challenging the obstructive behavior directly, this approach might motivate the witness to cooperate, notwithstanding his lawyer's behavior.

Inappropriate gestures by an adversary should be described for the record, and profane or otherwise inappropriate language highlighted on the record by asking the adversary to repeat his comments. The female lawyer might insist that all future deposition sessions with an adversary be video recorded. In general, the more outrageous the behavior, the greater the need for an affirmative response in order to maintain control. Indeed, the appearance of authority is the first step toward gaining and maintaining actual power.

Ideally, a woman lawyer should be versatile, with a number of styles and responses on which to draw. The strategic issue then becomes determining which response is appropriate in a particular situation. Obviously, many factors influence the decision, such as the gender and style of the defender and of others in the room, including the witness, other lawyers, any clients, and colleagues. Also relevant is the degree of inappropriateness of the behavior as well as the available responses. Finally, the impact of the behavior on the testimony and the client interests at stake must be considered.

Despite the tactical need to reassert authority in the face of a difficult adversary, a woman lawyer faces a double bind. To assert her authority, she must speak in a style our society associates with men.[59] Yet studies indicate that individuals who act contrary to cultural and societal expectations are often viewed negatively.[60] To further complicate the situation, women who have internalized these expectations may not want to act in the "male" manner.

Adding to the dilemma, if a woman speaks with certainty, makes bold statements of fact, interrupts others, and generally talks in an aggressive manner, she may be disliked by the witness.[61] In protesting any but the nastiest remarks, she may be viewed as humorless and oversensitive.[62] A woman who wants to be perceived as both powerful and likeable walks a particularly fine line. Hillary Rodham Clinton, for example, speaks from a position of power, but in media interviews she retains many markers of less powerful female communication—whether inadvertently or by design.[63]

In a deposition, unlike a jury trial (or a political campaign), maintaining control is more important than being popular. But a woman should not be quick to surrender the presumption of goodwill and fairness—the one dimension of speaker credibility in which she has an advantage over her male adversaries.[64] Even though being liked by an adversary or the witness is not the purpose of a deposition, being liked may be an effective way to gain an advantage over the adversary. Thus, when considering whether to object, keep silent, or retaliate against a difficult adversary, a female litigator must consider a number factors in deciding how to respond.

Suppose a female lawyer taking a deposition realizes that a male witness is becoming aggressive because he feels threatened by her authority. This perceived threat may arise either from her role as questioner and his as witness or from the woman's personal style. In either case, she may decide to cede some of the authority that naturally flows from her position as a taker. For instance, she might display a friendly demeanor or ask questions about a subject that is not threatening to the witness. To extract helpful testimony from a difficult witness, she may even resort to charm, thereby complying with societal expectations about how women should act. But, as already noted, it may be difficult to transform a "soft" demeanor into something more authoritarian.

Whether taking or defending a deposition, if a female lawyer encounters behavior egregious enough to warrant making a motion in response to her adversary's behavior, she should avoid saying anything on the record that would undermine her own credibility or integrity, either with the participants at the deposition or later when the record is presented to the judge. Any desire to express uncensored rage at her adversary usually should be suppressed.

Seeking Judicial and Other Intervention

Occasionally, nothing short of judicial intervention will rectify a situation with an abusive witness or adversary. When deciding whether to seek judicial intervention, a female lawyer must evaluate the behavior to determine how egregious it is. The watchword here is "caution": Judges generally do not favor discovery disputes, particularly motions for sanctions.[65] A female lawyer must also consider whether the judge is even likely to recognize gender discrimination.[66]

Judicial intervention for abusive deposition practices is authorized by statute, by rules of civil procedure, and by the court's inherent power. The methods by which a party may seek judicial intervention is thoroughly explored in Chapters 11, 14, and 16.

Few published opinions, state or federal, deal exclusively with the imposition of sanctions for abusive deposition behavior consisting solely of gender discrimination. Several cases, however, address the imposition of sanctions for such behavior. These cases provide persuasive precedent for a female lawyer seeking judicial intervention.[67]

In a New York appellate decision, *Principe v. Assay Partners*, for example, the offending behavior surfaced during the deposition of a fourth-party defendant represented by a female lawyer.[68] Quoting from the deposition transcript, the court cited the numerous comments made by plaintiff's counsel, including the comments quoted at the outset of this chapter.[69] In addition to verbal comments, the woman lawyer testified that these comments "were accompanied by disparaging gestures . . . dismissively flicking his fingers and waving a back hand at me."[70] In finding this behavior sanctionable, the court commented that "the words used here are a paradigm of rudeness, and condescend, disparage, and degrade a colleague on the basis that she is female."[71] The court noted that "the condemnation of such improper remarks springs from a growing recognition of the seriousness of gender bias and that bias of any kind cannot be permitted to find a safe haven in the practice of law."[72]

In another New York appellate decision, *In re Jordan Schiff*, the court sanctioned a lawyer representing the plaintiff at a deposition for his misbehavior toward a female defense lawyer. The court stated that the male lawyer "was unduly intimidating and abusive toward the defendant's counsel, and [that] he directed vulgar, obscene and sexist epithets toward her anatomy and gender."[73] In considering the recommendation of the Hearing Panel of the Departmental Disciplinary Committee, the court held that public censure was appropriate discipline for the lawyer's conduct, which was "inexcusable" and "intolerable," and that the conduct also violated New York's DR 1-102 of the Code of Professional Responsibility.[74] Unfortunately, the remedy of public censure did not help the female lawyer's client.

Since *Principe*, other courts have also issued sanctions based on displays of gender bias. In *Harthman v. Texaco*, an attorney who made a lewd gesture directed at a female adversary was held in contempt by the U.S. District Court for the Virgin Islands and suspended for a month. Although the judge observed that the attorney's obscene gesture "raise[d] the specter of animus,"[75] he found that the gesture constituted such a clear breach of "a lawyer's duty to treat with consideration all persons involved in the legal process" that sanctions would be imposed regardless of a finding of discrimination. One Maryland appellate court upheld the grant of attorney's fees and instituted a protective order against a male attorney who, in the course of defending a deposition in his client's tort claim, referred to the female opposing counsel as a "babe" and a "bimbo."[76]

In 2001, the Florida Supreme Court upheld a sanction of two years' probation against an attorney for unprofessional conduct designed to disparage a female opposing counsel and her client through sexist and racist comments. According to the court, the male attorney called female counsel a "bush leaguer," told her that "depositions are not conducted under 'girl's rules,'" and continually demeaned female counsel's legal knowledge and capabilities.[77]

In addition to seeking sanctions, female lawyers who encounter discriminatory behavior during litigation may take their complaints to their local boards of bar grievances or local bar associations. Indeed, a woman might find that a male adversary reprimanded by a body of his peers is more likely to behave himself in the future.

An increasing number of state bar associations and state and federal courts have stated that inappropriate and discourteous conduct will not be tolerated among members of the bar. Both state and federal courts, as well as bar associations, have promulgated rules aimed at ending abusive and outrageous conduct during litigation.[78]

But until civility in litigation becomes pervasive, women lawyers will continue to face special challenges at depositions. As an added problem, sex discrimination remains, in certain respects, the last publicly acceptable form of discrimination in our society.[79] Moreover, things said and done during litigation that are discriminatory may not be perceived as such by those involved and therefore may go uncorrected.[80]

Conclusion

As the first step in dealing with discrimination, lawyers—female and male alike—must be aware of its existence. Only then can the remedies suggested in this chapter be applied.

Notes

*In the first edition of this book, this chapter was co-authored by Lorna G. Schofield and Giuliana H. Dunham. Many thanks to Sarah Burg for her research assistance on this chapter for the second edition. Parts of this chapter are adapted from Depositions and the Gorilla Adversary, coauthored by Lorna G. Schofield & Jill A. Lesser, in THE WOMAN ADVOCATE (Am. Bar Ass'n, 1996).

1. Principe v. Assay Partners, 586 N.Y.S.2d 182, 184 (N.Y. Sup. Ct. 1992) (quoting deposition transcript in opinion in which court sanctioned male lawyer for misconduct); *see also infra* notes 45–48, 75–78, and accompanying text.

2. *Principe*, 586 N.Y.S.2d at 184.

3. Lilia M. Cortina et al., *What's Gender Got to Do With It? Incivility in the Federal Courts*, 27 LAW & SOC. INQUIRY 235, 236 (2002). *See, e.g., Eighth Circuit Gender Fairness Task Force, Final Recommendations of the Eighth Circuit Gender Fairness Task Force*, 31 CREIGHTON L. REV. 1 (1997); *Report of the New York Task Force of Women in the Courts, reprinted in* 15 FORDHAM URB. L.J. 3 (1986–87); *Massachusetts Gender Bias Study, Gender Bias in Courthouse Interactions*, 74 MASS. L. REV. 50 (1989); Kathleen L. Soll, *Gender Bias Task Forces: How They Have Fulfilled Their Mandate and Recommendations for Change*, 2 REV. L. & WOMEN'S STUD. 633, 634, 638 (1993); Deborah L. Rhode, *Gender and Professional Roles*, 63 FORDHAM L. REV. 39, 57–58 (1994) (finding that as result of these studies, gender bias has become more difficult to deny or dismiss).

4. Cortina et al., *supra* note 3, at 244.

5. Marilyn Price et al., *Gender Differences in the Practice Patterns of Forensic Psychiatry Experts*, 32 J. AM. ACAD. PSYCHIATRY & LAW 250, 250 (2004).

6. Lynn Hecht Schafran, *The Obligation to Intervene: New Direction from the American Bar Association Code of Judicial Conduct*, 4 GEO. J. LEGAL ETHICS 53, 63 (1990) (quoting respondent to Minnesota task force's lawyers' survey, who wrote, "I have personally on several occasions had opposing male counsel direct demeaning comments to me that appeared gender-based. This primarily occurs in depositions, negotiations, and settings outside the courtroom. The purpose usually seems to be to try to gain a tactical advantage by flustering an opposing woman attorney.").

7. ABA COMM'N ON WOMEN IN THE PROFESSION, A CURRENT GLANCE AT WOMEN IN THE LAW 2006, at 4 (2006), http://www.abanet .org/women/CurrentGlanceStatistics2006.pdf.

8. *Id.* at 2.

9. *Id.* at 4.

10. *See generally* Linda C. Morrison, *The National Association of Women Judges: Agents of Change*, 17 WIS. WOMEN'S L.J. 291 (2002).

11. Rhode, *supra* note 3, at 57–60. *Cf.* Marjorie Harness Goodwin, *Exclusion in Girls' Peer Groups: Ethnographic Analysis of Language Practices on the Playground*, 45 HUM. DEV. 392, 392 (2002) ("Forms of social exclusion in girls' groups call into question the notion that girls are fundamentally interested in cooperative interaction and a morality based on principles of relatedness, care, and equity.").

12. In addition to experiencing more gender bias, women are more likely to observe it. *See, e.g.*, Rhode, *supra* note 3, at 64 (finding that "virtually every bar commission and serious scholar in the field has documented persistent forms of discrimination, as well as substantial disparities in men's and women's perceptions of such behavior. In nearly all studies, between two-thirds and three-fourths of the women surveyed indicate that they have experienced some form of discrimination or bias, while only one-fourth to one-third of the men report observing such conduct.").

13. DEBORAH TANNEN, TALKING FROM 9 TO 5: HOW WOMEN'S AND MEN'S CONVERSATIONAL STYLES AFFECT WHO GETS HEARD, WHO GETS CREDIT, AND WHAT GETS DONE AT WORK 167 (1994); Rhode, *supra* note 3, at 65 & n.107 (finding that "[f]emale lawyers, particularly racial and ethnic minorities, frequently report that they lack the same presumption of competence that their white male colleagues enjoy") (citing Lynn Hecht Schafran, *Eve, Mary, Superwoman: How Stereotypes About Women Influence Judges*, 24 JUDGES J. 12, 15 (1985)); Special Comm. on Gender, D.C. Ct. App., Preliminary Report to the Task Force of the District of Columbia Circuit on Gender, Race and Ethnic Bias (May 1994); ABA MULTICULTURAL WOMEN ATTORNEYS NETWORK, THE BURDENS OF BOTH, THE PRIVILEGES OF NEITHER (1994); Deborah Ruble Round, Note, *Gender Bias in the Judicial System*, 61 S. CAL. L. REV. 2193, 2201 (1988); Edward A. Adams, *ABA Finds Minority Women in Law Face Twice the Hurdles*, N.Y.L.J., Aug. 8,

1994, at 1; Katrina M. Dewey, *A New Reality Sets In*, CAL. L. BUS., May 16, 1994, at 2024.

14.   TANNEN, *supra* note 13, at 167.

15.   *See* Minoru Hirano, Kiminori Sato & Keiichiro Yukizane, *Male-Female Difference in Anterior Commisure Angle*, *in* SPEECH PRODUCTION AND LANGUAGE 11 (Shigeru Kiritani et al. eds. 1997).

16.   *See* Christine Ericsdotter & Anna M. Ericsson, *Gender Differences in Vowel Duration in Read Swedish: Preliminary Results* 34–37 (Lund Univ., Dep't of Linguistics Working Papers No. 49, 2001).

17.   *See generally* DON KULICK & DEBORAH CAMERON, LANGUAGE AND SEXUALITY (2003). *See also* ANNA LIVIA & KIRA HALL, QUEERLY PHRASED: LANGUAGE, GENDER, AND SEXUALITY (1997).

18.   *See, e.g.*, Janet P. Humbert et al., *The Influence of Sexual Orientation on Vowel Production*, 116 ACOUSTICAL SOC'Y AM. J. 1905 (2004) (reporting findings consistent with the idea that innate biological factors influence lesbian, gay, bisexual, and transgender speech patterns indirectly by causing selective adoption of certain speech patterns characteristic of the opposite sex); Rudolf P. Gaudio, *Sounding Gay: Pitch Properties in the Speech of Gay and Straight Men*, 69 AM. SPEECH 30 (1994).

19.   *See, e.g.*, LANGUAGE, GENDER AND SOCIETY (Barrie Thorne et. al. eds., 1983). *But see* Bartley Christopher Frueh, *Gender Differences in Language Use: Implications for Impression Formation* (1990) (unpublished M. Psy. dissertation, Univ. of South Fla.) (finding that, despite growing body of evidence that significant gender differences in language usage exist, smaller body of research refutes these differences).

20.   *See, e.g.*, NANCY M. HENLEY, BODY POLITICS: POWER, SEX, AND NONVERBAL COMMUNICATION 73–75 (1977) (citing several studies). *But see* Matthias R. Mehl et al., Are Women Really More Talkative Than Men?, 317 SCIENCE 82 (2007) (finding in a study that college-age women emit 16,125 words per day, while college-age men emit 15,669).

21.   Candace West & Don H. Zimmerman, *Small Insults: A Study of Interruptions in Cross-Sex Conversations Between Unacquainted Persons*, *in* LANGUAGE, GENDER AND SOCIETY, *supra* note 19, at 102.

22.   ROBIN T. LAKOFF, TALKING POWER: THE POLITICS OF LANGUAGE IN OUR LIVES 205 (1990).

23.   Carmelia Suleiman & Daniel O'Connell, *Gender Differences in the Media Interviews of Bill and Hillary Clinton*, J. PSYCHOLINGUISTIC RES. (2007). The researchers observed that some of the gender differences were attributable to the gender of the interviewer. For example, male interviewers generally addressed Hillary Clinton by her first name, while female interviewers did not do so.

24.   *See generally* Md. Special Joint Comm., Gender Bias in Ct., *Report of the Maryland Special Joint Committee on Gender Bias in the Courts*, 260 (1989); Ann J. Gellis, *Great Expectations: Women in the Legal Profession, A Commentary on State Studies*, 66 IND. L.J. 941 (1991); Kathleen Reardon,

The Memo Every Woman Keeps in Her Desk, in REACH FOR THE TOP 75, 76–77 (Nancy A. Nichols ed., 1994).

25. TANNEN, *supra* note 13, at 277–79; LAKOFF, *supra* note 22, at 199.

26. Sherron B. Kenton, *Speaker Credibility in Persuasive Business Communication: A Model Which Explains Gender Differences*, 26 J. BUS. COMM. 143 (1989). For further discussion of how women are culturally primed to speak after men allocate so-called "speaking rights," see Penelope Eckert & Sally MacConnell-Ginet, *Organizing Speech, in* LANGUAGE AND GENDER 91 (2003).

27. Kenton, *id.* at 148.

28. *Id.* at 150. Kenton does not indicate whether men and women judge women the same way.

29. *Id.* at 150–52.

30. TANNEN, *supra* note 13, at 169–202.

31. *Id.* at 145–52.

32. *Id.* at 150.

33. The problem is intensified for women of color. A black woman partner at a major Chicago law firm reports that she has been mistaken for the court reporter at every deposition she has attended. ABA MULTI-CULTURAL WOMEN ATTORNEYS NETWORK, *supra* note 13, at 26.

34. West & Zimmerman, *supra* note 21. See also Chapter 15.

35. Kandis Koustenis, Note, *Sexual Trial Tactics: The Ability of the Model Code and Model Rules to Discipline Discriminatory Conflicts between Adversaries*, 4 GEO. J. LEGAL ETHICS 153, 153–56 (1990).

36. *Id.*; Lynn Hecht Schafran, *Abilities vs. Assumptions: Women as Litigators*, 19 TRIAL 37, 38 (1983).

37. Koustenis, *supra* note 35, at 156.

38. *Id.*

39. HENLEY, *supra* note 20, at 67–68 (finding that how people address one another can serve as status markers, while nonreciprocal usage of the status marker often indicates a status difference between the parties).

40. *See* LINDA BABCOCK, WOMEN DON'T ASK: NEGOTIATION AND THE GENDER DIVIDE 157–59 (2003).

41. Schafran, *supra* note 6, at 71–72 (recalling 1985 Florida State Bar Association annual meeting at which a male lawyer on panel told of a case in which he deliberately made a sexist remark to a female prosecutor to throw her off on cross-examination; the same lawyer stated it would never have occurred to him to make a racist remark to distract a minority adversary).

42. *See* Koustenis, *supra* note 35, at 156. *See also infra* note 79 and accompanying text (discussing promulgation of standards to regulate professional conduct between lawyers).

43. TANNEN, *supra* note 13, at 178.

44. *See, e.g.*, Koustenis, *supra* note 35, at 156–57.

45. West & Zimmerman, *supra* note 21. The bases for a proper instruction not to answer are limited. Federal Rule of Civil Procedure (FRCP) 30(c)(2) permits lawyers at depositions to instruct a witness not to answer only when claiming privilege as the basis of the objection, when seeking to enforce a limitation on evidence as directed by the court, or when seeking a protective order. See "Instructing a Witness Not to Answer" in Chapter 14.

46. Jean M. Cary, *Rambo Depositions: Controlling an Ethical Cancer in Civil Litigation*, 25 HOFSTRA L. REV. 561, 574 (1996).

47. Sherrill Kushner & Valerie Lezin, *Bias in the Courtroom*, 14 BARRISTER 9, 11 (1987).

48. *See* FED. R. CIV. P. 30(b)(3)(A); see also Chapter 17.

49. TANNEN, *supra* note 13, at 287.

50. *Id.*

51. ABA MULTICULTURAL WOMEN ATTORNEYS NETWORK, *supra* note 13, at 18.

52. See Chapter 14.

53. *See, e.g.,* HENLEY, *supra* note 20; West & Zimmerman, *supra* note 21; LAKOFF, *supra* note 22.

54. *See, e.g.,* Kenton, *supra* note 26.

55. *See* "Explaining the Deposition Process" in Chapter 7, discussing the importance of gaining the witness's confidence during witness preparation and "When Can You Instruct" in Chapter 14, discussing the importance of keeping the witness's confidence while defending.

56. See also Chapter 14 and Chapter 15.

57. The word "mention" is used as a value-neutral word. Women are taught not to boast; indeed "boasting" is viewed as negative behavior. "Strut," "swagger," and "swell," however, are male words that convey a distinctly different, if not entirely positive, meaning.

58. *See supra* note 45.

59. Frueh, *supra* note 19, at 9–10; TANNEN, *supra* note 13, at 170 (concluding that women are expected to hedge their beliefs as opinions, to seek opinions from others, and to be "polite" in their requests).

60. Frueh, *supra* note 19, at 9–10 (citing research); *see also* TANNEN, *supra* note 13, at 170, 193.

61. TANNEN, *supra* note 13, at 170.

62. ABA Comm. on Women in the Profession, *Report to the House of Delegates*, at 10 (1988).

63. Suleiman & O'Connell, *supra* note 23, studied review markers such as the number of syllables spoken (that is, the quantum of speech), use of the word "so" for emphasis, use of the hedge phrase "you know," and interruptions versus taking turns in interviews.

64. ABA Comm. on Women in the Profession, *Report to the House of Delegates, supra* note 62, at 6–8.

65. *See, e.g.,* Janet S. Kole, *When Bad Depositions Happen to Good Lawyers, in* THE WOMAN ADVOCATE 9 (1994); Sharon E. Grubin, *Calling the*

Judge for a Ruling during a Deposition or a View from the Other End of the Line: The Ten Commandments, in THE WOMAN ADVOCATE 16 (1994).

66. The judge who co-chaired the California Gender Bias Task Force wryly commented, "Until I was on this . . . Task Force, there never was any gender bias in my court." *The Final Report of the Ninth Circuit Gender Bias Task Force*, 67 S. CAL. L. REV. 727, 949 (May 1994).

67. Principe v. Assay Partners, 586 N.Y.S.2d 182 (N.Y. Sup. Ct. 1992); *In re* Jordan Schiff, 599 N.Y.S.2d 242 (N.Y. App. Div. 1993). For a general discussion of recent judicial attitudes regarding inappropriate and abusive conduct, see *Final Report of the Committee in Civility of the Seventh Federal Judicial Circuit*, 143 F.R.D. 441 (June 1992); *Bar Committee Begins Grappling with Lawyer Civility, in* BAR REP., D.C. BAR, Oct./Nov. 1993, at 4.

68. *Principe*, 586 N.Y.S.2d at 182, 187. The imposition of sanctions was based upon the violation of Rule 130 of the New York Rules of Court. Rule 130 permits sanctions to be imposed for behavior "undertaken primarily . . . to harass or maliciously injure another." Although a subjective standard is often used to review conduct under this rule, the judge in *Principe* analogized the language of Rule 130 to the federal rule (then FRCP 11; now FRCP 26(g)(1)(B)) and applied an objective standard for the imposition of sanctions. The court found that "the conduct at issue was not the conduct of a 'reasonable attorney.'"

69. *Principe*, 586 N.Y.S.2d at 184; see also *supra* text accompanying note 1 (for cited comments).

70. *Id.* at 184.

71. *Id.*

72. *Id.* at 185 (in finding behavior in this case inappropriate, court relied on several cases in which judges had been publicly disciplined and sometimes removed from the bench for sexually discriminatory conduct). *See, e.g.,* Ky. Bar Ass'n v. Hardesty, 775 S.W.2d 87 (Ky. 1989); *In re* Kivett, 309 S.E.2d 442 (N.C. 1983); *In re* Gelfand, 512 N.E.2d 533 (N.Y.), *cert. denied*, 484 U.S. 977 (1987).

Although this chapter does not cover gender bias in the courts, the fact that many judges have faced severe sanctions based on sexual harassment indicates a recognition of the seriousness of the problem of gender bias in the law. *See Report of the New York Task Force of Women in the Courts, reprinted in* 15 FORDHAM URB. L.J. 3 (1986–87); *Final Report of the Massachusetts Gender Bias Study: Gender Bias in Courthouse Interactions*, 74 MASS. L. REV. 50 (1989).

73. *Schiff*, 599 N.Y.S.2d at 242.

74. *Id.* (citing MODEL CODE OF PROF'L RESPONSIBILITY DR 1-102(A)(6) (1980)(a "lawyer shall not . . . engage in any . . . conduct that adversely reflects on his fitness to practice law"). Although the ABA Model Rules of Professional Conduct, which is adopted in 47 state jurisdictions, have no parallel provision, individual states have incorporated a standard similar

to that in the Model Code. *See, e.g.,* ALA. RULES OF PROF'L CONDUCT 8.4(g), MASS. RULES OF PROF'L CONDUCT 8.4(h). *See also* N.J. RULES OF PROF'L CONDUCT 8.4(h) ("It is professional misconduct for a lawyer to: . . . engage, in a professional capacity, in conduct involving discrimination (except employment discrimination unless resulting in a final agency or judicial determination) because of race, color, religion, age, sex, sexual orientation, national origin, language, marital status, socioeconomic status, or handicap where the conduct is intended or likely to cause harm.")

75. Harthman v. Texaco, 31 V.I. 175, 179–80 (D.V.I. 1994).

76. Mullaney v. Aude, 730 A.2d 759, 762 (Md. Ct. Spec. App. 1999).

77. Fla. Bar v. Martocci, 791 So. 2d 1074, 1075–76 (Fla. 2001).

78. *See, e.g.,* FINAL REPORT OF THE COMMITTEE ON CIVILITY OF THE SEVENTH FEDERAL JUDICIAL CIRCUIT (June 1992) (instituting standards of conduct addressed specifically to conduct at depositions); MODEL CODE OF PROF'L RESPONSIBILITY EC 7-10, EC 7-36, EC 7-37, EC 7-38, EC 7-39 (1989) (setting forth standards of conduct to which litigation counsel should adhere); Commercial and Fed. Litig. Section, N.Y. State Bar Ass'n, *A Proposal for Guidelines on Civility in Litigation* (June 1994) (recommending dissemination of guidelines specifically addressing standards of conduct at depositions); COLO. LOCAL R. 30.1C (imposing sanctions for abusive deposition conduct); KY. LOCAL R. (3)(b)(2)(E) (imposing sanctions for conduct unbecoming of officer of court); MO. SUP. CT. R. 61.01 (similar in form and content to FRCP 37); TEX. R. CIV. P. 186–215. For commentary on the Texas rule changes, see Alyson Nelson, *Comments, Deposition Conduct: Texas's New Discovery Rules End Up Taking Another Jab at the Rambos of Litigation,* 30 TEX. TECH L. REV. 1471, 1473 (1999) (arguing that although the Texas rules were not created solely to curtail uncivil behavior, their promulgation will actually meet that goal along with its other intentions).

Despite the Seventh Circuit's civility code, civility codes have not become widely implemented. For a discussion of the barriers to the implementation of civility codes and the failure of the legal profession to self-regulate, see Jonathan Macey, *Lawyers, Self Regulation, and the Idea of a Profession,* 74 FORDHAM L. REV. 1079 (2004).

79. Schafran, *supra* note 6, at 54–56 & n.6.

80. *See, e.g., id.* at 55.

CHAPTER 17

The Video Evolution: Pretrial and Trial Considerations

HENRY L. HECHT*

In the last forty years, video depositions have evolved from a rarely used and suspect medium to a powerful tool of the trial lawyer fully endorsed by the federal courts.[1] The use of video deposition testimony played back at trial changes how depositions are taken and defended and makes it essential for a witness to understand that deposition testimony carries the same probative weight as any testimony given at trial.

The government's use of extensive excerpts from the three-day video deposition of Bill Gates in the *United States v. Microsoft* bench trial showed that a video image can have far more impact than reading a transcript.

Here is how one commentator described Gates's video image:

He had combed his mop of hair straight down into bangs that hung unevenly across his pale forehead. Sipping from a Diet

Coke, he rarely looked up at his off-camera interlocutor and alternately rocked slowly back and forth or slouched forward, looking either bored or lost in thought. . . and took an interminable time to respond.[2]

Here is the video 's impact on the trial judge, Thomas Penfield Jackson:

Look at the witness's testimony. I've seen enough witnesses in nineteen years on the bench and eighteen in practice to know when witnesses are evasive, dissembling, defiant, and arrogant. All of those qualities were evinced in that deposition.[3]

And one Microsoft strategist even admitted the video had been a disaster:

One of the most monumental mistakes we made was not understanding how Bill Gates's deposition could be used. We never said, "So it's video taped. How will it be used?" We never focused on: "How did he look? How did he act?" We did him a disservice. And, to a certain extent, he did himself a disservice.[4]

With this in mind, the chapter first reviews the main reasons to record depositions on video, the currently available technology, and the effect of video recording on examination and defense techniques. The chapter then discusses how to best use a deposition video in case preparation, summary judgment practice, and settlement presentation. The chapter next identifies the steps to take when preparing to present video testimony at trial.[5] Finally, the chapter offers practical suggestions for showing video effectively, whether on a tight-budget basis or with a "spare-no-expense" approach.

Virtues of Using Video Pretrial

Video Is an Effective Check on Discovery Abuse by Both Counsel and Witnesses

When depositions are recorded on video, examiners are far less likely to bully witnesses, and defenders are less likely to make foolish objections, repeatedly confer with their witnesses, and coach them.[6] In addition, a video record serves as powerful evidence when you seek a court's intervention against an abusive taker or an obstreperous defender.

Video also discourages witnesses from taking lengthy pauses and seeking numerous conferences with their counsel. Furthermore, it captures and preserves for trial the witness's demeanor.[7]

Video Depositions Preserve the Testimony of an Unavailable Witness—for Better or Worse

Deposition testimony of an adverse party is admissible for any reason. Deposition testimony of unavailable witnesses, whether or not adverse, may also be presented at trial.[8] Presenting testimony on video can be far more powerful than presenting it by reading a transcript. The power of video has both pros and cons.

For example, deposition testimony on video of a terminally ill plaintiff can be the plaintiff's most potent weapon at trial.[9] But deposition testimony on video also can be incredibly damaging when it preserves the testimony of an adverse witness who looks better on video than in court. For this reason, if an adverse witness who is unavailable at trial appears especially sympathetic on video, you may prefer to read the deposition transcript—and hope another party does not request use of the video —rather than show the video yourself.[10]

Properly Presented at Trial, Video Depositions Are Far More Effective than a Dry Transcript Reading

When deposition testimony is presented at trial, portions are usually read directly into evidence. Alternatively, one lawyer can take the stand to act as the witness, while another reads the deposition questions.[11]

Reading a transcript is no substitute for a video of the witness, presented in living color—warts and all. (The video can also be used before a focus group or mock jury to get a sense of how the jury will react to the actual witness as opposed to using a transcript or having an actor present testimony.) On the screen, short pauses in answering questions seem to stretch out forever. Evasiveness, facial tics, inappropriate jokes, rolling of the eyes, sarcasm—on video, all are all magnified. Video also captures the true meaning of a witness's words. Read from a transcript, the answer "no" may sound unambiguous; when "no" is uttered on video, the meaning may be far different. The photographs in Figure 1 make the point.[12]

Figure 1
Video can be used in many ways to strengthen your case dramatically. On the printed page, "No" only means "No." On video, just as in person, you hear what's really being said. Like when the witness is reluctant, angry, or defensive. Video lets you read between the lines.

A Video Recording Synchronized to the Transcript Can Be Used Throughout the Discovery Process

Today's transcript management software, such as LiveNote, makes it easy for a lawyer to use a deposition video throughout the discovery process. In the past, a video often would not be synchronized to the transcript until it was certain that the case was going to trial. Even then, only video to be shown at trial was processed and prepared for presentation. Advances in transcript management software, combined with improvements in video technology, now enable an attorney to (1) play back the video from a previous deposition recording that has been synchronized to the official transcript, (2) create annotations in the transcript, and (3) e-mail video clips to experts or co-workers for strategic collaboration.[13]

By using transcript management software during the discovery phase of your case, you can easily become familiar with a witness's video testimony. In addition, you can annotate portions of written testimony with the corresponding video and then save the results as PowerPoint slides.[14] With PowerPoint slides—which are relatively easy to create—you can make a powerful video presentation where both the video excerpt and the actual transcript can be shown to the jury at the same time.[15] (See Figure 2.)

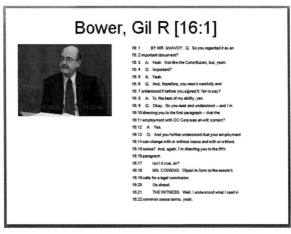

Figure 2

Friendly Witnesses (Especially Experts) Can Surprise Your Opponent by Giving Trial Testimony at Their Video Depositions

Your opponent may not realize it, but a video deposition of an adverse party or an unavailable trial witness may turn out to be the witness's trial testimony.[16] At a deposition, you can elicit testimony for use at trial; an unprepared defender, who is not thinking ahead, therefore risks preserving damaging testimony. In addition, recording a deposition for use at trial preserves trial testimony and thus frees up experts and other witnesses with busy schedules from having to testify at trial.

Demonstrations or Experiments Conducted During a Video Deposition Are More Effective than Courtroom Reenactments

Video reenactments of accidents at the site create a reality that cannot be duplicated in a courtroom.[17] One caveat,[18] however: Before you "officially" record a reenactment, conduct at least one trial run. That way, you avoid unpleasant surprises being memorialized on video.[19]

The production of a video reenactment is different from the production of a video deposition. A deposition recorded on video simply documents events on the day testimony was taken and recorded. A reenactment, on the other hand, allows both the attorney and the videographer more artistic license, although care must be taken to represent accurately the reenacted scene; otherwise, a court may not allow the video to be admitted into evidence at trial.[20]

Videos Are Powerful Tools for Impeachment

A prior inconsistent statement of a material fact captured on video at a deposition can be played back at trial to impeach a witness. Indeed, impeachment may be the most powerful use of video. Confronting a witness with contradictory testimony on a monitor inches from a witness's face can make even the most unflappable witness flinch.[21]

Video testimony can also prevent a witness from trying at trial to deny that an impeaching statement was made or trying at trial to "undo" the prior statement. A video prevents a witness from explaining away a prior inconsistent statement by disputing the accuracy of the written transcript or by blaming the examiner's pressure tactics for a prior inconsistent statement. In effect, the recorded video "puts the lie to the liar."

Video Excerpts Spice Up Opening and Closing Arguments

Consider the power of this opening statement:

> Ladies and gentlemen, you will see and hear the Defendant, John Jones, admit in his sworn testimony—recorded earlier in this case—that he was speeding at the time he injured the plaintiff.[22]

A short excerpt from the defendant's video deposition—with court approval—is then played for the jury.[23]

During closing arguments, video deposition testimony admitted into evidence can be replayed with the court's approval. Such use of a video recording is a powerful way to remind the jury of key evidence in the trial—and it does not ask them to rely on your recitation or their memories alone.[24]

Depositions Made Easy:
Noticing Requirements and Recording Logistics

Both federal and state courts have relaxed the rules governing video recording of depositions, and video has become more the norm than the exception.[25] In fact, the evolution of the Federal Rules of Civil Procedure (FRCP) regarding video recording illustrates how federal courts have shifted from suspicion of the medium to endorsement of it.

In 1970, the Federal Rules were amended to allow for the recording of testimony by "other than stenographic means." The changes were made to "facilitate less expensive procedures." [26] But the 1970 Advisory Committee noted that "[b]ecause these methods give rise to problems of accuracy and trustworthiness, the party taking the deposition is required to apply for a court order."[27]

Ten years later, the Federal Rules were again amended, this time to allow parties either to stipulate or to obtain a court order to record by other than stenographic means.[28] Still, electronic recording was not allowed "as a matter of course," because the 1980 Advisory Committee was "not satisfied that a case has been made for a reversal of present practice."[29]

With the 1993 amendments to the FRCP, electronic recording became a matter of right. Under amended FRCP 30, the noticing party may designate the method by which deposition testimony shall be recorded.[30] Unless the court orders otherwise, there are three methods: sound (audio), sound-and-visual (video), and stenographic.

The party taking the deposition bears the cost of the recording. Although a transcript need not be made at the time of the deposition, any party may arrange for a transcription to be made from a recording taken by nonstenographic means.[31]

But the power to choose the recording method is not the noticing party's alone. FRCP 30(b)(3)(B) provides that "[w]ith prior notice to the deponent and other parties, any party may designate another method for recording the testimony in addition to that specified

449

in the original notice."[32] Furthermore, under FRCP 26(c), any other party can object to the recording method and ask a court for a protective order.

The FRCP seem to envision that the decision to video a deposition must be made at the time of the notice.[33] But any party may have a second chance to designate the use of video. In one federal district court case, the judge allowed the noticing party to switch to video in the middle of a deposition and denied the deponent's motion for a protective order.[34]

Reasons to Have a Stenographic Record of a Video Deposition

Unless the parties agree otherwise, a video deposition, like any deposition, must be conducted before "an officer appointed or designated under Rule 28."[35] Although a contemporaneous stenographic record of a video deposition is not required, it is essential for several reasons. [36]

1. You will need a transcript if the video's sound track fails or is noisy, which could happen, for example, if papers were shuffled near a microphone.
2. A party may offer deposition testimony in stenographic or nonstenographic form in any court proceeding, but if a party offers deposition testimony in nonstenographic form, the party also must provide the court with a certified transcript of relevant portions, unless otherwise ordered.[37]
3. Under FRCP 26(a)(3)(A)(ii), a party expecting to use nonstenographic deposition testimony as substantive evidence at trial must provide other parties with a transcript before the trial. In addition, you will need a transcript to obtain rulings on admissibility before you assemble your final video presentation for trial.
4. As noted above, any party may request that deposition testimony offered for other than impeachment be presented in nonstenographic form, if available, unless the court orders otherwise.[38] Given the requirement that a transcript accompany the offer of nonstenographic testimony, your failure as taker to have a stenographic reporter present may send an undesired signal to the defender that you do not intend to use the deposition testimony at any stage in the proceeding.
5. When preparing for trial, it is easier first to review a written transcript and then designate the portions of the video

to be played.[39] As noted above, it is easier still to review a video synchronized to the transcript by transcript management software. Such software will allow you to search across multiple transcripts within a case, utilizing either key word searches or other search designations.[40]

6. If the witness is asked to review the deposition for errors, it is easier for the witness to do so with a transcript than with a video.[41]

Recording Requirements

The Federal Rules specify what must be said at the start and end of each deposition, unless the parties otherwise agree.[42] When a deposition is recorded on video, the rules also require that these items be repeated by the deposition officer at the beginning of each recording.[43] Rather then repeating the entire tedious statement before each segment, you may want to stipulate that a shorter version is used, such as "This is the beginning of recording number two in the deposition of Leslie Roberts. We are going back on the record at 2:30 PM." [44]

Although the rules specify what must be announced and who maintains custody of the recording, they provide little guidance on the actual recording. The rules state simply that "[t]he deponent's and attorney's appearance or demeanor must not be distorted through recording techniques."[45] Given the ease with which video can be manipulated to distort reality, pay careful attention both to recording mechanics and to examination and defense techniques.[46]

Recording Mechanics

It is best to reach agreement with opposing counsel on all aspects of the recording, including who records the testimony, the manner of recording, and the method of preserving the video.[47] Best practices include:

- The videographer should be a disinterested third party who is not an employee of anyone in attendance at the deposition;
- The equipment should be of professional standard quality and in good working condition;
- The camera should be mounted on a stable tripod or stand designed to hold a camera; and
- The camera should be directly across from the witness and level with—not above or below—the witness's eye level in

order to ensure that the camera angle will not distort the image or appearance of the witness.[48]

If you are defending a video deposition, remember that under the FRCP, you must raise any objection to the deposition officer or to the recording personnel (whether videographer or stenographic reporter). Object "before the deposition begins, or promptly after the basis for disqualification becomes known or, with reasonable diligence, could have been known." Otherwise, under the FRCP, the objection is waived.[49]

While it is the job of the videographer to record the image of the witness without distortion, it ultimately is the responsibility of the attorneys in attendance to ensure that the video fairly documents the witness and the deposition. Before the first question and answer, make sure everything is ready. Then, just as it is important in a "traditional" deposition to ensure that the stenographer is transcribing accurately, watch a portion of the video during a break to make certain the testimony is being accurately recorded.[50] Remember: FRCP 32(d)(3) provides that an objection to an error or irregularity at a deposition is waived if (1) "it is not timely made during the deposition" and (2) it relates to a matter that "might have been corrected at that time."[51] And FRCP 32(d)(4) provides that if a party detects "errors or irregularities" in the manner of transcription, a motion to suppress the deposition must be made with reasonable promptness; otherwise it will be waived.[52]

If you review a segment for any reason, make sure the videographer re-cues the video before you went off the record so that you do not record over testimony. Also remember that once an image is recorded, it will be impossible to re-create or adjust the angle of the camera.

Time-and-Date Information

Recording time-and-date information is a standard practice for video depositions. Originally, the time and date were recorded onscreen to prevent tampering with the recorded testimony. Today's cameras record this information into the data code (digital information imbedded into the recording), making an invisible, but absolute, record that is difficult to tamper with or destroy.[53]

Recording time-and-date information onscreen is thus an artifact of older technology and no longer necessary to ensure the integrity of the video record. In addition, it is no longer the most efficient way to find testimony. In fact, as camera technology further advances, the onscreen time-and-date function—considered by the camera industry to be a consumer function rather than a professional one—will cease to be available in high-end professional video cameras. Indeed, within the several next five years onscreen time-and-date information will no longer be available.[54]

Hiring the Videographer

Under the FRCP, you can use your own staff for the video recording. But you still need a deposition officer to administer the oath and make the mandatory announcements at both the start and end of the deposition.[55] And this officer cannot be your employee or have a financial interest in the suit.[56] Therefore, it may be easier to use an independent, professional videographer who is qualified to administer an oath, especially if there is no stenographic reporter who can serve as the required deposition officer. There are several professional legal video graphy training courses, and hiring a videographer with such certification[57] should ensure that you have a reliable, competent professional. In addition, an independent videographer will likely use a higher-quality camera for the recording.

Starting and Stopping the Recording

As discussed above, at the start of the deposition, the opening statement required by FRCP 30(b)(5) must be read into the record by the videographer. Whenever one attorney wants to go off the record, all participating attorneys must agree. If there is any disagreement, the videographer should not stop recording until an agreement is reached.

Understand that the video continues to record until the videographer physically stops the camera. Therefore, if you are not sure the recording has stopped, do not say anything you do not want to be part of the record. When going off the record, the videographer should state, "We are going off the record. The time is 3:30 PM." Then he should stop the recording and state, "Recording stopped," your cue that a recording no longer is being made. When going back on the record, the videographer should state, "Going back on the record; the time is 3:45 PM."

Streaming Video of the Deposition to Other Locations

As noted in the chapter on realtime transcription, technology such as LiveNote Video and Text Stream allow remote participants, including your trial team and your experts, to "attend" the depositions by viewing a live video feed.[58] If you attend a deposition where the video is being streamed to remote participants, remember that the audio and video may still be available to the remote participants—even when the deposition is off the record. Therefore, when the deposition is off the record, the videographer should turn down the audio feed so that no audio can be heard from the deposition room. If the videographer fails to do so, any conversation held in the room—from the mundane discussion of where to have lunch to important tactical information—may be heard by remote participants. In addition, the videographer should put the lens cap back on the camera and turn the iris down to black, or he should place a sign in front of the camera lens that simply states "deposition currently off the record" in order to prevent remote participants from viewing any "off the record" moments.

BlackBerrys and other devices that send information through radio frequencies interfere with the audio recording at depositions. This interference cannot be heard by participants at the deposition. But if the videographer and stenographic reporter use headphones, they may visibly jump when the interference occurs because it is very loud. More important, interference will plainly be heard when the recorded video is played back. In fact, it can be so loud that it drowns out all other audio, rendering it useless. The solution: Everyone at a deposition must turn off BlackBerrys and similar devices.[59]

Video Deposition Production Tips

Technology has advanced so that cameras can take good-quality pictures even under the most challenging conditions. Make sure, however, that the lighting and background do not make a friendly witness appear sinister.[60] Normal conference room lighting, such as overhead can lights or spotlights, can cast dark shadows on a witness's face, and overhead fluorescent lights may cause the skin tone of a light-skinned person to appear slightly greenish. The videographer should strive to make the lighting even, with as few shadows as possible. Throughout the deposition, continually monitor the lighting, noise, and other conditions to ensure the quality of the recording.[61] And, as suggested above, periodically check the videographer's playback monitor to make sure what is being recorded is a true representation of the deposition.

Instruct the videographer to turn off the camera's auto functions because functions such as "auto iris" can be very distracting. You will know when the video is being recorded with the auto iris function because the video image will brighten each time a white exhibit (most documents are on white paper) is passed to the witness. The brightening of the image will cause the face of the witness to darken as the camera automatically tries to compensate for the introduction of a bright white image.[62] Therefore, instead of using auto functions, the videographer should continually monitor the image.

The videographer should also "white balance" the image at the beginning of the deposition, at the lunch break, and at all other breaks during the day. (White balancing tells the camera what the color white should look like; the camera then can compensate for difficult lighting conditions, such as fluorescent lights.[63]) If white balancing is not performed, you will notice the witness progressively turning a different color (blue, most of the time) as sunlight shifts throughout the day.

In addition, make sure the videographer uses a neutral backdrop for each deposition. (The backdrop should be a mottled gray or blue with an indistinct background). Using the same backdrop throughout a deposition communicates continuity. Depositions taken in multiple locations on different days will then look the same—and the backdrop will create little to no distraction from the testimony. Furthermore, a neutral backdrop will improve the quality of the video encoding process; with less information to process, more bits can be spent on the important qualities of a video deposition, such as facial movements, and fewer bits need be spent on "set dressing," such as law books or law firm conference room wall art.[64]

When the setting of the deposition relates to the case, the setting will have an impact that goes beyond the purely visual. In one case, depositions were recorded on video in the Taiwanese defendants' expensive and sophisticated law offices. In exit interviews, jurors said that seeing the offices on video helped convince them that the law firm could not, as it claimed, have misplaced and lost numerous records.[65]

Expectations for the Videographer

Expect the videographer to arrive at least one hour before the deposition's scheduled start time. A true professional will want access to the conference room so that he can set up his equipment and perform test recordings to ensure that all components are working properly. By the time you arrive, the video equipment should be set up and lavaliere microphones should be available to all speaking parties.[66]

The videographer should record a master recording as well as a safety backup that can be used if the master malfunctions. The backup should be recorded in a different format than the master recording as an added protection.

Expect the videographer to interrupt the deposition to notify attendees of any technical problem. Should such a problem occur, go off the record immediately so that the videographer can resolve the problem without interrupting the testimony—or worse, potentially losing it. Once the issue has been resolved, if you are concerned that questions or testimony may have been lost or otherwise affected by the technical problem, ask to review the recording so you can determine whether that has happened. If this has happened, questions and testimony can be re-asked or read back into the record by the reporter.

The videographer should give his undivided attention to recording the deposition. You do not want a horror story caused by the videographer's unprofessional behavior. Therefore, the videographer should never:

- Read anything while recording the deposition, including books, newspapers, or text messages;
- Be otherwise occupied by any other technology, such as a laptop, BlackBerry, or Nintendo;
- Eat or chew gum;
- Talk on the phone; or
- Listen to anything other than the audio from the deposition recording.

Consider the Number of Cameras, Microphones, and the Use of Document Cameras[67]

The standard framing convention is called a "talking head," also known as a "head-and- shoulders" shot. With a "talking head" shot, the full frame of the video will consist almost entirely of a head-and-shoulders image, with little else in the frame. (See Figure 3.)

Some lawyers prefer to begin the recording with an "establishing" shot of all the participants. This wide-angle shot will set the context for the video and help the jury understand who was present and available to question.[68]

The typical video deposition shot is much different from the image seen in an edited television or film production. When watching an edited television or film production, the audience rarely

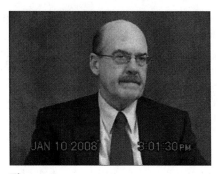

Figure 3
"Talking Head" Shot

sees a "talking head" shot for more than fifteen seconds—even in a news program. In a deposition, the camera does not move to a different shot; instead, the shot is static, providing the viewer with one angle of one image—the deponent. Depending on how you intend to use the video at trial, you may want to use multiple cameras, projectors, or document cameras during the deposition. When considering whether to use additional equipment, remember that current multimedia technology can do a great deal with a video image after it has been acquired (recorded) at the deposition site. Therefore, at a deposition, focus on recording the best image possible and wait until later to add special effects such as transitions, picture-in-picture, or side-by-side presentation of conflicting statements. If you think that at trial you may want to use split-screen images that include the examiner as well as the deponent and defender, consider using more than one camera. But remember that a split screen reduces the size of the witness's image.

A document camera—Elmo is the most popular brand—will record a video image of any exhibits or documents placed on its base. Document cameras can be connected to a recording deck or to a projector. When a document camera is connected to a recording deck, the images placed upon the base of the document camera will be recorded and can be edited into the deposition video later. Or the image can be used during the deposition with a split screen. In addition, using a document camera and a projector lets you project a large image of a document onto a screen in the deposition room, thereby allowing the witness to interact with the document in a way that will be visible to the jury during courtroom playback.

Of course, whatever you decision you reach about using a split screen must be discussed with opposing counsel. Tactically, the decision to use a split screen at a deposition depends on (1) whether you are the defender or the examiner, (2) the anticipated impact of the witness's testimony, and (3) the demeanor of the participants during the recording. Should you decide to use a split-screen recording during the deposition, make sure that the videographer is creating several recordings, including an independent master recording of only the deponent (again, a "talking head" shot is preferable), a recording of the split-screen image, and an independent recording of the secondary image. This three-master system will allow for maximum versatility in the postproduction process. And if the picture-in-picture image is not exactly what you want, you will have an opportunity to edit the video for settlement or trial playback purposes.

If you are defending an effective witness with a good camera presence, opt for a single camera so the jury can focus on the witness, not you. Conversely, if the witness may give damaging testimony or has an "image" problem, a split screen can diffuse any negative impact.[69] (With such a witness, a taker may want to object to use of a split screen.) In any event, trial presentation software gives you the ability to use both video image and documents, or scrolling text, to lighten the delivery of hurtful testimony by an image of only the witness.

Because video scenes can be manipulated, whether taker or defender, you should object if the videographer does anything without your agreement other than focus a single camera on the witness. If opposing counsel will not agree to a single camera and a fixed shot, you may need to seek a court order.

A word about microphones: Most home cameras with an internal microphone are sufficient to record loved ones, but they may not record the kind of high-end audio needed when the audio is to be played to a jury. A lavaliere microphone should be used for the witness and each of the speaking parties. A table microphone may be used when there are more parties in attendance than standard deposition equipment will serve, but it should be used only for secondary participants, not the main speaking parties. In any event, the camera's microphone should not be used for recording audio during a deposition. When using a table microphone, be careful not to tap the table or shuffle papers; otherwise, the audio portion of the recording may sound like a percussionist is being deposed. For this reason alone, lavaliere mics are preferable. Finally, the microphones should feed into a mixer, which will allow the videographer to adjust the recording levels of all attendees so that the recording accurately represents the audio levels of the speaking parties at the deposition.

Arrange for Custody of the Video Recording

Before the deposition, decide how you want custody of the recording to be handled. Deposition recordings are treated like stenographic transcripts, unless otherwise ordered by the court.[70] Absent a court order, the deposition recording, along with the officer's certificate, must "promptly" be sent "to the attorney who arranged for the transcript or recording." Under FRCP 5(d), federal courts no longer accept a deposition for filing unless first ordered by the court or used in the proceeding.[71]

The Federal Rules require the custodian to store the recording under conditions that protect it against "loss, destruction, tampering, or deterioration."[72] Upon payment of a reasonable fee, the recording also must be made available to any party or the deponent.[73] It is standard practice for the reporting firm or video company to maintain the master recording and provide copies from that master. If the master recording has been held by a disinterested third party, questioning the integrity of the recording will be difficult. Additionally, a video graphy firm will be more knowledgeable about proper archiving techniques.

Surprise! You're on Candid Camera: Video Depositions Can Demand Different Techniques by Both the Examiner and the Defender

In federal court, the deposition of any person may be used at trial if the deponent resides more than one hundred miles from the place of trial or is otherwise unavailable.[74] With video depositions, this provision presents a surprising opportunity for converting some depositions into trial testimony.

Therefore, if the deponent lives more than one hundred miles from the place of trial, be prepared to take a full video "trial deposition," which means asking the kind of questions you would ask the witness at trial on cross-examination. Why? Because you may not have the chance to question the witness at trial if she is beyond the court's subpoena power and unwilling to appear. Even if the witness lives close enough to be subject to that subpoena power, the witness's death, illness, or excused absence during trial may convert deposition testimony into trial testimony.[75]

Imagine this scenario: Your opponent notices the deposition of your expert, who resides more than one hundred miles from the place of trial.[76] At the deposition, your opponent conducts a typical discovery deposition of your expert, replete with open-ended questions. After your opponent finishes, you ask the witness a complete set of "trial-like" cross-examination questions. If your expert has performed well during the deposition, you have no obligation to tender the expert live at trial. Indeed, you can use the video deposition—which may have little or no cross-examination by opposing counsel. If, on the other hand, your expert "bombs" during the deposition, you can forgo calling him at trial. If you nevertheless decide to have your expert testify at trial, your opponent will have seen the expert's "dress rehearsal" at the deposition and will have ammunition for cross-examination. But at least you will be forewarned and can try to defuse the danger before "opening night."

Video thus changes the way in which depositions are taken—whether or not the witness is expected to be available for trial.[77] When a deposition is being recorded on video, the taker may not want to wait until trial to ask "hard" questions. Instead, the taker may want to confront the witness with trial-like cross-examination. If successful, the taker will have a record of evasion—or better yet dishonesty—as part of the available deposition record that can be played back for the jury.

But the decision is not an easy one because by asking trial-like cross-examination questions at a deposition you may tip off the witness to the hard questions normally reserved for trial and lose the element of surprise. On the other hand, if you do not confront a witness and the witness is unavailable for trial, the witness—who has not been asked the "hard" questions at her deposition—may seem more credible to a jury on video than she would in a courtroom.

Whether you are the taker or the defender, remember that once-minor issues take on new importance when a deposition is recorded on video.[78] Chewing gum, laughing at the wrong time, being sarcastic—all show badly on video. A good rule of thumb: always behave at a deposition as if you are being viewed by a jury on a large screen. (And this rule of thumb also applies to witnesses.)

At a video deposition, good examination techniques—important in every deposition—become more so. Even when a deposition is lengthy, the jury may see only short excerpts. Therefore, you must be sure that every deposition excerpt can stand alone in order to be effective at trial. As taker, avoid long questions and complex hypotheticals that are difficult for a jury to follow when shown as independent segments. If you sense that a particular segment of a deposition may be important at trial, be careful to ask self-contained questions to put the testimony in context, without reference to other portions of the testimony. Let the jury know, for example, that you are asking about "the contract of November 10, one year ago" or "the day after the head-on collision."

As a taker at a video deposition, you may need to clarify a witness's answer. For example, during a deposition, a witness often will refer to earlier testimony. If you ask a witness whether she has any document to support her testimony, she may reply, "None, other than those I referred to this morning." Although this answer may make sense to those attending the deposition, it might be incomprehensible when presented on video in a courtroom. So follow up this type of answer with something like, "Please remind me of the documents you referred to earlier in your deposition."[79]

As a taker, consider treating a deposition as having multiple parts.[80] Initially, conduct discovery, exploring areas where you do not know the answer. Then generate possible impeachment material.[81] Be sure to take notes or take advantage of the "rough" transcript made available through realtime transcription in order to help you to frame your follow-up questions. Later, start over, beginning with the witness's background just as you might at trial. Give clear sign-posts when the subject matter changes.[82] And confront the witness with impeachment material, as you would in court.

Be sure all references to exhibits are clear and unambiguous.[83] Identify all documents shown to the witness with a descriptive title that will be understood by the jury. Be specific about the parts of a document that are referenced, as a verbal picture will assist the jury. And, as suggested above, consider editing the video to include a full-screen image of the document or its relevant section with an inset picture of the witness testifying about it.[84]

Whether you are a taker or a defender, be careful about your own deposition behavior. As a defender, conferences with a witness—even for a legitimate reason such as determining privilege—can look sinister. In addition, nonverbal signals of any kind—even the most benign—look conspiratorial. Remember that whispered conferences with a witness may end up being recorded because the microphones used at deposition are extremely sensitive and even covering them will not completely keep them from capturing the audio. Make sure that you do not end up in the camera frame as a partial image. Conference-room chairs often swing and rock back; by sitting back in your chair, you could unintentionally insert yourself into the camera frame.

As a taker, if you anticipate an aggressive, disruptive defender, then video record the deposition—not so much to capture the witness, but to "cool off" the defender, who will be less likely to hinder a deposition with interruptions, comments, and lengthy objections that can be viewed on video by the judge and jury.[85] Similarly, as a defender, you can use the presence of the camera to control an overly aggressive examiner.[86] You may also need to revisit the usual defense strategy of not examining your own witness at the end of the deposition.[87] With a video deposition available to be played to the judge and jury, you may want the witness to clarify her answers rather than wait for trial.

The Use of Video Depositions at Trial

Setting the Stage

Two generations of Americans have been raised on television,[88] so the average juror is fairly sophisticated when it comes to video presentations. Take this into account when considering how to effectively present video at trial.

Properly planned, the presentation can be simple and relatively inexpensive. But it can also be complicated and costly, depending on the number of depositions, the number and complexity of exhibits, the use of graphics, the number and size of the monitors in the courtroom, and so on. If you hire an outside service to record a deposition and prepare it for use in the courtroom, agree with the service on a budget, but be flexible and expect changes.

The starting point for a good presentation is high-quality video.[89] Today's jury will not pay attention to a recording with poor video or audio quality. Moreover, your opponent may object to a poor-quality video. And that objection may be sustained by a trial judge who decides under Federal Rule of Evidence (FRE) 403 that the video 's prejudicial effect outweighs its probative value.[90] Again, using a professional videographer almost always eliminates this problem.

For a twelve-person jury, expect that two jurors can share one flat-screen monitor between them. In addition, provide the judge, witness, opposing counsel, and cross-examiner with their own flat-panel monitors. In larger courts, a large flat panel or projection device may be far more effective than a smaller screen.[91] Always make sure that all the equipment, particularly the wiring, fits easily into the courtroom.[92] In a smaller courtroom, you may want to use a projection television, with one large (forty-inch to seventy-two-inch diagonal) screen shared by the judge, jury, and all the participants.[93] Ultimately, your choice of monitors may have more to do with what you want to convey than with the size of the jury or the courtroom. For example, if you want to show a document on screen during the testimony or use graphics, a large screen may be essential.

Viewers are likely to be more forgiving of poor video quality than poor audio quality. The internal sound units in many television monitors will not sufficiently play audio in a courtroom. So make sure that you have access to the master control of the audio in the courtroom and that your presentation provider feeds the playback audio through the court's sound system. If the court does not have a sound system or if you do not have access to the court's sound system, place good-quality speakers throughout the courtroom; that way, everyone will be able to hear the audio. One set of speakers placed near the jury box should be sufficient for the jury, judge, and counsel. But if it is important for courtroom spectators to hear clearly, add a second set of speakers in front of the spectators' seating area.

Editing Video Depositions for Use at Trial

Now the real work begins—creating a video presentation for effective use at trial.[94] When the video testimony to be shown is continuous, there is no need for editing—except perhaps to omit testimony that the judge has ruled inadmissible. More typically, though, video segments are not continuous; instead, those of interest are out of order and contain objections that must be ruled upon before the video can be played. In addition, a video can have "quality" problems, with certain segments being hard to see or hear, or both.

In a world where media-wise juries are accustomed to high production values, you cannot afford "bad ratings" when you hit the play button. The video segments you wish to play must be easy for you to locate and easy for the jury to watch and understand. This is accomplished by editing, which requires the participation of opposing counsel and the approval of the court.

As a practical matter, establish procedures for regulating the editing process. If the court does not have a standard procedure, seek an order establishing one. These procedures should clarify how each side can offer evidence by video and provide a fair opportunity for objections. The procedures need to be adopted early enough so that each side has sufficient time to create its video presentation in a way that conforms to the rules of evidence and the parties' agreements, yet tells that story each side wants to tell.

In federal court, counsel must designate proposed testimony before trial, and all objections to the testimony must be made and ruled upon by the court in advance.[95] If you want to make a video presentation, press the court for a timely ruling on objections so that you have enough time to edit out segments ruled inadmissible.[96] Most trial judges allow video to present no more than could be presented if deposition transcripts were read.[97] When reading depositions at trial, most lawyers skip over objections and colloquy of counsel that would be inadmissible unless the court orders otherwise. Courts are likely to take the same approach for video. Therefore, edit out this extraneous material; otherwise, disruptions will occur at trial when you fast-forward through the inadmissible segments.[98]

In state court, where pretrial orders often are not required, you can use a pretrial motion in limine for this purpose. Regardless of your jurisdiction, have a strategy for dealing with last-minute court rulings that affect the video evidence you plan to offer.

But if a deposition is littered with sham objections and unfair commentary, consider coming to court with two versions of the video—one edited and one unedited. Then ask the judge to let the jury see how improper defense tactics hurt your examination.[99] When making this request, you might want to argue that such a sanction is far less severe than the one granted in *Kelly v. GafCorp*.[100] In that case, objections made at a crucial deposition by the prevailing party's lawyer were so numerous that the editing required to remove them destroyed the testimony's value.[101] Finding the edited video deposition a "hodgepodge, completely lacking in direction and continuity," the court sanctioned the prevailing party by granting the losing party's motion for a new trial.[102]

In addition to procedural issues, the trial preparation process raises issues of style. When preparing designations of deposition testimony, think of yourself as a movie director who wants the audience—the jury—to see a certain reality. You also want the jury to listen carefully. If the jury does not listen or cannot follow the presentation, showing the video is worse than not showing it at all.

Advances in transcript-management software and its capacity to play back the video synchronized to the transcript allow attorneys to create complete multimedia presentation packages without hiring expensive trial presentation technicians. Nevertheless, hiring a trial presentation company to prepare and present your multimedia at trial may be the most prudent course. Running trial presentation software requires some technical skill and can be stressful. And turning over the job to a professionally trained trial technician allows you to focus on the content of your case, not the playback.[103]

When it is time to play the deposition to the jury, be sure that all relevant testimony is easily accessible and ready for playback. Your playback files should have a naming convention that identifies the files and when they are to be used in the presentation. If you cannot easily and quickly locate testimony, you will lose your audience. (Recall the reaction you received the last time you asked even close family members to wait in a darkened room while you searched a video for that special scene from your child's first birthday party or your dream vacation.)

If you will be presenting edited video rather than synchronized video, consider creating your own DVD in order to present the video.[104] Using a video cassette recorder (VCR) to play back your presentation should be the last choice because an index of questions and answers based on the VCR's digital counter can be cumbersome. For one thing, a VCR's numeric counter is unique to that particular VCR model, and the index will not be compatible with another VCR.

When editing, remember that a video deposition consists mostly of static shots of the head and shoulders of a witness testifying while sitting at a table. In addition, a deposition will often include testimony about many documents. Therefore try to create more interest by inserting into the picture the part of the document about which the witness is testifying.[105] Another way to create interest is with animations and graphics, such as an accident reconstruction or a pie chart.[106] But remember: for such enhancements, you need the agreement of opposing counsel and the court's approval.

Jumping around to different segments of a witness's video testimony can confuse a jury, especially if you skip to different days of testimony. Therefore, to minimize confusion, consider using a gradual transition with a fade out to black and fade up from black between each segment. In addition, use titles—again, if permitted by the court—to help unify the flow. And before showing the video, be sure that all technical difficulties, both audio and video, were removed from the recording during the initial production process. (Techniques such as "audio sweetening" can be helpful in removing any annoying hums from the audio track—although again you may need court approval to use it.[107])

After editing, make a log of the segments that both you and your opponent have designated to be offered in evidence. During trial, carefully compare what is offered with what has been designated in advance. Careful scrutiny is required because errors can occur in the editing process after the court has ruled. Note those segments that are played and accepted into evidence so that during your closing argument you can establish a foundation for using those segments during your closing argument. Likewise, the absence of an entry on your log will help you demonstrate that segments you proffer for rebuttal have not already been shown to the jury. Finally, the log can be used to verify whether your opponent is playing the correct designations.

A final reminder about video depositions: Although video has been used in the courtroom for the last forty years, significant questions remain as to how much latitude a judge will permit in its presentation. For instance, courts disagree about whether and to what extent a party may reorder or integrate portions of video taken at a deposition to make the presentation match the chronology of events.[108] Some trial judges limit the use of integrated or "composite" Videos solely to the argument phase of a trial.[109] But when a particular use of video promotes clarity and efficiency, a trial judge will be more likely to permit it.[110]

Conclusion

Video technology adds a new dimension to trials. Used intelligently, this technology can make a tremendous impression on a judge and jury. But always remember Murphy's Law: If something can go wrong, it will. So be prudent. Regardless of how much confidence you have in technology, always have marked, back-up deposition transcripts ready to go.

Notes

*The author gratefully acknowledges William A. Brockett, who before his untimely death in 1996 first suggested, and then counseled me in, writing this chapter on the then-videotape "revolution" for the first edition of this book. The author also acknowledges Kathryn Filley Brown, whose technical expertise brought the chapter into the twenty-first century.

1.   In 1970, the Federal Rules of Civil Procedure were first amended to allow for recording testimony by nonstenographic means. *See infra* note 26 and accompanying text.

2.   Ken Auletta, World War 3.0: Microsoft vs. the U.S. Government, and the Battle to Rule the Digital Age 97 (2001).

3. *Id.* at 136. For a compilation of video excerpts of Bill Gates's deposition in *United States v. Microsoft Corp.*, see Gates Deposition Greatest Hits, http://www.youtube.com/watch?v=eKcPx2jD5to (last visited Feb. 8, 2009).

4. AULETTA, *supra* note 2, at 219.

5. This chapter focuses on the use of video depositions. FRCP 30(b)(4) provides that parties may stipulate or the court may, upon motion, order that a deposition be taken by telephone or other remote electronic means. For a discussion of telephone depositions, see Alexander R. Sussman & Edna R. Sussman, *Electronic Depositions*, LITIGATION, Summer 1989, at 26. For a discussion of audiotaping, see David M. Balabanian, *Medium v. Tedium: Video Depositions Come of Age, reprinted in* PRISCILLA A. SCHWAB & LAWRENCE J. VILARDO, THE LITIGATION MANUAL: DEPOSITIONS 96–97 (2006).

6. *See* Milwaukee Concrete Studios, Ltd. v. Greeley Ornamental Concrete Prods., Inc., 140 F.R.D. 373, 379–80 (E.D. Wis. 1991) (accepting argument that lawyers might avoid "long colloquys," "continuous interruptions," and "heated argumentation" if remaining depositions were recorded on video); Alexander v. F.B.I., 186 F.R.D. 123, 127 (D. D.C. 1998) ("video taping of depositions . . . allows the Court to observe how the attorneys conduct themselves in the depositions; which often becomes relevant on the issue of sanctions."). See also Chapter 15.

7. *See* Riley v. Murdock, 156 F.R.D. 130, 131 (E.D.N.C. 1994) (describing video recording as a "superior method" of conveying to fact finder the "full message" of witness's testimony). See also Chapter 11, note 91 and accompanying text, discussing the importance of nonverbal communication in conveying meaning.

8. FED. R. CIV. P. 32(a)(4). See also Chapter 25.

9. *See, e.g., In re* "Agent Orange" Prod. Liab. Litig., 28 Fed. R. Serv. 2d (Callaghan) 993 (E.D.N.Y. 1980) (allowing video taped deposition of plaintiff who claimed that Agent Orange caused him to develop a progressive brain tumor, which might leave him too ill to testify or dead by time of trial).

10. A party offering deposition testimony may offer it in stenographic or in nonstenographic form, unless otherwise ordered by court. However, on request of any party in a jury trial, deposition testimony offered for any purpose other than impeachment must be presented in nonstenographic form, if available, unless the court for good cause orders otherwise. FED. R. CIV. P. 32(c).

11. This dry recitation can become even more mind-numbing for a jury if the court permits only its own personnel to read the answers. See also *supra* note 10 and accompanying text.

12. The photographs pictured are adapted from advertisements copyrighted 1991 by Tearney & Tearney, Los Angeles, and created by Patti Cuthill and Associates. See also "Nonverbal Communication" in Chapter 11.

13. See *infra* note 89 and accompanying text, discussing the format in which video recordings are delivered.

14. LiveNote allows for export to PowerPoint as well as transfer to Sanction and Trial Director.

15. See *infra* note 89 and accompanying text, discussing presenting a video deposition at trial.

16. See *infra* notes 74 and 75 and accompanying text.

17. *See* Roberts v. Homelite Div. of Textron, Inc., 109 F.R.D. 664, 667 (N.D. Ind. 1986) (allowing defendant to reenact, during video taped deposition, lawn mower accident that caused plaintiff's injury); Emerson Elec. Co. v. Superior Ct., 946 P.2d 841, 845 (Cal. 1997) ("a demonstration or reenactment of an incident may well provide a more direct and accurate description than a verbal description of the same event").

18. Carson v. Burlington N., Inc., 52 F.R.D. 492 (D. Neb. 1971) (allowing video taped reenactment during video taped deposition of machine accident in blacksmith shop where injury occurred); Spraglin v. MHK Assocs., No. 877 Civil 1992, 1993 WL 83462, at *4 (Pa. Com. Pl. Oct. 19, 1993) (rejecting video reenactment because court found that accurately depicting automated cart striking plaintiff was too difficult and court was unwilling to rely on the "thespian talents of the plaintiff").

19. Does any lawyer need a greater reminder of the value of a trial run than the "glove experiment" in the O.J. Simpson murder trial? People v. Simpson, BA097211 (Cal. Super. Ct. L.A. Co. 1994).

20. When recording a reenactment, you can use available technology to produce a video with higher production value than required when recording a deposition.

21. Fanelli v. Centenary Coll., 211 F.R.D. 268, 270 (D.N.J. 2002) ("the use of video tape for impeachment purposes would give the fact finder the benefit of the witness's 'body language' in testifying at a deposition as compared to the 'body language' of the witness testifying in court"); Citizens for Responsibility & Ethics in Wash. v. Cheney, 580 F. Supp. 2d 168, (D. D.C. 2008) (noting that presentation of video deposition is typically helpful to weigh credibility of a witness). Impeachment with a video excerpt will be most effective if the segment is "cued up and ready to roll" and objections to the proffered portions have been resolved in advance. See *infra* text accompanying notes 95–102.

22. *See* Mark A. Neubauer, *Video taping Depositions*, LITIGATION, Summer 1993, at 60, 62 (suggesting this type of opening). Neubauer wisely cautions that because the segments of the deposition that are shown to the jury must be admissible, the desired sections should be "precleared" by the judge before trial. Indeed, most judges control the use during opening statement of any documents or deposition excerpts that are not admissible by stipulation.

23. Unless only a short "sound bite" is played during an opening statement, the impact of the video testimony may be lost when played

the second time during the trial. If an appropriate and brief section cannot be located, it may be wiser merely to refer to the testimony.

24.   Two authors suggest combining all or parts of various video depositions into one video in order to organize and highlight the testimony for the fact finder. Of course, the court's permission for such editing will be required. Sussman & Sussman, *supra* note 5, at 26, 27. See also *infra* text accompanying notes 108–10.

25.   This chapter focuses on the requirements of the Federal Rules. For a survey of state requirements governing video depositions, see GREGORY P. JOSEPH, MODERN VISUAL EVIDENCE (2004) (Appendix B, Summary Analysis of State Rules and Statutes Governing Video taped Depositions, and Appendix D, State Rules and Statutes Governing Video taped Depositions); Michael J. Henke & Craig D. Margolis, *The Taking and Use of Video taped Depositions: An Update*, 17 REV. LITIG. 1, 22–23 (1998).

26.   Indeed, history suggests that the experiment has been successful and the costs manageable. Recording a deposition on video is, however, not inexpensive. Currently, the cost of a videographer is about $1,300 per day. The cost should include the delivery of a digitized video, synchronized to the transcript with exhibits hyperlinked. Exhibit hyperlinking is an option available in transcript management software that allows for any reference to a particular exhibit in a transcript to be linked with the digital image (pdf or tiff file), so that when the hyperlinking is selected (by clicking the mouse on the differently colored area of text of the transcript), image viewer software will automatically open the referenced exhibit in the window.

27.   *See* FED. R. CIV. P. 30(b)(4) advisory committee's note (1970) (also noting court order is "to specify how the testimony is to be recorded, preserved, and filed, and it may contain whatever additional safeguards the court deems necessary").

28.   FED. R. CIV. P. 30(b)(4). The advisory committee noted that the 1980 amendments made explicit what may have been implicit in FRCP 29 regarding stipulations.

29.   The amendment allowing the parties to stipulate was made "so that conflicting claims with respect to the potential of electronic recording for reducing costs can be appraised in the light of greater experience." FED. R. CIV. P. 30(b)(4) advisory committee's note (1980).

30.   FED. R. CIV. P. 30(b)(3). For a discussion of the reasons for also making a contemporaneous stenographic record, see *infra* notes 36–41 and accompanying text.

31.   FED. R. CIV. P. 30(b)(3)(A).

32.   FED. R. CIV. P. 30(b)(3)(B). But note that the additional record or transcript shall be made at the designating party's expense, unless the court orders otherwise. *Id.*

33.   The federal rule does not specify the number of days of notice required if a party, other than the noticing party, desires to video the

deposition. *Compare* CAL. CIV. PROC. CODE § 2025.330(c) (West 2006) (requiring no less than three calendar days' written notice of intention to record by other than stenographic means).

34. *See* Riley v. Murdock, 156 F.R.D. 130, 131 (E.D.N.C. 1994).

35. FED. R. CIV. P. 30(b)(5)(A). See "Task 14: Arrange for a Deposition Officer, Court Reporter, Videographer (If Needed), and Room" in Chapter 4.

36. The rules provide that any party may arrange for the transcription from the recording. FED. R. CIV. P. 30(b)(3)(A).

37. FED. R. CIV. P. 32(c). To ensure an accurate record of the content of video played at trial, the court reporter, if not the judge, will insist on receiving transcripts of the video.

38. *Id.*

39. As discussed in "Using Litigation Support and Transcript Management Software to Manage Deposition Transcripts" in Chapter 24, transcripts are often made available in both "hard copy" and as an electronic file, allowing for easier computer searches. For purposes of a lawyer's review, the transcript need not be certified, and thus could be prepared in the lawyer's office.

40. As noted in the text, the ability to create multiple annotations containing transcript and video that can be played in a PowerPoint presentation is a powerful tool in preparing for trial.

41. See also "Reviewing and Correcting the Transcript" in Chapter 23.

42. FED. R. CIV. P. 30(b)(5). Among the requirements is a statement by the deposition officer, appointed under FRCP 28, that includes "(i) the officer's name and business address; (ii) the date, time and place of the deposition; (iii) the deponent's name; (iv) the officer's administration of the oath or affirmation to the deponent; and (v) the identity of all persons present." FRCP 28 further specifies that "[a]t the end of a deposition, the officer must state on the record that the deposition is complete and must set out any stipulations." See also "Opening Statement by the Deposition Officer" in Chapter 11, discussing the start of the deposition, and "Final Matters" in Chapter 23.

43. If practicing in a state that has not spelled out video recording requirements with similar specificity, a lawyer should consider using the FRCP as a starting place. See also *infra* note 47 and accompanying text.

44. See *infra* note 47 and accompanying text, discussing stipulations on recording a deposition.

45. FED. R. CIV. P. 30(b)(5)(B). *See* Henke & Margolis, *supra* note 25, at 22–23 (compiling state rules and court orders on motions under former FRCP 30(b)(4) concerning conditions for video recording).

46. In 1994, for example, more than thirty years after President John F. Kennedy's death, a movie was made in which the character Forrest Gump appears to speak with Kennedy. FORREST GUMP (Paramount Pictures 1994) (winner of six Academy Awards, including "Best Picture").

Similarly, anyone familiar with photo-editing software, such as Photoshop, knows how easy it is to edit a digital image. In *Campoamor v. Brandon Pest Control*, a Florida appellate court determined that Defendant's video tape, which showed his employee explaining the termination process along with a computer animation depicting it properly performed, was patently deceptive and should not have been admitted. 721 So. 2d 333 (Fla. App. 2 Dist. 1998).

47.　For useful areas to consider for stipulation, see the Uniform Audio-Visual Deposition Act, 12 U.L.A. 10 (1978) (approved by the National Conference of Commissioners on Uniform State Laws in 1978 and the American Bar Association at its midyear meeting in February 1979). *See also* JOSEPH, *supra* note 25, at App. A (Forms of Stipulation or Order Pursuant to Federal Rule of Civil Procedure 30(b)(4) and Cognate State Rules and Statutes).

48.　The technique of having the camera placed above or below eye level is often used in television documentary-type interviews. When the camera "eyeline" is below the "eyeline" of the interviewee, the illusion created is that the viewer is looking up to the person on camera, who is perceived as more important. When the camera is above the interviewee, the illusion is that the interviewee is below and therefore less important than the audience or the interviewer. As noted, both of these techniques should be avoided in deposition situations.

49.　FED. R. CIV. P. 32(d)(2).

50.　See "Opening Remarks and Stipulations" in Chapter 11, discussing a similar suggestion to have the stenographic reporter read back testimony early in the deposition to ensure its accuracy.

51.　FED. R. CIV. P. 32(d)(3)(B).

52.　The motion must be made "promptly after the error or irregularity becomes known or, with reasonable diligence, could have been known." FED. R. CIV. P. 32(d)(4).

53.　These data codes capture the camera and recording information, including date and time of the recording and camera settings, such as the F-stop (exposure rating), focal length, and timecode. Timecodes are the equivalent of digital frame numbering for video files and ensure that the images are in fact played one after the other in the same order they were created.

54.　In earlier years, when an onscreen time-and-date stamp was the norm, gaps in the time stamp sometimes left the fact finder wondering if something was missing. If you are using this technology and suspect that this problem may arise, ask the court to provide a single instruction to the jury about the editing process. To avoid the risk of the fact finder becoming skeptical, use technology that does not include onscreen time-and-date stamping.

55.　*See supra* note 42 and accompanying text.

56.　FED. R. CIV. P. 28(c).

471

57. Certifications for videographers include Certified Multimedia Expert (CME), Certified Legal Video Specialist (CLVS), and American Guild of Court videographers (AGCV).

58. For an overview of the evolving use of video streaming and real-time over the Internet, *see generally* Lisa DiMonte, *Electronic Depositions*, *in* MANAGING COMPLEX LITIGATION 2007: LEGAL STRATEGIES AND BEST PRACTICES IN "HIGH-STAKES" CASES (2007). See also "Realtime Video over the Internet" in Chapter 18, discussing video streaming.

59. Even placing such devices on the other side of the room, away from the video equipment, may not remedy the problem.

60. For example, check the background to see whether it is darker than the image of the witness; a window or a white wall can "wash out" the image or make the witness look sinister. Most cameras can be adjusted to become more light sensitive if the room is very dark or the lighting is poor. Extra lighting can always be used if necessary and, as an added bonus, extra lighting can be brought in to intimidate a witness and make them sweat (lights are hot and will raise the temperature in the room). Look for pictures displayed behind the witness's head; some would say that having a picture of former President Nixon as the backdrop could have made even Mother Teresa look bad.

61. Some statutes attempt to describe the nature of the site. *See, e.g.,* CAL. CIV. PROC. CODE § 2025.340(a) (West 2005) (area "shall be suitably large, adequately lighted, and reasonably quiet").

62. With the auto iris function off, the videographer will need to make sure the correct exposure is set.

63. This process is relatively quick and requires that the videographer place something white (usually paper) in front of the camera and set the camera to see that as white.

64. For the video to be synchronized to the transcript, it must first be converted to an electronic file. There are various file formats for video; however, only a few of these files will work with litigation software. The most useful file format is mpeg1. Mpeg1 files are computer files that permit viewing video with software such as Windows Media Player or most other litigation software such as LiveNote or Trial Director.

65. Wang v. Hsu, No. C-87-2981-THE (JSB), 1991 U.S. Dist. LEXIS 4398 (N.D. Cal. Mar. 1, 1991) (discussed in William A. Brockett, *Trial Run—The Video tape Revolution (Pretrial and Trial)*, 12 CEB CIV. LITIG. REP., Aug. 1990, at 190, and Nov. 1990, at 288.)

66. The audio cables should be taped to the underside of the deposition table and not placed across the table where they will be in your way.

67. *See* FED. JUDICIAL CTR., GUIDELINES FOR PRE-RECORDING TESTIMONY ON VIDEO TAPE PRIOR TO TRIAL, Pub. No. 76-3 (2d ed. 1976) (discussing camera operation and picture composition).

68. *See* Ernest Figari & Alan S. Loewinsohn, *Video taped Depositions Come to Court*, LITIGATION, Spring 1988, at 35, 38 (suggesting the initial wide-angle shot). Although it is a good idea, the judge may not allow it.

69. If the taker is adamant about not having a split screen, suggest the use of two cameras, one for the witness and one for counsel. With the use of two cameras, the jury will most likely remain focused on the monitor playing the witness's testimony.

70. FED. R. CIV. P. 30(f)(1) (unless otherwise ordered by the court, the deposition record is sealed and sent to the attorney who arranged the recording, who then stores the record to protect it from loss or damage). *See generally* Bruce Wessell & Wayne Hill, *Is That Me on YouTube? Ground Rules for Access, Use and Sharing of Digital Depositions*, Merrill Corp., *available for download at* http://www.trialpresentationblog.com/tags/Wayne-hill/.

71. *See* FED. R. CIV. P. 5(d)(1) (depositions "must not be filed until they are used in the proceeding or the court orders filing"); *see. e.g.*, M.D. N.C. CIV. LOCAL R. 7.3(e).

72. FED. R. CIV. P. 30(f)(1). Among the concerns with analog media (VHS tapes) are the temperature and humidity in the storage area as well as the need to store the tapes on "end" rather than flat. Analog media has a projected five-year life at best; digital media, on the other hand, has a projected 100-year life. Therefore, VHS tapes should be transferred to a digital format (DVD or digital tape) for archival purposes. But even digital files degrade. To increase their life span, maintain your media in a secure, climate-controlled environment.

73. FED. R. CIV. P. 30(f)(2)(A).

74. FED. R. CIV. P. 32(a)(4)(B). An exception to the "one hundred mile" rule is when the absence of a witness appears to have been procured by the party offering the deposition. See "How to Lay a Foundation for the Admissibility (or Inadmissibility) of a Document" in Chapter 13 and "Witness Unavailable under FRCP 32(a)(4)(A)–(D)" in Chapter 25, discussing the difference in the definition of "unavailability" between the FRCP and the FRE.

75. In some states, the video deposition of an otherwise available witness may be used if the intention is so stated in the notice. *See, e.g.*, CAL. CIV. PROC. CODE § 2025.620(d) (West 2005) (permitting use of video deposition of treating or consulting physician or of any expert witness, even though deponent available, if deposition notice reserved right to do so). Of course, parties also could so stipulate.

76. See Chapter 19.

77. *See* Videotape: Video Depositions: What You Don't Know Can Hurt You (ABA-CLE 1997). See also "The Video Deposition" in Chapter 10.

78. For a video deposition, the witness should have been instructed to dress as though for trial. See "The Video Deposition" in Chapter 10.

79.   Another solution would be the use of realtime transcription and the synchronization of the video using software such as West LiveNote or West Case Notebook. With such software, you can search across multiple transcripts, creating an easy and precise way to reference to other portions of testimony.

80.   Better yet, if the deposition is conducted over multiple days, try a different strategy each day. *But see* FED. R. CIV. P. 30(d)(1) (limiting depositions to one day of seven hours unless otherwise stipulated or ordered by the court).

81.   As an alternative to note taking, take advantage of the "rough" transcript made available through realtime transcription. See Chapter 18.

82.   Consider placecards to serve as "chapter headings." If you do not use chapter headings or otherwise signal changes in subject during the deposition, the court is unlikely to allow them to be added afterward. Video depositions can benefit from clear transitions, and even from chapter headings, because video presentations typically are shorter and more condensed than equivalent live testimony.

83.   See Chapter 12.

84.   The insertion of documents into the video will require agreement of counsel.

85.   *See supra* text accompanying note 6.

86.   Neubauer, *supra* note 22, at 61–62. Neubauer suggests that a defender consider requiring the use of a separate camera, at the defender's expense, to record the examining lawyer. The use of an additional camera would likely require agreement of the parties or a court order after a motion.

87.   See "Examining Your Own Witness" in Chapter 14.

88.   Lest this common perception be doubted as a myth perpetrated by overanxious parents, consider that the number of televisions in an average American household has grown from 1.5 in 1970 to 2.6 in 2005. *See* U.S. DEP'T COMMERCE, STATISTICAL ABSTRACT OF THE UNITED STATES at Table 1099 (2008).

89.   Digital tape mediums have become standard for video depositions. Formats such as DV, mini dv, and DVD ensure that the image recorded for your depositions will play back in high-quality image at trial. SVHS and VHS, although sometimes used in remote markets, are for the most part no longer viable recording or playback formats. Most courtrooms will support the playback of video on a DVD or computer through a projector or directly into the court's AV system.

90.   *See* Tsesmelys v. Doblin Truck Leasing, 78 F.R.D. 181, 185 (ED. Tenn. 1976) (court noting that it has, on several occasions, invoked provisions of FRE 403 to suspend or curtail testimony of witness being presented by means of video). "Although relevant, evidence may be excluded if its probative value is substantially outweighed by the danger

of unfair prejudice, confusion of the issues, or misleading the jury, or by considerations of undue delay, waste of time, or needless presentation of cumulative evidence." FED. R. EVID. 403.

91.   *See* Figari & Loewinsohn, *supra* note 68, at 38 (discussing advantages and disadvantages of large-screen presentations). Figari and Loewinsohn refer to the use of smaller monitors as the "traditional wisdom." They suggest that technological advances have offset the reasons why a large-screen format was not used in the past; namely, quality of the image and cost. *Id.*

92.   As with the use of any technology in a courtroom, such as an overhead projector or document projector, ask the court for permission to use it and confirm that the facilities, such as lighting and electrical capacity, are adequate.

93.   *Id.*

94.   Detailed discussion of editing a video deposition, including the use of trial presentation software, is beyond the scope of this book. *See, e.g.*, G. CHRISTOPHER RITTER, CREATING WINNING TRIAL STRATEGIES AND GRAPHICS (2004).

95.   *See, e.g.*, FED. R. CIV. P. 26(a)(3) (listing required information about evidence to be used at trial); FED. R. CIV. P. 16(c)(2)(C) (at pretrial conference, court can rule in advance on admissibility of evidence); W.D. PA. LOCAL R. 16.1.4(A)(4). See Chapter 25, discussing pretrial considerations in offering deposition testimony at trial.

96.   Time pressures have been reduced by the ability of current software to allow you to present video digitized and synchronized to the transcript and ready for playback. This technology allows for more freedom in the courtroom: For example, you now can decide "on the fly" which video and text segments to present as impeachment testimony.

97.   *See* Figari & Loewinsohn, *supra* note 68, at 38.

98.   Note, however, that there may be circumstances when you do not want pretrial rulings on objections. *See* Figari & Loewinsohn, *supra* note 68, at 38 (explaining that opponent may be intimidated or discouraged from objecting in front of jury). But use this strategy only if you have very little video to show because the court and jury will quickly lose their patience with your fumbling through video.

99.   See "How to Respond to Improper Speaking and Clarifying Objections" in Chapter 15, discussing using a pretrial motion to ask for the court's approval to show the video of opposing counsel's obstreperous tactics to the jury as one way to attempt to control problem counsel at a deposition.

100.   115 F.R.D. 257 (E.D. Pa. 1987).

101.   *Id.* at 258.

102.   *Id.* at 257.

103. In addition, both LiveNote and West Case Notebook software allow you to select any portion of synchronized transcript and video and then export the selected portion of testimony to PowerPoint.

104. Most courthouses are now equipped with a DVD player and monitor. You can save multiple video clips onto a DVD and then randomly access the clips using a menu and remote control. In addition, DVDs can be preprogrammed to run different sequences of video files or edited clips. Soon DVDs should replace the use of edited video tape in most courtroom situations because they provide more flexibility and less chance of operator error in playback.

105. *See supra* note 84 and accompanying text.

106. *See supra* note 82 and accompanying text. Animation for trial presentation has become quite sophisticated due to the overall improvement in computer-generated graphics. For example, animation can be used to demonstrate a complicated construction defect in 3D with a time-lapse visual illustrating the evolution of the defect and the resulting failure. In addition, computer graphics can be highly effective in demonstrating accident reconstructions that would otherwise be too difficult to re-create in a "live" format. Computer graphics also allow for the presentation to be shown from several different angles and perspectives. Static graphics can also be very persuasive, having gone beyond simple pie charts and bar graphs to illustrate complex information displayed in a visually attractive fashion for the jury.

107. Audio sweetening is the process of cleaning up or enhancing an audio file. This technique can help when a witness is speaking at a low volume and his audio level needs to be increased, or when there is an interference in the audio, such as noise from a ventilation system, that can be reduced by removing that frequency from the audio track.

108. *See* Mark IV Props. Inc v. Club Dev. & Mgmt. Corp., 12 B.R. 854, 859–60 (Bankr. S.D. Cal. 1981) (allowing video taped depositions of numerous corporate officers, which had been prepared and edited by defendant without participation of plaintiff). *But see* Beard v. Mitchell, 604 F.2d 485, 503 (7th Cir. 1979) (upholding trial court's decision not to admit integrated deposition testimony on ground that presentation created confusion and false inference).

109. *See* ETSI Pipeline Project v. Burlington N., No. B-84-979-CA (E.D. Tex. Mar 16, 1988) (unpublished pretrial order) (allowing both parties to use composite, rearranged video taped deposition testimony but only during argument), *reprinted in* Michael Henke, *The Taking and Use of Video taped Depositions*, 16 AM. J. TRIAL ADVOC. 151, 167–70 (1992).

110. *See* Henke & Margolis, *supra* note 25, at 17.

CHAPTER 18

The Realtime Advantage: Using Realtime Transcription for More Effective Depositions

HAL S. MARCUS

Introduction

Since the early 1990s, advances in court reporting technology have offered new ways for savvy litigators to attain even more effective results from their depositions.

Using realtime transcription technology, attorneys—both takers and defenders—can see the deposition transcript appear on their computer screens as it is generated by the reporter, literally as it is being spoken. They can pause, scroll back, and review the day's testimony at will. They can be sure that they received a satisfactory answer to the question asked, that a question is not compound, and that a significant opportunity for an objection is not missed. Simply put, realtime transcription can remove the guesswork at a deposition.

Software tools enabling the receipt of a realtime transcript have become standard issue at hundreds of law firms nationwide. A leading realtime tool, LiveNote, has been named the most widely used litigation software among the top 200 U.S. law firms.[1] Thousands of litigation professionals use realtime transcription technology daily at depositions, arbitrations, and trials across the United States, and the numbers are growing steadily, both domestically and internationally.

Used properly, a realtime connection can help a taker achieve greater control over the proceedings, a more comprehensive final transcript, and a more impressive demonstration of competence to opposing counsel. Used improperly, realtime transcription can cause a taker to become distracted and even self-conscious. This chapter provides guidance to help you achieve maximum benefit from realtime transcription without any of its potential pitfalls.

How Does It All Work?

Stenography

For some decades, most court reporters have used transcription devices commonly referred to as "steno machines" (also called "Stenowriters" or other brand name variations) to generate transcripts more efficiently. Steno machines contain three banks of keys (24 to 26 keys in total) that are pressed by the reporter in combined keystrokes. The seemingly endless permutations of these combinations theoretically enable reporters to "write" any word in the English language far faster and with fewer keystrokes than would be required if they had to type individual letters.

The end product is a shorthand record that eventually must be translated into English text. Historically, the steno machine would ink the "steno notes" onto long, narrow strips of paper to be translated at a later time. However, the advent of laptop computers (which could easily be brought to deposition sites) created the potential for a more efficient process.

CAT Software

Computer-aided transcription (CAT) software enables a court reporter's work product to be transcribed into English text at the deposition site—in "real time." CAT software imports the reporter's steno text and instantly compares it with an ever-growing, user-specific dictionary maintained on the laptop, which associates specific steno markings with the words they are intended to represent. Experienced realtime reporters diligently maintain and augment dictionaries of more than 50,000 words; sometimes these dictionaries emphasize a particular type of litigation, such as medical malpractice or construction defect.

When necessary, CAT software accesses words in a dictionary. The software then displays the translated text in real time on the court reporter's laptop, giving the reporter both instant visual confirmation and the ability to edit so that she can correct errors or fill in blanks while the testimony is fresh in her mind.

In addition to helping the reporter prepare a final, certified transcript faster, this technology also enables her, at any time, to export and distribute her "notes"—that is, the rough transcript in English. For years, many reporters have offered clients—for an additional fee—a floppy diskette at the end of the day's testimony that contains an electronic copy of the uncertified transcript. Such a disk is usually called a "rough ASCII" or "dirty disk." This practice continues today, though such files are now commonly burned to CDs or sent to attorneys as e-mail attachments.[2]

Realtime Recipient Software

Starting in the early 1990s, software products began giving attorneys the ability to view and annotate, in real time, the rough transcript that appears on the reporter's CAT laptop. A number of products, such as CT Summation, CaseView, RealLegal Binder, Bridge, and TranscriptManagerPro, offer realtime capabilities, with LiveNote being the most widely used.

Most attorneys now bring a laptop computer to the deposition with realtime recipient software preinstalled. Using computer cables, an Internet connection, or (occasionally) wireless technology, the court reporter will establish a connection from her CAT laptop to the attorney's computer.[3]

The Realtime Display

Using realtime recipient software, the attorney receives an instant visual display of the transcript as it is created. Additional functions available to the user depend on the realtime software used and/or the service provider chosen.

The software may display the incoming transcript in different increments, from several characters at a time, to bunches of words, to an entire line of testimony. Generally, the display screen will scroll down as it fills up so that the most recent lines of testimony are always displayed, though the user can usually pause the incoming display and scroll back up at any time. Some products enable a user to manipulate the look and feel of the realtime screen—including text fonts, sizes, and colors. Most products retain the realtime transcript on the recipient's computer as it comes in, thereby providing unlimited reference at breaks during the deposition or at a later time.

Interactivity with the Transcript—Quick Marks

The user usually has some degree of interactivity with the testimony—for example, the ability to annotate key testimony, assign issues, enter notes, run searches, and generate reports. The most basic kind of annotation is commonly referred to as a Quick Mark—a generic highlight in the margin next to a particular line of testimony (see Figure 1).

Most realtime software inserts a Quick Mark with a simple tap on the laptop's spacebar. Some software also enables the association of specific issues with the transcript text, also with a single keystroke.[4]

Generally, Quick Marks and other annotations entered on an attorney's laptop will not be shared with other users in real time; such annotations are maintained privately on the attorney's computer in the standard realtime configuration. Nevertheless, such annotations can be shared in realtime with other members of the attorney's team if the attorney connects to a realtime feed from a case saved on a local area network (LAN), such as a shared network drive at the law firm. For example, using LiveNote software, an attorney can send an annotation to a colleague via Instant Messaging.[5]

Usually, the realtime transcript, along with any Quick Marks or other annotations entered by the attorney, is automatically saved on the attorney's laptop. Such entries need not be discarded when the final transcript arrives; many realtime tools enable the user to update the realtime transcript to the final transcript—replacing rough text with final text—without displacing entered annotations.

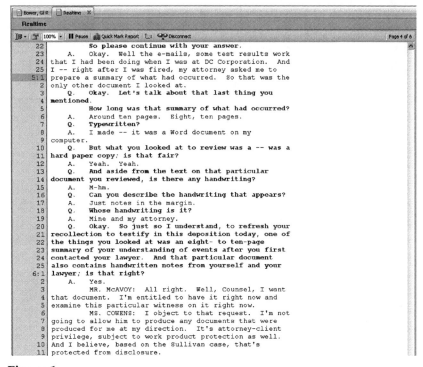

Figure 1

Realtime transcript as it appears in recipient software on an attorney's computer. The attorney has entered a Quick Mark at page 5, line 1.

Interactivity with the Transcript—Word Index

Some realtime recipient software features an interactive word index (see Figure 2) that updates regularly in realtime. The index is effectively a list of every word in the transcript with references

Figure 2

The realtime word index updates several times per minute.

to each page and line that the word appears (much like the concordance often provided to attorneys in hard copy by court reporters along with the final transcripts).[6]

With LiveNote, moving the cursor over a page/line reference will show a "pop-up" with some context around the selected word (for example, a set number of lines above and below, or a surrounding question and answer). A single click will take the user to that reference in the realtime transcript text.

Avoiding Distraction

First time users of realtime transcription sometimes report that they find the scrolling text distracting, particularly when they are the taker. They find themselves staring self-consciously at the screen and watching their words appear, rather than focusing on their questions and maintaining eye contact with the deponent (see Figure 3).

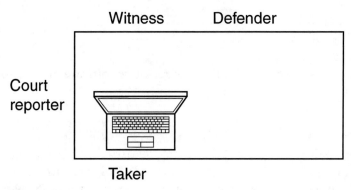

Figure 3
Non-recommended position for the taker's realtime laptop; it may promote distraction and poor eye contact with the witness.

A simple technique will avoid this pitfall: move the laptop computer away from its traditional position directly in front of you to the side. In a standard deposition setting, this usually means placing the laptop between the taker and defender. That placement should encourage you to look at the witness, rather than your laptop (compare Figures 3 and 4).

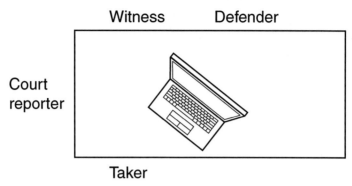

Figure 4
Recommended position for the taker's realtime laptop, fostering good eye contact and minimizing distraction, while still enabling ready access to the keyboard for entering marks.

In a video deposition, the taker often must move down along his side of the table to make room for the videographer, camera, lighting, and other possible equipment. Nevertheless, to avoid distraction, the realtime laptop should still be placed to the side of the taker rather than directly in front of him (see Figure 5).

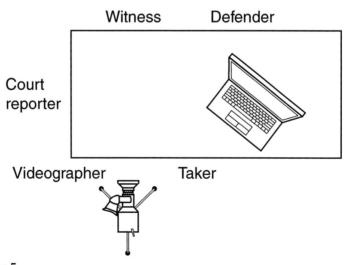

Figure 5
Recommended positioning for a video recorded deposition recorded on video.

483

The taker may benefit even more by tilting down the laptop screen so that the text is barely visible; this removes the temptation to use the realtime screen as a "virtual" crutch, instead encouraging its use as a valuable reference aid. Most attorneys report that with just a little practice or a reasonable proficiency with computers, real time is a comfort, not a distraction, at a deposition.

Accessing Other Transcripts

The attorney may have all the other deposition transcripts from the matter saved on her computer as well, enabling her to quickly retrieve and compare testimony, or even read prior testimony into the current record as part of a question. Some realtime software tools make it simple to access historical transcripts even while connected to the realtime transcript.

Benefits for the Taker

Stay More Focused on the Deponent

Maintaining strong eye contact with the witness and avoiding distraction is critical for the taker to achieve her goals for the deposition. Tools like the Quick Mark feature can be particularly helpful in achieving this goal.[7] With Quick Mark, the need to take handwritten notes is reduced; Quick Mark also provides a far more exact reference than an attorney's handwritten notes provide. The simple hand gesture of tapping the spacebar requires no diversion of one's eyes; the spacebar, the largest key on a keyboard, is easily found by touch.

Maintain a Poker Face

A taker may prefer not to call attention to her interest in a particular answer. With Quick Marks, annotation can be entered surreptitiously with a quiet tap on the space bar that others in the room may not notice. At a minimum, this technique can be far subtler than looking down at a legal pad to write notes, checking one's watch to jot down the time the answer was given (so it can be located later in a 300-page transcript) and then finally looking back up at the witness to continue.

Ask Better Questions

Even a simple "Yes" or "No" answer gleaned from a witness will not achieve its desired objective if the taker did not phrase the question clearly and concisely. With a realtime transcript, the taker can refer back to any asked question—immediately, at lunchtime, or during a break—to be sure she has asked the right question and secured the response needed to establish her case.

Respond More Effectively to Objections

Often, the taker may find she can more respond more effectively to—and minimize the frequency of—certain objections by immediately referring back to earlier parts of the record. For example, objections of "asked and answered" may be challenged by reading back the exact words that were actually asked and answered.[8] Confronted in this way, the defender may become more selective as he considers making future objections.

With certain software tools, the taker can highlight all objections as they appear on her screen. Alternatively, she may be able to find all objections with a simple word search through the transcript. She may also be able to generate an automatic report of all objections complete with context and page/line indicators—a powerful reference guide when dealing with a particularly obstreperous defender.[9]

Neutralize Stalling Tactics

A common defense technique designed to break the taker's flow and challenge her control over the proceedings is to ask the court reporter for a "readback" of the question before the witness answers. This requires the reporter to (1) enter a notation that she is going off the record, (2) refer back to the earlier testimony on the CAT laptop, (3) read back the question, and then (4) enter a notation that she is going back on the record. This tedious procedure gives the witness a moment to breathe and reflect, and gives the defender a chance both to reassert his own presence with the witness and to slow down the taker.

Using realtime, there is no need to go off the record: the taker can happily ask the question again herself—verbatim from the transcript or rephrased—aided by the computer screen at her side.

Generate a More Complete Record

Sometimes a taker needs to refer back to earlier testimony to ensure she has not missed an opportunity provided by an unexpected answer, neglected to secure a fully responsive answer to an important question, or failed to exhaust the deponent's recollection on a topic. By "Quick Marking" the critical points and then referring back to them at lunchtime or on a break, the taker can avoid such pitfalls.[10]

Intimidate a Less-than-Forthcoming Witness

"Quick Marking" may also be used as an intimidation tactic. A witness who keeps responding "I don't recall" or gives answers of questionable veracity may become more forthcoming when he sees the taker's noticeable—maybe even aggressive—tap on the space-bar after each such answer. Evasive witnesses have been known to cringe visibly each time the taker reaches for the spacebar.

Pin Down (and Wound) the Witness

Challenging a witness with prior inconsistent testimony is a powerful way not only to exert greater influence over the proceedings but also to generate candid, more complete responses from a recalcitrant witness. Confronted with potentially inconsistent testimony, the witness may decide to explain herself more fully, thus generating a more fluid and productive dialogue. Realtime transcription users often cite the value of being able to refer back to a witness's earlier testimony or to the testimony of other witnesses.

Some takers even bring a projector to depositions. This enables them to project a witness's evasive or questionable responses against the wall—side by side with inconsistent testimony from other transcripts. This tactic can have a profound psychological impact on the witness.

As noted above, some realtime software enables a taker to access and search other transcripts without disconnecting from the realtime connection. This technique works particularly well when the taker is assisted by a "second chair," attending either onsite at the deposition or remotely via the Internet.[11]

Share Information Rapidly with Colleagues or Clients

Many takers use realtime software to mark all useful bits of testimony over the course of the day. Then, shortly after the deposition, they generate and e-mail a report of all the marked testimony to the client or co-counsel. Sharing such reports can be a very efficient way for a taker to brief her client and her colleagues on the salient points of testimony provided that day. Most realtime software provides the ability to generate reports of Quick Marked testimony, including some context around each mark (for example, several lines above and below, multiple surrounding question and answer pairs, or even entire pages), thereby generating a more effective report.

Organize the Testimony in Advance for Quick Analysis Later

Using annotative features in simple ways can cut down preparation time and facilitate case analysis. For example, certain software enables a user to assign predefined issues to the realtime text with a single keystroke. The user thus creates customized "issues" pertinent to the case and then organizes them in a numerical list, perhaps giving each issue a distinct color. By simply pressing the corresponding number key on the computer keyboard, the user can then enter a colored-coded mark next to the pertinent line of testimony, and the software logs the issue association. Sometimes referred to as Issue Marks, this feature enables the taker to easily sort testimony by issue and create customized reports.

The taker can use Issue Marks in three beneficial ways:

1. The taker can enter an Issue Mark when starting a new line of questioning (for example, press the appropriate number key for the "Damages" issue when starting a new line of questioning related to damages calculations). Issue marks make each section easy to find when reviewing the testimony later and even enable rough calculations of the amount of time spent on a particular topic.

2. The taker can enter an Issue Mark when a particularly telling answer is given that touches on a key issue (for example, press the appropriate number key for the "Awareness" issue when the deponent's answer indicates he was aware of a key fact). These references can then be easily grouped together in a report on the issue, and all pertinent testimony can be easily shared with a client or co-counsel.

3. The taker can enter an Issue Mark every time a particular objection is made by the defender (for example, press the appropriate number key for the "Objection: Privilege" issue whenever the defender claims privilege and instructs the witness not to answer a question). The annotation can then be used to challenge the witness at the deposition or to facilitate drafting a motion or brief at a later date.

Though attorneys sometimes express concern that they will be too distracted entering Issue Marks in realtime, they often find this technique much simpler than expected. If just a handful of significant issues (say ten or fewer) are set up in advance, applying them to testimony with a single keystroke is only marginally more challenging than tapping the spacebar, yet can yield far greater advantages.

Many realtime software products retain Quick Marks and Issue Marks with the transcript text until deleted by the user. The marks remain in place even when—as recommended—the user later updates the realtime text to conform it to the final certified text delivered by the court reporter. Thus, Quick Marks and Issue Marks serve as a powerful road map for attorneys and paralegals to navigate and easily "mine" even lengthy transcripts for the most valuable information.

Benefits for the Defender

Follow the Questioning Better

Realtime text can help a defender stay focused and analyze the flow of questions. The written record may help to identify what listening alone may not reveal: what has been covered and where the questioning is leading.

Help the Witness Follow and Respond

A witness who is struggling to comprehend a line of questioning may be more likely to over-answer, speculate, or otherwise provide unsolicited information. By referring to the realtime record and by showing the screen to the witness as needed, a defender can help anchor the witness and ensure that his testimony remains on track and limited to the question asked.

Monitor and Correct the Deponent's Manner of Answering Questions

Using realtime, a defender can Quick Mark the places in the testimony where the witness over-answered a question, speculated unnecessarily, failed to pause and consider an answer before responding, or violated any of the other principles discussed during witness preparation.[12] At a break, the defender can show the realtime transcript to the witness to illustrate the problematic behavior in the witness's own words.

Formulate Better Objections

Viewing the realtime transcript can help a defender identify questions that are compound, vague, have been asked and answered, may violate privilege, and the like. Recurring questioning patterns

488

may become more obvious in print, helping the defender to both anticipate opportunities to object and tailor objections more effectively. And using the Issue Mark or word index can help a defender identify all the similar objections over the course of the transcript. [13]

Defend the Witness from Harassment and Intimidation

When the taker engages in intimidating tactics, such as mischaracterizing the witness's testimony, the defender can use realtime testimony to protect her client. Using the onscreen word index, the defender can identify and read into the record the taker's aggressive or misleading comments and then show the contrast by reading back the deponent's actual testimony. Faced with such an exacting and well-substantiated objection, and the threat of a well-founded motion, the taker may be more restrained as the deposition continues.

Share Information Quickly with Colleagues and Clients

The defender may benefit as much as or more than the taker by generating Quick Mark reports during or immediately after the deposition and e-mailing them to colleagues, co-counsel, or clients. For example, when the witness is a key executive from the client's corporation, the defender may feel greater-than-usual pressure to keep the client well-apprised of testimony, which may affect both litigation strategy and business decisions. Realtime reports make such communication more efficient and more accurate by reducing the likelihood that the defender's oral summary will be misinterpreted.

Benefits for All Involved

Even adversaries sometimes have overlapping interests. By increasing efficiency and accuracy in the deposition discovery process, realtime transcription generally benefits all parties in a case.

Facilitate Foreign Language Translation

Depositions of foreign language deponents can pose significant logistical challenges; even the most talented, well-trained, professional interpreters will sometimes struggle with dialects and idioms. These difficulties may lead to delays, confusion, and an unreliable record that is further undermined when the witness later submits a lengthy list of corrections.[14]

Viewing a realtime transcript on a computer can help interpreters on both sides function far more quickly and capably. Armed with realtime transcription, an interpreter can read the English questions before translating, and then confirm that his translations of the answers are accurate. Given these capabilities, many litigators always use realtime transcription for depositions of a foreign-language deponent.

Facilitate Scientific Depositions

When a deposition is replete with complicated language (as typically occurs in litigation involving issues of medicine, intellectual property, computer science, biotech, and the like) realtime transcription yields numerous benefits. Attorneys without scientific specialization may find it much easier to follow the testimony and challenge evasive responses. Witnesses may be less likely to misspeak and then submit corrections later. Even the reporter will benefit from receiving onsite corrections and clarifications from the participants, these giving her a head start in preparing the final transcript.

Serial Versus Internet-Based Realtime

Overview of Serial (or "Traditional") Realtime

Most realtime connections are currently "serial-based," meaning that they are provided by connecting a 9-pin serial cable from the court reporter's CAT laptop directly to the attorney's laptop (see Figure 6). Realtime reporters commonly carry multiline devices that can take a single output and provide connections to as many as five recipient laptops. At depositions with more attendees, multiple multiline devices can be used to provide dozens of connections.

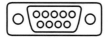

Figure 6
Sketch of a 9-pin serial port on a computer into which the serial cable is inserted.

Laptops Without Serial Ports

Lighter, slimmer laptop designs often lack 9-pin serial ports; instead, they have smaller, more adaptable USB ports. To enable serial realtime connections, attorneys with such laptops should use serial-to-USB adapters (see Figure 7). Such adapters are small, inexpensive, and generally available at computer hardware stores. A serial-to-USB adapter comes with a driver (a small software program) that should be preinstalled on the attorney's laptop and ideally tested with the attorney's realtime software before the first deposition at which it will be used. Because not all serial-to-USB devices work well with all realtime software products, check with your realtime software provider for recommendations before purchasing a device.

Figure 7
A serial-to-USB adapter cable, necessary for laptops without serial ports.

Configuration of the Recipient Laptop

To successfully connect to a court reporter using a serial and/or USB cable, the user's laptop computer must have an available communications (or "COM") port ready to receive the feed. Most laptops have this port. But the software used to synchronize a BlackBerry, Palm, or similar device may already be occupying the necessary COM port, potentially blocking the feed. This issue usually can be easily resolved by simply turning off the synchronization program, typically by clicking on the icon for such a program in your operating system's toolbar (which usually appears in the bottom right of the computer screen, near the time display). Some—though certainly not all—realtime court reporters are well versed in helping the recipient configure his computer to solve problems like this.

Realtime recipient software products may also require the recipient to identify which court-reporting CAT software the reporter is using, so the software can properly reformat the incoming feed. Again, well-versed court reporters are aware of this requirement and can guide attorneys who are onsite—if not beforehand.

Checklist: Common Serial Realtime Connection Issues and Suggested Solutions

- COM port is not available due to BlackBerry or other PDA (personal data assistant) synchronization software. Solution: Turn off synchronization software or select a different COM port, if available, in the recipient software settings.
- COM port is not available due to "infrared" feature on laptop (infrared technology enables a user to wirelessly print or to synchronize BlackBerrys or other PDAs to the laptop). Solution: Turn off infrared, usually from the Windows Control Panel.
- Serial-to-USB adapter is not installed properly or not compatible with realtime recipient software. Solution: Install adapter's driver software on laptop; check with software provider regarding compatibility.
- Realtime recipient software is set to wrong CAT system output or baud rate settings. Solution: Change the settings in realtime recipient software per reporter's instructions.[15]
- Court reporter hardware problems, such as (1) CAT system not set properly for realtime output; (2) serial "send & receive" cables not functioning; or (3) multiline device not functioning. Solution: Cannot be resolved by the recipient; the court reporter or her agency must repair or replace the malfunctioning equipment.

Streaming Realtime Deposition Text over the Internet

Realtime deposition connections can also be established over the Internet, opening the door to greater functionality and broader participation by one's legal team in the deposition process.

The technological model is fairly straightforward. Instead of—or in addition to—using serial-to-USB cables to connect the reporter to the recipients, the Internet is used as a delivery system. The court reporter connects the CAT laptop (or a secondary computer if he prefers not to install extra programs on his CAT laptop) to the Internet via an ethernet cable or phone connection. As he writes, he transmits the realtime transcript feed to a hosted computer server, which makes it available to both onsite and remote users, anywhere in the world, who have an authorized username and password for that session.

First introduced to the industry in the late 1990s, Internet-based realtime transcription is far from new. Until recently, however, its use has been limited largely to two scenarios: (1) depositions where one or more participants need to view the live transcript from a remote location, or (2) multiparty depositions where the sheer number of realtime connections in the room makes using serial cables a serious logistical challenge. Today, the use of Internet-based real time is more common, encompassing a far broader range of depositions, trials, and arbitrations.

Recipient Tools

Depending on the Internet realtime service used, a transcript may be received into a user's realtime recipient software, or it may be viewed in an Internet browser. The specific functionality available to the user varies, depending on the service chosen; however, the advent of realtime access without the need to preinstall software has opened up significant new possibilities, allowing lawyers and clients to "attend" depositions from remote locations.[16]

Internet Realtime Use on the Rise

A number of factors have led to substantial growth in the adoption of Internet-based real time. Internet connectivity is now routinely available in law firm conference rooms and hotels nationwide. Realtime streaming technology has adapted to network firewalls (security systems that historically blocked many transmissions into corporate servers), while still providing high standards of privacy and security. Perhaps most important, attorneys and paralegals have achieved a substantially higher comfort level with online meetings and other strategic uses of the Internet in their daily practice.

In addition, Internet-based real time has become, in many ways, easier to use and more reliable than serial real time. With Internet-based real time, the recipient need not be concerned with COM port availability, serial-to-USB adapters, cabling problems, CAT output, or baud rate options.[17] As long as Internet access is available and the user has the right username and password, a trouble-free connection should follow.

Realtime Video over the Internet

Today, more and more depositions are recorded on video at the taker's request in order to preserve the witness's testimony in a visual medium.[18] This live deposition video and audio may now be streamed over the Internet to remote attendees along with the written realtime transcript. For this to happen, the videographer's camera must be connected to a digital encoding device (a box usually about the size of a video game console) that converts the deposition video to a digital file suitable for streaming over the Internet. The remote recipient uses either an installed software product or a Web browser to monitor the video virtually in real time, within seconds of the live action.

Video streaming creates the closest simulation of the onsite experience, enabling the end user to detect the deponent's tone, demeanor, and body language.[19] It also offers the potential for a busy remote attendee to monitor the deposition audibly, much like listening to the news on a television playing in the background while completing other tasks.

Video streaming from a deposition is very different from traditional videoconferencing technology. Video streaming provides a direct feed from a full-size video camera that is recording the witness, rather than from a secondary, smaller, movable camera elsewhere in the room. The video feed is unidirectional from the deposition room, so the remote recipients cannot be seen, nor can the camera's view be expanded for a broader view of the attorneys or others in the room. This has an advantage over videoconferencing, because a second, audibly moving camera serves as a regular reminder to all present that they are being watched and video recorded.

Video streaming thus provides recipients a realtime view of what a judge or jury will see later if the deposition video is played at trial. Recipients view the same deposition video that may be synchronized to the final transcript for convenient playback in transcript management or trial presentation software.[20]

Instant Messaging During Depositions

A further benefit of Internet-based realtime connections is the availability of Instant Messaging (IM)—sometimes also referred to as "Chat"—technology. It can be—as IM users in both business and personal settings know—a very effective way to get quick answers and share time-sensitive information with others.

In the context of a deposition, it is increasingly common to find paralegals or second-chair attorneys "attending" depositions over the Internet while actually offsite back at their offices. IM allows remote attendees to support their onsite colleagues, providing useful quotes from other transcripts, translations of complicated terms, or document references related to the deponent's testimony. For example, an onsite taker can send an IM to a paralegal back at the office requesting examples of inconsistent testimony. (This is easily done because the paralegal is watching the same realtime testimony; thus, by typing a single word—"Conflicting?"—into an IM, the taker makes a request.) The paralegal can then search through the other transcripts in the case and send a reply with the inconsistent testimony. When ready, the taker can read the conflicting excerpt directly into the record from her computer screen and impeach the witness, ask for an explanation, or take any other action she deems strategically advisable.

In addition to paralegals and second-chair attorneys, other remote attendees might include (1) experts, who can help the taker navigate overly technical language and look for unresponsive answers; (2) co-counsel representing related parties, who can monitor the deposition to see if their clients are mentioned by the witness and can, if necessary, contribute additional questions; and (3) clients, who not only can monitor the status of their case but may also be able to help their attorney identify inaccurate or misleading testimony.

In the deposition context, IM can yield far more effective results than typical e-mail. For example, with IM it is easy to see which remote colleagues are online and connected to the deposition at a given moment. Having this capability should prevent messages from being sent futilely to a user who has logged off from the session; it also encourages greater responsiveness to requests from the deposition site.

Security and Privilege Considerations of IM

Privilege issues raised by progressive technologies (such as fax or e-mail) generally have focused on whether the parties to a communication have a reasonable expectation of privacy.[21] Using this standard, most communications conveyed over IM in a deposition setting are likely to be privileged.

But before using IM as a deposition tool, consider whether the security and retention policies of the IM service provider realistically include an expectation of privacy. For example, LiveNote's IM service is secured using 128-bit SSL RSA encryption (the maximum level of encryption provided by most Web sites) and does not save the content, or even log the existence, of Instant Messages. Still, LiveNote users can choose to save their Instant Messages on their own computers or networks; consequently, even though a potentially producible record may be created, privacy is ensured.

Of course, even otherwise privileged communications can become subject to discovery if the privilege is waived because of how the communication is used. For example, if a defender shows a privileged IM to a witness to refresh her recollection, the taker could argue that the defender has waived the privilege and the IM may now be discoverable.[22]

Rules, Regulations, and Realities

Notification Requirements for Realtime

The Federal Rules of Civil Procedure are silent on the matter of realtime transcription, as are nearly all of the state codes.[23] Despite the substantial adoption of realtime transcription in most parts of the United States, California is the only state whose code addresses the realtime process.

California Code of Civil Procedure § 2025.220(a)(5) requires that the noticing party indicate in the deposition notice "any intention to record the testimony by stenographic method through the instant visual display of the testimony." This section also provides guidelines to ensure that the court reporter is notified in advance of the realtime requirement and is prepared to offer equivalent services at equivalent rates to all parties involved:

> If the deposition will be conducted using instant visual display, a copy of the deposition notice shall also be given to the deposition officer. Any offer to provide the instant visual display of the testimony or to provide rough draft transcripts to any party which is accepted prior to, or offered at, the deposition shall also be made by the deposition officer at the deposition to all parties in attendance. Any party or attorney requesting the provision of the instant visual display of the testimony, or rough draft transcripts, shall pay the reasonable cost of those services, which may be no greater than the costs charged to any other party or attorney.

Despite the absence of such rules outside of California, logistics require that the reporting agency be told in advance that realtime service is required so it can supply an onsite reporter with the necessary skills and equipment. Because reporters and agencies have a financial incentive to offer realtime services to attendees other than the taker, they almost always will notify the defender that real time will be used.[24] Thus, even without a requirement of formal notice, the defender will learn of the taker's plan to use real time and have a reasonable opportunity to use it as well.

What If Only the Defender Wants to Use Realtime?

A problem can arise when the taker has not indicated any plan to use real time but the defender wants to use it. The defender will first need to contact the taker to let him know that real time will be used and then make appropriate arrangements. A defender who makes arrangements through the taker may not achieve his goals, so most defenders will make arrangements directly with the reporting agency. In any event, the request for realtime services may require a change in staffing from the taker's preferred non-realtime reporter or agency, which may affect the rates charged to the taker for basic stenography services.[25]

To avoid such uncertainties, counsel on both sides should agree early in the deposition discovery phase to address the specific reporting services to be made available. For example, in matters involving multiple depositions, attorneys on different sides might agree to hire the same court reporting agency for all depositions, thereby ensuring consistency in the delivery of realtime and other reporting services.

Deposing a Witness Remotely Using Realtime

When a witness is located far enough away from the lawyers that an in-person deposition is inconvenient (and especially when the witness's testimony may be relatively insignificant), it makes sense to conduct the deposition from a remote location. The Federal Rules of Civil Procedure allow for this contingency, and many state codes follow suit. FRCP 30(b)(4) provides:

> The parties may stipulate—or the court may on motion order—that a deposition be taken by telephone or other remote means. For the purpose of this rule and Rules 28(a), 37(a)(2), and 37(b)(1), the deposition takes place where the deponent answers the questions.

In the typical scenario, the court reporter—serving as the deposition officer—appears onsite with the witness to administer the oath and manage the exhibits.[26] A speakerphone is used for open, two-way communication. In such situations, the offsite taker can be aided greatly by video recording the deposition using realtime transcription and streaming both over the Internet.

Requesting Realtime Reporting Services

Reporter Certifications and Standards

Of the roughly 40,000 practicing court reporters nationwide, only about 10,000 to 12,000 hold themselves out as capable of providing interactive realtime transcription.[27]

Of these, only 2,500 are Certified Realtime Reporters (CRRs).[28] The CRR certification means that the reporter has demonstrated to the National Court Reporting Association the ability to create a realtime transcript that is at least 96 percent accurate at a speaking speed of 180 words per minute. Though generally considered a notable credential, the CRR distinction is neither required by law nor universally sought by reporters. In an industry already replete with various certification levels, many highly competent and successful reporters do not view the CRR distinction as valuable enough to warrant taking another test.

In addition, while it demonstrates a high degree of accuracy, the CRR distinction does not indicate whether the reporter has been trained or tested on the technology used to provide and troubleshoot realtime connections. Thus, even though a CRR-certified reporter should be able to create a quality realtime transcript, she may not be capable of sharing it successfully in realtime with clients.[29]

Confusion over What "Realtime" Means

When scheduling deposition services, be aware that there is some confusion about the term "realtime reporter." Some reporters will declare that they are "realtime reporters" because they use CAT systems and can provide a "rough ASCII transcript," even though they are not equipped to provide an instant visual display of a transcript. So be specific when requesting realtime services and indicate which realtime software tool you will be using.

Building a Dictionary in Advance

For depositions that may involve a great deal of technical terminology or an unusual number of proper names, it is wise to provide a list of such terms and names to the court reporter or agency several days before the deposition.[30] The list will allow the reporter to expand her dictionary before the deposition to include these words for proper translation in real time.

Nontranslatable words may appear in a realtime transcript either with phonetic spelling ("Rockefeller" might appear as "rock a fell her") or as incorrect words with similar sounds (in one deposition, the term "per stirpes" translated as something to do with "herpes"). Nontranslatable words may also appear as gibberish text in all capital letters ("CKGHXXP"). Providing a list to the reporter will reduce the incidence of such problems and thus avoid distractions in realtime and ensure the accuracy of the final transcript.

Checklist: Requesting Realtime Reporting Services

- Make clear your desire to *connect* to real time, not merely to receive a rough transcript at the end of the day.
- Identify which realtime software tool you will use and request a court reporter who has been trained and tested on how to successfully establish connections using that software.
- If desired, ask for a reporter who has been trained and is set up to provide an Internet-based realtime connection.
- When planning to use IM, specify which attendees should be able to communicate in the same IM group.
- Provide the agency or reporter with a list of proper names and other specialized terms that may appear in the transcript. Often you can accomplish this by providing a word index from a previous transcript or providing a copy of the deposition notice.

Additional Costs of Realtime Reporting

Though widely considered a worthwhile expenditure, using realtime transcription can add to the cost of the deposition process. Here are a few cost items to consider.

Cost of Realtime Software

Cost and pricing plans for realtime software vary. Some software manufacturers offer perpetual licenses; others offer subscriptions for a fixed monthly fee. Some licenses may trigger additional costs for each realtime use, but such products typically can be licensed on an "unlimited use" basis. When comparing software products, consider their different functionality and ease of use, as well as the extent to which they are known and supported by your preferred court reporters.

Court Reporter's Realtime Writing Fee

Realtime transcription generally triggers additional fees for the court reporter. Realtime reporters charge a premium because of the additional skill and pressure involved in creating a quality realtime transcript, along with the need to ensure that it is delivered successfully to the recipients. These costs vary by geographical region and may also be affected by the availability of realtime reporters at a given time; typically a realtime writing fee will add 25 to 35 percent to the reporter's page rate.

Be sure you find out what services are included with the realtime writing fee. For example, a daily rough transcript will often be provided—typically as an e-mail attachment—within hours after the deposition. This will enable you to update the saved realtime transcript text to a cleaner version. But sometimes this daily rough transcript service is not included. If requested, this service will cost as much as the realtime writing fee.

Many, though not all, court reporters charge an additional premium if you want Internet-based real time instead of serial-based real time. But as real time use increasingly moves away from serial or USB connections and toward Internet technology, the costs will likely decrease.

Court reporting fees are often negotiable, particularly for matters with a large number of planned depositions. Multiple-party depositions may warrant even greater price elasticity because they offer a reporter or an agency the prospect of additional realtime connections and transcript copy purchases. But be sure you understand what services are included for a reduced fee; when a reduced fee also means reduced services, the value of the reduction may be little or nothing.

Possible Cost Savings from Realtime Reporting

Despite its additional costs, realtime reporting services ultimately can produce cost savings for both clients and then attorneys.

Avoiding the Need for "Expedited" Transcripts

An attorney who leaves a deposition with the reporter's rough transcript on her laptop may have less need to expedite the creation and delivery of the final transcript. Typically, getting a final transcript on an expedited one-day turnaround basis costs about double the page rate, and getting a final transcript in fewer than ten days is likely to result in a surcharge that may exceed the additional realtime writing cost.

Of course, if you need to quote from a transcript in a time-sensitive motion or brief, then you still need an expedited final transcript to ensure that the cited testimony, as well as the corresponding page and line numbers, conform to the certified record.

Avoiding Digesting Fees

As noted above, after Quick Marks or other annotations have been entered in the realtime transcript, you can automatically generate a report of the testimony's salient points.[31] By using this tool, you can avoid the cost associated with having a paralegal or third-party service create a digest or summary of the transcript.

Some attorneys find the transcript report not only to be more cost-effective but also more useful as well. A digest is created by an editor who paraphrases all the testimony in the record. By contrast, a transcript report contains the precise questions and answers in the record, but only those deemed significant by the reviewing attorney.

Avoiding Unnecessary Travel

Internet-based real time can reduce costs by eliminating the need to travel to participate in a deposition. These savings can include travel costs, the reduction of unproductive time, and expert and other professional fees. As noted above, the growing availability of realtime video and audio streaming—along with the transmission of transcript text—is enabling attorneys to take a broader range of depositions remotely and more cost-effectively.

What to Expect in the Future

Predicting the future of digital technology in a hardcopy medium is a precarious endeavor. Still, certain trends seem inevitable. Realtime transcription technology will continue to become richer in features, easier to use, and easier to administer. Over time, it will become more readily available and more cost-effective, even though, as noted above, a national shortage of realtime court reporters may trigger short-term price fluctuations.

As attorneys become more comfortable working with digital exhibits instead of exclusively with hardcopy, all deposition attendees—remote and onsite—will be able to view not only the transcript of the testimony but also the marked exhibits in real time.

In addition, as the legal industry continues to expand its use of online meeting technology, the deposition process is likely to become more virtual as well. Indeed, we may even see a gradual erosion of the distinction between onsite and offsite appearances at depositions.

Ultimately, though, realtime innovations are likely to emerge and be adopted only to the extent they deliver tangible competitive advantages to litigators within the tense—and sometimes fragile—framework of a deposition.

Notes

1. *See* AmLaw Tech Surveys 2004, 2005, 2006, and 2007 (Am. Lawyer Media).

2. See also Chapter 24, discussing the format in which transcripts are produced to counsel.

3. See *infra* section "Serial Versus Internet-Based Realtime" for specific hardware and logistical requirements of a realtime connection.

4. See *infra* discussion of Issue Marks in "Benefits for the Taker."

5. See *infra* section "Streaming Realtime Deposition Text over the Internet."

6. See "Managing Transcripts and Exhibits" in Chapter 24, discussing a concordance summary, and Exhibit A to that chapter.

7. See *supra* section "Interactivity with the Transcript—Quick Marks."

8. See also "Opening Remarks and Stipulations" in Chapter 11 and "Reactions by the Taker to the Defender's Tactics" in Chapter 14.

9. See also Chapter 15.

10. See *supra* section "Interactivity with the Transcript—Quick Marks."

11. See *infra* section "Streaming Realtime Deposition Text over the Internet."

12. See "Twenty Guidelines for Deposition Testimony" in Chapter 7.

13. See *supra* section "Benefits for the Taker."

14. See "Reviewing and Correcting the Transcript" in Chapter 23.

15. The correct settings for CAT output format and baud rate vary, depending on the court reporter's choice of CAT software and equipment. The most common settings are "CaseView" for CAT output format

and "2400" for baud rate; consequently, these are the default settings in some realtime recipient software tools.

16. See *infra* section "Instant Messaging During Depositions."

17. See *supra* section "Configuration of the Recipient Laptop."

18. *See generally* Bruce Wessell & Wayne Hill, *Is That Me on YouTube? Ground Rules for Access, Use and Sharing of Digital Depositions*, Merrill Corp., *available for download at http://www.trialpresentationblog.com/tags/Wayne-hill/*.

19. See "Nonverbal Communication" in Chapter 11.

20. See also "Video Synchronization" in Chapter 24.

21. See "Confidentiality and Waiver of Privilege" in Chapter 6.

22. See Chapter 9.

23. See "Securing Attendance of the Deposition Witness" in Chapter 3, discussing notification requirements for depositions.

24. See *infra* section "Additional Costs of Realtime Reporting."

25. See *id.*

26. Although the Advisory Committee Notes to FCRP 30(b)(4) indicate that the record may be taken by less expensive means than stenography (for example, mechanical, electrical, or photographic means), the taking party must apply for a court order to use such potentially less accurate and less trustworthy recording methods. The court may, in turn, prohibit the use of such methods or require that they be used only in conjunction with additional safeguards.

27. E-mail from Marshall Jorpeland, Dir. of Commc'ns, Nat'l Court Reporters Ass'n, to the author (Feb. 18, 2009) (on file with the author).

28. *Id.*

29. By contrast, the Certified LiveNote Reporter (CLR) distinction demonstrates that a reporter has been trained and tested on how to support the hardware and software used to transmit a realtime transcript. Over 800 reporters have achieved CLR status and may be retained via various reporting agencies across the United States.

30. See "Preparing to Take a Deposition" in Chapter 4, discussing the value of providing a glossary to the court reporter.

31. See Chapter 24, discussing transcript summarization in detail.

CHAPTER 19

Expert Witness Depositions

RAOUL KENNEDY*

"In these times when it is impossible to know everything, but becomes necessary for success in any vocation to know something of everything and everything of something, the expert is more and more called upon as a witness both in civil and criminal cases. In these days of specialists their services are often needed to aid the jury in their investigations of questions of fact relating to subjects with which the ordinary man is not acquainted."

—*Francis L. Wellman,*
The Art of Cross-Examination, 94 (4th ed. 1936).

Had Wellman been possessed of clairvoyance, he could have added, "And all the foregoing is going to increase exponentially during the twentieth century and into the twenty-first century." Today, the pervasiveness of experts in litigation is exceeded only by the daunting task of the lawyer who must master enough of the expert's—frequently arcane—area of expertise either to effectively (1) depose the hostile expert or (2) prepare and present testimony of a friendly expert.

This chapter addresses both challenges. First, it discusses the rules governing expert discovery in light of the 1993 and 2000 amendments to the Federal Rules of Civil Procedure (FRCP). Second, it provides a checklist of tips and pointers for effectively preparing one's own expert for deposition. Finally, it presents the ten subjects that should be covered to allow a lawyer with even minimal experience in taking depositions and with little or no knowledge of the expert's field to discover effectively and efficiently an opposing expert's opinions and the underlying bases for those opinions.

Rules Governing Expert Discovery

Federal Rule of Evidence (FRE) 702 permits an expert trial witness to testify in the form of an opinion if the testimony is related to scientific, technical, or other specialized knowledge and if that testimony would assist the trier of fact to understand the evidence. The opposition is then entitled to cross-examine the expert fully about the bases and reasons for each opinion.[1]

Amendments to FRCP 26

Despite considerable controversy surrounding changes to the FRCP that were proposed by the Supreme Court in 1993 (including changes to FRCP 26), significant amendments took effect on December 1, 1993, because Congress failed to pass legislation to block the revisions.[2] The 1993 amendments radically altered the manner of disclosing experts' identities and the means of discovering their opinions in four principal ways:

1. The identities of all expert trial witnesses must be disclosed well in advance of trial;
2. Testifying experts must provide comprehensive written reports of their expected testimony and additional information about themselves;
3. Depositions of experts are conducted as a matter of right; and
4. A party has a continuing duty to supplement material changes in an expert's basis for testimony.

Further amendments to FRCP 26 were enacted in 2000 to ensure that these revisions would be adopted and observed uniformly in the federal courts. The most important 2000 amendment was the abandonment of the 1993 "opt out" provision, which authorized courts to alter or reject the new disclosure requirements.

Through these changes, the amendments ensured that expert information would be available in every case, on a different timetable, and in a changed format from the former regime.[3] This chapter focuses on the current requirements of FRCP 26, beginning with a brief discussion of practice under the former FRCP 26.

Discoverability of the Opinions of Testifying and Nontestifying Experts

Before 1970, federal courts were divided regarding the discoverability of expert opinions.[4] In 1970, the FRCP were amended to set forth a specified procedure for discovering both facts known and opinions held by experts that the experts acquired or developed in anticipation of litigation or for trial.

The basic scheme established by the 1970 amendments upholds one of the fundamental purposes of the work-product rule, which is to prevent one side from laying back, doing nothing, and then taking advantage of the opponent's industry.[5] In furtherance of that goal, case law following the 1970 amendments provides that, in the absence of exceptional circumstances, the only retained experts who can be discovered are those who will actually testify at trial.[6] Conversely, when an expert has not been retained to assist in the defense or prosecution of a case, there are no work-product considerations, and that individual's expertise is subject to discovery even when the individual had no interest or stake in the litigation.[7]

The 1970 amendments to FRCP 26(b)(4) subdivided experts into four categories for purposes of discovery. The first category is experts a party expects to use as witnesses at trial; that is, testifying experts. The second category encompasses three types of nontestifying experts:

- Experts retained or specially employed in anticipation of litigation or preparation for trial, who are not expected to testify;
- Experts informally consulted in preparation for trial, but not formally retained; and
- Experts whose information was not acquired in preparation for trial; that is, in-house experts, percipient experts, and research scholars.

These categories retain their relevance even after the 1993 amendment, and each is addressed in turn below.

Testifying Experts

Mandatory Disclosure Under FRCP 26

Identity of Testifying Experts

Under the current FRCP 26, parties are *required* to disclose to other parties the identity of any expert witnesses to be used at trial to present evidence under FRE 702, 703, or 705.[8] The timing of the disclosure is set by court order or stipulation of the parties. Absent such order or stipulation, the disclosure must be made at least ninety days before trial or the date the case is to be ready for trial. If the expert testimony is intended only for the purpose of contradicting or rebutting evidence offered by another party on the same subject, the disclosure must be made within thirty days after the disclosure made by the other party.[9]

Written Report

Disclosure of a witness who has been "retained or specially employed to provide expert testimony in the case or one whose duties as the party's employee regularly involve giving expert testimony" must include a written report prepared and signed by the witness.[10] The report required by FRCP 26(a)(2)(B) must contain:

(i) a complete statement of all opinions the witness will express and the basis and reasons for them;

(ii) the data or other information considered by the witness in forming them;

(iii) any exhibits that will be used to summarize or support them;

(iv) the witness's qualifications, including a list of all publications authored in the previous 10 years;

(v) a list of all other cases in which, during the previous four years, the witness testified as an expert at trial or by deposition; and

(vi) a statement of the compensation to be paid for the study and testimony in the case.[11]

FRCP 26(b)(5)(A) requires a party to notify other parties if material subject to disclosure is being withheld based on a claim of privilege or work-product protection. The party must describe the nature of the documents, communications, or things not produced or disclosed in a manner that, without revealing information itself privileged or protected, will enable other parties to assess the applicability of the privilege or protection.

Depositions

Under FRCP 26, a party is entitled to depose any expert who has been identified as one who will offer his or her opinions at trial. The deposition is to take place after the required report disclosing the expert's opinions has been provided.[12] According to the Advisory Committee's Note on the 1993 amendments to the rule, "Since depositions of experts required to prepare a written report may be taken only after the report has been served, the length of the depositions of [those] experts should be reduced, and in many cases the report may eliminate the need for a deposition."[13] Because experts are not parties, technically they need to be subpoenaed.[14] In practice, however, experts are almost always made available for deposition on a reciprocal basis without the necessity for a subpoena.

Duty to Supplement

FRCP 26 also contains a duty to supplement that is broader in scope than under the previous rules. Under FRCP 26(e)(1), a party has the duty to supplement or correct the expert's report and deposition responses " (A) in a timely manner if the party learns that in some material respect the disclosure or response is incomplete or incorrect, and if the additional or corrective information has not otherwise been made known to the other parties during the discovery process or in writing; or (B) as ordered by the court."[15] Such supplemental disclosures are to be made at least thirty days before trial.

Nontestifying Experts

The mandatory disclosure requirements of the 1993 amendments do not affect practice concerning nontestifying experts. Discovery practices regarding such experts, therefore, follow the practice preceding the 1993 amendments. The following categories of nontestifying experts will be discussed in this section: (1) retained or specially employed experts, (2) informally consulted but not retained experts, and (3) experts whose information was not acquired in preparation for trial, such as in-house experts, percipient experts, and research scholars.

509

Retained or Specially Employed Experts

Discoverable on Showing of Exceptional Circumstances

A separate procedure exists for discovering the identity and learning the opinions of experts who have been retained or specially employed but who are not expected to be called as witnesses at trial. Traditionally, facts known or opinions held by such experts are discoverable only on a showing of exceptional circumstances; that is, a showing that it is impracticable for the party seeking discovery to obtain facts or opinions on the same subject by other means.[16]

Nothing in the former rules or the accompanying advisory committee's note explained precisely what constitutes "exceptional circumstances." Professor Albert Sacks, a reporter to the committee, has suggested that such circumstances include those in which one party has had the opportunity to conduct experiments or tests concerning an item or piece of equipment that is no longer available, or in which the number of experts in a field is small and those available have already been retained by other parties in the case.[17]

The courts are divided over whether exceptional circumstances must be shown to discover the identity of a retained or specifically employed expert or only when a party seeks to discover facts known or opinions held by a retained or specially employed expert,[18] or whether exceptional circumstances must be shown to discover even the identity of such an expert.[19]

These conflicting lines of cases were considered by the Tenth Circuit Court of Appeals in *Ager v. Jane C. Stormont Hospital & Training School for Nurses.*[20] The court concluded, after carefully analyzing the Advisory Committee's note to FRCP 26, that exceptional circumstances must be demonstrated to ascertain either the identity of, or other collateral information concerning, a retained or specially employed expert who is not expected to be called as a witness at trial.[21]

Unfortunately, the *Ager* decision does not provide counsel with any guidance on how to learn enough about a retained or specially employed expert to establish that there are exceptional circumstances justifying revelation of his or her name and knowledge. This information can be obtained, however, through interrogatories such as the following:

1. Have you retained or specially employed any experts in anticipation of litigation whom you do not expect to call at trial?

510

2. If yes, please describe the types of experts retained (in other words, their fields of expertise) and the nature of the services that they performed in anticipation of litigation or preparation for trial.

Interrogatories drafted in this manner avoid the *Ager* court prohibition against seeking the specially retained expert's identity without a showing of exceptional circumstances. Such interrogatories also avoid offending the prohibition against seeking facts known or opinions held by a specially retained expert absent a showing of exceptional circumstances.[22]

What Constitutes "Exceptional Circumstances"?

Most courts have interpreted the "exceptional circumstances" requirement as meaning an inability to obtain equivalent information from other sources.[23]

In particular, cost alone has generally been found insufficient to satisfy the requirement. For example, in *Shell Oil Refinery*,[24] the plaintiffs' expert opined that it would cost from $230,000 to $315,000 to duplicate tests performed by Shell employees, who the court concluded were retained or specially employed in preparation for trial. The court held that because the plaintiffs were capable of duplicating those tests, cost alone did not constitute exceptional circumstances.

In *Coates v. AC&S, Inc.*,[25] the court ruled that exceptional circumstances were present even though both the plaintiff and the defendants had been provided with tissue samples from the plaintiff's decedent. Both sides had sent the samples to multiple experts in an effort to ascertain whether the death was due, as the plaintiff alleged, to mesothelioma. The court ordered the parties to disclose the identity of all doctors to whom the samples had been sent, regardless of whether the doctors would be called as witnesses at trial. The court justified this order as being needed to prevent "shopping" of the samples, and on the ground that examination of tissue samples from a deceased person was sufficiently analogous to an independent medical examination to entitle all parties to the type of discovery permitted in the independent medical examination arena.[26]

The defendants protested that sending samples to more than one doctor was reflective not of "shopping" but of the difficulty of rendering a definitive diagnosis of mesothelioma. The court rejected this argument, stating, "The reality for the situation is that if a number of other experts have been consulted herein, but who could not make a definitive diagnosis, and these experts are not called as witnesses, then the jury could be misled regarding the truth of plaintiff's condition."[27] The court failed to explain how this differs from any other situation in which a party has consulted multiple experts before finding one who would offer an opinion favorable to that party's position. It is, in short, difficult to reconcile the *Coates* decision with philosophy underlying the work-product rule.

In *Pearl Brewing Co. v. Joseph Schlitz Brewing Co.*,[28] the plaintiff's experts, who were not expected to testify at trial, had created a complicated computer program concerning beer marketing. Another plaintiff's expert, who was expected to be called at trial, based his conclusions on this program. The defendant protested that its expert would be unable to understand the program without an explanation of certain undefined shorthand codes. The court granted discovery from the nontestifying experts, but only for the code explanations, emphasizing that the defendant was not trying to use the plaintiff's efforts to establish its own case but was instead attempting only to expedite analysis of the proffered testimony of the plaintiff's experts.

Informally Consulted Experts

A separate category of nontestifying experts includes those informally consulted in preparation for trial but not retained or specially employed.

Neither the identities nor the opinions of informally consulted experts are discoverable, even if exceptional circumstances exist.[29] Relying on *Ager*, the presiding United States Magistrate Judge *in Kuster v. Harner*[30] explained that the restriction on discovery of nontestifying experts constitutes a specific limitation on the general rule of discovery found in the former FRCP 26(b)(1). As a result, the judge denied a motion to compel a response to an interrogatory seeking the identity of all persons consulted or retained in anticipation of litigation or preparation for trial who were not expected to be called as trial witnesses.[31]

Based on *Ager*, the task confronting an opposing party is to confirm whether an expert who is purportedly of the informally consulted variety does, in fact, fall within that category. The decision in *Ager* enumerated the following factors that should be considered in determining whether a given expert was informally consulted, or retained or specially employed:

1. The manner in which the consultation was initiated;
2. The nature, type, and extent of information or material provided to, or reviewed by, the expert in connection with his or her review;
3. The duration and intensity of the consultative relationship; and
4. The terms of the consultation, if any (for example, payment or confidentiality of test data).

Counsel should be able to discover this information through variations of the interrogatories suggested above, such as:

1. Have you had any contact of any sort with any experts other than those whom you have identified as potential trial witnesses or described in response to questions (1) and (2) concerning retained or specially employed experts?[32]
2. If your answer to the preceding interrogatory is in the affirmative, please state separately, for each such expert, the following:
   - The manner in which consultation was initiated;
   - The precise nature, type, and extent of information or material provided to the expert in connection with his or her review;
   - The precise nature, type, and extent of material, if any, reviewed by the expert in reaching an opinion;
   - The duration of the consultative relationship, including, but not limited to, the date of the first contact with the expert, the date of the last (or most recent) contact, the total number of contacts, and the total number of hours expended by the expert on the matter; and
   - The terms of the consultation, including, but not limited to, terms of payment; amount of payment, if any; confidentiality of test data or opinions reached by the expert; and the plans, if any, for the expert to render any future services.

The In-House Expert

The distinction among the categories of nontestifying experts becomes blurred when an expert, who has been employed or has served as a consultant for one of the parties and has acquired a certain amount of expertise as a consequence of that employment, acquires additional expertise as a nontestifying consultant who assists in the preparation of a lawsuit.

513

The cases that have dealt with this problem have permitted discovery when a party's "in-house" expert had investigated a matter as part of his or her regular duties and not in anticipation of litigation.[33] Applying a similar test, the court in *Grinnell Corp. v. Hackett*[34] permitted discovery concerning a master's degree thesis that had been written by an in-house expert for one of the parties. On the other hand, in *USM Corp. v. American Aerosols, Inc.*,[35] the court disallowed discovery for work done by an in-house expert who was not to testify at trial and who was merely consulted informally concerning a matter in litigation.

One district court judge has adopted a dramatically different rule. He found that an expert is someone who not only possesses expertise but is also in a position to testify "neutrally and not as a partisan." He then found that employees are necessarily partisans, can never be experts, and are, therefore, subject to discovery on the same basis as any other ordinary witness.[36]

Most courts that have addressed the question have concluded that "retained or specially employed" means "something more than simply the assignment of a current employee to a particular problem raised by current litigation."[37]

Additional criteria that tend to move an employee into the retained or specially employed category—with the potential for discovery—include having the employee's work directed by lawyers or by the legal department, having the employee report only to the legal department or outside counsel, and having the employee's written report directed only to the legal department or outside counsel. On the other hand, the fact that the employee did not receive any additional compensation for the particular work is generally nondeterminative. Finally, the mere fact that the employee's work is used not only to defend a lawsuit but also to improve the company's products or operations does not, without more, preclude an employee from falling within the retained or specially employed category.[38]

In *Marine Petroleum Co. v. Champlin Petroleum* Co.,[39] the court found that the expert in question had been operating as a general consultant and was subject to discovery up to the point when the employer received an "issue letter" from the Federal Energy Administration, advising that the company might be in violation of petroleum price regulations. The court found that from that point on, the expert was a specially employed expert and his work was not discoverable.

In *Inspiration Consolidated Copper Co. v. Lumbermen's Mutual Casualty Co.,*[40] the court was confronted with the task of determining the discoverability of opinions held by an accountant who had performed three separate functions: (1) regular auditor for one of the parties; (2) consultant for one aspect of a complex, interrelated case; and (3) trial witness concerning another aspect of the dispute.

The parties conceded that the information acquired in the third category was discoverable. The court held that the second category of information fell within general work-product protection and was discoverable only on a showing of exceptional circumstances. The first category was found not to enjoy any work-product protection whatsoever and was subject only to the relevancy standards that govern discovery generally.[41]

An even more complex separation task arose in two personal injury cases, in which the same expert demonstrated a remarkable penchant for switching sides. In *Barkwell v. Sturm Ruger Co.,*[42] the plaintiff claimed that there were defects in the safety of a gun manufactured by the defendant. The defendant hired a consultant who had testified for the plaintiff's lawyer in previous gun safety defect cases. When the plaintiff attempted to notice the deposition of his former expert, the defendant objected, explaining that it had no intention of calling the expert as a witness at trial and that the plaintiff had failed to demonstrate "exceptional circumstances" that would justify deposing the expert in his role as consultant.[43]

The court had little difficulty in finding that the plaintiff was not entitled to depose the expert concerning information he had developed as a consultant in the present case. The more troublesome question was whether the expert could be deposed concerning the opinions formed or facts learned while employed by the plaintiff's counsel in connection with previous cases. Although this information had been acquired in anticipation of litigation, the court held that the work-product rule was intended only to prevent a party from taking advantage of the efforts of an adversary, and therefore did not apply to opinions held or facts learned in connection with other litigation. Hence, the court ruled that the expert could be questioned concerning the expertise he developed while working with the plaintiff's counsel on earlier cases.[44]

This same expert surfaced again in *Sullivan v. Sturm, Ruger & Co., Inc.,*[45] in which counsel for the plaintiff sought to depose him. The defendant objected and a motion to compel by the plaintiff ensued. In ruling on the motion, the judge noted that in 1976 the defendant had retained the expert as a consultant in the *Sullivan* case. Thereafter, the expert wrote to counsel for the plaintiff in the *Barkwell* case, discussed above, indicating that he desired to work for the plaintiff in that action. Subsequently, Sturm retained this expert for a second time as a consultant in the *Sullivan* matter. The defendant argued that because it employed this expert both before and after his employment by Barkwell, his employment by the defendant was entitled to protection from discovery. The judge was neither persuaded nor amused. He held that the expert could be deposed concerning facts known and opinions held by him before his employment by the defendant the second time. The court also found that defendant was responsible for making the expert available for deposition and made clear that sanctions would be imposed if the defendant persisted and contended that it had no control over him.[46]

Percipient-Witness Experts

Percipient witnesses who also are experts (for example, treating physicians) and who possess information that was not acquired in preparation for trial are not subject to the discovery available under FRCP 26(b)(4)(A). These witnesses can be deposed, however, like any other percipient witness. For example, defendant-physicians are allowed to testify concerning their medical opinions relating to their treatment of a plaintiff without providing the plaintiff's counsel with their written expert reports.[47]

If a percipient expert witness is not listed in response to an interrogatory seeking the identity of experts that the other party intends to call as witnesses, whether that expert can testify as an expert or only as a percipient witness depends on the facts. In *Baran v. Presbyterian University Hospital*,[48] for example, the court held that the defendant-physicians who treated the plaintiff fit into the category of "actors or viewers" and not the category of experts retained for purposes of litigation, and thus could testify about their medical opinions without providing information required by FRCP 26(b)(4)(A).[49] The district court also pointed out that the plaintiff had deposed both defendant-physicians before trial and could have asked them for their ultimate opinion concerning the malpractice issue.

When a party's expert is a percipient witness as an expert who has a relationship with the other side, the conflict may preclude the witness's testimony. For example, in *Miles v. Farrell*,[50] a doctor who treated the plaintiff both before and after being retained by one of the defendants was not permitted to testify either as an expert or a treating doctor because of the conflicting roles he had played in the case.

The Research Scholar

There are a growing number of disputes concerning the right to depose the "research scholar," an expert who has no percipient information concerning the case and who has no desire to work for any of the parties, but who has relevant knowledge or expertise gained only through research or otherwise. Compelling disclosure of subpoenaed information from a research scholar may be denied or restricted when compliance would force an unreasonable burden on the scholar from whom production is sought. The reported decisions discussed below have employed a balancing test, weighing the need and the relevance of the requested information against the harm or burden on the research scholar, in deciding whether to quash or modify a subpoena in this context.

In *Wright v. Jeep Corp.*,[51] one of the parties to a personal injury action arising out of a rollover accident attempted to subpoena a professor and research scientist who was the principal author of a report on rollover accidents. The professor had no firsthand knowledge of the case and had not been retained as an expert by either side. He objected to the subpoena on numerous grounds: the First Amendment protects him, as a researcher and writer, from having to testify against his will; a professor can claim academic privilege; the subpoena sought privileged and confidential documents; testifying would be burdensome; and forcing him to testify would have a chilling effect on future research.[52]

Though expressing sympathy for the professor's plight, the court held that "[t]he solution is not to cover up the information or its data . . . but to use the tools available to lessen the burden and to permit the information to become available,"[53] and to ensure that the professor is properly compensated. The court specifically found that compelling the professor to testify did not violate any First Amendment rights and would not tend to chill scientific research.[54]

In *Dow Chemical Co. v. Allen*,[55] the government threatened Dow with cancelling its right to manufacture herbicide, based on the government's reaction to studies published by the University of Wisconsin finding animal toxicity in such herbicides. Dow sought copies of all notes, reports, working papers, and raw data relevant to the university's research, arguing such materials were necessary to evaluate whether earlier completed studies were accurate and whether proper protocol and methodology were followed.

The university argued that disclosure of such information would be unduly burdensome with respect to both the present state of the study and its future efficacy as a medical research project. Specifically, the university argued that dissemination of the data into the public domain would invalidate the usefulness of such studies as a basis for further scientific research and papers; that years of research effort, professional reputations, and credibility would be lost by such forced disclosure; and that the capacity of an academic institution to be free from unwarranted intrusion disclosure would jeopardize, resulting in the stifling of academic freedom.

In evaluating the competing interests, the district court found that the hardship such disclosure would place on the university outweighed the need for such information. In so deciding, the court considered the issue raised by Dow in support of disclosure: first, whether Dow had sufficient access to enough relevant data that if confronted with adverse material at trial, it could test the validity of the studies; and second, whether the data were essential to raise a negative inference that if undisclosed information revealed changes in protocol, Dow could argue that earlier studies were flawed or erroneous.

Evaluating both factors, the appellate court affirmed the lower court's determination that the plaintiff had failed to show the requisite necessity. Because the undisclosed research that had been requested would not be relied upon at trial, the plaintiff's alleged need for this material was unwarranted.

In *In re Snyder*,[56] the same research scientist who had been subpoenaed in *Wright* was again subpoenaed for deposition and production of data that led to his rollover report. As in *Wright*, the expert was not a party or otherwise retained as an expert. The court in *Snyder* agreed with *Wright* that there is no general academic privilege that protects an expert from being either subpoenaed to testify or required to produce documents in his or her possession. Nevertheless, the court found that the former FRCP authorized issuance of a protective order to quash the subpoena if it was unduly burdensome. The court quashed the subpoena, finding it to be unduly burdensome because of the breadth of the documentation that it sought.

The *Snyder* court was equally concerned about the potential chilling effect on scientific research of the indiscriminate issuance of subpoenas to involuntary, nonparty expert witnesses to testify and produce documents in litigation. The court found that the potential for harassment through the discovery process might deter members of the public from studying defects in products or practices. The court thus recommended that members of both the legal and research communities propose amendments that would increase certainty in the scope of discovery from involuntary expert witnesses.

The Second Circuit addressed the same subject in a thoughtful opinion in *Kaufman v. Edelstein*,[57] holding that the factors to be considered in determining whether an unwilling expert should be compelled to testify include

1. The extent to which the expert is being called because of his or her knowledge of facts relevant to the case rather than to give opinion testimony;
2. The extent to which the testimony sought pertains to a previously formed and expressed opinion or to a new one;
3. The uniqueness of the witness's knowledge;
4. The extent to which the party seeking the testimony is unable to obtain a comparable witness willing to testify; and
5. The extent of the oppression the witness will suffer by being required to testify.

The Second Circuit was again confronted with the research scientist's duties in *Mount Sinai School of Medicine v. American Tobacco Co.*[58] That case arose out of a number of product liability suits in which the plaintiffs alleged that their decedents had died from a combination of cigarette smoking and exposure to asbestos. Although no one from Mount Sinai was expected to testify as an expert in any of those cases, the plaintiffs planned to present expert witnesses who would rely on seminal studies that had been done by members of the Mount Sinai staff.

Initially, the tobacco company defendants served a sweeping subpoena duces tecum on Mount Sinai, in a case that was pending in the New York State court system. Mount Sinai successfully moved to quash.[59] The tobacco companies then served a somewhat narrower subpoena on Mount Sinai in connection with cases pending in federal court in Louisiana and Pennsylvania. Mount Sinai filed a motion to quash in the district court in New York, alleging that (1) the subpoenas were barred by res judicata and collateral estoppel; (2) under New York law there is an absolute privilege that applies to a scholar's work; and (3) even if there is no absolute privilege, researchers enjoy a qualified privilege, and the tobacco companies failed to demonstrate that their interest outweighed those of the researchers. Mount Sinai moved, in the alternative, for a protective order allowing the subpoenaed documents to be redacted to eliminate potential matters of privacy.

The district court denied the motion to quash but issued a protective order designed to ensure the privacy of the individuals who participated in the studies. On appeal, the Second Circuit affirmed, emphasizing that because the subpoenaed matters consisted largely of computer tapes and other support documentation, the burden to produce them was less. In addition, the parties had agreed that when necessary to protect the anonymity of study participants, pertinent identifying information could be redacted. The court also noted that the tobacco companies were not seeking to compel any member of the Mount Sinai staff to testify or prepare a report.

Against that background, the court considered, and rejected, each of Mount Sinai's specific objections:

- First, because the subpoena in the federal-court action was narrower than the one that had been quashed in the state-court action, the court found that the state court ruling did not have any preclusive effect.
- Second, the court found that there was no absolute privilege covering production of the requested documents. The decision indicates that New York law might have resulted in a different ruling had the tobacco companies sought to compel any of the Mount Sinai staff to testify.
- Third, the court acknowledged that the Seventh Circuit recognizes a qualified scholar's privilege, but found no indication that New York had done so. Further, the court found that even if the existence of such a qualified privilege were assumed, its underlying basis is to eliminate the possibility that research results discovered before publication would be vulnerable to preemptive or predatory publication by others. Because, the results of the materials in question had all been published years before, this consideration was absent.

The Second Circuit did, however, recognize the need for an appropriate protective order to protect the confidentiality of the studies' participants.

In *Bluitt v. R.J. Reynolds Tobacco Co.*,[60] a district court upheld a magistrate judge's decision to quash a subpoena issued by tobacco manufacturers. The discovery sought all raw data underlying a study published by a university relating tobacco smoke to cancer in women. The university was neither a party to the case nor retained by either side. It sought to quash the subpoena on the basis that some of the underlying information sought was privileged, confidential, and/or proprietary under Louisiana state law.

In upholding the decision to quash the subpoena, the district court found the following: (1) the information the university sought to withhold was confidential,[61] and (2) the tobacco company failed to show the requisite need for the information to overcome the confidentiality of the documents. In support of the second finding, the court concluded that all the standard criteria by which scientific research normally is evaluated had been fully presented and disclosed. Moreover, the court noted that although in *Wright* there was a "high probability"[62] that the results of the author's research would be used in the instant case, there were twelve other environmental tobacco smoke lung-cancer studies available to the tobacco manufacturers. The court did not find it necessary to reach the issue of whether the university's documents were protected by an absolute privilege.

Privileges Relating to Expert Witnesses

If you do not understand the scope of the attorney-client privilege and the work-product rule as they relate to communications with experts, you may unwittingly lose their protections. As a general rule, communications between counsel and their experts, unlike communications between counsel and their clients, are *not* protected by the attorney-client privilege—because the relationship does not satisfy the "client" prerequisite and the communication may not satisfy the "confidential communication" prerequisite. Similarly, the work-product privilege, which protects counsel's mental impressions and conclusions prepared in anticipation of litigation, does not, in all circumstances, protect an expert's mental impressions and conclusions prepared in anticipation of litigation. These privileges as they apply to communications with experts are discussed next.[63]

Expert Attorney-Client Privilege and the In-House Expert

As noted above, communications between lawyers and their experts are generally not protected by the attorney-client privilege. A special issue arises, however, when the expert is an employee of a corporate client. Under such circumstances, is the communication from the employee-expert protected under the attorney-client privilege?

In *Upjohn Co. v. United States*,[64] the Supreme Court refused to "lay down a broad rule or series of rules to govern all conceivable future questions in this area," but did endorse a subject-matter approach to the issue of whether such communications are privileged. The Court considered the subject matter about which counsel's advice was sought by the corporation and whether the communication was made by an employee in the performance of his or her duties of employment.

In *Upjohn*, the Court rejected the "control group" test, under which the ability of the corporate employee to control decision making in the area in which the lawyer was advising the corporation was the key. The court noted that lower-echelon employees frequently possess information that counsel needs, and it reasoned that the purpose of the privilege can therefore be achieved only if relevant communications by such employees are protected. The court reasoned that, in fact, the lawyer's advice will frequently be more significant to noncontrol-group members than to those who officially sanction the advice, and the control-group test makes it more difficult to convey full and frank legal advice to the employees who will put into effect the client corporation's policy. After analyzing the varying, and frequently inconsistent, results that courts have reached in trying to determine control-group membership, the Court also rejected the control-group test because it lacks the degree of certainty necessary if the privilege is to function effectively.[65] Thus, under *Upjohn*, an employee-expert's communication may be privileged, depending upon the subject matter of the communication.

Expert Witnesses and the Work-Product Rule

In dealing with experts, you must be aware that what you transmit to your expert may be the subject of attempted discovery and that the results of such attempts may be successful. Otherwise, you may find the other side using your own work product to its advantage.

The mental impressions, conclusions, opinions, or legal theories of any lawyer or other representative of a party concerning litigation clearly are protected, unless shared with third parties, including experts.[66] All other work product is only conditionally protected; it is discoverable on a showing that the party seeking discovery has substantial need of the materials in preparation for that party's case and is unable, without undue hardship, to obtain the substantial equivalent of the materials by other means.[67]

Work-Product Rule and Categories of Experts

As discussed above, there are four types of expert witnesses recognized under the FRCP, and separate work-product considerations apply to each type. There is no specific litmus test for determining the discoverability of conditionally protected materials, and in each situation, counsel must examine case law to determine how the work-product rule has been applied.[68]

Trial Witnesses

A common question in determining whether conditionally protected materials are discoverable concerns the status accorded the work product that is created before the expert is designated as a trial witness. Generally, work done by an expert when acting as a consultant or as a percipient witness becomes discoverable when the witness is designated as a testifying expert.[69] And work done by an expert once that expert is designated as a trial witness is not protected.

Nonwitness Experts Retained or Specially Employed

Although a nontestifying consultant's opinion generally is not discoverable, you should keep in mind that if a consultant renders an opinion and shares that opinion with an expert who testifies at trial, and if the trial expert concedes that he or she relied in part on the consultant's report, the consultant's report and opinion may then become subject to cross-examination under FRE 703 and 705.[70]

Informally Consulted Experts

Neither the identities nor the opinions of informally consulted experts are discoverable, even if exceptional circumstances exist.[71]

Percipient Experts

Experts whose information was not acquired in preparation for trial are the federal equivalent of percipient experts under state practice. Their knowledge does not constitute work product, and they can be either contacted informally or deposed like any other third-party witness under FRCP 30.

Duration and Extent of Work-Product Protection

The reported federal decisions are split three ways on how long the work protection applies to materials used by experts. The three positions may be summarized as follows:

- At one extreme are the cases such as *In re Murphy*[72] and *Duplan Corp. v. Moulinage et Retorderie de Chavanoz*,[73] finding perpetual protection of work product.
- At the opposite extreme are cases holding that work product is protected only during, and in connection with, the case in which the protected work product was prepared.[74]
- A third, intermediate position is that work-product protection applies only in the case for which the material was prepared or in a second, closely related case.[75]

In *Federal Trade Commission v. Grolier, Inc.*,[76] the Supreme Court adopted the first approach and held that attorney work-product protection applied under FRCP 26(b)(3)(A), even though the litigation had terminated six years earlier and there was no related litigation involved. The decision in *Grolier*, however, also rested independently on an interpretation of Exemption 5 of the Freedom of Information Act,[77] which may limit the applicability of the ruling.[78]

Waiver of Work-Product Protection

One line of cases holds that the transmission of documents to an expert, without more, does not waive work-product protection and does not render discoverable portions of documents containing the most highly protected work product: a lawyer's mental impressions, conclusions, opinions, and legal theories.[79] Facts contained in such transmissions, however, may be discoverable on a showing under FRCP 26(b)(3)(A)(ii) of substantial need and unavailability from other sources without undue hardship.

Other cases have taken the position that anything that is transmitted to an expert who will actually testify at trial could conceivably have influenced the expert's opinion and, therefore, is discoverable.[80] For example, *Bogosian v. Gulf Oil Corp.*[81] was rejected, albeit with "trepidation," in *Intermedics, Inc. v. Ventritex, Inc.*, when the court held that a lawyer's work product disclosed to an expert who will testify at trial is discoverable, unless an extraordinary showing of unfairness is made that goes well beyond interests generally protected by the work-product doctrine.[82] One of the primary concerns that the court in *Intermedics* had with *Bogosian* was the threat that the lawyer's communications with his own expert could affect the independence of the expert's thinking. The court found that communications from a lawyer could not only influence the expert's opinion, but could also furnish the expert with the opinion itself; because such communications would reflect directly on the credibility and reliability of the expert, they were held to be discoverable.[83]

In a federal case, the court suggested the lawyer opposing a claim of waiver of work-product protection for material given to an expert should ask the judge to conduct an in camera inspection if the transmissions contain a combination of lawyer opinion, work product, and facts.[84] In *National Steel Products Co. v. Superior Court*,[85] a California state court outlined a three-step process by which a judge could conduct an in camera inspection to rule on a claim of work-product privilege. First, the judge determines if the report reflects lawyer impressions, opinions, conclusions, legal research, or theories. Second, the judge determines whether the material is advisory. If the material is advisory, it is protected by the conditional work-product privilege; if it is not advisory, the material is discoverable. Third, if portions of the material are not privileged, the judge should determine whether other good cause for discovery outweighs the policy underlying a conditional work-product privilege.[86]

Scientific Expert Testimony

Pre-*Daubert* Standard

For many years, the test used by federal courts to determine the reliability of scientific testimony proffered at trial was that established in the 1923 seminal case of *Frye v. United States*.[87] In *Frye*, a district court held that lie-detector results[88] were inadmissible in a criminal action:

> Just when a scientific principle or discovery crosses the line between the experimental and demonstrable stages is difficult to define. Somewhere in this twilight zone the evidential force of the principle must be recognized, and while courts will go a long way in admitting expert testimony deduced from a well recognized scientific principal or discovery, the thing from which the deduction is made must be sufficiently

established to have gained general acceptance in the particular field in which it belongs.[89]

Under *Frye*, a party was precluded from offering scientific expert testimony unless it could show that the expert had relied on scientific techniques that had gained "general acceptance" in the particular field in which the technique was offered.[90] This requisite showing of general acceptance for purposes of reliability was based on a presumption that courts were ill-equipped to make such determinations.[91] Accordingly, courts were needed to gauge expert "consensus" in order to rule on whether the proffered evidence was sound and reliable; this practice would often lead to the unfortunate result that relevant evidence was excluded.[92] The *Frye* test, or some modified version thereof, remains in force in various state jurisdictions.

The *Daubert* Standard

In *Daubert v. Merrell Dow Pharmaceuticals, Inc.*,[93] the U.S. Supreme Court in 1993 addressed the question of whether a petitioner's unpublished recalculations of previously published scientific data met the acceptable standard of reliability for admissible evidence. The Supreme Court determined that, in fact, the role of the trial court was not to decide whether the proffered scientific testimony or the information on which it is based had acquired "general acceptance" in the scientific community. Instead, the trial judge faced with a proffer of scientific expert testimony must decide whether it is relevant and reliable.[94]

The proffered evidence is relevant and reliable under *Daubert* if the court determines that it is "scientific knowledge" (reliable) that will "assist the trier of fact to understand the evidence or to determine a fact in issue" (relevant).[95] In order to qualify as scientific knowledge as opposed to "junk science," an inference or assertion must be derived by the scientific method.[96] The ultimate inquiry under the holding of *Daubert* is thus not whether the expert's conclusions are correct, but whether his or her methodology is sound.[97]

The *Daubert* court identified four factors for determining whether a particular inference, theory, or technique is scientific knowledge; that is, whether it is reliable:

1. Whether it can be and has been tested;
2. Whether it has been subjected to peer review and publication;

3. Its known or potential rate of error; and

4. Whether the theory or technique has acquired "general acceptance," because, although that standard is not controlling, it is still an important factor in determining admissibility, particularly if it has been satisfied.[98]

The *Daubert* standard quickly came to be first clarified and then expanded. In *General Electric Co. v. Joiner*,[99] the Supreme Court held that because it was principally in the trial court's domain to exclude unreliable expert testimony, the proper standard of review of a trial court's *Daubert* rulings was merely abuse of discretion. In *Kumho Tire Co. v. Carmichael*,[100] the Supreme Court further expanded the scope of the trial court's "gatekeeping function" outlined in *Daubert* to apply not only to testimony from scientific experts, but also from technical and other specialized experts as well. Together the *"Daubert* Trilogy"—*Daubert, Joiner*, and *Kumho Tire*—and its progeny compose the modern federal standard for admissibility of expert testimony.

In 2000, FRE 702 was amended to reflect the *Daubert* standard, with its focus on reliability:

If scientific, technical, or other specialized knowledge will assist the trier of fact to understand the evidence or to determine a fact in issue, a witness qualified as an expert by knowledge, skill, experience, training, or education, may testify thereto in the form of an opinion or otherwise, if (1) the testimony is based upon sufficient facts or data, (2) the testimony is the product of reliable principles and methods, and (3) the witness has applied the principles and methods reliably to the facts of the case.[101]

In assessing the admissibility of proffered scientific testimony, attorneys should be mindful of other potentially applicable provisions as well, such as FRE 703 (expert opinions may be based on otherwise inadmissible hearsay if based on facts or data of a type reasonably relied on by experts in the field), FRE 706 (trial judge may appoint an expert of the court's own choosing), and FRE 403 (relevant evidence may be excluded if its probative value is outweighed by danger of unfair prejudice, confusion, or misleading jury).[102]

Familiarity with the *Daubert* factors is, therefore, essential to planning what questions are appropriate to ask of an expert at a deposition.

Preparing One's Own Expert for Deposition

The key to a successful deposition of your client's expert is careful preparation. This includes anticipation of the types of questions and the areas of inquiry the expert is likely to encounter. The carefully prepared expert should be able to function at the deposition with only minimal assistance from the lawyer for the party who retained the expert. An expert who is not carefully prepared will likely perform inadequately at the deposition, regardless of how actively you attempt to interject.

The task of preparing your own expert is simplified immeasurably by remembering that the deposition's primary purpose is to discover *all* the expert's opinions and *all* the bases for those opinions.[103]

Need for Preparation

Preparing experts to testify should begin during the auditioning process. By the time you are required to designate expert witnesses, you should have determined whether the selected experts have jury appeal, respond to instructions, can explain their areas of expertise clearly to the jury, and can stand up well to cross-examination.[104]

Under FRCP 26(b)(4)(A), experts who are expected to be witnesses are subject to deposition before trial. The deposition of an expert who is required by the disclosure provisions of FRCP 26(a)(2)(B) to provide a written report, however, may not be taken until the report has been served.[105] Thus, under FRCP 26, lawyers are forced to begin preparation of their experts well before trial.[106]

When scheduling a deposition preparation session, tell the expert what work you expect the expert to have completed by the time you meet. For example, before the preparation session, you will probably want the expert to (1) have read all materials counsel has sent;[107] (2) have completed the tests, experiments, and other work that you have requested; and (3) have thought through all important aspects of the case, particularly possible questions from the opposition and how to respond to them.

You should divide the preparation process for your own experts into procedural and substantive aspects. Prepare checklists for each of these two areas (or use the checklists below), and then check off items as they are accomplished. This not only simplifies preparation of the expert, but also reduces the risk of overlooking an important aspect of preparation. Such checklists provide a valuable tool for testimony, both during the deposition and at the actual trial. Appropriate checklists may include the following items:

Procedural Checklist

- Location of deposition or trial
- What to wear
- Purpose of expert's testimony at deposition or trial
- Deposition and trial procedures; for example, where to sit, questions by judge or jurors
- Objections, how to respond, and areas about which you recommend the expert not testify at deposition or trial
- The parties and lawyers who will be there, and their interests in the litigation
- Handling hypothetical questions
- Habits and idiosyncrasies of other lawyers who will be at deposition or trial
- How to avoid arguments with other counsel

Substantive Checklist

- Compensation
- Expert's qualifications
- Nature of expert's assignment
- Materials consulted or relied upon; every document that expert should review before testifying
- Attorney-client or work-product problems
- Expert's file contents; what to bring to deposition or trial and what not to bring
- Work already performed on case and any work still to be performed
- Opinions reached and bases for them
- Inconsistencies and how explained
- Anticipated scope of opposing counsel's cross-examination of expert
- Review of how expert will explain technical concepts and language
- Review of points that you want the expert to make and that will be established in whole or in part through the expert's direct examination at trial
- Expert's view of opposing experts, what their testimony will probably be at deposition or trial, and the strengths and weaknesses of their testimony

- Expert's education of you about technical concepts about which you are unclear
- If desired, jury consultant session with expert to improve expert's presentation[108]

Explaining Deposition Procedures to an Expert

Purposes of a Deposition

Both experienced and inexperienced counsel often overlook the possibility that the expert may not be fully conversant with the nature and purposes of a deposition.[109] Even with experienced experts, you should explain how the expert's testimony fits into the overall framework of the particular case and exactly what is expected of the expert at the deposition.

You must make clear to the expert whether you want to use the deposition as a vehicle for persuading the other side of the correctness of your position in the hope that the case can be settled before trial, or whether you want to reveal as little about the case as possible during the deposition so that your position is a surprise at the time of trial.

If you follow the former approach, the expert should be encouraged to adopt an advocate's stance; that is, fully explain answers, volunteer testimony that may not be specifically called for by the opponent's questions, and, in general, try to "sell" your side of the case at every available opportunity. If the latter approach is followed, you should remind the expert to respond only to the particular questions asked; to use "yes" or "no" answers whenever possible; to resist the temptation to elaborate on answers; and, in general, to avoid assisting opposing counsel with insights or observations not directly called for by the examiner's queries.

Deposition Procedures

When dealing with experts who are relatively inexperienced with testifying, your deposition preparation should include the same information that is covered with lay witnesses. You should familiarize the witness with deposition procedures, as well as the nature and purpose of a deposition, so that you and the expert approach the deposition with the same understanding. Those procedures include the following:

- The expert is under oath.
- The expert should be sure that he or she understands a question before answering it. The expert can ask for clarification if necessary.
- The expert should not talk at the same time as another person because the reporter cannot transcribe more than one person's words at a time.
- All parties may review the deposition transcript. Opposing counsel may comment on revisions to the transcript.

Objections

If the expert is not an experienced witness, you should explain the purpose of objections in lay language.[110] Explain that objections may be made to the form or the substance of questions, including, as discussed below, certain hypotheticals. In addition, explain that if an objection is made only to the form of the question, the expert will be required to answer.

The expert should be told to listen carefully to the objections because they frequently contain clues from you that indicate what the expert should do in responding to questions or that provide the expert with a basis for not answering questions. For example, if you object to a question as vague and ambiguous because it is indefinite about time, the expert should be encouraged to explain her inability to answer the question as phrased because of the vague time frame. You should tell the expert that when you raise your hand, it is a signal for the expert to listen to the forthcoming objection before attempting to respond.

Any areas in which you do not want the expert to answer questions should be discussed ahead of time, and the expert should be told to notify you before responding to a question when the answer would disclose such material. You should explain that you cannot instruct the expert not to answer a question, but that you should suggest (or advise) that the expert not answer, and the expert can follow this advice.[111]

Throughout the preparation session, remember that your communication with the expert will seldom be protected by the attorney-client privilege. Some communications may enjoy work-product protection, although this protection rarely survives the deposition stage of the case.[112]

Distinguishing Friend from Foe

The expert should be able to distinguish friend from foe, especially in multiple-plaintiff and multiple-defendant cases. He must know which lawyer represents which party and how each lawyer's interests coincide with, or differ from, those of the expert's employer. The expert must distinguish when to be wary and when not to frustrate the efforts of an ally. It is most important for you to acquaint the expert with potential questions and how they relate to the lawsuit.

The expert should be provided with, or shown, each party's FRCP 26(a)(2) disclosure statements (or responses to interrogatories concerning experts), so that the expert knows who are the opposing and allied experts. You should ask for the expert's view of the other experts. If your expert is friendly with, or has high regard for, an opposing expert, you should anticipate a question regarding that friendship or esteem, and you should help the expert determine how to disagree with the views of the friend, mentor, or idol.

Habits and Idiosyncrasies of Other Counsel

Lawyers employ various tactics in examining witnesses, ranging from charm (in hope of getting the witness to drop her guard) to abuse (in hope of intimidating the witness). You should prepare the expert witness for any tactics you know the opposition is likely to use. For example, through design or otherwise, lawyers frequently ask an expert a long list of questions that the expert knows nothing about, either because the questions have nothing to do with the case or because they concern areas that are unrelated to the expert's singular role in the case. During deposition preparation, experts should be counseled not to be embarrassed or disconcerted if they must repeatedly answer, "I do not know."

Avoiding Arguments with Other Counsel

Because expert witness depositions are concerned largely with opinion testimony, the risk of argument is greater than in the depositions of factual witnesses. The expert should be instructed to resist the temptation to argue with the other lawyers, particularly if the expert has an argumentative nature. Tell the expert that her credibility and ability to persuade may be undermined if she is perceived as an advocate. In addition, tell her that when tempers flare, she is more likely to blurt out a damaging or poorly conceived answer.

Identifying Nature of Assignment

The expert must understand, and should be able to articulate, her assignment in the case, preferably in twenty-five words or less. It is embarrassing when an expert at the deposition stage of a case cannot succinctly state what work she has performed on a file. Moreover, an expert who has a solid understanding of her assignment can better control the deposition, distinguish relevant from irrelevant questions, and avoid answering questions that do not relate directly to her assignment in the case.

In framing the expert's assignment, it is frequently helpful to look at relevant jury instructions for the elements that must be satisfied to prevail in the case, and then to select the particular elements that the expert will be relied on to establish or disprove. The expert will then know which questions call for information the expert has not been hired to address. In addition, knowing the scope of the assignment can be important as the case proceeds, for an expert who offers opinions at trial in an area not included in the expert witness's disclosure statement may create reversible error.[113]

The value of the expert knowing the scope of the assignment is well illustrated by the following example. In a products liability case involving a claim of defective manufacture (as opposed to defective design), the plaintiff may be required to prove that the product differed from the manufacturer's intended result or from other similar products. Neither the plaintiff nor the plaintiff's expert is obligated to redesign the product in a nondefective form or to conceive of an optimum product. It is sufficient, for example, if the plaintiff's expert has determined that a particular failed metal part has a greater number of voids or fissures than are contained in its nondefective counterparts. The expert who understands the limited nature of the assignment can deflect questions such as, "What is the minimum number of voids and fissures that you think a part of this kind should have to be nondefective?" by stating that he or she has not been called on to make such a determination, but has focused entirely on analyzing the differences between the failed part and its nondefective counterparts.

Another example: In multidefendant tort litigation, the individual defendants are not responsible for establishing how the accident occurred; rather, counsel for a particular defendant need only show that the accident was not caused by an act or omission by his client. Thus, when it is alleged that an automobile accident occurred because of excessive speed and inattention on the part of various drivers, as well as a malfunctioning traffic light, counsel for the defendant that manufactured or maintained the signal light need only show that the light was performing properly. The assignment of the expert for the manufacturer could thus be limited in scope to determining whether the signal light was properly functioning at the time of the accident. If the expert is then asked her opinion concerning the driving of some other defendant, the design of that traffic signal as contrasted with other traffic signals, or anything other than the expert's precise assignment, the expert can respond without hesitation that the question relates to areas that she has not been called on to consider.

File Contents

In state courts that do not require predeposition disclosures, during the deposition preparation session, you should ensure that the expert's entire file is assembled so that it can be produced at deposition, if required.

The expert should make a written notation in the file of any items that are temporarily unavailable because of size or that have been removed. In that way, the expert need not rely on her recollection when asked about the contents of the file at the deposition. Similarly, if the expert's file contains anything that you believe should not be produced because of privilege or other considerations, this material should be removed from the file and put in a safe place so there will be one less housekeeping detail to worry about during the actual deposition. But, as discussed above, keep in mind that any privileged work-product material provided to, and referred upon by, your expert is no longer protected and must be produced.

Compensation

The amount of compensation paid to the expert is almost certain to come up during deposition,[114] and experts should be prepared to deal with it. Federal courts generally agree that FRCP 26(a)(2)(B) requires disclosure of more than simply the expert's hourly rate, although there is no agreement on the threshold standard that must be met in order to compel disclosure of other information related to compensation.[115] If experts do not bring their time records to the preparation session, they should at least consult those records before testifying so that they can give a reasonably accurate estimate of the total amount of time spent on the case, a breakdown of how the time was spent, and an estimate of the total charges incurred. Experts who try to estimate hours worked and dollars billed may guess wrong and thus provide the opposition with a basis for cross-examination at trial, while experts who profess not to have such estimates may seem unprofessional or evasive.

Work Performed on Case, Opinions Reached, and Bases for Them

The expert should be prepared to delineate the substantive work he has performed on the case and the approximate amount of time spent on each activity.

When asked for his opinions, the expert should be prepared to give them precisely and with confidence. If a report has not already been prepared, which may be the case in state court proceedings, numerous or complex opinions should be written and made a part of the file so the expert can refer to them. The expert also should be able to recite the particular facts or other matters on which each opinion is based.

Inconsistencies

The expert should be prepared to deal with whether he has encountered anything that is either inconsistent or not fully consistent with the opinion reached. For example, if there is contradictory eyewitness testimony and the expert has adopted the testimony of one witness while excluding that of the other, the excluded testimony must be regarded as inconsistent and the expert should be prepared to justify the reasons for rejecting that testimony. If inconsistencies are numerous or if, during preparation, the expert has difficulty remembering inconsistencies, a written record should be made of them and incorporated in the file.

Hypothetical Questions

Although hypothetical questions are permissible both on direct and cross-examination of experts,[116] they are difficult to frame in a non-objectionable manner. Most hypothetical questions asked at a deposition omit one or more essential foundational elements, assume facts not in evidence, or are otherwise objectionable as to form.[117] Cautious counsel whose expert is being deposed will frequently object on foundational grounds to every hypothetical question. The witness should be alerted to this strategy before the deposition.

Hypothetical questions are used frequently to try to draw concessions from experts. Therefore, explain to the witness that you will object to incomplete hypotheticals or hypotheticals assuming facts not established during discovery.

An expert who answers an incomplete hypothetical, or one that the evidence does not support, typically will either be speculating or creating an avenue for potential impeachment. A proper objection, vigorously adhered to, either will get a better-framed question or will avoid the risk of an imprecise answer.

If you fail to object at the deposition to a hypothetical question that is defective because it assumes facts not in evidence, the objection may be waived. Therefore, before the deposition begins, advise your expert not to volunteer answers to these questions when you object.

Questions Outside Expert's Area of Expertise

Because the expert is not your client, you ordinarily do not have the right to instruct her not to answer a question.[118] But you can, and should, inform the expert that she is not obligated to answer questions—or guess or speculate—about matters outside her field of skill or expertise.

Questions Outside Expert's Designated Area of Expertise

An expert will frequently have expertise beyond that of her *designated* area of testimony. In addition, lawyers often use multiple experts with overlapping fields of expertise, electing to limit the intended testimony of each to avoid needless duplication or potential conflict. For a variety of tactical purposes (such as catching the expert unprepared, or creating a conflict between the testimony of the expert and another expert who has been designated to testify in that area), opposing counsel frequently ignore these limitations and attempt to depose the expert in areas outside the designated scope of intended testimony. In response to such questions you should argue that opposing counsel's proposed examination is in violation of the designated scope of expertise.

As noted above, a lawyer generally has no right to instruct an expert not to answer a question on any ground. There is, however, nothing to prohibit counsel from *advising* the expert that she should not feel obligated to respond to questions that are outside the designated area of testimony and to which the expert is unprepared to give a definite response. You should obtain the expert's agreement in advance that the expert will heed such advice. If the expert is uncomfortable with this, you should advise her of the area of expertise in which she has been disclosed and that tell her she has the right to confine her opinions to that area. If the expert remains uncomfortable with your directive, and her gratuitous testimony is likely to hurt your case, you should consider withdrawing the expert as a trial witness.

Preparing to Depose One's Own Expert

In preparing the expert for deposition, you should alert your witness that you may wish to conduct your own examination after your opponent finishes his questioning.

Examining one's own expert is relatively rare but should be considered if there is a substantial possibility that the expert will not be available to testify at trial. Examining one's own expert requires the same preparation that is needed for direct examination at trial.[119]

Remember to question the expert on her qualifications. This foundation will be necessary to permit the introduction of the deposition at trial; the trial court must be satisfied that the expert has the requisite qualifications to offer an opinion on the disputed issue.[120]

In addition, if you intend to offer your expert's deposition at trial, before beginning the deposition, think of all possible objections that may be made at trial. Use that information to help you elicit unobjectionable testimony from your own expert at the deposition.

Deposing the Opponent's Expert

Purpose of Expert's Deposition

To be sure, the expert may be discredited during the deposition, but that is generally not the deposition's primary purpose. The questioner's ultimate goal is usually not to impeach or impugn the expert to gain tactical advantage regarding the expert's credibility, but rather to focus on learning *everything* the expert thinks about the case, has been told or learned about it, and has done or plans to do in connection with it. By following the format outlined in this chapter, even the most inexperienced questioner can make sure that these objectives are accomplished.

How *Not* to Depose an Expert

All too many examiners begin an expert's deposition with no clear plan. Lacking any other organizational framework, they simply begin with the top paper in the expert's file (or the first line in the expert's report), ask the expert about that item, and then proceed through the balance of the file, item by item. Not only is this procedure time-consuming, but it does not ensure that the questioner has learned everything the expert thinks about the case and the basis for each conclusion the expert has reached. Using this approach, the questioner can come away from the deposition without a full and complete understanding of all of the work the expert has already performed and the precise basis for each of the expert's opinions. This approach also fails to establish whether the expert has any plans for doing further work and, if so, the nature of that work.[121]

Other questioners skip around haphazardly in an apparent effort to trick the expert with a nonsequential questioning technique. Although this method may reveal useful inconsistencies or contradictions in the witness's testimony, it also fails to fulfill the questioner's intention of learning everything about the expert's work on the case. Still other lawyers begin by asking for the expert's ultimate opinion and then become so confused or overwhelmed that they fail to inquire systematically into the factual or other evidentiary bases and underlying reasoning of each element of the opinion.

It may be helpful for the questioner to imagine himself as a psychiatrist and the expert witness as a patient. As with the psychiatrist, the questioner's goal is to get the patient to talk freely, with a minimum of interruption and interjection by the questioner. Unlike the approach used on cross-examination at trial—keeping the opposing expert tightly constrained and restricted to giving yes and no answers—the aim of most depositions is to get the expert to talk openly and give complete explanations without holding anything back.

How to Depose an Expert: Ten Subjects That Should Be Covered

Although there are exceptions, an expert ordinarily should be questioned about each of the following ten subjects, discussed in turn below.[122]

1. Education and Employment Background

Start with the expert's formal education, other training and experience, awards, employment history, and experience as a trial consultant and witness. Why? Because you need this information to determine whether the expert is qualified to testify, to avoid surprise at trial, and to evaluate whether different or more experts are needed to compete favorably with the opposition's expert.[123]

For example, in a case involving a handling problem with an automobile, the questioner can explore whether the expert has ever participated in competitive driving or racing, in addition to the expert's employment background. As another example, in a medical-malpractice action involving the general removal of a cataract, the questioner should find out how many cataract operations the witness has performed or assisted in and compare this information with the professional experience that the questioner's expert may be able to catalog for the jury.[124]

Background information can be elicited in succinct form by asking the expert, "Please state your educational background, starting at the high-school level." You should then ask whether the expert has had any other training (for example, correspondence courses or seminars) that bears in any way on the work performed or to be performed in the present case.

Next, ask questions about the expert's employment history in chronological order, beginning with the first full-time job and including details of any military experience. You should ask questions about part-time or temporary jobs because this information also may shed light on the expert's work on the present case. For example, if the case involves a claimed automobile defect, ask whether the expert has ever worked for an automobile manufacturer, participated in designing the part of the vehicle in question, or worked as an automobile mechanic.

Depending on the area of expertise, ask whether the expert has any other relevant qualifications. For example, when deposing a doctor, ask whether he is board certified, and, if so, in what specialty. When deposing an engineer, ask the deponent to identify the states where he is licensed.

Finally, ask about any other relevant information, such as whether the expert has done the following:

- Maintained membership in any professional societies or organizations;
- Taught or lectured in a relevant area;
- Written any articles, books, or papers in the area;
- Participated in drafting any relevant legislation, such as a regulation, or testified before any legislative body that has considered legislation or regulations relevant to the case; and
- Done anything else that may have had a bearing on the expert's work on the case.

Generally—but as discussed below, not necessarily—you should not cross-examine the expert regarding any of this background information during the deposition. Learning about it is all that is necessary. Moreover, it is probably better not to give the witness a practice session in responding to your cross-examination before the trial.

Although you must learn the witness's educational and employment background at some point before trial, tactical considerations may militate against your developing this information at the deposition. For example, suppose you know the expert will be unavailable to testify in person at trial, and the deposition is being video recorded. You may want to ignore qualifications altogether or, to make your strategy less obvious, touch on them only briefly when questioning the witness. Your hope is that opposing counsel will neglect to qualify the expert at the deposition and that the absence of a *qualified* expert will increase your client's settlement value or weaken the opposition's case at trial. You might try the same strategy if the expert is from out of state or makes such a poor personal appearance that opposing counsel may try to introduce the deposition at trial instead of calling the expert as a live witness. Absent such tactical considerations, however, you should thoroughly explore the expert's qualifications. Note, however, that even if you fail to explore the expert's qualifications, opposing counsel will generally rectify these omissions by properly qualifying the expert by asking appropriate questions during her portion of the deposition.

Also consider the situation where the expert has been deposed, and neither examining nor opposing counsel has questioned the expert concerning her qualifications. If it later develops that the expert will not be available to testify at trial, *opposing* counsel should consider calling another expert—for the sole purpose of establishing the qualifications of the unavailable expert—so that the unavoidable expert's deposition transcript can be read at trial. But be forewarned: This may require designation of an additional expert under FRCP 26(e).[125]

2. Prior Experience as Expert

Having learned about the expert's overall educational and employment background, the questioner next should ascertain the witness's prior experience in litigation as an expert. If the witness has never before been retained as an expert, this phase of the deposition will be extremely brief. When the expert has been retained in other cases, substantial interrogation is needed to learn the following:

- How long has the expert been testifying in litigation matters on either a part-time or a full-time basis?
- During that time, in how many cases has the expert been contacted as a consultant, given a deposition, testified at trial, or otherwise given expert testimony under oath in a hearing or other judicial or legislative proceeding?
- In what percentage of *each* category given above has the expert worked for the plaintiff or the defendant, respectively? Many experts work almost entirely, if not exclusively, for one side or the other in litigation, but are understandably reluctant to reveal this fact. A general estimate of the overall breakdown of cases in which the expert has been hired is insufficient. If the witness's responses in this area seem to be ambivalent, counsel should press for the specific names and locations of past cases in which the expert has actually testified at a deposition or in court for each side.
- How many of the expert's prior cases, if any, have involved the same fact situation or issue as in the present case? For example, this may be the first case involving a bus that an expert in automobile accident cases has encountered.
- In what other types of cases has the expert been consulted, been deposed, or testified at trial? This question is particularly germane to the professional accident-reconstruction expert, who estimates accident speeds and time of impact one day, criticizes the design of a helicopter the next day, and, in between, attacks or defends the coefficient of friction of a bathtub. With this expert, the questioner should develop as many different areas as possible to later show that the expert will offer opinions on almost any subject.
- Has the expert previously testified on behalf of the same law firm or defendant? Many defendants, and lawyers on both sides, fall into the habit of repeatedly using the same expert. The questioner should find out the total number of cases in which the expert has been retained—not just those in which she has testified—by both the opposing lawyer and the opposing party.

Learning about an expert's prior litigation experience may help to show potential bias. Experts may be examined concerning fees earned in prior cases.[126] If this information cannot be obtained from any source other than the expert's tax returns, then the examining party is entitled to copies of the returns.[127] In addition, an expert may be examined about (and required to produce) specific documents and writings reviewed for purposes of the case. Additionally, when the expert's opinion is based on experience as an expert witness in similar cases, the expert may be required to retrieve and produce such documents, although the examining party may be required to share in the accompanying cost.[128]

Although the federal courts have yet to address the question, some jurisdictions have imposed limits on this line of inquiry. For example, in *Allen v. Superior Court*,[129] counsel was permitted to examine a medical expert regarding the percent of time and amount of compensation derived from his work as an expert. But the details of his billing and accounting, and the specifics of his prior testimony at trial and depositions, were considered proper subjects of a protective order. In the court's view, "Exact information as to the number of cases and amounts of compensation paid to medical experts is unnecessary for the purpose of showing bias."[130]

When an expert testifies at a deposition or trial, her opinions become a matter of public record and are the proper subject matter for impeachment. However, there is still an open question whether, and to what extent, opinions reached and reports prepared by the expert in previous cases are discoverable. Are they discoverable when the expert was designated as an anticipated trial witness, but the case was settled before the expert was deposed? When the expert did additional work after being deposed, but the case was settled before the expert testified at trial? When the expert was designated to testify in a prior case and reached opinions, but was not actually called at trial?

3. Assignment in Present Case

The questioner should learn the date on which the expert was first contacted, if not already disclosed as required by FRCP 26. The opinions of an expert who was retained on the eve of the required disclosures are frequently subject to attack as not being the product of considered study and analysis. The opinions of an expert who was retained after initial disclosures are subject to attack on credibility grounds. Was the lawyer who disclosed the expert before retention simply clairvoyant and able to argue that the expert would support counsel's case without even knowing the facts, or did counsel have reason to believe that the expert was sufficiently "malleable" that he would be able to testify for whoever was paying the bill?

You should also ascertain the circumstances of the original contact (for example, letter, telephone call, personal visit) and the nature of the assignment. Significantly, many experts cannot answer this last inquiry because the expert never asked, and the lawyer never explained, exactly the assignment was.

Finally, if the expert was retained in writing, or if there are notes on some of the written materials given the expert by the lawyer, you should review them to see whether they contain compromising admissions or give the expert a distorted view of the case.

4. How Time on the Case Has Been Spent

To ensure that all work the expert has completed on the case is examined during the deposition, there is no substitute for breaking down the expert's time into hours. You should ask how many hours the expert has spent on the case, starting with the date the expert was retained. If the expert professes to be unable to answer this question, establish that the expert is being paid on an hourly basis and continue to press for a best estimate of hours. If adequate disclosures about compensation have not been made, demand production of the expert's time sheets.[131]

Next, determine by general category the way in which the expert's time has been spent on the case and the approximate number of hours expended on each category:

- Hours spent reading and the nature of what has been read—for example, deposition transcripts, interrogatories, answers, other pleadings, or file materials, as well as secondary sources such as books, articles, reports, studies, and medical records.
- Hours spent discussing the case and with whom—for example, opposing counsel, the opposing party, other experts, and independent third parties, as well as the nature of the discussion with each.
- How the balance of the time has been spent. The nature of the inquiry will depend on the nature of the case, but will frequently include such matters as visiting the accident scene, examining and testing parts, examining exemplars or competitive products, doing calculations, and research-

ing comparable properties, businesses, or other similar facts, circumstances, or conditions.

Finally, this is an opportune time in the deposition to inquire about the expert's rates, charges, and manner of billing. Look for any discrepancy between the billing rate or method for time spent at a deposition noticed by the client and the fees, including those at trial, charged to the party who retained the expert.[132]

5. File and Reports

The questioner should next turn to the expert's file. You should first have the expert provide a general inventory of the file and identify the categories included—for example, deposition transcripts, photographs, calculations, medical records, and notes. Generally, it is not necessary at this early stage to go through each item in the file, page by page or line by line. Rather, it suffices to have the general categories identified and the materials marked as exhibits to the deposition. As discussed above, under FRCP 26(a)(2)(B), a report also should have been submitted at the time of disclosure.

6. Assistance the Expert Has Received

Ideally, the breakdown of how the expert's time has been spent will have disclosed whether anyone assisted the expert. To eliminate all uncertainty, however, you should specifically inquire into this area. The identity of each assistant and the precise nature of the work performed by each must be established for several reasons.

- First, it may be desirable or even necessary to depose the assistant to understand fully the nature of the opposition's case. Even if this step is not necessary, it may be worth doing. Frequently, an assistant has had little or no experience testifying and may be far easier to impeach or otherwise discredit than the designated expert.
- Second, the assistant may not fully concur with all the expert's opinions or may otherwise disagree with the expert in some respect.
- Third, particularly in cases in which a significant portion of the work in the file has been done by an assistant, it may be desirable for tactical reasons to demonstrate that the designated expert is actually just a "front" chosen for his or her appearance, manner, or ability to withstand cross-

examination. (By doing so, you can discredit the designated testifying expert.)

7. Expert's Opinions

The questioner is now in a position to move on to the opinions that the expert has reached in the case. This information should be contained in the FRCP 26(a)(2)(B) disclosure statement, but such statements often contain only broad generalities. The deposition provides an opportunity to pin the expert down on the precise opinions, and subopinions, she has reached.

For example, does the expert believe that an automobile part failed before or after the accident? Does the expert feel that the doctor's failure to diagnose cancer was negligent? Does the expert have an opinion concerning the total loss of support and contribution suffered by the decedent's survivors? When the question is less obvious, you should simply say, "Please tell us each opinion you have reached as a result of your work on this case."

But before moving on to the next area in which the expert may have formed an opinion, make sure no opinions have been overlooked by asking close-out questions such as, "Are there any other opinions or conclusions you have reached in this case that you have not already told us about? What are they?"[133]

8. Bases for Each Opinion

The questioner should then ask the expert to state separately for each opinion all facts or other information on which the opinion is based. Again, this information should—but not necessarily will—be contained in the FRCP 26(a)(2)(B) disclosure statement. You should resist the temptation to quarrel with the expert or challenge the basis for the opinion. Rather, strive to give the expert an unfettered opportunity to explain everything on which the opinion or conclusion is based.

At appropriate intervals, ask whether there is "anything else" not previously discussed that forms the basis for each opinion in order to make sure nothing has been omitted. The strategy behind this tactic is twofold. First, it minimizes the risk that the expert will be able to change the factual basis for that opinion at the time of trial, and it certainly renders the expert subject to impeachment if such a change occurs. Second, it may develop facts, lines of reasoning, or other matters that you and your own experts have overlooked and that may have to be taken into account—or that even undermine or destroy your theory of liability or defense. Problems in your case can be dealt with far more effectively if they are discovered during the deposition rather than at trial.

The kinds of information an expert will offer to support her opinions vary widely.[134] Generally, however, the examiner should try to elicit the following:

- Any admissible evidence—for example, photographs, records, tests, experiments, or statements—on which the expert relies;
- Any inadmissible or arguably inadmissible data—for example, subsequent remedial measures held inadmissible under FRE 404—on which the expert relies;
- All assumptions, conjectures, or reasoning that forms the basis for the opinion;
- Corroboration, if any, for the opinion; and
- Any other reasons the expert may have for reaching or holding the opinion, including any books, articles, or treatises[135] that the expert contends support the opinion.

9. Inconsistencies with Each Opinion

The examiner should ask whether the expert has encountered any fact, article, or other matter—whether contained in material relied upon or elsewhere—that is either inconsistent or not fully consistent with each opinion reached. Assuming the expert is truthful and candid, this line of questioning should apprise you of any weaknesses in the opposition's case, some of which may not have occurred to either you or your own experts.

In addition, answers to these questions frequently provide good ammunition for impeachment of the expert at trial. For example, if at the deposition the expert acknowledges having read certain conflicting or inconsistent testimony, the expert who claims at trial that he has encountered nothing that is inconsistent with the opinions reached will have some explaining to do. Likewise, you may be able to impeach an expert witness with relevant learned treatises, even if the expert has not commented upon them.[136]

10. Other Contemplated Work

Under FRCP 26(e)(1), an expert is required to supplement disclosures made pursuant to FRCP 26(a)(2)(B), and thus this information already may be available. In addition, ascertain whether there is anything further that the expert is scheduled to do in the case—for example, additional reading, calculations, or experiments. Also find out whether the expert has additional work planned or contemplated, even though not presently scheduled, and the nature of this work. Finally, ask whether, assuming an unlimited budget and ample time, the expert would like to do any additional work to further test, corroborate, or solidify any opinions expressed.

Additional Six Questions That May Be Appropriate

All questions necessary to fulfill the questioner's goal at an expert's deposition—that is, to learn everything the expert thinks about the case and has done or plans to do in connection with the case—have now been discussed. The inexperienced examiner often is well advised to stop there and not attempt further questioning. Depending on the nature of the case and the skill, goals, and experience of the examiner, however, several other areas may be worth pursuing.

1. Trial-Type Cross-Examination

In some instances, it may be beneficial to test weaknesses in the expert's opinions or reasoning by using trial-type cross-examination to discredit the witness at the deposition. This may serve to fluster an inexperienced expert or let opposing counsel know, for purposes of possible settlement, just how weak his client's case might be. As a general rule, however, profitable areas of cross-examination are best left for trial. Otherwise, the expert gets a preview of your intended cross-examination and can learn how to meet it at trial.

2. Assume the Expert Is Correct

An often-effective technique is for the questioner to assume that the opposing expert is correct. For example, in the typical slip-and-fall case, if the plaintiff's expert claims that the plaintiff slipped not because of some foreign substance on the pavement or flooring, but because the surface itself had too low a coefficient of friction that caused it to be slippery, you might ask a line of questions that assume that the floor really was as slippery as claimed. Then you can ask whether the expert has heard of any other similar incidents where there was a low coefficient and someone slipped. If the answer is "no," you can ask how the expert accounts for the seeming lack of consistency.

On a products liability case, where the defendant's expert contends an accident happened because of the plaintiff's habitual misuse of the product, ask questions such as the following: "Why wasn't the plaintiff injured when misusing the product on an earlier occasion? Why have other misusers of the product escaped injury?"

3. Make the Expert Go to the Extreme

When the expert's opinion seems questionable, the examiner can make it appear ludicrous by applying it to similar but more extreme facts. For example, if an expert states that no automobile gas tank should suffer a fuel loss in a 50 miles per hour accident, you might ask if the expert feels the same way about an accident at 60, 80, or 100 miles per hour.

This line of questioning creates a dilemma for the expert: either commit to some fixed, arbitrary speed (for example, 62.8 miles per hour) above which fuel loss is expected but below which it should not occur, or claim an inability to answer the question without more data. But the expert who needs more data still may not be out of the woods. For example, one expert testified that even in a 300-mile-per-hour accident, he would have to examine the wreckage of the vehicles to know for sure whether the resulting fuel loss had been caused by a defective gas tank.

An expert who can be led to take such an extreme position in deposition testimony will suffer a loss of credibility in the jury's eyes, and opposing counsel will have a strong basis for arguing at trial that the expert—far from being an objective scientist—is simply an advocate seeking to be hired to testify in as many cases as possible. Furthermore, if this information can be developed in deposition, it may have an effect on the settlement value of the litigation in advance of trial.

4. Is the Expert Too Consistent?

Although the professional expert who has testified dozens of times in similar or identical cases may appear abundantly qualified, this experience can often be the expert's greatest weakness. The examiner should fully explore the expert's prior testimony and work performed in earlier related cases.

Suppose, for example, that you learn in thirty previous failure-to-diagnose-cancer cases, the expert testified that the failure to diagnose was not negligent. If you can elicit deposition testimony from the expert that the previous cases occurred in different states, involved different doctors with different levels of experience, and involved different kinds of cancer and different claims of delay, at trial you can point out that the only consistency in the case is that the defendant's expert always finds a lack of negligence. The plaintiff's expert who travels around the country attacking a particular product or condition is subject to similar impeachment.

Consider another example: The expert who has testified for years—and been paid to testify—about the same supposedly dangerous condition also may be vulnerable to attack before judge or jury if she has done nothing to eliminate the condition. Many judges and jurors expect a well-intentioned person who spends a considerable portion of time testifying about a problem to do something about it.

5. Does the Expert Really Fit the Case?

An expert may offer an opinion at the deposition in an area in which she does not appear to have sufficient expertise. In such instances, the examiner should return to the expert's qualifications to determine whether they qualify her to give that particular opinion.

For example, an accident-reconstruction expert who is qualified to render opinions concerning stopping distances and interpretation of skid marks may try to offer opinions concerning automobile design or the driver's subjective reaction to danger. Under these circumstances, you may want to find out whether the expert has:

1. Ever been qualified by a court in the relevant jurisdiction to render such an opinion;
2. Rendered such an opinion in a previous deposition;
3. Obtained a degree or other formal training in vehicle design, psychology, human factors, or other disciplines that would seem to cover the area of opinion being expressed;
4. Read or written on the subject; and
5. Achieved any other expertise in that particular area.[137]

6. What Would Satisfy the Expert?

It is sometimes a good strategy at the deposition to ask what the expert contends the opposing party should have done to avoid the expert's judgment of fault. For example, in a product liability action involving failure to warn of a danger, the defendant's lawyer could ask the expert exactly what kind of warning would have to be given to make the product defect-free. Would the warning have to be in writing? If so, precisely what wording should it contain? And where should it be placed, distributed, or otherwise disseminated?

Similarly, counsel for a plaintiff, whom the defense has accused of having failed to take proper steps to mitigate damages (be they physical, financial, or otherwise), should consider asking the expert what alternative measure the plaintiff should have taken.

Compelling an Expert to Answer Deposition Questions

It is sometimes necessary for counsel to move to compel an expert to answer questions asked at the deposition. Situations in which this occurs include the following:

- The lawyer for the party retaining the expert has instructed the expert not to answer questions, as if the expert were a client.
- The retaining lawyer refuses to allow the expert to answer a hypothetical question because an essential element is missing or misstated. (Note that the examining party should demand specification of the omission or misstatements.)
- The expert does not bring his complete file to the deposition.
- The expert refuses to answer questions concerning similar pending lawsuits.

When these or similar problems arise during the deposition, you have the option of adjourning it.[138] Generally, however, you should continue questioning the expert. Your position will not benefit from refusing to proceed because the expert or opposing counsel has improperly blocked inquiry in a particular area. Because expert depositions are usually taken close to the trial date, it is imperative that you glean as much information as possible from expert witnesses as soon as possible.

You should then move to compel further discovery responses after the deposition has been completed. The court should be more sympathetic to an examiner who can represent that everything possible was done to minimize the need for the motion. (Notice of the motion must be given to all parties and to the deponent either orally at the examination or by subsequent service in writing.[139]) If the motion to compel is granted, you will have the opportunity to redepose the expert—albeit often uncomfortably close to the time of trial.

Notes

*Portions of this chapter are drawn from California Expert Witness Guide (2d ed. 2007), Chapters 11–12, copyright by the Regents of the University of California. Used with permission of Continuing Education of the Bar–California.

1. *See* FED. R. EVID. 705.
2. See also "The Federal Discovery Scheme" in Chapter 2.
3. *See* John C. Koski, *Mandatory Disclosure*, 80 A.B.A. J. 85 (1994).
4. *See, e.g.*, Ager v. Jane C. Stormont Hosp. & Training Sch. for Nurses 622, F.2d 496, 500 (10th Cir. 1980). *See generally* 8 CHARLES A. WRIGHT & ARTHUR R. MILLER, FEDERAL PRACTICE AND PROCEDURE § 2029 (1970).
5. See "Work-Product Privilege" in Chapter 6, discussing the balance between discovery and work-product protection.
6. *See, e.g.*, Pearl Brewing Co. v. Joseph Schlitz Brewing Co., 415 F. Supp. 1122, 1134 (S.D. Tex. 1976).
7. *See, e.g.*, Wright v. Jeep Corp., 547 F. Supp. 871 (E.D. Mich. 1982).
8. FED. R. CIV. P. 26(a)(2)(A).
9. FED. R. CIV. P. 26(a)(2)(C)(ii).
10. FED. R. CIV. P. 26(a)(2)(B).
11. FED. R. CIV. P. 26(a)(2)(B)(i)–(vi).
12. FED. R. CIV. P. 26(b)(4)(A).
13. FED. R. CIV. P. 26(a)(2) advisory committee's note (1993). *See also* FED. R. CIV. P. 26(b)(4)(A).
14. See "Subpoenas to Nonparties" in Chapter 3.
15. FED. R. CIV. P. 26(e)(1)(A).
16. *See, e.g.*, Marsh v. Jackson, 141 F.R.D. 431 (W.D. Va. 1992).
17. *See, e.g.*, Lewis v. United Air Lines Transp. Corp., 32 F. Supp. 21 (W.D. Pa. 1940). *See also* JAMES L. UNDERWOOD, A GUIDE TO FEDERAL DISCOVERY RULES (2d ed. 1985).
18. *E.g.*, *In re* Folding Carton Antitrust Litig., 83 F.R.D. 256 (N.D. Ill. 1979).
19. *E.g.*, Guilloz v. Falmount Hosp. Ass'n, 21 Fed. R. Serv. 2d (Callaghan) 1367 (D. Mass. 1976); Perry v. W.S. Darley & Co., 54 F.R.D. 278 (E.D. Wis. 1971); *see also* Note, *Discovery of Retained Nontestifying Experts' Identities Under the Federal Rules of Civil Procedure*, 80 MICH. L. REV. 513 (1982).
20. 622 F.2d 496, 503 (10th Cir. 1980).
21. *See In re* Pizza Time Theatre Sec. Litig., 113 F.R.D. 94 (N.D. Cal. 1986) (following *Ager*, holding that identities of nontestifying experts should be subject to same standard as discovery of their opinions—that of "exceptional circumstances"); Hermsdorfer v. Am. Motors Corp., 96 F.R.D. 13 (W.D.N.Y. 1982) (following *Ager*, rejecting counsel's attempt to circumvent FRCP 26(b)(4)(B) by arguing that defendant's experts were retained to assist in product development, not in anticipation of litigation

or preparation for trial; and reasoning that experts might also have been retained in anticipation of litigation or preparation for trial).

22. On the other hand, such questions elicit the information necessary to satisfy the "exceptional circumstances" hypotheticals proposed by Professor Sacks. *See* UNDERWOOD, *supra* note 37, § 1.04(e).

23. *In re* Shell Oil Refinery, 132 F.R.D. 437, 442 (E.D. La. 1990) (and cases cited therein).

24. *Id.*

25. 133 F.R.D. 109 (E.D. La. 1990).

26. *Pizza Time Theatre*, 113 F.R.D. at 110.

27. *Id.* at 111.

28. 415 F. Supp. 1122 (S.D. Tex. 1976).

29. *See Ager*, 622 F.2d at 501. *See also* Kuster v. Harner, 109 F.R.D. 372 (D. Minn. 1986).

30. 109 F.R.D. 372 (D. Minn. 1986).

31. *Kuster* also includes an especially insightful analysis of the discussion in the Advisory Committee's note to the 1970 amendment to FRCP 26 on discovery of the identity of persons who will not testify.

32. For questions (1) and (2), see the interrogatories set forth in *supra* section "Retained or Specially Employed Experts."

33. *See, e.g., In re* Sinking of Barge Ranger I., 92 F.R.D. 486 (S.D. Tex. 1981).

34. 70 F.R.D. 326 (D.R.I. 1976).

35. 631 F.2d 420 (6th Cir. 1980).

36. Va. Elec. & Power Co. v. Sun Shipbuilding & Drydock Co., 68 F.R.D. 397 (E.D. Va. 1976).

37. Kan.-Neb. Nat. Gas Co., Inc. v. Marathon Oil Co., 109 F.R.D. 12, 16 (D. Neb. 1985); *Shell Oil Refinery*, 132 F.R.D. at 437.

38. Hermsdorfer v. Am. Motors Corp., 96 F.R.D. 13, 15 (W.D.N.Y. 1982).

39. 641 F.2d 984 (D.D.C. 1980).

40. 60 F.R.D. 205 (S.D.N.Y. 1973).

41. *Id.* at 209. *See also In re* Shell Oil Refinery, 134 F.R.D. 148 (E.D. La. 1990) (limiting discovery to opinions formulated by employee-experts in their preparation for trial testimony and foreclosing discovery about their opinions formulated as members of defendant's postaccident investigation team).

42. 79 F.R.D. 444 (D. Ala. 1978).

43. *Id.* at 446.

44. *Id.*

45. 80 F.R.D. 489 (D. Mont. 1978).

46. For an overview of treatment by the federal courts of the discoverability of the identity and opinions of nontestifying experts under the FRCP, see Douglas Alan Emerick, *Discovery of the Non-Testifying Expert*

Witness's Identity Under the Federal Rules of Civil Procedure: You Can't Tell the Players Without a Program, 37 HASTINGS L.J. 201 (1985).

47. *See* Baran v. Presbyterian Univ. Hosp., 102 F.R.D. 272 M.D. Pa. 1984); Keith v. Van Dorn Plastic Mach. Co., 86 F.R.D. 460 (E.D. Pa. 1980).

48. 102 F.R.D. 272 (W.D. Pa. 1984).

49. *Id.* at 273.

50. 549 F. Supp. 82 (N.D. Ill. 1982).

51. 547 F. Supp. 871 (E.D. Mich. 1982).

52. *Id.* at 873.

53. *Id.* at 877.

54. *Id.* at 875. *But cf.* Michigan v. Ewing, 474 U.S. 214 (1985) (affirming dismissal of student from institution of higher learning based on court's "responsibility to safeguard . . . academic freedom, a special concern of the First Amendment"); Sweeny v. New Hampshire, 354 U.S. 234, 262 (1957) (Frankfurter, J., concurring) ("The dependence of a free society on free universities means the exclusion of governmental intervention in the intellectual life of a university . . . whether such intervention occurs avowedly or through action that inevitably tends to check the ardor and fearlessness of scholars, qualities at once so fragile and so indispensable for fruitful academic labor."); Brown v. Trs. of Boston Univ., 891 F.2d 337, 350–51 (1st Cir. 1989) (upholding inadmissibility of statements made by university officials unrelated to tenure review of individual because of "the chilling effect that admission of such remarks could have on academic freedom").

55. 672 F.2d 1262 (7th Cir. 1982).

56. 115 F.R.D. 211 (D. Ariz. 1987).

57. 539 F.2d 811 (2d Cir. 1976).

58. 880 F.2d 1520 (2d Cir. 1989).

59. *In re* R.J. Reynolds Tobacco Co., 518 N.Y.S.2d 729 (Sup. Ct. 1987).

60. No. 94-2318, 1994 U.S. Dist. LEXIS 16933, at *4 (E.D. La. Nov. 22, 1994).

61. FED. R. CIV. P. 45(c)(3)(B).

62. *Bluitt*, 1994 U.S. Dist. LEXIS 16933, at *4.

63. See the discussion later in this chapter concerning the impact of the loss of attorney-client privilege and work-product protection on communications with an expert. See also Chapter 6.

64. 449 U.S. 383, 386 (1981). See "Applying the Attorney-Client Privilege When the Client Is a Corporation" in Chapter 6, discussing the *Upjohn* case.

65. For further insight into the assertion of the federal attorney-client privilege by a corporation and the circumstances under which that privilege can be waived, see *Commodity Futures Trading Comm'n v. Weintraub*, 471 U.S. 343 (1985) (holding voluntary disclosure by trustee of corporation in bankruptcy waived debtor corporation's attorney-client privilege for communications that occurred before bankruptcy

petitions filed). *See also In re* Coordinated Pretrial Proceedings in Petroleum Prods. Antitrust Litig., 658 F.2d 1355, 1361 (9th Cir. 1981) (protections of *Upjohn* extended to include "orientation sessions" before depositions with ex-employee witnesses who were not employees of company at time sessions held).

66. Fed. R. Evid. 26(b)(3).

67. *Id.* See "How to Avoid Putting Privileged Documents at Risk" in Chapter 9, discussing work-product protection in the context of FRE 612.

68. *See* James L. Underwood, A Guide to Federal Discovery Rules 24 (2d ed. 1985). *See also* Lewis v. United Air Lines Transp. Corp., 32 F. Supp. 21 (W.D. Pa. 1940). *See generally* 8 Wright & Miller, *supra* note 4, §§ 2021–2050.

69. *See, e.g.,* Berkey Photo, Inc. v. Eastman Kodak Co., 603 F.2d 263, 306 (2d Cir. 1979) (allowing limited admissibility of key 1915 consent decree in antitrust action, when sole expert witness had studied decree and advised lawyers he was unable to reconcile it with defendant's claims; not relevant that expert had analyzed and expressed misgivings about decree before he was designated prospective trial witness). *See* Baran v. Presbyterian Univ. Hosp., 102 F.R.D. 272 (W.D. Pa. 1984) (holding defendant-physicians fit into category of "actors or viewers," not experts retained for purposes of litigation; therefore, they should have been allowed to testify about their medical opinions relating to their treatment of plaintiff without providing plaintiff's counsel with their written expert reports).

70. *See, e.g.,* Lewis v. Rego Co., 757 F.2d 66, 74 (3d Cir. 1985) (holding cross-examination concerning conversations between consultant and trial expert should have been permitted).

71. Fed. R. Civ. P. 26(b)(4)(B) advisory committee's note (1970). See also the related discussion earlier in this chapter.

72. 560 F.2d 326 (8th Cir. 1977).

73. 487 F.2d 480, 484 (4th Cir. 1973).

74. United States v. Leggett & Platt, Inc., 542 F.2d 655, 660 (6th Cir. 1976); United States v. Int'l Bus. Mach. Corp., 66 F.R.D. 154, 178 (S.D.N.Y. 1974).

75. Republic Gear Co. v. Borg-Warner Corp., 381 F.2d 551, 557 (2d Cir. 1967); Hercules, Inc. v. Exxon Corp., 434 F. Supp. 136, 153 (D. Del. 1977); Midland Inv. Co. v. Van Alstyne, Noel & Co., 59 F.R.D. 134, 138 (S.D.N.Y. 1973). *See also* 8 Wright & Miller, supra note 4, § 2024.

76. 462 U.S. 19 (1983).

77. 5 U.S.C. § 552 (2002).

78. *See, e.g.,* Powell v. United States, 584 F. Supp. 1508 (N.D. Cal. 1984) (dictum) (questioning government's reliance on Grolier in asserting work-product privilege in response to Freedom of Information Act request for information on criminal proceeding that had terminated twenty years earlier).

79. *See* Bogosian v. Gulf Oil Corp., 738 F.2d 587, 593 (3d Cir. 1984); Hamel v. Gen. Motors Corp., 128 F.R.D. 281 (D. Kan. 1989); Carter-Wallace, Inc. v. Hartz Mountain Indus., 553 F. Supp. 45 (S.D.N.Y. 1982).

80. Gilhuly v. Johns-Manville Corp., 100 F.R.D. 752 (D. Conn. 1983); Boring v. Keller, 97 F.R.D. 404 (D. Colo. 1983); James Julian, Inc. v. Raytheon Co., 93 F.R.D. 138 (D. Del. 1982); Berkey Photo, Inc. v. Eastman Kodak Co., 74 F.R.D. 613 (S.D.N.Y. 1977). *See also* Elm Grove Coal Co. v. Dir., Office of Workers' Comp. Programs, 480 F.3d 278, 301–03 (4th Cir. 2007); William Penn Life Assur. Co. v. Brown Transfer & Storage Co., 141 F.R.D. 142 (W.D. Mo. 1990); Occulto v. Adamar, Inc., 125 F.R.D. 611 (D.N.J. 1989).

81. 738 F.2d 587 (3d Cir. 1984).

82. 139 F.R.D. 384, 387 (N.D. Cal. 1991).

83. *Id.* at 397.

84. *See Hamel,* 128 F.R.D. at 284.

85. 210 Cal. Rptr. 535 (1985).

86. *Id.* at 489–90.

87. 293 F. 1013 (D.C. Cir. 1923).

88. *Id.* The court refers to a "systolic blood pressure deception test," a precursor to the modern polygraph test.

89. *Id.* at 1014.

90. *Id.*

91. *See id.* ("[T]he opinions of experts or skilled witnesses are admissible in evidence in those cases in which the matter of inquiry is such that inexperienced persons are unlikely to prove capable of forming a correct judgment upon it, for the reason that the subject-matter so far partakes of a science, art, or trade as to require a previous habit or experience or study in it, in order to acquire a knowledge of it.").

92. *See* People v. Leahy, 8 Cal. 4th 587, 601–02 (Cal. 1994).

93. 509 U.S. 579 (U.S. 1993).

94. *Id.* at 589.

95. *Id.* at 590.

96. *Id. See also* Cabrera v. Cordis Corp., 134 F.3d 1418, 1420 (9th Cir. 1998).

97. Daubert v. Merrell Dow Pharms., Inc., 43 F.3d 1311, 1318 (9th Cir. 1995) (*Daubert II*) (reviewing *Daubert* case on remand); United States v. Arnold, 3 Fed. Appx. 614, 616 (unpublished opinion) (9th Cir. 2001) (*Daubert* factors not relevant to expert's testimony regarding *modus operandi* of alien smuggling because testimony's reliability depends on knowledge and experience of expert rather than methodology or theory behind it).

98. *See Daubert,* 509 U.S. at 593–95.

99. 522 U.S. 136, 142–43 (U.S. 1997).

100. 526 U.S. 137, 141 (U.S. 1997).

101. FED. R. EVID. 702.

102. *See Daubert,* 509 U.S. at 595.

555

103.   See *infra* section "Purposes of a Deposition." See also "Purposes of a Deposition" in Chapter 2.

104.   FRCP 26(b)(4)(C) provides that "[u]nless manifest injustice would result, the court must require that the party seeking discovery: (i) pay the expert a reasonable fee for time spent in responding to discovery [under this subdivision]." This language differs significantly from that of various state statutes. For example, California Code of Civil Procedure, section 2034.430(b), limits the fees recoverable from the opposition to the time the expert actually spent at the deposition. Under FRCP 26, a party seeking discovery from an expert must reimburse the expert not only for actual time spent in deposition, but also for time spent in preparation, particularly in complex cases. S.A. Healy Co. v. Milwaukee Metro. Sewage Dist., 154 F.R.D. 212 (E.D. Wis. 1994). FRCP 26(b)(4)(C)(ii) provides that when exceptional circumstances justify discovery of a percipient or specially retained witness who is not expected to testify at the trial, the non-discovering party must "pay the other party a fair portion of the fees and expenses it reasonably incurred in obtaining the expert's facts and opinions."

105.   FED. R. CIV. P. 26(b)(4)(A).

106.   See "Preparation Sessions: When, Where, How Often, and with Whom" in Chapter 5.

107.   In the process, you should assume that anything given to an expert witness may become the subject of discovery if that witness is disclosed as a trial witness.

108.   Such a session is not privileged. See *supra* section "Privileges Relating to Expert Witnesses."

109.   See Chapter 7.

110.   See "Making Objections" in Chapter 14.

111.   See later sections of this chapter concerning questions outside the expert's designated area of expertise.

112.   See *supra* section "Privileges Relating to Expert Witnesses."

113.   *See, e.g.*, Smith v. Ford Motor Co., 626 F.2d 784 (10th Cir. 1980) (discussed in text accompanying notes 21–24); Weiss v. Chrysler Motor Corp., 515 F.2d 449 (2d Cir. 1975).

114.   FRCP 26(a)(2)(B)(vi), for example, requires that experts disclose in their written report the compensation to be paid for their work and testimony in the case.

115.   *Compare* Cary Oil Co. v. MG Ref. & Mktg., Inc., 257 F. Supp. 2d 751, 757 (S.D.N.Y. 2003) (requiring requesting party to show "reasonable suspicion" that compensation arrangement "materially changed" expert's opinion) *with* Amster v. River Capital Int'l Group, LLC, No. 00 Civ. 9708 (DC) (DF), 2002 U.S. Dist. LEXIS 16595, at *3 (S.D.N.Y. Sept. 4, 2002) (requiring requesting party to show "plausible argument" that total amount of compensation could be relevant to showing of bias) *and* Boselli v. Se. Pa. Transp. Auth., 108 F.R.D. 723, 726 (E.D. Pa. 1985) (permitting

requesting party to obtain compensation information because it would be "useful" for purposes of effective cross-examination).

116.   *See, e.g.*, Rohrbaugh v. Owens-Corning Fiberglass Corp., 965 F.2d 844 (10th Cir. 1992); Trademark Research Corp. v. Maxwell Online, Inc., 995 F.2d 326 (2d Cir. 1993).

117.   See *supra* section "Explaining Deposition Procedures to an Expert: Objections," concerning how to explain the nature of objections to an expert. *See* FED R. CIV. P. 32(d)(3)(A), 32(d)(3)(B). *See, e.g.*, Cordle v. Allied Chem. Corp., 309 F.2d 821 (6th Cir. 1962) (because hypothetical questions on same subject matter could have been substituted for questions actually asked of expert if proper objection had been made at deposition, grounds for objections to testimony at trial waived for failure to make them at deposition). See also "The Question Calls for Speculation" in Chapter 14, discussing objections to a hypothetical.

118.   See "Instructing a Witness Not to Answer" in Chapter 14.

119.   See "Surprise! You're on Candid Camera: Video Depositions Can Demand Different Techniques by Both the Examiner and Defender" in Chapter 17, discussing the value of video recording an expert who is not expected to be available for trial.

120.   Compare this suggestion with the next section in this chapter, discussing the strategic considerations in deposing an opposing expert about his or her qualifications.

121.   See *supra* note 15, discussing the possibility that additional work by an expert after his or her deposition may require a supplemental report by the expert (see FRCP 26(e)(1)) and may be the basis for an argument that the deposition should be reopened (see FRCP 30(d)(1)).

122.   When an expert has provided a written report as required under FRCP 26(a)(2)(B), some of the ten points may already be covered in whole or in part.

123.   Among other things, the examiner needs to learn during the deposition whether to bring a *Daubert* motion to limit or exclude the expert's testimony. See *supra* section "The *Daubert* Standard."

124.   It is not necessary to object at the deposition to the witness's competence to testify as an expert. Counsel can wait until trial to do so. Objections to the competency of an expert witness, or to the relevance or materiality of testimony and the like, are not waived by failure to make them before or during the deposition. FED. R. CIV. P. 32(d)(3)(A). See also "Objections That Are Preserved" in Chapter 14.

125.   *See, e.g.*, Price v. Seydel, 961 F.2d 1470, 1474 (9th Cir. 1992) (holding court may exclude testimony of witness not listed in pretrial witness list, based on evaluation of the surprise or prejudice to opposing party, opposing party's ability to cure prejudice, whether waiver of rule against calling unlisted witness would disrupt order by trial of case, and evidence of bad faith or willfulness in failing to list witness).

126.   Collins v. Wayne Corp., 621 F.2d 777, 783 (5th Cir. 1980).

127. Hawkins v. S. Plains Int'l Trucks, Inc., 139 F.R.D. 679 (D. Colo. 1991). *See also* Terwilliger v. York Int'l Corp., 176 F.R.D. 214, 216–20 (D. Va. 1997).

128. *Hawkins*, 139 F.R.D. at 681.

129. 198 Cal. Rptr. 737 (1984).

130. *Id.* at 453, 198. *See also* Russell v. Young, 452 S.W.2d 434 (Tex. 1970).

131. Although FRCP 26(a)(2)(B)(vi) requires disclosure of "the compensation to be paid for the study and testimony," this often produces nothing more than the expert's hourly rate in the case. See *supra* note 116, discussing discovery about compensation to be paid.

132. As noted, FRCP 26(a)(2)(B)(vi) requires only that the expert disclose "compensation." Thus, counsel will need to develop this detailed information in the deposition.

133. See "Closure" in Chapter 11.

134. *See* FED. R. EVID. 703 (Bases of Opinion Testimony by Experts):

> The facts or data in the particular case upon which an expert bases an opinion or inference may be those perceived by or made known to the expert at or before the hearing. If of a type reasonably relied upon by experts in the particular field informing opinions or inferences upon the subject, the facts or data need not be admissible in evidence in order for the opinion or inference to be admitted. Facts or data that are otherwise inadmissible shall not be disclosed to the jury by the proponent of the opinion or inference unless the court determines that their probative value in assisting the jury to evaluate the expert's opinion substantially outweighs their prejudicial effect.

135. See "Learned Treatise" in Chapter 13.

136. *See* FED. R. EVID. 803(18) (Learned Treatises).

137. Information about the expert's previous trial experience can also be obtained from jury verdict reporting services, which typically index lower-court cases by name and type of expert. Useful data about experts and their publications can be located using computer-assisted research services, such as LEXIS/NEXIS and Westlaw. Depending on the individual's field of expertise, information can also be found on specialized research services, such as Index Medicus (for doctors) and Knight-Ridder's Dialog Information Services, Inc. (for other fields).

138. See "Concluding the Testimony" in Chapter 23, discussing the adjournment of depositions. See also "How Long May the Deposition Last?" in Chapter 3, discussing the limitation of a deposition in federal practice to one day of seven hours, absent agreement or court order (FRCP 30(d)(1)). Counsel frequently reach agreement to allow a deposition of more than one day in cases where the expert's report is particularly voluminous and complicated.

139. See Chapter 15, discussing motions to compel and for sanctions.

CHAPTER 20

Taking and Defending the Deposition of the Class Representative

GEORGE DONALDSON

Because of the nature of class actions, the deposition of a class representative presents special problems and opportunities for both takers and defenders. Before courts will certify a class action, they require the plaintiff seeking to represent the class, sometimes called the "named plaintiff,"[1] to meet several tests or requirements, the principal two of which are adequacy and typicality.[2]

These two requirements ensure that absent members of the class are afforded due process in the adjudication of their claims, and, accordingly, that the judgment rendered in the class action is binding.[3] To make sure these requirements are met, the law allows a scope of questioning at the deposition of a named plaintiff that is broader than ordinarily permitted at the deposition of a plaintiff

559

in non-class litigation. Indeed, many of the areas about which a plaintiff may be questioned in a class action are completely irrelevant in non-class actions.

This chapter begins by reviewing the adequacy and typicality requirements. The chapter next shows how the two requirements expand the scope of the named plaintiff's deposition. Finally, the chapter explains the practical significance of this expanded inquiry for both takers and defenders.

Special Features of Class Actions

A principal benefit of the class action lawsuit is the conservation of judicial resources. In such a lawsuit, one or more persons represent a larger group of persons possessing claims or defenses similar to those of the representative parties.[4] Whether or not favorable to the class, any judgment in the lawsuit binds all class members who do not exclude themselves or "opt out" of the class.[5] Thus, among other benefits, a class action permits a single adjudication of a multitude of similar claims.[6]

Because a class judgment binds all class members, courts will not "certify" a lawsuit as a class action unless certain fundamental due process protections are in place.[7] Under Federal Rule of Civil Procedure 23, as well as the parallel law of many states,[8] these due process protections, insofar as they relate to the class representative, boil down to two requirements: adequacy and typicality.[9]

As for adequacy, under FRCP 23(a)(4), the class representative must "fairly and adequately protect the interests of the class."[10] In *Eisen v. Carlisle & Jacquelin*, a leading case on class actions, the United States Court of Appeals for the Second Circuit explained this requirement as follows:

> [A]n essential concomitant of adequate representation is that the party's attorney be qualified, experienced and generally able to conduct the proposed litigation. Additionally, it is necessary to eliminate so far as possible the likelihood that the litigants are involved in a collusive suit or that plaintiff has interests antagonistic to those of the remainder of the class.[11]

As for typicality, the claims or defenses of the class representative must be "typical" of the claims or defenses of the class.[12] This requirement is met by a showing that the plaintiff's claim "stems from the same event, practice, or course of conduct that forms the basis of the class claims and is based on the same legal or remedial theory."[13] As long as there is such a showing, the presence of immaterial factual differences between the claims of the class and those of the class representative are of little significance.[14]

Expanded Scope of Discovery Permitted in Class Actions

Because adequacy and typicality are designed to protect the due process rights of absent class members, courts are careful to ensure that both requirements are met.[15] For that reason, at the deposition of a named plaintiff in a class action, the taker is allowed wide latitude in asking questions that may bear on the two requirements.

However, even though courts look at such depositions from the standpoint of due process, class action defendants generally have a different perspective. Although purporting to ensure proper class representation, the defendant's goal often is to use the deposition of a named plaintiff to defeat class certification and thereby limit their exposure to liability.[16]

Indeed, because a class action almost always poses a threat of far greater liability than an individual action alleging similar misconduct, defendants are highly motivated to defeat the certification of the class action. Demonstrating that the named plaintiff fails to meet the adequacy and typicality requirements is certainly a means to this end.[17]

In any event, given concerns about adequacy and typicality, courts permit certain questions during the deposition of a named class action plaintiff that would be off limits or irrelevant in other depositions. The types of questions permitted are discussed next.

Questions About Adequacy

The adequacy requirement involves three considerations: (1) whether the named plaintiff will vigorously prosecute the action, (2) whether the named plaintiff has retained counsel experienced and competent in class litigation, and (3) whether the named plaintiff's interests are antagonistic to, or in conflict with, those of the class.[18]

Vigorous Prosecution

In attempting to show that the named plaintiff will not be a vigorous advocate for the class, a deposition taker will often try to elicit testimony indicating the plaintiff's ignorance of even the most rudimentary facts concerning the action. For example, in *Lubin v.*

Sybdeon Corp., a federal district court rejected the adequacy of a named plaintiff who, at his deposition,

> testified that he had never read or seen either the original complaint or the amended complaint, that he did not even recognize the names of many of the defendants, that he had never seen or read the prospectus, that he does not understand how much he has invested in the limited partnership, that he misunderstands the nature of the complaint's fraud allegations, that he is not willing to fund the costs of the suit (if necessary), and that he has never discussed the tax consequences of this suit with any of the prospective class members.[19]

Thus, as *Lubin* demonstrates, deposition testimony establishing a named plaintiff's ignorance of critical facts surrounding the action can sometimes succeed in disqualifying a class representative.[20]

But *Lubin* is clearly the exception, not the rule. So long as the named plaintiff testifies to an understanding of the *general* outlines of the action, he or she is not likely to be disqualified because of purported ignorance.[21] The reason is obvious: Laypersons cannot be expected to have more than a general overview of the complex legal issues generally arising in class actions. Courts, therefore, are reluctant—if not flatly unwilling[22]—to disqualify a proposed class representative or deny class certification simply because a named plaintiff does not demonstrate a detailed understanding of these issues.[23] In short, to prove inadequacy, the defendant must show that the named plaintiff has an "alarming unfamiliarity" with the case.[24]

Nevertheless, if you are defending a class representative's deposition, make sure he has a basic understanding of the case. Have your client read the complaint before it is filed, and have him read it again during the preparation session. In addition, prepare the witness to testify, at least in a general way, about (1) the purpose of the case, (2) the nature of the claimed injuries and damages, (3) the identity of the defendants, and (4) their alleged wrongdoing. Prepare the witness to testify about his general understanding of class actions, the responsibilities of a class representative, and why he is willing to be a class representative.

Conversely, if you are taking the deposition of a named plaintiff, you should be prepared to examine the witness on each of these topics, as well as any others that test and probe the witness's knowledge of the case, the nature of the claims asserted, and the identity and role of the defendants.[25] Your goal in asking such questions is to lay a foundation for opposing a certification motion by arguing that the class plaintiff is not truly the interested party but simply the pawn of counsel.[26]

Another aspect of "vigorous prosecution" is whether the class plaintiff has taken, or will take, an "active role" in the litigation.[27] If you are the deposition taker, try to establish that the named plaintiff has done little more than lend her name to the action. Ask whether she reviewed the complaint *before* it was filed. A negative answer can be used to show that the named plaintiff is just a stakeholder for her lawyer. Ask whether the plaintiff has actively participated in litigation decisions and, if so, how. But remember, if the witness's testimony indicates some meaningful involvement in, or awareness of, the progress of the litigation, that testimony will hurt your subsequent effort to disqualify.[28]

As the taker, you may want to ask questions about certain of the named plaintiff's personal circumstances, as these may bear on adequacy in general and her ability to vigorously prosecute in particular. Suppose a named plaintiff's standing is based on his status as a legal representative (for example, as a trustee or other fiduciary). In that case, try to show that the named plaintiff lacks the legal authority to assert claims on behalf of anyone other than the beneficiary that he is expressly authorized to represent.[29] Testimony showing a lack of such authority may support a finding of inadequacy.[30]

Another area to explore is past misconduct by a named plaintiff. Courts have disqualified representatives whose integrity as fiduciaries has been impugned,[31] or when a potential conflict exists between the named plaintiff's duties as a class representative and those as a fiduciary.[32] Similarly, although past bad acts, including a prior felony conviction, are not automatically disqualifying,[33] a plaintiff's past record of misconduct may lead to a finding of inadequacy.[34]

In a similar vein, defendants also may seek to undermine the credibility of the class representative by pointing out inconsistencies in the representative's deposition testimony or between such testimony and the allegations of the complaint. Again, the purpose of this is to cast doubt on the suitability of the named plaintiff to act as a champion for the class.[35]

A deposition taker will also want to ask about a named plaintiff's physical condition, illness, incapacity, and advanced age. The answers to these questions may demonstrate that the plaintiff has physical limitations that might prevent active participation in, or the exercise of independent control over, the action. But physical limitations usually will not result in a finding of inadequacy, especially if there is no other reason to disqualify the plaintiff as the class representative.[36]

The taker should also explore the class representative's understanding of the financial burdens of a class action,[37] as well as the representative's willingness and capacity to repay the costs of pursuing the action.[38] Depending on the nature of the case and size of the class, these costs can be enormous and far in excess of the named plaintiff's individual damages. A named plaintiff's failure to acknowledge any financial responsibility for the action, or her reluctance or refusal to agree to the requisite financial commitment (for example, to pay the costs of litigation or the costs of defense if there is an adverse disposition), occasionally results in, or contributes to, denial of class status.[39]

Be aware, however, that for several reasons questions about financial burden have become increasingly pointless when attempting to demonstrate inadequacy. First, as a practical matter, class action lawyers—not the representatives—almost always bear the costs of class litigation. Second, courts usually sharply restrict questioning in this area to avoid a general fishing expedition into the plaintiff's finances.[40] Finally, and perhaps most important, the ethical rules governing lawyers in many jurisdictions cast considerable doubt on whether any inquiry in this area continues to be relevant, even in the class action context.[41] In fact, many jurisdictions now permit lawyers to advance the costs and expenses of litigation and make the repayment of such costs and expenses contingent on the outcome.[42] Accordingly, if a representative in a class action in such a jurisdiction has such an arrangement, the representative does not have, and should not have to testify about, *any* financial responsibility for costs.[43]

However, the law on costs is not uniform. Thus, when preparing to depose a class representative, both the taker and the defender should review the ethical rules of the jurisdiction where the suit is filed to determine if questions about financial responsibilities continue to be relevant.

In jurisdictions where the client remains ultimately liable for the costs of litigation regardless of outcome, such questions will no doubt continue to be allowed. If you are defending a deposition in such a jurisdiction, when you prepare your witness, remind her that named plaintiffs are ultimately responsible for costs, even if advanced by counsel. And remind her to be prepared to testify to a "willingness" to assume such financial responsibilities.[44]

If a taker persists in asking such questions in jurisdictions where such questions should be irrelevant under the governing ethical rules, a defender should instruct the class representative not to answer such questions. If necessary, the defender should seek a protective order barring the inquiries on the ground that they are irrelevant, harass the witness, and invade the witness's privacy.[45]

Ordinarily, the class representative is not entitled to special compensation for acting as class representative unless a court orders such compensation as an "incentive award," or for incurring costs on behalf of the class, or for rendering extraordinary service to the class.[46] It is at least unethical—and under certain circumstances arguably illegal—for a class representative to share in the fees awarded to class counsel upon successful prosecution of the case.[47] For example, in federal securities cases, the payment of extra compensation to a class representative has been statutorily prohibited, or at least substantially restricted, since passage of the Private Securities Litigation Reform Act (PSLRA) by Congress in 1995.[48] As a taker in these cases, it is thus entirely proper to ask the class representative questions to determine whether she reached any such improper agreement with counsel for the putative class.

Qualifications of Class Counsel

The second prong of the adequacy test requires the plaintiff to retain counsel who is competent and experienced in class litigation.[49] According to courts and commentators alike, "the single most important factor considered . . . in determining the quality of the representative's ability and willingness to advocate the cause of the class has been the caliber of the plaintiff's attorney."[50]

Obviously, the general experience, competence, and reputation of plaintiff's counsel, and whether plaintiff's counsel may have a conflict of interest, are relevant to this issue.[51] Information about these attributes, however, is usually developed outside the arena of a class representative's deposition. Nevertheless, at the named plaintiff's deposition, the taker may, and should, ask questions about aspects of the attorney-client relationship, including whether class counsel has acted unethically. Although such questions would be inappropriate in non-class litigation, they are allowed in a class action deposition, subject to the attorney-client privilege.

For example, it has become routine to ask the class representative about how she came to become a plaintiff,[52] whether she was solicited,[53] and, if so, the nature of the solicitation.[54] Although in recent years the scope of permissible solicitation has expanded significantly,[55] solicitation may still be improper,[56] and evidence of it may be grounds for disqualifying the class plaintiff's counsel.[57]

Therefore, when preparing a named plaintiff for a deposition, the defender should discuss with the witness the sequence of events by which the action was initiated and, if pertinent, issues that may arise concerning solicitation.[58] Although disqualification for ethical reasons, including those involving solicitation, is extremely rare and arises only when a lawyer's conduct is gross and goes to the heart of adequacy of representation, it is nevertheless possible and should not be overlooked.[59]

Antagonistic Interests

The third prong of the adequacy test looks at whether the interests of the proposed class representative conflict with those of the class.[60] This factor focuses on the named plaintiff rather than counsel,[61] and "considers whether the named plaintiffs' interests are sufficiently aligned with the absentees'."[62]

The existence of a conflict does not automatically result in a finding of inadequacy.[63] To be disabling, the conflict must concern core issues and not be merely speculative or potential.[64] The conflict must also involve issues common to the class.[65]

Given these parameters, disabling conflicts are relatively rare. When they do arise, it is usually because of a relationship between the class representative and the defendant or its affiliate that may interfere with the representative's obligation to provide undivided loyalty to the class.[66] Suppose, for example, the daughter of the named plaintiff is also an employee of the defendant. This situation presents a potentially disabling conflict because the named plaintiff may eventually decide, out of loyalty to his child, to be a less-than-zealous class representative.

Conflicts involving loyalty can arise in a variety of settings. Consider a class action against a corporation in which the named plaintiff is a dissident shareholder seeking to take over the corporation. If the plaintiff is using the lawsuit primarily for reasons of self-interest, this fact may result in disqualification because the plaintiff does not have undivided loyalty to the class.[67]

Disabling conflicts may also surface when the class is defined in a manner that creates the potential for an intraclass conflict. Suppose the named plaintiff belongs to a subgroup of the class that stands to gain a disproportionate benefit from a proposed settlement of the action.[68] In that situation, a disabling conflict might exist between the representative and members of the class not in that subgroup.

Yet another situation in which disabling conflicts may arise is one discussed above—namely, when the class representative has an agreement with counsel to obtain compensation in excess of that available to other class members. Such an arrangement may place the representative's own interests in conflict with his duty to the class, and, as noted above, may be unethical or even potentially illegal.[69] Contrast this arrangement with the payment of an incentive award to the class representative. These awards are perfectly proper and are frequently permitted. In fact, at the conclusion of the litigation, the court may reward a representative for his or her efforts in creating a common fund for the class.[70] Such awards are typically modest in amount (for example, $10,000), bear no relation to the attorney's fees awarded to class counsel (so as not to constitute an improper sharing of fees), and reflect the extra effort and time expended by the class representative for the benefit of the class.[71]

Questions About Typicality

Unlike adequacy, the second prerequisite to class certification—typicality—does not focus on the circumstances of the class representative or her counsel. Instead, typicality looks at whether the class representative's claim or defenses differ in some material way from those of the class as a whole.[72] As one federal district court explained, "This 'requirement focuses less on the relative strengths of the named and unnamed plaintiffs' cases than on the similarity of the legal and remedial theories behind their claims."[73]

Claims

The representative's claims are typical if they stem from the same event or practice that forms the basis of the class claims.[74] Put another way, the representative's claims must share common characteristics with the claims of the absent class members. But the claims need not be identical.[75] Regardless of how this class action prerequisite is phrased, "it is not a demanding one."[76]

Nonetheless, at a class representative's deposition, the taker can and should ask questions aimed at uncovering and exploiting any differences between the class claims alleged in the complaint and the named plaintiff's individual claims. However, if differences exist, they must be material for typicality to be wanting.

Damages are a good example. Damages suffered by individual class members almost always vary. Yet these variations are immaterial because they do not affect the underlying claims and will not by themselves destroy typicality.[77] Liability issues, in contrast, are more likely to affect typicality. Consider a discrimination class action: The named plaintiff will often seek to redress a whole range of grievances, including ones that she did not suffer individually. Provided that the overall misconduct challenged by the suit is similar to the misconduct alleged by the plaintiff, class certification will be appropriate.

In analyzing the typicality of claims, the law requires courts to apply "a rigorous analysis" and not to make presumptions based on conclusory allegations of similarity.[78] As a result, deposition takers will usually ask questions that focus on whether the named plaintiff's individual injuries stem from conduct *substantially similar* to that sought to be remedied in the class action. If the similarity is there, differences between the class plaintiff's individual claims and those of the class will not be fatal. Takers, of course, can be expected to frame questions that magnify the differences.

Typicality problems can also surface around the question of the named plaintiff's standing to sue. For example, a named plaintiff with no individual standing to sue a particular defendant—perhaps because she suffered no injury by virtue of the defendant's conduct or because she is unable to establish harm from a conspiracy in which the defendant participated—generally cannot represent a class that can assert such claims.[79] In other words, a named plaintiff may not "bootstrap" class allegations into standing to sue individually. The reason for this rule: "A class representative must be part of the class and 'possess the same interest and suffer the same injury' as the class members."[80]

In cases in which standing may be an issue, the deposition taker will usually ask questions about the extent to which the representative can state an individual claim against a particular defendant. The named plaintiff must be prepared to respond because if such claims cannot be articulated, she may lack standing to sue that defendant on behalf of the class, and her claims may be deemed atypical.

Defenses

Typicality also can become an issue because of potential defenses facing the class representative.[81] Suppose the named plaintiff's claims are time-barred or subject to a serious statute of limitations challenge. In this situation, the named plaintiff may face a defense that is unique to him and prevents him from pressing the claims of the class. Because a complaint often does not include enough facts to resolve a statute of limitations issue, the class representative's deposition becomes the forum for ferreting out these facts. At the deposition, the taker should ask questions about potential defenses; before the deposition, the defender, of course, should prepare the witness to respond to such questions.

In a fraud case, the taker should explore whether the named plaintiff's claims of misrepresentation are predicated on standardized written representations made to the class as a whole, as opposed to oral representations made to the named plaintiff, but not to the class as a whole.[82] If the latter, the named plaintiff may be subject to a unique class certification defense, which, in turn, might destroy his typicality.[83]

In securities class actions, the class representative also may have purchased securities both before and after discovering the defendant's alleged misrepresentations. If so, the class representative, unlike other members of the class, may be peculiarly subject to a reliance defense.[84] Again, because such facts do not usually emerge from the complaint, the class deposition is the perfect vehicle for exploring these issues.

Typicality concerns may also arise in cases in which the named plaintiff has been a frequent litigant. In fact, because of concerns about so-called "professional plaintiffs" who had a history of bringing similar securities class actions while owning an extremely small number of shares of stock in the defendant, the PSLRA restricts the number of securities actions in which one can act as a class representative.[85] A parallel judicial concern, addressed in part by the restrictions found in the PSLRA, is that the frequent litigant faces atypical defenses.[86] Consequently, when the named plaintiff in a class action has frequently acted as class representative, the taker should ask about this circumstance.[87]

Conclusion

The filing of a class action raises issues of adequacy and typicality. Both requirements must be satisfied before a court will certify a

class action. For this reason, questions that bear on the two requirements are fair game at the deposition of a named plaintiff. To properly take, prepare a witness for, or defend such a deposition, you
need to understand how these two requirements work and what
types of questions they are likely to generate at the deposition.

Notes

1.   In this chapter and in the case law, the representative or named
plaintiff is also sometimes referred to as the "class representative" or the
"class plaintiff."

2.   FED. R. CIV. P. 23(a); *see also infra* note 9.

3.   Hansberry v. Lee, 311 U.S. 32, 40–43 (1940).

4.   *See, e.g.,* Supreme Tribe of Ben-Hur v. Cauble, 255 U.S. 356, 363–
64 (1921).

5.   FED. R. CIV. P. 23(c)(2)(B)(v) & (c)(3)(B); Laskey v. Int'l Union
(UAW), 638 F.2d 954, 956 (6th Cir. 1981). In certain types of class actions,
absent class members have no right to exclude themselves. *See* FED. R.
CIV. P. 23(c)(2)(A) & (3)(A). Also, in class actions where an "opt out" right
is afforded and a settlement is reached after the class has been originally
certified, the court may allow a new "opt out" opportunity to those class
members who did not previously exercise their "opt out" right. FED. R.
CIV. P. 23(e)(4).

6.   *See* FED. R. CIV. P. 23(a); *Supreme Tribe of Ben-Hur,* 255 U.S. at
363–64.

7.   *See Hansberry,* 311 U.S. at 40–43.

8.   *See, e.g.,* CashCall, Inc. v. Super. Ct., 159 Cal. App. 4th 273, 284
(2008); Richmond v. Dart Indus., Inc., 629 P.2d 23, 28 (1981); City of San
Jose v. Super. Ct., 525 P.2d 701, 712–13 (1974).

9.   In addition to the requirements of adequacy and typicality,
FRCP 23(a) also requires common questions of law or fact and a class so
numerous that joinder is impracticable. Because these latter two factors
generally do not involve issues arising or developed during the course of
the named plaintiff's deposition (except as they may overlap with adequacy and typicality concerns), they are not analyzed separately in this
chapter.

10.   FED. R. CIV. P. 23(a)(4).

11.   391 F.2d 555, 562 (2d Cir. 1968); *accord* Hoxworth v. Blinder, Robinson & Co., Inc., 980 F.2d 912, 923 (3d Cir. 1992); Richards v. FleetBoston
Fin. Corp., 235 F.R.D. 165, 169–70 (D. Conn. 2006).

12.   FED. R. CIV. P. 23(a)(3).

13.   Jordan v. County of Los Angeles, 669 F.2d 1311, 1321 (9th Cir.),
vacated on other grounds, 459 U.S. 810 (1982); *see also* Multi-Ethnic Immi-
grant Workers Org. Network v. City of Los Angeles, 246 F.R.D. 621, 631–32

(C.D. Cal. 2007); Dura-Bilt Corp. v. Chase Manhattan Corp., 89 F.R.D. 87, 99 (S.D.N.Y. 1981) ("[t]he proper inquiry is whether other members of the class have the same or similar injury, whether the action is based on conduct not special or unique to the named plaintiffs, and whether other class members have been injured by the same course of conduct").

14.   *See* Dukes v. Wal-Mart Stores, Inc., 222 F.R.D. 137, 150 (N.D. Cal. 2004) (citing Shipes v. Trinity Indus., 987 F.2d 311, 316 (5th Cir. 1993)), *aff'd*, 509 F.3d 1168 (9th Cir. 2007), *reh'g en banc granted*, 556 F.3d 919 (9th Cir. 2009); *accord* Weinberger v. Thornton, 114 F.R.D. 599, 603 (S.D. Cal. 1986); Schwartz v. Harp, 108 F.R.D. 279, 282 (C.D. Cal. 1985); Vasquez v. Super. Ct., 484 P.2d 964, 969 (1971).

15.   *See Hansberry*, 311 U.S. at 40–43.

16.   *See, e.g.*, Sley v. Jamaica Water & Util., Inc., 77 F.R.D. 391, 393–94 (E.D. Pa. 1977); R. Kirby, *A Proposal Regarding Rule 23(a)(4): Adequacy of Representation in Class Actions*, 6 CLASS ACTION REP. 210, 212–13 (1980).

17.   Showing that the named plaintiff is inadequate or atypical, however, may not be enough to defeat the class action. Courts often allow the substitution of another plaintiff who satisfies these requirements and, in so doing, permit the action to proceed as a class action. *E.g., CashCall*, 159 Cal. App. 4th at 287.

18.   *See* Lerwill v. Inflight Motion Pictures, Inc., 582 F.2d 507, 512 (9th Cir. 1978); Wetzel v. Liberty Mut. Ins. Co., 508 F.2d 239, 247 (3d Cir. 1975); *In re* Wal-Mart Stores, Inc. Wage & Hour Litig., 2008 WL 413749, at *12 (N.D. Cal. Feb. 13, 2008); Florence v. Bd. of Chosen Freeholders of County of Burlington, 2008 WL 800970, at *10–11 (D.N.J. Mar. 20, 2008).

19.   688 F. Supp. 1425, 1462 (S.D. Cal. 1988) (citation omitted).

20.   *See Lubin*, 688 F. Supp. at 1462; Kassover v. Computer Depot, Inc., 691 F. Supp. 1205, 1213–14 (D. Minn.1987), *aff'd*, 902 F.2d 1571 (8th Cir. 1990); Scott v. New York City Dist. Council, 224 F.R.D. 353, 356–58 (S.D.N.Y. 2004); *see also* Koenig v. Benson, 117 F.R.D. 330, 337 (E.D.N.Y. 1987).

21.   *See, e.g.*, Stuart v. Radioshack Corp., 2009 WL 281941, at *10 (N.D. Cal. Feb. 5, 2009); Harrington v. City of Albuquerque, 222 F.R.D. 505, 514–15 (D.N.M. 2004); Lewis v. Nat'l Football League, 146 F.R.D. 5, 10 (D.D.C. 1992); Kaplan v. Pomerantz, 131 F.R.D. 118, 121–22 (N.D. Ill. 1990); Lerner v. Haimsohn, 126 F.R.D. 64, 67 (D. Colo. 1989); *In re* Diasonics Sec. Litig., 599 F. Supp. 447, 452–53 (N.D. Cal. 1984).

22.   Alaska Elec. Pension Fund v. Pharmacia Corp., 2007 WL 276150, at *3 (D.N.J. Jan. 25, 2007) ("[t]he level of knowledge of the class representative is not a relevant inquiry in this Circuit" (citations omitted)).

23.   *See* Nathan Gordon Trust v. Northgate Exploration, Ltd., 148 F.R.D. 105, 107 (S.D.N.Y. 1993) ("it is familiar law that a class representative need not have personal knowledge of the evidence and the law involved in pursuing a litigation"); Chakejian v. Equifax Info. Servs. LLC, __ F.R.D. __ , 2009 WL 764656, at *6 (E.D. Pa. Mar. 25, 2009). As the Supreme Court has noted, the FRCP, including FRCP 23, "were designed

in large part to get away from some of the old procedural booby traps which common-law pleaders could set to prevent unsophisticated litigants from ever having their day in court." Surowitz v. Hilton Hotels Corp., 383 U.S. 363, 373 (1966).

24. *Stuart*, 2009 WL 281941, at *10; Fernandez v. K-M Indus. Holding Co., Inc., 2008 WL 2625874, at *3–4 (N.D. Cal. Jun. 26, 2008); Moeller v. Taco Bell Corp., 220 F.R.D. 604, 611–12 (N.D. Cal. 2004); *Koenig*, 117 F.R.D. at 337.

25. *See, e.g.*, *Scott*, 224 F.R.D. at 356–58 (failure to read complaint, no idea of what a class representative is, no knowledge of allegations of complaint); Levine v. Berg, 79 F.R.D. 95, 97 (S.D.N.Y. 1978) (lack of familiarity with complaint, inability to articulate claims); Weisman v. Darneille, 78 F.R.D. 669, 671 (S.D.N.Y. 1978) (inability to describe claim and identify defendants); Greenspan v. Brassler, 78 F.R.D. 130, 133–34 (S.D.N.Y. 1978) (inability to identify defendants, lack of knowledge of elements of complaint); Seiden v. Nicholson, 69 F.R.D. 681, 688 (N.D. Ill. 1976) (failure to read amended complaints, lack of knowledge about allegations and size of proposed class). *But see In re* Cooper Cos., Inc. Sec. Litig., 254 F.R.D. 628, 637 (C.D. Cal. 2009) (distinguishing *Darneille*).

26. It is often said that the members of the proposed class are "entitled to more than blind reliance on counsel." *In re* Storage Tech. Corp. Sec. Litig., 113 F.R.D. 113, 118–19 (D. Colo. 1986); *see also* Kirkpatrick v. J.C. Bradford & Co., 827 F.2d 718, 726–27 (11th Cir. 1987) (named plaintiff's disqualification appropriate only if his or her conduct is so minimal as to have abdicated conduct of the case to his or her lawyers); Eufaula Drugs, Inc. v. TDI Managed Care Servs., 250 F.R.D. 670, 677 (M.D. Ala. 2008); *but see* Eslava v. Gulf Tel. Co., 2007 WL 2298222, at *2–3 (S.D. Ala. 2007) (restricting holding in *Kirkpatrick* only to securities cases and refusing to establish a standard of general application); London v. Wal-Mart Stores, Inc., 340 F.3d 1246, 1254 (11th Cir. 2003) (stringent examination of adequacy required in non-securities cases).

27. Castano v. Am. Tobacco Co., 160 F.R.D. 544, 551 (E.D. La. 1995), *rev'd on other grounds*, 84 F.3d 734 (5th Cir. 1996).

28. Of course, it is important for the defender not to waive privileged communications by permitting substantive answers to questions that require the deponent to disclose communications she had about such matters with counsel. Such questions are to be distinguished from general inquiries that are aimed at testing the named plaintiff's knowledge of the case, the answers to which do not involve privileged communications with counsel.

29. *See* First Interstate Bank of Nev. N.A. v. Chapman & Cutler, 837 F.2d 775, 781 (7th Cir. 1988); *In re* AM Int'l, Inc. Sec. Litig., 108 F.R.D. 190, 198 (S.D.N.Y. 1985) (custodian found to be inadequate representative after his status changed upon child's maturity); *In re* Luxoticca Group, S.p.A. Sec. Litig., 2004 WL 2370650, at *6–7 (E.D.N.Y. Oct. 22, 2004); *In re*

FleetBoston Fin. Corp. Sec. Litig., 253 F.R.D. 315, 324–25 (D.N.J. 2008); *see also* Plum Tree, Inc. v. Rouse Co., Inc., 58 F.R.D. 373 (E.D. Pa. 1972).

30. *See In re AM Int'l, Inc. Sec. Litig.*, 108 F.R.D. at 198; *see also* Landy v. Amsterdam, 96 F.R.D. 19, 20–21 (E.D. Pa. 1982); *In re* LTV Sec. Litig., 88 F.R.D. 134, 150 (N.D. Tex. 1980).

31. *See* Tedesco v. Mishkin, 689 F. Supp. 1327, 1337 (S.D.N.Y. 1988); Folding Cartons, Inc. v. Am. Can Co., 79 F.R.D. 698, 703 (N.D. Ill. 1978).

32. *See First Interstate Bank*, 837 F.2d at 781; Schatzman v. Talley, 91 F.R.D. 270, 273–75 (N.D. Ga. 1981).

33. *See, e.g., In re* Activision Sec. Litig., 621 F. Supp. 415, 429 (N.D. Cal. 1985); Jones v. Ford Motor Credit Co., 2005 WL 743213, at *9 (S.D.N.Y. Mar. 31, 2005).

34. *E.g.*, Hively v. Northlake Foods, Inc., 191 F.R.D. 661, 668 (M.D. Fla. 2000); McCall v. Drive Fin. Servs., L.P., 236 F.R.D. 246, 251–52 (E.D. Pa. 2006); *In re* Proxima Corp. Sec. Litig., [1993–1994 Transfer Binder] Fed. Sec. L. Rep. (CCH) ¶ 98,236, at ¶¶ 99,626–27 (S.D. Cal. 1994) (proposed class representative admitted having participated in fraud); Maddox & Starbuck, Ltd. v. British Airways, 97 F.R.D. 395, 396–97 (S.D.N.Y. 1983); Green v. Carlson, 653, F.2d 1022 (5th Cir. 1981); Cobb v. Avon Prods., Inc., 71 F.R.D. 652, 654–55 (W.D. Pa. 1976), *appeal dismissed without opinion*, 565 F.2d 151 (3d Cir. 1977); Jones v. Pac. Intermountain Exp., 24 Fed. R. Serv. 2d (Callaghan) 95, 96 (N.D. Cal. 1977) (convicted, incarcerated murderer deemed inadequate).

35. *See* Norman v. Arcs Equities Corp., 72 F.R.D. 502, 505 (S.D.N.Y. 1976).

36. *See, e.g.*, CV Reit v. Levy, 144 F.R.D. 690, 698 (S.D. Fla. 1992); McGlothlin v. Conners, 142 F.R.D. 626, 634 (W.D. Va. 1992); Moskowitz v. Lopp, 128 F.R.D. 624, 635–36 (E.D. Pa. 1989); Fickinger v. C.I. Planning Corp., 103 F.R.D. 529, 533 (E.D. Pa. 1984). A class representative's responsibilities are simply too narrow in scope (attending a deposition; participating in other, limited pretrial discovery; and possibly offering testimony at trial) for most physical limitations to cause disqualification. For that reason, only the most feeble class representatives will be disqualified; even then, substitute class representatives may be available to replace or bolster the existing representation.

37. For example, in *Eisen v. Carlisle & Jacquelin*, 417 U.S. 156, 178–79 (1974), the Supreme Court held that in a FRCP 23(b)(3) class action, individual notice must be provided when class members may be identified through reasonable efforts, and the plaintiff must pay notice costs. *See also In re* ML Lee Acquisition Fund II, L.P. & ML Lee Acquisition Fund (Ret. Accounts) II, L.P. Sec. Litig., 149 F.R.D. 506, 508–09 (D. Del. 1993); Liberty Lincoln Mercury, Inc. v. Fund Mktg. Corp., 149 F.R.D. 65, 79 (D.N.J. 1993).

38. *See* Palmer v. BRG of Ga., Inc., 874 F.2d 1417, 1421 (11th Cir. 1989), *rev'd on other grounds*, 498 U.S. 46 (1990).

39. *E.g.*, Fruchter v. Fla. Progress Corp., 2002 WL 1558220, at *7 (Fla. Cir. Ct. Mar. 20, 2002); Brooks v. S. Bell Tel. & Tel. Co., 133 F.R.D. 54, 58–59 (S.D. Fla. 1990); Lohse v. Dairy Comm'n of State of Nev., 1977-2 Trade Cas. (CCH) ¶ 61,805 (D. Nev. 1977); Murphy v. Alpha Realty, Inc., 1977-2 Trade Cas. (CCH) ¶ 61,566 (N.D. Ill. 1977); Tomkin v. Kaysen, 69 F.R.D. 541, 543–44 (S.D.N.Y. 1976); Strong v. Ark. Blue Cross & Blue Shield, Inc., 87 F.R.D. 496, 510–11 (E.D. Ark. 1980); Parker v. George Thompson Ford, Inc., 83 F.R.D. 378, 380–81 (N.D. Ga. 1979); Nat'l Auto Brokers Corp. v. Gen. Motors Corp., 376 F. Supp. 620, 638 (S.D.N.Y. 1974), *aff'd*, 572 F.2d 953 (2d Cir. 1978); Blumenthal v. Great Am. Mortgage Investors, 74 F.R.D. 508, 513 (N.D. Ga. 1976).

40. *See, e.g.*, Sanderson v. Winner, 507 F.2d 477, 479–80 (10th Cir. 1974); Sayre v. Abraham Lincoln Fed. Sav. & Loan Ass'n, 65 F.R.D. 379, 382–84 (E.D. Pa. 1974), *amended*, 69 F.R.D. 117 (E.D. Pa. 1975); *but see In re* Sheffield, 280 B.R. 719, 721–22 (Bankr. S.D. Ala. 2001); Porter v. Nationscredit Consumer Discount Co., 2004 WL 1753255, at *2 (E.D. Pa. Jul. 8, 2004); Royhouse v. Miller, 2007 WL 2220386, at *1 (W.D. Okla. Jul. 30, 2007).

41. *See* Rand v. Monsanto Co., 926 F.2d 596, 600–01 (7th Cir. 1991); *In re* WorldCom, Inc. Sec. Litig., 219 F.R.D. 267, 284–85 (S.D.N.Y. 2003).

42. *See, e.g.*, MODEL RULES OF PROF'L CONDUCT R. 1.8(e) (2004); CAL. RULES OF PROF'L CONDUCT R. 4-210 (A)(3); *In re* THQ, Inc. Sec. Litig., 2002 WL 1832145, at *8 (C.D. Cal. Mar. 22, 2002), and cases cited therein; *see also* Boccardo v. Comm'r of Internal Revenue, 56 F.3d 1016, 1019 (9th Cir. 1995) ("[i]n a federal class action, a state prohibition against the lawyer picking up the tab for costs has been invalidated as frustrating the Federal Rules of Civil Procedure, Rule 23"); *In re WorldCom*, 219 F.R.D. at 284–85.

43. Indeed, a number of courts have effectively so held. *See, e.g.*, United Nat'l Records, Inc. v. MCA, Inc., 101 F.R.D. 323, 327 (N.D. Ill. 1984).

44. Simon v. Westinghouse Elec. Corp., 73 F.R.D. 480, 485 (E.D. Pa. 1977); *In re* Indep. Gasoline Antitrust Litig., 79 F.R.D. 552, 557 (D. Md. 1978).

45. *See Rand*, 926 F.2d at 600–01; *see also infra* note 48. See also "Instructing a Witness Not to Answer" in Chapter 14 and "Improper Instructions Not to Answer" in Chapter 15.

46. *See In re* Dun & Bradstreet Credit Servs. Customer Litig., 130 F.R.D. 366, 373–74 (S.D. Ohio 1990); Hadix v. Johnson, 322 F.3d 895, 897 (6th Cir. 2003), and cases cited therein.

47. A prominent class action law firm, three of its partners, a former partner, and several of the firm's clients were indicted for allegedly entering into such arrangements. The partners and some of the firm's clients pled guilty to charges relating thereto. *See* U.S. Dep't of Justice Release No. 07-114 (Sept. 18, 2007); U.S. Dep't of Justice Release No. 08-030 (Mar. 20, 2008). The law firm entered into a nonprosecution agreement requiring it, inter alia, to pay a $75 million fine. *See* Jonathan D. Glater, *Big*

Penalty Set for Law Firm, but Not a Trial, N.Y. TIMES (June 17, 2008). These developments will no doubt lead to even more aggressive questioning in this area.

48.   *See* 15 U.S.C. §§ 78u-4 *et seq.* Subsection (a)(2)(A)(vi) provides that the plaintiff must declare under oath that, inter alia, he will not accept any payment for serving as a class representative beyond his pro rata share of any recovery, except reimbursement for reasonable costs and expenses (including lost wages) awarded by the court. Moreover, in addition to restricting payments to class representatives, the PSLRA imposes special requirements on class representatives that are likely to give rise to other questions at the class representative's deposition:

> Each plaintiff seeking to serve as a representative party on behalf of a class shall provide a sworn certification, which shall be personally signed by such plaintiff and filed with the complaint, that—
>
> (i) states that the plaintiff has reviewed the complaint and authorized its filing;
> (ii) states that the plaintiff did not purchase the security that is the subject of the complaint at the direction of plaintiff's counsel or in order to participate in any private action arising under this chapter;
> (iii) states that the plaintiff is willing to serve as a representative party on behalf of a class, including providing testimony at deposition and trial, if necessary;
> (iv) sets forth all of the transactions of the plaintiff in the security that is the subject of the complaint during the class period specified in the complaint;
> (v) identifies any other action under this chapter, filed during the 3-year period preceding the date on which the certification is signed by the plaintiff, in which the plaintiff has sought to serve as a representative party on behalf of a class.

15 U.S.C. § 78u-4(a)(2)(A)(i)–(v). This latter requirement is tied to another provision of the PSLRA that restricts the number of actions in which one can serve as a class representative to five in any three-year period unless the court permits otherwise, thus attacking the use of so-called "professional plaintiffs." 15 U.S.C. § 78u-4(a)(3)(B)(vi).

49.   Brame v. Ray Bills Fin. Corp., 85 F.R.D. 568, 575 (N.D.N.Y. 1979); Turner v. A.B. Carter, Inc., 85 F.R.D. 360, 364 (E.D. Va. 1980).

50.   Symposium on Class Actions, *The Class Representative: The Problem of the Absent Plaintiffs,* 68 Nw. U. L. REV. 1133, 1136 (1974). *See also* Ferrell v. Busbee, 91 F.R.D. 225, 233 (N.D. Ga. 1981).

51.   *See, e.g.,* Wrighten v. Metro. Hosps., Inc., 726 F.2d 1346, 1351–52 (9th Cir. 1984); Sweet v. Pfizer, 232 F.R.D. 360, 371 (C.D. Cal. 2005);

Cullen v. New York State Civil Serv. Comm'n, 435 F. Supp. 546, 560, 563 (E.D.N.Y.), *appeal dismissed*, 566 F.2d 846 (2d Cir. 1977).

52.　*See* Norman v. Arcs Equities Corp., 72 F.R.D. 502, 505–06 (S.D.N.Y. 1976); *Tomkin*, 69 F.R.D. at 543.

53.　*In re* Stavrides v. Mellon Nat'l Bank & Trust Co., 60 F.R.D. 634, 636–38 (W.D. Pa. 1973).

54.　*See Stravrides*, 60 F.R.D. at 636–38; Harris v. Gen. Dev. Corp., 127 F.R.D. 655, 662 (N.D. Ill. 1989).

55.　*See* Shapero v. Ky. Bar Ass'n, 486 U.S. 466, 472–76 (1988).

56.　*Id*. at 479–80.

57.　*But see* Busby v. JRHBW Realty, Inc., 513 F.3d 1314, 1323–24 (11th Cir. 2008) ("only the most egregious misconduct on the part of plaintiffs' lawyer could ever arguably justify denial of class status") (quoting Halverson v. Convenient Food Mart, Inc., 458 F.2d 927, 932 (7th Cir. 1972)); Kennedy v. United Healthcare of Ohio, Inc., 206 F.R.D. 191, 197–98 (S.D. Ohio 2002).

58.　*See* Carlisle v. LTV Electrosystems, Inc., 54 F.R.D. 237, 240 (N.D. Tex. 1972); *see also* Wagner v. Lehman Bros. Kuhn Loeb, Inc., 646 F. Supp. 643, 659–62 (N.D. Ill. 1986) (violations of ethical rules bar lawyer from serving as class counsel); Ward v. Nierlich, 2006 WL 5412626, at *6 (S.D. Fla. Sep. 18, 2006); Simon v. Merrill Lynch, Pierce, Fenner & Smith, 16 Fed. R. Serv. 2d (Callaghan) 1021, 1022 (N.D. Tex. 1972); Korn v. Franchard Co., [1970–1971 Transfer Binder] Fed. Sec. L. Rep. (CCH) ¶ 92,845 (S.D.N.Y. 1970); Efros v. Nationwide Corp., 98 F.R.D. 703, 706–07 (S.D. Ohio 1983).

59.　*See Carlisle*, 54 F.R.D. at 240; Korn v. Franchard Corp., 456 F.2d 1206, 1208 (2d Cir. 1972).

60.　*See* Sosna v. Iowa, 419 U.S. 393, 403 (1975); Mazza v. Am. Honda Motor Co., 254 F.R.D. 610, 618 (C.D. Cal. 2008).

61.　*See In re* Joint E&S Dist. Asbestos Litig., 133 F.R.D. 425, 431–32 (E.D. & S.D.N.Y. 1990); Shankroff v. Advest, Inc., 112 F.R.D. 190, 194 (S.D.N.Y. 1986). Note that as long as there is at least one class representative who is not affected by the antagonism or conflict, the case may proceed on a class basis.

62.　*Mazza*, 254 F.R.D. at 618; *In re* Gen. Motors Corp. Pick-Up Truck Fuel Tank Litig., 55 F.3d 768, 800 (3d Cir. 1995).

63.　*See* Marshall v. Holiday Magic, Inc., 550 F.2d 1173, 1177 (9th Cir. 1977), *abrogated on other grounds*, Phillips Petroleum Co. v. Shutts, 472 U.S. 797 (1985).

64.　Soc. Servs. Union, Local 535 v. County of Santa Clara, 609 F.2d 944, 948 (9th Cir. 1979); Buus v. WAMU Pension Plan, 251 F.R.D. 578, 585 (W.D. Wash. 2008); Edmondson v. Simon, 86 F.R.D. 375, 381–82 (N.D. Ill. 1980), *vacated on other grounds*, 33 Fair Empl. Prac. Cas. (BNA) 943 (N.D. Ill. 1982).

65.　*See In re* Corrugated Container Antitrust Litig., 643 F.2d 195, 208 (5th Cir. 1981); Strube v. Am. Equity Inv. Life Ins. Co., 226 F.R.D. 688, 696 (M.D. Fla. 2005).

66. *See Shankroff*, 112 F.R.D. at 194; *In re* Gulf Oil/Cities Serv. Tender Offer Litig., 112 F.R.D. 383, 388 (S.D.N.Y. 1986); Freeman v. Motor Convoy, Inc., 700 F.2d 1339, 1345–47 (11th Cir. 1983).

67. *See* William Penn Mgmt. Corp. v. Provident Fund for Income, Inc., 68 F.R.D. 456, 459–60 (E.D. Pa. 1975) (plaintiffs sought management contract); *see also* duPont v. Wily, 61 F.R.D. 615, 622 (D. Del. 1973); Puharich v. Borders Elecs. Co., Inc., 11 Fed. R. Serv. 2d (Callaghan) 510, 511 (S.D.N.Y. 1968); DeLeo v. Swirsky, 2002 WL 989526, at *3 (N.D. Ill. May 14, 2002). Put another way, the named plaintiff's motives may be disqualifying if they are found to jeopardize the interests of the class. Sperry Rand Corp. v. Larson, 554 F.2d 868, 874 (8th Cir. 1977); *see also William Penn*, 68 F.R.D. at 458–59; Esler v. Northrop Corp., 86 F.R.D. 20, 36 (W.D. Mo. 1979).

68. *See In re Gen. Motors Corp.*, 55 F.3d at 800–01 (intraclass conflict between individual vehicle owners and fleet owners who were members of settlement class).

69. *See* discussion *supra* note 47. This issue affects the adequacy of both class counsel and the class representative.

70. *See In re* SmithKline Beckman Corp. Sec. Litig., 751 F. Supp. 525, 535 (E.D. Pa. 1990); *In re Dun & Bradstreet*, 130 F.R.D. at 373–74; Bogosian v. Gulf Oil Corp., 621 F. Supp. 27, 32 (E.D. Pa. 1985).

71. *Id.; see also* discussion *supra* note 48.

72. *See* Gen. Tel. Co. of Sw. v. Falcon (Falcon), 457 U.S. 147, 158 n.13 (1982); De la Fuente v. Stokley-Van Kamp, Inc., 713 F.2d 225, 232 (7th Cir. 1985); Vulcan Golf, LLC v. Google, Inc., 254 F.R.D. 521, 525–26 (N.D. Ill. 2008).

73. *Castano*, 160 F.R.D. at 550–51 (citations omitted).

74. *See supra* note 13.

75. *See* Allen v. Chi. Transit Auth., 2000 WL 1207408, at *7 (N.D. Ill. Jul. 31, 2000) (one common issue will suffice); Allen v. City of Chi., 828 F. Supp. 543, 553 (N.D. Ill. 1993); Martin v. Ark. Arts. Ctr., 28 Fed. R. Serv. 2d (Callaghan) 695 (E.D. Ark. 1979).

76. *Castano*, 160 F.R.D. at 551.

77. *See In re Activision*, 621 F. Supp. at 428.

78. *Falcon*, 457 U.S. at 157–59, 161.

79. *See* O'Shea v. Littleton, 414 U.S. 488, 494 (1974) ("[i]f none of the named plaintiffs purporting to represent a class establishes the requisite of a case or controversy with the defendants, none may seek relief on behalf of himself or any other member of the class" (footnote omitted)); Portis v. City of Chi., 347 F. Supp. 2d 573 (N.D. Ill. 2004); La Mar v. H&B Novelty & Loan Co., 489 F.2d 461, 465 (9th Cir. 1973). However, if defendants are jurisdictionally linked through, inter alia, contract, conspiracy, or concerted scheme, some courts have held that the plaintiff would have the requisite standing to sue a defendant with whom he or she had not dealt directly. *E.g., La Mar*, 489 F.2d at 465; Payton v. County of Kane, 308

F.3d 673, 678–83 (7th Cir. 2002); Matte v. Sunshine Mobile Homes, Inc., 270 F. Supp. 2d 805, 824–28 (W.D. La. 2003); *In re* Tri-State Crematory Litig., 215 F.R.D. 660, 685–87 (N.D. Ga. 2003). *But see In re* FEMA Trailer Formaldehyde Prods. Liab. Litig., 570 F. Supp. 2d 851, 855–56 (E.D. La. 2008) (casting doubt on validity of conspiracy/concerted scheme allegations as establishing standing); Harry v. Circus Circus Casinos, 223 F.R.D. 541, 543–44 (D. Nev. 2004).

80.   *Falcon*, 457 U.S. at 156 (quoting E. Tex. Motor Freight Sys., Inc. v. Rodriguez, 431 U.S. 395, 403 (1977)).

81.   *See* Gary Plastic Packaging Corp. v. Merrill Lynch, Pierce, Fenner & Smith, 903 F.2d 176, 179–80 (2d Cir. 1990), *cert. denied*, 498 U.S. 1025 (1991) (class certification improper when representative subject to unique defenses that might become focus of litigation). "[I]f it is predictable that 'a major focus of the litigation will be on an arguable defense unique to the named plaintiff or a small subclass, then the named plaintiff is not a proper class representative.'" Wofford v. Safeway Stores, Inc., 78 F.R.D. 460, 489 (N.D. Cal. 1978) (quoting Koos v. First Nat'l Bank of Peoria, 496 F.2d 1162, 1164 (7th Cir. 1974)). A disputed defense, however, may not destroy typicality, *see* Dupler v. Costco Wholesale Corp., 249 F.R.D. 29, 38–39 (E.D.N.Y. 2008), nor is there a lack of typicality where the defense is not the likely "focus" of the litigation, Steinberg v. Nationwide Mut. Ins. Co., 224 F.R.D. 67, 74 (E.D.N.Y. 2004).

82.   *See, e.g.*, Williams v. Balcor Pension Investors, 150 F.R.D. 109, 114–15 (N.D. Ill. 1993) (claims of named plaintiff, who relied on oral representations of investment adviser not traceable to written prospectus distributed to class, found not to be typical).

83.   This is a situation that typically may overlap with the class action prerequisite requiring predominance of common questions. Using this example, if each class member received different oral misrepresentations, questions relating to reliance and other elements of fraud may not be common as between the named plaintiff and other class members.

84.   *See, e.g.*, Rocco v. Nam Tai Elecs., Inc., 245 F.R.D. 131, 135–36 (S.D.N.Y. 2007); Kovaleff v. Piano, 142 F.R.D. 406, 408 (S.D.N.Y. 1992); Kline v. Wolf, 88 F.R.D. 696, 699 (S.D.N.Y. 1981), *aff'd*, 702 F.2d 400, 403 (2d Cir. 1983); *see also Blumenthal*, 74 F.R.D. at 513. *But see, e.g., In re* Rent-Way Sec. Litig., 218 F.R.D. 101, 114 (W.D. Pa. 2003); Rosen v. Textron, 369 F. Supp. 2d 204, 208–09 (D.R.I. 2005).

85.   15 U.S.C.§ 78u-4; *see also supra* note 48.

86.   *See, e.g.*, Hanon v. Dataproducts Corp., 976 F.2d 497, 508 (9th Cir. 1992); Hoexter v. Simmons, 140 F.R.D. 416, 422–23 (D. Ariz. 1991); Shields v. Smith, [1991–1992 Transfer Binder] Fed. Sec. L. Rep. (CCH) ¶ 96,449, at ¶¶ 91,967–98 (N.D. Cal. 1991).

87.   *See Hanon*, 976 F.2d at 508; *In re* Harcourt Brace Jovanovich, Inc. Sec. Litig., 838 F. Supp. 109, 114 (S.D.N.Y. 1993).

CHAPTER 21

Deposition Perjury by Your Witness

HENRY L. HECHT

Someday, you may find yourself in a deposition where the client you are representing commits perjury. Though perjury at a deposition may seem less dramatic than perjury at a trial, it can have devastating effects on a case. It also can result in severe consequences for both you and your untruthful client.

This chapter examines the special problems that arise when a defender learns her client is committing, or has committed, perjury at a deposition. The issues that arise when a lawyer learns a client intends to commit perjury at a future deposition are covered in Chapter 8.[1]

This chapter begins by examining how a lawyer's duties of candor to the court and confidentiality to the client sometimes conflict in cases of client perjury. It first discusses how the American Bar Association (ABA) and a majority of jurisdictions have resolved this conflict in favor of candor to the court—whether the perjury occurs during a deposition or a trial. In either setting, if a client will not rectify the perjury, the lawyer must disclose the perjury to the court. The section next discusses the minority approach, which does not require disclosure, but instead allows the lawyer to withdraw. This section concludes with a brief discussion of the Federal Rules of Civil Procedure (FRCP), which in some instances also require a lawyer to rectify a client's deposition perjury.

The second section of the chapter considers two threshold questions that a lawyer must answer before determining whether she must rectify a client's false testimony during a deposition. The first question is whether the lawyer "knows" the client has testified falsely. The second is whether the false testimony is material to the case.

The third section discusses ways in which a lawyer might prevent or minimize deposition perjury by her client. It also reviews the remedial steps a lawyer must take once she has determined that the client has committed perjury during a deposition.

The final section of the chapter reviews the adverse consequences to both lawyer and client that can result if perjury at a deposition is not rectified properly.

Source and Nature of a Lawyer's Duty

Suppose you are about to prepare Leslie Roberts, the plaintiff in the *Scoops* case, for her deposition. One issue you need to address is whether she remembers telling Terry Blake, Defendant Business-Aide's salesperson, that she was applying for a bank loan and planned to use accounting software to prepare her loan application. If she remembers saying these things, her testimony will strengthen her claim that Business-Aide knew of her accounting software needs and nevertheless, negligently or intentionally, sold her software unsuited for those needs.

Imagine that during deposition preparation you have the following exchange with your client:

Q. Leslie, did you personally tell Terry Blake that you needed accounting software because you were applying for a bank loan?

A. I don't remember if I said anything about the bank loan.

Q. You can't remember one way or the other?

A. No.

Q. What's your best recollection?

A. Well, I suspect that I didn't say anything about the bank loan because I thought Frank Fuller, my employee, had already reviewed my business's needs with Ms. Waller. I didn't think I needed to repeat everything.

Q. Are you sure you didn't say something to Terry about the loan?

A. I can't be absolutely sure, but I probably didn't say anything about the bank loan.

Q. Can you think of any document or person that might aid your memory?

A. No. I didn't take any notes during my meeting with Terry or make any notes afterward.

Q. Since your meeting with Terry, have you asked Frank whether you said anything to him about that meeting?

A. No. When I met Terry, Frank was no longer employed at the store, so there was no one I'm aware of who knew what I said to Terry other than Terry and myself.

You leave the preparation session slightly disappointed. If this question is asked at her deposition, Roberts will have to testify that she could not recall telling Blake about the loan application. That testimony is not fatal to her lawsuit. But her legal position would be far stronger if she could testify that she told Blake about the loan.

Later, at Leslie Roberts' deposition, the following exchange takes place:

Q. Did you tell Mr. Blake that you intended to apply for a bank loan and wanted accounting software for that purpose?

A. Yes, of course, I did.

The response catches you by surprise. What should you do now?

ABA Model Rules

Under the ABA Model Rules of Professional Conduct (Model Rules), a lawyer who knows his client has offered perjured testimony or falsified evidence during a judicial proceeding cannot ignore the misconduct. Instead, the lawyer must take remedial action.[2]

Model Rule 3.3 provides in part:[3]

Candor Toward the Tribunal

(a) A lawyer shall not knowingly:

(1) make a false statement of fact or law to a tribunal or fail to correct a false statement of material fact or law previously made to the tribunal by the lawyer; [or]

. . . .

(3) offer evidence that the lawyer knows to be false. If a lawyer, the lawyer's client, or a witness called by the lawyer has offered material evidence and the lawyer comes to know of its falsity, the lawyer shall take reasonable remedial measures, including, if necessary, disclosure to the tribunal. A lawyer may refuse to offer evidence, other than the testimony of a defendant in a criminal matter, that the lawyer reasonably believes is false.

(b) A lawyer who represents a client in an adjudicative proceeding and who knows that a person intends to engage, is engaging or has engaged in criminal or fraudulent conduct related to the proceeding shall take reasonable remedial measures, including, if necessary, disclosure to the tribunal.

(c) The duties stated in paragraphs (a) and (b) continue to the conclusion of the proceeding, and apply *even if* compliance requires disclosure of information otherwise protected by Rule 1.6.

(d) In an ex parte proceeding, a lawyer shall inform the tribunal of all material facts known to the lawyer that will enable the tribunal to make an informed decision, whether or not the facts are adverse.[4]

Because acquiescing in a client's perjury is tantamount to assisting a criminal or fraudulent act by the client,[5] and assisting a client in offering false evidence,[6] Model Rule 3.3 requires a lawyer to rectify known perjury.[7]

But, as noted above, if the lawyer reveals the perjury, she may also be disclosing otherwise confidential communications protected by Model Rule 1.6.

Model Rule 1.6 provides:

Confidentiality of Information

(a) A lawyer shall not reveal information relating to the representation of a client unless the client gives informed consent, the disclosure is impliedly authorized in order to carry out the representation or the disclosure is permitted by paragraph (b).

(b) A lawyer may reveal information relating to the representation of a client to the extent the lawyer reasonably believes necessary:

(1) to prevent reasonably certain death or substantial bodily harm;

(2) to prevent the client from committing a crime or fraud that is reasonably certain to result in substantial injury to the financial interests or property of another and in furtherance of which the client has used or is using the lawyer's services;

(3) to prevent, mitigate or rectify substantial injury to the financial interests or property of another that is reasonably certain to result or has resulted from the client's commission of a crime or fraud in furtherance of which the client has used the lawyer's services;

(4) to secure legal advice about the lawyer's compliance with these Rules;

(5) to establish a claim or defense on behalf of the lawyer in a controversy between the lawyer and the client, to establish a defense to a criminal charge or civil claim against the lawyer based upon conduct in which the client was involved, or to respond to allegations in any proceeding concerning the lawyer's representation of the client; or

(6) to comply with other law or a court order.[8]

The conflicting duties of candor (Model Rule 3.3) and confidentiality (Model Rule 1.6) are fundamental to our justice system. The duty of candor helps find the truth and preserves public confidence in the courts. The duty of confidentiality facilitates competent representation, encourages people to seek early legal advice, and may itself ultimately serve the search for truth.[9]

But as noted above and as Model Rule 3.3(c) explicitly acknowledges, the candor required by Model Rule 3.3 may conflict with the confidentiality protected by Model Rule 1.6. The conflict arises in a perjury situation because the lawyer's knowledge of his client's perjury often comes from confidential communications with the client, rather than from an independent source.

In Formal Opinion 353[10] (based on the 1987 version of Model Rule 3.3), the ABA Standing Committee on Ethics and Professional Responsibility (Ethics Committee) considered these competing duties in the context of perjury during a trial. Applying the express language of Model Rule 3.3, the opinion resolved the conflict in favor of candor. The Ethics Committee noted in its Opinion that Model Rule 3.3(b) (now Rule 3.3(c)) explicitly requires compliance with Model Rule 3.3(a), even when compliance requires disclosure of otherwise protected information. Thus, the Opinion found that "[i]t is now mandatory, under [Model Rule 3.3(a) and 3.3(b)], for a lawyer who know[s] the client has committed perjury, to disclose this knowledge to the tribunal if the lawyer cannot persuade the client to rectify the perjury."[11]

Model Rule 3.3 and Formal Opinion 353 radically altered the ABA's earlier position on client perjury. Until 1987, under both the Model Code and the Canons of Professional Ethics (Canons),[12] a lawyer who learned that a client had committed perjury had to remedy the perjury by remonstrating with the client and by withdrawing if necessary.[13] If the client refused to rectify the perjury, the lawyer could disclose the perjury to the court or to other parties *only if* knowledge of the perjury did not come from a client "confidence" or "secret."[14]

Because knowledge of client perjury most often comes from a confidential communication with the client, disclosure was rarely required by the Model Code or Canons.[15] Therefore, as the committee noted in Formal Opinion 353, Model Rule 3.3 represented a "major policy change" in a lawyer's duty when a client testifies falsely.[16]

In our hypothetical from the *Scoops* case, the client's perjury occurs during a deposition, a proceeding conducted under the auspices of a tribunal, but not before the tribunal.[17] Until 1993, it was unclear whether the duties arising from courtroom perjury also apply to deposition perjury. After all, Model Rule 3.3 is titled "Candor Toward the Tribunal," and Formal Opinion 353 addressed only perjury during trial; the Opinion did not decide whether the duty of disclosure also applied to perjury during a deposition.

In 1993, in Formal Opinion 376, the Ethics Committee addressed the issue.[18] The Opinion found that Model Rule 3.3 applies as much to deposition perjury as it does to trial perjury. Additionally, the Committee noted that Comment 10 to Rule 3.3 requires a lawyer to take "reasonable remedial measures" if the lawyer "knows of the falsity of testimony elicited from the client during a deposition." If withdrawal or remonstration is not effective, then the lawyer must reveal the information, even if it would otherwise be confidential.[19] Therefore, a lawyer in a civil case who discovers that a client lied while being deposed must take all reasonable steps to rectify the fraud, including disclosure to the court, if necessary.[20]

The facts of Formal Opinion 376 illustrate the issue. A lawyer represented an insurance agent in a suit by an insured against both the agent and the insurance company. The insured's policy required proof of claim within sixty days of loss. The insured alleged that he had mailed the proof of claim one day before the deadline. At the agent's deposition, the plaintiff tried to prove timely mailing to, and receipt by, the insurer. When the agent was asked if he had received proof of claim by the sixtieth day, he replied that he had not. As confirmation, he produced a copy of his office mail log, which was marked as a deposition exhibit.

The agent signed the deposition transcript, and his lawyer started preparing a motion for summary judgment based upon the plaintiff's failure to provide timely proof of claim. Several days later, the lawyer ran into the agent at the airport. For the first time, the agent told his lawyer he had lied at his deposition about the proof of claim. He told his lawyer that he had received the proof of claim on the sixtieth day and his secretary had entered its receipt in the mail log. But the agent later destroyed the proof of claim and altered the log.

In determining that Model Rule 3.3 applied to perjury at a deposition, the Ethics Committee noted the serious damage caused by false discovery responses:

> [W]e think that even before these [deposition] documents are filed there is potential ongoing reliance upon their content which would be outcome determinative, resulting in an inevitable deception of the other side and *a subversion of the truth finding process which the adversary system is designed to implement.*[21]

The Majority Position: Disclosure Required

Even before Formal Opinion 376, many jurisdictions and courts had already decided that a lawyer must inform the court of a client's deposition perjury, even if disclosure required the revelation of confidences. In *Committee on Professional Ethics v. Crary,*[22] for example, the Iowa Supreme Court disbarred Crary for failing to stop a deposition in a divorce proceeding when it became clear his client was lying. Crary knew his client was lying because the lies concerned the client's whereabouts at times when she had been with him on an adulterous rendezvous. Like the Ethics Committee in Formal Opinion 376, the *Crary* court focused on the serious damage perjury inflicts on the judicial process:

The attorney functions at the heart of the fact-finding process, both in trial and in pre- and post-trial proceedings. If he knowingly suffers a witness to lie, he undermines the integrity of the fact-finding system of which he himself is an integral part.[23]

Thus, the court concluded, whether in a deposition or at a trial, "an attorney must not knowingly permit a witness to lie."[24]

The court rejected the lawyer's argument that the attorney-client privilege forbids disclosure of the perjury. Client perjury, the court said, falls outside the attorney-client relationship.[25] Although a client may expect a lawyer to assist him to the best of the lawyer's ability, the client "may not expect . . . that the attorney will tolerate lying or any other species of fraud in the process."[26]

Other jurisdictions also have required disclosure of a client's perjury even though knowledge of the perjury could have come only through confidential communications.[27] For example, the Minnesota Supreme Court in *In re Mack*[28] suspended a lawyer for an additional twenty-three months because he failed to rectify a client's deposition perjury. As in *Crary*, the Minnesota court rejected the lawyer's claim that the attorney-client privilege precluded disclosure of the client's false testimony.[29] The court noted that Rule 3.3 of the Minnesota Rules of Professional Conduct, which is based on ABA Model Rule 3.3, required disclosure despite the competing, relevant duty of confidentiality.[30]

The vast majority of jurisdictions currently follow the ABA Model Rules regarding rectification of client perjury. Presumably, those courts would reach results similar to the ones in *Crary* and *Mack*.[31] However, each jurisdiction has its own rules of professional conduct, and these may vary from those of the ABA. In addition, courts interpret these rules differently, so it is always prudent to check applicable disciplinary rules and relevant case law to determine the precise scope of a lawyer's duties in the face of deposition perjury, particularly when the duty of confidentiality is involved.

The Minority Position: Client Confidences Cannot Be Revealed

The vast majority of jurisdictions, as noted above, require the disclosure of client confidences if necessary to rectify perjury. But several jurisdictions do not follow ABA Model Rule 3.3 and do not permit a lawyer to reveal client confidences, even in the face of client perjury.[32]

For example, the District of Columbia and California have rules of professional conduct that forbid a lawyer from remedying client perjury in ways that reveal client confidences.[33] The District of Columbia permits withdrawal but not the disclosure of client confidences.[34]

Similarly, the general rule in California is that an attorney owes a duty of confidentiality to the client, except to prevent a crime that could result in substantial bodily injury or death.[35] Several California ethics opinions have opined that an attorney *does not* have a duty to let the court know that a client has committed testimonial perjury.[36] Instead, the attorney must first ask the client to consent to rectification. If the client refuses, the attorney must warn the client about the consequences of perjury, including the fact that the attorney cannot rely upon or refer to any of the perjured testimony. If the client still refuses, the attorney must make a motion to the court to be allowed to withdraw from the case, without disclosing the testimonial perjury unless the client consents.[37] As an interesting alternative, California State Bar Formal Opinion 74 noted that the attorney may seek, without explanation, a stipulation from opposing counsel to strike the perjured testimony, thereby remedying the problem. If that stipulation is agreed to, the court may strike the testimony. If the stipulation is not agreed to, the attorney must move that the testimony be stricken, stating whatever grounds exist, but again without disclosing its perjurious nature unless the client consents.[38]

Federal Rules of Civil Procedure

The Federal Rules are another source of an attorney's affirmative duty to correct deposition perjury. This duty is found in the requirements of FRCP 26(e) relating to supplementation of discovery responses; it is also found in the mandates of FRCP 11. Failure to comply with these rules leaves both lawyer and client vulnerable to sanctions.[39]

FRCP 26(e) requires a party to supplement responses to formal discovery requests whenever the party learns that prior disclosures are materially incorrect or incomplete. The 1993 advisory committee's note to FRCP 26(e) indicates that the duty to supplement does not "ordinarily [extend] to deposition testimony." However, FRCP 26(e)(2) explicitly extends the duty to supplement to the deposition of *expert* witnesses. If an expert offers an opinion at a deposition that is materially incorrect or an opinion that subsequently changes, then the deposition must be supplemented to reflect the correct information or change at least thirty days before trial, unless otherwise directed by the court.

The Federal Rules, as noted above, can also be read as imposing a duty to rectify deposition perjury. Among other things, FRCP 11 requires a lawyer to certify by signature on every pleading, including motion papers, that to the best of the lawyer's knowledge, information, and belief, formed after a reasonable inquiry, every allegation or factual contention in the pleading has evidentiary support or is likely to have evidentiary support after reasonable discovery. Similarly, denials of factual contentions must be based on the evidence or must be reasonably based on a lack of information or belief.

The circuits are split on whether FRCP 11 imposes a continuing duty on lawyers to investigate the factual basis of a suit when discovery casts doubt on earlier positions. Many circuits hold that FRCP 11 does not impose a continuing obligation on the signer to update, correct, or withdraw a pleading or motion that, when signed, satisfied the requirements of FRCP 11.[40] Other circuits have rejected this position in favor of a more expansive reading of FRCP 11.[41] As amended in 1993, Rule 11 now specifies that a lawyer may be sanctioned "whether by signing, filing, submitting, or *later advocating*" a pleading or written motion.[42]

As an example of the later view, in *Battles v. City of Ft. Myers*, the Eleventh Circuit upheld an FRCP sanction taxing costs to a lawyer, noting that the "1993 amendment to Rule 11 emphasizes an attorney's continuing obligations to make inquiries, and thus the rule allows sanctions when an attorney continues 'insisting upon a position after it is no longer tenable.'"[43] Similarly, in *Phonometrics v. Economy Inns of America*, the Federal Circuit upheld a trial court's order sanctioning a plaintiff who continued to assert legal theories to recover for alleged patent infringement despite a recent appellate decision that made his theories untenable. The trial court concluded that once he was on notice that his claim no longer had legal or evidentiary support, he had a duty to discontinue the claim.[44]

By analogy, a lawyer's discovery of client perjury might have the same effect on the factual basis of a claim or defense. Recall the facts of Formal Opinion 376: When the lawyer discovered that the insurance agent lied at his deposition about receipt of the proof of claim, she probably also realized that one of her client's defenses no longer had the evidentiary support that appeared available when the answer was signed and filed. In those circuits that find a continuing obligation, the lawyer's failure to correct the original answer could result in FRCP 11 sanctions.

Requirements of Knowledge and Materiality

In the previous section, we assumed that Leslie Roberts testified at her deposition that she told Terry Blake, the computer salesperson, that she intended to apply for a bank loan and wanted accounting software for that purpose. If that testimony is false, do you have a duty to take remedial action?

As discussed above, every jurisdiction requires some remedial action by a lawyer who knows that his client committed deposition perjury. A lawyer has this duty whenever (1) the lawyer knows the client has testified falsely and (2) the falsity concerns a material fact.[45] These two predicates will be discussed in turn.

Knowledge

Suppose that as you listen to Leslie Roberts's deposition testimony about what she told Blake, you are certain the testimony is false. You carefully reviewed this point with Roberts during her deposition preparation session, and she told you that she had not said anything to Blake about a bank loan. At the preparation session, Roberts also said she knew of no one and no document that could refresh her memory. Now, listening to Roberts at her deposition, you know of no reason for the change in testimony.[46] Do you *know* enough to trigger the duties of disclosure or withdrawal?

Model Rule 3.3 provides that a lawyer shall not "knowingly" permit client fraud.[47] In Formal Opinion 353, discussed above, the Ethics Committee emphasized that Model Rule 3.3's obligation to reveal client perjury is "strictly limited" to circumstances in which the lawyer *knows*, rather than merely suspects, that the client's testimony is false. Such knowledge, the committee suggested, ordinarily comes from the client's own admissions. The Terminology Section of the Model Rules, however, adds that "knowledge" also may be "inferred from circumstances."[48]

Although some jurisdictions have addressed the knowledge issue, no single standard exists for determining how much a lawyer must *know* before remedial measures are required. Most courts and state professional codes, though, require a lawyer to have more than a mere suspicion that a client has committed perjury.[49] Some jurisdictions require a lawyer to rectify or reveal a client's fraud only when the lawyer has actual knowledge of a witness's fraud. For example, the Virginia Code of Professional Responsibility requires that the witness expressly acknowledge the perjury before the lawyer has a duty to disclose.[50] Similarly, the Fourth Circuit found no duty to disclose even when a lawyer had a strong belief that his client was going to lie.[51] In that case the lawyer's belief was based on his client's "[f]arfetched" story that was "dramatically outweighed by other evidence."[52]

Professor Monroe Freedman raises the "actual knowledge" requirement even higher. He argues that "knowingly" in Model Rule 3.3 should be read to mean "willfully." Given that reading, a lawyer would not violate Model Rule 3.3's mandate to disclose or withdraw if he did not offer a witness's perjury in "bad faith and with an evil intent."[53] In Freedman's view, a lawyer can avoid offering perjury in bad faith by making a good-faith effort—even if unsuccessful—to dissuade the client from testifying falsely. In that situation, argues Freedman, the perjured evidence is not offered willfully but rather under the compulsion of the adversary system.

Freedman's interpretation of Model Rule 3.3 is difficult to reconcile with the clear holding of Formal Opinion 376. In that opinion, as discussed above, the Ethics Committee stated that "if efforts to persuade the client to rectify fail, the lawyer must herself act to see that a fraud is not perpetrated on the tribunal."[54] In such circumstances, the committee added, "[d]irect disclosure . . . may prove to be the only reasonable remedial measure in the client fraud situations most likely to be encountered in pretrial proceedings."[55] Furthermore, contrary to Freedman's view, Model Rule 3.3 seems to apply equally to innocent and intentional false statements. Regardless of a client's or a lawyer's intentions, under Model Rule 3.3, offering material false evidence is forbidden and must be rectified.

In contrast to an actual knowledge requirement, some courts have suggested that a "reasonable suspicion" of perjury may be enough to place the lawyer under a duty to investigate further.[56] What is more, that suspicion can come from some source other than a client's verbal admission. That is what happened in *Crary*. The lawyer knew his client was lying about her whereabouts at certain times because, as noted above, at those times she had been on an adulterous rendezvous with him.[57] Still other courts have found circumstantial evidence to be a sufficient basis for knowledge of impending perjury.[58]

In those situations where the information impugning a client's testimony comes from a source other than the client, a lawyer should consider carefully its authenticity and verifiability.[59] A court that later investigates the perjury probably will not accept the lawyer's statement that he did not have actual knowledge. Instead, the court is likely to consider whether a reasonable practitioner would have recognized the fraud.

The attorney-client relationship, of course, should not be built on suspicion. Ordinarily, a client is entitled to a lawyer's trust. According to Professor Freedman, a lawyer should be a client's "champion in a hostile world."[60] Yet, as an officer of the court, a lawyer cannot hide behind an actual knowledge requirement nor engage in willful ignorance when circumstances call for further investigation.[61]

Similarly, a lawyer should not rely on such philosophical hairsplitting as "no one can ever *really* know." The consequences of ostrich-like inaction in the face of a client's fraud can be severe for both the lawyer and the client.[62] Willful ignorance, the Ethics Committee warned in its Formal Opinion 353, may violate professional standards:

> The Committee notes that some trial lawyers report that they have avoided the ethical dilemma posed by Rule 3.3 because they follow a practice of not questioning the client about the facts in the case and, therefore, never "know" that a client has given false testimony. Lawyers who engage in such practice may be violating their duties under Rule 3.3 and their obligation to provide competent representation under Rule 1.1.[63]

Professor Charles Wolfram has written that minimal standards of lawyer competence probably require "such investigation as is necessary to determine the extent to which cross-examination or other impeachment of a client's intended testimony would effectively rebut the testimony."[64] From a strategic standpoint, to allow a client's questionable deposition testimony to stand without any further inquiry could be disastrous for the prosecution or defense of a case. As previously discussed, failure to investigate may also violate FRCP 11, which can be interpreted to require a continuing duty to investigate when a lawyer gains knowledge that casts serious doubt on the legitimacy of a claim or defense.

Suppose a lawyer believes a client's story is false, but even after investigating does not know for sure. Under Model Rule 3.3(a)(3), "[a] lawyer may refuse to offer evidence, other than the testimony of a defendant in a criminal matter, that the lawyer reasonably believes is false."[65] However, although a lawyer may refuse to offer such evidence, a lawyer may not reveal client confidences in the process. Disclosure of client confidences is strictly limited to situations in which the lawyer *knows* the testimony is false.

Once again, a cautionary note: The knowledge standard is not uniform across jurisdictions. Therefore, always check the applicable rules of professional conduct and relevant case law in your jurisdiction to determine what level of knowledge triggers a duty to take remedial steps.

Materiality

In considering materiality, the second prong of the test, recall the hypothetical: You know that Leslie Roberts falsely testified at her deposition that she told Blake about the bank loan. You also know this testimony is material because the defendant's knowledge at the time the alleged false representation was made is a key issue. But frequently, materiality is not so clear. Some client misstatements will border on the trivial or irrelevant. Thus the question: When is a falsehood "material" so that it triggers a duty to take remedial action?

Several appellate opinions have addressed the issue of materiality in criminal cases where defendants have been convicted for making a false statement under oath in a prior civil deposition.[66] But the definition of materiality in this context does not necessarily define a lawyer's professional responsibility to take remedial action for perjury at a deposition. Nevertheless, these cases provide some guidance for a lawyer who needs to determine whether a client's false statements are sufficiently material to require notification.

When perjury at a deposition is at issue, courts are split over the definition of materiality. The Ninth and Sixth Circuits follow a relatively narrow standard: False testimony is material if it has a tendency to affect the outcome of the underlying suit for which the testimony was taken.[67] The Second and Fifth Circuits take a far more expansive view that parallels the civil standard defined in FRCP 26(b)(1).[68] According to these courts, a misstatement is material not only when it might affect the outcome of a lawsuit, but also when "a truthful answer might reasonably be calculated to lead to the discovery of evidence admissible at the trial of the underlying suit."[69] Thus, in the Second and Fifth Circuits, a fact is material if it is within the scope of discovery as broadly defined by FRCP 26(b)(1).

Model Rule 3.3 addresses only misstatements of material fact.[70] And like the Ninth and Sixth Circuits, the Ethics Committee appears to favor a restrictive view of materiality. In Formal Opinion 376, the committee noted that the insurance agent's misstatements regarding receipt of the proof of claim "relate to a material fact, in that a necessary element of plaintiff's case is at issue."[71] The opinion also speaks of the "outcome determinative" nature of the agent's fraud.[72]

If you need to decide whether a misstatement is material, keep in mind three critical points. First, some courts have sanctioned lawyers for remaining silent even when a client's misstatement probably was not outcome determinative. In fact, one court sanctioned a lawyer even though opposing counsel knew the actual facts and was not fooled by the perjury.[73] While the perjury did not affect the outcome of the lawsuit, the perjurious client had hoped the falsehood would have that effect. In the interest of deterring such attempts, a court may decide to sanction both successful and unsuccessful perjury, and sanctions may be imposed against both the lawyer and the client. Indeed, at least one court has ordered the public reprimand of a lawyer who failed to correct misstatements made by a deposed client even though the court noted the misstatements were not material.[74]

Second, a court may find false testimony material because it reflects on the issue of a witness's credibility. This is especially true when the witness is a party.[75]

Third, because of discovery's crucial role in litigation, courts are increasingly concerned about truthfulness in the discovery process, regardless of the nature of the perjury. This concern permeates Formal Opinion 376.

Obviously, a client inclined to perjury will be motivated to lie about material facts rather than "immaterial" ones. But clients often guess wrong about what is important in a case and therefore may slip into dishonesty over trivial matters. Because materiality is fact-specific, treat each intentional misstatement independently and with caution. Just as important, when determining whether a misstatement is material, consult the applicable rules of professional conduct and relevant case law.

Preventing and Remedying Client Perjury

In our *Scoops* hypothetical, Leslie Roberts's deposition perjury caught you, the defending lawyer, by surprise. Indeed, such misconduct can be difficult to anticipate. Nonetheless, there are steps you can take to prevent perjury at a deposition and, after it has occurred, to limit the damage.

For starters, when preparing a deposition witness, emphasize the importance of truthfulness.[76] Tell the witness that there are many good reasons to tell the truth: moral, ethical, and strategic.

If a witness appears to be straying dangerously close to perjury during a deposition, there are several steps you can take. First, decide whether an ambiguity in the question may be causing an apparently false response. If so, object to the question if you have a legitimate basis to do so.[77] The objection may cause the examiner to rephrase the question so that the answer is no longer suspicious. Or the objection may signal to the witness that you are concerned about the answer.

A second step, taken after an apparently false answer is given but before any further false testimony is offered, is to seek a break and confer with your witness.[78] During this conference, ask the witness why her deposition testimony differed from the version she provided during witness preparation. Hold this "off the record" conversation before any other action is taken; that way you can decide whether there is a reason for the change in the witness's story or whether perjury has occurred or is likely to occur.

Suppose the witness has no reasonable explanation for the change in her testimony, and you believe additional false testimony will be offered. At this point, bluntly warn your client of perjury's serious consequences and tell the client about your ethical obligations. Explain that if the client persists in committing perjury or refuses to rectify perjury that already has occurred, you must withdraw, disaffirm the evidence, and, depending on the jurisdiction, may even be required to disclose the perjury to the opposing party and to the court.[79] If your client still intends to testify in a manner you believe to be false, suspend the deposition before additional perjury can occur.[80] This step will prevent additional damage while possibly allowing you to reopen the deposition after further discussion with the client.

Once the deposition has been suspended, decide whether rectification is required for any false statement already on the record. If rectification is necessary, you have several options. One is to resume the deposition and have the witness correct her testimony. Another is to resume the deposition and clarify the record by questioning your witness after opposing counsel has finished his direct examination.[81]

Suppose you learn about the perjury only after the deposition is over. In that situation, case law and Formal Opinions of the ABA Ethics Committee largely agree both on the remedial steps required and the order in which they should be taken. (Remember, as a threshold matter, you must know that a material misstatement was made by the witness.)

Initially, take steps that least invade your client's expectation of confidentiality.[82] Talk to the client confidentially and urge him to correct the perjurious testimony immediately. A witness may avoid a perjury prosecution by recanting false testimony before it (1) substantially influences the proceeding or (2) becomes apparent the falsity would have been exposed anyway.[83] Immediate recantation also demonstrates the type of good faith that can salvage a judge's goodwill. Therefore, urge the witness to recant before opposing counsel can confront the witness with incriminating documents or questions.

There may also be ways to fix the problem without damaging the client's credibility. Depending on the rules of the relevant jurisdiction and the nature of the evidence, you may be able to rectify the perjury without divulging the client's wrongdoing or breaching the client's confidence.[84] Some jurisdictions, for example, allow you to supplement or amend incomplete or incorrect answers to deposition questions in a number of ways that rectify the perjury without directly disclosing it to the court. If the deposition has concluded, you could offer the witness for an additional deposition at which time the witness can correct the testimony.[85] If the witness has not corrected the earlier testimony by the end of this additional direct examination, you can clarify the record by questioning your own witness.

As an alternative, after the deposition, a witness can correct the false testimony by making changes to the deposition transcript.[86] Such changes, however, leave a witness open to both comments at trial about the corrections to the transcript and also cross-examination at trial.[87]

As discussed above, when a client refuses to rectify perjury, you must take independent steps to prevent the fraud. At a minimum, you must cease representation and withdraw.[88] Of course, withdrawal is a severe remedy that may alert the court and the other party that something is amiss with your case. But withdrawal alone may not be sufficient because withdrawal does not necessarily notify the court or the other parties of the specific false evidence. In fact, Formal Opinion 353 states that "withdrawal can rarely serve as a remedy for a client's perjury."[89] And a lawyer's duty to alert the court to a client's fraud probably continues to the conclusion of the proceeding, even if the lawyer has withdrawn before that.[90]

If withdrawal is not sufficient, another option—short of full disclosure—is withdrawal and disaffirmance of evidence or documents. In this situation, a lawyer withdrawing from representation repudiates any evidence or document he knows to be based wholly or partly on false evidence. He makes this repudiation, however, without saying anything about the disaffirmed item other than that he no longer stands behind it. Absent such disaffirmance, a client might continue to use the tainted evidence, and its use could be construed as a de facto continuation of representation by the lawyer.[91] Withdrawal and disaffirmance, though less intrusive on the attorney-client relationship than direct disclosure to the tribunal, will help to limit the prejudice to the other party that otherwise would result from the fraud.[92]

Ultimately, if none of the foregoing steps fully rectifies the fraud, a lawyer must disclose the perjury to the other party and sometimes even to the court.[93] Indeed, Formal Opinion 376 states that disclosure "may prove to be the only reasonable remedial measure in the client fraud situation most likely to be encountered in pretrial proceedings."[94]

Adverse Consequences to Client and Lawyer

Suppose the preventive and remedial measures discussed above do not work. What are the consequences for the client? For the lawyer?

For one thing, a client whose perjured deposition testimony is discovered may face a motion to compel and possible sanctions under FRCP 37.[95] Under Rule 37(a)(4), an evasive or incomplete disclosure, answer, or response is treated as a failure to disclose, answer, or respond. Because a false response to a deposition question is undoubtedly an evasive and incomplete response, the examining party has a basis to move to compel a response under FRCP 37(a)(1). If the motion is granted or the correct response is made after the motion is filed, the court may require the witness, his lawyer, or both to pay the moving party's reasonable expenses, including attorney's fees incurred in making the motion, unless the response was substantially justified or other circumstances make an award of expenses unjust.[96]

In addition, FRCP 37(c)(1) provides for sanctions when a party fails to correct an error in the deposition testimony of an expert witness as required by FRCP 26(e)(2).[97] In *United States v. Shaffer Equipment Co.*,[98] a federal district court imposed monetary sanctions on two government lawyers who failed to reveal what they knew of their expert witness's perjury during a deposition. In imposing the sanctions, the court found that FRCP 26(e) furnished "fair warning" of its power to punish the lawyers' misconduct in a "manner it finds appropriate."[99]

The *Shaffer* court also noted that apart from FRCP 26, the lawyers' conduct violated their duty of candor to the tribunal and could be sanctioned under the court's inherent power. The court stated that it "has the inherent authority to discipline all attorneys who appear before it and 'the inherent power extends to the full range of litigation abuses.'"[100] So beware: Although FRCP 26(e) does not apply on its face to a nonexpert's deposition testimony, the failure to supplement a client's perjured deposition testimony may be a "litigation abuse" sanctionable under a court's broad inherent power to regulate discovery.

Sanctions authorized by FRCP 37(c)(1) can be severe. A party who without substantial justification fails to disclose information required by FRCP 26(e)(1) cannot use that information to supply evidence on a motion, at a hearing, or at trial, unless the failure is harmless. In addition, the court may require payment of reasonable expenses, including attorney's fees. And a court may inform the jury of the failure to make the disclosure and impose certain of the sanctions found in FRCP 37(b)(2)(A)(i)–(vi). These include an order that certain facts will be considered established, an order refusing to allow the disobedient party to support or oppose certain claims or defenses, an order striking pleadings or dismissing the action, and a default judgment against the disobedient party.

An FRCP 37 sanction is only one of several possible adverse consequences for both a witness and his lawyer. For the witness, the discovery of perjury will result in impeachment and loss of credibility. It can also lead to a contempt citation.[101] And, although criminal prosecution for perjury is rare, an irate opposing party or an active judge may pursue this option.[102] Perjury also exposes a client to a motion to overturn a perjury-tainted judgment and to a suit for damages.[103] Furthermore, deposition perjury is likely to alienate the very judge who will rule on future motions and may preside at trial.

For the lawyer, the most immediate effect of permitting perjury is the loss of reputation. Financial loss also may result because perjury can destroy a lawsuit that may have survived without the falsity. Criminal prosecution, though infrequent, is not without precedent. And disciplinary proceedings are a real threat.[104]

Another potential problem for the lawyer is that a client facing a claim of perjury may accuse her lawyer of suborning perjury— whether or not true.[105] In a California appellate case, *Blain v. Doctor's Company*,[106] a physician who had been sued for medical malpractice filed a legal malpractice action against his insurer. The physician claimed the defense lawyer hired by the insurer encouraged him to lie at his deposition. The physician also claimed that by following his lawyer's advice, he suffered emotional distress, was exposed to greater liability, and had his medical practice destroyed.

The *Blain* court concluded that the doctrine of unclean hands required dismissal of the physician's claim. It was unlikely, the court noted, that a client could be confused by his lawyer about "the legality of lying in the teeth of the oath just sworn."[107] At least one court, however, permitted a client to bring a suit seeking the recovery of fees paid to the lawyer who allegedly suborned perjury.[108]

Deposition perjury may have other consequences. For example, it can jeopardize a settlement or favorable trial result. It also can provide grounds for an independent tort action against the lawyer. In a Second Circuit case, *Cresswell v. Sullivan & Cromwell*,[109] plaintiffs sued the law firm of Sullivan & Cromwell on the grounds that the firm had acted fraudulently or with gross negligence when it failed to produce documents requested during discovery in earlier litigation in which the firm had been the opposing counsel. Had they received the documents, the plaintiffs alleged, they would not have settled the earlier suit for such a small amount.[110] The trial court ruled in favor of Sullivan & Cromwell on the tort claims. But the Second Circuit reversed, allowing the suit to proceed in equity as an independent action to relieve the plaintiffs from the settlement.[111]

Cresswell involved fraud in connection with document production. By analogy, a lawyer who knowingly acquiesces in a client's perjury at a deposition could be vulnerable to the same attack. The opposing party could claim that the perjured testimony deprived him of material facts that, if known, would have led to a more favorable settlement. *Cresswell* suggests that a court might upset the settlement and even award money damages.

Formal disciplinary proceedings probably pose the most likely—and hence most menacing—threat to a lawyer who fails to rectify a client's known perjury. As already noted, suspension and disbarment have resulted.[112] Public reprimand is likely.

Conclusion

When a lawyer discovers that her client has committed perjury at a deposition, the competing duties of candor to the tribunal and confidentiality to the client can put the lawyer between the proverbial rock and hard place. Given the position of the ABA and many courts, lawyers and clients should not expect leniency. Therefore, a lawyer must be ready to act. And that means knowing, and strictly complying with, the applicable standards of professional conduct and the rules in the relevant case law.

Notes

1. See Chapter 8. Similarly, this chapter does not address directly the problems that arise when deposition perjury is committed by individuals other than the client, such as adverse parties or third-party witnesses. Thus, it does not address the alternatives open to a lawyer who takes the deposition of a perjurious witness. *See* Jonathan Liebman & Joel Cohen, *Perjury and Civil Litigation*, LITIGATION, Summer 1994, at 43 (discussing remedies available to taker confronted with perjurious deposition witness); *In re* Grievance Comm. of the U.S. D. Ct., D. of Conn., 847 F.2d 57 (2d Cir. 1988) (considering culpability of lawyer who did not report opposing party's perjury). Nor does it address the duties of a lawyer who is neither taking nor defending the deposition at which she is present, yet who knows perjury is occurring. Finally, this chapter does not treat the full range of issues, including constitutional considerations that arise when the client is a criminal defendant. For a discussion of a defense lawyer's duty in the face of perjury by a criminal defendant, see Nix v. Whiteside, 475 U.S. 157 (1986).

2. For more than one hundred years, the professional standards of the ABA have served as models of the regulatory law governing the legal profession. The Canons of Professional Ethics were first adopted in 1908 and underwent occasional revision until the adoption of the Model Code of Professional Responsibility in 1969. The Model Code stood as the disciplinary code of a great majority of states and federal districts until it was formally superseded by the introduction of the Model Rules in 1983. As of April 2009, all states except California and Maine have adopted professional standards based on the Model Rules. Those jurisdictions that have not yet adopted the whole of the current Model Rules, however, are still likely to follow standards derived from the Model Code.

A federal district court usually adopts the disciplinary rules of the state in which the district court sits. There are no uniform federal rules of professional conduct, however, and some federal districts have adopted local rules that vary from the state standards. *See, e.g.*, Rand v. Monsanto Co., 926 F.2d 596, 601–03 (7th Cir. 1991) (cataloging various disciplinary standards of federal district courts).

3. The Model Rules underwent a revision and renumbering in 2002. Among the changes, Rule 3.3 now imposes a duty on lawyers to correct prior statements made to the court that the lawyer later discovers were false. Also, Rule 1.6 now permits disclosure to rectify substantial injury resulting from a client's serious abuse of the lawyer's services.

4. MODEL RULES OF PROF'L CONDUCT R. 3.3 (2008) (emphasis added).

5. Perjury is a criminal or fraudulent act. The federal statute that makes perjury a crime reads as follows: "Whoever under oath . . . in any proceeding before or ancillary to any court or grand jury of the United States knowingly makes any false material declaration . . . shall be fined under this title or imprisoned not more than five years, or both." 18 U.S.C. § 1623(a) (2008). Every state has a similar law prohibiting perjury.

6. *See In re* Mack, 519 N.W.2d 900 (Minn. 1994) (lawyer's failure to correct false deposition testimony constituted violation of Minnesota Rules of Professional Conduct 3.3(a)(2) and 3.3(a)(4), which are patterned after ABA Model Rules).

7. Model Code of Prof'l Responsibility (Model Code) DR 7-102, the predecessor to Model Rule 3.3, also imposes a duty of candor upon the lawyer. As explained in this chapter, however, the scope of remedial action required by Model Rule 3.3 is broader than that required by DR 7-102. *See infra* text accompanying notes 13–16.

8. MODEL RULES OF PROF'L CONDUCT R. 1.6 (2008).

9. *See, e.g.*, Charles P. Curtis, *The Ethics of Advocacy*, 4 STAN. L. REV. 3 (1951); Stephen McG. Bundy & Einer Richard Elhauge, *Do Lawyers Improve the Adversary System? A General Theory of Litigation Advice and Regulation*, 79 CAL. L. REV. 313, 403–04 (1991) (arguing persuasively that confidentiality ultimately increases amount of information reaching tribunal).

10. ABA Comm. on Ethics and Prof'l Responsibility, Formal Op. 353 (1987). ABA formal opinions address ethical questions of general interest. Formal and informal opinions are promulgated by the ABA Standing Committee on Ethics and Professional Responsibility, which has existed, in one form or another, since 1913. The committee is composed of prominent bar members. Although the opinions are not law, courts frequently cite them. Court decisions are the only authoritative interpretation of professional rules. GEOFFREY C. HAZARD, ET AL., THE LAW AND ETHICS OF LAWYERING 16 (4th ed. 2004).

11. Formal Op. 353, *supra* note 10.

12. *Supra* note 2.

13. ABA Comm. on Ethics and Prof'l Responsibility, Formal Op. 287 (1953); ABA Comm. on Ethics and Prof'l Responsibility, Formal Op. 341 (1975).

14. *See* Formal Op. 287, *supra* note 13 ("[T]here should be perfect freedom of consultation by client with attorney without any apprehension of a compelled disclosure by the attorney. . . ." (quoting Formal Opinion 91 (1933))); Formal Op. 341, *supra* note 13.

15. *See* Charles Wolfram, *Client Perjury*, 50 S. CAL. L. REV. 809, 864–65 (1977).

16. Formal Op. 353, *supra* note 10.

17. *See* FED. R. CIV. P. 30(c).

18. ABA Comm. on Ethics and Prof'l Responsibility, Formal Op. 376 (1993).

19. MODEL RULES OF PROF'L CONDUCT R. 3.3 cmt. 10 (2008).

20. Although Model Rule 3.3 requires, under specified conditions, the disclosure of confidential communications, Model Rule 1.6 continues to forbid the disclosure of many criminal and fraudulent acts by a client when the wrongdoing does not fall under the provisions of Model Rule 3.3. For example, a lawyer may almost never disclose past wrongful acts by the client that form the basis of the representation. A full discussion of Model Rule 1.6 and its exceptions is not possible here. For a discussion of confidentiality in other contexts, see Model Rule 1.2 (Scope of Representation) and Model Rule 1.6 (Confidentiality of Information), as well as the comments to those rules.

21. Formal Op. 376, *supra* note 18 (emphasis added). In Formal Opinion 376, the committee also mentions Model Rule 4.1 (Truthfulness in Statements to Others) as another rule that could guide the lawyer's conduct in the face of deposition perjury. Unlike Model Rule 3.3, Model Rule 4.1 does not contain a provision explicitly trumping the duty of confidentiality in Model Rule 1.6. Because the committee ultimately rested its decision on Model Rule 3.3, it did not reach the extent of any independent duty imposed by Model Rule 4.1.

22. 245 N.W.2d 298 (Iowa 1976).

23. *Id.* at 305.

24. *Id.*

25. *Id.* at 306; *see also* United States v. Carbone, 798 F.2d 21, 28 (1st Cir. 1986); *In re* King, 322 P.2d 1095, 1097 (Utah 1958) ("We cannot permit a member of the bar to exonerate himself from failure to disclose known perjury by a self-serving statement that in his judgment he had a duty of non-disclosure.").

26. *Crary*, 245 N.W.2d at 306.

27. *See, e.g., Carbone*, 798 F.2d at 28 (if lawyer knew client committed perjury, he had a duty to inform judge immediately); McKissick v. United States, 379 F.2d 754, 761–62 (5th Cir. 1957) (even if the client specifically directed lawyer not to reveal perjury, the lawyer was still under professional, ethical, and public duty to report it).

28. 519 N.W.2d 900 (Minn. 1994). At the time the attorney, Mack, was informed of his client's deception, he was already embroiled in previous disciplinary action for knowingly submitting a client's false answer to an interrogatory, which resulted in his suspension. *Id.* at 903.

29. *Id.* at 902.

30. *Id.*

31. *See* THOMAS D. MORGAN & RONALD D. ROTUNDA, 2009 SELECTED STANDARDS ON PROF'L RESPONSIBILITY 150–65 (2009) (state-by-state analysis of ethics rules relating to client confidences).

32. Those jurisdictions that have not adopted ABA Model Rule 3.3 still follow ethical standards based on the earlier ABA Model Cole. *See supra* text accompanying note 2.

33. Notably, New York, which had followed a version of the prior Model Code, adopted a new set of Rules of Professional Conduct, effective April 1, 2009. The new rules, which adopt most but not all of the ABA Model Rules, will for the first time bring New York more in line with other states' ethics codes.

34. D.C. RULES OF PROF'L CONDUCT R. 3.3(b) (2007). For a well-stated argument in favor of nondisclosure of client confidences even in the face of client perjury, see MONROE H. FREEDMAN, LAWYERS' ETHICS IN AN ADVERSARY SYSTEM 1–8, 27–41 (1975).

35. CAL. BUS. & PROF. CODE § 6068(e) (West 2003).

36. Cal. State Bar, Formal Op. 74 (1983); Cal. State Bar, Formal Op. 146 (1996).

37. *Id.*

38. Cal. State Bar, Formal Op. 74 (1983).

39. Due to the 1993 amendments to the FRCP, discovery violations are sanctioned according to the provisions of FRCP 26 through FRCP 37. They are no longer within the purview of FRCP 11. FED. R. CIV. P. 11(d). Nevertheless, FRCP 11 may be applicable in instances of deposition perjury. *See* cases cited *infra* notes 40–41. For further discussion of FRCP 37 sanctions, see *infra* text accompanying notes 96–100.

40.   *See, e.g.*, Edwards v. Gen. Motors Corp., 153 F.3d 242, 245 (5th Cir. 1998); *In re* Mroz, 65 F.3d 1567, 1572 (11th Cir. 1995).

41.   *See, e.g.*, Battles v. City of Ft. Myers, 127 F.3d 1298 (11th Cir. 1997).

42.   FED. R. CIV. P. 11(b) (emphasis added).

43.   *Battles*, 127 F.3d at 1300 (quoting the advisory committee's note to FRCP 11).

44.   Phonometrics, Inc. v. Econ. Inns of Am., 349 F.3d 1356–65 (Fed. Cir. 2003).

45.   *See* MODEL RULES OF PROF'L CONDUCT R. 3.3(a)(3) (2008) ("A lawyer shall not *knowingly* . . . offer evidence that the lawyer knows to be false. If a lawyer, the lawyer's client, or a witness called by the lawyer has offered material evidence and the lawyer comes to know of its falsity, the lawyer shall take reasonable remedial measures, including, if necessary, disclosure to the tribunal." (emphasis added).

46.   Of course, before deciding that the testimony is false, it is always best to ask the witness in an off-the-record conference, assuming one is permitted, why she has a newfound recollection. *See infra* text accompanying note 78.

47.   Compare former Model Code DR 7-102(B)(1) (1983), which provided that a lawyer's duty was triggered when he or she received information *clearly establishing* that a client has perpetrated a fraud upon the tribunal.

48.   MODEL RULES OF PROF'L CONDUCT R. 1(f) (2008).

49.   *See, e.g.*, Sigma-Tau Industrie Farmaceutiche Riunite, S.p.A. v. Lonza, Ltd., 48 F. Supp. 2d 16, 20 (D. D.C. 1999) (finding lawyer's surprisal by his client's in-court testimony does not equate to actual knowledge that the testimony is false); *In re* Grievance Comm. of the U.S. D. Ct., D. of Conn., 847 F.2d 57 (2d Cir. 1988) (refusing to impose sanctions on a lawyer who did not alert the court of an *opposing* party's deposition perjury, reasoning that the lawyer "must clearly know, rather than suspect" fraud before he has a duty to report it); *see also* Whiteside v. Scurr, 744 F.2d 1323, 1328 (8th Cir. 1984) (mere suspicion or inconsistent statements insufficient to establish that defendant's testimony would have been false), *rev'd on other grounds sub. nom.* Nix v. Whiteside, 475 U.S. 157 (1986); Witherspoon v. United States, 557 A.2d 587, 592 (D.C. 1989) (requiring a lawyer to have a "firm factual basis" for believing his client will testify falsely before taking measures to prevent the presentation of perjured testimony); United States ex rel. Wilcox v. Johnson, 555 F.2d 115, 122 (3d Cir. 1977).

50.   VA. RULES OF PROF'L CONDUCT R. 1.6(c)(2) (2008).

51.   United States v. Midgett, 342 F.3d 321, 326–27 (4th Cir. 2003).

52.   *Id.*

53.   Monroe Freedman, *Getting Honest About Client Perjury*, 21 GEO. J. LEGAL ETHICS 133, 138 (2008).

54. Formal Op. 376, *supra* note 18.

55. *Id.*

56. *See, e.g.*, State v. Zwillman, 270 A.2d 284, 289 (N.J. 1970) (lawyer does not need to decide falsity of client's representations unless he has actual knowledge or unless from facts within his personal knowledge or professional experience he should know or reasonably suspect that representations are false).

57. *See supra* text accompanying notes 22–26.

58. People v. Flores, 538 N.E.2d 481 (Ill. Sup. Ct. 1989); People v. Bartee, 566 N.E.2d 855 (Ill. App. Ct. 1991); People v. Taggart, 599 N.E.2d 501 (Ill. App. Ct. 1992); Cooper v. Oklahoma, 71 P.2d 1168 (Okla. Crim. App. 1983).

59. *See* Wolfram, *supra* note 15, at 842–43.

60. FREEDMAN, *supra* note 34, at 24.

61. *Id.* In this connection, Judge Frankel has observed that "[t]he sharp eye of the cynical lawyer becomes at strategic moments a demurely averted and filmy gaze," leaving the lawyer "unfettered by clear prohibitions that 'actual knowledge of the truth' might expose." Marvin E. Frankel, *The Search for Truth: An Umpireal View*, 123 U. PA. L. REV. 1031, 1039 (1975).

62. *See, e.g.*, Fla. Bar v. McCaghren 171 So. 2d 371, 372 (Fla. 1965) (lawyer suspended after failing to make inquiry into suspicious circumstances surrounding client's gathering of evidence); see also *infra* section "Adverse Consequences to Client and Lawyer," discussing the adverse consequences of unrectified perjury to both the lawyer and the client; *but see* Jawa v. Rome Dev. Disabilities Servs. Office, No. 97-CV-1346, WL 288661, at *4 (N.D.N.Y. May 5, 1999) (finding that absent "obvious indications of the client's fraud or perjury, the attorney is not obligated to undertake an independent determination before advancing his client's position.")

63. Formal Op. 353, *supra* note 10, at n.9. See also "Proper Practice Versus Improper Coaching" in Chapter 7 and "Ethical and Practical Constraints" in Chapter 8.

64. Wolfram, *supra* note 15, at 843 n.126. Also see "Witness Preparation and Preparing to Examine Witnesses at Trial" in Chapter 23, discussing impeachment of a witness by prior inconsistent statements.

65. MODEL RULES OF PROF'L CONDUCT R. 3.3(a)(3) (2009). *See also* MODEL RULES OF PROF'L CONDUCT R. 3.3.(a) (2009) (commenting on the standard for determining whether a lawyer knows that evidence is false).

66. For a general treatment of prosecutions of civil perjury, see *Two Cheers for Lying (About Immaterial Matters)*, 5(3) PROF'L LAWYER 1 (May 1994). *See infra* notes 67, 69.

67. United States v. McKenna, 327 F.3d 830, 839 (9th Cir. 2003) (upholding conviction for perjury under 18 U.S.C § 1621 and making a

false declaration under oath under 18 U.S.C. § 1623(a)); United States v. Sassanelli, 118 F.3d 495, 499 (6th Cir. 1997) (affirming perjury conviction under 18 U.S.C. § 1621). The key elements of perjury under 18 U.S.C. § 1621 are (1) testimony under oath (2) concerning a material matter (3) with the willful intent to provide false testimony. Similarly, 18 U.S.C. § 1623(a) makes it unlawful to (1) knowingly make a (2) false (3) material declaration (4) under oath (5) in a proceeding before or ancillary to any court of the United States.

68. FED. R. CIV. P. 26(b)(1) provides that information sought in discovery "need not be admissible at the trial if the discovery appears reasonably calculated to lead to the discovery of admissible evidence."

69. United States v. Kross, 14 F.3d 751, 754 (2d Cir. 1994) (affirming conviction under 18 U.S.C. § 1623(a) for making a false declaration under oath and applying a broad standard for materiality similar to the civil standard in FRCP 26(b)(1)); United States v. Holley, 942 F.2d 916, 924 (5th Cir. 1991) (reversing conviction for making a false declaration under oath and stating that when "assessing the materiality of statements made in a discovery deposition, some account must be taken of the more liberal rules of discovery").

70. "A lawyer shall not knowingly . . . fail to correct a false statement of *material* fact or law previously made to the tribunal by the lawyer," and if "a lawyer . . . has offered *material* evidence and comes to know of its falsity, the lawyer shall take reasonable remedial measures, including . . . disclosure." MODEL RULES OF PROF'L CONDUCT Rs. 3.3(a)(1), 3.3(a)(3) (2008) (emphasis added).

71. Formal Op. 376, *supra* note 18.

72. *Id.*

73. *Crary*, 245 N.W.2d 298 (1976); Wolfram, *supra* note 15, at 844.

74. Attorney Grievance Comm'n of Md. v. Sperling, 463 A.2d 868 (Md. 1983).

75. Liebman & Cohen, *supra* note 1, at 43.

76. See "1. Always Tell the Truth" in Chapter 7.

77. Liebman & Cohen, *supra* note 1, at 43. In our hypothetical, there would appear to be no good-faith basis for an objection to the examiner's question. See "When Can You Instruct?" in Chapter 14, discussing the defender's role and FRCP 30(c)(2).

78. This tactic would be unavailable if a break and conference with the witness for any purpose other than determining privilege are not permitted in the applicable jurisdiction. In addition, taking a break is a sure signal to the questioner of a problem in the examination. See "Taking Care of the Preliminaries" in Chapter 14, discussing witness and defender conferences.

79. Giving your own client a "Miranda" warning can have a damaging effect on the lawyer-client relationship. *See* Jay Sterling Silver, *Truth, Justice and the American Way: The Case Against the Client Perjury Rules*, 47

Vand. L. Rev. 339, 395 & n.191 (1994). The client, however, is entitled to know that you cannot knowingly assist in perpetrating a fraud and that you may be obligated to disclose incriminating information to the court. *See* Model Rules of Prof'l Conduct R. 1.4(a)(5) (2008) (A lawyer shall "consult with the client about any relevant limitation on the lawyer's conduct when the lawyer knows that the client expects assistance not permitted by the Rules of Professional Conduct or other law.").

80. *Crary*, 245 N.W.2d at 307 (lawyer should not have allowed deposition to continue in face of client's perjury, nor allowed it to resume two days later).

81. See "Examination of Your Own Client at the Deposition on Cross-Examination" in Chapter 10 and "Examining Your Own Witness" in Chapter 14.

82. Formal Op. 376, *supra* note 18.

83. *See* 18 U.S.C. § 1623(d) (2008).

84. As previously noted, some jurisdictions explicitly forbid disclosure of the perjury when that disclosure will reveal confidential communications. *See supra* text accompanying notes 31–34.

85. Absent court order, a person may not be deposed more than once during the same case without the written stipulation of the parties and, in some circumstances, only with approval of the court. Fed. R. Civ. P. 30(a)(2)(A)(ii). In addition, as a practical matter, few lawyers want to open up their witnesses to further questioning beyond the seven-hour time limit imposed under FRCP 30(d)(1).

86. Fed. R. Civ. P. 30(e).

87. See "Reviewing and Correcting the Transcript" in Chapter 23.

88. *See* Model Rules of Prof'l Conduct R. 1.16(a)(1) (2008) (withdrawal mandatory when continued representation would result in violation of rules of professional conduct).

89. Formal Op. 353, *supra* note 10.

90. Model Rules of Prof'l Conduct R. 3.3(c) (2008).

91. Disaffirmance cannot be prevented by a quick dismissal of the lawyer by the client. "Whenever circumstances exist that would otherwise require a lawyer to withdraw, disaffirmance may be in order even if the client fires her before she has a chance to do so." ABA Comm. on Ethics and Prof'l Responsibility, Formal Op. 366 (1992) (providing extensive discussion of withdrawal and disaffirmance of lawyer's work product).

92. Formal Opinion 376 (1993) does not entirely resolve whether it is necessary to disclose *why* previously provided information is being altered or disaffirmed. On the one hand, the opinion suggests that alteration or supplementation may be possible without disclosing the reasons for the change. On the other hand, the opinion notes that disaffirmance alone may not provide a satisfactory remedy because it "does not necessarily put either successor counsel or the opposing party on notice as to why the documents are being disaffirmed." Formal Op. 376, *supra* note 18.

93. This assumes, of course, that the jurisdiction requires or permits such disclosure.

94. Formal Op. 376, *supra* note 18.

95. *See supra* note 39 (regarding applicability of FRCP 37 to discovery sanctions).

96. Fed. R. Civ. P. 37(a)(5)(A). See also *supra* "Adverse Consequences to Client and Lawyer."

97. *See supra* text accompanying note 39.

98. 158 F.R.D. 80 (S.D.W.V. 1994).

99. *Id.* at 87.

100. *Id.* (quoting United States v. Shaffer Equip. Co., 11 F.3d 450, 457 (4th Cir. 1993)).

101. Wolfram, *supra* note 15, at 814 n.15.

102. Liebman & Cohen, *supra* note 1, at 44, 46; *see also* Mark Curriden, *The Lies Have It*, A.B.A. J., May 1995, at 68 (discussing growing prevalence of perjury and lack of prosecutions).

103. Wolfram, *supra* note 15, at 814 n.15.

104. *See, e.g.*, Nix v. Whiteside, 475 U.S. 157, 173 (1986) ("[a] lawyer who would . . . cooperate [with client perjury] would be at risk of prosecution for suborning perjury, and disciplinary proceedings, including suspension or disbarment.")

105. See "Proper Practice Versus Improper Coaching" in Chapter 7.

106. 272 Cal. Rptr. 250 (Ct. App. 1990).

107. *Id.* at 258.

108. Feld & Sons v. Pechner, Dorfman, Wolfee, Rorinick & Cabot, 458 A.2d 545 (Pa. Super. Ct. 1983).

109. 922 F.2d 60 (2d Cir. 1990).

110. *Id.* at 65.

111. *Id.* at 72; *see also* Maddox v. State, 613 S.W.2d 275, 280–81 (1980.)

112. *See, e.g.*, *Crary*, 245 N.W.2d 298 (Iowa 1976) (disbarment); *In re* Mack, 519 N.W.2d 900 (Minn. 1994) (continued twenty-three month suspension); *In re* Jagiela, 517 N.W.2d 333 (Minn. 1994) (six-month suspension).

CHAPTER 22

What to Do When the Fifth Amendment Pays Civil Litigation a Visit

Michael J. Shepard

Many years ago, the Fifth Amendment almost always was a privilege for gangsters and their ilk. Among lawyers, the Fifth Amendment's declaration that no person "shall be compelled in any criminal case to be a witness against himself" created issues only in the world of criminal defense attorneys and prosecutors. But the privilege may be asserted in civil cases as well as criminal cases,[1] and with the rise in white-collar criminal cases and in civil litigation that parallels those proceedings, the Fifth Amendment now plays a significant and increasingly frequent role in civil litigation and, more specifically, in depositions.[2]

Over time, more and more practitioners in civil cases have found themselves facing Fifth Amendment issues when clients who are compelled to provide discovery also face the risk of criminal liability for conduct related to the civil litigation. Most commonly, this situation arises in securities fraud and antitrust cases, where there often is civil and/or administrative litigation pursued at the same time as a criminal investigation. But given the breadth of criminal fraud statutes,[3] the situation can arise in a wide variety of civil cases. Whatever the subject matter, the issue might arise starkly, when in the midst of preparing for a deposition or responding to a discovery request, a lawyer learns that her client has potential criminal liability. All of a sudden, the routine process of preparing for a deposition becomes anything but routine, as the lawyer and client grapple with issues such as whether the client should answer the potentially incriminating questions, what risk of prosecution may arise from those answers, and what the consequences are if the client declines to answer.

This chapter addresses the four primary practical issues facing lawyers when their client or the adverse party might risk incrimination by responding to civil discovery, and particularly to deposition questions: (1) how to decide whether to assert the privilege; (2) how to assert the privilege; (3) how the assertion of the privilege plays out at a civil trial or on dispositive motions (both for plaintiffs and for defendants); and (4) how (and whether) the assertion of the privilege, as well as any inferences that flow from such an assertion, can be avoided or lessened through alternatives such as grants of immunity or stays of discovery.

How to Decide Whether to Assert the Privilege

Deciding whether a client should assert the Fifth Amendment privilege—especially when the decision needs to be made quickly and often when little is known about the case—is one of the most difficult decisions for a client that a lawyer can participate in making. Sometimes even identifying the need to make the decision— that is, identifying that the client may face a risk of criminal liability so that a decision whether to assert the privilege needs to be made—takes work, requiring a full airing of the underlying facts by the client and some digging by the lawyer to learn additional facts, both about the underlying case and about the possibility of government investigations. But whether the need to make the decision was immediately apparent or took some inquiry, it is the sort of decision that a client should make only in consultation with an experienced practitioner, specialized in the field.

The reason the decision often is so delicate is that it can force clients to choose between two highly valued sets of assets, neither of which they want to give up. The first is an uncompromised ability to present their best defense in a future criminal case, a case that could send them to jail for a substantial period of time. The second, opposing set of assets is their reputation in the community and their ability to prosecute or defend the civil litigation, especially civil litigation that could impose a meaningful financial burden. Protecting the first asset would favor asserting the privilege; protecting the second set of assets would counsel in favor of answering questions.

Testifying at a deposition or otherwise providing discovery before trial in a civil case can compromise a client's ability to present the best defense in a criminal case because one of the few advantages a criminal defendant has is the ability to remain silent until all the prosecution's evidence is presented—and to do so without suffering the penalty of any adverse inference from that silence in the criminal case. Remaining silent until the prosecution has presented its case allows criminal defendants to have their recollections fully refreshed and to understand the evidence against them before they testify—a significant advantage in a world in which one bad answer can doom a defendant to conviction. It also lessens the risk of incurring perjury or obstruction of justice charges. But asserting the privilege often becomes a public event and can unfairly cause severe damage to the client's reputation. And even if the assertion of the privilege never becomes public (subject to the successful use of the alternatives to that assertion described in the last section of this chapter), refusing to answer questions will in some jurisdictions cripple the client's ability to prosecute or defend civil litigation.

In making this delicate decision, most experienced practitioners start with the wisdom of the iconic criminal defense lawyer Edward Bennett Williams. He advised that whenever a criminal investigation or charge is in progress or can be anticipated, "you'd have to be a complete idiot to do anything other than take the Fifth Amendment."[4] Heeding this advice, start with the presumption that clients who are or have a material chance of being subjects or targets of a criminal investigation should assert their privilege, and deviate from that presumption only when you are firmly convinced it is safe to do so.

How can you feel sufficiently safe to allow your client to testify at a deposition instead of invoking the privilege? The decision will turn primarily on whether there is a real risk of criminal prosecution. To assess that risk, you need to thoroughly gather the facts and to apply them to the potential theories of prosecution. Learn as much as possible about the matters under investigation from the client and from any other witnesses who might be willing to share information, using a joint defense or information-sharing agreement if appropriate.[5] If a criminal case is known to be on the prosecutor's radar screen, ask the prosecutor for as much information about the investigation as possible, including a statement of whether your client is a witness, subject, or target of the investigation. But keep in mind that disclosure from the prosecutor is likely to be frugal and that the prosecutor's assessment may be subject to change. If civil discovery is available to gather more facts, use it.

Delay can be your ally if you can put off any response to a deposition notice or other discovery in the civil case (and thereby the decision whether to assert the privilege) until you have more information. Therefore, if delay is possible, by all means delay. Such delays can sometimes be negotiated. If not, a delay can sometimes be achieved by winning a motion to a stay discovery.[6] In the alternative, if your client has already asserted his Fifth Amendment privilege, you can ask the court to allow your client to "undo" his earlier assertion of the privilege and answer questions or provide previously missing discovery later in the case, assuming your opponent cannot make a showing of material prejudice.[7]

Another factor to assess in deciding whether to assert the privilege is the client's level of tolerance for risk, including any perceived job-related need for the client to appear to be open and cooperative. As part of this assessment, consider whether a truthful statement by your client would, if it reached the public, tell a story that would help the client's reputation in the court of public opinion. But if there is a real risk of criminal prosecution, it requires exceptional circumstances for the interest of the client in civil litigation and in his personal reputation to outweigh that risk. For example, a sitting president may need to address allegations about an alleged affair with an intern and about alleged false statements in a deposition about that affair. And it appears such considerations led President Clinton to decide to testify before a grand jury about Monica Lewinsky, rather than assert his privilege.[8] For more ordinary clients, the assertion of the privilege will not attract similar levels of media or congressional scrutiny. But few clients are totally disinterested in their reputation and standing in the community, and most clients understandably feel that their standing will be adversely affected by a Fifth Amendment assertion. Therefore, your clients must weigh the impact on reputation against a more draconian risk—jail.

The privilege against self incrimination may be asserted any time a witness has "reasonable cause to apprehend danger of criminal liability"—even if no criminal investigation has begun,[9] even if the witness has already been convicted but has not yet been sentenced,[10] and even after sentencing if there is a risk of additional prosecution.[11] The privilege covers not only testimony in a civil case but also the act of producing documents, because that act can have testimonial aspects.[12] Just as the privilege may be asserted at any stage of a feared or actual criminal proceeding, so too may it be asserted at any stage of, and in any type of, civil or administrative proceeding.[13] Although the text of the Fifth Amendment speaks of no person being compelled "to be a witness against himself" in "a criminal case," the courts have extended its protection "to all areas where the government seeks to compel testimony from an individual in whatever forum."[14]

How to Assert the Privilege

If, after engaging in this delicate balancing, you and your client decide to assert the Fifth Amendment privilege, there is no magic language that must be used. Whether in response to an interrogatory, a deposition question, or any other inquiry or disclosure, the client simply states that she declines to answer based on her Fifth Amendment privilege. Sometimes, lawyers fence about whether the invocation must include a reference to the potential for self-incrimination, but the word "incrimination" is not in the amendment itself. Therefore, referring to the Fifth Amendment should suffice.

The most important consideration in asserting the privilege is to make sure the assertion is in a timely manner and is not waived. The Fifth Amendment operates on a "use it or lose it" basis; and, except when a client is questioned while in the government's custody, the privilege can be lost without any warning that a response risks waiver.[15] About all that can be said to mitigate a waiver is that it is limited to the proceeding in which the waiver occurred.[16]

Those asserting the privilege would prefer merely to announce their intention to do so and thereby avoid having to repeat the incantation in response to each deposition question. In fact, they would prefer to avoid having to show up for the deposition at all. But if challenged by the opposing party, the witness will not be able to make a "blanket" assertion. The reason: there may be questions the deponent can answer without risk of incrimination.[17] As a result, the privilege must be asserted on a question-by-question basis so that the propriety of invoking the privilege as to each question can be ascertained by the court.[18] Pursuant to the Federal Rules of Civil Procedure (FRCP) 37(a), if a deponent refuses to answer a question, the examiner may either ask about other matters or adjourn the deposition; in either case, the examiner may later apply to the court for an order compelling the witness to answer.

But this rationale for disfavoring "blanket" assertions is questionable given that most courts are loathe to interfere with the assertion of the Fifth Amendment privilege[19] and that the standards for asserting the privilege are fairly lax. Courts generally will sustain a blanket assertion as long as the witness has "reasonable cause to apprehend danger of criminal liability"[20] and the answer may provide a clue leading investigators to discover "a link in the chain" of evidence needed to prosecute the witness.[21] The ease with which the standard for asserting the privilege can be met should also serve as a warning to those who might think they do not need to assert it: The standard for accepting the assertion is easily satisfied because the smallest admission, even such seemingly innocuous testimony as identifying an old telephone number or confirming the existence of a personal relationship, can turn out to provide a material link in the government's proof in a criminal case.[22] If there are genuine questions about whether this standard is met, the best procedure is for the court to review the assertions in camera.[23]

As a result of these standards, rather than using a question-by-question approach to challenge the witness's assertion of the privilege, most deposition takers instead will ask extremely leading and possibly argumentative questions in response to which they fully expect the witness to assert the privilege. Then, at trial or as part of summary judgment motion, the examiner will argue that specific, powerful inferences should be drawn from the assertion of the privilege in response to those questions.[24]

Therefore, if you believe there is value to asking such questions in order to make the inferences as specific as possible—a question that is open to dispute—you probably do not want to call the opposition in advance to attempt to obtain an agreement to allow a "blanket" assertion. Calling in advance would allow the party asking the questions to anticipate the privilege assertion and to prepare more specific, inference-favorable questions in advance. As a practical matter, however, a party's assertion of the privilege often comes only after requests for delays and a stay of discovery that leave little doubt that an assertion of the privilege is at least a real possibility. As a result, a party intending to assert the privilege can usually assume that the party asking the questions will be prepared for it.

Trying to pick and choose among the questions asked—answering some and asserting the privilege in response to others—is likely to be a mistake. Despite the contrary impression that might be drawn from the judicial requirement of a question-by-question approach, such selective assertions will not produce much benefit at trial because, as a general matter, a single assertion of the privilege will bring with it much if not all of the possible prejudice the trier of fact might attach to a blanket assertion of the privilege against self-incrimination. And a selective, question-by-question approach creates two real risks: First, without a crystal ball, you may permit your client to answer a question that will turn out to assist in a prosecution against her; and second, your client may answer a question that will be deemed to have waived the privilege.[25] Therefore, unless there is a good reason not to do so, assert the privilege for all questions beyond an introductory few such as name.[26]

How the Assertion of the Privilege Plays Out at a Civil Trial and on Dispositive Motions

In most jurisdictions, a party in a civil case is entitled to bring to the attention of the trier of fact its opponent's assertion of the Fifth Amendment privilege and to argue that the trier of fact should draw an adverse inference against the opponent based on that assertion. The Supreme Court has held that the United States Constitution does not preclude such adverse inferences in civil proceedings, as long as the inference is not mandatory, is only one of the factors considered by the trier of fact, and is given no more probative value than the facts of the case warrant.[27]

Exactly why the Supreme Court permits this inference is subject to question. After all, the Court has itself "condemn[ed]" the practice of imputing a sinister meaning to the exercise of a person's constitutional right under the Fifth Amendment,[28] declaring that one of the Fifth Amendment's "basic functions" is "to protect *innocent* men . . . who might otherwise be ensnarled by ambiguous circumstances."[29] Moreover, such inferences usually are not allowed from the assertions of other privileges, such as the attorney-client privilege.[30] And some jurisdictions treat the assertion of the Fifth Amendment privilege like other privileges, and do not allow it to be brought to the attention of the trier of fact or to be the basis of an adverse inference.[31] But the party asserting the privilege in those jurisdictions must realize that the opposing party is allowed to, and will likely, comment on the absence of evidence offered, though the comment may not tie that absence or evidence to, or mention, the fact that the party had asserted the Fifth Amendment privilege. These jurisdictions appear to assume that without specific comment on a Fifth Amendment assertion, a jury will not figure out the reason why there is an absence of evidence. This assumption may well be accurate, but it has never been tested empirically.

But most jurisdictions permit evidence of the assertion to be presented at a civil trial and permit the trier of fact to draw an adverse inference from that assertion. Cases so holding cite to different language and rationales from the Supreme Court, such as the Court's observation that silence in the face of an accusation is a "relevant fact" and is "often evidence of the most persuasive character."[32] Assessing how the inference can be most effectively exploited—and how such exploitations can be limited—depends to some extent on whether it is raised before trial (where sometimes a distinction is drawn between plaintiffs who assert the privilege and defendants who do so) or at trial. And both before trial and at trial, there are issues about drawing inferences from the assertions of nonparties.

While these three different contexts—assertion before trial, at trial, and by nonparties—raise different issues, some rules and strategies apply in every context. First, generally an adverse inference from the assertion of the privilege is not by itself sufficient for a finding of liability;[33] in fact, some cases go so far as to declare that an adverse inference should be drawn only if there is other probative evidence on the issue.[34] Second, the court can decline to draw an adverse inference or refuse to allow the jury to draw one, if the danger of unfair prejudice substantially outweighs the probative value of the inference or there are other ways to establish the proposition that the inference is offered to support.[35] Third, the question of whether the jury should draw the inference is one that can be litigated, and argued, not just with the court, but with the jury as well.[36] In that instance, the parties will likely try to offer expert testimony on whether, in the circumstances in which the privilege was asserted, an innocent person would have done the same thing so that no inference should be drawn. Fourth, even where the inference may be drawn, Federal Rule of Evidence (FRE) 403 (which excludes relevant evidence when its probative value is substantially outweighed by the danger of unfair prejudice) can be used to limit the emphasis on the invocation or to limit argument that the decision of the trier of fact should be based solely on that invocation.[37]

Drawing Inferences Before Trial

Issues about inferences from assertions of privilege in depositions, as well as other discovery or response pleadings, may first arise before trial in dispositive motions. In the past, courts frequently distinguished between whether the assertion was made by the plaintiff or the defendant: Courts reasoned that the plaintiffs came to court "voluntarily," and, as a result, should not be allowed to initiate litigation and then decline to answer questions or to provide discovery.[38] The more modern view, however, is that plaintiffs do not automatically waive their Fifth Amendment rights when they bring litigation to enforce other rights.[39]

When the defendant asserts the privilege—despite rules providing that allegations of a complaint that are not specifically denied in an answer to the complaint are deemed admitted[40]—courts will treat a defendant's assertion of the privilege in an answer as the equivalent of a specific denial and will require the plaintiff to prove the allegation covered by this constructive denial.[41] Beyond these basic principles, which offer some protection to both plaintiffs and defendants, courts generally decide the consequences of privilege assertions when ruling on pretrial motions by a balancing process that allows considerable room for case-specific arguments on specific issues identified below.

Assuming that the court has not stayed discovery from the party asserting the privilege, the court will analyze a plaintiff's assertion of privilege, by balancing the desire to avoid punishing possible exercises of the privilege against the defendants' need for information to defend the case. For example, the court will examine (1) the extent to which the information that is withheld on privilege grounds is significant to the opposing party's claim or defense; (2) whether the opposing party has an alternative means to obtain the information it needs; and (3) whether there is any effective, alternate remedy other than a judgment in favor of the opposing party.[42] An adverse inference has been found to satisfy these standards in many cases, but the issues remain hotly contested.[43] In preparing its argument counsel should focus on a case-specific analysis of those three questions—especially on the question of denial of access to key information on a pivotal issue[44]—but should not lose sight of the fact that, like jurors, many judges have an emotional reaction against letting someone who has asserted a privilege against self-incrimination "get away with something." Therefore, provide the court, to the extent possible, with all the facts bearing on the question of whether in this case the privilege assertion is one of those instances when it is, as the Supreme Court predicted in *Grunewald*, "to protect innocent men."[45]

Dismissal is not an available remedy when the defendant asserts the privilege. Rather, in such cases, the battle is fought over the following issues, addressed in the remainder of this chapter: (1) whether the case can or should be stayed; (2) whether an adverse inference should be drawn at summary judgment or trial; and (3) whether parties whose view of the risks of prosecution often change during the course of the litigation may "undo" their assertion of the privilege and be allowed to testify at trial. On these issues too there is often an advantage for the party who can prevail on the issue of whether the privilege assertion was "protect[ing] innocent men" as described in *Grunewald*[46] or whether it instead was allowing a criminal to "game" the system.

Drawing Inferences at Trial

There are no reported cases addressing requests by parties to offer expert testimony on whether an adverse inference should be drawn. Likewise, there are no reported cases addressing requests by parties to preclude their opponent from arguing an adverse inference on the ground that the probative value of the inference is substantially outweighed by the unfair prejudice it would create. The argument against the inference may be made to the trier of fact by motion, with or without supporting testimony by an expert. The essence of the argument is that when an investigation is pending, most criminal defense lawyers will counsel a client to assert his privilege, and remind the client that the privilege was designed to protect the innocent. Asking for an adverse inference based on a privilege assertion, the argument continues, is therefore an appeal to the unjustified bias that anyone who asserts the privilege must be guilty. As a result the risk of creating unfair prejudice from the unjustified bias outweighs any probative value of the adverse inference. The parties seeking the adverse inference would respond that this judgment is the sort of judgment about a party's motivation that finders of fact are typically asked to make and that there is nothing unfairly prejudicial about drawing an adverse inference under these circumstances.[47]

Drawing Inferences from Privilege Assertions by a Nonparty Witness

Less common, but potentially considerably more important, is the question of whether an adverse inference may be drawn against a party when a nonparty witness asserts the privilege. This issue most frequently arises when the privilege is asserted by employees or former employees of a corporation that is a defendant in civil litigation. Numerous cases have allowed nonparties to be called to the witness stand in a civil trial to assert their Fifth Amendment privilege and to permit the trier of the fact to draw an adverse inference against a party based on that assertion.[48]

Some recent cases have questioned that approach. The knee-jerk acceptance of the inference against a corporation for an assertion of the privilege by, for example, a former employee is particularly suspect given the shift by corporations away from the "we're all family" corporate response to government investigations by corporations of the 1950s to the current "look out for number one and toss employees to the wolves" approach fostered by the incentives for cooperation in the Sentencing Guidelines that govern the sentencing of corporations in federal court.[49] In the current environment, the lack of any relationship or, all too often, a contentious relationship between a corporation and a former employee during a government investigation undermines an essential premise in the logic of permitting an adverse inference against a party based on the assertion of the privilege by a nonparty. The premise that the party has a close enough relationship with the nonparty witness that the party can control the witness' decision to assert the privilege—or at least that the witness's "self-interest would counsel him to exculpate the employer if possible"[50]—no longer seems viable.

Given the emphasis on retaining flexibility in applying the rules of privilege on a case-by-case basis reflected in FRE 501, courts have been reluctant to establish firm rules about allowing an adverse inference from a nonparty's invocation of the privilege; instead, courts rely on the common law interpreted "in the light of reason and experience."[51] For that reason arguments about whether the invocation of privilege by a nonparty should result in an adverse inference against a party will focus on a series of considerations: (1) the nature of the relevant relationships, including questions such as loyalty and the likelihood that the witness would act to damage the relationship; (2) the degree of control the party has over the non-party witness; (3) the compatibility of the interests of the party and the nonparty witness in the outcome of the litigation; and (4) the role of the nonparty witness in the litigation, including questions such as whether the witness played a controlling role in the events under-lying the litigation.[52] And, for assertions of the privilege by former employees, some courts have added a fifth consideration: "factors suggesting that a former employee retains some loyalty to his for-mer employer." For example, if the employer is paying the non-party's attorney's fees, at least in the absence of an ironclad obli-gation to do so, such payments "would reduce the chance that the former employee would falsely cast blame on the former employer"[53] and might be seen as a reason to permit an adverse inference.

The arguments for allowing an adverse inference usually are case-specific. Faced with the possibility of an adverse inference against your corporate client, in this and all other instances, be pre-pared first to persuade the court that an adverse inference should not be drawn, and then, as a backup, be prepared to offer evidence to the jury that "could rebut any adverse inference that might attend the employee's silence," including the production of "contrary testi-monial or documentary evidence."[54] For example, the significance of the corporation's payment of an employee's attorney's fees might be neutralized by proof that payment is required by a statute[55] or by an indemnification agreement. Regardless of this argument, before a corporation agrees to pay an employee's legal fees, you as coun-sel for the corporation need to assess not only the strength of the claimed entitlement to payment of fees[56] but also balance the ben-efits of access to information and possible input or influence on deci-sions against the risk of an adverse inference. Extra scrutiny should be given to arrangements in which the corporation not only pays for counsel but also uses the same lawyer or firm to represent both the corporation and the employees or former employees. Although this arrangement has unquestioned benefits of cost and efficiency, it may increase the chances a court will permit an adverse inference because the arrangement generates the appearance—if not the reality—that the corporation is controlling the representation.[57]

How to Avoid the Assertion of the Privilege as Well as How to Avoid or Lessen Adverse Inferences

Given the difficult choices faced by parties asserting their Fifth Amendment privilege, careful attorneys will consider alternative approaches to avoid the need to compromise the ability of their clients to present their best defense in a criminal case, to avoid negative impact on their reputation, and to allow them to prosecute or defend civil litigation. One alternative—seeking immunity—has not found success in any reported civil cases, primarily due to the deference courts give to the prosecutor's discretion to decide who does and does not get immunity. But another alternative—seeking a partial stay of discovery—has generated at least some success in recent years.

Obtaining Immunity from Prosecution

Obtaining immunity might seem like an appealing solution for parties forced with asserting the privilege. But unless the prosecutor chooses to grant immunity because it would advance the government's interest in its criminal investigation or prosecution, it is not an available solution. Courts in all civil actions and in almost all criminal cases are unwilling to grant parties immunity either because of the absence of statutory authority to do so[58] or because they do not want to interfere with decisions by the executive branch of government and possibly undermine potential prosecutions.[59] For these reasons, although courts have granted immunity in a few federal criminal cases when they found that the government violated due process in a way that could only be corrected by a grant of immunity,[60] they have not, as noted above, ordered immunity in any reported civil cases. Some states acknowledge the possibility that a civil trial court may order immunity but only if the prosecutor has been given notice and an opportunity to object.[61]

In addition, seeking an immunity order in a criminal case in an effort to force the deponent to testify in the civil case is not necessarily a viable solution because even if the court presiding over the grand jury or criminal trial entered an immunity order, the witness still retains the right to assert the privilege in a civil case and therefore cannot be compelled to testify. As a result, immunity granted in criminal proceedings provides no protection for testimony given in private civil actions.[62] While, as a practical matter, a prosecutor who has granted immunity to a witness may be unlikely to prosecute that witness, a risk of prosecution—even if theoretical—remains. As a result, even immunized witnesses will be loath to testify in a civil case without an express agreement with the prosecutor that the civil testimony will not be used against them. Furthermore, counsel must remember that immunity orders do not provide protection against a charge that testimony procured through immunity was perjured.[63]

There are also no reported cases of success in obtaining something akin to immunity through a protective order under FRCP 26(c)(1)(A) that would preclude disclosure of the party's testimony. In the end, it has been held in other contexts that a grand jury subpoena trumps a civil protective order purporting to preclude disclosure of the testimony.[64] As a result, a protective order in a civil case will not in the end protect the party asserting the privilege. Therefore counsel should not allow—nor should courts compel—testimony in exchange for an unenforceable protective order precluding its disclosure.[65] In addition, such protective orders have also been rejected as a solution to avoid the negative publicity that results from a public awareness of privilege assertion.[66]

Obtaining a Stay of Discovery

A party may have more success in avoiding adverse consequences from privilege assertions by trying to delay discovery or stay a deposition. While there is no constitutional right to a stay, federal courts have discretion to control the sequence of discovery and to decide whether to delay discovery in the face of other proceedings.[67] Under the law of some states, a stay may even be favored.[68] But regardless of any presumptions about stays in cases in which prosecutors do not take a position, stays in civil cases can be very hard to obtain when the prosecutors seek to intervene and oppose a stay, given the deference most courts show to prosecutors.[69]

Deciding whether to seek a stay—and predicting whether a stay will be granted—hinge on a series of practical and strategic factors. First, despite occasional admonitions by the Supreme Court to minimize the costs of asserting the privilege,[70] stays are often denied. In addition, seeking a stay may expose your client's intention to assert the privilege or expose details about the criminal investigation that the opponent may not otherwise know—at least not at that point in the litigation. You also need to consider that the court's decision on your request for a stay will not be based solely on the benefit to your client who seeks to avoid asserting the privilege. Instead, the court will consider (1) the opponent's interest in continuing the litigation and the burden the opponent will incur as a result of the proposed delay; (2) the burden on the defendant of having to defend in two different forums; (3) the burden on the court and nonparties; and (4) any public interest.[71] While prosecutors frequently—but not always—obtain stays of civil actions upon request, the batting average of private parties seeking a stay of civil litigation is significantly lower.[72]

Second, parties seeking to avoid asserting the privilege still might on balance be better off without a stay. Criminal prosecution generally carries with it a far greater wallop than that of civil litigation, including not only possible jail time and fines but also orders of restitution that can be enforced by "victims" just like a civil judgment.[73] And parties in criminal investigations and prosecutions have limited or no discovery rights.[74] Therefore, despite the negative impact on a civil case, it may turn out to be better to forgo a stay, suffer any adverse consequences in the civil case, allows discovery to proceed, and use the discovery, including depositions of key prosecution witnesses to aid in the defense of the criminal case.[75]

Another strategy for a party seeking to avoid asserting the privilege would be to allow discovery in general to proceed and seek only a limited stay in order to postpone the few depositions or other discovery that would necessitate asserting the privilege. But before going down this road, it is important to determine the extent to which witnesses who will later testify for the government in the criminal case will themselves be able to assert their Fifth Amendment privilege in response to civil discovery and, as a result, eliminate the expected benefit of conducting discovery in the hope that it will help in the defense of the criminal case. Even witnesses who have pled guilty and agreed to cooperate retain their right to their Fifth Amendment privilege until they are sentenced. And both the witness and the prosecutor will want to postpone the sentencing until after any criminal prosecution of your client in order to prevent you from deposing the witness who has already pled guilty as part of your client's effort to gain an advantage in preparing to cross-examine that witness at your client's criminal trial.

Third, even if the court is willing to stay civil proceedings until the statute of limitations has run in the criminal case,[76] the calculation of when the statute of limitations expires can be extremely difficult. A client can be prosecuted in multiple jurisdictions; and, in each jurisdiction, there may be multiple potential offenses with statutes of limitation of varying lengths.[77] Even after the temporal limits of the governing statutes of limitation are identified, determining when the criminal conduct ended can be very challenging and perilous: For example, in a situation where there are allegations of an ongoing conspiracy, the government's deadline to bring charges may be extended. In addition, for some federal statutes such as mail and wire fraud,[78] the time runs not from the last of the fraudulent statements themselves but from the last act in furtherance of the fraud, which may include wires or mailings long after the last fraudulent statement. In the end, neither the clients, nor their party opponents, nor even the court supervising the civil litigation may know with certainty the last day your client can be prosecuted.

These complications drive some parties who may plan to assert their Fifth Amendment privilege to try to delay depositions and responses to other discovery until late in the discovery process. In some cases, the opponent may be willing to accept a discovery delay based on the needs of its own witnesses or may accept a delay to avoid the risk of having a longer stay imposed by the court. If a delay is impossible, a party may decide to assert the privilege with the hope that the status of the criminal proceedings will improve before the close of civil discovery and with the further hope that it will be able to "undo" the privilege assertion and testify. But, as noted above, that strategy runs the risk that the court may not allow the party to "undo" the privilege assertion and testify.[79] But that risk may be easier to swallow than the alternatives.

Conclusion

The delicate considerations identified in this chapter help explain why the decisions faced by parties contemplating the assertion of the Fifth Amendment privilege are among the most challenging that lawyers help their clients to make. While never easily made, those decisions—as well as those made by your opponents—can be better made with knowledge of the various moves that each side can take and with a strategy that from the outset anticipates the possible risks and benefits. Even then, with careful planning with a party who may need to assert the privilege, an outcome without adverse consequences cannot be guaranteed.

Notes

1. *See infra* note 11.

2. Although there is no means of tracking invocations of the Fifth Amendment privilege (either in civil cases or anywhere else), its increased use in civil cases is reflected by the increased attention given to the subject in publications directed to civil practitioners. *See, e.g.*, Albritton, *Presumption of Guilt: Taking the Fifth in Civil Proceedings*, LITIGATION, Fall 2007; Scheff, Coffina & Baisinger, *Taking the Fifth in Civil Litigation*, LITIGATION, Fall 2002; Auspitz, *Asserting the Fifth Amendment Privilege Against Self-Incrimination in Parallel Proceedings*, in PARALLEL PROCEEDINGS IN SECURITIES CASES 2008 (PLI, 2008).

3. *See, e.g.*, 18 U.S.C. §§ 1341, 1343.

4. Quoted in Raphaelson, Cohen & Stuckwisch, *Legislate in Haste, Report and Probe at Leisure*, NAT'L L.J., Mar. 10, 2003.

5. See "Representation of Corporate Affiliates and Their Employees" in Chapter 6, discussing the joint-defense doctrine.

6. See *infra* section "How to Avoid the Assertion of the Privilege as Well as How to Avoid or Lessen Adverse Inferences," describing motions for a stay.

7. "Undoing" an assertion has been allowed in some cases but not in others. *See* SEC v. Graystone Nash, Inc., 25 F.3d 187, 190–92 (3d Cir. 1994). An argument can be made that allowing the "undoing" of an assertion is the preferred procedure, at least when it can be done in a way that eliminates any prejudice to the party-opponent, because it seeks to minimize the possibility that sanctions will be imposed from the assertion of the privilege as the Supreme Court has sometimes urged. *See, e.g.*, Spevack v. Klein, 385 U.S. 511, 515 (1967).

8. *See, e.g.*, Woodward, *A President's Isolation*, WASH. POST, June 13, 1999, at A1.

9. Hoffman v. United States, 341 U.S. 479 (1951).

10. Mitchell v. United States, 526 U.S. 314, 323–24 (1999).

11. *See, e.g.*, *In re* Grand Jury Proceedings (Samuelson), 763 F.2d 321 (8th Cir. 1985); United States v. Smith, 245 F.3d 538 (6th Cir. 2007).

12. *See, e.g.*, Baltimore City Dep't of Soc. Servs. v. Bouknight, 493 U.S. 549, 555 (1990).

13. *See* Rogers v. United States, 340 U.S. 367, 373, 375, 378 (1951); Malloy v. Hogan, 378 U.S. 1 (1964); McCarthy v. Arndstein, 266 U.S. 34 (1924). Corporations cannot assert the privilege because the Fifth Amendment is written to apply to "persons."

14. Albritton, *Presumption of Guilt: Taking the Fifth In Civil Proceedings*, LITIGATION, Fall 2007, at 20.

15. *See, e.g.*, United States v. Kordell, 397 U.S. 1 (1970); SEC v. Graystone Nash, Inc., 25 F.3d 187 (3d Cir. 1994).

16.   *See, e.g.*, United States v. James, 609 F.2d 36 (2d Cir. 1979); United States v. Licavoli, 604 F.2d 613 (9th Cir. 1979). *But see* United States v. Miller, 904 F.2d 65 (D.C. Cir. 1990).

17.   WRIGHT, MILLER & MARCUS, FEDERAL PRACTICE & PROCEDURE, CIVIL § 2018; *see, e.g.*, N. River Ins. Co. Inc., v. Stefanou, 831 F.2d 484, 487 (4th Cir. 1987).

18.   *See* Nat'l Life Ins. Co. v. Hartford Accident & Indem. Co., 615 F.2d 595 (3d Cir. 1980); *In re* Morganroth, 718 F.2d 161, 167 (6th Cir. 1983); Baker v. Limber, 647 F.2d 912, 916 (9th Cir. 1981); Doe *ex rel.* Rudy-Glanzer v. Glanzer, 232 F.3d 1258 (9th Cir. 2000); *In re* Grand Jury Subpoena, 739 F.2d 1354, 1359 (8th Cir. 1984).

19.   *See, e.g.*, Scheff, Coffina & Baisinger, *Taking the Fifth in Civil Litigation*, LITIGATION, Fall 2002, at 36; LAFAVE, ISRAEL, KING & KERR, CRIMINAL PROCEDURE 239 (3d ed. 2008) ("courts are to give the witness every benefit of the doubt in reviewing his assertion of the privilege").

20.   *See, e.g.*, Hoffman v. United States, 341 U.S. 479 (1951).

21.   *See, e.g.*, Kastigar v. United States, 406 U.S. 441 (1972); Pillsbury v. Conboy, 459 U.S. 248, 265 (1983). *See also* Marchetti v. United States, 390 U.S. 38, 53 (1968).

22.   Robert Heidt, *The Conjurer's Circle: The Fifth Amendment & Privilege in Civil Cases*, 91 YALE L.J. 1062, 1071–72 (1982).

23.   United States v. Grable, 98 F.3d 251 (6th Cir. 1996).

24.   Parties with interests similar to that of the witness, such as co-defendants, might respond by asking equally slanted questions in *their* favor, leaving the record uncertain as to what inference should be drawn. *See generally* WRIGHT & GRAHAM, FEDERAL PRACTICE & PROCEDURE, EVIDENCE § 7753 (4th ed. 2000).

25.   *See, e.g.*, Klein v. Harris, 668 F.2d 274, 287 (2d Cir. 1981) (establishing waiver standards); Nutramax Labs., Inc. v. Twin Labs., Inc., 32 F. Supp. 2d 331 (D. Md. 1999).

26.   *See, e.g.*, Osterhoudt, *Representing a Grand Jury Witness*, 16 LITIGATION 6, 9 (1990). *But see* Hiibel v. Dist. Court, 542 U.S. 177 (2004) (Stevens, J., dissenting).

27.   *See, e.g.* Baxter v. Palmigiaro, 425 U.S. 308 (1976); Lefkowitz v. Cunningham, 431 U.S. 801 (1977). For these purposes "civil proceedings" have been held to include deportation proceedings and habeas corpus proceedings. *See* United States v. Solano-Gordines, 120 F.3d 957, 962 (9th Cir. 1997); Reasonover v. Washington, 60 F. Supp. 2d 937, 960 (E.D. Mo. 1999). Although private actors are not barred from taking action against employees based on their assertions of the Fifth Amendment privilege, there is a line of cases limiting sanctions that state actors can impose based on invocations of the privilege, at least under certain circumstances. *See, e.g.*, Garrity v. N.J., 385 U.S. 493 (1967); Lefkowitz v. Cunningham, 431 U.S. 801, 807–09 (1977); Swan v. City of Boston, 329 F.3d 275, 279–82 (1st Cir. 2003).

28. Slochhower v. Bd. of Educ., 350 U.S. 551, 557 (1956). *See* State Farm Life Ins. Co. v. Gutternman, 896 F.2d 116, 119 (5th Cir. 1990) ("The assertion of the privilege, particularly on the advice of counsel, is an ambiguous response."). In criminal cases, of course, no such inference is permitted. *See, e.g.*, Griffin v. California, 380 U.S. 609 (1965).

29. Grunewald v. United States, 353 U.S. 391, 421 (1957) (emphasis in original). Some parties offer expert testimony from experienced criminal defense lawyers in an attempt to contest the inference.

30. *See, e.g.*, CAL. EVID. CODE § 913; UNIF. R. EVID. 512; Proposed Federal Rule of Evidence 513. (The proposed rules were approved by the Supreme Court on November 20, 1972, but not accepted by Congress. *See* 1974 U.S.C.C.A.N. 7051, 7052, 7053, 7058.) The traditional argument in favor of the adverse inference is that in criminal cases, the privilege seeks to avoid government abuse and forcing the defendant to choose between "the 'cruel trilemma' of perjury, self incrimination, or contempt in the face of possible incarceration," but in civil cases the opponent is merely "another litigant with whom it is presumably on an equal footing" and the threat of criminal prosecution is more attenuated. Scheff, Coffina & Basinger, *Taking the Fifth in Civil Litigation*, LITIGATION, Fall 2002, at 70. *See* RAD Serv. Inc. v. Aetna Cas. & Sur. Co., 808 F.2d 271, 275 (3d Cir. 1986).

31. *See, e.g.*, CAL. EVID. CODE § 913; KY. R. EVID. 511; *In Interest of L.S.*, 748 S.W.2d 571, 575 (Tex. App. 1988).

32. Baxter v. Palmigiano, 425 U.S. 308, 319 (1976).

33. *See, e.g.*, Lefkowitz v. Cunningham, 431 U.S. 801, 808 (1977); SEC v. Colello, 139 F.3d 674, 678 (9th Cir. 1988); *Custody of Two Minors*, 396 Mass. 610, 616 (1985).

34. *See* Hasbro, Inc. v. Serafino, 958 F. Supp. 19, 25 (D. Mass. 1997).

35. *See, e.g.*, FED. R. EVID. 403; Doe v. Glanzer, 232 F.3d 1258 (9th Cir. 2000).

36. *See, e.g.*, Brink's Inc. v. City of New York, 717 F.2d 700, 707 (2d Cir. 1983) (assertion of privilege by former and present employees held to be admissible evidence and relied upon in closing argument).

37. Cerre Gordo Charity v. Fireman's Fund, 819 F.2d 1471, 1482 (8th Cir. 1987).

38. *See, e.g.*, Lyons v. Johnson, 415 F.2d 540–41 (9th Cir. 1969) (allowing plaintiff to proceed after asserting her privilege in discovery would "convert the privilege from a shield to a sword").

39. Pillsbury v. Conboy, 459 U.S. 258, 263–64 (1983) (courts cannot give parties or witnesses assurances of immunity); Curtis v. Duval, 124 F.3d 1, 9 (1st Cir. 1997); United States v. Mackey, 117 F.3d 24, 28 (1st Cir. 1997); United States v. Angiulo, 897 F.2d 1169, 1190–93 (1st Cir. 1990); United States v. Hooks, 848 F.2d 785, 799 (7th Cir. 1988); United States v. Quintanilla, 2 F.3d 1469 (7th Cir. 1993); *In re* Grand Jury Proceedings, 995 F.2d 1013, 1017 (11th Cir. 1993); United States v. Tindle, 808 F.2d 319,

325 (4th Cir. 1986); United States v. Pennell, 737 F.2d 521, 526–29 (6th Cir. 1984); United States v. Turkish, 623 F.2d 769, 773–74 (2d Cir. 1980); United States v. Westerdahl, 945 F.2d 1083, 1086 (9th Cir. 1991). 18 U.S.C.A. §§ 6001–6005 (West 2006); United States v. Moussaoui, 382 F.3d 453, 466 (4th Cir. 2004); Robert Heidt, *The Conjurer's Circle: The Fifth Amendment Privilege in Civil Cases*, 91 YALE L.J. 1062, 1100–02 (1982). Gov't of Virgin Islands v. Smith, 615 F.2d 964, 973–74 (3d Cir. 1980); United States v. Morrison, 535 F.2d 223 (3d Cir. 1976). United States v. Herman, 578 F.2d 1191, 1204 (3d Cir. 1978). These cases flow from the Supreme Court's reasoning in cases such as *Garrity v. New Jersey*, 385 U.S. 493 (1967), and *Spevack v. Klein*, 385 U.S. 511 (1967), which addressed the issue of imposing consequences on the assertion of constitutional privileges.

40.   *See, e.g.*, FED. R. CIV. P. 8(b)(6).

41.   *See, e.g.*, Indus. Indem. Co. v. Niebling, 844 F. Supp. 1374 (N. Ariz. 1994).

42.   *See, e.g.*, SEC v. Graystone Nash, Inc., 25 F.3d 187, 192 (3d Cir. 1994). Note that traditional discovery sanctions should not be available because the discovery rules deal only with information that is not priviliged. *See* FED. R. CIV. P. 26(b)(1), (2).

43.   *See, e.g.*, Wehling v. Columbia Broad. Sys., 608 F.2d 1084 (5th Cir. 1980).

44.   *Id.*

45.   *Grunewald*, 353 U.S. at 421.

46.   *Id.*

47.   *See generally* LiButti v. United States, 107 F.3d 110, 124 (2d Cir. 1997).

48.   *See, e.g.*, Brink's Inc. v. City of New York, 717 F.2d 700, 707–10 (2d Cir. 1983); RAD Servs., Inc. v. Aetna Cas. & Sur. Co., 808 F.2d 271, 175–77 (3d Cir. 1986).

49.   *See, e.g.*, U.S. SENTENCING GUIDELINES MANUAL § 8C2.5(g).

50.   RAD Servs., Inc. v. Aetna Cas. & Sur. Co., 808 F.2d 271, 275 (3d Cir. 1986).

51.   Federal Rule of Evidence 501 provides in pertinent part that except as otherwise required, privilege issues "shall be governed by the principles of the common law as they might be interpreted by the court of the United States in the light of reason and experience."

52.   *See, e.g.*, LiButti v. United States, 107 F.3d 110, 123–24 (2d Cir. 1997); LoRusso v. Borer, No. 3:03CV504 (MRK), 2006 U.S. Dist. LEXIS 16623, at *21–22, 35 (D. Conn. Feb. 28, 2006). Differences between the interest of an employer and those of its allegedly wrongdoing former employees have been recognized with increasing frequency in recent decisions. *See, e.g.*, United States v. Stein, No. S1-05, 2006 WL 2060430, at *14 (S.D. N.Y. July 25, 2006).

53.   Fed. Deposit Ins. Corp. v. Fid. & Deposit Co. of Md., 45 F.3d 969, 978 n. 4 (5th Cir. 1995).

54. RAD Servs., Inc. v. Aetna Cas. & Sur. Co., 808 F.2d 271, 273 (3d Cir. 1986).

55. *See, e.g.,* CAL. LABOR CODE § 2802 (requiring employers to indemnify employees "for all that the employee necessarily expends or loses in direct consequence of the discharge of his duties as such, or of his obedience to the directions of the employer, even though unlawful, unless the employee, at the time of obeying such directions, believed them to be unlawful." *See* Douglas v. Los Angeles Herald-Exam'r, 50 Cal. App. 3d 449 (1975).

56. The California statute, for example, which is similar to many forms of indemnification, provides that there is no obligation to pay fees if employees believed the directions under which they were operating were unlawful. CAL. LABOR CODE § 2802.

57. Such an arrangement raises conflict of interest issues. In the event the corporation is a target or subject of a criminal investigation as those terms are defined in the United States Attorney's Manual § 9-11.511, but the individuals are not subjects or targets, or vice versa, there may be an actual conflict and the prosecutors may oppose common representation.

58. *See, e.g.,* Pillsbury v. Conboy, 459 U.S. 258, 263–64 (1983); United States v. Doc, 465 U.S. 605 (1984).

59. *See, e.g.,* Curtis v. Duval, 124 F.3d 1, 9 (1st Cir); United States v. Moussaoui, 382 F.3d 453, 466 (4th Cir. 2004); Heidt, *The Conjurer's Circle: The Fifth Amendment Privilege in Civil Cases,* 91 YALE L.J. 1062, 1100–02 (1982).

60. These cases generally address immunity for witnesses helpful to defendants rather than for the defendants themselves. *See, e.g.,* Gov't of Virgin Islands v. Smith, 615 F.2d 964, 973–74 (3d Cir. 1980); United States v. Duran, 189 F.3d 1071, 1087 (9th Cir. 1999). The Third Circuit has discussed a broader theory allowing judicially ordered immunity when a defendant needs a witness's testimony to provide for an effective defense as guaranteed by the Sixth Amendment, *see id.,* but this theory has been widely rejected elsewhere. *See, e.g.,* Curtis v. Duval, 124 F.3d 1 (1st Cir. 1997). A panel of the Ninth Circuit loosened its rule somewhat by holding that a defendant seeking immunity for a witness who has relevant testimony that directly contradicts the testimony of an immunized prosecution witness—the only potentially viable theory in the Ninth Circuit—must show only that the prosecution's selective denial of immunity had the *effect* of distorting the fact-finding process, as opposed to having to show that the prosecutor's *purpose* in denying immunity to the defense witness was to distort the fact-finding process. *See* United States v. Straub, 538 F.3d 1137, 2008 WL 3547541 (9th Cir. Aug. 15, 2008).

61. *See* Daly v. Superior Court of San Francisco, 19 Cal. 3d 132 (1977).

62. *See* Pillsbury Co. v. Conboy, 459 U.S. 248 (1983).

63. *See, e.g.,* 18 U.S.C. § 6002 (providing for use immunity—"no testimony or other information compelled under the order (or any

information directly or indirectly derived from such testimony or other information) may be used against the witness in any criminal case"—but expressly excepting "a prosecution for perjury, giving a false statement, or otherwise failing to comply with the order").

64. *See, e.g., In re* Grand Jury Subpoena, 62 F.3d 1222 (9th Cir. 1995); *In re* Grand Jury Subpoena, 836 F.2d 1468 (4th Cir. 1988).

65. Andover Data Servs. v. Statistical Tabulating Corp., 876 F.2d 1080, 1084 (2d Cir. 1989) (trial court compelled testimony from a witness who had asserted his Fifth Amendment privilege due to the "strong need" for the testimony and entered a protective order limiting access to the testimony and imposing nondisclosure obligations on persons with knowledge of the testimony; Court of Appeals reversed, reasoning that the district court's order "provides no guarantee that compelled testimony will not somehow find its way into the government's hand for use in a subsequent criminal prosecution").

66. *See, e.g.,* Gumowitz v. First Fed. Sav. & Loan Assoc. of Roanoke, No. 90 Civ. 8083 (MBM), 1994 U.S. Dist. LEXIS 8713 (S.D. N.Y. June 29, 1994).

67. *See, e.g.,* United States v. Kordell, 397 U.S. 1 (1970); Pacers v. Superior Court, 162 Cal. App. 3d 686 (1984); Fed. R. Civ. P. 26(f).

68. California law, for example, precludes comment on the exercise of the Fifth Amendment privilege in civil cases, *see* Cal. Evid. Code § 940, and has been interpreted by at least one appellate court to require that "when both civil and criminal proceedings arise out of the same or related transactions, an objecting party is *generally entitled* to a stay of discovery in the civil action until disposition of the criminal matter," and that a court requested to enter such a stay must "weigh the . . . competing interests . . . with a view toward accommodating the interests of both parties" (emphasis added). Pacers v. Superior Court, 162 Cal. App. 3d 686 (1984). *But see generally* Avant! Corp. v. Superior Court, 79 Cal. App. 4th 876 (2000); Fuller v. Superior Court, 87 Cal. App. 4th 299 (2001).

69. *See, e.g.,* Shepard and Buehler, *No Security: Internal Investigations into Violations of the Securities Laws, in* Internal Corporate Investigations 414, 417 (3d ed. 2007); *see generally* Campbell v. Eastland, 307 F.2d 478, 487 (5th Cir. 1962) (court determines key "public interest" factor in granting stay to be based on "a government policy determination of priority"). *But see* Order Granting the United States' Motion to Stay Certain Discovery, Aronson v. McKesson HBOC, Inc., No. 99 CV 40743 (N.D. Cal., entered Oct. 21, 2004).

70. *See, e.g.,* Lefkowitz v. Cunningham, 431 U.S. 801, 808 n. 5 (1977); Spevack v. Klein, 385 US. 511, 515 (1957).

71. *See, e.g.,* Keating v. Office of Thrift Supervision, 45 F.3d 322, 324–25 (9th Cir. 1995).

72. *See, e.g.,* Scheff, Coffina & Baisinger, *Taking the Fifth In Civil Litigation,* Litigation, Fall 2002, at 39.

73. *See, e.g.,* 18 U.S.C. § 3664.

74. For example, in federal court and most state courts, criminal defendants cannot depose the witnesses against them absent exceptional circumstances. *See* FED. R. CRIM. P. 15.

75. *See, e.g.,* Order Granting the United States' Motion to Intervene and Denying Without Prejudice Its Motion to Stay Certain Discovery, Aronson v. McKesson HBOC, Inc., No. 99 CV 40743 (N.D. Cal., entered Oct. 21, 2004).

76. *See, e.g.,* Wehling v. Columbia Broad. Sys., 608 F.2d 1084 (5th Cir. 1980).

77. Several states, for example, have six-year statutes of limitation for fraud, *see, e.g.,* MASS. GEN. LAWS ch. 277 § 63; MICH. COMP. LAWS § 767.24; OHIO REV. CODE § 2901.13; WIS. STAT. § 939.74, one year longer than the most typical federal statutes. *See, e.g.,* 18 U.S.C. § 3282(a). But, in some instances, certain federal statutes have longer limitation periods. *See, e.g.,* 18 U.S.C. § 1031(f).

78. *See, e.g.,* 18 U.S.C. §§ 1341, 1343.

79. *See, e.g.,* United States v. 4003–4005 Fifth Ave., 55 F.3d 78, 84–85 (2d Cir. 1995); *see generally* FED. R. CIV. P. 16, 26.

CHAPTER 23

The End of the Deposition

MARK D. PETERSEN*

When is the deposition over? And when it is over, is it *really* over?

The end of a deposition presents numerous issues for parties and their lawyers—whether takers or defenders—and initiates a new series of pretrial considerations and concerns. Lawyers must be as well prepared for the conclusion of a deposition as they are for any argument or presentation, because failing to consider the issues that may arise as a deposition is ending can jeopardize your client's rights. Concerns such as how late in the day the examination should go, whether all the lawyers have finished their questioning, and whether further questioning may be limited or monitored by the court—perhaps through a special master—all should be considered *before* it is time to make these decisions. Anticipating the unexpected will set you apart from other lawyers.

After a deposition has concluded, the lawyers involved need to reassess their cases, mull over possible motions, and reevaluate their strategy. They need to report to clients and update their databases. And they need to use what they learned at the deposition to prepare for trial. One of the main reasons for conducting discovery—including taking depositions—is to give you the information you need to present the best case at trial. Deposition transcripts will be essential in preparing your witnesses to testify at trial. They also will be essential in helping you prepare to depose other witnesses.[1]

This chapter examines the conclusion of the deposition, first from the taker's perspective and then from the defender's perspective. The first section discusses matters that each lawyer should address as the deposition is ending; it also looks at the rights that should be reserved to keep open all possible forms of further discovery.[2] The next section reviews the tasks that should be accomplished immediately after the deposition, again from the taker's perspective and then from the defender's. The chapter then turns to the pretrial uses of depositions, including case assessment, witness preparation, and motions. The chapter concludes with a discussion of how to use a deposition transcript at trial. Because every case and every witness is unique, there are few hard-and-fast rules. What works in one situation often will be inappropriate in another, so in every case be flexible and adjust your approach—including tactics and strategy—whenever necessary to achieve your goals.

Concluding the Testimony

The Taker's Role

Most lawyers want their depositions—like a good book—to have good endings: a clear break, a mutual understanding of the status of the deposition (was it completed or adjourned to another time?), and a sense of how to resolve open issues, such as documents not produced and questions not answered. Though it may seem easier at the time to avoid some issues and hope they will work themselves out, it is usually far more important for your client's rights—and less expensive—to address these issues before leaving the deposition room.

As the examining lawyer, this is "your" deposition. Know what you want from it. When preparing for it, consider and decide how to handle the various issues that might arise at the deposition, including those that may arise at the end of the deposition.

It Ain't Over 'Til . . .

Whether a deposition is finally over may seem on its face to be obvious and not susceptible to misunderstanding. But far too often, at the apparent end, there is a question about the status of the deposition.

Never walk away from a deposition without a clear under-standing of its status. This is important for several reasons. First, absent stipulation or leave of court, Federal Rules of Civil Proce-dure (FRCP) 30(a) limits a party to one deposition per witness and restricts each side to a total of ten depositions.[3] Second, absent stipulation or leave of court, FRCP 30(d)(1) limits a deposition to one day of seven hours. You may be able to obtain an exception in your case, but only on an individual-witness basis and only by agreement or court order.[4]

In addition, the date for the cutoff of discovery may affect the scheduling and length of depositions and whether it is possible to put off completion of the deposition. For instance, if other depo-sitions cannot be taken before completion of particular examina-tion and the discovery cutoff is looming, it may not be possible to adjourn for the day and resume the next week.[5]

Are you really finished questioning this witness? This may be your only chance to examine the witness before trial, so you must be certain that you have covered all areas of inquiry before decid-ing that you are done and before releasing the witness. To pre-pare for the point when you will announce that you are finished, ask some "catch-all" questions as you come to a close: "Do you want to change any of the answers you have given here today? Are there any questions that you answered that you now think you did not understand? Have you been able to recall anything in response to those questions or about those subjects to which you had no recollection?" There may be other questions you can ask for this purpose as well, depending on the case and how the wit-ness responded throughout the course of the deposition. There-fore, take a break when you are just about finished. Review your notes and any relevant documents or exhibits. You may find that you made a note to yourself to go back and question the witness further about some topic, but have forgotten to do so.

There are no magic words that will automatically protect your right to continue the deposition at some point in the future. Some local practices may have specific terms with meaning for local lawyers, but there is no universally accepted term of art. There-fore, make clear on the record what is happening: either that you are through for now, subject to resuming again at a date and time to be determined; or that you are through pending the resolution of some issue, such as a motion to compel or for a protective order; or that you have completed deposing the witness.

635

Even if you are done and thus apparently relinquishing your right to depose this witness further before trial, it is usually best to note on the record that you intend to question the witness again should circumstances arise that would permit you to do so (such as a supplemental discovery response pursuant to FRCP 26(e)). In a computer trade-secrets case, for example, you might announce, "Although I am now concluding the deposition, if further discovery indicates that this witness has any knowledge about the programming codes—which he has denied today—I am reserving my right to conduct further examination." Concede nothing, and anticipate that new developments might allow you to reopen the deposition.

In considering your options as the end of the day approaches, remember the deposition notice itself. Lawyers used to notice depositions "to continue from day to day until completed." But FRCP 30(d)(1) now provides that "[u]nless otherwise stipulated or ordered by the court, a deposition is limited to 1 day of 7 hours." Therefore, absent stipulation or leave of court, you no longer can expect, as under former practice, that a deposition will resume the next day if not completed.

Sometimes, however, lawyers will agree to a longer deposition if there is a good reason for adjourning and resuming on a mutually acceptable schedule. For the record, you might say something like this: "I cannot resume tomorrow because of a long-standing meeting out of town, but we are prepared to resume the next day and I understand that this is acceptable." As taker, it is usually better to ask about the witness's availability early in the day so that no one is surprised when you ask for agreement to continue the next day or at a future date.

If counsel have agreed to a deposition lasting longer than seven hours, it is not uncommon for the witness and the defender to request to complete the deposition in one day, regardless of the time ("We are prepared to stay here tonight as late as necessary to finish the deposition"). However, a deposition should not be an endurance contest.[6] If you think that you can complete your questioning in a reasonable time—and if all in attendance, including the court reporter, are able and willing to stay—then consider staying late. But as the evening wears on and you, the witness, and the court reporter start to tire, your goals for the deposition may be at risk. If you need the evening to prepare for further examination, or if you are concerned that your questioning or the testimony elicited might suffer due to fatigue, stop.

Continuing the Deposition for Specific Purposes

Sometimes depositions are continued to another time even though general questioning is complete. The lawyers might agree, for example, to reconvene the deposition for inquiry into a specific subject matter, perhaps after additional documents have been produced or a court order has been issued.[7] In this situation, however, the taker must be extremely cautious about limiting her right to further examination in order to avoid foreclosing a subject area that could have been explored before the decision to reconvene. Given the acrimony that occasionally arises during depositions, it might seem expedient to avoid conflict by limiting further examination to a single discrete subject. However, if you do this, you may find that once you question the witness on this subject, additional avenues of exploration now are cut off. So consider something like the following exchange in a case involving notification of a dangerous condition:

> DEFENDER: I understand that the deposition now is concluded for all matters, except that we have agreed that you can depose my client on the limited issue of notice, should further discovery indicate that an effort was made to provide notice to the general manager of the facility.
>
> TAKER: I agree that the deposition is concluded for now. But I am reserving my right to question this witness further on all subjects relevant to notice if further discovery indicates that any efforts were made to notify the general manager.

Further Examination upon Additional Discovery

To some extent, the idea of examining the witness again after later discovery sounds like trying to have your cake and eat it too. The defender usually will not agree to a wide-open request, but the above exchange illustrates a situation in which both lawyers might agree to additional questioning on a narrow subject or perhaps questioning related to a new issue in the case.[8]

A variation on this idea involves documents. During the examination, the taker may have asked the witness to look for additional documents. If the testimony indicated that materials responsive to an outstanding request to produce may exist but have not yet been produced,[9] the taker must do two things: (1) remember to leave the deposition open for further inquiry about such materials that might become available later and (2) must state clearly on the record that she intends to depose the witness on these matters when the documents are produced. It may be that no additional documents are located, or that after reviewing the new documents, the taker has no further questions, but leaving that option open is important—and in some cases may be pivotal. Suppose, for example, that after the deposition a critical document is produced. It can be explained only by this now "completed" witness. Although an interrogatory or two might provide additional information, it is no substitute for live testimony and the chance to dissect the witness's explanation of the newly produced document.

If during a deposition the deponent or the defender agreed to produce or look for additional documents, be careful to follow up after the deposition to ensure that the witness complies.[10] It is entirely appropriate to ask the court reporter to make a list of the documents requested during the deposition, and it is often wise to ask the reporter to mark areas of testimony where the witness agreed to produce additional documents so that these passages can be located quickly at the end of the day. It is always prudent to write a letter to the defender reiterating her agreement (or her client's agreement) to produce additional documents. A document request also can be served for materials identified by the witness in the deposition—indeed, this is usually the safest way to proceed—because it ensures accountability and a procedure for compelling production if it is not completed within the time allowed by FRCP 34. Your relationship with your opponent may dictate what action is appropriate; but if this is unclear, take the safest route.

Continuing the Deposition Pending a Court Order

The deposition might also remain open pending the outcome of a court ruling. For example, if the witness failed to answer appropriate questions—whether or not so instructed by her lawyer—the taker may file a motion to compel the witness to answer. Or if a witness was unwilling to answer a question—perhaps to guard a trade secret or the privacy of another person—the defender might seek a stipulation or file for a protective order to avoid the need to answer. Or the taker might seek an order permitting examination of the witness in this area. In either case, the deposition may be suspended or concluded pending a ruling on the motion.

If the deposition is concluded, the taker should state on the record that she has completed her questioning except for those areas that may be properly explored after the court has resolved the dispute.[11] But do not assume that a protective order will also give you the right to reopen the deposition.

If instead of finishing the deposition, you suspend it to seek guidance from the court—such as by asking for a protective order—state clearly on the record that the deposition is not over but rather adjourned until the issue is resolved. FRCP 30(d)(3)(A) permits the taker to suspend the deposition for the time necessary to file a motion "[i]f the objecting deponent or party so demands." Do not get frustrated and simply walk out, announcing, "That's it!" You may intend to merely suspend the deposition to seek a court order, but if you do not clearly make that demand on the record, the deposition might be deemed concluded.[12]

In general, it is better to avoid interrupting or suspending a deposition to seek a court order. Therefore, do not hesitate to ask opposing counsel if a disputed issue can be resolved informally. In any event, a conference with opposing counsel (not necessarily in person) is required before you can move for a protective order.[13] Such conferences often produce a stipulated agreement, which can, if needed, be turned into a protective order.

As an alternative, at the end of the deposition, ask the witness and the defender if they will reconsider an instruction not to answer certain questions. This question gives them an opportunity to rethink their position and signals your intent not to drop this point. Many defenders believe that their opponents will not carry through on their threat to bring a motion to compel, so they stick to instructions not to answer even when their legal position is weak. If you threaten a motion to compel testimony and the other side refuses to budge, make the motion; otherwise, you will lose credibility. Sometimes, the bravado that prompted the defender's instruction not to answer will have waned by the end of the day, and reason will prevail over obstinate positioning.

Handling Documents at the End of the Deposition

Deposition notices often include a request for the witness to produce documents, creating another potential for an issue at the end of the day.[14] Although the taker may have brought copies of other documents to be marked as exhibits, the witness might also show up with original documents about which you want to ask questions.

It is common for the producing party to permit inspection and copying of these documents at the deposition. FRCP 30(f)(2)(A) provides that such documents must be marked as exhibits and annexed to the transcript if requested by any party. The rule also permits copies of the documents (or the originals) to be bound with the transcript after all parties have had the opportunity to inspect and copy the documents. If copies are to be included with the transcript, the parties must be given the opportunity to confirm that the copies are identical to the originals. And if any party is concerned about the preservation of the originals (or about the usefulness of copies), FRCP 30(f)(2)(B) permits that party to ask the court to order that the originals be attached to the transcript "pending final disposition of the case." Thus, at the end of the deposition, be diligent in ensuring that any newly produced documents you believe to be relevant are appended to the original transcript.[15]

Requesting Review of the Deposition Transcript

Another matter that the taker should address on the record at the end of the deposition is the opportunity for the deponent to review and correct the transcript. This usually is an issue for the witness's lawyer, so as the taker, you may not wish to raise it. FRCP 30(e) gives a witness 30 days after notice that the transcript is available to review the transcript and make changes *if requested* by the witness or another party *before completion of the deposition*.[16] But professional courtesy suggests that the taker raise this issue even if the defender does not; that way, if the tables are turned, there is a reasonable expectation of similar treatment. If no one requests that the witness have time to review and correct the transcript or, if a request is made but no changes are submitted, the deposition transcript will be deemed satisfactory for use as is, and the witness will not need to sign it.[17]

Final Matters

The taker must tend to some housekeeping matters at the conclusion of the examination. FRCP 30(b)(5)(C) requires that the officer before whom the deposition is conducted state on the record that the deposition is complete and set forth any stipulations of counsel regarding custody of the transcript, exhibits, and other relevant matters. Some court reporters will put the statement at the end of the transcript automatically—without confirming with you that the deposition is over. Because the rule requires the statement to be made "at the end of the deposition," make sure that the deposition officer (typically the court reporter) does not indicate the deposition is complete when that is not your intention. Otherwise, if there is any question about whether you are entitled to examine the witness further, your opponent may argue that the reporter indicated that the deposition was over. Most reporters will not assume anything unless they have received precise instructions from the taker, but do not become complacent and leave yourself vulnerable to an embarrassing situation.

Before you leave the deposition room, ask the court reporter whether she has any questions; for example, about the spelling of names or any terms unique to the case.[18] You will also want to ensure that the reporter has all the documents that are to be appended to the transcript; it is all too easy for exhibits to get mixed in with the lawyers' papers and taken back to the office.

In sum, the taker should think about the following points as the deposition concludes:

- Is the deposition completed?
- Are there pending issues, contingencies, or potential changes that should cause you to reserve your right to further question this witness?
- Will your opponent reconsider instructions not to answer?
- Is the witness to look for, or produce, additional documents?
- How will documents marked at the deposition be handled?
- Does the witness want time to review and perhaps correct the transcript?

The Defender's Role

As should now be obvious, it is critical to have an unambiguous record about the status of the deposition at the end of the seven-hour day or at the end of the testimony. In fact, the defender should be concerned about many of the same issues that concern the taker and have just been discussed. Is the deposition finished? Is it continued until another day and time? Are there other open issues that might subject the witness to further examination? Even if you and your opponent cannot agree about whether there is to be further testimony, make your position clear on the record; that way, a court can evaluate it properly if a motion to compel or a motion for a protective order is made.

Examining Your Own Witness

If the other parties' lawyers have completed deposing your witness, consider examining her yourself.[19] Although the general rule is to not examine your own witness at deposition, sometimes unique circumstances necessitate a short examination.[20] For example, a case may involve a particularly complex transaction, and the taker's questions may have obscured the issues, leaving your opponents with a misunderstanding about matters critical to their proper evaluation of the case. Having your witness carefully unravel the essential points at the end of her deposition—through your skillful questioning—could avoid needless discovery triggered by the taker's failure to obtain clear testimony about complicated matters.

You may also want to examine your own witness when the taker has failed to question your witness about a critical point, such as an expert report prepared for your client before the filing of her lawsuit—especially if you have already disclosed the report. You might decide that some testimony from your witness about this report would be timely and enhance the prospects of settlement. Or you may anticipate filing a motion for which deposition testimony from your witness would be more powerful than just a declaration or affidavit. If the taker has not examined on this subject, you may want to ask some questions yourself, even though the taker will then have the opportunity to reexamine the witness on this point. As noted, on matters that your opponent has not explored, deposition testimony is usually more persuasive than sworn statements in a self-serving declaration.

If you have not prepared the witness before her deposition for your examination, take a break and discuss with her your reasons for questioning her. But be careful not to ask questions that would yield gratuitous testimony or inadvertently disclose your strategy, especially if you have good reason to believe the other side has little interest in being reasonable. Resist the temptation to have your witness explain her view of the facts just because you or the witness feels that she did not have the chance to tell the full story.

Reconsidering Instructions Not to Answer

As noted above, when a deposition is concluding, a taker may offer you the opportunity to reconsider any instructions to not answer questions. Even if the taker does not make this offer, take a moment to reconsider such instructions before leaving the deposition. Defenders often give them in the heat of the moment, without thinking carefully about the question or the implications if the witness refuses to answer. Therefore, take a break just before the conclusion of the deposition, review any instructions not to answer and, if appropriate, avoid a possible motion to compel (which could lead to sanctions if your instruction was not warranted) by allowing your witness to respond.[21]

Handling Documents at the End of the Deposition

The general rules for handling documents produced at the deposition are discussed above. If you have produced originals, it is generally best to make clear to the lawyers present that they can inspect the documents and make copies but that you intend to keep the originals.[22] Although other parties can ask the court to order that the originals be annexed to the transcript in accordance with FRCP 30(f)(2)(B), you may be able to avoid such an order by offering to stipulate on the record that the originals will be kept safely by you and produced if necessary for trial or further hearings, and that other parties may use copies as though they were originals. Even if your offer does not prevent a motion to attach the originals to the transcript, your willingness to agree to these procedures will strengthen your opposition to the motion.

During the deposition, your witness may have been asked to look for certain documents, and often a response to this request is deferred until the end of the deposition. It is generally better not to agree at the deposition to look for or produce additional documents, but rather to take the matter under advisement.[23] You can, for instance, promise to tell your opponent within a day or two whether you and your client will agree to look for and produce additional materials. This approach can lead to a motion to compel; it also can lead to the deposition being extended beyond the seven-hour time limit in order for the taker to ask questions about newly produced documents. Nevertheless, you often are better off running these risks and having time to consider the request rather than assuming an obligation that was unnecessary.

If a request for documents is appropriate, look for the requested documents during a break or overnight if the deposition is continuing to another day. These materials then can be produced immediately so the examination is not delayed or extended. Of course, your ability to do the search will depend on the scope of the request, the quantity of the requested materials, and the time needed to review the documents before producing them. The taker may want to suspend the examination to review newly produced documents. But unless the materials are voluminous or unusually complex (such as a technical report on an offering circular), insist that the taker proceed with the deposition as scheduled.

Requesting Review of the Deposition Transcript

Corrections to a deposition transcript can be a crucial issue for a witness and her defender. As noted above, FRCP 30(e) governs this issue and allows 30 days to review and correct the transcript *if requested* by the witness or someone else *before completion of the deposition*. In most circumstances, this will be the witness's only opportunity to make changes to her testimony; therefore, as a defender, *always* make this request. If the deposition is particularly long, or if other circumstances will make it difficult to review the transcript within 30 days, lawyers will usually stipulate to a longer time or to a specified date. In any event, the record should be clear on this is point, eliminating any possibility that the witness might inadvertently waive her right to review the transcript and make corrections.[24]

Additional Issues for Both Taker and Defender

There are some administrative issues at the conclusion of a deposition about which both takers and defenders must be concerned. These include custody of the original transcript, expediting the transcript, and obtaining copies of the transcript in some form other than a typed or printed transcript (such as a copy of the video recording or disk if the testimony was recorded electronically).[25]

Maintaining the Original Transcript

FRCP 30(f)(1) provides that "[u]nless the court orders otherwise, the officer must seal the deposition in an envelope or package bearing the title of the action and marked 'Deposition of [witness's name]' and must promptly send it to the attorney who arranged for the transcript or recording." Under FRCP Rule 5(d), depositions are no longer filed with the court unless they are used in a proceeding or the court orders filing. Even then, only those parts actually used need be filed.[26]

As noted above, FRCP 30(b)(5)(C) directs that when the depositions ends, "the officer must state on the record that the deposition is complete and must set out any stipulations made by the attorneys about custody of the transcript or recording and of the exhibits, or about any other pertinent matters." But do not assume that the court reporter intends to provide the transcript to the lawyer who noticed the deposition.[27] Make sure the record reflects the understanding about who will maintain the original transcript.

If you are the lawyer who is supposed to maintain the original transcript, understand your responsibilities and take them seriously. FRCP 30(f)(1) requires that you store the original transcript "under conditions that will protect it against loss, destruction, tampering, or deterioration." The reporter will provide you with the transcript sealed in an envelope; do not open the envelope, but instead store it in a place where it cannot be damaged or mixed in with other discovery materials.[28] Ask for a copy of the transcript in addition to the original, just as you would if the original transcript were to be filed with the court. This allows you to have a working copy (to be copied again for your client or to be annotated) without having to break into the sealed original. If the original transcript is eventually presented to the court (for instance, at the beginning of trial) and it appears that the sealed envelope has been opened, you can expect criticism from the other lawyers in the case, even if the reason the seal was broken is innocuous.

Expediting the Transcript

It is often necessary to obtain the transcript of a deposition by a particular date—perhaps because of an impending motion or in preparation for another deposition. Therefore, it is always prudent to ask the court reporter when you can expect to receive the transcript and to request an expedited transcript if necessary. Court reporters charge a premium for expediting transcription, so this cost, which typically is passed along to the client, should be balanced against need. But when having the testimony available is crucial for an impending hearing or submission, the extra cost may well be worth it. If multiple parties want an expedited transcript, the cost can be apportioned; but cost sharing should be discussed ahead of time with the other lawyers.

Many court reporters today can provide a "rough" transcript for counsel's use at the end of each day of testimony. This will be an unofficial transcript that the reporter has not yet reviewed or corrected for transcription errors. Sometimes reporters provide rough transcripts at no additional cost. Check with the reporter to see whether she offers this service; if she does (whether free or not), consider making arrangements with other counsel to use it. The defender might object to using a rough transcript because her witness has not had an opportunity to review the testimony, but this rough version will give the lawyers on both sides a good sense of the witness's testimony. It should prove useful in exploring topics and clarifying areas of examination if the deposition is continued.

If a rough transcript is to be used for some other purposes, such as in support of or opposition to a motion, ask the other parties to agree that the rough transcript may be used. Although using a rough transcript may avoid the cost of ordering an expedited version, in the long run the savings may not be worth it. For one thing, other parties may object to using a rough testimony. In addition, depending upon the skill of the court reporter, a rough transcript may be so inconsistent or error-laden that its value is lost.[29] If the testimony is crucial to your case and you need it to support or oppose a critical motion, you are well advised to pay extra for an expedited official transcript (even if not reviewed by the witness), rather than run the risk that a rough version will detract from your legal arguments.

Computer Disks and Other Forms of Testimony

In today's world of computers and law-specific software, lawyers in a deposition often want not only a hard copy (or a copy in some other medium, such as on video), but also a computer disk with the testimony.[30] Such a disk, with the appropriate software, will allow a lawyer to review the testimony on a computer, search for specific words or phrases, and even annotate the electronic version of the transcript without affecting the pagination or line numbers in the original. Some software even allows lawyers to copy text directly from the transcript into pleadings or other documents (such as a witness preparation memorandum or an examination outline). Therefore, ask the court reporter for a computer disk at the end of the deposition—which most reporters provide without additional cost—and specify in which format you want the disk prepared.[31] If you do not know what format your particular software uses, ask for an ASCII version of the transcript, as most software programs can either use this format or easily convert it to the proper form.[32]

Most court reporters can also provide a "condensed" transcript, which you should also request (or confirm a previous request for) at the end of the deposition. A condensed transcript consists of many pages of testimony (sometimes ten) on one piece of paper. This form of transcript is easier for some lawyers and witnesses to review, and it certainly makes traveling with deposition transcripts easier.[33] Some reporters will also create a concordance or word list with the condensed transcript, showing how often and where words in the testimony have been used. For instance, in a construction case, the list might show that the word "defect" was used 22 times during a deposition: at page 8, lines 14–18; at page 12, line 6; and so forth.

If the deposition was recorded on audio or video, issues may arise about the desired format of the recording.[34] This is usually a subject that the taker will address with the reporter before the deposition begins. Because a videographer may be able to provide the recorded testimony in various formats, if you have a particular need, request it at the start of the deposition and then confirm your request at the end.

FRCP 30(b)(3)(A), read in conjunction with 30(f)(3), provides for handling of video recordings in a manner similar to stenographically recorded testimony. But you can negotiate other mutually acceptable arrangements with the other lawyers if this is important for your particular situation. For example, when a deposition was recorded both by a stenographer and by a videographer, you might ask the other lawyers to stipulate that subject to the court's approval, either the written transcript or the video recording may be used as the official record of the testimony.[35]

Failure of the Witness or a Lawyer to Appear or Proceed

One day you may find yourself at a deposition at which the noticing lawyer either does not appear, or appears but does not proceed with the deposition. Or the defender or his witness may fail to attend, perhaps because she was not subpoenaed as required.[36] FRCP 30(g) provides for sanctions in these situations.

If the noticing lawyer does not show up or fails to proceed with the deposition, the court may order that lawyer to pay the reasonable expenses, including attorney's fees, incurred by a party for her and her lawyer to attend. If you have noticed a deposition, therefore, be sure to give adequate notice for any postponement, or you will risk sanctions.[37] Make a careful record if you are not going to proceed, showing explicitly why your decision is warranted and why you should not be compelled to pay other parties' costs or attorney's fees. Here is an example of a statement that the taker might make on the record, explaining why he is not going forward:

DEPOSING LAWYER: We are here today for the deposition of Arthur Jackson, who is not a party to this litigation. A deposition notice was served, and Mr. Jackson was properly subpoenaed. I will ask the court reporter to mark a copy of the deposition notice and subpoena as Exhibits A and B. Mr. Jackson is here today and states that he has retained a lawyer for this deposition, but his lawyer is not present. Mr. Jackson knows of no reason why his lawyer is not here but says that he is prepared to proceed without his lawyer. We have made at least five attempts to call Mr. Jackson's lawyer, and each time his secretary has said that he is not in and that she does not know how to reach him. Due to these circumstances, I believe that it would be inappropriate to proceed with the deposition today even though Mr. Jackson is willing to proceed, and we will reschedule the deposition tentatively for Thursday morning at 9 AM. I have left a message to this effect for Mr. Jackson's lawyer, and I will fax him a letter in this regard as well. The defendant's lawyer has stated that he will seek his fees and costs against me for not proceeding; but given the circumstances as I have stated them, I believe it would be unfair to Mr. Jackson and inappropriate to proceed at this time.

A statement such as this one may protect you if any other party attempts to impose sanctions against you for failing to proceed with the deposition.

A similar situation arises if a witness fails to appear for a deposition because the noticing lawyer failed to serve the required subpoena. Other lawyers and parties who attend that deposition may seek reasonable expenses, including attorney's fees, against the noticing lawyer for costs incurred for the witness and her defender to attend. The lawyers involved should make clear statements on the record setting forth the facts underlying the witness's failure to appear. This statement or statements will likely be submitted to the court in support of, or in opposition to, a motion for sanctions.

After the Deposition

Once the deposition is over, all the lawyers who participated in the process must consider several matters. There will be reports to the client, reassessment of the case, and related motions—whether or not the deposition was taken for these purposes. These matters will be discussed in the following sections, first from the taker's perspective and then from the defender's.

Tasks for the Taker

Reporting to the Client

One of the first things you should do after a deposition is report to your client. It is the client who is paying for this work, and she is entitled to know what is happening. A deposition is a relatively important event during the course of pretrial work, and the client will want to know whether it was a valuable exercise and what it means for her case. Model Rule of Professional Conduct 1.4(a) requires lawyers to keep their clients "reasonably informed about the status" of their matters, and virtually all states have similar provisions in their rules of professional conduct.[38] One of the most frequent complaints that bar associations receive from clients is that their lawyers failed to communicate with them.[39] Reporting to the client is important at all stages of litigation—and depositions are no exception.

Your report to the client should include a summary of the deposition, particularly key testimony directly affecting the case. Even if your client was the witness or otherwise attended the deposition, you should still provide her with this summary because the importance of certain questions and answers may not have been as obvious to her as they were to you. It is usually best to organize your summary by topic rather than by just rehashing the testimony in the order that it occurred. The reason: During a complex deposition, the taker often jumps from topic to topic, not necessarily in chronological order, many times returning to certain subjects. The taker changes topics to avoid signaling to either the witness or her lawyer the intent of any particular line of questioning. Later, the taker will put the pieces of this testimonial puzzle together to create a complete picture that was not so obvious during the examination. It is this complete, reassembled picture that you want to "paint" for your client in your postdeposition report.

In addition to summarizing the testimony, your report should also assess the impact of the witness's testimony on the case. Whether the witness testified as expected, whether she helped or harmed your case, and the kind of witness she was (for example, cooperative, obstructionist, believable, or unsympathetic), are all points that should be addressed. Remember, your client expects you not only to report on what happened, but to analyze its impact on her case.

A witness's deposition testimony may trigger other considerations, all of which you should bring to your client's attention. For instance, the deposition may have identified new witnesses who need to be contacted, subpoenaed, and deposed. Because this development may change your discovery plan and increase the budgeted cost for the case, inform your client immediately. New theories of liability or defense may also have become obvious or more (or less) tenable, and the strategy for proceeding given these new matters must be discussed with your client. Make recommendations, or at least offer alternative courses of actions, so your client can evaluate her situation and make decisions accordingly.

Reviewing Deposition Testimony

Once the transcript is prepared, the taker—and, as discussed below, the defender—should review it for accuracy. If questions, answers, or objections have been transcribed incorrectly, the court reporter should be notified and asked to correct the offending matters. Depending on how the deposition ended, there may be additional opportunities to cross-examine the witness. If there is, you will need to carefully review the previous testimony to prepare for further examination. In addition, the impact of certain testimony cannot always be fully assessed during a deposition. Carefully putting together the pieces of the puzzle with the transcript will yield a much better understanding of the testimony's impact and any need to develop further evidence. If your review of the transcript changes your initial assessment of the impact of a witness's testimony, prepare a supplemental report to your client.

In addition to the deposition summary normally prepared for the client immediately after the testimony, each lawyer usually should prepare a summary of the testimony. Some lawyers do this themselves; others have legal assistants or an outside service prepare the summary.[40] Unless the deposition is unusually brief, it is essential to have some sort of summary if the deposition is to be useful at trial.

Motions Regarding the Deposition

Another matter to consider immediately after the deposition is whether to make any motions based on the witness's testimony—or, in some cases, lack of testimony. As a part of the reassessment process, it may now be clear that a motion to amend the complaint or answer is necessary, because the witness has opened the door to a new theory that must be preserved.[41] In other situations, the testimony may give rise to a cross-complaint or a counteraction. If such steps seem warranted, plan to move quickly so that you do not waive whatever rights you have to take such action and prevent a party from claiming it was prejudiced by delay.

Compelling Testimony

If the witness refused to answer certain questions—whether instructed not to answer or otherwise—the taker must consider a motion to compel answers. FRCP 37(a)(3)(B) lays out the basic procedure, and FRCP 37(a)(1) specifically requires that any such motion include a certification that the moving party made a good-faith effort to obtain the testimony without court action.[42] It may be sufficient to make this effort at the deposition itself by asking the deponent or her lawyer to reconsider the decision to refuse to answer, making the record clear that this is your effort to resolve the issue and that a motion to compel will follow if the witness continues to refuse. A conference with opposing counsel (although not necessarily in person) is also required before a motion to compel will be granted. FRCP 37(a)(1) provides that a motion to compel must "include a certification that the movant has in good faith conferred or attempted to confer with the person or party failing to make disclosure or discovery in an effort to obtain it without court action."[43]

The motion should establish why the question at the deposition was appropriate and why the refusal to answer was unjustified. Include as an exhibit to the motion a copy of the transcript showing the question and the deponent's refusal to answer, as well as the transcript pages detailing your efforts to resolve the issue informally. Any later efforts to resolve the problem should also be described in a declaration, with any relevant correspondence attached. In addition, make contemporaneous records of these later attempts to resolve the matter because you may need to prove them as a prerequisite to obtaining relief on a motion to compel.[44]

FRCP 37(a)(5)(A) provides that if the motion is granted or the information is provided after the motion is filed, the court *must* sanction the offending party or her lawyer or both by ordering them to pay the moving party its reasonable expenses, including attorney's fees. The court will not sanction the offending party, however, if the moving party fails to certify a good-faith effort to resolve the issue prior to a request for court intervention or if the failure to respond was "substantially justified, or other circumstances make an award of expenses unjust."[45] Therefore, if you intend to file a motion to compel testimony, consider your grounds carefully and be certain that you have made the necessary efforts to resolve the issue informally. If the motion is denied, the court can enter a protective order and require the moving party or her lawyer or both to pay the reasonable costs and attorney's fees of the party or witness who opposed the motion.[46]

Production of Documents

After the deposition, it may be prudent to serve a new FRCP 34 request to produce documents or to follow up on the FRCP 30(b)(2) request for documents that had been made with the deposition notice. The witness's responses—to questions about previous document requests or subpoenas, documents already produced, efforts to comply with previous requests, and offers to search for additional documents—might make it imperative to make a formal request for additional documents to ensure that some important piece of evidence is not inadvertently missed. Local rules or case-specific discovery orders may limit a party's right to request documents. Therefore, be sure that your decision to serve a new request based on deposition testimony is consistent with such restrictions.[47] If document requests are limited, try to show during the examination that the documents at issue fall within the categories of materials previously demanded or should have been voluntarily produced at the beginning of the case.[48] In this situation, a motion to compel production, rather than a new production request, is more appropriate and avoids any restriction on FRCP 34 requests.

Reopening the Deposition

Finally, at some point you may consider re-noticing the deposition of a witness. Assuming that the examination was not simply adjourned to another time, FRCP 30(d)(1) provides, as noted above, that a witness may be deposed only once in any action and only for one day of seven hours. However, there are times when you may have the opportunity to depose the witness again.[49] Probably the most common situation is when an employee of a party, who was a percipient witness to the actions giving rise to the lawsuit, is later designated as an expert for that party as well. In this situation, the other parties would generally be permitted to depose this witness again, but only in her capacity as an expert. This situation requires a new notice of deposition rather than merely resending the original notice.[50]

Reopening a deposition may be permitted when an already-deposed witness appears to have knowledge about a newly added claim or defense that had not been presented at the original deposition. Your effort to depose this witness again will likely meet with opposition, but depending on the facts of a particular situation, you often will be able to make a good argument that reopening the deposition is justified.[51] "Like most discovery disputes, the availability of a second deposition is left to the discretion of the trial court."[52]

If a deposed witness reviews her deposition testimony and then makes substantial changes to it, these changes may also provide grounds for reopening the deposition.[53] But before seeking leave of court to reopen the deposition, ask opposing counsel if she will permit further examination in light of these changes. If not, then a motion will be necessary. But do not conclude that you must depose a witness again just because she substantially revises her testimony after it is transcribed. You might get more mileage out of these changes by commenting upon them at trial to show that the witness's testimony is not trustworthy.[54]

Tasks for the Defender

Reporting to the Client

As suggested above for the taker, the importance of reporting to the client cannot be overemphasized. Even if your client was the witness or otherwise attended the deposition, you should still report to her about the deposition for at least two reasons. First, it provides a record that you are communicating with your client about the status of her case. Second, even if your client attended the deposition, she may not have a complete understanding of the impact of the testimony. Although you may have explained some of this to your client during breaks or over lunch, it is still critical to give her a full report after the deposition is complete so that she understands what occurred and how it affects her case.

Remember, do not just report—analyze. That is what your client is paying you to do. She should be advised not only about what was said, but also about what actions may be required as a result of the testimony. Changes in strategy or case theory, amendments to pleadings or new pleadings, and additional discovery (for example, from newly identified witnesses) should all be addressed.

If your client has insurance coverage, a report to the carrier at the end of the deposition may also be advisable. New facts elicited at the deposition may now provide a basis for coverage that was not apparent before. If so, this would be the time to notify potential carriers by tendering the defense of your client based on the deposition testimony, or to retender the case if coverage was previously denied.[55]

Reviewing and Correcting the Transcript

Assuming a proper request was made by the deponent or a party before the end of the deposition, the witness will have 30 days from the time the transcript is made available to read her testimony and make corrections.[56] This 30-day period runs from notification by the court reporter to the deponent or her lawyer that the deposition transcript is available to review, and the changes must be transmitted to the reporter within this time. Expect this time limit to be strictly enforced.[57] Send the transcript to the witness with a letter requesting that she carefully review her testimony, looking not only for errors in transcription, but also for incomplete or wrong answers. Advise your witness to note proposed changes on a separate sheet of paper so that her copy of the transcript remains clean. This will prevent problems that might arise if the other side sees your client's copy of her deposition transcript—at trial, for instance—and finds proposed changes that ended up not being submitted.

Review the deposition testimony carefully. Ensure that all your objections were accurately recorded so that they will be preserved for trial and appeal. Court reporters focus primarily on the witness and the taker. So occasionally they miss an objection, especially one made at the same time as the witness was beginning to answer.[58] If you fail to insert objections (or other corrections) that were made at the deposition, they will be waived under FRCP 32(d)(4). And untimely changes may not be permitted.[59]

Also review the transcript for errors in recording the questions. If you know from your notes or memory that a question in the transcript was not recorded as asked, request that it be changed. If the deposition was recorded on video, you have an easy record to review in order to verify the actual question that was posed. Absent a recording or an agreement by counsel that the question is not accurately transcribed, you must at least ensure that your request to correct the question is appended to the record or it will be waived.

Suppose you or your witness finds errors in the transcript, or you find answers that should be modified or changed. There is a split of authority about the scope of permitted changes to a deposition transcript. Some courts do not allow changes in the substance of testimony and permit only changes that clarify or correct clerical errors.[60] Other courts hold that the deponent may make any type of changes, provided a reason is given for each change.[61]

Deciding whether to make changes may pose a dilemma. Changes to the transcript (unless they are minor, such as correcting typographical errors) will likely elicit commentary from opposing counsel at trial.[62] But if you do not make the changes and your witness testifies differently at trial than she did at her deposition, opposing counsel can impeach her with her deposition testimony. Moreover, if you make some changes to the transcript but fail to catch all the answers that should have been corrected or modified, you will face a double dilemma: impeachment and the possible embarrassment of having changed testimony after the deposition. If some changes were made, your witness will not be able to explain credibly her new testimony at trial by saying that she overlooked it when reviewing her deposition transcript: the fact that she made other changes to the transcript when she initially reviewed it will make such an excuse seem feeble.

What to do in the face of this dilemma? If the changes to the transcript are relatively minor (a vague and ambiguous phrase you must define for yourself in each case), then by all means submit them. But what do you do if your witness now wants to make *significant* changes affecting the substance of her testimony? There are a number of ways to proceed, but an approach that works best for one situation may not work as well for another. Consider the following ideas whenever this problem arises.

Carefully analyze the witness's proposed changes. Are they really changes to her testimony, or are they more in the nature of further explanation? If they are only elaboration, then perhaps they are not necessary. And a discussion with your client about the consequences of adding new testimony may persuade her that she answered the questions adequately during the deposition. Moreover, if the taker failed to follow up sufficiently, your witness should save her ammunition for trial.[63]

If you conclude that the proposed changes are more than just elaboration, then question your witness carefully about them. Did your witness misunderstand the question when it was asked, or has she now decided that the question calls for a different answer? Did she forget some facts during the deposition, or is this an effort to word her testimony more artfully to lessen (or strengthen) its impact? Try to determine what is going on. Then, when you discuss with your client her view of the accuracy of her testimony and the consequences of modifying or augmenting it now, she may conclude that many (or all) of her proposed changes are not needed.

If you conclude, however, that portions of the recorded testimony—whether transcribed or taped—are inaccurate or misleading, you have an ethical obligation to correct the transcript.[64] Work closely with your witness to craft the changes in a manner that both accurately reflects her real testimony and minimizes the negative impact of making the changes. Make sure that your witness has finished reviewing her entire testimony very carefully before making any changes so that there is little risk of her testimony at trial deviating from her corrected deposition transcript.

If there are "changes in form or substance," FRCP 30(e)(1)(B) requires the deponent "to sign a statement listing the changes and the reasons for making them."[65] The witness's lawyer normally submits the changes to the deposition transcript in a letter to the court reporter, indicating the page and line where the correction is to be made. This is sometimes called an "errata sheet." If one or more of the changes is difficult to explain, it may be better for that change to include an annotated copy of the appropriate page from the transcript, showing what is intended. And, of course, send a copy of your letter to the court reporter and to all the lawyers in the case. The officer before whom the deposition was conducted "must note in the certificate prescribed by Rule 30(f)(1) whether a review was requested and, if so, must attach any changes the deponent makes during the 30-day period."[66]

Resisting Efforts to Reopen the Deposition

Depending upon how the deposition ended, the taker may wish to examine your witness at another time. Unless you agreed at the deposition to produce your witness again for further examination (for example, on a limited subject), you may want to take steps to prevent opposing counsel from getting another "bite of the apple."

One course of action might be simply to refuse to produce the witness for further testimony, forcing the other side to file a motion to compel. But before refusing, consider the consequences of having your witness testify again, and weigh these against the possible benefits. For instance, you might agree to make your witness available in exchange for another chance to depose one of the other side's witnesses. If you believe that you would profit from such a trade, discuss the benefits, the risks, and the costs with your client and make your recommendation accordingly.

When you feel your opposition to a second deposition is correct, it can be emotionally satisfying to just say "no." But remember, if you lose the taker's motion to compel, FRCP 37(a)(5)(B) empowers the court to impose sanctions, including attorney's fees, for improperly refusing to produce the witness. And ordinarily a lawyer cannot simply refuse to produce a witness but instead must affirmatively seek a protective order in the face of efforts to take further testimony.[67]

Always check the custom in your jurisdiction and proceed accordingly. The safest approach is usually to seek a protective order. Before taking that step, however, evaluate the strength of your position in recognition of the court's power to sanction lawyers seeking protective orders if their motions are not well founded.[68]

Pretrial Uses of Depositions and Preparing for Trial

Once the immediate postdeposition tasks have been completed, the lawyers for both sides have the opportunity to use the witness's testimony in pretrial activities. Reevaluating the merits and problems of the case, updating the case files, preparing witnesses, and considering possible motions—all need to be addressed.

Case Assessment

Evaluating the impact of the testimony on the case is an obvious reason for reviewing the transcripts and reporting to clients. Clients are entitled to your analysis of the testimony, including how it affects claims, defenses, and settlement prospects. The importance of reassessing the case in light of new deposition testimony cannot be overemphasized.

After each witness is deposed, all lawyers involved in the case should consider a host of issues to determine the effect of that testimony on their respective positions. Think through the following questions:

- Did the witness testify as expected?
- Was the witness credible?
- Will the deponent make a good witness at trial (that is, will she be sympathetic, likable, particularly believable, and so forth)?
- Will your opponent make the same assessment?
- Was the deponent's testimony consistent with that of other witnesses?
- Was the deponent's testimony consistent with your theme and theory of the case?
- Has the deponent's testimony supported some element(s) of your case, weakened your case, or left it unaffected?
- If the testimony strengthened or weakened your case, is it appropriate to reevaluate your settlement position?
- Do you need additional discovery because of this testimony?
- What steps can you and should you take to bolster your case following this testimony?

Think carefully about each of these questions and any others that seem appropriate to the particular facts of your case. A good way to test your analysis is to discuss it with others, perhaps another lawyer in your office or even an attorney for a similarly situated party, to see whether they share your assessment.[69]

As depositions proceed, all the lawyers should continually check to see whether they are amassing the evidence and testimony necessary to support each element of their case. At the least, this means ensuring that there are witnesses to authenticate each document and other evidence to be introduced at trial.[70] Most lawyers maintain some form of proof chart (discussed below), identifying all the elements of each claim or defense that must be proved at trial, together with the testimony and other evidence expected to make that proof. Maintaining and updating a proof chart as depositions proceed is a valuable way to prepare for trial and to evaluate what further discovery you need as the close of discovery approaches and what impact each witness's deposition testimony has on the case.

It is also possible that new theories of the case may emerge as a result of deposition testimony. If so, you may need to conduct additional legal research to understand what testimony or other evidence is needed to support or oppose these theories. Your research may, in turn, suggest additional discovery, including new depositions and document requests that need to be scheduled quickly. The discovery cutoff date may affect these decisions.

Finally, evaluate whether you need damage control following a witness's testimony. If the witness's testimony hurt your case, what steps should you take to counter it? Work with your client on this so that she understands how the witness's testimony has affected her position. Ask your client to help you identify other witnesses or other evidence to shore up her case. Working with your client will also help keep her both informed about the status of the case and aware of the risks of proceeding.

Updating Your Database

Most lawyers maintain some form of database for each case. This may be a series of notes or files or some form of computer database that organizes the information learned in discovery and from other pretrial work. In addition to preparing the reports and summaries recommended above, update your database with information learned from every deposition. Update both the file for the deponent and any other file her testimony affects. Updating will be especially important as you prepare to take or defend upcoming depositions.

Witness Preparation and Preparing to Examine Witnesses at Trial

When it is time to start preparing for trial, there are at least two significant uses for deposition transcripts: (1) preparation of witnesses to testify, and (2) preparation of outlines for conducting direct and cross-examination of witnesses. Your deposition summaries will now be invaluable for locating crucial testimony and sensitive areas that must be covered either in witness preparation or examination.

Familiarity with your witness's deposition will help you prepare your direct-examination outline. For example, during direct examination at trial you may want to defuse certain weak areas of your witness's testimony. Opposing counsel's examination at the deposition will help you decide how to approach this task. In preparing your own witness for trial, review and practice both direct testimony and her answers to likely questions on cross-examination. Practicing her answers to your questions on direct will help you and the witness spot areas where sloppy responses could open the door to troubling cross-examination.

Although direct examination is important, equally important is your understanding of potential cross-examination areas. A witness's deposition testimony should provide a road map of potential cross-examination areas. In preparing your witness to testify, use her deposition transcript to illustrate the areas of inquiry and the types of questions that she will likely encounter on cross-examination. She then can practice answering likely cross-examination questions in a manner consistent with her deposition testimony and as supportive of your case as possible. Reviewing her deposition testimony will also help the witness understand how her trial testimony will open her up to impeachment if her trial testimony is inconsistent with her deposition testimony. Be sure your witness knows exactly what she said at her deposition so that the topics of her examination and her testimony are less likely to become confused. And review any corrections made to the transcript and the reasons given for making them.

Be sure that your client and other friendly witnesses understand the impact of their answers to questions at deposition and how those answers might be used at trial. Questions and answers that seemed innocent enough at the time of deposition can become devastating in the hands of a skilled trial lawyer, so prepare all your witnesses for the ways in which their answers might be turned against them. This preparation should help them listen carefully to the questions asked at trial and understand how they fit in with questions asked at their deposition.

When preparing a witness, review other deposition transcripts in the case. Opposing counsel may have formulated new attack strategies or new theories as discovery proceeded. These new ideas might be revealed by the questions and subjects of inquiry explored in the more recent depositions. Moreover, never assume that cross-examination of any witness at trial will be limited to areas explored at her deposition. In addition, make sure the testimony of your witnesses is consistent. Reviewing every deposition transcript will help you avoid the testimonial weak link that opposing counsel will otherwise seize upon in trying to derail your case. Consistency may be the hobgoblin of little minds, but for lawyers it is the glue that can hold together an otherwise tenuous position.[71]

In preparing to examine a witness at trial, most lawyers will craft an outline of the examination, together with a proof chart.[72] This chart generally can be put together directly from the deposition summary (unless the summary is too detailed or expansive). The trial chart usually includes columns to indicate any evidentiary problems and your response if you are faced with that objection during trial.

A proof chart for a witness in a sexual-harassment case might look like the one in Figure 1. The references to page and line numbers in the deposition transcript allow the trial examiner to refresh recollection or impeach the witness if she cannot remember important facts or if her testimony at trial strays from that offered at her deposition. Impeaching a trial witness with prior inconsistent deposition testimony can significantly undermine the witness's credibility and is often a dramatic event—and sometimes a tipping point at the trial. The impact is muted, however, if the impeaching lawyer cannot quickly find the conflicting deposition testimony.

Topic	Testimony	Page/Line	Objection	Response
Intimacy	He told me about his separation from his wife.	26:8–28:11	Hearsay	FRE 801(d)(2) Admission not hearsay
Knowledge	I knew that he was dating another woman in the firm.	58:14–26	No foundation	Transcript 11:14–12:3

Figure 1
Sample Proof Chart

Motions Supported by Deposition Testimony

Sometimes, deposition testimony creates a need for motions. Motions to compel further testimony or for protective orders have already been discussed. But there are other motions that deposition testimony might necessitate. And one of the goals for some depositions is securing testimony that will support a critical motion, such as an issue- or case-dispositive one.

Summary Judgment

Lawyers often aim their discovery not only at trial preparation but also at gaining the evidence needed for a summary judgment motion. Before deposing a witness as discussed above, it is important to understand the law governing every claim and the elements or evidence to which the court will look to rule that one party or another is entitled to judgment as a matter of law. With that knowledge in hand, takers try to elicit testimony from witnesses consistent with the law governing the case.

FRCP 56(a) suggests—but does not require—that motions supporting or opposing summary judgment be supported by concurrently filed affidavits. The rule also permits affidavits to be supplemented by deposition transcripts (among other things) or to be opposed by depositions.[73] Indeed, FRCP 56(f) provides that if a party opposing a summary judgment motion shows by affidavit that it cannot present facts essential to its opposition, the court may order, among other remedies, that depositions be taken.[74] In any event, facts submitted to a court in support of a motion for summary judgment must be admissible evidence.[75] Of course, the fact that a witness testified to some matter in a deposition does not make that testimony automatically admissible. Therefore, if you plan to use deposition excerpts in support of your summary judgment motion, be sure that your excerpts are admissible or find a way to put that evidence in admissible form.

Likewise, FRCP 32 makes clear that the use of deposition testimony in court proceedings, including trial and hearings on motions,[76] is limited by the requirement that it be admissible under the rules of evidence.[77] Federal Rule of Evidence (FRE) 804(b)(1) provides that testimony at a deposition is not hearsay "if the party against whom the testimony is now offered . . . had an opportunity and similar motive to develop the testimony by direct, cross, or redirect examination."

Provisional Remedies

Temporary restraining orders, preliminary injunctions, writs of attachment, and other provisional remedies often are additional situations in which deposition testimony may be used to support and oppose the requested relief.[78] Given the typical fast-paced schedule for such motions, courts will often permit expedited discovery—including depositions—to be completed before the hearing on the application. The use of depositions at a hearing is governed by FRCP 32 and FRE 804, and the testimony offered through depositions must otherwise be admissible as though at trial. Indeed, FRCP 65(a)(2) permits the court to advance the trial of the matter and have it consolidated with the hearing on the application for a preliminary injunction. But even if the trial is not advanced, evidence admitted at the hearing (including testimony through depositions) becomes a part of the trial record.

Motions in Limine

Motions in limine—made just before trial for, among other reasons, limiting or preventing the introduction of prejudicial, irrelevant, or inadmissible evidence or testimony—usually are based on legal arguments without the kind of factual support typically required for a preliminary injunction or summary judgment motion. But deposition testimony will provide lawyers with some sense of what a witness will say during trial or how she may answer certain questions, and that will often alert the astute lawyer to a need or opportunity to limit the testimony through a motion in limine.

For example, a witness may be prepared to testify at trial that she received notice of a certain dangerous condition that existed on public property. But if the law requires the plaintiff to prove that the public entity had notice before the incident, and if a witness does not know when the incident occurred or when she received the notice, it may be appropriate to exclude her testimony on this point (at least until the foundational timing element has been established). Exclusion of the testimony would prevent prejudice if the jury failed to understand that the notice the witness said she received was not timely and therefore did not matter.

Your review of the deposition transcripts thus has another purpose. Each time you study the deposition testimony, ask yourself what elements of the case each portion supports or undermines and how this testimony might be limited by a motion in limine. As you think generally about motions in limine, your deposition summaries will help you locate offending testimony that might be avoided by such motions.

As with the other motions mentioned above, the Federal Rules require that deposition testimony used to support motions in limine must be admissible in evidence. It could be disastrous to lose a valid motion because you failed to comply with the requirements for getting admissible evidence and testimony before the court.

Using Depositions at Trial

Assume you have completed a deposition, made the appropriate changes to the transcript, reported to your client, updated your database, followed up with motions, and prepared your witness examinations for trial. Now what do you need to do to be able to use the deposition transcripts during the trial? Do you file the transcripts, lodge them with the court, or simply bring them with you? What do you do if the deposition was taped but not stenographically recorded, and how do you proceed if the original transcript is not available?

As an initial matter, plan on having all deposition transcripts available to file or lodge with the court, whether or not you think you will need them during trial. There is always some chance—for example, a witness becoming unavailable unexpectedly—that you may need each transcript. Avoid agonizing; bring them all. But under FRCP 5(d), you file only those to be "used in the proceeding."[79]

Assume that the deposition in question was stenographically recorded and thus a written transcript was prepared. Who has the original transcript? As discussed above, it should be with the lawyer who arranged for the deposition unless otherwise agreed or ordered by the court.[80] Once you have determined who has custody of the original, write and request that she lodge the transcript or file it with the court or give to you so that you can lodge or file it. It is unlikely that you will meet any resistance to this request, but if you do, calling the court's attention to the matter—by letter or motion—should resolve it quickly.

Filing deposition transcripts is no different from filing any brief or pleading. The transcript is presented to the clerk, who stamps it as "filed" and thereby makes it a part of the official court record. Many courts, however, prefer that deposition transcripts be "lodged" rather than filed.[81] Lodging simply means that the original deposition transcripts are presented to the court (usually the clerk of the courtroom where the trial is scheduled), with a short pleading advising that the original transcripts have now been provided to the court for trial:

> Defendant XYZ Corporation, in preparation for the trial of this matter, hereby lodges with this Court the original transcripts of the deposition testimony of the following witnesses:
>
> > George Washington
> > Abraham Lincoln
> > Franklin D. Roosevelt

The court's local rules or pretrial orders usually prescribe the method and time for lodging or filing transcripts.[82] If you have any questions or concerns about this procedure, a phone call to the courtroom clerk will usually provide the information you need.[83]

If for some reason the original transcript of a deposition is no longer available (for instance, because it has been lost, destroyed, or misplaced), you must make arrangements for a copy to be accepted by the court. As previously noted, the starting point in this effort is a request that all lawyers stipulate that a copy of the deposition transcript may be used in lieu of the original at trial. Usually, this will solve the problem, and such a stipulation often is made on the record at the end of the deposition to avoid such problems.[84] However, if all the lawyers will not agree to such a stipulation, then a request must be made to the court. This issue usually arises just before a deposition transcript must be provided to the court, when someone first realizes that the original is missing. Therefore, typically there is little time to act. If that is the case, an immediate motion is warranted, together with an application for an order shortening the time on which the matter can be heard. Depending on when the problem arises, you can also raise this issue with the court at the final pretrial conference. The judge can often be more persuasive than you in convincing other parties to accept a copy if the original transcript is no longer available.

If the deposition was not stenographically recorded, you must provide the court with a copy of the video recording or audiotape in the same way transcripts are provided—by lodging or filing them. If you intend to use a video to present the testimony of a witness at the trial, you must also provide a transcript of those portions of the deposition testimony that you intend to present in this way.[85]

What if the witness never signed the transcript? Are you precluded from using it at trial without this signature? If changes were submitted to the transcript in accordance with FRCP 30(e), then the witness was required to sign a statement regarding those changes, which the reporter then appends to the transcript. The signed statement regarding changes fulfills the requirement for a signed transcript. If no review was requested or if no changes were made during the review period, then the transcript can be used unsigned as if it had been signed.[86] As suggested earlier in this chapter, the lawyer taking the deposition should state that if no changes are made, the transcript can be used unsigned without limitation.

Conclusion

So is the deposition over? The answer: "That depends." The careful lawyer will consider the various issues raised in this chapter in order to best protect her client and advance the client's interests. For a taker, this might mean laying the groundwork to reopen the deposition if justified. For a defender, this might mean ensuring that all avenues for an additional deposition session are closed. Most important, however, is that all options have been thought through well before the last question of the day so that you do no harm to your client or her case.

Notes

*The author gratefully acknowledges the contributions of David Phillips of Farella Braun + Martel LLP, in helping to revise this chapter for the second edition.

1. A transcript technically is not required when a deposition is video recorded, but one is almost always requested anyway, and it will be required if the video recording is to be used at trial. *See* FED. R. CIV. P. 32(c). "[T]here is no requirement that a party taking a deposition by non-stenographic means provide a written transcript of the entire deposition to other parties." Hudson v. Spellman High Voltage, 178 F.R.D. 29, 31 (E.D.N.Y. 1998). "Any other party is free to prepare a written transcript of the tape recorded deposition, however, the party noticing the deposition does not have that obligation." *Id.*

2. See also Appendix 9, summarizing considerations for takers and defenders at the end of the deposition.

3. Provisions in Rule 30 allowing "opt-outs" from these discovery restrictions by local rule were abrogated when the Federal Rules were revised in 2000.

4. Obviously, the Court will allow more than seven hours "if needed to fairly examine" the plaintiff. FRCP 30(d)(1). However, the better practice is for the deposition to go forward to determine how much is able to be covered in the seven hours and, then, if additional time is needed, for counsel to stipulate to extend the deposition for a specific additional time period. If the parties cannot reach a stipulation, then Court intervention may be sought. Malec v. Trs. of Boston Coll., 208 F.R.D. 23, 24 (D. Mass. 2002).

In *LaPlante v. Estano*, counsel was allowed to continue a deposition beyond the seven-hour limit when the other side was "recalcitrant and uncooperative in their refusal to answer questions" and curtailed the deposition without justification. 226 F.R.D. 439, 440 (D.Conn. 2005).

Similarly, in *Miller v. Waseca Medical Center*, the court stated:

> The mere fact that these cases might have proceeded separately does not establish that 14 hours is the appropriate length for a deposition of a witness common to both cases. By the same logic, the fact that the two cases have now been consolidated into one also does not establish that it is proper that no deposition last more than seven hours. Rather, the Court is called upon in each case to make a fact intensive inquiry as to whether a particular witness should or should not be required to submit to questioning which exceeds seven hours in length. The Notes of the Advisory Committee to the 2000 amendments suggest some of the factors to consider, but their most important advice is in a single sentence: "Preoccupation with timing is to be avoided."

205 F.R.D. 537, 540 (D. Minn. 2002).

5. Different jurisdictions handle discovery cutoff in different ways, so lawyers must understand the local procedure and how it will affect rights to depose witnesses. For instance, United States Court for the Northern District of California Local Rule 26-2 states explicitly that the discovery cutoff is that date "by which all responses to written discovery are due and by which all depositions must be concluded." Without a stipulation between lawyers or permission of the court, a party may not be able to submit deposition testimony taken after the discovery cutoff date to support motions or in place of live testimony if the witness is unavailable at trial.

6. See Chapter 11 and Chapter 14, discussing the taker's and defender's perspectives on trying to complete a deposition in one day.

7. Even if the deposition is concluded, there may be opportunities to reopen it later. Changes made to the testimony upon review of the transcript by the witness (FRCP 30(e)) or by a supplement to a prior discovery response (FRCP 26(e)) might permit further inquiry. See discussion later in this chapter.

667

8. Reopening the deposition to examine a witness concerning a topic about which he denied knowledge ultimately may not be the best strategy. If the witness has lied or otherwise damaged his credibility, it may be better not to give the witness the opportunity to explain before he gets in front of a judge or jury.

9. FRCP 26(a) requires lawyers to exchange certain documents and other information as "initial disclosures" without the need for a specific discovery request. The parties are also under a continuing obligation to supplement discovery responses when further investigation reveals potentially relevant evidence. FED. R. CIV. P. 26(e). See also "The Federal Discovery Scheme" in Chapter 2.

10. See "Receipt of Documents" in Chapter 11, discussing requests for documents discovered during the deposition from the taker's perspective, and "Defender's Response to Document Requests During a Deposition" in Chapter 14.

11. Time limits for the completion of a deposition, such as the seven-hour rule imposed by FRCP 30(d)(1), make risky any delay in fully completing the deposition. But Rule 30(d)(1) permits the court to allow additional time if necessary for a fair examination or if a party impedes or delays the deposition. Sanctions may also be imposed under FRCP 37 if the conduct of lawyers or parties has been improper. *See, e.g.,* FED. R. CIV. P. 30(d)(2); S.D. FLA. R. 30.1.

12. When questioning is conducted oppressively or in bad faith, FRCP 30(d)(3)(A) specifies that counsel may halt the deposition and apply for a protective order. *See, e.g.,* Redwood v. Dobson, 476 F.3d 462, 467–70 (7th Cir. 2007) (counsel "would have been entitled to stalk out of the room" when questioning was "designed to harass rather than obtain information"). But such a situation is exceptional, and counsel would be well advised to think carefully, and perhaps call a brief calming-down recess, before suspending the deposition. See also "Problems for the Defender in Controlling the Examiner" in Chapter 15.

13. See *infra* section "Motions Regarding the Deposition." FRCP 26(c)(1) provides that a motion for a protective order must "include a certification that the movant has in good faith conferred or attempted to confer with other affected parties in an effort to resolve the dispute without court action." *See also* FED. R. CIV. P. 37(a)(1) (same requirement regarding motion to compel).

14. FED. R. CIV. P. 30(b)(2), 45(a)(1)(C).

15. Although parties attending the deposition can get copies of documents—those produced at the deposition or otherwise used as exhibits—during the deposition, they frequently just ask for a copy of the transcript with the appended documents at the end of the deposition. This raises another issue concerning documents at the end of the deposition. Do all those in attendance want copies of all the materials introduced? If the

exhibits are modest in number and length, then there is usually no issue, and the court reporter will include copies of all documents with the copies of the transcript. But concerns arise when the documents are voluminous (for instance, hundreds of pages of offering circulars in a securities case) or oversized (like plans or blueprints in a construction case). The cost of reproducing these documents may be substantial, so lawyers often will agree that not all documents appended to the original transcript need to be copied. Other arrangements are then made for those materials, such as a central document/exhibit repository to which all parties have access.

16.   FRCP 30(e)(1)–(2) states in full:

> (1) On request by the deponent or a party before the deposition is completed, the deponent must be allowed 30 days after being notified by the officer that the transcript or recording is available in which:
> (A) to review the transcript or recording; and
> (B) if there are changes in form or substance, to sign a statement listing the changes and the reasons for making them.
> (2) The officer must note in the certificate prescribed by Rule 30(f)(1) whether a review was requested and, if so, must attach any changes the deponent makes during the 30-day period.

17.   See *infra* section "Using Depositions at Trial," discussing unsigned transcripts.

18.   See "Task 15: Pack a Bag Carefully" in Chapter 4, discussing providing a glossary to the court reporter at the start of a deposition.

19.   See also "Examining Your Own Witness" in Chapter 14.

20.   See Chapter 14, note 1.

21.   *See, e.g.*, Resolution Trust Corp. v. Dabney, 73 F.3d 262 (10th Cir. 1995) (sanctions imposed for improper instruction not to answer on ground of privilege); Starlight Int'l, Inc. v. Herlihy, 186 F.R.D. 626, 646 (D.Kan. 1999) (same).

22.   Clients generally prefer to keep their original documents or at least have their lawyers keep them.

23.   See "Defender's Response to Document Requests During a Deposition" in Chapter 14.

24.   See *infra* sections "Reviewing Deposition Testimony" and "Reviewing and Correcting the Transcript."

25.   *See* FED. R. CIV. P. 30(f). Also consider what happens if the noticed deposition does not go forward as scheduled.

26.   *See* FED. R. CIV. P. 5(d) advisory committee's note (2000).

27.   The lawyer who noticed the deposition may turn out to have a relatively minor role in the deposition, while another party's lawyer ends up really being the lead "taker." In that case, the primary taker may

be the appropriate lawyer to maintain the original transcript. *See* FED. R. CIV. P. 30(f).

28.   See *infra* section "Using Depositions at Trial," discussing how to get the original transcripts before the court for use at hearings or trial.

29.   Court reporters tend to build their "dictionaries" of the case over the course of depositions, and therefore later transcripts in rough form are usually more accurate than earlier transcripts in rough form. The skill of the court reporter involved may also affect the quality of the rough transcript.

30.   See Chapter 24, discussing the use of computer technology as part of the deposition process. See also Chapter 18.

31.   You may have raised the need for a computer disk or electronic file with the reporter at the beginning of the deposition or even when you arranged for the reporter to cover the deposition. It still is good practice to confirm this request with the reporter at the end of the deposition so she can annotate the transcript or her notes with this request.

32.   Pronounced "as-key," ASCII stands for American Standard Code for Information Interchange. As long as you know how to pronounce it, your court reporter will know what you want. See Chapter 22, note 3.

33.   Of course, if you requested computer disks or electronic files of the testimony and have a laptop computer, you might not need to travel with hard copies of transcripts.

34.   See Chapter 17.

35.   FRCP 32(c) provides that, except as otherwise directed by the court, a party offering deposition testimony at a hearing or trial "must provide a transcript of any deposition testimony the party offers, but may provide the court with the testimony in nontranscript form as well."

36.   If the witness is a party, no subpoena is necessary to compel attendance at the deposition under FRCP 30. If the witness is not a party, however, attendance should be secured by the issuance and service of a subpoena in accordance with FRCP 45. See Chapter 3, for a detailed discussion on securing the attendance of a witness.

37.   In *Barrett v. Brian Bemis Auto World*, 230 F.R.D. 535 (N.D. Ill. 2005), for instance, the deponent appeared for his deposition with the documents he was supposed to have produced earlier. The lawyer conducting the deposition cancelled it because she had not had the documents before the deposition to prepare. The court awarded sanctions against her under FRCP 30(g)(1).

> While defense counsel may have very well believed she was prejudiced by the late production of the . . . documents, at the very least, counsel should have started the deposition on the topics she was prepared for and continued the deposition to reserve the opportunity to question Plaintiff's expert on the new disclosures if it became necessary. It was also incumbent

> upon defense counsel to alert Plaintiff's counsel to the fact
> that she did not intend to proceed with the deposition due to
> the delayed production before the day of the deposition.

Id. at 537.

38. *See, e.g.*, Cal. Rules of Prof'l Conduct R. 3-500 ("A member shall keep a client reasonably informed about significant developments relating to the employment or representation. . . .").

39. For example, in March 2000, the Intake Unit of the State Bar of California's Chief Trial Counsel did a study of complaints to the bar's toll-free complaint line. Nearly one-fourth of the calls alleged a failure to adequately communicate, more than any other category of complaint category. *See* State Bar of Cal., Investigation and Prosecution of Disciplinary Complaints Against Attorneys in Solo Practice, Small Size Law Firms and Large Size Law Firms 17 (2001), *available at* http://www.calbar.ca.gov/calbar/pdfs/reports/2001_SB143-Report.pdf.

40. See "Types of Summaries" in Chapter 24, describing deposition summaries more fully, including some sample forms and suggestions for undertaking this task.

41. Leave to amend a complaint is, in general, liberally granted if there is no prejudice to the other side. Forman v. Davis, 371 U.S. 178, 182 (1962); Sides v. City of Champaign, 496 F.3d 820, 825 (7th Cir. 2007); Int'l Ass'n of Machinists & Aerospace Workers v. Republic Airlines, 761 F.2d 1386, 1390 (9th Cir. 1985); Fed. R. Civ. P. 15(a).

42. FRCP 37 permits the examining lawyer either to complete the deposition or adjourn it before bringing a motion to compel.

43. *See also* Fed. R. Civ. P. 26(c). The certification required for a motion to compel is no different from what would be required if the witness instead sought a protective order.

44. *See, e.g.*, RLI Ins. Co. v. Conseco, Inc., 477 F. Supp. 2d 741 (E.D.Va. 2007).

45. Fed. R. Civ. P. 37(a)(5)(A).

46. Fed. R. Civ. P. 37(a)(5)(B); *see also* Fed. R. Civ. P. 26(c).

47. *See, e.g.*, D. Md. R. 104(1) (no more than thirty requests for production per party); D. Mass. R. 26.1(C) (limit of two separate sets of requests for production "for each side (or group of parties with a common interest)").

48. FRCP 26(a)(1)(A)(ii) requires that the parties produce "a copy—or a description by category and location—of all documents, electronically stored information, and tangible things that the disclosing party has in its possession, custody, or control and may use to support its claims or defenses, unless the use would be solely for impeachment." Some local rules are even more explicit. *See, e.g.*, E.D. Tex. R. CV-26(d).

49. For example, in *Arctic Cat, Inc. v. Injection Research Specialists, Inc.*, 210 F.R.D. 680 (D. Minn. 2002), where the plaintiff company's

designated expert could not answer deposition questions because he needed documentation that he did not bring with him and that had not been expressly demanded in the deposition notice, the court allowed an additional seven hours of deposition time.

50. *See., e.g.,* McCulloch v. Hartford Life and Accident Ins. Co., 223 F.R.D. 26 (D. Conn. 2004) (deposition notice requesting person with knowledge of negotiation and execution of reinsurance agreement did not duplicate second notice requesting representative with knowledge of factual basis for insurer's denials of request to admit). See "Exceptions to the 'Only Once' Rule" in Chapter 3.

51. *See, e.g.,* Estell v. Williams Scotsman, Inc., 228 F.R.D. 668 (N.D. Okla. 2005) (second deposition of key witness allowed after another witness withdrew key admission); Quality Aero Tech., Inc. v. Telemetrie Elektronik GmbH, 212 F.R.D. 313, 319 (E.D.N.C. 2002) (newly discovered information, the proffered rationale for the second notice, would have been sufficient for finding of good cause under Rule 30); Zamora v. D'Arrigo Bros. Co. of Cal., 2006 WL 3227870, at *2 (N.D. Cal. 2006) ("discovery sought is not unreasonably cumulative or duplicative, because the 2004 witness could not have answered questions about data produced in 2006"); Mishkin v. Peat, Marwick, Mitchell & Co., 1988 U.S. Dist. LEXIS 11,753 (S.D.N.Y. 1988) (deposition reopened for questions on subsequently produced documents); Christy v. Pa. Tpk. Comm'n, 160 F.R.D. 51 (E.D. Pa. 1995) (plaintiff may be deposed second time on new allegations in amended complaint); *but cf.* Evan v. Estell, 203 F.R.D. 172 (M.D. Pa. 2001) (second deposition on physical condition not permitted when no change in condition alleged); Graebner v. James River Corp., 130 F.R.D. 440 (N.D. Cal. 1989) (second deposition not permitted when, despite amended complaint, issues in case had narrowed since first deposition); FED. R. CIV. P. 30(a)(2)(A)(ii).

52. Innomed Labs, LLC v. Alza Corp., 211 F.R.D. 237, 239 (S.D.N.Y. 2002).

53. *Compare* Bonner v. Guccione, 1996 U.S. Dist. LEXIS 6516 (S.D.N.Y. 1996), *and* Sec. & Exch. Comm'n v. H.K. Freelance & Co., 1992 U.S. Dist. LEXIS 17,838 (S.D.N.Y. 1992) (reopening when changes significant), *with* Lugtig v. Thomas, 89 F.R.D. 639 (N.D. Ill. 1981), *and* Hawthorne Partners v. AT&T Techs., Inc., U.S. Dist. LEXIS 4966 (N.D. Ill. 1994) (no reopening unless changes make deposition "incomplete or useless without further testimony"). *Cf., e.g.,* Gipson v. Wells Fargo Bank, N.A., 239 F.R.D. 280 (D. D.C. 2006) (additional one-hour deposition permitted, even without motion to reopen, in light of "ambiguity" in telephone conference call); Herring v. Teradyne, Inc., 2002 WL 32068318 (S.D.Cal. 2002), at *4 (two nontechnical clarifying changes would not be stricken, when opposing party could "seek to reopen the examination . . . in order to further investigate any ambiguity that [deponent] might have created by changing his

answers"). For a good discussion of this problem, see *DeLoach v. Philip Morris Cos., Inc.*, 206 F.R.D. 568 (M.D. N.C. 2002).

54. The original answer will remain part of the record and may be used to impeach the witness on cross-examination. Eicken v. USAA Fed. Sav. Bank, 498 F. Supp. 2d. 954, 961 (S.D. Tex. 2007); Lugtig v. Thomas, 89 F.R.D. 639, 641–42 (N.D. III. 1981); Sec. & Exch. Comm'n v. H.K. Freelance & Co., 1992 U.S. Dist. LEXIS 17,838 (S.D.N.Y. 1992). The possibility of commenting at trial about a witness's changes to the deposition transcript should be balanced against the fact that fewer than 2 percent of all civil cases go to trial. See Chapter 1, note 2. Saving this attack for a trial that never happens will not be very effective or satisfying.

55. The decision—and the strategy—of tendering or retendering your client's defense to an insurance carrier depends on many other factors. If the possibility of tendering has not arisen until the time of deposition testimony, there may be an issue of delay in notifying the carrier. This is generally a matter of state law, but typically you must show that the carrier has not been prejudiced by the late notice. You might want to clear up this issue by asking your own witness a question at the end of the deposition to establish that there has been no prejudice (for example, by showing that the condition giving rise to the tender argument has just occurred or manifested itself).

56. *See* FED. R. CIV. P. 30(e).

57. *See, e.g.*, Welsh v. R.W. Bradford Transp., 231 F.R.D. 297 (N.D. Ill. 2005) (striking errata sheet completed within thirty-day period but not transmitted to reporter in time).

58. If you have any question during the deposition about whether your objection was recorded, promptly ask the reporter. This will avoid the inevitable disagreement with opposing counsel when you try to insert the objection following review of the transcript. A video recording will make the objection easier to spot.

59. The "procedural requirements of Rule 30(e) must be adhered to." Agrizap, Inc. v. Woodstream Corp., 232 F.R.D. 491, 493 (E.D. Pa. 2006) (declining to permit changes where review was not timely requested).

60. *See, e.g.*, Hambleton Bros. Lumber Co. v. Balkin Enters., Inc., 397 F.3d 1217, 1226 (9th Cir. 2005) ("Rule 30(e) is to be used for corrective, and not contradictory, changes." As one court put it: "A deposition is not a take home examination. . . . If that were the case, one could merely answer the questions with no thought at all, then return home and plan artful responses." Greenway v. Int'l Paper Co., 144 F.R.D. 322 (W.D. La. 1992); *accord* Rios v. Bigler, 847 F. Supp. 1538 (D. Kan. 1994)).

61. *See, e.g.*, Lamarche v. Metro. Life Ins. Co., 236 F. Supp. 2d 34, 41 (D. Me. 2002) (allowing change in answer from "no" to "yes" after deponent explained that he had misunderstood the question, was exhausted after hours of questioning without a lunch break, and was a diabetic).

For a thoughtful expression of the broader view of the Rule, see *Reilly v. TXU Corp.*, 230 F.R.D. 486, 490 (N.D. Tex. 2005). ("As written, the Rule makes provision for changes in substance that are made for legitimate reasons, such as to correct a misstatement or honest mistake. This furthers the purpose of the discovery process—to allow the parties to elicit the true facts of a case before trial.") *See also, e.g.*, Lugtig v. Thomas, 89 F.R.D. 639 (N.D. Ill. 1981); Duff v. Lobdell-Emery Mfg. Co., 926 F. Supp. 799, 803 (N.D. Ind. 1996).

62. See "Foundational Questions" in Chapter 11. The deposing lawyer probably admonished the witness at the beginning of the deposition that if she makes changes to the recorded transcript, he will be allowed to comment on those changes at trial. You should instruct your witness about this as well when you are preparing her for the deposition. There is little to be gained by having the witness try to avoid difficult questions during the deposition with the hope of crafting something clever during review of the transcript. *See also supra* notes 52–53.

63. Also see *supra* section "Examining Your Own Witness."

64. *See, e.g.*, MODEL RULES OF PROF'L CONDUCT R. 3.3 (2008); CAL. RULES OF PROF'L CONDUCT R. 5-200; *cf. supra* notes 52–53 (regarding scope of permissible changes to transcript); see also Chapter 21.

65. Note that "a party may always move to amend a deposition response if new and different information surfaces post-deposition." Wilson v. Lakner, 228 F.R.D. 524, 530 (D. Md. 2005).

66. FED. R. CIV. P. 30(e)(2).

67. *See, e.g.*, FED. R. CIV. P. 37(d); Henry v. Gill Indus., Inc., 983 F.2d 943, 947 (9th Cir. 1993); Robinson v. Transamerica Ins. Co., 368 F.2d 37 (10th Cir. 1966); see also "Task 1: Review the Notice and/or Subpoena for Procedural Compliance and Follow Its Commands" in Chapter 4, discussing options for a defender in receipt of a defective deposition notice.

68. Sanctions are available under FRCP 26(c), FRCP 37(a)(5), and FRCP 11. Sanctions may also be awarded under 28 U.S.C. § 1927 when an attorney's conduct, "viewed objectively, manifests either intentional or reckless disregard of the attorney's duties to the court." Tenkku v. Normandy Bank, 348 F.3d 737, 743–44 (8th Cir. 2003).

69. Be careful to ensure that discussions with co-counsel will be privileged. Obviously any such discussion with another lawyer in the case would be undertaken only under an expectation of confidence. In this regard, it is always advisable to have a joint prosecution or joint defense agreement, which should ensure that your conversations are protected. *See, e.g.*, John Morrell & Co. v. Local Union 304A of United Food & Commercial Workers, AFL-CIO, 913 F.2d 544, 555–56 (8th Cir. 1990) (joint defense); Waller v. Fin. Corp. of Am., 828 F.2d 579, 583 n.7 (9th Cir. 1987) (same); Sedlacek v. Morgan Whitney Trading Group, Inc., 795 F. Supp. 329, 331 (C.D. Cal. 1992) (joint prosecution). If you have any concerns about the loss of privilege, talk only to a lawyer in your office

about your assessment, so that there will not be any problem regarding confidentiality. See also "Representation of Corporate Affiliates and Their Employees" in Chapter 6, discussing attorney-client privilege and the joint defense doctrine.

70. See also "How to Lay a Foundation for the Admissibility (or Inadmissibility) of a Document" in Chapter 13.

71. "A foolish consistency is the hobgoblin of little minds, adored by little statesmen and philosophers and divines." Ralph Waldo Emerson, *Self-Reliance, in* Essays 57 (1841).

72. See also "Preparing to Take a Deposition" in Chapter 4, discussing case analysis and the use of outlines in preparing to take a deposition.

73. FRCP 56(e)(1) states that the court "may permit an affidavit to be supplemented or opposed by depositions, answers to interrogatories, or additional affidavits."

74. FRCP 56(f) states:

> If a party opposing the motion shows by affidavit that, for specified reasons, it cannot present facts essential to justify its opposition, the court may:
>
> (1) deny the motion;
> (2) order a continuance to enable affidavits to be obtained, depositions to be taken, or other discovery to be undertaken; or
> (3) issue any other just order.

75. FRCP 56(e)(1) states that a "supporting or opposing affidavit must be made on personal knowledge, set out facts that would be admissible in evidence, and show that the affiant is competent to testify on the matters stated."

76. See also Chapter 25.

77. FRCP 32 is entitled "Using Depositions in Court Proceedings." The rule provides extensive direction concerning this issue.

78. FRCP 65 governs injunctions.

79. The Advisory Committee note to the 2000 revision to this subsection cautions: "because the filing requirement applies only with regard to materials that are used, only those parts of voluminous materials that are actually used need be filed."

80. *See* FED. R. CIV. P. 30(f).

81. *Compare* S.D. FLA. R. 26.1(D) (filed at "outset" of trial) *and* D. ME. 26(c) ("complete original of the transcript or the discovery material to be used" to be filed seven days before trial) *with* C.D. CAL. R. 32-1 (lodged "on or before the first day of a trial"). In *United States v. Novelli*, 381 F. Supp. 2d 1125 (C.D. Cal. 2005), the court refused to consider partial transcripts lodged instead of the complete transcript required by Local Rule 32-1. The time for filing or lodging required by local rules is often different for motions than for trials.

82.   *See supra* note 68. Remember, if you intend to present testimony through a witness's deposition, FRCP 26(a)(3) requires that the witness be so designated to all other parties (unless the deposition testimony is to be used only for purposes of impeachment). If the deposition was not stenographically recorded, the rule requires that a transcript of the pertinent portions of that deposition testimony be provided. FED. R. CIV. P. 26(a)(3)(ii).

83.   The clerk and deputy of the courtroom to which you are assigned are usually an invaluable resource and know how things are to be done. If they like you, they can provide you with assistance and answers to questions that might otherwise seem unobtainable. Therefore, give such persons every reason to like you. Be courteous, treat them with respect, and always pay close attention to what they say.

84.   FRE 1004 permits lawyers to use other evidence of a writing if the original has been lost or destroyed and if the loss or destruction was not the result of bad faith. Though no case has been found directly on point, this rule would seem to permit the use of a copy of the deposition transcript if the original were lost or destroyed. Note also that FRE 1007 allows use of deposition testimony to prove the contents of writings, recordings, or photographs "without accounting for the nonproduction of the original."

85.   FED. R. CIV. P. 26(a)(3)(ii)–(iii). The exception to this rule is if the recorded testimony is to be used only to impeach witnesses who will testify in person. See also Chapter 17, discussing reasons to also record a video recorded deposition stenographically and how to present video recorded testimony at trial.

86.   FRCP 32(d)(4) states that irregularities in the signing (among other things) of a deposition transcript are waived "unless a motion to suppress [the deposition] is made" within a reasonable time after the problem was or should have been discovered.

CHAPTER 24

Managing, Summarizing, Indexing, and Searching Depositions: The Role of Paralegals and Computer Software

Christine Bergren Greene

Many litigation tasks once done by lawyers are now done by paralegals.[1] Two of the most important tasks are summarizing deposition transcripts and using computers to manage and search transcripts and exhibits. This chapter provides templates for deposition summaries, ideas for outsourcing summaries, and background information on software tools to supplement, summarize, and manage transcripts and exhibits.

The first section of the chapter describes four methods for summarizing deposition testimony, with examples of each method. It also discusses alternatives to in-house summarizing and handling of deposition transcripts and exhibits. The second section describes how computer technology can be used to review, locate, and organize deposition testimony and deposition exhibits.

Types of Summaries

Why Summaries Are Important

A deposition summary compresses the language of the transcript, thereby facilitating fast and reliable access to testimony. The job of summarizing, sometimes called digesting, can be tedious and time-consuming. Yet summaries are essential. Among other things, they help lawyers to: (1) prepare for subsequent depositions and pretrial motions, such as motions for summary judgment; (2) prepare subsequent discovery responses and demands, including interrogatories, requests for production, and requests for admissions; (3) prepare for witness examination at trial; and (4) locate deposition testimony for witness impeachment at trial.

Deposition summaries also can help highlight significant testimony and issues, locate exhibits, and cross-reference testimony concerning particular issues or exhibits. Finally, they can be used for cross-referencing testimony among several deponents, eliminating the time-consuming job of reviewing hundreds of pages of deposition transcripts.

There are four basic methods for summarizing depositions: (1) traditional page-line, (2) topical index, (3) issue-category, and (4) narrative, each discussed in order below. (Special types of depositions, such as video recorded depositions, use special methods of summarizing.[2])

Regardless of the method used, a summary should always begin with the following:

- Case name and number;
- Name of the deponent and title of the summary (such as "Summary of the Deposition of Leslie Roberts");

- Time, date, and location of the deposition; and
- Names of all the lawyers and others present at the deposition.

Traditional Page-Line Summary Method

The page-line summary is the most common of the four methods. It is an abridged, compressed version of the original transcript and covers the subject matter page by page as it appears in the transcript. Citations are to the page and line where testimony appears, providing a quick reference to the actual transcript. Major topics, exhibits, and changes in examining lawyers are highlighted for easier visual access.

The page-line summary method provides excellent access to the deposition transcript. Because topic headings are included in the summary, it can be quickly perused to locate an area of interest. And, because the summary follows a chronological, page-by-page pattern, it is easy to understand.

The following is a sample page-line summary based on the deposition of Plaintiff Leslie Roberts in the *Scoops v. Business-Aide, Inc.* case.

Sample Page-Line Summary

Leslie Roberts, dba Scoops v. Business-Aide, Inc.
Superior Court of HLH
Eastern District
No. 10—1234 CMY

SUMMARY OF THE DEPOSITION OF LESLIE ROBERTS

Taken July 1, one year ago
Commencing at 10:00 AM
Taken before James Smith, CSR and Notary Public

Present at Deposition: Leslie Roberts, Deponent
Rose Yuspa, Lawyer for Plaintiff
Emily B. Carter, Lawyer for Defendant
    Business-Aide, Inc.
Wanda Castillo, Paralegal for Ms. Carter

679

Page: Line	Summary
4:2	Witness sworn in by court reporter [also serving as deposition officer]. Introductory comments and instructions by Ms. Carter to deponent.
6:9	Commencement of direct examination by Ms. Carter.
6:12	**Personal Background:** Born in St. Paul, MN. Graduated Wheaton College seven years ago; art history major. Married Jim Donaldson, grad. student at Harvard. Divorced after 3 years. Current residence: 33 Green Street, Cambridge, MA. Single-family residence owned solely by deponent. Mortgage held by Cambridge S&L.
8:7	**Employment History Before Scoops:** Seven years ago to three years ago—Painting, odd jobs (for example, waitress, illustrator, short-order cook).
10:15	**History of Scoops Ice Cream Business:** Deponent enjoyed making desserts, especially homemade ice cream. Borrowed $5,000 (5% interest) from friends to help lease storefront and rent ice-cream-making equipment (blending tanks, holding tanks, batch freezers). Opened Scoops three years ago.
12:5	**Pre-Computer Accounting & Management Procedures at Scoops:** No separate corporate identity. Operation runs out of checking account, which deponent maintains in store's name. Deponent prepared tax returns without assistance (1040, with a Schedule C, Profit and Loss from Business or Profession). Scoops's income and expenses were reported on cash basis.
16:14	**Accounting & Management Problems:** After expansion of business two years ago, deponent had trouble coordinating sales and inventory. For example, August, two years ago, batch of cream spoiled because deponent bought too much for available orders.

Page: Line	Summary
19:14	**Accounting & Management Problems:** As of two years ago, 30% sales on cash basis; 70% bulk sales, on credit, to restaurants. Expenses: 80% cash basis, 20% credit basis. Deponent unable to regularize cash flow. Two years ago, deponent borrowed an additional $2,000 from friends (5% interest) to meet unexpected bills.
22:24	**Frank Fuller's Role at Scoops:** June, two years ago: hired Frank Fuller as assistant. $265/week. No formal job description. Duties included serving ice cream, drafting correspondence, and keeping the books.
25:24	**Pre-Computer Accounting & Management Procedures:** Collected cash each day and deposited it in Scoops's checking account. Fuller and deponent prepared handwritten bills for credit sales, placed in folder labeled "Sales." Bills were placed in folder labeled "To Be Paid." Fuller prepared checks monthly for deponent to sign.
26:9	**Initial Interest in Purchasing a Computer:** September, two years ago, deponent attended Chamber of Commerce seminar on use of computers as a management tool.
26:26	**Ex. 1: Sept., two years ago:** Deponent's notes taken during Chamber of Commerce Seminar. Ex. 1 is marked.

Topical-Index Summary Method

Of the four summarizing methods, the topical index method is the easiest to prepare and the least detailed. It lists the main subjects by page and line reference, and it can be used alone or to provide access to the original transcript and the page-line summary.

In fact, it is a good idea to create a topical index for each page-line summary. With a topical index, cross-referencing to multiple deposition summaries is easy. Suppose you or your paralegal want to locate testimony about an exhibit used at several depositions. Simply review the topical index for each deposition; note the pages where the exhibit is mentioned and then go to the page-line summaries or the original transcripts where the testimony appears.

681

The topical index also provides an overview of the contents of a deposition—a useful resource for reviewing a multivolume deposition transcript because it enables you to identify the relevant volume quickly.

Sample Topical-Index Summary

Leslie Roberts, dba Scoops v. Business-Aide, Inc.
Superior Court of HLH
Eastern District
No. 10—1234 CMY

TOPICAL INDEX TO SUMMARY OF
THE DEPOSITION OF LESLIE ROBERTS

Taken July 1, one year ago
Commencing at 10:00 AM
Taken before James Smith, CSR and Notary Public

Present at Deposition: Leslie Roberts, Deponent
Rose Yuspa, Lawyer for Plaintiff
Emily B. Carter, Lawyer for
   Defendant Business-Aide, Inc.
Wanda Castillo, Paralegal for
   Ms. Carter

Topic	Summary Page	Transcript Page
Personal Background	1	6:12
Employment History Before Scoops	1	8:7
History of Scoops Ice Cream Business	1	10:15
Pre-Computer Accounting & Management Procedures at Scoops	1	12:5
Accounting & Management Problems	1	16:14
Accounting & Management Problems	2	19:14
Frank Fuller's Role at Scoops	2	22:24

Pre-Computer Accounting & Management Procedures	2	25:24
Initial Interest in Purchasing a Computer	2	26:9
Ex. 1: Sept., two years ago, Deponent's Notes Taken During Chamber of Commerce Seminar	2	26:26

Issue-Category Summary Method

The issue-category summary is a more complex and detailed method than the traditional page-line summary. Its purpose is to group together either full quotations or compressed, summary versions of testimony about a particular subject matter. This method works well for lengthy depositions, especially when they include numerous exhibits and the witness has been examined by several lawyers. In addition, the preservation of full quotations can be a valuable tool for impeaching a witness at trial.

An issue-category summary can be prepared with a word processing program. However, it is more efficient to use a transcript management software program. (These software programs are discussed in the second section of this chapter.)

Sample Issue-Category Summary

Leslie Roberts, dba Scoops v. Business-Aide, Inc.
Superior Court of HLH
Eastern District
No. 10—1234 CMY

ISSUE-CATEGORY SUMMARY OF
THE DEPOSITION OF LESLIE ROBERTS

Taken July 1, one year ago
Commencing at 10:00 AM

Taken before James Smith, CSR and Notary Public

Present at Deposition: Leslie Roberts, Deponent
Rose Yuspa, Lawyer for Plaintiff
Emily B. Carter, Lawyer for
    Defendant Business-Aide, Inc.
Wanda Castillo, Paralegal for
    Ms. Carter

Subjects and Statements (Page/Line)

Accounting & Management Problems
Deponent experienced trouble coordinating sales and inventory beginning two years ago. For example, Aug., two years ago, a batch of cream spoiled because deponent bought too much for available orders. (16:14–17:26)

Also, two summers ago, deponent unable to regularize cash flow. Sales were 30% cash basis, 70% credit basis. Expenses, on other hand, were 80% cash basis, 20% credit basis. As a result, deponent borrowed additional $2,000 from two friends at 5% interest to meet unexpected bills. (19:14–20:23)

Computer Acquisition: Initial Interest
Attended Chamber of Commerce seminar on using computers to manage a business. (See Ex. 1, Sept., two years ago, Deponent's Notes Taken During Chamber of Commerce Seminar.) (26:9–28:2)

Knowledge of Computers
Deponent knew nothing about computers or how to acquire a computer. She did not personally research the subject of acquiring a computer because she felt intimidated by the subject matter. She assigned Fuller the task of researching the subject, based on his experience (one computer course in college) and her notes from the Chamber of Commerce seminar in September, two years ago. (28:3–32:15)

Narrative Summary Method
Many lawyers also want a narrative summary as a companion to the traditional page-line summary. The narrative summary is not a tool for accessing the transcript. Instead, it is a report on the

684

testimony, telling the deponent's story in a format that is easier to read than the page-line format. For this reason, narrative summaries are often attached to client status reports.[3]

A narrative summary can be either a detailed report or a cursory overview, depending on the needs of a case or a client. In some cases, a narrative summary might be the only summary prepared, particularly in a large case in which dozens of depositions are taken and the cost of preparing page-line summaries for every deposition would be prohibitive.

Sample Narrative Summary

Leslie Roberts, dba Scoops v. Business-Aide, Inc.
Superior Court of HLH
Eastern District
No. 10—1234 CMY

NARRATIVE SUMMARY OF
THE DEPOSITION OF LESLIE ROBERTS

Taken July 1, one year ago
Commencing at 10:00 AM
Taken before James Smith, CSR and Notary Public

Present at Deposition: Leslie Roberts, Deponent
                           Rose Yuspa, Lawyer for Plaintiff
                           Emily B. Carter, Lawyer for
                               Defendant Business-Aide, Inc.
                           Wanda Castillo, Paralegal for
                               Ms. Carter

Personal and Educational Background
Leslie Roberts was born and raised in St. Paul, Minnesota. Seven years ago, she graduated from Wheaton College, where she was an art history major. After college, she married Jim Donaldson, a graduate student in English at Harvard and lived in a house they jointly purchased. The mortgage for the house was held by the Cambridge Savings & Loan Association.

Ms. Roberts divorced Mr. Donaldson four years ago. She remained in their house in Cambridge and assumed full liability for the mortgage.

Work Experience

After graduating from Wheaton College, Ms. Roberts had a variety of odd jobs for three years. She did some painting and illustrating, but also worked as a waitress and short-order cook. She had no prior experience working with computers.

History of Scoops Ice Cream Business: Formation

Ms. Roberts enjoyed making ice cream and, based on her interest and urging of friends, decided to sell it commercially. After the divorce, two friends loaned her $5,000, at 5% interest, to help her lease a storefront and rent ice-cream-making equipment. Three years ago, she opened a small ice cream outlet called "Scoops."

History of Scoops Ice Cream Business: Accounting & Management Procedures and Problems

Initial accounting and management procedures were simple. Accounts, both revenue and expenses, were handled using a simple checking account. No accounting ledgers were kept. Ms. Roberts prepared tax returns herself, filing a Schedule C with her personal Form 1040. Income and expenses were reported on a cash basis.

Receipts were deposited daily. Credit sales were placed in a folder labeled "Sales." Credit sales were not logged on an accounting ledger. Bills were collected and placed in a folder labeled "To Be Paid" and paid by check on a monthly basis. Accounts receivable did not always match accounts payable. As a result, cash problems developed within a year of the beginning of the business.

Alternatives to In-House Deposition Summarizing

As noted above, summarizing a deposition is labor-intensive. As a rule of thumb, an experienced paralegal working at peak efficiency can summarize ten to fifteen pages of a complex transcript per hour. Therefore, a one-hundred-page deposition transcript might require eight to fifteen hours of paralegal time, depending on the skill of the paralegal.

When a case has a large number of depositions, using in-house paralegals to summarize the transcripts can create problems. For one thing, if paralegals spend most of their time summarizing, they will not be able to perform other critical tasks on a case. In addition, although paralegals are billed at lower rates than lawyers, the cost of using an in-house paralegal to summarize a typical one-hundred-page deposition transcript can be significant; and many clients balk at paying these added charges.

To minimize such problems, some firms hire temporary employees who work part- or full-time summarizing the depositions in a case. Sometimes referred to as "digesters" or "abstractors," these "temps" are typically trained by the in-house paralegal assigned to the case or by the firm's paralegal manager. Digesters are typically law clerks, paralegal students, freelance legal assistants, or graduate students from a local university.

The downside to using digesters is that they are not as familiar with the case as the paralegals working on it. For this reason, if you use digesters, be sure to implement a quality-control system to review their work product.

As an alternative to hiring temporary staff as digesters, some law offices use vendor digesting services.[4] These services advertise on the Internet, in state and local bar magazines, through local paralegal association newsletters, and in national paralegal magazines. In addition, many court reporting firms and litigation support firms offer deposition-summarizing services.

Here are some criteria to consider when deciding whether to use a digesting service:

1. How long has the service been in business?
2. Will the service provide a list of references? If so, what do the references report?
3. Whom does the service hire to digest? Are the digesters experienced paralegals? Are they familiar with the discovery process?
4. Does the service train its digesters?
5. Have samples of the service's work been provided?
6. Is the service's work product as readable, thorough, complete, and professional-looking as in-house work product?
7. Will the service summarize transcripts with the transcript management software program you prefer?
8. Does the service provide summaries in both hard copy and electronic format?

687

9. Does the service give a money-back guarantee or at least promise to redo an unsatisfactory summary?
10. What steps does the service take to protect confidential work product and avoid conflicts?
11. What kind of turnaround time does the service offer?
12. What is the extra cost for "expedited" service?

Managing Transcripts and Exhibits

In addition to summarizing deposition transcripts, paralegals can organize and keep track of voluminous transcripts and exhibits. They can also assist in preparing witness files, which can be very useful both during depositions and when preparing for trial. A typical witness file includes the following items:

- Notice of deposition;
- Transcript (certified copy, if necessary);
- Word index to the transcript, also known as a "concordance," provided by court-reporting firm (see Exhibit A at the end of the chapter);
- Condensed version of the transcript provided by court reporter (see Exhibit B at the end of the chapter);
- Summary of deposition;
- Correspondence concerning deposition logistics (for example, steps taken to track down a witness, attempts to set up convenient time for deposition, and so forth);
- If applicable, correspondence concerning corrections made to transcript by deponent;
- If applicable, video recording of the deposition; and
- Deposition exhibits or, if applicable, other media containing images of deposition exhibits.

When a deposition has numerous exhibits, say fifty or more, they should be indexed. For depositions with fifty to one hundred exhibits, a word processing or spreadsheet program is usually sufficient for creating the index. Once the number of exhibits exceeds one hundred, a database program, probably a litigation-support indexing software program, may be required. In many law offices, paralegals, not lawyers, design the database and code exhibits for it. Examples of industry standard litigation support software include Thomson West's Summation, LexisNexis's Concordance, and LexisNexis's CaseMap.

One advantage of a database is that exhibits can be sorted in different ways: by exhibit number, by deponent, by date, by volume number, by page and line number when first marked for identification, by lawyer examining the witness, by topic, by issue, or by virtually any database field (category) you need or want. When exhibits are sorted using a database, it takes only a few minutes to get an answer to a search request such as: "List all deponents who testified concerning exhibits 25, 62, 153, and 202, and list where the testimony on those exhibits begins."

Using Computers to Index and Search Depositions

Suppose you have a complex contracts case going to trial in a week. Fifty witnesses have been deposed, and all their depositions are summarized. Half of the witnesses testified about a disputed contract provision, and you now need their testimony located and summarized in a hurry.

With computer and litigation support software, hundreds—even thousands—of deposition pages can be searched in a relatively short time.

Using Litigation Support and Transcript Management Software to Manage Deposition Transcripts

Litigation support software is designed to help lawyers and paralegals manage litigation information, especially discovery documents, whether they have been produced in hard copy or electronic format. For deposition management, this software typically includes features such as realtime capabilities, sophisticated search engines, transcript database organization, and exhibit linking. LexisNexis's Concordance and CaseMap and Thomson West's Summation all include these features.

A subset of litigation support software, known as transcript management software, is designed to be used as a transcript tool. Thomson West's LiveNote and RealLegal and LexisNexis's Text-Map are good examples of this software.[5] They provide the features listed above, and some also provide streaming video and audio, online repository services, specialized reporting capabilities, issue tracking, and integration with litigation support software.

In many law offices, paralegals, generally in collaboration with litigation support staff and attorneys, play a major role in deciding which software program to use or buy; and, typically, it is a paralegal's job to manage the transcript software by arranging for a realtime feed at the deposition, uploading the transcripts and exhibits into the program when back at the office, and working closely with the law firm's information technology (IT) staff to ensure that the software will work properly on the firm's computer network. A paralegal may also train, either formally or informally, a firm's lawyers and other paralegals to use the litigation support software. Paralegals often work closely with court reporting firms that offer additional training and technical support.

Litigation support and transcript management software programs are very useful. But they can be expensive, and they can end up sitting in their shrink-wrap on a shelf if the law office is unwilling to provide support and training to use them effectively. Therefore, before purchasing this software, determine whether the new technology will improve an existing process or system and whether your law office can provide sufficient litigation and IT support services to properly install and manage the software.

Getting Started: Order Deposition Transcripts in Electronic Format

The starting point for using litigation support or transcript management software is having the deposition transcript in electronic format. Court reporters routinely provide deposition transcripts in electronic format as part of their deposition service. The standard format is ASCII,[6] a plain computer format recognized by a wide range of software programs. But while ASCII is commonly used, you need a particular ASCII format with page and line numbers hard-coded into the file. Your court reporter will handle this distinction for you. The advantage of the ASCII format is that it allows the computerized transcript to be used with a variety of transcript tools, from WordPad to more advanced word processing programs to sophisticated litigation support programs.

Many court reporters provide the electronic copy of the transcript in E-Transcript[7] format, which has greater functionality than an ASCII file; E-Transcript makes the file user-friendly because it is equipped with a viewer and search engine to open, browse, search, print, or e-mail the file. Court reporters often will provide E-Transcript at low cost or for free. An E-Transcript is compatible with other litigation support and transcript management software systems and includes a utility to convert the file to ASCII.

Using Word Processing Programs to Search and Manage Transcripts

A word processing program such as WordPad is handy to open, view, and print a transcript from an ASCII file. The program provides basic search capabilities as well. But using word processing programs to search transcripts yields limited benefits, particularly when it comes to searching transcripts or managing a group of transcripts. For example, when relying on a word processing program to conduct searches, the search command must be repeated for each key word searched. In addition, word processing programs are not equipped with robust search engines capable of creating a list of key words to be searched and then searching for them sequentially. Moreover, most word processing programs, unlike litigation support programs, are not designed to search using "wildcards." (An example of a wildcard is the search command "t*n," which will find *ton*, *tan*, and *tin*.)

When relying on word processing programs to search transcripts, each transcript must be searched separately for the desired key words. Although word processing programs can provide a list of documents where a key word is found, they cannot automatically provide a list of page and line numbers where the key word is located in several transcripts. And word processing programs may threaten document integrity. In the process of cutting and pasting pertinent text into a summary document, it is easy to rewrite the record or lose testimony.

Given all of these problems, as a practical matter word processing programs work well only for limited searches; that is, searches for a few key words (say five to ten) in a small number of transcripts (say two to three). For anything more, you need litigation support or transcript management software. Even if your law practice involves small cases (ten or fewer transcripts), transcript management software may be a wise investment if your cases are closely related to one another. With the software, for example, you can quickly compare expert witness testimony, whether given in the same or different cases, to see how an expert testified on similar issues.

Using Adobe Acrobat to Search and Manage Transcripts

Although Adobe Acrobat is not commonly considered a litigation support or transcript management tool, it can be useful. If the transcripts are provided by the court reporter in portable document format (PDF) or are converted by the paralegal into PDF format, Adobe Acrobat provides a robust search engine for searching key words in a single transcript or across an electronic folder containing multiple transcripts. However, when reporters provide a transcript in PDF, it is virtually impossible to do anything else with the transcript because you cannot remove the formatting and then import the file into any other program besides Adobe. Even if you can extract the text, the page and line numbers are lost.

Using "Generic" Full-Text Search Programs to Search and Manage Transcripts

A "generic" full-text software program refers to a search program that has potential for wide use in the law office but is not specifically designed for transcripts. An example of such a program is the well-known ISYS Search Software.[8] It indexes all the words in an electronically stored document or all of the documents in a folder, whether the document was created in a word processing program, spreadsheet, Adobe Acrobat PDF format, PowerPoint, or other software program. Its features include natural language (plain English) searching, categorization, and results-clustering of hits. You can attach text notes and link to documents, such as scanned deposition exhibits. Programs like ISYS are often used to index briefs, interrogatory responses, pleadings, and electronic discovery information. They are also popular for indexing a law firm's brief bank or as a search engine on a law office's intranet. In that regard, they are sometimes referred to as knowledge-management programs.

A generic full-text search program is superior to a word processing program when it comes to deposition transcript search technology. Full-text search programs like ISYS can simultaneously search several transcripts, can search for multiple key words and synonyms, can annotate the search results, and can track relevant "hits" in a separate file.

But generic full-text search programs have limitations when it comes to managing transcript information. To create a document summarizing your deposition search hits, you must go to each hit individually; highlight and copy the relevant material; and then paste it into a separate file. This can be time-consuming when many transcripts must be searched and summarized. On the other hand, a transcript management software program, as described above, does that automatically and is usually more effective. In addition, transcript management programs offer specific transcript-related features such as realtime capture, which allows for instantaneous access to, and display of, the testimony. As a result, many law offices support both a full-text search program for their brief banks along with a transcript management software program for their transcripts.

Using Transcript Management Software

Selecting the right litigation support or transcript management software is not difficult. Most of the programs are industry standards and have been successfully used by law offices for many years. In evaluating whether a particular program will work for your law office, you may need to consider several factors, including:

- What type of staffing and support will be required to successfully use the program?
- How easy is the program to use?
- What training or other "hotline" support is available from the software company?
- What is the single-user cost and the network (multiple-user) cost?
- What other uses can the software program provide to the law office?

Litigation support programs such as Concordance, CaseMap, and Summation provide transcript management features and are more robust than stand-alone transcript management programs. They also provide sophisticated document and electronic document management, are linked to imaging software, and are integrated with trial presentation software. But, because they are more robust, they are more complex to implement and manage.

Transcript management programs such as LiveNote, RealLegal, and TextMap are "transcript-centric." They provide sophisticated search engines that can search for words and phrases, can conduct searches across multiple transcripts, and can annotate transcripts. Both LiveNote and RealLegal are designed to be used in the courtroom during realtime transcription. They provide customizable transcript printed reports—from a simple listing of page and line numbers of all the "hits" in each deposition to a complex listing of each hit with verbatim text in question-and-answer format. In addition, the list of hits these programs produce can be organized and printed in deponent order, date order, or issue-code order.

They also integrate with the most popular litigation support programs, such as Concordance, CaseMap, and Summation.

Unlike generic full-text search programs such as ISYS, transcript management programs search for key words or phrases through multiple transcripts and can do so in sequential order across the collection of transcripts. When a global search through multiple transcripts is necessary, this feature can save tremendous amounts of time.

Best Practices at Depositions

Full-text searching can sometimes be frustrating—for example, when your search for a key word yields either no or too few hits. This problem often is not caused by the software or by the choice of search terms, but as a result of the richness of the English language, which enables the same word or concept to be described in multiple ways. Consider a deposition concerning an automobile accident. If you search only for the words "automobile accident," you may get no hits. In the deposition, the accident may have been referenced any number of ways, including "event," "incident," "crash," or "that unpleasant experience." One cure for this problem is to use a full-text program that searches synonyms, and many of the most commonly used transcript management software programs provide that feature. Even a full-text program search, however, is only as good as the synonyms already programmed into the software or added by the lawyer or paralegal.

Given the richness of the English language, the best practice is to determine and list key words before the deposition that can be used when searching for relevant testimony. Use these key words during the deposition when asking questions or clarifying a witness's answers. And, as you question the witness after the deposition, make a running list of the words you or the witness use when referring to a particular event or situation. Your list, developed before and during the deposition, can then be used to develop your search terms.

Inconsistencies in our speech patterns provide another obstacle to effective searches. One example: Instead of using the same term over and over, such as "plaintiff" or "defendant," a lawyer may alternate between this form of reference and a person's name. Later, a full-text search for the person's name will account for only a portion of the possible hits. Therefore, before the deposition, list the synonyms that you may use so that later you will be able to capitalize on the power of full-text search software.

Other Tools for Reviewing Transcripts

Key Word or Concordance Index

A "key word" or "concordance" index is an index of all the words in the deposition, in alphabetical order, with page and line references to where in the transcript they can be found, as well as the number of occurrences of each word.[9] Court reporters routinely provide such an index, generally without charge. Always order one from the court reporter unless your own deposition software includes a concordance-reporting feature that allows you to create your own index. Transcript management tools provide this index report in electronic version as well. The index can be a valuable tool for deciding which search terms to use.

Condensed Transcripts

Many court reporters provide a condensed transcript along with the traditional version. Using available software, the court reporter can condense a 150-page transcript into twenty or thirty pages. When printed on both sides, the condensed version takes up far less space, depending on how many columns of transcript you want per page and the size of the typeface. These printouts are almost universally provided in four-pages-on-a-page format, but they can be even more condensed.

There are several reasons for ordering and using a condensed transcript. First, because it is much smaller than the standard version, you can pack more transcripts into a binder or briefcase. Second, condensed transcripts can sometimes be easier to read because most of the "white space" of a standard twenty-five line, double-spaced transcript has been eliminated. Finally, it is easier to make notations in the margins of a condensed transcript because it can be formatted with a two-to-three-inch column for that purpose.[10]

Transcript management software programs such as LiveNote, RealLegal, and TextMap are able to produce condensed transcripts. Many judges prefer the condensed version over the traditional paper version because it reduces the number of pages they have to review and possibly store in their chambers. Nevertheless, before delivering any transcript to the judge's chambers, check with the court clerk on the judge's preferred style and format.

Hyperlinked Exhibits

Court reporters routinely offer to scan paper-based deposition exhibits and link them directly to the electronic version of the transcript. Both the transcripts and exhibits are copied to a disk or attached as an electronic file. "Clickable" hyperlinks are then created in the transcripts, so that you need only to click the hyperlink to view the referenced exhibit in the E-Transcript file provided by the court reporter. Court reporters may charge extra for this service; therefore, ask your reporter before the deposition what will be provided and at what cost. As an alternative, your paralegal can scan the exhibits back at the law office and, as discussed above, use transcript management software to link exhibits to the text. Because litigation support software tools such as Concordance, Summation, LiveNote, TextMap, and RealLegal are integrated with one another, exhibits linked in one program can also be linked to other support software.

Realtime Reporting[11]

Court reporters can also record depositions (and trials) in real time. The reporter's computer-assisted transcription machine is connected to a computer with software capable of instantaneously translating the stenographic notes into an ASCII file. Thus, as the reporter records the testimony, a transcript of the testimony is created simultaneously, visible on the computers of those attending the deposition.

A court reporter's first realtime transcript is often called a "dirty copy" (or "dirty ASCII") because it has not been cleaned up and proofread by the reporter. Nevertheless, given the recording skills of most reporters,[12] the number of misspelled and untranslatable words in a "dirty" transcript is usually so few that they do not prevent an effective key-word search with a full-text search program.

One obvious advantage of real-time reporting is that at the end of a day, you have a transcript of the day's testimony—though not a perfect one. That transcript makes it easier to prepare for the next deposition or the continuation of the current one. But remember, you will need a certified copy of the transcript if the deposition is to be offered in evidence, whether in support of a pretrial motion or at trial.[13]

A second advantage of realtime reporting is that by using a laptop computer and realtime software, such as LiveNote, you can have a copy of the realtime transcript appear on your laptop while you are examining the witness or defending her. (During the deposition, the testimony is typically displayed on the court reporter's computer monitor as well as those of the attorneys present.) Seeing the questions and the witness's answers can help you be more effective, whether as examiner or defender. Of course, you will need to learn to deal with the possible distractions associated with realtime transcripts. Fortunately, help is available: most court reporters will visit your office well before a deposition to demonstrate and train you in using realtime software.

Using realtime technology, you can mark text and make notes while the witness is speaking. Your marks and notes are confidential. They appear only on your laptop; neither the court reporter, the witness, nor opposing counsel has access to them. Back at your office, you can print out the entire transcript or just the marked and annotated testimony.

Realtime transcription is also available for Internet depositions where the court reporter provides realtime text over the Internet using software such as LiveNote. In these situations, the lawyer typically takes the deposition over the telephone while the court reporter sends the realtime feed via the Internet. Other remote listeners or observers (for example, co-counsel and experts) can be similarly connected.[14]

Two caveats: First, although realtime reporting has become popular for use at depositions and trials, some courtrooms are not equipped to handle it. Therefore, confirm with the court reporter and the court clerk that the necessary equipment is available. Second, when using realtime technology, expect to pay an additional charge for the service.

Video Synchronization

Video synchronization allows a court reporter to link video recorded testimony to the transcript.[15] The result is that the reporter—whether at a deposition or in the courtroom—can provide both an electronic transcript and a copy of the video deposition synchronized with the transcript.

Data from video synchronization can be imported into software programs such as Trial Director, Summation, and LiveNote. You can search for words and phrases in the transcript. When you have a "hit," the exact point in the video where the word or phrase has been spoken is automatically located. Using a split-screen display, you can view the video of the witness on one side of your computer monitor while the written transcript appears on the other side. During a multiday deposition or trial, replaying prior testimony in this manner can help refresh a witness's memory or impeach a witness with a prior inconsistent statement.

Video synchronization can be expensive, however. Court reporters typically charge an additional fee for each hour of video synchronized to the transcript. Charges increase if overnight turnaround is requested. And there will be a separate fee for the videographer who recorded the deposition.

Conclusion

Litigation paralegals are critical members of the litigation team. They often are instrumental in finding—at a moment's notice—a critical piece of information, testimony, discovery, or evidence. They must be computer literate and have the skill, aptitude, and knowledge to select, manage, and use litigation support technology tools, including transcript management software. For this reason, they play a vital role in managing transcript testimony so that it is accessible and usable to the litigators.

Notes

1. In this chapter, the term "paralegal" is used instead of "legal assistant." Many law firms use the terms interchangeably or use other terms such as "legal analyst." The American Bar Association's definition of paralegal/legal assistant is "a person qualified by education, training, or work experience who is employed or retained by a lawyer, law office, corporation, governmental agency, or other entity who performs specifically delegated substantive legal work for which a lawyer is responsible."

2. *See* C.B. GREENE, DEPOSITION MANUAL FOR PARALEGALS 215 (2d ed. 1994) (providing a detailed discussion of how to prepare deposition summaries.)

3. See "Reporting to the Client" in Chapter 23.

4. State bar associations in a number of jurisdictions have issued ethics opinions about outsourcing legal work. These opinions have concluded that outsourcing—whether to nonlawyers and lawyers outside the state jurisdiction of the hired attorney, or to nonlawyers and lawyers not within the country of the hired attorney—is acceptable and does not aid the unauthorized practice of law, as long as certain guidelines are followed. *See, e.g.,* NYCBA Formal Op. 2006-3 (stating "A lawyer may ethically outsource legal support services overseas to a non-lawyer if the lawyer (a) rigorously supervises the non-lawyer, so as to avoid aiding the non-lawyer in the unauthorized practice of law and to ensure that the non-lawyer's work contributes to the lawyer's competent representation of the client; (b) preserves the client's confidences and secrets when

outsourcing; (c) under the circumstances described in this Opinion, avoids conflicts of interests when outsourcing; (d) bills for outsourcing appropriately; and (e) under the circumstances described in this Opinion, obtains the client's informed advance consent to outsourcing.")

5.   In 2006, Thomson West acquired LiveNote along with the Real-Legal, LLC brand, and LexisNexis acquired CaseSoft's CaseMap and TextMap.

6.   ASCII stands for American Standard Code of Information Interchange.

7.   E-Transcript was developed by RealLegal, LLC.

8.   ISYS Software is a product of ISYS Search Software, a supplier of desktop, network, Web site, and intranet search solutions for business and government.

9.   See Exhibit A, at the end of the chapter, for a sample key word or concordance index.

10.   See Exhibit B, at the end of the chapter, for a sample condensed transcript with a column for marginal notes.

11.   See Chapter 18.

12.   Some added skills are needed to provide realtime transcription services, so care must be taken in selecting a qualified realtime reporter.

13.   See "Handling Documents at the End of the Deposition" in Chapter 23, discussing the need for a transcript at the end of the deposition.

14.   If your opponent objects to other persons being connected by computer, remember that under Federal Rule of Civil Procedure 30(c)(1), automatic witness exclusion under Federal Rule of Evidence 615 does not apply. A protective order under FRCP 26(c)(1)(e) must be sought for exclusion. See also "Task 11: Consider Whether You Need a Protective Order" in Chapter 4, discussing the need for a protective order permitting only certain persons to attend a deposition.

15.   See "A Video Recording Synchronized to the Transcript Can Be Used Throughout the Discovery Process" in Chapter 17.

Exhibit A
Sample Key Word or Concordance Index

Deponent: John Doe, date   Doe v. Smith

Exhibit B
Sample Condensed Transcript

Deponent: John Doe, date   Doe v. Smith   VOLUME I

Page 54	Page 56
1 Q. It is.	1 to a fiber per cubic centimeter, you're limited to a
2 A. Transit pipe facility which basically used	2 maximum exposure in a day of 30 minutes in that kind of
3 asbestos structural fibers in the material itself. And	3 environment.
4 there are -- it's known now that there are a great number	4 Q. Did you come to any other general conclusion
5 of people -- nobody ever monitored exposure levels. They	5 regarding the toxicology of asbestos when working at
6 just worked with asbestos. Nobody was paying any	6 Hanford?
7 attention to it. And there were a great many people that	7 A. No.
8 have been diagnosed with lung cancers and mesothelioma	8 Q. Have you since come to any other general
9 that were there.	9 conclusions regarding any other --
10 Since then the work that's gone on to try to	10 A. The problem is a chronic one rather than an acute
11 quantify what levels are hazardous are the things that	11 one. This is different than exposure to, let's say,
12 have produced the current existing exposure limit	12 acetone vapors, which is an acute problem.
13 standards. And it's on those things that my understanding	13 Q. You've described to me your work in December of
14 about the toxicology is based. Now --	14 last year, and you've described to me the testimony you
15 Q. Right. But --	15 gave at a hearing in Placerville.
16 A. Can a few brief exposures, if they were	16 A. No. Oh, okay. Yes. The testimony in December
17 continuous over years, yes, I think they could.	17 hearing in Placerville was different.
18 Q. I was trying to just get from you how you're	18 Q. Two different things. Other than those two
19 using those words.	19 cases, instances, bits of work, have you done -- and the
20 A. Chronic meaning continuous exposure every workday	20 Hanford, have you done other work regarding asbestos?
21 over a great many years. In principle, if NIOSH and OSHA	21 A. The Hanford work was never done in any legal
22 are correct and the concentration is less than a tenth of	22 context other than just supervisory oversight.
23 a fiber per cc's, which is a hundred thousand fibers per	23 Q. Right. I'm trying to get a sense of what your
24 cubic meter, if that concentration is at that level or	24 work on asbestos has been.
25 less, then you could be exposed to it eight hours a day	25 A. None. I think this report here will also make

Page 55	Page 57
1 every day of the year and suffer no long-term	1 some reference to asbestos because the Webber Creek Quarry
2 consequences.	2 had serpentine rock in it and was a potential source of
3 Q. Is that your understanding what the exposure	3 asbestos exposure.
4 limit is designed to mean?	4 MR. FUCHS: I'm handing you what will be marked
5 A. Yes. There are -- the standards for asbestos are	5 as Exhibit 6.
6 two. There's what's called the TWAS, time weighted	6 (Defendant's Exhibit 6 was marked for
7 average standard. That's the one that's the tenth of a	7 identification.)
8 fiber per cc, point one fibers per CC. And that's what's	8 BY MR. FUCHS:
9 called a PEL-TWA, permissible exposure limit dash TWA,	9 Q. I'll represent to you that I pulled this off the
10 time weighted average.	10 web when I Googled you as well. Does this look familiar
11 And that means you can be exposed to that	11 to you?
12 particular concentration eight hours a day on average,	12 A. Yes, very familiar.
13 eight hours a day for your whole lifetime and never have	13 Q. Good. So I didn't make this one up either.
14 any adverse effects.	14 A. Nope. It's -- 15 talks about the work that I did
15 They also have a STEL, which is a short-term	15 with Freda.
16 exposure limit. That's a PEL-STEL, and that's a 30-minute	16 Q. Before we start talking about this specifically,
17 exposure at which the average is one fiber per cubic	17 this is a document with your name at the top, again with
18 centimeter or a million fibers per cubic meter.	18 Ted in quotes, and it's called, I guess, Forensic
19 If you're in an extremely dusty area where the	19 Analytical Work For Attorneys, right?
20 concentration gets up to a fiber per cubic centimeter,	20 A. Yes.
21 then you have to limit the exposure to such a person -- if	21 Q. Good. Okay. Did you prepare this document at
22 you're wearing protection, respiratory protection, none of	22 some point?
23 these things count because you're breathing them anyway,	23 A. Yes, I did.
24 the respirator is stopping it.	24 Q. Good. And did you post it to the web or did
25 If you're unprotected and the concentration gets	25 somebody get a hold of it or what?

CHAPTER 25

Using Depositions at Trial

DONALD W. CARLSON
ROBERT M. PETERSON

This book started with the premise that because over 98 percent of all civil cases filed in federal courts resolve by way of settlement or pretrial adjudication, depositions, not trials, are at the heart of dispute resolution.[1] But you need to be prepared to try each case. And to be prepared, you must understand the uses of deposition testimony at trial.

Although there are many ways to use deposition testimony at trial, this chapter will focus on the five most typical uses: (1) as a substitute for a witness's in-court testimony; (2) to impeach a hostile witness's in-court testimony with prior inconsistent deposition testimony; (3) to rehabilitate a witness's testimony by the introduction of prior consistent deposition testimony; (4) to refresh a witness's recollection; and (5) to establish a past recollection recorded when the trial witness's memory cannot be refreshed.

This chapter discusses the legal requirements governing the admissibility of deposition testimony under the Federal Rules of Civil Procedure (FRCP) and the Federal Rules of Evidence (FRE), along with strategic considerations.

Depositions as Substitute Testimony

All trial lawyers prefer to present their cases through the live testimony of witnesses at trials.[2] The dry reading of lengthy deposition testimony seldom holds the jury's interest and lacks the dramatic flair necessary to make a lasting impression. And, for better or worse, when deposition testimony is read at trial, the jury cannot evaluate the witness's demeanor to determine credibility.

Certain situations, however, such as death, illness, mental infirmity, or unavailability, make live testimony impossible. In the limited circumstances discussed below, trial counsel may decide for tactical reasons to present testimony by reading deposition testimony rather than by putting a live witness on the stand. Accordingly, as trial counsel, you need a firm understanding of the legal requirements for the admissibility of deposition testimony as a substitute for live testimony.

General Legal Requirements

The use of deposition testimony as evidence in federal civil trials is governed by FRCP 32 and by FRE 801 through FRE 804. Both the FRCP and the FRE distinguish between the use of deposition testimony of an adverse party, which can be used for any purpose, and the use of deposition testimony of a witness who is not an adverse party, which can be used only when the witness is unavailable. These distinctions are discussed below.

Adverse Party's Deposition

Under FRCP 32(a)(3), a party's deposition (or the deposition of the party's director, officer, managing agent, or designee under FRCP 30(b)(6) or 31(a)(4)), may be used by an adverse party for any purpose. The rule permits a party to introduce the deposition of an adversary as part of its substantive proof, regardless of the adversary's availability to testify at trial.[3] FRE 801(d)(2) provides parallel authority for introducing an adverse party's deposition testimony as direct, adoptive, or authorized admissions.[4]

Because FRCP 32(a)(3) allows an opposing party's deposition to be used for any purpose, it is not necessary to establish the witness's "unavailability." In fact, the adverse party may even be present in the courtroom when his deposition testimony is read. Therefore, although most trial lawyers prefer to confront an adverse party during live cross-examination with his deposition testimony, a trial lawyer may instead choose to read portions of the adverse party's deposition during the presentation of her client's case.

For example, if the opposing party has given a particularly damaging or inflammatory answer during his deposition, the trial lawyer should consider reading (or showing a video) of that portion of the deposition testimony even though the adverse party witness is not on the stand. This tactic prevents the adverse witness from immediately explaining away the testimony. If the adverse witness later takes the stand to explain his deposition testimony—either in his case-in-chief or in rebuttal—he not only highlights the testimony but also presents opposing counsel with another opportunity to cross-examine.

Nonparty's Deposition

Deposition testimony is more commonly used as substitute testimony for nonparties. FRCP 32(a)(4) permits a party to introduce *any* witness's deposition for any purpose upon demonstrating that (1) the witness is absent and over one hundred miles from the place of hearing or trial; or (2) the witness is unable to testify due to age, illness, infirmity, death, or imprisonment; or (3) the party offering the deposition has been unable to procure the witness's attendance by subpoena; or (4) exceptional circumstances justify introduction of the witness's deposition.

Witness Unavailable Under FRCP 32(a)(4)(A)–(D)

The "unavailability" requirements of FRCP subparagraphs 32(a)(4)(A)–(D) for using a witness's deposition overlap many of the grounds under which a witness is deemed unavailable under FRE 804 (Hearsay Exceptions; Declarant Unavailable).[5] But in one way, FRCP 32(a)(4) provides broader grounds for the admission of deposition testimony than those specified in FRE 804.

Subparagraph B of FRCP 32(a)(4) permits the introduction of deposition testimony upon demonstration that the witness is over one hundred miles from the place of trial or outside the United States, as long as the court determines that the witness's absence was not procured by the proponent of the testimony. By contrast, under FRE 804(a), a witness's deposition testimony is admissible only if the witness is deemed "unavailable." Apart from illness, infirmity, death, imprisonment, or extraordinary circumstances, FRE 804(a)(5) provides that a witness will be considered unavailable only if the proponent can show that his presence at trial cannot be secured by process or other reasonable means. Because a subpoena may be effectively served anywhere within the state in which a federal district court sits or within one hundred miles of the place of trial, the fact that the witness is one hundred miles or more from the place of trial does not necessarily mean that the witness cannot be subpoenaed and therefore is unavailable under FRE 804(a)(5).[6] For example, a witness in Los Angeles is more than one hundred miles from the Northern District of California's federal court in San Francisco, but is certainly subject to subpoena within California.

FRCP 32(a)(4)(B)'s relatively less stringent requirements for admissibility are highlighted in *Daigle v. Maine Medical Center*.[7] In *Daigle,* the appellant contended that the FRCP requires an evidentiary showing of unavailability as a predicate to the introduction of a witness's deposition. The appellant also asserted that a witness, though more than one hundred miles from the place of trial, is not unavailable if, with reasonable efforts, he might be persuaded to attend trial.[8]

The Court of Appeals for the First Circuit rejected both contentions. The court held that the FRCP does not require that the witness be "unavailable" within the meaning of the FRE before his deposition can be used at trial. Rather, "[d]istance is the decisive criterion: so long as a witness is shown to be more than one hundred miles from the place of trial, the admissibility of deposition testimony under the aegis of [the Rule] is not contingent upon a showing that the witness is otherwise unavailable."[9]

Establishing the Foundation for Admissibility Under FRCP 32(a)(4)(A)–(D)

The decision to admit a deposition as substitute testimony generally rests in the sound discretion of the trial court.[10] Because a witness's absence at trial is not enough to warrant admission of deposition testimony, the prudent lawyer will marshal all necessary witnesses and documentary evidence to meet FRCP 32(a)'s prerequisites for the introduction of deposition testimony. When you are the offering party, be prepared to introduce a death certificate if the witness is dead, or an affidavit from an infirm witness's treating physician, or evidence that the witness's place of residence is more than one hundred miles from the trial, or an affidavit of a process server who diligently, but unsuccessfully, attempted to serve the witness with a subpoena.

The Need to Explain a Witness's Absence

The need for an explanation is illustrated in *Moore v. Mississippi Valley State University*.[11] In *Moore*, the trial court refused to admit the deposition testimony of a Mr. Lewis, a critical witness in a civil rights action. Though Lewis was listed on the pretrial order as a witness for the appellants, he failed to appear at trial. Because the proponent failed to explain the reason for the witness's absence, the appellate court affirmed the trial court's exclusion of Lewis's deposition testimony.[12]

After reviewing the grounds for the admissibility of Lewis' deposition testimony under both FRCP 32 and FRE 804, the *Moore* court explained that

> [t]he trial court cannot act spontaneously [to admit deposition testimony] in these circumstances. Rather, it must be given a reason that conforms to Rules 804(a)(5) and [32(a)(4)] to allow in the deposition. The burden is on the offering party to supply such justification. In this case, Moore offered nothing except the plain assertion that Lewis was unavailable. Moore made no effort to explain the reason for Lewis' unavailability or offer some explanation to the trial court and thus failed to meet her burden.[13]

The availability of a deponent depends upon the conditions as they exist at the time the deposition is offered.[14] A letter by the witness to the court or to a lawyer concerning the witness's location has been found sufficient to establish his presence over one hundred miles from court at the time of the trial.[15] The testimony of a live witness with personal knowledge of the location of the deponent can also establish the witness's location. The witness's unavailability may even be established by the witness's own deposition testimony.[16]

Similarly, a witness's inability to attend due to age, illness, infirmity, or imprisonment can be established by an affidavit of the witness, his treating physician, or both. A certified certificate of death or the testimony of a witness with personal knowledge of the deponent's death should be sufficient to establish that the witness is dead and obviously unavailable.

Exceptional Circumstances

When a trial lawyer cannot show unavailability under FRCP 32(a)(4)(A)–(D), it still may be possible to use a deposition as substitute testimony. FRCP 32(a)(4)(E) permits the admission of deposition testimony at trial upon notice to the opposing party, if the proponent establishes that exceptional circumstances compel the introduction of such testimony.

Courts have found the following situations to be "exceptional circumstances" meriting the admission of deposition testimony: (1) an expert witness's in-court testimony would have resulted in an inordinate expense;[17] (2) a doctor serving as an expert witness had such a busy schedule that his video recorded deposition was taken in anticipation of offer at trial;[18] and (3) an expert's in-court testimony would have confused the jury.[19]

Practical Considerations and Tactics in the Introduction of Deposition Testimony at Trial

Notice and Objections

For deposition testimony to be admissible at trial, FRCP 32(a)(1) requires that it be "admissible under the Federal Rules of Evidence" applied as "if the deponent were present and testifying." But objections that might be obviated, removed, or cured if promptly presented—such as objections to the form of questions—are waived unless made during the deposition.[20] In contrast, objections to the competency, relevancy, or materiality of testimony are not waived by failure to assert them at the deposition unless the ground for the objection could have been cured at the deposition.[21]

Given the provisions of FRCP 32(a), a deposition taker who wants to preserve testimony for trial must carefully consider each objection and attempt to cure well-founded objections by rephrasing questions until the witness testifies without an objection.[22] Similarly, lawyers who are adverse to the party taking the deposition must be attentive and prepared to assert succinct, specific objections to deposition questions. This is particularly true of party-deponents, whose depositions may be used at trial for any purpose. For example, on cross-examination of an adverse party at trial, an objection to the cross-examiner's question might be sustained by the trial judge. If, however, the cross-examiner asked the same party the same question at the deposition and no objection was made, the cross-examiner may then simply read the deposition question and answer at trial.

Most federal pretrial orders require precise identification of deposition testimony to be offered in the case-in-chief.[23] In the absence of pretrial identification of deposition testimony, you should advise the court and opposing counsel, outside the presence of the jury, of the deposition testimony that you wish to offer. This testimony should be identified by page and line number. After the proffered testimony has been identified, opposing counsel can then review it to determine whether to renew any objections made during the deposition and ask for a ruling on those objections. At that time, opposing counsel may also assert those objections reserved for trial, such as hearsay and relevance. Whenever possible, objections to deposition testimony being offered at trial should be stated succinctly in writing and filed with the court. Objections to the admissibility of deposition testimony are then resolved by the judge in a hearing outside the presence of the jury.

When to Introduce Deposition Testimony at Trial

Ideally, trial counsel will consider the introduction of deposition testimony at trial as carefully as she considers the strategic decision of when to call a particular live witness. But that is not always possible. Trial counsel sometimes must use deposition testimony to fill in gaps created by other live witnesses' schedules or incorrect time estimates. Thus, regardless of pretrial requirements, you should have any deposition testimony that you may want to offer completely prepared for presentation to the fact finder before the trial begins.

There are no strict guidelines on when to use deposition testimony. However, trial counsel should consider the duration of the testimony and whether it will produce any dramatic impact. For example, you would not want to conclude trial on Friday evening with key deposition testimony needed to establish a foundational predicate. You also should analyze whether the deposition testimony is necessary to establish the admissibility of live testimony or documents or whether the testimony will be relied upon by expert witnesses. If so, you will want to read the necessary deposition testimony before the live testimony for which it is the foundational predicate.

How to Present Deposition Testimony as Substitute Testimony

Before the deposition testimony is read to the jury, you should educate the jury about the nature and legal consequences of deposition testimony and the reasons why it will be read in lieu of live testimony.[24] For example, when you know before trial that deposition testimony will be used as substitute testimony, you should mention that in your opening statement. In addition, immediately before the first reading of deposition testimony, ask the trial judge to preinstruct the jury by explaining the nature of a deposition, the fact that deposition testimony is given under oath, and the fact that deposition testimony deserves no greater or lesser weight than any other form of evidence.

If you intend to play deposition testimony recorded on video, ask the trial judge to preinstruct the jury that the questions and answers shown on video were the same questions asked and answers given at the deposition. With the advent of digital photography and computer-enhanced imagery, many jurors now question whether photographs and video recordings have been edited and truthfully represent the image depicted.[25] Therefore, ask the judge to tell the jury that what they will see is exactly what took place at the deposition.

Typically, stenographic deposition evidence is presented by trial counsel reading the transcribed questions with an associate, staff member, or other reader sitting in the witness chair reading the transcribed responses of the deponent. But give some thought to selecting the person playing the role of the witness. If possible, the sex and age of the deponent and the "reader/witness" should match. If you must assume both roles in reading deposition testimony, be sure to distinguish the interrogator's questions from the deponent's answers so the jury will not be confused.

Trial judges vary on how much voice inflection or histrionics they will tolerate from the reader/witness. If the judge allows latitude, favorable testimony obviously should be read by a "witness" who appears honest, open, and appealing; in contrast, testimony from adverse witnesses might be read by individuals whom the jury will remember for their furtive glances and insincere veneer. But be careful not to risk a sustained objection from opposing counsel or, even worse, a stern warning from the court for an overly dramatic or otherwise misleading reading of deposition testimony.

Lengthy deposition testimony—whether read or recorded on video—can be tedious for the trier of fact. Edit the deposition carefully and, when possible, try to enliven the reading of deposition testimony by using enlargements or transparencies of exhibits referenced in the deposition.

Tactics

When a deponent is truly "unavailable" under either FRCP 32 or FRE 804, trial counsel *must* use the deposition to get the witness's testimony before the trier of fact. But in some limited circumstances—such as when the witness lives over one hundred miles from the place of trial but is still within the subpoena power of the court, or when a friendly witness lives beyond the subpoena power of the court but would come to trial if asked—a trial lawyer can make tactical decisions to present the testimony either through the deposition transcript or by the live witness.

The rule of thumb is that a live witness is preferable. But sometimes that is not the case. For example, some honest, decent people make terrible impressions on a jury for one reason or another. Suppose you have a friendly witness who would not present well at trial and resides beyond the subpoena power of the court. Even when that friendly witness is willing to appear voluntarily at trial, the advantage of live testimony may be outweighed by the disadvantage of that witness's physical appearance or demeanor. If the deposition transcript of the witness reads well, you may want to have a more presentable, appealing person read the deposition testimony at trial rather than have the actual witness testify in person.

You also may want to use deposition testimony in lieu of live testimony when a friendly witness who gave useful testimony at the deposition may be vulnerable to a damaging, well-planned cross-examination at trial. This is particularly true when the friendly witness resides outside the subpoena power of the court and therefore cannot be called to trial by opposing counsel.

Another occasion on which reading deposition testimony may be tactically advantageous is when a hostile witness, who resides more than one hundred miles from court, has given useful testimony at deposition and you anticipate that the witness may be prepared to qualify that testimony at trial. Even though that witness, if residing within the state, can be subpoenaed, you may want to read the deposition testimony. Of course, opposing counsel can later call the witness to explain his deposition testimony, but that explanation may not be as effective as it would be if given under live cross-examination.

The Rule of Completeness

Trial counsel usually wants to introduce only selected portions of a deposition transcript; rarely will a witness's entire testimony be helpful to one side or another. But FRCP 32(a)(6) provides that if only part of a deposition is offered in evidence by a party, an adverse party may require the offeror to introduce any other part that in fairness ought to be considered. FRE 106 has a similar provision. Moreover, fairness dictates that opposing counsel should be able to introduce other portions of the deposition that qualify, or provide context for, the proffered testimony. It has been held to be error not to permit the opposing party to read other relevant parts of the deposition, at least at the conclusion of the initial reading of the deposition testimony.[26]

If opposing counsel designates portions of the transcript that he intends to read into evidence during "cross-examination," the lawyer offering the testimony must first decide whether the counterdesignations are sufficiently damaging to render the deposition testimony she planned to offer neutral, confusing, or harmful. If so, the proponent may elect to withdraw the deposition testimony altogether. If the proponent nevertheless elects to proceed with introducing deposition testimony, she almost always should introduce those portions counterdesignated by opposing counsel during the "direct examination" of the reader/witness. If the proponent reads only a portion of the deposition and then permits opposing counsel to read relevant portions on cross-examination, the proponent will appear unfair for failing to provide the complete picture and the deponent's direct examination may be less credible. On the other hand, because counsel and the reader of a deposition on direct examination control the tempo and inflection of the reading, introducing damaging or unfavorable portions of the deposition during direct should reduce the negative impact on the jury. In addition, the deponent's testimony may impact the proffering party more favorably when there is no cross-examination.

Using Depositions to Contradict or Impeach the Trial Testimony of a Witness

Deposition testimony can provide extremely damaging ammunition for cross-examination. There is no better way to impeach a witness than with his own words given under oath at his deposition. Unlike the use of depositions as substitute testimony, where the evidentiary rules are complex and the presentation relatively straightforward, the evidentiary rules for using deposition testimony to impeach are simple and the presentation is complex. Different trial lawyers use different approaches with different degrees of effectiveness.

Legal Requirements

FRCP 32(a)(2) allows trial counsel to impeach a witness's trial testimony with an inconsistent statement made during deposition. And any trial witness, not just an adverse party, may be impeached with inconsistent deposition testimony. Under FRE 801(d)(1)(A), prior inconsistent statements in a deposition are not hearsay and may be considered by the trier of fact as substantive evidence.

To be admissible, prior inconsistent statements need not be diametrically opposed to the witness's trial testimony. All that is required is that the relevant deposition testimony, taken as a whole, differs from the witness's in-court testimony, either by what was said or what was not said.[27]

Tactics and Illustrations of Impeachment by Deposition Testimony

Although there are many ways to impeach a witness with a deposition transcript, all methods generally include three fundamentals.[28] First, the trial witness must be pinned to a particular statement so that the prior inconsistency is readily apparent to the fact finder. Second, in jury trials, the trial lawyer's cross-examination must inform the jury about the circumstances surrounding the deposition testimony, including the fact that the deposition testimony was under oath. Finally, the trial lawyer must confront the witness with the inconsistent deposition testimony and convey that inconsistency to the fact finder. Each fundamental is discussed and illustrated below.

Pinning Down Trial Testimony

To impeach a witness effectively with deposition testimony, it is essential to pin the witness to a particular statement that is clearly inconsistent with his trial testimony. If the inconsistency is unequivocal—for example, testimony on direct examination at trial that the light was green versus deposition testimony that the light was red—there is little more to do than have the witness state the inconsistency on the stand; that is, "the light was green."

713

But when the inconsistency is not obvious, the trial lawyer must shape the testimony to bring out the inconsistency; otherwise it may be lost on the jury or, worse yet, not appear inconsistent at all. For example, assume that on direct examination a witness testifies that the car was moving "a little too fast," but in his deposition testified that the car was traveling fifty miles per hour in a twenty-five-mile-per-hour zone. To effectively impeach this witness, you would need to set up the inconsistency as follows:

Q. On direct examination you testified that the car was traveling "a little too fast."

A. Yes, I did.

Q. By "a little too fast," did you mean "a little" above the speed limit?

A. Yes.

Q. And the speed limit is twenty-five miles per hour, isn't it?

A. Yes.

Q. You would not consider driving fifty miles per hour in a twenty-five-mile-per-hour zone as going only "a little too fast," would you?

A. No. I would not.

Q. In fact, wouldn't you say that driving fifty miles per hour in a twenty-five-mile-per-hour zone is very fast?

A. Yes.

After this exchange, the witness is ready to be impeached with his deposition testimony that the car was traveling fifty miles per hour. If the lawyer did not first pin down the inconsistent deposition statement, the witness might successfully explain that there was no inconsistency because "a little too fast" and "fifty miles per hour" were synonymous. The trial lawyer's goal is to make the witness's trial testimony as directly contrary to the prior deposition testimony as possible in order to prevent the witness from circumventing the impeachment with a plausible explanation.

Foundational Questions

At some point during an impeachment with prior inconsistent deposition testimony, most trial lawyers ask foundational questions about the time, place, and circumstances of the deposition. The purpose is to educate the jury about the formality of the deposition process and the significance of sworn deposition testimony. Some lawyers prefer not to interrupt the flow of cross-examination; instead, they first impeach the witness and then ask questions about the circumstances of the deposition. Other lawyers believe that jurors give more weight to the impeachment if they are first made aware of the circumstances surrounding the deposition; these lawyers use foundational questions at the outset to add drama and suspense to the ensuing confrontation.

Regardless of which approach is used, the foundational questions should be asked only once of each witness. Thus, trial lawyers should consider deferring the more dramatic inconsistencies until after the jury learns about the deposition process, when the foundational questions need not be repeated.

An effective way to educate the jury about the deposition process is to ask a series of questions concerning the deposition, which the witness must answer affirmatively:[29]

Q. Sir, was your deposition taken in this case on June 18, one year ago, at my office?
A. Yes.
Q. Were you represented by counsel at that deposition?
A. Yes.
Q. Was your testimony given under oath at that deposition?
A. Yes.
Q. Was it the same oath that you took here at trial?
A. Yes.
Q. And did I advise you that any inconsistency between your deposition testimony and your testimony at trial could be brought to the attention of the jury?
A. I believe you did, yes.

If the witness made corrections in his deposition transcript or signed it, the lawyer might continue as follows:

Q. Did you later read the transcript testimony?
A. Yes.
Q. Did you make any corrections in your testimony?
A. Yes.
Q. Did you sign your deposition transcript?
A. Yes.
Q. And you signed your deposition after reviewing it because your answers were true and correct?
A. Yes.

These or similar foundational questions are asked in order to demonstrate to the jury the formality and fairness of the deposition process.

Confronting the Witness with the Inconsistency

After the witness has been pinned to the inconsistency, counsel must confront the witness with the inconsistency. There are at least three ways to confront a witness with deposition testimony.

Under the first method, a lawyer confronts the witness with an inconsistent deposition statement by first showing the witness the transcript and then reading from it. For example:

> CROSS-EXAMINER: I now show you the original transcript of your deposition. [If signed, ask if it is the witness's signature.] Will you now please read to yourself lines 6 through 9 on page 12? [Hand the deposition transcript to witness.]
>
> Q. Were you asked, "How fast was the car traveling?"
> A. Yes.
> Q. And did you answer, "Fifty miles per hour"?
> A. Yes.

Showing the witness a transcript first gives the appearance of fairness, but it also gives the witness additional time to collect his thoughts and prepare an explanation. Some witnesses will even try to look at additional pages of the transcript in an effort to place the impeaching testimony in context. Thus, most trial lawyers do not like this method because it is cumbersome and gives too much control to the witness.

Under prior law, trial counsel was required to show or tell the witness about a prior inconsistent statement before impeaching him.[30] FRE 613(a) changed the long-standing rule and provides that trial counsel is no longer required to show or tell the witness about the inconsistent statement before impeaching him with it, although counsel is required "on request" to show or disclose the statement to opposing counsel.

Because of this change in the law, many lawyers now prefer the second impeachment method: reading directly from the transcript after the witness has been pinned to the inconsistent statement. By reading the deposition questions and answers, trial counsel streamlines the examination and, equally important, controls the tempo and inflection of the reading.

Under the third method of impeachment, after pinning down the inconsistent statement, trial counsel simply asks the witness either whether he testified differently under oath before trial or whether he testified to the prior inconsistent testimony. There are only three answers to these questions: "Yes;" "I do not recall;" or "No." Regardless of the answer, trial counsel can read the inconsistent testimony from the transcript.

The advantage of this third approach is that trial counsel has complete control of the impeachment. When trial counsel, armed with the deposition transcript in full view of the jury, asks a witness whether he has testified differently under oath, the jury will recognize immediately that the deposition testimony is inconsistent with the trial testimony. This third approach may even lead to a "double impeachment." If the witness answers "no," the trial lawyer impeaches not only the substantive statement but also the witness's denial that he ever said it. For example, the cross-examiner might confront the witness with inconsistent deposition testimony as follows:

Q. You stated under oath before this trial that the car was going fifty miles per hour; is that correct?

A. No, I did not.

CROSS-EXAMINER: I now read to you from the transcript of your testimony in our deposition at page 12, lines 6 through 9. Question: "How fast was the car going?" Answer: "Fifty miles per hour."

Q. That was your testimony at your deposition. Is that correct?

A. Yes, it was.

The witness may try to explain his answer by testifying that he did not give the recorded answer or that his answer was inaccurately reported. One way to counter such a response is to establish that the witness signed or corrected the deposition transcript. However, if the deposition was not corrected or signed, or if the witness contends either that he overlooked that particular response when signing the deposition or that the deposition testimony was inaccurately reported, it may be necessary to call the deposition reporter as a witness to testify to the accuracy of the transcript.[31]

Finally, after confronting the witness with the inconsistent deposition testimony, the trial lawyer must decide whether to ask the witness why he has changed his testimony. As with most trial strategy, there are no rigid guidelines that will ensure the correct result. Still, the following rule of thumb can be helpful: Generally, avoid the "why" question because you cannot possibly know if the witness will have a plausible explanation for the inconsistency. But if you are confident the inconsistency cannot convincingly be explained, the "why" question will present the witness with yet another opportunity to appear dishonest before the jury.

Using Depositions to Rehabilitate a Trial Witness

By Showing Prior Consistent Statement

Under FRE 801(d)(1), deposition testimony of a witness—whether or not a party to the action—can be used to rehabilitate the witness's testimony if (1) evidence of a prior inconsistent statement outside the courtroom is admitted to attack his credibility (for example, during cross-examination), (2) a prior consistent statement in the witness's deposition was made *before* the alleged inconsistent statement, and (3) the deposition testimony is offered to rebut an express or implied charge of a recent fabrication or improper influence or motive. The prior consistent statement must have been made before the motive to fabricate arose.[32]

Counsel might attempt to rehabilitate a witness during redirect examination in the following manner:

Q. Sir, when I was questioning you earlier, did you testify that the car was going fifty miles per hour?

A. Yes.

Q. And then when opposing counsel was cross-examining you, you said that about two years ago, you told an investigator that you were not sure how fast the car was going; is that correct?

A. Yes.

Q. Sir, do you recall coming to my office and having your deposition taken?

A. Yes.

Q. Did you make your statement to the investigator before or after you had given that deposition testimony?

A. After.

Q. About how long after?

A. Several months.

Q. Did you receive a letter from Plaintiff's counsel threatening to sue you as the owner of the car?

A. Yes.

Q. Did you receive that letter before or after you gave your deposition?

A. After.

EXAMINER: Your Honor, at this time I would like the witness to read lines 6 through 9 on page 12 of the transcript of his deposition that was taken on February 3, one year ago.

WITNESS: [Reading from deposition] Question: "How fast was the car going?" Answer: "Fifty miles per hour."

Q. Was that your testimony at that time?

A. Yes, it was.

Q. Sir, can you tell the jury why you said something different to the investigator when you spoke with him?

A. [Witness states reasons.]

The last question in this dialogue should be asked only by a lawyer who is confident that the witness's answer would enhance his credibility.

By Additional Deposition Testimony

As discussed above, the "rule of completeness," as codified in FRCP 32(a)(6) and FRE 106, provides that if only part of a deposition is offered in evidence by a party, an adverse party may require the offeror to introduce any other part that in fairness ought to be considered. The rule of completeness applies when deposition testimony is used as substitute testimony due to the witness's unavailability. The rule also applies when a witness is impeached with deposition testimony at trial. In other words, when a witness is impeached at trial on cross-examination with a prior inconsistent statement in his deposition, the lawyer calling the witness may then read other portions of the deposition in an effort to rehabilitate the witness. Although the rule of completeness applies whenever deposition testimony is read, strategic considerations are different when the deponent is present at trial than when the deponent is unavailable.

Many judges prefer that the rehabilitating testimony be read after cross-examination has been concluded and during redirect examination. But when the cross-examiner has impeached the witness by reading a portion of her deposition taken out of context, the effectiveness of the rehabilitating testimony on the jury may be lost if the reading is delayed too long. In this situation, the lawyer who called the witness usually should object and request that he be permitted to read the rehabilitating testimony immediately following the impeachment so the jury is not misled. For example:

Q. You testified on direct examination that you had a series of meetings with my client in March, two years ago, relating to the contract in issue in this suit; is that correct?

A. Yes, that is correct.

Q. You testified in your deposition that you never even met my client until June, two years ago, two months after the alleged meetings about the contract. Is that correct?

A. I don't remember that, sir.

Q. I refer you to page 32, line 16, of your deposition, where you make the statement that you first met my client in June, two years ago. That was your testimony; is that correct?

OPPOSING COUNSEL: Objection, your Honor. If counsel will refer to line 2 of the following page, he will see that Ms. Smith corrected her testimony and said that she first met counsel's client in June, three years ago, instead of June, two years ago.

CROSS-EXAMINER: Your Honor, opposing counsel will have the opportunity to rehabilitate his witness when my cross-examination has been completed.

OPPOSING COUNSEL: Your Honor, by that time the rehabilitation will be too late to be effective and the jury may be misled. In fairness to Ms. Smith, counsel should read to the jury the deposition testimony on the following page, where Ms. Smith corrected her answer.

THE COURT: Counsel, I believe that in fairness to the witness, you should read the testimony on the following page.

Of course, when a witness's deposition contains impeaching testimony and does not contain any rehabilitating testimony on the same issue, the witness should be prepared, if possible, to explain in a forthright manner why the deposition and trial testimony are inconsistent.

Using Depositions to Refresh Recollection

Everybody in the world forgets. Some people forget because of time; others forget because they have poor memories in the first place. Some of the best-prepared witnesses forget important facts simply because their sheer terror on the witness stand results in mental paralysis. Every trial lawyer has experienced a witness who simply draws a blank, no matter how skillfully the lawyer attempts to conjure an accurate recollection by asking provocative questions. Fortunately, FRE 612 permits a witness to use a writing, including a deposition, to refresh recollection. If, instead of drawing a complete blank, the witness "forgets" by testifying incorrectly, FRE 607 permits trial counsel to impeach her own witness.

The memory of any witness—whether or not a party to the action—can be refreshed while he is on the stand. To use a deposition to refresh a witness's recollection in court, counsel must first show that the witness has no recollection of the subject of the inquiry. Suppose a witness who is asked on direct examination, "What color was the car?" answers, "I don't remember." The witness can then be asked to read to himself a specified portion of his deposition testimony and then answer the question. Counsel might proceed as follows:

Q. Do you remember going with me to opposing counsel's office on September 16, two years ago, and giving a deposition under oath?

A. Yes.

Q. Were the details of the accident fresher in your mind then than they are now?

A. Yes.

EXAMINER: Your Honor, with your permission, I would like to show the witness the transcript of the deposition that he gave on September 16, two years ago.

THE COURT: Go ahead.

Q. Sir, please read to yourself lines 4 through 11 on page 27 of your deposition transcript. [Witness reads to himself.] Now, does that refresh your memory about the color of the car that hit you?

A. Yes.

Q. What color was it?

A. Red.

A more difficult problem is presented when a favorable witness testifies at trial inconsistently with his deposition testimony. Trial counsel may elect to impeach her own witness by using his deposition to establish a prior inconsistent statement. But doing so may highlight the impeaching material and possibly destroy any ability to rehabilitate the witness effectively. In this situation, the best strategy may be to ask for a recess before direct examination has been concluded. During the recess, you can use the deposition transcript to refresh the witness's memory. The witness then can return to the stand, retract the erroneous testimony, and explain why it was originally given.

Using Depositions as Past Recorded Recollection

Before trial, review how to use depositions as past recorded recollection under FRE 803(5). Taking this step will help you avoid even the slightest case of nerves when your effort to refresh your witness's recollection with deposition testimony fails, with the witness apologizing, "No, I'm sorry; I just don't remember."

Recall the witness in the preceding section who on direct examination could not remember the color of a car. Knowing that the witness testified at deposition that the car was red, trial counsel properly tried to nudge the witness's memory by refreshing it with deposition testimony. If the witness read the deposition transcript but still could not remember the color of the car, trial counsel could have offered the deposition testimony as a past recorded recollection.

Under FRE 803(5), the past recorded recollection of a witness is admissible as an exception to the hearsay rule.[33] Therefore, deposition testimony can be admitted as a past recorded recollection.[34]

The foundational requirements for the admission of past recorded recollection are (1) the witness claims an inability to recollect the matter about which the examiner has inquired; (2) the recorded information relates to the inquiry; (3) the witness had knowledge of the subject information; and (4) the information was fresh in the mind of the witness at the time it was recorded.[35] In *United States v. Patterson*,[36] grand-jury testimony given ten months after the conversation at issue in the trial was deemed admissible when it was established that the prior testimony was given while still fresh in the witness's mind. The same considerations apply to the introduction of deposition testimony.

In contrast to FRE 612 (Writing Used to Refresh Memory), which allows only an adverse party to introduce writings used to refresh recollection, FRE 803(5) allows any party to read into evidence a past recorded recollection upon the establishment of a proper foundation.[37]

For example, after unsuccessfully attempting to use deposition testimony to refresh the witness's recollection about the color of the car, counsel might proceed as follows:

Q. Sir, were you present at the scene of the accident?
A. Yes, I was.
Q. At the scene of the accident, did you personally observe the color and make of the car?
A. Yes, I did.
Q. And did you testify at your deposition about your knowledge of the make and color of the car?
A. Yes, I did.
Q. After your deposition was completed, did you have an opportunity to read and sign the deposition transcript?
A. Yes, I did.
Q. Sir, can you identify the signature at the back of the deposition transcript?
A. Yes, that is my signature.
EXAMINER: Your Honor, I would now like to read to the jury the deposition testimony at page 27.
THE COURT: Go ahead.

Under FRE 803(5), the deposition testimony is read into evidence, but not received as an exhibit unless offered by opposing counsel.

Conclusion

In a perfect world, you would never need to use a deposition transcript at trial. On direct examination, your witness would testify eloquently and effectively, never wavering from her prior, firm grasp of the facts. Nor would you ever need to impeach a witness with a deposition; on cross-examination, every hostile witness would readily admit the logic of your penetrating questions. But in the real world, you always will need to use deposition transcripts at trial. Indeed, the outcome of your trial may depend on how well you prepared for a deposition, on whether you ably took or defended a deposition, and on whether you know how and when to use a deposition at trial.

Notes

1. See Chapter 1, note 2.

2. But see "Virtues of Using Video Pretrial" in Chapter 17, discussing the use of video recorded depositions at trial and, in particular, the possible advantages of using video recorded testimony rather than a live witness.

3. Brazos River Auth. v. GE Ionics, Inc., 469 F.3d 416, 434 (5th Cir. 2006) (citing Coughlin v. Capitol Cement Co., 571 F.2d 290, 308 (5th Cir. 1978)).

4. *See* FRE 801(d)(2):

(d) A statement is not hearsay if—

. . .

(2) The statement is offered against a party and is
(A) the party's own statement in either an individual or representative capacity or
(B) a statement of which the party has manifested an adoption or belief in its truth, or
(C) a statement by a person authorized by the party to make a statement concerning the subject, or
(D) a statement by the party's agent or servant concerning a matter within the scope of the agency or employment, made during the existence of the relationship, or
(E) a statement by a conspirator of a party during the course and in furtherance of the conspiracy.

5. FRE 804(a) reads in part as follows:

(a) Definition of unavailability. "Unavailability as a witness" includes situations in which the declarant—
(1) is exempted by ruling of the court on the ground of privilege from testifying concerning the subject matter of the declarant's statement; or
(2) persists in refusing to testify concerning the subject matter of the declarant's statement despite an order of the court to do so; or
(3) testifies to lack of memory of the subject matter of the declarant's statement; or
(4) is unable to be present or to testify at the hearing because of death or then existing physical or mental illness or infirmity; or
(5) is absent from the hearing and the proponent of a statement has been unable to procure the declarant's attendance . . . by process or other reasonable means.

A declarant is not unavailable as a witness if exemption, refusal, claim of lack of memory, inability, or absence is due to the procurement or wrongdoing of the proponent of a statement for the purpose of preventing the witness from attending or testifying.

6. *See* Scott E. Perwin, *Use of Depositions in Federal Trials: Evidence or Procedure?* 16 Litigation 37, 38 (Fall 1989).

7. 14 F.3d 684, 691 (1st Cir. 1994). At the time of this decision, subparagraph B was contained within FRCP 32(a)(3).

8. *Id.*

9. *Id.* at 692 (citing Carey v. Bahama Cruise Lines, 864 F.2d 201, 204 n.2 (1st Cir. 1988)).

10. Thomas ex rel. Smith v. Sheahan, 556 F. Supp. 2d 861, 875 (N.D. Ill. 2008) (citing Smith v. Equitable Life Assur. Soc. of U.S., 67 F.3d 611, 617 n.3 (7th Cir. 1986)); *Daigle, supra* note 7, at 690.

11. 871 F.2d 545 (5th Cir. 1989).

12. *Id.* at 552.

13. *Id.*

14. *See* 8A Charles Alan Wright et al., Federal Practice and Procedure § 2146 (2008) (footnote omitted).

15. *Daigle, supra* note 7, at 691.

16. *Id.*; Hartman v. United States, 538 F.2d 1336, 1345–46 (8th Cir. 1976) (affirming trial court's admission of deposition testimony solely upon deponent's uncontradicted statement seven months before trial that he lived more than one hundred miles from courthouse).

17. Borchart v. United States, 133 F.R.D. 547, 547–48 (D. Wis. 1991); *but see* Bobrosky v. Vickers, 170 F.R.D. 411 (W.D. Va. 1997) (finding large expense to defendant in personal injury suit in taking depositions of several physicians does not constitute exceptional circumstance).

18. Reber v. Gen. Motors Corp., 669 F. Supp. 717, 720 (E.D. Pa. 1987); *but see* Angelo v. Armstrong World Indus., Inc., 11 F.3d 957, 963–64 (10th Cir. 1993) (doctor's "extremely busy" schedule was not an "exceptional circumstance").

19. Lebeck v. William A. Jarvis, Inc., 145 F. Supp. 706, 724–25 (E.D. Pa. 1956).

20. Fed. R. Civ. P. 32(d)(3)(B). See also "Making Objections" in Chapter 14.

21. Fed. R. Civ. P. 32(d)(3)(A).

22. See Chapter 11 and "Reactions by the Taker to the Defender's Tactics" in Chapter 14..

23. See Appendix 10-A, listing topics for consideration in a pretrial.

24. See Appendix 10-B for a model format for the introduction of deposition testimony at a jury trial, including preinstruction of the jury.

25. See Chapter 17.

26. Westinghouse Elec. Corp. v. Wray Equip. Corp., 286 F.2d 491, 494 (5th Cir. 1961); *but see* Thompson v. Austin, 272 Fed. Appx. 188 (3d Cir. 2008) (finding it was within court's discretion to exclude a portion of witness's deposition testimony in personal injury case).

27. *In re* A.H. Robins Co., Ind., 575 F. Supp. 718 (D.C. Kan. 1983); *see also* United States v. Matlock, 109 F.3d 1313, 1319 (8th Cir. 1997) (noting

that inconsistent statements can be found in "evasive answers, inability to recall, silence, or change of position").

28. See Appendix 11, discussing the steps to impeach a witness at trial by prior inconsistent deposition testimony.

29. See "Opening Questions" in Chapter 11, discussing the use of foundational questions during the deposition.

30. Queen Caroline's Case, 129 Eng. Rep. 976 (1820).

31. The reporter will testify to his occupation, experience, certification, presence at the deposition, administration of the oath, and method of transcription, as well as the witness's opportunity to review and sign the deposition and the accuracy of the transcript.

32. Tome v. United States, 513 U.S. 150 (1995).

33. *See* FRE 803(5): The following are not excluded by the hearsay rule, even though the declarant is available as a witness:

> (5) A memorandum or record concerning a matter about which a witness once had knowledge but now has insufficient recollection to enable the witness to testify fully and accurately, shown to have been made or adopted by the witness when the matter was fresh in the witness' memory and to reflect that knowledge correctly. If admitted, the memorandum or record may be read into evidence but may not itself be received as an exhibit unless offered by an adverse party.

34. United States v. Arias, 575 F. 2d 253 (9th Cir. 1978) (transcript of prior trial testimony admissible as past recorded recollection).

35. United States v. Edwards, 539 F.2d 689 (9th Cir. 1976); Rush v. Ill. Cent. R.R. Co., 399 F.3d 705, 719 (6th Cir. 2005).

36. 678 F.2d 774 (9th Cir. 1982).

37. Baker v. Elcona Homes Corp., 588 F.2d 551 (6th Cir. 1978).

APPENDIXES

APPENDIX 1

EXHIBIT A
Sample Notice of Deposition
and Request for Production of Documents
Henry L. Hecht

ROSE YUSPA, ESQ.
YUSPA & FOX, LLP
One Central Plaza
Boston, MA 02111
Telephone: (617) 555-5221

Attorneys for Plaintiff
LESLIE ROBERTS, dba SCOOPS

SUPERIOR COURT OF HLH
EASTERN DISTRICT

LESLIE ROBERTS, dba SCOOPS,	
Plaintiff,	Civ. Action No. 10-1234 CMY
v.	
BUSINESS-AIDE, INC.,	NOTICE OF DEPOSITION AND REQUEST FOR THE PRODUCTION OF DOCUMENTS
Defendant	

TO DEFENDANT BUSNIESS-AIDE, INC.
AND ITS ATTORNEYS OF RECORD:

PLEASE TAKE NOTICE that, pursuant to Rule 30 of the Federal Rules of Civil Procedure, Plaintiff Leslie Roberts, dba Scoops, by and through its attorneys of record, will take the deposition on oral examination of the Custodian of Records of Defendant Business-Aide, Inc. This deposition will take place at the law offices of Yuspa

729

1 & Fox, LLP, One Central Plaza, Boston, MA 02111, commencing at

2 [time], on [date], unless the parties mutually agree to hold the depo-

3 sition on a different date and time or at a different location.

4   This deposition will be taken by both stenographic and audiovi-

5 sual (video) means before an officer authorized to administer oaths

6 and will continue from day to day until completed. The deposition

7 will be taken for the purposes of discovery, for use at trial in this

8 matter, and for any other purpose permitted under the Federal

9 Rules of Civil Procedure.

10   PLEASE TAKE FURTHER NOTICE that, pursuant to Rules 30

11 and 34 of the Federal Rules of Civil Procedure, the deponent is to

12 produce at the deposition the documents identified in Exhibit B

13 attached to this Notice.

14

15 Dated: _____   YUSPA & FOX, LLP

16   By: _____

17   Rose Yuspa, Esq.

18   Attorneys for Plaintiff
LESLIE ROBERTS, dba SCOOPS

19

20

21

22

23

24

25

EXHIBIT B
Schedule of Documents to Be Produced

Definitions

A. The term "PERSON" includes without limitation any natural person, firm, association, partnership, corporation, or any other form of legal entity.

B. The terms "YOU" and "YOUR" mean Defendant Business-Aide, Inc., including each of its current and former agents, employees, attorneys, consultants, investigators, accountants, and all other persons acting on its behalf.

C. The term "PLAINTIFF" means Plaintiff Leslie Roberts, dba Scoops, including each of her current and former agents, employees, attorneys, consultants, investigators, accountants, and all other persons acting on her behalf.

D. The term "COMMUNICATION" or "COMMUNICATIONS" means any transmission of information from one person to another, including without limitation by personal meeting, telephone, letter, telegraph, electronic mail, electronic bulletin boards, electronic "chat rooms," and other similar forms of electronic correspondence, teleconference, facsimile, or telex.

E. Consistent with Rule 34(a) of the Federal Rules of Civil Procedure, the term "DOCUMENT" or "DOCUMENTS" means all physical or "hard copy" documents, including, but not limited to, writings, drawings, graphs, charts,

1 photographs, letters, files, memoranda, calendars, and
2 reports.

3 F. The term "ELECTRONICALLY STORED INFORMA-
4 TION" means native files (including all embedded files and
5 metadata) of electronic data stored in any medium, includ-
6 ing, but not limited to, e-mail, voicemail, word processing
7 documents and spreadsheets, audio and video recordings,
8 and any other electronically stored files regardless of the
9 storage medium in which they reside, including, but not
10 limited to, computer hard drives (for example, laptops, desk-
11 tops, and servers), removable storage media (for example,
12 tapes, disks, cards, and flash memory devices), PDAs, net-
13 worked drives, and optical storage devices such as CDs and
14 DVDs. This term also includes information contained on
15 backup tapes and all other recovery and archival systems.
16 To the extent that YOU possess data in nonstandard formats
17 (including legacy data), YOU shall translate such informa-
18 tion into a reasonably usable format and produce both the
19 source nontranslated data and the translated version.

20 G. The term "RELATING TO" or "RELATE TO" means con-
21 stituting, comprising, pertaining to, referring to, record-
22 ing, evidencing, containing, setting forth, reflecting,
23 showing, disclosing, describing, explaining, summariz-
24 ing, supporting, contradicting, refuting, or concerning,
25 whether directly or indirectly.

732

1   H.   The term "LAWSUIT" means the above-captioned action.

2   **Instructions**

3   I.   Unless otherwise specified, the time period covered by each

4   document request is from January 1, 2000, to the present.

5   J.   Each request contained herein extends to all documents

6   in YOUR possession, custody, or control.

7   K.   These requests require the production of all responsive

8   documents, including all responsive information stored

9   electronically, regardless of the data storage medium

10   or system on which the electronic data resides. These

11   requests thus should be understood to encompass, and

12   YOUR responses should include ELECTRONICALLY

13   STORED INFORMATION.

14   L.   All ELECTRONICALLY STORED INFORMATION that

15   does not exist in a standard file format shall be translated

16   by YOU into a reasonably usable format. For example, leg-

17   acy data that can be read only by using obsolete hardware

18   systems and software shall be translated into contempo-

19   rary formats.

20   M.   To the extent that YOU contend that YOU need not pro-

21   vide discovery of certain responsive ELECTRONICALLY

22   STORED INFORMATION on the ground that the infor-

23   mation is not readily accessible, YOU shall identify with

24   particularity: (1) the information that is not reasonably

25   accessible; (2) the reasons why the information is not rea-

733

1   sonably accessible; and (3) the precise burden and cost

2   associated with production of the information.

3   N. YOU must identify, by category or type, any sources

4   containing potentially responsive ELECTRONICALLY

5   STORED INFORMATION that YOU are not searching.

6   This identification should provide enough detail to enable

7   Plaintiff to evaluate the burdens and costs of providing

8   the discovery and the likelihood of finding responsive

9   information on the identified sources.

10   O. If YOU claim, for any reason, that certain electronic data

11   sources need not be searched or that data from certain

12   sources need not be produced, YOU shall make reason-

13   able data samples available to Plaintiff's counsel and pro-

14   vide access to the data sources for testing and analysis at

15   a time and in a manner convenient for the parties.

16   P. The identification obligations contained in Instructions M

17   and N do not relieve YOU of any common law or statutory

18   duty to preserve evidence in this LAWSUIT. YOU should

19   preserve all relevant and potentially relevant information

20   regardless of the source of that information.

21   Q. YOU shall take measures to ensure that any processes

22   by which potentially relevant information could be auto-

23   matically deleted or overwritten shall be suspended until

24   such time as the parties have come to an agreement about

25   the treatment of such automatic computer processes.

734

R. If certain documents exist in both searchable and non-searchable formats, YOU must not remove or degrade the ability of ELECTRONICALLY STORED INFORMATION to be searched, and YOU must provide native text-searchable copies of documents.

S. If documents exist in both electronic and nonelectronic form or if multiple copies of the same document exist in the same form, YOU shall produce all copies and may not selectively choose which format or version to produce.

T. To the extent that YOU contend that potentially relevant documents might reside on dynamic databases or other nonstatic computer systems, YOU shall specify all such databases or systems and identify the types of potentially relevant documents that might reside on such databases or systems.

U. If YOU assert any privilege in responding to any request, describe in detail in each instance the type of privilege asserted, the basis for the assertion, and all facts relied upon to support or related to the claim of privilege and identify, to the fullest extent short of waiver, all information for which YOU claim a privilege.

V. If privileged or protected information YOU may by timely notice assert the privilege or protection and YOU may obtain return of the materials without waiver. For this reason, YOU may not avoid or delay production

1   obligations based on blanket, nonspecific assertions of

2   privilege or other protection.

3   W. If, after making your initial production and inspec-

4   tion, YOU obtain or become aware of any further

5   DOCUMENTS or ELECTRONICALLY STORED INFOR-

6   MATION responsive to these requests, YOU are required

7   to produce such additional documents to Plaintiff's

8   counsel in this LAWSUIT pursuant to Rule 26(e) of the

9   Federal Rules of Civil Procedure.

10 X. In construing any request, the singular form of a word

11 shall be interpreted as plural and plural as singular as

12 necessary to bring within the scope of the request any

13 information or documents that might otherwise be con-

14 strued to be outside its scope.

15 Y. In construing any request, whenever appropriate, "and"

16 as well as "or" shall be construed either disjunctively or

17 conjunctively as necessary to bring within the scope of

18 the request any information that might otherwise be con-

19 strued to be outside its scope; and "all" shall mean "any

20 and all" unless the context requires otherwise.

21 Z. Each request shall be construed independently and not

22 with reference to any other request herein for purposes of

23 limitation unless a request so specifies.

24 //

25 //

736

Documents to Be Produced for Inspection and Copying

A. All DOCUMENTS and ELECTRONICALLY STORED INFORMATION between Leslie Roberts, dba Scoops, or any employee thereof, and Business-Aide, Inc., or any employee thereof.

B. All DOCUMENTS and ELECTRONICALLY STORED INFORMATION discussing, referring to, or relating to any oral communications, including but not limited to telephone conversations, between any employee of Leslie Roberts, dba Scoops, and any employee of Business-Aide, Inc.

C. All DOCUMENTS and ELECTRONICALLY STORED INFORMATION constituting, discussing, referring to, or relating to, any business transactions between Leslie Roberts, dba Scoops, and Business-Aide, Inc., including but not limited to a purchase by Leslie Roberts, dba Scoops, of computer hardware and/or software from Business-Aide, Inc.

EXHIBIT C
Proof of Service

I, Wanda Castillo, declare:

I am employed in the City of Boston, County of Suffolk, Massachusetts in the office of a member of the bar of this court at whose direction the following service was made. I am over the age of 18 years and not a party to this action. My business address is Yuspa & Fox, LLP, One Central Plaza, Boston, Massachusetts 02111.

On [*month, day, and year*], I served a true and correct copy of Plaintiff's Notice of Deposition of, and Request for Production of Documents by, the Custodian of Records of Defendant Business-Aide, Inc., as well as this Proof of Service by consigning the documents to an express mail service for guaranteed next day delivery to the following person:

> Emily B. Carter
> Straus & Carter, LLP
> 1 Clancy Street
> Boston, MA 02111

I declare under penalty of perjury under the laws of the United States of America that the above is true and correct.

Executed on [*month, day, and year*], at Boston, Massachusetts.

By: _____
Wanda Castillo

APPENDIX 2-A

Federal Subpoena Form:
Subpoena to Testify at a Deposition
or to Produce Documents in a Civil Action

Note to the Reader: The following form AO 88A is occasionally updated. The current version of the form can be downloaded at http://www.uscourts.gov/forms/uscforms.cfm?ShowAll=Yes.

AO 88A (Rev. 01/09) Subpoena to Testify at a Deposition or to Produce Documents in a Civil Action

UNITED STATES DISTRICT COURT
for the

	)	
_____	)	
Plaintiff	)	
v.	)	Civil Action No. _____
	)	
_____	)	(If the action is pending in another district, state where:
Defendant	)	

SUBPOENA TO TESTIFY AT A DEPOSITION
OR TO PRODUCE DOCUMENTS IN A CIVIL ACTION

To:

    ❐ *Testimony:* **YOU ARE COMMANDED** to appear at the time, date, and place set forth below to testify at a deposition to be taken in this civil action. If you are an organization that is *not* a party in this case, you must designate one or more officers, directors, or managing agents, or designate other persons who consent to testify on your behalf about the following matters, or those set forth in an attachment:

Place:	Date and Time:

    The deposition will be recorded by this method: _____

    ❐ *Production:* You, or your representatives, must also bring with you to the deposition the following documents, electronically stored information, or objects, and permit their inspection, copying, testing, or sampling of the material:

    The provisions of Fed. R. Civ. P. 45(c), relating to your protection as a person subject to a subpoena, and Rule 45 (d) and (e), relating to your duty to respond to this subpoena and the potential consequences of not doing so, are attached.

Date: _____

        CLERK OF COURT

                               OR

_____   _____
   Signature of Clerk or Deputy Clerk   *Attorney's signature*

The name, address, e-mail, and telephone number of the attorney representing *(name of party)* _____
_____ , who issues or requests this subpoena, are:

AO 88A (Rev. 01/09) Subpoena to Testify at a Deposition or to Produce Documents in a Civil Action (Page 2)

Civil Action No.

PROOF OF SERVICE
(This section should not be filed with the court unless required by Fed. R. Civ. P. 45.)

This subpoena for *(name of individual and title, if any)*

was received by me on *(date)*   .

☐ I personally served the subpoena on the individual at *(place)*

_____ on *(date)* _____ ; or

☐ I left the subpoena at the individual's residence or usual place of abode with *(name)*

_____ , a person of suitable age and discretion who resides there,

on *(date)* _____ , and mailed a copy to the individual's last known address; or

☐ I served the subpoena on *(name of individual)* _____ , who is

designated by law to accept service of process on behalf of *(name of organization)*

_____ on *(date)* _____ ; or

☐ I returned the subpoena unexecuted because _____ ; or

☐ Other *(specify):*

Unless the subpoena was issued on behalf of the United States, or one of its officers or agents, I have also tendered to the witness fees for one day's attendance, and the mileage allowed by law, in the amount of

$ _____ .

My fees are $ _____ for travel and $ _____ for services, for a total of $ 0.00   .

I declare under penalty of perjury that this information is true.

Date: _____   _____

Server's signature

_____

Printed name and title

_____

Server's address

Additional information regarding attempted service, etc:

| Print | Save As... | Attach | Reset |

741

AO 88A (Rev. 01/09) Subpoena to Testify at a Deposition or to Produce Documents in a Civil Action (Page 3)

Federal Rule of Civil Procedure 45 (c), (d), and (e) (Effective 12/1/07)

(c) Protecting a Person Subject to a Subpoena.

(1) *Avoiding Undue Burden or Expense; Sanctions.* A party or attorney responsible for issuing and serving a subpoena must take reasonable steps to avoid imposing undue burden or expense on a person subject to the subpoena. The issuing court must enforce this duty and impose an appropriate sanction — which may include lost earnings and reasonable attorney's fees — on a party or attorney who fails to comply.

(2) *Command to Produce Materials or Permit Inspection.*

(A) *Appearance Not Required.* A person commanded to produce documents, electronically stored information, or tangible things, or to permit the inspection of premises, need not appear in person at the place of production or inspection unless also commanded to appear for a deposition, hearing, or trial.

(B) *Objections.* A person commanded to produce documents or tangible things or to permit inspection may serve on the party or attorney designated in the subpoena a written objection to inspecting, copying, testing or sampling any or all of the materials or to inspecting the premises — or to producing electronically stored information in the form or forms requested. The objection must be served before the earlier of the time specified for compliance or 14 days after the subpoena is served. If an objection is made, the following rules apply:

(i) At any time, on notice to the commanded person, the serving party may move the issuing court for an order compelling production or inspection.

(ii) These acts may be required only as directed in the order, and the order must protect a person who is neither a party nor a party's officer from significant expense resulting from compliance.

(3) *Quashing or Modifying a Subpoena.*

(A) *When Required.* On timely motion, the issuing court must quash or modify a subpoena that:

(i) fails to allow a reasonable time to comply;

(ii) requires a person who is neither a party nor a party's officer to travel more than 100 miles from where that person resides, is employed, or regularly transacts business in person — except that, subject to Rule 45(c)(3)(B)(iii), the person may be commanded to attend a trial by traveling from any such place within the state where the trial is held;

(iii) requires disclosure of privileged or other protected matter, if no exception or waiver applies; or

(iv) subjects a person to undue burden.

(B) *When Permitted.* To protect a person subject to or affected by a subpoena, the issuing court may, on motion, quash or modify the subpoena if it requires:

(i) disclosing a trade secret or other confidential research, development, or commercial information;

(ii) disclosing an unretained expert's opinion or information that does not describe specific occurrences in dispute and results from the expert's study that was not requested by a party; or

(iii) a person who is neither a party nor a party's officer to incur substantial expense to travel more than 100 miles to attend trial.

(C) *Specifying Conditions as an Alternative.* In the circumstances described in Rule 45(c)(3)(B), the court may, instead of quashing or modifying a subpoena, order appearance or production under specified conditions if the serving party:

(i) shows a substantial need for the testimony or material that cannot be otherwise met without undue hardship; and

(ii) ensures that the subpoenaed person will be reasonably compensated.

(d) Duties in Responding to a Subpoena.

(1) *Producing Documents or Electronically Stored Information.* These procedures apply to producing documents or electronically stored information:

(A) *Documents.* A person responding to a subpoena to produce documents must produce them as they are kept in the ordinary course of business or must organize and label them to correspond to the categories in the demand.

(B) *Form for Producing Electronically Stored Information Not Specified.* If a subpoena does not specify a form for producing electronically stored information, the person responding must produce it in a form or forms in which it is ordinarily maintained or in a reasonably usable form or forms.

(C) *Electronically Stored Information Produced in Only One Form.* The person responding need not produce the same electronically stored information in more than one form.

(D) *Inaccessible Electronically Stored Information.* The person responding need not provide discovery of electronically stored information from sources that the person identifies as not reasonably accessible because of undue burden or cost. On motion to compel discovery or for a protective order, the person responding must show that the information is not reasonably accessible because of undue burden or cost. If that showing is made, the court may nonetheless order discovery from such sources if the requesting party shows good cause, considering the limitations of Rule 26(b)(2)(C). The court may specify conditions for the discovery.

(2) *Claiming Privilege or Protection.*

(A) *Information Withheld.* A person withholding subpoenaed information under a claim that it is privileged or subject to protection as trial-preparation material must:

(i) expressly make the claim; and

(ii) describe the nature of the withheld documents, communications, or tangible things in a manner that, without revealing information itself privileged or protected, will enable the parties to assess the claim.

(B) *Information Produced.* If information produced in response to a subpoena is subject to a claim of privilege or of protection as trial-preparation material, the person making the claim may notify any party that received the information of the claim and the basis for it. After being notified, a party must promptly return, sequester, or destroy the specified information and any copies it has; must not use or disclose the information until the claim is resolved; must take reasonable steps to retrieve the information if the party disclosed it before being notified; and may promptly present the information to the court under seal for a determination of the claim. The person who produced the information must preserve the information until the claim is resolved.

(e) Contempt. The issuing court may hold in contempt a person who, having been served, fails without adequate excuse to obey the subpoena. A nonparty's failure to obey must be excused if the subpoena purports to require the nonparty to attend or produce at a place outside the limits of Rule 45(c)(3)(A)(ii).

742

APPENDIX 2-B

Federal Subpoena Form:
Subpoena to Produce Documents, Information, or Objects or to Permit Inspection of Premises

Note to the Reader: The following form AO 88B is occasionally updated. The current version of the form can be downloaded at http://www.uscourts.gov/forms/uscforms.cfm?ShowAll=Yes.

AO 88B (Rev. 01/09) Subpoena to Produce Documents, Information, or Objects or to Permit Inspection of Premises

UNITED STATES DISTRICT COURT
for the

_____	)
Plaintiff	)
v.	)
	)
_____	)
Defendant	)

Civil Action No. _____

(If the action is pending in another district, state where:

SUBPOENA TO PRODUCE DOCUMENTS, INFORMATION, OR OBJECTS
OR TO PERMIT INSPECTION OF PREMISES

To:

    ❏ *Production:* **YOU ARE COMMANDED** to produce at the time, date, and place set forth below the following documents, electronically stored information, or objects, and permit their inspection, copying, testing, or sampling of the material:

Place:	Date and Time:

    ❏ *Inspection of Premises:* **YOU ARE COMMANDED** to permit entry onto the designated premises, land, or other property possessed or controlled by you at the time, date, and location set forth below, so that the requesting party may inspect, measure, survey, photograph, test, or sample the property or any designated object or operation on it.

Place:	Date and Time:

    The provisions of Fed. R. Civ. P. 45(c), relating to your protection as a person subject to a subpoena, and Rule 45 (d) and (e), relating to your duty to respond to this subpoena and the potential consequences of not doing so, are attached.

Date: _____

        CLERK OF COURT

                          OR

_____   _____
   Signature of Clerk or Deputy Clerk   *Attorney's signature*

The name, address, e-mail, and telephone number of the attorney representing *(name of party)* _____
_____ , who issues or requests this subpoena, are:

FEDERAL SUBPOENA FORM, TO PRODUCE DOCUMENTS

AO 88B (Rev. 01/09) Subpoena to Produce Documents, Information, or Objects or to Permit Inspection of Premises (Page 2)

Civil Action No.

PROOF OF SERVICE

(This section should not be filed with the court unless required by Fed. R. Civ. P. 45.)

This subpoena for *(name of individual and title, if any)*

was received by me on *(date)*   .

❏ I personally served the subpoena on the individual at *(place)*

on *(date)*   ; or

❏ I left the subpoena at the individual's residence or usual place of abode with *(name)*

, a person of suitable age and discretion who resides there,

on *(date)*   , and mailed a copy to the individual's last known address; or

❏ I served the subpoena to *(name of individual)*   , who is

designated by law to accept service of process on behalf of *(name of organization)*

on *(date)*   ; or

❏ I returned the subpoena unexecuted because   ; or

❏ other *(specify):*

Unless the subpoena was issued on behalf of the United States, or one of its officers or agents, I have also tendered to the witness fees for one day's attendance, and the mileage allowed by law, in the amount of

$.

My fees are $ for travel and $ for services, for a total of $ 0.00   .

I declare under penalty of perjury that this information is true.

Date:

_____
Server's signature

_____
Printed name and title

_____
Server's address

Additional information regarding attempted service, etc:

| Print | Save As... | Attach | | Reset |

Federal Rule of Civil Procedure 45 (c), (d), and (e) (Effective 12/1/07)

(c) Protecting a Person Subject to a Subpoena.

(1) *Avoiding Undue Burden or Expense; Sanctions.* A party or attorney responsible for issuing and serving a subpoena must take reasonable steps to avoid imposing undue burden or expense on a person subject to the subpoena. The issuing court must enforce this duty and impose an appropriate sanction — which may include lost earnings and reasonable attorney's fees — on a party or attorney who fails to comply.

(2) *Command to Produce Materials or Permit Inspection.*

(A) *Appearance Not Required.* A person commanded to produce documents, electronically stored information, or tangible things, or to permit the inspection of premises, need not appear in person at the place of production or inspection unless also commanded to appear for a deposition, hearing, or trial.

(B) *Objections.* A person commanded to produce documents or tangible things or to permit inspection may serve on the party or attorney designated in the subpoena a written objection to inspecting, copying, testing or sampling any or all of the materials or to inspecting the premises — or to producing electronically stored information in the form or forms requested. The objection must be served before the earlier of the time specified for compliance or 14 days after the subpoena is served. If an objection is made, the following rules apply:

(i) At any time, on notice to the commanded person, the serving party may move the issuing court for an order compelling production or inspection.

(ii) These acts may be required only as directed in the order, and the order must protect a person who is neither a party nor a party's officer from significant expense resulting from compliance.

(3) *Quashing or Modifying a Subpoena.*

(A) *When Required.* On timely motion, the issuing court must quash or modify a subpoena that:

(i) fails to allow a reasonable time to comply;

(ii) requires a person who is neither a party nor a party's officer to travel more than 100 miles from where that person resides, is employed, or regularly transacts business in person — except that, subject to Rule 45(c)(3)(B)(iii), the person may be commanded to attend a trial by traveling from any such place within the state where the trial is held;

(iii) requires disclosure of privileged or other protected matter, if no exception or waiver applies; or

(iv) subjects a person to undue burden.

(B) *When Permitted.* To protect a person subject to or affected by a subpoena, the issuing court may, on motion, quash or modify the subpoena if it requires:

(i) disclosing a trade secret or other confidential research, development, or commercial information;

(ii) disclosing an unretained expert's opinion or information that does not describe specific occurrences in dispute and results from the expert's study that was not requested by a party; or

(iii) a person who is neither a party nor a party's officer to incur substantial expense to travel more than 100 miles to attend trial.

(C) *Specifying Conditions as an Alternative.* In the circumstances described in Rule 45(c)(3)(B), the court may, instead of quashing or modifying a subpoena, order appearance or production under specified conditions if the serving party:

(i) shows a substantial need for the testimony or material that cannot be otherwise met without undue hardship; and

(ii) ensures that the subpoenaed person will be reasonably compensated.

(d) Duties in Responding to a Subpoena.

(1) *Producing Documents or Electronically Stored Information.* These procedures apply to producing documents or electronically stored information:

(A) *Documents.* A person responding to a subpoena to produce documents must produce them as they are kept in the ordinary course of business or must organize and label them to correspond to the categories in the demand.

(B) *Form for Producing Electronically Stored Information Not Specified.* If a subpoena does not specify a form for producing electronically stored information, the person responding must produce it in a form or forms in which it is ordinarily maintained or in a reasonably usable form or forms.

(C) *Electronically Stored Information Produced in Only One Form.* The person responding need not produce the same electronically stored information in more than one form.

(D) *Inaccessible Electronically Stored Information.* The person responding need not provide discovery of electronically stored information from sources that the person identifies as not reasonably accessible because of undue burden or cost. On motion to compel discovery or for a protective order, the person responding must show that the information is not reasonably accessible because of undue burden or cost. If that showing is made, the court may nonetheless order discovery from such sources if the requesting party shows good cause, considering the limitations of Rule 26(b)(2)(C). The court may specify conditions for the discovery.

(2) *Claiming Privilege or Protection.*

(A) *Information Withheld.* A person withholding subpoenaed information under a claim that it is privileged or subject to protection as trial-preparation material must:

(i) expressly make the claim; and

(ii) describe the nature of the withheld documents, communications, or tangible things in a manner that, without revealing information itself privileged or protected, will enable the parties to assess the claim.

(B) *Information Produced.* If information produced in response to a subpoena is subject to a claim of privilege or of protection as trial-preparation material, the person making the claim may notify any party that received the information of the claim and the basis for it. After being notified, a party must promptly return, sequester, or destroy the specified information and any copies it has; must not use or disclose the information until the claim is resolved; must take reasonable steps to retrieve the information if the party disclosed it before being notified; and may promptly present the information to the court under seal for a determination of the claim. The person who produced the information must preserve the information until the claim is resolved.

(e) Contempt. The issuing court may hold in contempt a person who, having been served, fails without adequate excuse to obey the subpoena. A nonparty's failure to obey must be excused if the subpoena purports to require the nonparty to attend or produce at a place outside the limits of Rule 45(c)(3)(A)(ii).

APPENDIX 3

Supplies to Take to a Deposition

HENRY L. HECHT

1. Caption page for the court reporter
2. If the deposition is a continuation, notation for the court reporter of the date of the last deposition, the page number of the last transcript, and the last exhibit number
3. If realtime transcription is to be used, any necessary computer requirements for the court reporter and your own computer, including software, serial-to-USB adapter, and cables
4. If the testimony is to be recorded on video, any necessary equipment for the videographer
5. Instructions for the court reporter on when, where, and how (that is, in what format) to deliver the transcript
6. Glossary of relevant terms and the spelling of any difficult words for court reporter
7. Applicable rules of civil procedure and evidence, as well as any local rules and standing orders of the presiding judge governing discovery
8. Contact information for the Judge, Magistrate Judge, or Special Master who will decide discovery disputes
9. Available dates for discovery motions to be heard
10. Personal calendar for scheduling purposes
11. Copy of the notice, subpoena, written stipulation, or court order that secured the attendance of the witness
12. List and text of any proposed stipulations
13. Copy of any discovery orders, including protective orders, that might apply to the deposition
14. Copy of the pleadings
15. Outline of questions
16. Copy of model questioning formats; for example, see Appendix 6, Model Questions for Discovery About a Conversation: The 4 C's, and Appendix 7, Model Questions for an Examination About a Document

17. Documents, placed in a witness folder, with at least four copies of each: one to be marked at the deposition, shown to the witness, and attached to the transcript; one for the opposing counsel (plus additional copies if other counsel will be present); one for the court reporter; and one annotated copy that you will use when questioning the witness
18. Standard English dictionary

APPENDIX 4

A Lawyer's Guide to Preparing a Deposition Witness

Henry L. Hecht

Few lay witnesses know what a deposition is; even fewer have ever testified at one. The following guidelines are designed to assist you in explaining the deposition process to a witness. Because witnesses and cases vary, these guidelines should be adapted for each witness and circumstance. Always be careful not to overload a witness with more advice and "rules" than the witness is likely to remember and apply.

Although these guidelines are drafted as if they could be sent—with appropriate modifications—to a witness, deliver them orally. With rare exceptions, written instructions should never be given to a witness because of the danger that they will be misunderstood or discovered by your opponent.

I. What is a deposition?

A. A deposition is part of the discovery process by which parties learn the facts from each other during litigation but before trial.

B. A deposition is testimony taken under oath, usually in an informal setting, such as a conference room. (Your deposition is scheduled to start at [*time*] on [*date*], at [location]. It is expected to end at [*time*].)

C. A court reporter will be present to transcribe your testimony. (You may want to show the witness an actual transcript.) It is important to tell the truth, not only because you will have sworn to tell the truth but also because your deposition testimony can be used at trial.

D. Sometimes depositions are video recorded. If your deposition will be video recorded, I will let you know because special guidelines that I will discuss with you will apply. (See Section IX below regarding video recorded depositions.)

E. In addition to the opposing party's lawyer, who will ask you questions, I will be there. (See Sections VI and VII below regarding the role of the defender.)

F. Do not be surprised if the other party is present; the other side has a right to be there.

II. Tell the truth.

A. There is no more important rule.

B. You will only hurt the case if you do not do so.

III. Listen carefully to the question.

A. Wait until the question is completed before answering. (See Section IV.A below about pausing before answering.) If you did not hear all of a question clearly or you want to hear it again, ask the examiner to repeat the question. If I think it will help you, I will ask the reporter to "read back" the question.

B. If a question is confusing or ambiguous, or uses unfamiliar terms, ask the examiner to clarify it.

In particular:

1. If a question contains a false or uncertain assumption, even a minor one, do not answer it. Point out the false assumption.

2. Do not answer hypothetical questions, particularly if they are incomplete. Stick to the facts.

3. Be careful with leading questions, which usually start with, "Is it correct that ... ?" Leading questions may include assumptions that you do not want to accept, and they usually require a carefully explained answer, not just a "yes" or "no" response.

4. Be careful with questions that include conclusory terms and adjectives such as "agreement," "frequently," "important," and the like. Ask the examiner for a definition of the word. If you do so, expect the examiner to ask you for your definition of the word. Answer with the facts; do not accept the examiner's characterizations, which are likely to be in his or her interest.

750

5. Be careful of questions that start with words such as "Is it fair to say. . . ?" Again, answer with the facts; do not accept the examiner's characterization.

6. Do not adopt an examiner's summary or paraphrase of your testimony. Disagree if it is inaccurate.

IV. Form your answers carefully.

A. Pause before you respond to a question. There are five reasons to do so: (1) to be sure you have the question in mind; (2) to be sure you understand the question; (3) to formulate your answer; (4) to give me time to object; and (5) to be sure your answer is correct in light of my objection. Try counting (perhaps to five) after the question is asked and before you answer. If the deposition is being video recorded, you may want to shorten the length of your pause. (See Section IX below regarding video recorded depositions.)

B. Stick to your first-hand knowledge and do not offer more than a question specifically asks for.
In particular:

1. Do not volunteer information; answer only the question asked.
   For example:
   Question: "Did you communicate with Ms. Miller in September regarding the availability of widgets?"
   Wrong Answer: "No, but in September, I spoke with the president of A regarding our license agreement with B." (Such an answer is not required. It goes beyond the question asked.)
   Correct Answer: "Yes," "No," or "I do not recall." (Brief, truthful answers are appropriate. It is the examiner's job to follow up. Your job is to answer only the question asked.)

2. Do not speculate. Answer questions only on the basis of your personal knowledge; that is, what you learned directly through your senses.
   For example:
   Question: "Who was present at the meeting in September?"
   Wrong Answer: "I assume that Ms. Miller was at the meeting. This is the type of meeting that she usually attends."

751

Correct Answer (assuming you were not physically present at the meeting or do not have any other reason to know): "I do not know."

Question: "Did anyone tell you who was present at the meeting?"

Correct Answer (if true): "Yes." (Do not volunteer who told you or who was present because the question does not call for this additional information; it calls for a "Yes" or "No." It is the examiner's job to follow-up.)

3. Do not guess. Do not give an answer based upon opinion or surmise, no matter how well-informed you believe you are. If you do not know or cannot recall something, say so.

   For example:

   Question: "Did the officers of A and B meet in September to discuss licensing widgets?"

   Wrong Answer: "I suppose so because a license agreement between them was signed in September, so they must have met."

   Correct Answer: "Yes," "No," "I do not recall," or "I do not know" (whichever is true).

4. Do not interpret the question; answer what is asked, not what you think the examiner is trying to ask. (This is especially important advice for professionals, such as doctors, who often must interpret incorrectly worded questions from their patients.)

5. Do not volunteer the names of other persons unless the names are requested.

   For example:

   Question: "Did you speak to Ms. Miller of B concerning the availability of widgets?"

   Wrong Answer: "No, but Mr. Carter did."

   Correct Answer (if true): "No."

6. Do not use speculative words and phrases such as "possibly," "probably," "in all likelihood," and "it must have been." Be especially careful if asked to "estimate" something. Remember the admonitions not to guess or speculate.

7. Do not give absolute, definitive answers that cannot be modified or supplemented at a later time; try to

qualify your answers so that you "leave the door open." Avoid words such as "never" and "always"; they have a way of coming back to haunt you.

For example:

Question: "Have you told us everything that was said between you and Ms. Miller at that meeting in September?"

Wrong Answer: "Yes, I have told you absolutely everything that was said."

Correct Answer: "Yes, as far as I can recall (as I sit here today)." (If you later recall additional things said, it will be easier to supplement this answer.)

8. Do not volunteer when you answer that you reviewed documents in preparation for your deposition. (See also Section V.E below regarding documents and depositions.)

For example:

Question: "Were you aware of any communications between A and B in September?"

Wrong Answer: "No, but I recently saw a memorandum indicating that some officers of A were in contact with the president of B, so I assume there must have been some communication."

Correct Answer: "Yes," "No," or "I do not recall," (whichever is true).

9. Answer a question with "I do not recall," "I do not remember," or a similar phrase if you once knew the answer but have forgotten it at the time of the deposition. This is a valid, understandable response, especially when many of the events in question occurred long ago and may have held no special significance to you when they occurred.

10. When you have finished your answer, stop. Do not try to fill a "void of silence" with an answer. Wait for the next question. If the examiner then asks whether that is all you recall, answer "Yes," if that is true. But remember the admonition to avoid absolute, definitive answers.

11. Do not try to "help" the examiner. The examiner is not there to help you. And, as a general rule, this is not your chance to tell your side of the case.

C. Everyone makes mistakes. Do not be upset if you forget a fact or misstate a date. If you realize your mistake during the deposition, correct it. (If you are unsure whether you have made a mistake or whether you should change your answer, you may want to discuss it privately with me before testifying further.) (See Section VII below regarding breaks and conferences.)

D. At the end of your deposition and after we have conferred, I am entitled to ask you questions, but I probably will not do so.

E. Mistakes discovered after a deposition may be corrected when you review your transcript (after we have discussed whether you should make any corrections).

V. Treat documents cautiously.

A. Do not be surprised if the examiner shows you documents with your name on them. During discovery we produced (gave) many documents to the other side. I will review many of them with you when preparing you for your deposition.

B. Read each document carefully and completely that you are shown by the examiner. Even if the document is familiar, do not skim it. If the examiner asks you a question about a document without giving you time to read it, ask for time. If you do not ask, I will.

C. After reading a document, especially a lengthy one, ask the examiner to repeat the question. If I think it is useful, I will ask the court reporter to "read back" the question. In particular:

1. Because your or another person's name is on a document as a recipient, do not assume that you or the other person ever received it or read it.

   For example:

   Question: "Did you receive Ms. Miller's letter of May 23?"

   Wrong Answer: "I must have because it is addressed to me."

   Correct Answer (if you do not recall having received the document): "I do not recall."

2. If you do not recall having seen a document, say so before you answer any question about it.

3. If you wrote (authored) a document, you may explain the meaning of its wording if you are asked. Do not try to explain how those who received the document may have interpreted it. That would be speculation.

4. If you received a document, you may explain your understanding of its language. Do not try to explain the intentions of its author. Do not try to explain what the author meant by his or her words. That would be speculation.

D. If the examiner asks you a question about a document without showing it to you, ask to see it. If you do not ask, I will.

E. If you are asked about a document that is not being shown to you and you are certain that it already has been produced to the other side, ask to see a copy if you think the document would help you answer the question. But be careful not to refer to documents you reviewed with me that you do not think the examiner has already seen.

NOTE: At this point in the preparation session, consider explaining to the witness that a document that is used to prepare a witness by refreshing recollection but that has not been provided to opposing counsel may become discoverable.

F. Do not agree to supply documents requested by the examiner. The request should be addressed to, and handled by, me.

G. Do not bring any documents with you to the deposition unless you already have discussed doing so with me. If the examiner learns about a document you brought with you, you will be asked to produce it.

VI. Listen carefully to me (your lawyer) during your deposition.

A. If I object to a question, listen to what I say. You may learn something about the question and how it should be answered. Having heard my objection, consider whether you are still able to answer the question. Even if I object, you may still be required to answer the question. But answer the question only if you understand it and it contains no ambiguities or hidden assumptions. (See Section IV above regarding formulating answers carefully.)

NOTE: At this point in the preparation session, consider reviewing some common deposition objections and explaining what they mean and what they intend to convey, using examples.

B. If the examiner does not rephrase a question after I object, I may ask the reporter to "read it back" before you answer in order to be sure that you have it in mind.

C. If I instruct you not to answer a question, *do not answer it*. Do not be intimidated if the examiner threatens you with sanctions for refusing to answer.

D. If you are unsure whether you have to answer a question, ask me.

VII. Take breaks or confer with me when needed.

A. Call for a break whenever you are tired. Do not remain in the room; use the opportunity to discuss privately any problems with me. If you do not ask for a break, I will ask for one if I think one is needed.

B. Before a question is asked or after you have answered it, you are allowed to confer privately with me, unless I tell you otherwise. If the matter requires extended consultation with me, suggest a break. But do not ask for a break too often; it may create the impression you are being coached.

C. If a question is pending (that is, you have not answered it), I will let you know if you are permitted to confer privately with me before you answer.

NOTE: Depending on the witness and the case, you may want to describe the various privileges such as attorney-client, work-product, spousal, or physician-patient.

D. If you are unsure whether a privilege applies, ask me before you answer.

E. There is no such thing as saying something "off the record." When you say anything within earshot of opposing counsel, expect to be asked about it on the record.

VIII. Do not discuss your preparation session with anyone.

A. Conversations with me or any of your attorneys are privileged and cannot be discovered. If you discuss our conversations with others, the privilege may be lost.

NOTE: At this point in the preparation session, consider describing the attorney-client privilege, in what situations it applies, and how it can be lost.

B. If you are asked at your deposition "Did you meet with your attorney before your deposition?" answer "Yes" (if true). You also may be asked about the length of your preparation session and who was present. You may answer these three questions. Say no more unless I instruct you to do so. Do not be embarrassed by the fact that we met; it is perfectly proper.

C. If you are asked by anyone, including family members, about your preparation session with me, answer that your attorney told you not to discuss it. That should end the discussion.

IX. Video recorded depositions.

A. If your deposition will be video recorded, I will let you know.

B. Your video can be shown to (played for) the jury, so there are some special considerations when you testify.

1. Dress as if you are attending a formal business meeting. No business casual.

2. Look directly at the camera, not at me. You do not want to create the impression that you are being coached. The jury will be constantly judging your credibility.

3. Pause before you answer, but do not pause as long as you might for a stenographically recorded deposition. Even a short pause can look like it is "forever" on video.

4. You are entitled to breaks and to confer with me. But remember that leaning over to talk to me will be captured by the camera and may create the impression that you are being coached. Again, that may hurt your credibility.

X. Final reminders.

A. Please meet me before your deposition at [*time*] and [*place*]. If anyone else is there when you arrive, remember not to discuss the case.

NOTE: It usually is advisable to meet your witness before the deposition somewhere other than the deposition site, which is typically in the examiner's office. This meeting will give you a chance to offer final reminders and to answer any last-minute questions.

B. Whether or not your deposition will be video recorded, dress in something suitable for a formal business meeting. The examiner will be judging everything about you.

C. Do not drink any alcohol or take any drugs (prescription or otherwise) before testifying without letting me know. These substances could affect your ability to testify. In addition, the examiner may ask whether you did so.

APPENDIX 5

Starting the Deposition

HENRY L. HECHT

1. Initial considerations
   a. Arrange for transcription, if required, and video recording, if requested.
   b. If realtime transcription is being used, confirm that the necessary computer connections have been made and test the connections.
   c. If the deposition is being recorded on video, have the videographer test the set-up.
   d. Confer with the reporter regarding the number of copies as well as the format and timing for the delivery of the transcript, if necessary.
   e. Provide reporter with a caption page and a glossary, if necessary. (See also Appendix 3, Supplies to Take to a Deposition.)
   f. Decide on the location, seating, and persons present.
   g. Anticipate a request for a protective order.
2. Stipulations and how to enter into them
   a. Consider which stipulations to offer.
   b. Consider the pros and cons of using only the applicable procedural rules.
   c. Decide how to deal with an offer of the "usual" stipulations.
3. Opening statement by the deposition officer
4. Swearing of the witness by the deposition officer
5. Opening remarks to the witness (optional)
6. Opening questions to the witness (optional)
   a. Establish a foundation for subsequent impeachment.
   b. Consider alternative starts and tone.
7. Receipt of documents pursuant to a request for production or subpoena
   a. Mark documents that are produced.
   b. Review the scope of the search for documents.

      c.   Ask questions about electronic discovery ("e-dis-
          covery").

      d.   Ask questions about any objections to production by
          the responding party.

8.   Conducting a background examination

      a.   Ask about personal background information.

      b.   Ask about education.

      c.   Ask about work experience.

APPENDIX 6

Model Questions for Discovery About a Conversation: The Four "Cs"

Henry L. Hecht

Stage One: Context

A. How many conversations occurred? (Once established, take each separately.)
B. When did the conversation occur?
C. Where did the conversation occur? (For example, did it occur in person? Did it occur over the telephone?)
D. How long did the conversation last?
E. Who participated in the conversation? How can they be located?
   1. If the witness did not participate, how does the witness know about the conversation?
   2. If the witness's knowledge is based on information provided by others, how do they know about the conversation? How can they be located?
   3. If the witness's knowledge is based on information provided by a document, what is that document? Has it been produced? If not, why not? (If the document was not produced, follow up with a demand for production.)
F. Was the conversation documented? (See Stage Four, Corroboration, below.)

Stage Two: Content

A. What was discussed or said—verbatim or in substance?
   1. Consider using a chronological approach.
   2. Consider using a topical approach.
B. Use the "T-funnel" technique.
   1. Use open-ended questions: the "five W's" (Who, What, When, Where, and Why) and the "one H" (How?).

2. Use the witness's last answer to formulate your next question ("looping").
3. Use narrow questions for elaboration and clarification.
4. Use leading questions to suggest the answer.
5. Use closure and summary questions to foreclose a later, credible change in testimony. (See Stage Three, Closure, below.)

C. Use active listening.
   1. Listen for content.
   2. Listen for feeling (use of empathy).
D. Use and recognize nonverbal communication (signals).
   1. Be aware of your own nonverbal signals.
   2. Interpret signals from the witness.
   3. Use and recognize paralanguage: tone, pace, inflection, pitch, and volume.
   4. Remember the dangers of misinterpretation.

Stage Three: Closure

A. Use the "anything else" question to exhaust recollection; consider alternative formulations.
B. Use silence ("the pause"); wait for the witness to fill the void.
C. Use a summary question to recapitulate.
D. Deal with lack of recall.
   1. Think about whether a lack of recall is helpful to your case because it may limit the witness's ability to dispute your side's version.
   2. Determine the meaning of "I do not recall."
      a. Does it mean the witness has no recollection because the conversation did not occur?
      b. Does it mean the conversation may have happened, but the witness does not recall what was said?
   3. Attempt to foreclose a credible, newly found recollection.
      a. Determine whether any document would help the witness's memory (refresh recollection). If so, what document? Has it been produced? If not, why not? (If the document was not produced, follow up with a demand for production.)

    b. Determine whether any person would help refresh recollection. If so, who? How can this person be located?

    c. Establish habit, custom, or routine practice and compare with this event.

    d. As foundation for a later argument that a new-found recollection is not credible, ask what the witness did in preparation for the deposition.

Stage Four: Corroboration

A. Were notes taken at the time (or was the conversation recorded in any manner)? If so, by whom? If so, has the document or recording been produced? If not, why not? (If the document or recording has not been produced, follow up with a demand for production.)

B. Were notes or a memorandum prepared after the conversation? If so, by whom? If so, has that document been produced? If not, why not? (If the document was not produced, follow up with a demand for production.)

C. Was any action taken as a result of the conversation? If so, by whom?

D. Was the action documented? If so, by whom? If so, has that document been produced? If not, why not? (If the document was not produced, follow up with a demand for production.)

E. Was the conversation discussed with anyone afterward? If so, with whom? If so, was the discussion documented? If so, has that document been produced? If not, why not? (If the document was not produced, follow up with a demand for production.)

F. Who knows about the conversation? How do they know about it? How can they be located?

APPENDIX 7

Model Questions for an Examination About a Document

HENRY L. HECHT

Marking a Document

1. Have the reporter mark the exhibit for identification (give it a document number and refer to the production control number or "Bates stamp" identification number, if available).
2. Provide the marked exhibit to the witness and a copy to opposing counsel.
3. Ask the witness to review the exhibit and let you know when she has completed her review before asking any questions.
4. After you have determined that the witness has finished reviewing the document, identify the document for the record or ask the witness to do so.
5. Ask whether the witness reviewed the document before the deposition (anticipate an objection based on a claim of attorney-client privilege and work-product protection).
   a. Ask whether the witness had a lack of recollection before reviewing the document.
   b. Ask whether the document refreshed the witness's recollection.
6. Authenticate the document.
7. Lay the foundation for the ultimate admissibility of the document into evidence (optional).
8. Question the witness about the document, always referring to the document by exhibit number.

Questions for the Author of a Document

1. When was the document prepared?
2. If the witness does not recall when the document was prepared, follow up with questions about whether the

witness (or his employer) has a regular practice or procedure for preparing such documents.

3. Why was the document prepared?
4. Who prepared the document?
   a. If the named author did not prepare the document, who did?
   b. Did anyone help the author prepare the document? If so, who?
   c. Follow up with questions about whether there is a regular practice or procedure concerning who prepares such documents.
5. How was the document prepared?
   a. How much time was spent in preparation?
   b. What sources of information were used?
   c. Were any other documents used in preparing the document in question?
   d. If so, have those documents been produced? If not, why not? (Follow up with a document request.)
6. Were there any prior drafts of the document?
   a. How many?
   b. Are there any underlying notes?
   c. If so, have those documents been produced? If not, why not? (Follow up with a document production request.)
7. Who reviewed the drafts?
   a. Were any comments made about prior drafts? Were the comments made in writing? Were they made by another means?
   b. Were the comments retained?
   c. If so, have those documents been produced? If not, why not? (Follow up with a document production request.)
8. Where is the original? If the original is not available, why not? (Follow up with a document request.)
9. To whom was the document sent? Follow up with questions about whether the witness (or his employer) has a regular practice or procedure for distributing or routing such documents.
10. What does the author mean by the words used in the document?

Questions for the Recipient of a Document

1. When was the document received?
2. Was anything attached to the document?
   a. If so, have the attachments been produced? If not, why not? (Follow up with a document production request.)
   b. Is anything missing?
3. Did the witness read the document upon receipt?
   a. If not, when was it read?
   b. If not, why not? Follow up with questions about whether the witness (or employer) has a regular practice or procedure for distributing or routing such documents.
4. Did the witness communicate with others after receiving the document?
   a. Was the communication documented?
   b. Has the documentation been produced? If not, why not? (Follow up with a document production request.)
5. Did the witness take any action after receiving the document?
   a. Was the action documented?
   b. Has the documentation been produced? If not, why not? (Follow up with a document production request.)
   c. Did anyone else take any action?
6. Was there a response to the document?
   a. Was the response in writing? If so, has the response been produced?
   b. If not, why not? (Follow up with a document production request.)
7. Is the document the witness received accurate?
   a. If not, in what way is the document inaccurate?
   b. Did the witness make any corrections?
   c. Did anyone else find any inaccuracies?
   d. Was the author informed of the inaccuracies?
   e. By whom? In what manner?
8. How does the witness interpret the document and the words in the document? (What is the witness's understanding of the document?)

APPENDIX 8

Objections at a Deposition in Federal Practice

HENRY L. HECHT

I. Deciding Whether to Object

A. Is the question objectionable?

    1. FED. R. CIV. P. 30(c)(1):

> The examination and cross-examination of a deponent proceed as they would at trial under the Federal Rules of Evidence, except Rules 103 and 615.

    2. FED. R. CIV. P. 30(c)(2):

> An objection must be noted on the record . . . , but the examination still proceeds; the testimony is taken subject to any objection.

B. Will the objection be waived if not made at the deposition? Or will it be preserved until trial?

    1. FED. R. CIV. P. 32(d)(3)(A):

> An objection to a deponent's competence—or to the competence, relevance, or materiality of testimony—is *not waived* by a failure to make the objection before or during the deposition, *unless* the ground of for it might have been corrected at that time. (Emphasis added.)

    2. FED. R. CIV. P. 32(d)(3)(B):

> An objection to an error or irregularity at an oral examination *is waived* if: (i) it relates to the manner of taking the deposition, the form of a question or answer, the oath or affirmation, a party's conduct or other matters that might have been corrected at that time; and (ii) it is *not timely* made during the deposition. (Emphasis added.)

C. Even if the question is objectionable, is it strategically wise to object?
1. Will the objection help the witness answer the question?
2. Will the objection educate opposing counsel?
3. Will the witness be available at trial? Do you think the examiner will try to use the testimony at trial?
4. Will your objections create a record of obstreperous defense when considered by a judge?

II. How to State An Objection

FED. R. CIV. P. 30(c)(2):

An objection must be stated concisely in a nonargumentative and nonsuggestive manner.

III. What Happens After an Objection?

FED. R. CIV. P. 30(c)(2):

An objection at the time of the examination—whether to evidence, to a party's conduct, to the officer's qualifications, to the manner of taking the deposition, or to any other aspect of the deposition—must be noted on the record, but the examination *still proceeds; the testimony is taken subject to any objection.* (Emphasis added.)

IV. Three Grounds on Which to Instruct Not to Answer

FED. R. CIV. P. 30(c)(2):

A person may instruct a deponent not to answer only when necessary [1] to preserve a privilege, [2] to enforce a limitation directed by the court, or [3] to present a motion under FRCP 30(d)(3) (to limit or terminate the deposition on the ground that it is being conducted in bad faith or in a manner that unreasonably annoys, embarrasses, or oppresses the deponent or party).

V. Appropriate Objections to the Form of a Question or Answer

NOTE: After such an objection, the examiner usually will try to cure the error unless the examiner only wants to gather information and is not concerned about admissibility.

A. Ambiguous, vague, or unintelligible—FED. R. EVID. 611(a)(1)
B. Argumentative—FED. R. EVID. 611(a)(1)

NOTE: Argumentative questions are those designed to persuade witnesses or to be contentious, rather than to elicit an independent answer.

C. Asked and answered—FED. R. EVID. 611(a); see also FED. R. EVID. 403

NOTE: Faced with this objection, experienced examiners will argue that it is inappropriate because the purpose of a deposition is to gather information. The objection should be used when the same question is asked so often that it becomes cumulative, burdensome, and repetitious. See also FED. R. EVID. 403, FED. R. CIV. P. 26(b)(1), FED. R. CIV. P. 26(c), and FED. R. CIV. P. 26(g).

D. Assumes facts not in evidence or in dispute—See FED. R. EVID. 611(a)(1)

NOTE: Faced with this objection, experienced examiners will argue that it is inappropriate because no testimony or item is "in evidence" at a deposition. Expect experienced counsel to carefully frame the same question as a hypothetical so that the testimony can be used when and if each element needs to be established at trial. Often, the more appropriate objection is lack of foundation. See Section VI.C below.

E. Compound or complex—FED. R. EVID. 611(a)(1)
F. Leading—FED. R. EVID. 611(c), Fed. R. Civ. P 30(c)

NOTE: This objection usually is appropriate when the deponent is not a hostile witness, an adverse party, or a witness identified with an adverse party. But the objection is inappropriate when the question is (1) designed to establish preliminary (or foundational) matters; (2) designed to refresh recollection; (3) designed to aid witnesses, such as children or the infirm, who require help in testifying; (4) directed to an expert witness; or (5) related solely to identifying exhibits (a preliminary or foundational matter).

G. Mischaracterizes the prior testimony or misstates the evidence—FED. R. EVID. 611(a)(1)

771

H. Calls for a narrative response or is overly broad—FED. R. EVID. 611(a)(1)

NOTE: Faced with this objection, experienced examiners will argue that this objection is inappropriate because the concern at trial about potentially objectionable testimony by a witness is not present at a deposition. Expect experienced counsel to persist in seeking a response.

I. Nonresponsive answer—FED. R. EVID. 611(a)(1)

NOTE: After a nonresponsive answer, the examiner should object to the answer and move to strike (although such a motion may damage any rapport already established with the witness). The right to move to strike is generally thought to belong to the examiner.

J. Calls for speculation—FED. R. EVID. 602, FED. R. EVID. 701, FED. R. EVID. 702, and FED. R. EVID. 703

NOTE: This objection is proper when a question seeks information not in a witness's personal knowledge. It often is used interchangeably with an objection that no foundation has been established to show the witness has knowledge about the subject about which he is being questioned. See Sections VI.A and VI.C below. The objection can also be used when the question calls for an improper lay or expert opinion.

VI. Appropriate Objections to the Substance of a Question

NOTE: Objections to the substance of a question usually are preserved until trial; that is, the failure to raise them at the deposition does not waive them at trial. But if the defect in the question could be corrected at the deposition, the objection must be timely made or it will be waived. See Section I.B above.

A. Competency of the witness—FED. R. EVID. 601, FED. R. EVID. 602, FED. R. EVID. 701

NOTE: This objection is often used interchangeably with an objection that there is no foundation establishing that the witness has personal knowledge of the matter he or she is being asked about. Faced with this objection, experienced examiners will attempt to establish the competency of the witness. See also Sections V.J above and VI.C below.

B. Inadmissible opinion or conclusion—FED. R. EVID. 701; see also FED. R. EVID. 704(a)

NOTE: This objection is commonly raised when a lay witness is asked for a legal conclusion. Faced with this objection, experienced examiners will attempt to establish the competency of the witness. See also Section VI.A above.

C. Insufficient or lack of foundation—FED. R. EVID. 703

NOTE: This objection is often used in place of an objection that a hypothetical posed to an expert is incomplete. Faced with this objection, experienced examiners will demand that the defender state the missing elements of the hypothetical so that the defect can be cured. The defender should continue to object and advise the expert not to answer if the question relates to materials the expert did not actually consult, consider, or rely on in forming an opinion. See also Section V.D above.

D. Improper rehabilitation
E. Limitation on evidence directed by the court—FED. R. CIV. P. 30(c)(2); see also FED. R. CIV. P. 26(c)(1).
F. Privileges—FED. R. CIV. P. 26(b)(l); FED. R. CIV. P. 30(c)(2); FED. R. EVID. 501

NOTE: Under Fed. R. Civ. P 26(b)(1) "Parties may obtain discovery regarding any *non-privileged* matter that is relevant to any party's claim or defense. . . ." (Emphasis added.) See also FED. R. CIV. P. 26(c) and FED. R. CIV. P. 30(b)(3)(B) for limitations on the scope of discovery by the court.

If a question violates a privilege and the witness is a client, the defender should object and instruct the witness not to answer; otherwise the privilege may be waived. If the witness is not a client, the defender should object and advise the witness not to answer. See FED. R. CIV. P. 30(c)(1) on the right to instruct. In response to this instruction, experienced examiners will likely seek preliminary (or foundational) facts establishing when, where, and to whom the alleged privileged communications were made. See FED. R. CIV. P. 26(b)(5)(A)(i) and (ii) for the required disclosures after a claim of privilege or protection of trial preparation materials, and see FED. R. CIV. P. 26(b)(5)(B) about handling claimed privileged material on notification by the producing party (the "clawback" provision).

FED. R. EVID. 501 incorporates the laws of the various states on privilege. Among the most commonly asserted privileges are the following:

1. Attorney-client—See FED. R. CIV. P.26(b)(1)
2. Work product—FED. R. CIV. P. 26(b)(3)
3. Physician-patient
4. Confidential marital communications
5. Privilege not to testify against a spouse
6. Trade secrets

   NOTE: Consider objecting and seeking a protective order. See FED. R. CIV. P. 6(c)(1)(G) and FED. R. CIV. P. 30(c)(2).

7. Fifth Amendment privilege against self incrimination—U.S. Constitution, Amendments V and XIV
8. Privacy
9. Penitent-clergy

G. Unfair prejudice, harassment, or undue embarrassment—FED. R. EVID. 403, FED. R. EVID. 611(A)(3)

NOTE: A defender should consider an objection and instruction not to answer if the question appears to be asked in bad faith or to unreasonably annoy, embarrass, or oppress the deponent or opposing party, and a protective order cannot be secured before the questioning. See FED. R. CIV. P. 26(c); FED. R. CIV. P. 30(c)(2); and FED. R. CIV. P. 30(d)(3).

VII. Inappropriate Objections to the Substance of a Question

NOTE: Typically, the objections in this category go to the admissibility of the evidence sought rather than to its discoverability. Given the broad scope of discovery, these objections are preserved until trial and usually should not be made at the deposition. See Section I.B above.

A. Original writing requirement ("not the best evidence")—FED. R. EVID. 1002; but see FED. R. EVID. 1003; FED. R. EVID. 1004; and FED. R. EVID. 1005

B. Hearsay—FED. R. EVID. 801; FED. R. EVID. 802; FED. R. EVID. 805; but see FED. R. EVID. 803; FED. R. EVID. 804; FED. R. EVID. 805; FED. R. EVID. 80, and FED. R. EVID. 807 for exceptions

C. Offer to compromise or compromise payment—FED. R. EVID. 408; see also FED. R. EVID. 407 and FED. R. EVID. 409

D. Relevance—FED. R. EVID. 401; FED. R. EVID. 402; FED. R. EVID. 403; and FED. R. CIV. P. 26(b)(1)

E. Subsequent remedial measures—FED. R. EVID. 407

F. Existence of liability insurance—FED. R. EVID. 411; see also FED. R. CIV. P. 26(a)(1)(A)(iv) regarding its discoverability

APPENDIX 9

Adjourning the Deposition in Federal Practice

HENRY L. HECHT

1. Review your notes.
2. Ask whether the witness or defender wishes to reconsider an instruction not to answer.
3. Consider whether to ask any final questions or make any closing remarks as a foundation for subsequent impeachment.
4. Decide whether to conclude, continue, or suspend the Deposition:
    a. Conclude the deposition ("no further questions");
    b. Continue to a date certain, including day to day until completed;
    c. Continue to a date to be agreed upon by counsel;
    d. Conclude, pending a motion to compel further answers or production of documents and for sanctions (see also FED. R. CIV. P. 37(a)(4) regarding award of expenses, including attorney's fees, incurred in relation to the motion);
    e. Suspend, pending a motion to terminate or limit or for a protective order or to compel further answers or to produce documents and for sanctions—FED. R. CIV. P. 30(d)(4); or
    f. Conclude or suspend, pending an order for additional time due to frustration of "fair examination"—FED. R. CIV. P. 30(d). See also FED. R. CIV. P. 26(b)(2) regarding limitations on discovery and FED. R. CIV. P. 30(d)(2) regarding limitation to one day of seven hours.
5. Allow for examination by the witness's own counsel if requested.
6. Determine whether original deposition exhibits will be retained by the reporter and annexed to the transcript

or whether the person who produced them will keep the originals—FED. R. CIV. P. 30(f)(2).

7. Determine if the witness wishes time to review, correct, and sign the transcript—FED. R. CIV. P. 30(e)(1):
   a. Pros and cons of making corrections;
   b. Effect of failure to correct and sign; and
   c. Deposition officer to note if review requested and attach any changes made by the deponent—FED. R. CIV. P. 30(e)(2).

8. Make arrangements for a transcript, confirm the format of the transcript, make arrangements for delivery and custody of the transcript, and make arrangements for storage of the original, certified transcript and annexed exhibits. See FED. R. CIV. P. 30(e) and 30(f).

9. Be aware of the duty to supplement discovery disclosures—FED. R. CIV. P. 26(e). See also FED. R. CIV. P. 37(c) regarding failure to disclose.

10. Allow for closing statement by the deposition officer—FED. R. CIV. P. 30(b)(5)(C).

APPENDIX 10-A

Introduction of Deposition Testimony at Trial: Pretrial Considerations

HENRY L. HECHT

1. What deposition testimony is to be offered in evidence
2. Basis for the offer—FED. R. CIV. P. 32(a)
3. Objections to the basis for the offer or admissibility of the testimony—FED. R. CIV. P. 32(a) and 32(b)
4. Objection to the use of the deposition of an unrepresented party
5. Objection to the use of a deposition subject to a protective order—See FED. R. CIV. P. 26(c)
6. Objections to specific questions and answers offered
   a. Objections made at the time of the deposition—FED. R. CIV. P. 32(d)
   b. Objections required to be "timely" made during the deposition that were not made and are therefore waived—FED. R. CIV. P. 32(d)(3)(B)
   c. Objections preserved that need to be made at time of the offer into evidence—FED. R. CIV. P. 32(d)(3)(A)
7. Additional portions of the deposition to be offered by the adverse party—FED. R. CIV. P. 32(a)(6)
8. Courtroom presentation
   a. Jury versus judge (bench) trial
   b. Unless the court orders otherwise, a party must provide a transcript of any deposition testimony the party offers, but may provide the court with the testimony in nontranscript form (such as a video recording) as well; on any party's request, deposition testimony offered in a jury trial for any purpose other than impeachment must be presented in nontranscript form, if available, unless the court for good cause orders otherwise—FED. R. CIV. P. 32(c)
9. Request for preinstruction of the jury (See Appendix 10-B, Model Format for a Jury Trial.)

APPENDIX 10-B

Introduction of Deposition Testimony at Trial: Model Format for a Jury Trial

HENRY L. HECHT

OFFERING COUNSEL: Your Honor, at this time we would like to read portions of the deposition testimony of [*witness*] taken in this matter pursuant to the Federal Rules of Civil Procedure.

I will read the questions and an associate in my office, [*name*], will assist me by reading the answers.

At this point, Your Honor, we ask that you instruct the jury concerning the reading of the deposition.

THE COURT: A deposition is the sworn testimony of a witness taken before trial. The witness is placed under oath and sworn to tell the truth. The lawyers for each party may ask questions. The questions and answers are recorded. When a person is unavailable to testify at trial (or is an opposing party in the lawsuit), the deposition of that person may be used at the trial.

The deposition of [*witness*] was taken on [*date*]. You should consider the deposition testimony you are about to hear in lieu of live testimony in the same way as if the witness had been present to testify.

OFFERING COUNSEL: The following questions were asked of [*witness*] at the deposition:

[THE DEPOSITION TESTIMONY IS THEN READ TO THE JURY.]

OFFERING COUNSEL: Your Honor, I have no further portions to read from the deposition.

OPPOSING COUNSEL: Your Honor, in fairness, at this point we offer the following additional portions of the deposition testimony of [*witness*].

[THE ADDITIONAL PORTIONS ARE THEN READ TO THE JURY.]

APPENDIX 11

Impeachment by Prior Inconsistent Deposition Testimony: The Three "Cs"

Henry L. Hecht

Step One: Confirm the Present Testimony

1. You testified on direct: _____. Is that correct?
2. Or, if the witness has given an answer on cross-examination that is inconsistent with what you expected: Are you now testifying that _?

Step Two: Credit the Prior Deposition Statement

1. You testified at a deposition in my office, is that correct?
2. You testified under oath, is that correct?
3. It was the same oath you took today, is that correct?
4. You were told that your deposition testimony could be used as evidence at trial, is that correct?
5. You were told at your deposition to ask me to rephrase a question if you did not understand it, is that correct?
6. You had an opportunity to review your deposition testimony, is that correct?
7. You made _____ corrections to your deposition testimony, is that correct? (If no corrections were made: You did not make any corrections, is that correct?)
8. You then signed your deposition transcript as correct (if true), is that correct?
9. You had prepared for your deposition with your attorney, is that correct?
10. Your attorney was present at your deposition, is that correct?
11. The attorney who represented you at your deposition is the same attorney who represents you in the courtroom today (if true), is that correct?

Step Three: Confront the Witness with the Prior Inconsistent Deposition Testimony

1. To the Court: May I approach the witness?
2. I show you a copy of your deposition transcript, which has been marked as Exhibit A for identification.
3. I refer you and your counsel to page _____ and lines _____.
4. Let me know when you have finished reviewing it.
5. At your deposition, I asked you the following question: _____, is that correct?
6. At your deposition, you gave the following answer under oath: _____, is that correct?

   NOTE: As a general rule, do not ask a follow-up question, such as "Which answer is true?" because you do not know what the witness will say. Let the inconsistency stand on its own. If the judge insists that you ask a follow-up question, ask: Did I read that question and your answer correctly?

Alternatives to Using the Three "Cs"

1. If the deponent is a party witness, the prior inconsistent deposition testimony may be read into evidence without asking any questions of the witness.
2. Rather than show the deposition transcript to the witness before reading the prior inconsistent answer to the jury, read the question and answer and show the transcript only if the witness claims, "I do not remember that question and answer," or says, "I am not sure that is what I said."
3. A third alternative—more dangerous, but also more dramatic: "My question to you at your deposition was: 'What color was the light?' Please read your previous deposition answer to the jury." This technique has the danger of a garbled reading by the witness and an unwelcomed attempt by the witness to explain his answer.

Table of Cases

800

Index

ABOUT THE PRINCIPAL AUTHOR AND EDITOR

Henry L. Hecht is co-founder of The Hecht Training Group, consultants on skills training for lawyers (www.HechtTrainingGroup .com), and on the faculty of the University of California, Berkeley, School of Law (Boalt Hall) (www.law.berkeley.edu).

From 1973 until 1983, he had an active litigation practice, first with the Watergate Special Prosecution Force as an Assistant Special Prosecutor, and then with Heller Ehrman LLP of San Francisco, California.

Since 1983, in addition to teaching at the Law School, he has designed and conducted in-house training programs at more than 65 law firms, corporate law offices, government agencies, firms of consulting experts, and bar associations across the country. Using the "learning by doing" method, he has presented workshops on deposition, negotiation, motion practice, and trial skills.

In 1991, he co-founded The Hecht Training Group, which brings together a group of attorneys as trainers who each have taught lawyering skills for more than 20 years.

Mr. Hecht has lectured and written extensively for the American Bar Association (ABA), the American Law Institute-American Bar Association (ALI-ABA), the Practising Law Institute (PLI), California Continuing Education of the Bar (CEB), and the National Practice Institute (NPI). In addition, he is a member of the Advisory Board of ALI-ABA In-House CLE and an elected member of the American Law Institute (ALI).

His publications include a book, *Effective Depositions*, 2nd ed. (ABA 2010); two mock case files, *Scoops v. Business-Aide, Inc: A Liability and Damages Case File*, 5th ed. (2009) and *Donna Taylor v. Shape-Up Stores, Inc.: A Damages Case File*, 2nd ed. (with V. O'Brien) (2009); and three multi-media CD-ROMs, *Mastering Motions: Mechanics and Techniques* (with T. Hallahan) (PLI 1999), *Taking Effective Depositions: Mechanics and Techniques* (PLI 1997), and *Defending Depositions: Mechanics and Techniques* (PLI 1997).

Mr. Hecht is a graduate of Harvard Law School (J.D. cum laude 1973) and Williams College (B.A. magna cum laude 1968).

ABOUT THE CONTRIBUTORS

Donald W. Carlson is the Senior Founding Partner of Carlson, Calladine & Peterson LLP, and has spent the last 30 years trying a wide variety of complex cases for both plaintiffs and defendants. Mr. Carlson is a Fellow of the American College of Trial Lawyers, a Fellow of the Academy of International Trial Lawyers, and a member of the American Board of Trial Advocates (ABOTA), the three most prestigious invitation-only organizations that recognize plaintiff and defense attorneys who have successfully tried numerous jury cases while demonstrating excellence and professionalism. As well as authoring numerous articles on trial procedure and trial tactics, he often is asked to teach trial skills to the legal community.

G. Richard Dodge, Jr. is a partner in the Litigation Department in the Washington, D.C., office of Dewey & LeBoeuf. His practice includes civil litigation, internal investigations, and white-collar criminal defense. Mr. Dodge received his J.D. from Georgetown University Law Center in 1998, where he was a member of the *American Criminal Law Review.*

Diana S. Donaldson served as the managing partner of Schnader Harrison Segal & Lewis LLP for six years and is a member of its Litigation Department. She graduated from the Ohio State University College of Law, where she was Order of the Coif and Articles Editor of the *Ohio State Law Journal.* She served as a law clerk for the Honorable Max Rosenn of the United States Court of Appeals for the Third Circuit.

Ms. Donaldson has spoken and written about litigation strategies, and in particular about depositions. She co-authored with Dennis R. Suplee *The Deposition Handbook,* now in its fourth edition.

George Donaldson is a practicing attorney, specializing in class and complex business litigation, who founded his own firm in 1987. He has been a lecturer for the Business Law Section of the California State Bar, the California Continuing Education of the Bar (CEB), the American Trial Lawyers Association (ATLA), the American Bar Association (ABA), and the International Association for Financial Planning, and he has written articles for Practising Law Institute and *Trial Magazine*. He is a member of the bars of California, Virginia, the District of Columbia, and numerous federal courts. Mr. Donaldson received his J.D. from The George Washington University in 1976.

Stuart W. Gold is a practicing trial lawyer and member of Cravath, Swaine & Moore LLP in New York. He has litigated all varieties of complex cases and has argued before the United States Supreme Court. Mr. Gold attended New York University School of Law, receiving his J.D. in 1972. After law school, he clerked for the Honorable Edward Weinfeld of the United States District Court for the Southern District of New York.

Christine Bergren Greene is the Chief of the Legal Support Operations Branch of the Office of the Attorney General, California Department of Justice. The Legal Support Operations Branch provides office management, legal secretarial, clerical, business, and office services to the legal professionals in the six legal offices of the Office of the Attorney General. Prior to her current position, Ms. Greene served as a litigation paralegal and as a manager of the Litigation Support Section in the Office of the Attorney General. She is the author of *Deposition Manual for Paralegals* (2nd ed. 1993). She received her B.A. in History from the University of California at Berkeley and her M.B.A. in Finance from The George Washington University in Washington, D.C.

Peter Gruenberger is a retired Partner of, and a consultant to, the global law firm Weil Gotshal & Manges LLP, headquartered in New York. At the firm, he was the long-time head of both the National Litigation Training and the Ethics Committees. From 1969 to date, his trial practice has involved securities, antitrust, bankruptcy, and other complex litigation matters.

Mr. Gruenberger is now a member and principal of The Hecht Training Group (www.HechtTrainingGroup.com). He has designed and conducted in-house training programs for law firms, in-house legal departments, firms of consulting experts, and bar associations on ethics and professional responsibility, evidence, trial skills, and depositions.

He has written and lectured for the Federal Judicial Center, the New York City, New York County, and American Bar Associations as well as the *Columbia University Law Review*, ALI-ABA, Law Journal Press, and the *University of Texas Review of Litigation*. He was a founding member and officer of the ABA's Section of Litigation.

After graduating from Columbia College and Columbia University School of Law (where he was Editor of the Law Review), Mr. Gruenberger served as a Judge Advocate General Officer in the United States Army.

Raoul D. Kennedy is a partner in the San Francisco office of Skadden, Arps, Slate, Meagher & Flom LLP, where he handles civil litigation at both the trial and appellate levels. He is a graduate of the University of California, Berkeley, School of Law. Mr. Kennedy is a member of the American College of Trial Lawyers, the American Board of Trial Advocates, the International Academy of Trial Lawyers, the International Society of Barristers, and the American Academy of Appellate Lawyers, and is past president of the California Academy of Appellate Lawyers. He is the co-author of the *California Expert Witness Guide* (California CEB).

Hal S. Marcus is a principal at iCyte, Inc., a leading provider of web research management and collaboration tools. At the time he wrote this chapter, Mr. Marcus was Vice President of Litigation Product Management at Thomson Reuters, providers of Westlaw and LiveNote software. A graduate of the University of Michigan Law School, he worked as a litigator at New York's Mudge Rose Guthrie Alexander & Ferdon before commencing a career in business and product development and becoming a regular industry speaker on the application of technology to legal practice. Over the years, Mr. Marcus has trained and consulted with thousands of legal professionals, many of whom have informed his contribution to this publication.

Paul C. Palmer is the CEO and General Counsel of Bluecher U.S.A., Inc. Prior to his current position, he was a member of the Litigation Department of Debevoise & Plimpton in Washington, D.C. Mr. Palmer received his B.A. from Tufts University in 1977 and his J.D. from The George Washington University in 1980, where he was the Executive Editor of *The George Washington Law Review*. He is a contributing author of *Effective Depositions* (ABA 1997) and the co-author of "Preparing a Witness to Testify" in *Taking and Defending Depositions in Commercial Cases* (Practicing Law Institute 1993) and in *Taking Successful Depositions in Commercial Cases* (Practicing Law Institute 1992).

Mark D. Petersen is a partner in the San Francisco law firm of Farella Braun + Martel LLP. He specializes in complex commercial litigation, including securities fraud, construction disputes, and entertainment lawsuits. Mr. Petersen received his B.S. in 1974 from the United States Naval Academy and his J.D. in 1983 from University of California, Hastings College of Law. He has taught deposition and trial skills with the National Institute of Trial Advocacy and the University of San Francisco Intensive Advocacy Program.

Robert M. Peterson is a founding partner of Carlson, Calladine & Peterson LLP and over his 28 year career has tried many high stakes cases, lasting from three weeks to three months. Mr. Peterson represents businesses and individuals in high exposure, complex cases, including insurance bad faith, corporate fraud, unfair competition, professional liability, class actions, and catastrophic injury lawsuits.

Mr. Peterson is nationally known for his expertise in insurance bad faith and punitive damages issues, and he has tried or litigated insurance bad faith cases in more then 20 states. He has authored over a dozen articles on topics such as punitive damages, class actions, and litigation and trial techniques. He is a frequent speaker at industry seminars and has taught trial deposition techniques to California lawyers.

Mr. Peterson is a graduate of University of California, Hastings College of Law, San Francisco (J.D. 1981) and Cornell University, Ithaca, New York (A.B., English, 1978).

Eve Saltman is currently the Vice President, Legal at OnLive, Inc., in Palo Alto, California, where she leads all the day-to-day legal affairs of the company. Prior to OnLive, Ms. Saltman held a variety of legal roles at Autodesk, Siebel Systems, and LiveOps. She started her legal career Orrick, Herrington & Sutcliffe LLP, in San Francisco and Silicon Valley.

Lorna G. Schofield is a partner with Debevoise & Plimpton LLP in the firm's New York office. She has spent most of her career doing complex commercial civil litigation and trials, the most widely reported of which was her defense of TV celebrity Rosie O'Donnell in a dispute with the publisher of *Rosie* magazine. In the past few years Ms. Schofield has spent the majority of her time representing clients in regulatory and criminal investigations, following up on her earlier work as a federal prosecutor. Ms. Schofield is currently the Chair of the American Bar Association's Section of Litigation. She has served in many other positions with the section, including co-chair of the task force that developed the Civil Discovery Standards, which provide guidelines to lawyers and judges in areas not addressed by the rules.

Michael J. Shepard is a partner in the San Francisco office of Hogan & Hartson LLP. A trial lawyer, his practice includes white-collar criminal defense and related proceedings, civil trials, and internal investigations. He is a graduate of Princeton University and Stanford Law School, where he was Senior Articles Editor of the *Stanford Law Review* and Order of the Coif. He served as a federal prosecutor in Chicago, trying thirty cases involving public corruption, financial fraud, and other federal offenses, and eventually serving as Interim United States Attorney there as well as Chief of the Public Integrity Section of the Criminal Division of the Justice Department in Washington D.C. Since returning to private practice in 1994, Mr. Shepard has conducted many internal investigations and tried numerous cases, both civil and criminal, some of which have actually raised the issues addressed in his chapter.

David A. Sonenshein is a Professor of Law at Temple University School of Law and a graduate of Cornell University and the New York University School of Law. Professor Sonenshein teaches evidence, civil procedure, and trial advocacy at the law school and has taught trial advocacy, evidence, and deposition practice in law firms throughout the country. The author of dozens of articles and books, Professor Sonenshein also served as the Director of the American Institute for Law Training within the Office (AILTO), the in-house training organization of ALI-ABA, and teaches evidence to Federal Judges for the Federal Justice Center. He is the co-author with the late Irving Younger and Michael Goldsmith of the evidence casebook, *Principles of Evidence*. Professor Sonensheim was named Temple University's Great Teacher in 2007, and he has been named the Outstanding Professor at the Law School six times.

Dennis R. Suplee, a graduate of the University of Pennsylvania Law School, is a partner in the Philadelphia office of Schnader Harrison Segal & Lewis LLP. His practice concentrates on commercial litigation, including insurance coverage cases, patent and trademark litigation, antitrust litigation, and defense of mass tort cases. Mr. Suplee is a Fellow and former Regent of the American College of Trial Lawyers, and a Fellow and Past President of the International Academy of Trial Lawyers.

He is co-author of two standard works on litigation practice, *The Deposition Handbook*, now in its fourth edition, and *The Expert Witness: A Handbook for Litigators*, and speaks frequently on effective litigation techniques.

Judge Jeffrey S. White is a United States District Court Judge for the Northern District of California, San Francisco Division. Before his appointment to the bench in 2003, Judge White was a partner and chair of the Litigation Department of Orrick, Herrington & Sutcliffe LLP, in San Francisco, California. Judge White is a lecturer in civil trial advocacy at the University of California, Berkeley, School of Law (Boalt Hall). He received his J.D. at State University of New York at Buffalo School of Law in 1970.